S0-ANE-152

THE AUTHORS

RAY G. PRICE, a professor at the University of Minnesota, is in charge of business teacher education at that institution. His interest in consumer and economic education dates back thirty-five years when he started his teaching career in the public high schools of Indiana. In addition to his many writings, his activities in this area include membership on the Board of Trustees of the Joint Council on Economic Education; chairmanship of the Committee on Economic Education at the University of Minnesota; and secretaryship of the Minnesota State Council on Economic Education. Dr. Price has served as an advisor to the Consumer Education Study of the National Association of Secondary School Principals; as a consultant on economic education to the Minneapolis Public Schools; and both as a director of, and consultant to, numerous economic education workshops.

VERNON A. MUSSELMAN is a professor of business education at the University of Kentucky. Dr. Musselman has taught in both junior and senior high schools, in junior colleges, and at the university level. He has had practical experience and is the author of many articles published in a variety of professional business education journals as well as of several books in the field of business education. He has served the profession actively for many years as an officer in regional and national professional business education associations.

J. CURTIS HALL is dean of the School of Business at Virginia Commonwealth University, Richmond, Virginia. Basic education in business and economics has been his major interest throughout his career in high school, college, and university teaching. His writings in this field have appeared in numerous professional publications. In addition he is a coauthor of a book on business organization and management. He currently is serving as the general business editor of a national professional journal. Dr. Hall is a member of the Economic Education Committee of the Virginia Chamber of Commerce. He has participated in economic workshops at the local, state, regional, and national levels and has served as consultant on business and economic education throughout the South.

EDWIN E. WEEKS, JR., is assistant superintendent for administration in the City School District of Syracuse, New York. Formerly, as City Supervisor of Business Education in Syracuse, Dr. Weeks received wide recognition for his establishment of a city-wide curriculum that stressed the importance of general and basic business education in the vocational business program. The American Economic Foundation in 1963 honored him with an award for this achievement. In addition to classroom teaching on the high school, adult, and collegiate levels, he has had office and management experience in business and industry and in the Armed Forces. An active member and officer in many educational and business organizations on local, state, and national levels, Dr. Weeks is currently on the Board of Directors of the Eastern Business Teachers Association.

GENERAL BUSINESS FOR EVERYDAY LIVING

GENERAL BUSINESS FOR EVERYDAY LIVING

THIRD EDITION

RAY G. PRICE

VERNON A. MUSSELMAN

J. CURTIS HALL

EDWIN E. WEEKS, JR.

Gregg Division

McGRAW-HILL BOOK COMPANY

New York St. Louis Dallas San Francisco Toronto London Sydney

GENERAL BUSINESS FOR EVERYDAY LIVING,
Third Edition

Library of Congress Catalog Card No. 65-18748

8 9 0 DODO 9 8 7 6 5 4 3 2

ISBN 07-050841-0

Book Design: BETTY BINNS

PREFACE

A DISTINGUISHING feature of a free enterprise system is that its guiding force is the sum total of the millions of individual decisions that all of us make as consumers, producers, and voters. The preservation of this kind of system depends on the ability of individuals to make wise decisions. For everyone living in a free enterprise system, therefore, a knowledge of business and the economic system within which it operates is an important need. That this need has not adequately been met is a matter of grave concern not only to leaders in education but also to leaders in business, labor, agriculture, and government.

With few exceptions, the only students in our secondary schools enrolled in courses about business are those majoring or planning to major in business. One reason is that textbooks used in courses about business have been written primarily for that particular group of students, in spite of claims to the contrary. *General Business for Everyday Living, Third Edition,* is truly an exception. It provides an opportunity for *all* students to become effective economic citizens.

OBJECTIVES AND FEATURES

The objective of this edition of *General Business for Everyday Living* is essentially the same as that of earlier editions—to raise the level of economic understanding among the nation's youth by giving them an overall view of the place and purpose of business in our society. Like its predecessors, this edition is divided into a logical sequence of 12 units, comprising 50 parts. Extensive changes have been made, however, both in the organization and content.

Teachers who have used earlier editions will find this one upgraded yet easier to understand. It is upgraded in that it covers important topics more fully. In other words, it concentrates on making significant concepts clear and meaningful to young learners. On the other hand, some topics of a specific vocational nature have been eliminated.

The text is easy to understand because explanations are carefully worded in terms that students can grasp. In addition, every effort has been made to help students acquire a business and economic vocabulary consisting primarily of those terms most frequently used in the press. All such terms are fully defined when first introduced and repeated often enough so that students become confidently familiar with them. For easy reference, terms defined in the text are also included in the glossary.

TEACHING AND LEARNING AIDS

The activities suggested at the end of each part serve both to implement and supplement what has been learned from reading the text. These end-of-part materials are divided into sections as follows:

Building Your Vocabulary

To understand the world of business, one must understand the language of business. The vocabulary exercises in this end-of-part section help students to master the important terms that are defined in the text. Terms included in the vocabulary exercises appear in bold-face italics where defined in the text.

Checking Your Reading

The questions in this section are all answered in the text. Thus, they serve a twofold purpose. Students will find them a valuable study guide since they follow the order of the text. Teachers will find them a valuable means of determining how well students have mastered the content of each part.

Sharing Your Opinion and Experience

The questions in this section vary in purpose. Some are designed to stimulate discussion; some, to uncover what students already know; some, to provide opportunities for students to apply what they have learned. None of the questions are answered in the text before they appear in this section; therefore, all serve to extend learning by pushing students beyond the text.

Projects and Problems

In this section teachers will find an abundance of meaningful activities. For example, since business information is often presented by means of charts, graphs, and tables, there are numerous problems involving the use of these. There are problems that give students practice in obtaining information from newspaper reports and problems designed to help students relate what they learn to their own communities. And there are many problems involving arithmetic. But they are not arithmetic problems put there for the sake of arithmetic. Like all problems in this section, they tell a story that helps students to understand better the concepts presented in each part.

Challenge Problems

The questions and activities in this section are an invitation to students to engage in supplementary learning experiences requiring a greater degree of sophistication than those provided in the other end-of-part sections.

INTENDED USE

General Business for Everyday Living, Third Edition, is the answer to a growing demand on the part of teachers for a textbook that deals with important economic concepts. But it is not an economics text. Rather it is one approach to economic understanding. It is intended for use as an introductory business course. It is an ideal foundation for advanced basic business courses such as consumer economics and economics and, if so used, will maximize the effectiveness of those courses. On the other hand, students who do not have an opportunity to take advanced courses will find their study of this text of inestimable value.

ACKNOWLEDGMENTS

The authors take this opportunity to thank the many teachers throughout the country who have used earlier editions of the text and contributed suggestions for its improvement. They also publicly acknowledge the many letters received from student-users of the book. Constructive criticism as well as praise from this source aided in the development of a better product. The authors are especially grateful to the businessmen and organizations who served as advisers during preparation of the manuscript. Included in this group are Harlan B. Miller, Director of the Educational Division, Institute of Life Insurance; Earl G. Nicks, Educational Director of the Insurance Information Institute; Jerry Miller, Health Insurance Institute; Edward G. Mayers, Senior Economist, Department of Economics, McGraw-Hill Publications; Second Northwestern National Bank of Minneapolis; Household Finance Corporation; the Business and Economics Department of the Minneapolis Public Library; and the United States Chamber of Commerce.

RAY G. PRICE
VERNON A. MUSSELMAN
J. CURTIS HALL
EDWIN E. WEEKS

CONTENTS

CONTENTS OF UNIT 1

Unit 1 / What Business Does for You

PART 1
WE LIVE IN A BUSINESS WORLD

Courtesy Union Carbide and Carbon Corp.

ONE thing that people everywhere have always had in common is wants. They want food to eat, clothes to wear, and homes to live in because these are needed for survival. Most of us also want things like phonograph records, skates, and skis—if only for the pleasure they afford.

In the stories you read as a child, wants were often satisfied in magical ways. When Cinderella wanted to go to the ball, a wave of her godmother's wand brought her everything she needed for that occasion. The good shoemaker and his wife prospered from the nightly visits of several hard-working elves. Other heroes and heroines of story-book fame obtained their hearts' desires simply by wishing.

In real life, however, people count on business to satisfy most of their wants. True, business has none of the mystery that surrounds the storybook methods. But if you say that it also lacks magic, you could be wrong. It may be that because you do business with business many times every day, its magic escapes you. Yet what other system of satisfying wants has enabled so many people to live as well as we do in the United States?

WHAT IS BUSINESS?

Business is our principal means of satisfying human wants. Suppose, for example, that some afternoon on your way home from school you feel hungry. When you begin to think how good a fudge sundae would taste, you feel even hungrier. Hurriedly you count your money; and, if you have enough, you head for the nearest soda fountain. Within minutes after the idea first occurred to you, you are enjoying a frosty dish of ice cream and chocolate. Magic? Well, hardly. Business made it possible for you to have that sundae. And it is doubtful whether any system of magic could satisfy a want in much less

THERE ARE 9 MILLION BUSINESSES IN THE UNITED STATES.

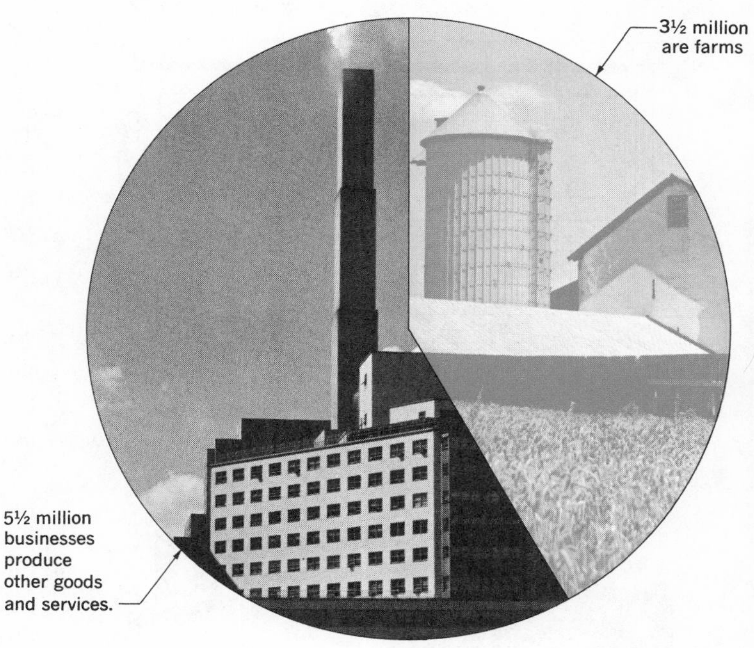
3½ million are farms
5½ million businesses produce other goods and services.

time. When you consider that now there are approximately 198,000,000 people in the United States with wants to be satisfied, you may begin to realize how important business is.

Business Supplies Us with Goods and Services

Even though you may never have wanted a fudge sundae, you certainly have plenty of wants. Some of them can be satisfied with material objects like typewriters, books, and cameras. These things that you can see and feel are ***goods.*** Some of your other wants are satisfied with ***services,*** like having your hair cut, your picture taken, or your car repaired. Whether you want a good or a service, however, you usually count on business to supply it. You depend on business for the food you eat, the clothes you wear, the home you live in. You depend on business for movies and other forms of entertainment. You even depend on business for the newspapers and magazines you read.

Business Provides Jobs

What was the first thing you did when you thought about wanting a fudge sundae? You counted your money. And where did the money come from? You or someone had to earn it. Unlike primitive man who satisfied his wants directly by hunting and fishing, people today buy the goods and services they want. In most cases they buy them with money earned working at jobs provided by business. During a recent year business provided work for seven out of every eight persons employed. The number of workers needed by business at any one time depends on the extent to which people buy the goods and services produced. The greater the demand for goods and services, of course, the more workers business is able to employ.

BUSINESS ORGANIZES TO PRODUCE

More than 9 million separate business organizations

95 PERCENT OF BUSINESSES EMPLOY FEWER THAN 20 PERSONS.
SHOE REPAIR
BARBERSHOP
small business

produce goods and services in the United States. Each of these organizations is a *business enterprise*. About three and a half million of them are farms. The rest produce goods and services of every kind. Together these 9 million enterprises turn out 90 percent of all goods and services produced in this country.

A business enterprise may be just one individual like your shoe repairman, a neighborhood dressmaker, or someone your age who operates a lawn-mowing service. Or a business may be an extremely large organization like the American Telephone and Telegraph Company, which has nearly three million owners and employs almost one million workers.

Enterprises that produce similar products make up what is called an ***industry.*** All automobile manufacturers, for example, make up the automobile industry. The dry-cleaning industry is made up of the nation's many dry cleaners. There is a steel industry, mining industry, food industry, and so on.

Most Business Enterprises Are Small

The size of a business may be measured in several ways. One is by the number of workers it employs. If you consider a business that employs fewer than 500 workers small, then at least 97 percent of the nonfarm enterprises in the United States are small. In fact, 95 percent of them have fewer than twenty workers each. Among these small enterprises are most of the places where you or your family does business, like the stores and repair shops in your community, the bank, the movie theater.

Large enterprises, although few in number, produce more than half of all goods and services produced by business. One reason is that small businesses, as a rule, serve only those who live nearby. Most large business enterprises, on the other hand, sell their goods or services nationwide. Steel, petroleum products, automobiles, and electrical equipment are typical examples of goods produced by large businesses. Some of the services provided by large businesses are railroad transportation, telephone communication, and life insurance protection.

BOTH WORKERS AND ENTERPRISES ARE PRODUCERS

Any person or enterprise that produces a good or service for the purpose of selling it to others is a ***producer.*** If you do work for which you are paid—like baby-sitting, delivering newspapers, or mowing lawns—then you are a producer. For some part of your life you will undoubtedly work full-time, producing a good or service that others will buy. In that way you will earn the money you need to buy the things you want. How much you can buy will depend on how much you earn.

Note that business enterprises are also producers; in other words, a person employed by a business firm is a producer, but so is the firm that employs him.

CONSUMERS ARE IMPORTANT TO BUSINESS

Anyone who buys or uses the goods and services of business is a ***consumer.*** This means that all of us are consumers. You are consuming when you read this book; use pencils, ink, and paper; ride a bus; or have a tooth filled.

As a consumer you are important to business because the way consumers spend their money largely determines the kinds of goods and services that enterprises produce. The purpose of business, remember, is to satisfy people's wants. The enterprise that produces a good or service people do not buy cannot stay in business for long.

Suppose that you and all your friends preferred potato chips to any other kind of snack. You would show this preference by spending your money for potato chips rather than for peanuts, pretzels, cheese crackers, and the like. In order to stay in business, the companies that produced these other snacks would make potato chips instead. Or suppose large numbers of young people bought records instead of going to the movies. If continued, this practice would lead to more records and fewer movies being produced.

Picture how your community might have looked fifty or more years ago. Many of the changes that have taken place since then hinged on the decisions of consumers. If people had rejected electric lights, for example, we might still be using gaslight or kerosene lamps.

BUSINESS PRODUCES TWO KINDS OF GOODS

The word "goods" is sometimes used to mean both goods and services. Goods and services that satisfy human wants directly are called ***consumer goods.***

Examples of Producer and Consumer Goods
The cement mixer and the computer are producer goods. The shoes and rings are consumer goods.

Courtesy Burroughs, Linde Air Products Co., and Sears, Roebuck and Co.

These are things—such as food, refrigerators, furniture, medical care, and television repairs—for which individuals and families spend their money. Two-thirds of all goods and services produced in this country are consumer goods.

Goods used in producing other goods are ***producer goods.*** The business enterprise that produced your fudge sundae used a soda fountain in producing it. The soda fountain, therefore, is a producer good. The farmer's seed and tractor, the photographer's camera, the newsboy's bicycle are all producer goods because they are used to produce other goods or services.

The purpose for which a good is used determines whether it is a producer or consumer good. A car used by a salesman in calling on his customers is a producer good. The car a family buys for its own personal use is a consumer good.

WHY CALL BUSINESS A SYSTEM?

The millions of separate business enterprises producing goods and services in this country are *interdependent.* That means they depend on one another. The soda-fountain owner who supplied your fudge sundae, for example, had to have the cooperation of many other producers.

One was the farmer who supplied the milk and cream needed. Another was the enterprise that produced the ice cream. Before these two could do their work, however, trucks had to be manufactured to haul the milk to the ice-cream plant and the ice cream to the soda fountain. In addition, roads had to be paved. Docks had to be constructed for the ships that brought the sugar from Hawaii and cacao beans for chocolate from West Africa. The construction of those docks depended on businesses that supply wood, steel, cement, and nails. Each of these was dependent in turn on still others. So it is with all business enterprises in the United States. Not one can operate without the help of others. Together they form a system that produces billions of dollars worth of goods and services each year.

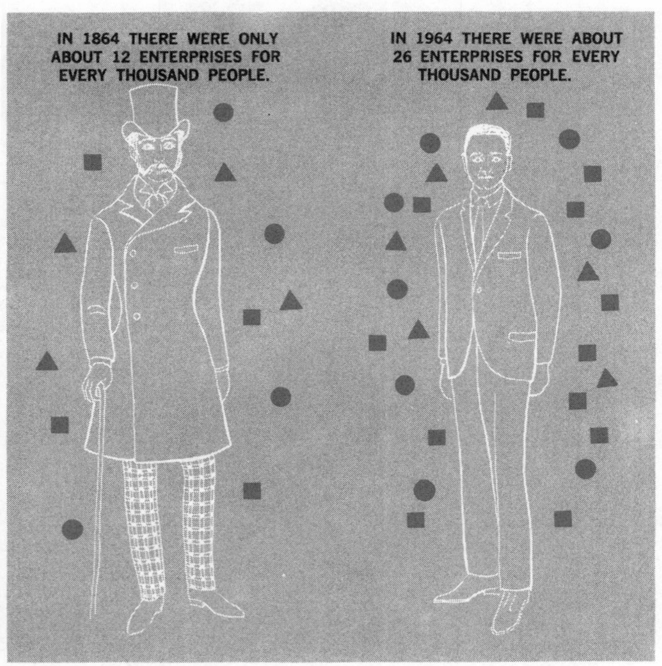

IN 1864 THERE WERE ONLY ABOUT 12 ENTERPRISES FOR EVERY THOUSAND PEOPLE.
IN 1964 THERE WERE ABOUT 26 ENTERPRISES FOR EVERY THOUSAND PEOPLE.

BUSINESS IS A GROWING SYSTEM

One of the most impressive facts about our business system is the way it has increased in size. In 1864 it included about 350,000 nonfarm enterprises. By 1964, one hundred years later, the number of nonfarm enterprises had increased to almost 5 million.

Perhaps you are thinking that this was only natural since our population also increased during the same century. True, the more people there are with wants to be satisfied, the greater the need for business. But business more than kept up with the rise in population. It surpassed it. In 1864 when our population was around 30 million, there were fewer than 12 nonfarm business enterprises for every 1,000 persons. By 1964 our population had reached 192 million. Yet for every 1,000 persons there were better than 26 nonfarm enterprises.

IT IS IMPORTANT TO UNDERSTAND OUR BUSINESS SYSTEM

As you can see, our everyday lives are closely linked to business in more ways than one. We depend on it for the goods and services we cannot do without. And most of us depend on business for the jobs we need in order to buy those goods and services. Certainly it is no exaggeration to say that part of understanding the world in which we live is to understand business.

Many people think that because they have daily contacts with business they know all they need to know about it. But you can buy goods and services from business without understanding how it operates, just as you can drive a car without a knowledge of what makes it run. Our business system is also like a car in that both have changed over the years. Some of these changes were brought about by law; others, by custom. In both cases, the influence of the people of that time brought about the changes. In a similar way the future development of our business system will depend on the actions of those living today. Isn't this argument enough in favor of understanding it?

NOTE TO STUDENT

Throughout this text you will be asked to set up tables or forms and to write answers to questions in the section entitled Projects and Problems as well as in the section entitled Challenge Problems. Whenever you are asked to do this, use a separate sheet of paper or your *Student Activity Guide.* Do not write in the textbook.

BUILDING YOUR VOCABULARY

List the figures 1 to 7 on a sheet of paper, numbering down. Read the seven statements given below at the right; then, for each statement, select from the column at the left the term that best matches it in meaning. Write this term next to the appropriate number.

consumer	1. Material objects, such as books or cameras
consumer goods	2. Things others do for us, like cutting our hair or repairing our cars
goods	3. A group of business enterprises that produce similar products or provide similar services
industry	4. A person or enterprise that makes goods or provides services
producer	5. Anyone who buys or uses the goods and services of business
producer goods	6. Goods and services that satisfy human wants directly
services	7. Goods used to produce other goods or services

CHECKING YOUR READING

1. What is the purpose of business?
2. Explain two ways in which people are dependent on business.
3. What determines the number of workers needed by business?
4. Nearly one-third of the business enterprises in the United States are of one kind. What kind are they?
5. What percent of this country's goods and services is produced by business?

6. Compare large and small business enterprises in terms of number, amount of goods produced, and so on.
7. What is the relationship between an individual's role as a producer and his role as a consumer?
8. Why are consumers important to our business system?
9. For whom are most goods and services produced in the United States?
10. Explain why the millions of separate business enterprises in this country are called "our business system."
11. Compare the growth of our business system with the growth of our population during the century from 1864 to 1964.
12. Why is it important to understand our business system?

SHARING YOUR OPINION AND EXPERIENCE

1. Do you think there is any "magic" in our business system? Explain your answer.
2. As stated in the text, business enterprises turn out approximately 90 percent of the goods and services produced in the United States. Who produces the remaining 10 percent?
3. Carefully examine this textbook and name at least three different kinds of businesses that might have helped to produce it.
4. Give examples of articles that may be either consumer goods or producer goods.
5. Explain how growth in population increases the need for business enterprises. What are some other things that might give rise to new businesses?
6. Bill Wright maintains that people were more independent in earlier times than they are today. Do you agree? What do you think he means?
7. Primitive man satisfied his wants in a direct manner. Today people satisfy their wants in an indirect manner. Explain.

PROJECTS AND PROBLEMS

1. Write the following items in the left-hand column of a form like that shown below: clothing, electric power, gasoline, hotel accommodations, haircut, insurance, air transportation, telegraph message, truck repair, desk lamp. Place a check mark (√) in the appropriate column to indicate whether it is a good or a service.

Item	Good	Service
Example: Book	√	

2. On a form similar to the one shown on page 9, list five businesses in your community that produce goods. For each business, list one item it produces. Place a check mark (√) in one or both of the other columns to indicate whether the item is for producers, consumers, or both.

Name of Business	Item Produced	For Producers	For Consumers
Example: Banner Box Company	*Paper cartons*	√	

3. Using a form similar to the one you ruled for project No. 2 on page 8, list five businesses in your community that produce services. In the second column write the kind of service produced. Place a check mark (√) in one or both of the last two columns to indicate whether it is a service for consumers, producers, or both.
4. Name five types of businesses—either manufacturing or service—on which each of the following depends: filling station, barbershop, grocery store, lumberyard.
5. What types of business enterprises are listed in your telephone directory that you did not know existed in your community? Limit your list to ten.
6. Business information is often presented by means of tables, charts, or graphs in order to show comparisons or relationships. For example, the table below shows five of the largest companies in the United States during a recent year, measured by the number of employees.

FIVE OF THE LARGEST BUSINESS FIRMS IN THE UNITED STATES
(measured by number of employees)

Company	*Number of Employees*
Ford Motor Company	**160,181**
United States Steel	**225,081**
General Motors	**595,000**
Standard Oil Company of New Jersey	**140,000**
General Electric Company	**250,621**

Prepare a table similar to that above, listing the companies in order of their size, as measured by employees. Begin with the largest.

CHALLENGE PROBLEMS

1. Another way of measuring the size of a business is by its sales of goods or services. In a recent year five of the largest companies from the standpoint of sales were: General Electric—$4,200,000,000; Standard Oil of New Jersey—$8,000,000,000; General Motors—$12,700,000,000; United States Steel—$3,700,000,000; Ford Motor Company—$5,200,000,000.

   Prepare a table showing this information. List the companies in the order of size as measured by sales. Begin with the largest. If you wish, you may write the sales figures in decimal form. For example, $4,200,000,000 would be written $4.2. You would then need to indicate this in your column heading.

Company	Sales (in billions)

2. Select one of the companies listed in the table you prepared for the preceding problem and explain why it has to be big.
3. Is business able to satisfy all human wants? Why?

PART 2
BUSINESS SATISFIES YOUR WANTS THROUGH PRODUCTION

Courtesy General Motors Corp.

NATURE provides everything needed for human survival, but not so people can satisfy their wants without effort. Land for growing food must be plowed, planted, and cultivated; trees must be cut down; and metals must be mined. Food crops must be harvested; trees must be sawed into boards; and metals must be refined and made into new shapes. Finally, these goods must be transported to places where those who want them can buy them. Changing the form or location of natural things to satisfy human wants is ***production.*** It is the principal function of business.

ALL BUSINESSES ENGAGE IN PRODUCTION

Some people mistakenly think that production is limited to making things like refrigerators, or growing things like grain or potatoes. But turning out goods is only one kind of production. The purpose of production is to satisfy human wants. All activity, therefore, which contributes to this purpose, either directly or indirectly, is production.

In order to satisfy a human want, goods must not only be in the shape or form wanted, they must also be where they are wanted, when they are wanted. If you wanted a loaf of bread, would wheat growing in a field satisfy your want? Of course, not! The wheat would first have to be ground into flour; the flour, mixed with other ingredients to make bread; and the bread, be on your grocer's shelf when you went to buy it. This means that in addition to making goods, production includes transporting and selling them as well. It also includes other services, such as those performed by doctors, lawyers, dry cleaners, photo studios, and the like, because these too satisfy people's wants. Production, then, is the function of all business enterprises.

ALL ACTIVITY IN WHICH PEOPLE ENGAGE TO SATISFY HUMAN WANTS IS PRODUCTION.

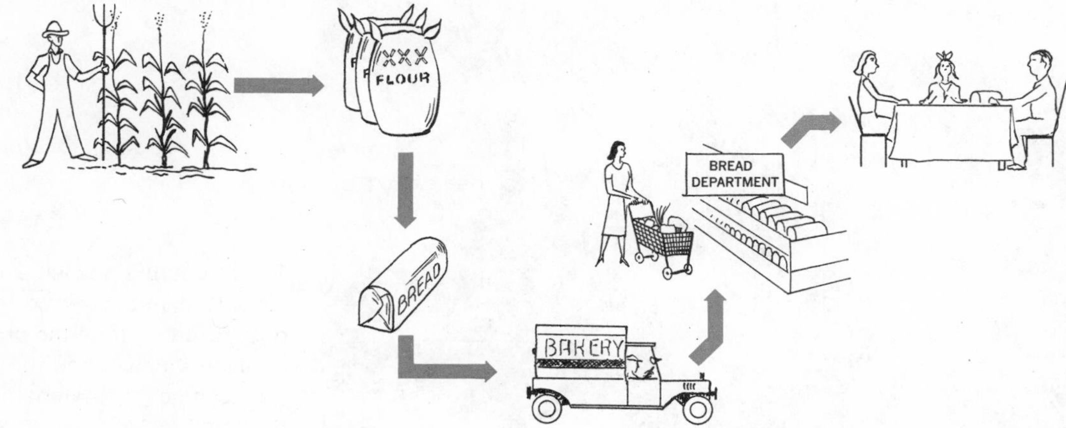

WHAT IS NEEDED FOR PRODUCTION?

Think a moment about the different kinds of businesses in your community. What are some of the things they must have in order to produce their goods or services? Take the service station, for example. It needs gasoline and the pumps for putting it into cars. It must have air hoses, grease racks, and an assortment of parts. The bakery must have ovens, mixers, pans, and showcases. It must also have a supply of ingredients used in baking, such as flour, eggs, sugar, butter, and milk. The variety store must have merchandise to sell, counters, a cash register, wrapping paper, and string or tape. All of them must have places in which to do business and someone to do the work.

These things that business enterprises use in producing goods and services are called *factors of production.* All of them belong to one of three groups. They are either natural resources, labor, or capital.

Natural Resources

Production of every kind really begins with natural resources. ***Natural resources,*** of course, are the things nature gives man to work with—land, soil, water, wildlife, forests, coal, oil, iron, and so on. These gifts of nature contribute to production in several ways. The most obvious one is by providing raw materials, such as copper, lead, lumber, and iron that business uses in producing goods. But natural resources have other important uses as well. For example, coal, oil, natural gas, uranium, and water supply the power needed to run the machines used in production. Nature also provides waterways for transporting goods and furnishes climate favorable to growing certain kinds of crops.

Labor

The second factor of production is labor. ***Labor*** is the human effort that goes into production. Sometimes it is called "human resources." In the business world all work done for pay is labor, whether the work draws on the physical or mental abilities of the worker.

Capital

The third factor of production is capital. ***Capital*** is simply another name for producer goods. It includes the man-made things used in production, like tools, machinery, trucks, factories, railroad cars, and office buildings. Goods of this kind which can be used over and over again are called *fixed capital.* Goods used up in production, like raw materials, office

Trees, a natural resource, are being converted into plywood. The sawdust resulting from the process will be used for fuel, and the log cores will become raw material for papermaking.

Courtesy St. Regis Paper Co.

supplies, or fuel, are called *working capital.* A business must replace its working capital continually. In time even its fixed capital wears out and has to be replaced.

The term "capital" is often used to mean the money needed to buy producer goods. When someone says that he would go into business if he had enough capital, he usually means money. To distinguish between the goods used in production and the money needed to obtain such goods, the goods themselves are called *capital goods.* The money to buy them is *money capital.*

WHAT DOES PRODUCTION COST?

Every business uses the factors of production in some way although it is not always easy to recognize how. All draw on natural resources, if only for the land they occupy. Every business must have labor even if the owner himself provides it. True, some businesses require little capital; but it would be impossible to produce much of anything without capital of some kind. Even primitive man probably wove a basket of grasses before starting out to gather wild fruits and berries. Production, as you should begin to see, is the result of combining labor with natural resources and capital.

What a business pays for the factors of production is what it costs that business to produce. In other words, the prices paid for the use of land, for materials, for labor, for tools or other equipment are the costs of production.

PRODUCTION IS ACHIEVED THROUGH SPECIALIZATION

For centuries production was largely a family or tribal affair. Even the pioneer families of our own country produced almost everything they consumed. Each household grew its own food, built its own house, and wove the cloth used to make its own garments. Children were taught at an early age to churn butter, to make candles, and to whittle nails from wood. In those days everyone had to be a jack-of-all trades. What a family could not produce for itself, it usually had to do without.

Today it would be hard to find anyone who produced more than a small fraction of all goods and services he consumes. Most workers specialize in one kind of production. Jill Hanson's father is a dairy farmer. Jan Milligan's parents operate a clothing store. Jerry Stein's dad is a dentist. Millions of other people work at different jobs to produce the countless goods and services wanted. Altogether there are more than 24,000 ways by which the people of this country earn a living. Dividing the work of production in this manner is called ***specialization,*** or the *division of labor.*

Specialization May Be Simple or Complex

A simple division of labor is one in which each worker engages in a single trade or profession. Some might be dairy farmers like Mr. Hanson; some, store owners like the Milligans; and some, dentists like Dr. Stein. Others work as teachers, lawyers, truck drivers, plumbers, and so on. In some kinds of production, however, the division of labor is more complex. With our present manufacturing methods, for example, no one worker makes a complete product from start to finish. Instead the work is divided into many separate tasks, and each worker performs only one. Mark Haney's father, who works in a factory that makes refrigerators, sprays the finish on the doors. Other workers spray paint the refrigerator cabinets. Others fasten the doors on the cabinets.

If you have ever watched an automobile moving through a jiffy car wash, you may have noticed a similar division of labor. As one worker cleans the inside front of a car, another cleans the inside back. At the same time a third is cleaning a section of the outside; a fourth, a different section; and so on. Then the car moves along to another group of workers whose job is to scrub the wheels. Finally the car comes to the last group of workers who rub it dry. Altogether the work of washing a single car may be divided among as many as 20 workers. The complete job takes an average of 5 minutes. As a car moves from one stage of the washing process to the next, however, another car is moved into its place. Each worker performs the same task on every car. This means that several cars are being handled at one time. With this system a whole line of cars can be washed at the rate of one a minute.

Specialization May Be Geographic

Sometimes a division of labor is the result of natural differences among regions. Most of the iron miners in this country live in an area around Lake Superior where the largest ore deposits are. The major corn producers are found in the Central Plains region because that area has the fertile soil, long growing season, and summer rain needed to grow corn. Fishing provides employment for people living in coastal communities. A division of labor caused by the location of natural resources or raw materials is called *geographic specialization.*

RESULTS OF PRODUCTION ARE SHARED BY MEANS OF INCOME

When production centered in the home, dividing what had been produced was no problem. Each family's share of goods and services was as much or as little as it had produced. But when workers specialize, there has to be some way of dividing what is produced. As you can understand, it would be impossible to divide the goods and services themselves. Instead, part of the money received from the sale of the goods and services is divided among the workers who contributed to their production. Workers then buy the goods and services they want.

Money received by business from the sale of goods and services is ***income.*** Out of this income business must pay the costs of production. The share of income that workers receive is called *wages* or *salary.* Income, like goods and services, is the result of production. Total income depends on total production. How much income (goods and services) there is to divide depends on how much has been produced.

PRODUCTION DEPENDS ON SPENDING

In Part 1 you learned how consumers help to determine what is produced by the way they spend their money. In the same manner consumers help to determine how much is produced. The more goods and services consumers buy, the more goods and services business produces. Consumers, however, do not do all the spending. Business enterprises and governments also buy goods and services. Their spending encourages further production, the same as spending by consumers. The buying of all three groups—consumers, business, and government—determines total production.

Spending is sometimes referred to as *demand*. ***Demand*** is the amount of a good or service that will be bought at a particular price. A businessman might say that there is no demand for a certain product. He means that people do not buy enough of it to make its production worthwhile.

HOW IS PRODUCTION MEASURED?

The total amount that a nation produces during any year is its ***gross national product.*** Gross national product, called GNP for short, is always expressed in dollars. In 1964, for example, the gross national product of the United States was $623 billion. This means that when the prices of all goods and services produced during 1964 were added together, the total amount was $623 billion.

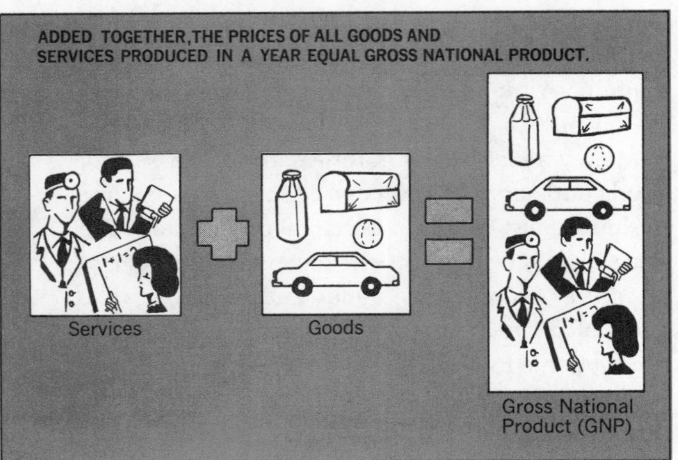
ADDED TOGETHER,THE PRICES OF ALL GOODS AND SERVICES PRODUCED IN A YEAR EQUAL GROSS NATIONAL PRODUCT.
Services
Goods
Gross National Product (GNP)

Why is production measured in prices? Because this nation produces a tremendous number and variety of items. How else could you add together such different things as bathtubs, movies, candy bars, paint, shoes, and airplane rides?

PRODUCTION DETERMINES OUR STANDARD OF LIVING

Standard of living is a term used to describe the way a family or the people of a nation live. How well a family or a people live is measured by the number and kinds of goods and services they have. Families that live in comfortable homes, drive cars, educate their children, own life insurance, and take vacation trips have a high standard of living. Families that are poorly fed, clothed, and housed, on the other hand, have a low standard of living. A nation's standard of living is high or low depending on the way most of its people live.

This means that a nation's standard of living is closely tied to its total production, or gross national product. The more goods and services a nation produces in proportion to its population, the higher its standard of living. A nation's standard of living also depends on how the income resulting from production is divided. In some countries there are extremes of poverty and wealth. A small number of families live in luxury, while the majority are desperately poor; and there is no middle class. In other countries, the United States for one, the majority live well.

BUILDING YOUR VOCABULARY

List the figures 1 through 10 on a sheet of paper, numbering down. Read the ten statements given below at the right; then, for each statement, select from the column at the left the term that best matches it in meaning. Write this term next to the appropriate number.

capital
demand
factors of production
gross national product
income
labor
natural resources
production
specialization
standard of living

1. Changing the form or location of natural things to satisfy human wants
2. Natural resources, labor, and capital
3. Things in existence that man did not produce, such as timber, oil, and iron
4. The human effort that goes into production
5. Man-made things used in production
6. A way of dividing production, so that each worker performs only one job
7. Money received by business from the sale of goods and services
8. The amount of a good or service that will be bought at a particular price
9. The total amount that a nation produces in a year
10. The way a family or the people of a nation live

CHECKING YOUR READING

1. What is the purpose of production?
2. Explain the statement that "all businesses engage in production."
3. In what ways do natural resources contribute to production?
4. What is another term for labor?
5. Explain the difference between fixed capital and working capital.
6. How do capital goods differ from money capital?
7. What are the costs of production?
8. Explain or describe the different kinds of specialization.
9. When workers specialize, what method is used to divide what they produce?
10. What is the workers' share of a company's income called?
11. What determines total income?
12. What determines total production?
13. Why is GNP always expressed in dollars?
14. Explain how a nation's standard of living is closely related to its GNP.
15. What other important factor influences the standard of living of a nation?

SHARING YOUR OPINION AND EXPERIENCE

1. Joan Wilson earns extra spending money by baby-sitting after school and on weekends. Is Joan engaged in production? Why?
2. Why is farmland considered a natural resource?

3. Mary's father is a lawyer who works for a chemical company. Is his work *labor*? Why?
4. One important difference between fixed capital and working capital is that one can sometimes be substituted for labor. Which one? Explain or give examples.
5. Explain the statement, "Today production is based on teamwork."
6. Does the division of labor help to increase production? How?
7. Is there geographic specialization where you live? If so, what are the conditions that encourage the specialization?
8. How would you describe your community? Is it known as an agricultural area, a trade center, or a manufacturing center?

PROJECTS AND PROBLEMS

1. Select an article manufactured in your community and list the raw materials needed to produce it.

   Example: Raw materials needed to produce shirts
   1. *cotton cloth*

2. List six types of production being carried on in your community by young people about your age.
3. Name four kinds of labor that require mostly physical effort, four that depend primarily on mental effort, and four that require both physical and mental effort.
4. Make a list of capital goods that might be used by one of the following kinds of business enterprises: clothing store, shoe-repair shop, railroad, mining company.

   Example: Capital goods required for a clothing store
   1. *display cases*

5. What goods and services do *you* believe a family must have in order to have a high standard of living? Limit your list to twelve items.

CHALLENGE PROBLEMS

1. If nature provides everything needed for human survival, why do people in some parts of the world die of malnutrition?
2. The following item appeared in newspapers around the nation on or about October 22, 1963. Read it carefully, then answer the questions below.

U.S. OUTPUT GAINS

Washington, D.C. A gain of $8.9 billion in production last quarter carried national output to a record rate of $588.5 billion a year.

The gain almost assured a GNP of $600 billion a year by early 1964. The increase in production was the largest in any quarter since the fall of 1961.

▪ *a.* What does the term "output" refer to? ▪ *b.* Write $8.9 billion without using the decimal. ▪ *c.* What is meant by an $8.9 billion gain in production? ▪ *d.* How long a period of time is a quarter? ▪ *e.* Up to the time the above item was written, had our gross national product ever been higher than $588.5 billion a year? ▪ *f.* According to the above report, is our gross national product increasing or decreasing? ▪ g. How does a change in GNP affect the nation as a whole?

PART 3 BUSINESS MARKETS GOODS

WHAT do you think of when you hear the word "market"? The neighborhood grocery perhaps? Or a suburban supermarket where your family shops for food and household supplies? True, these are markets. But a market need not be a special place. In business a "market" is any meeting between a buyer and a seller for the purpose of exchanging goods or services. If you buy an article from a salesman who comes to your door, your doorstep serves as a market. If you order goods by mail, you take part in an exchange; and there is a market. Many agreements between buyers and sellers are made over the telephone.

To market goods and services simply means to sell them. The process of moving goods from producers to consumers is ***marketing.*** Since goods cannot satisfy human wants until people have them in their possession, marketing goods is as much a part of production as making goods.

HOW ARE CONSUMER GOODS MARKETED?

Marketing can be a complex process or it can be a simple one. Marketing occurs in its simplest form when goods pass directly from their original producer to the consumer. The farmer who sells his fruits and vegetables to passing motorists from a roadside stand is marketing them directly.

Only a small portion of the goods consumers buy, however, is obtained directly from those who make or grow them. A manufacturer who turns out goods by the hundreds or thousands must also sell them in large quantities. The same is true of the farmer who grows many acres of grain, peas, potatoes, or other food products. Most consumer goods, therefore, are bought from business enterprises not directly involved in their production. An enterprise of this kind is called a ***middleman.*** Why "middleman" do you suppose?

Courtesy Kaiser Steel Corp.

THREE MAIN WAYS OF MARKETING GOODS

ONE-STEP MARKETING

TWO-STEP MARKETING

THREE-STEP MARKETING

Most Consumer Goods Are Marketed Through Retailers

The middlemen that consumers know best are retailers. A ***retailer*** is a seller who deals directly with consumers. Your neighborhood grocer is a retailer. So is your shoe repairman, baker, and druggist. Big-city department stores that carry a wide variety of merchandise and mail-order houses that sell thousands of items through catalogs are all retailers. The service station where you buy gasoline for the family car, the local movie theater, and the dry cleaner are all retailers. Not only do retail businesses outnumber other kinds of business enterprises in the United States, they also market most of the consumer goods and services sold.

Suppose that instead of marketing his fruits and vegetables from a roadside stand, the farmer sold them all to a retail grocer in a nearby city or town. The grocer in turn would sell them in small quantities to his customers. Instead of one buyer and seller as before, this method of marketing involves two buyers and two sellers. The goods change hands not once, but twice.

Retailers Obtain Consumer Goods from Wholesalers

In some cases retailers do obtain their goods directly from those who make or grow them. Large mail-order houses often have manufacturers produce items especially for them. Generally, however, retailers buy their merchandise from wholesalers. A ***wholesaler*** is a merchant who buys goods in large quantities and resells them in smaller lots. One wholesaler, for example, might purchase a thousand jackets from one or more manufacturers and sell them in turn to several retailers. Most wholesalers specialize; that is, they handle just one line of merchandise, such as food, clothing, or drugs.

Now imagine a large farm enterprise that could supply ten or more retailers with fruits and vegetables. Rather than take time from his work to find that many grocers willing to buy his products, the farmer sells his entire crop to a wholesale merchant. Then it becomes the wholesaler's job to find retail grocers who will buy the farmer's fruits and vegetables. With this method there are three buyers and three sellers.

Although marketing may involve still more buyers and sellers, most goods are marketed in one of the three ways just described: producer to consumer; producer to retailer to consumer; or producer to wholesaler to retailer to consumer. How goods are marketed depends on the kind of goods they are, how they are produced, and where they are produced.

HOW MUCH DOES MARKETING COST?

As you know, the price you pay for any item must cover all costs of producing it, including marketing. But did you also know that in some cases the cost of marketing goods exceeds the cost of making them? It is estimated, for example, that 62 cents out of each dollar spent for food products is their marketing cost. One reason food marketing costs are high is that many food items like vegetables, fruit, milk, and eggs are perishable. Losses resulting from spoiled goods are part of the cost of marketing them. On the average about half of the total amount spent for consumer goods represents their marketing cost.

Marketing Functions Determine Cost

The purpose of marketing is to make goods available to consumers when and where they want them. The retailer does his part by keeping in stock hundreds of items consumers want. In a big department store, for example, you can buy clothing, cosmetics, household equipment, sporting goods, books, and countless other articles. In addition to fruits and vegetables that may have been grown nearby, the typical retail grocer handles numerous items from distant places, like bananas from Central America, tea from India, sardines from Norway, and spices from the East Indies. Think how long it would take to shop if you had to go to a different store for each item you wanted, or if you had to obtain each item directly from its original producer.

Wholesalers serve retailers in much the same way that retailers serve consumers. A wholesaler of coats and sweaters, for example, might also carry hats, mittens, skirts, and shirts. Through wholesalers, retailers are able to obtain with a single order the goods of several producers. Wholesalers also serve producers of goods. What about the farmer who produced enough fruits and vegetables to supply ten or more retailers? Wouldn't he save time by selling them all to one wholesaler?

In the process of moving goods from the original producer to the point of final sale, middlemen perform numerous other tasks. These are known as the ***functions of marketing.*** The cost of marketing any one item depends on how many of these functions must be performed. Some may be performed more than once. As you read about the marketing functions described below, you might ask yourself these questions: Is it a necessary service? If the function were not performed, would it make a difference in how well consumers' wants were satisfied?

Transporting Goods. Many of the goods you buy or use travel long distances to reach you. The cacao beans for chocolate from West Africa and the bananas from Honduras are only two examples. Automobiles manufactured in Detroit may be bought by a family living in Arizona. Even farm products grown nearby must be hauled to town. Transporting goods is one of the major marketing functions.

THE COST OF MARKETING VARIES WITH THE TYPE OF PRODUCT.

Motor vehicles
Marketing 12.4% of product cost

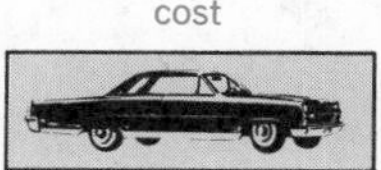

Office equipment
Marketing 20.2% of product cost

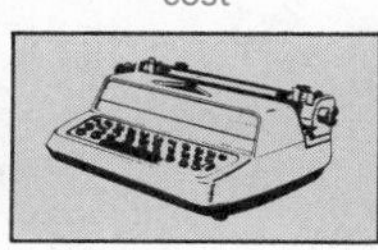

Food
Marketing 62% of product cost

Courtesy Cities Service Company

Wholesalers need large storage plants for storing their goods before sending them to retailers.

Packaging Goods. Next time you go shopping, notice how many items come to market in cartons, cans, or wrappers of some kind. Packaging makes goods easy to handle and to store. Packaging also reduces waste by keeping goods clean and fresh until consumers buy them. In 1964 it was estimated that 13 billion dollars was spent on packaging, and the amount is said to be increasing at the rate of one billion dollars a year. Frequently it is the package that sells the product.

Food, both hot and cold, can be purchased from these convenient vending machines.

Courtesy The Vendo Company

Processing Goods. The milk a creamery buys from the dairy farmer is raw. Before it can be delivered to your door, it must be pasteurized. Large quantities of fresh fruits and vegetables are canned or frozen, so that they can be enjoyed the year round. Changing the form of things already produced in order to sell them is *processing.* Potatoes are a good example.

Consumers will buy only so many raw potatoes. But additional potatoes can be sold when they are processed in different ways. One of the most popular ways is to make them into potato chips. Potatoes are also processed and packaged for use as mashed potatoes, scalloped potatoes, and potato salad. Cake mixes are another example of how processing can increase sales. Since cake mixes were first introduced, the sale of cake flour has nearly doubled. Much of the present work of processing involves the performing of services that people once did for themselves.

Storing Goods. Some goods are not wanted at the time they are first produced. Strawberries picked in June may be wanted for shortcake in January. To meet the demand for toys at Christmas, producers must make toys all year round. Until these things are wanted, they must be stored. As goods move from producers to consumers, it is sometimes necessary to store them several times. Finished goods are stored by the manufacturer until wholesalers buy them. They may then be stored by wholesalers until retailers buy them. And retailers must keep a supply of goods on hand to meet the needs of their customers.

Different types of goods call for different types of storage. Wheat, as you may know, is kept in grain elevators; oil, in large metal tanks. Frozen foods must be put into cold storage. Providing storage facilities for goods is the business of some enterprises.

Advertising Goods. If you had never heard of motor scooters, cameras, or airplane trips, would you want any one of them? Aren't most of the things you want products that you know about? That is why producers advertise. They want you to know about the goods and services they have for sale. And they want you to buy their goods and services, rather than those of another producer. Advertising is a form of salesmanship. It is perhaps the best-known of the marketing functions.

CONVENIENCE IS IMPORTANT

Sometimes goods are sold only because consumers do not have to go out of their way to buy them. For this reason producers are always looking for new ways to market their goods and services. Door-to-door salesmen bring merchandise right into your home. Many goods and services are sold through vending machines. Food, soft drinks, stamps, and ice cream are only a few examples of goods that are marketed in this way. There is the familiar jukebox that plays your favorite record when you deposit a coin. And there are vending machines that issue insurance policies, shine shoes, and take pictures.

More and more businesses offer customers drive-in service. Among them are banks, eating places, movie theaters, laundry and dry-cleaning establishments. The purpose of all these methods of marketing is to sell more goods by making it convenient for consumers to buy them.

MARKETING CONTRIBUTES TO OUR STANDARD OF LIVING

Every day you use goods produced in other parts of the country or in other countries of the world; therefore, you take these things for granted. But not too many years ago people had only what could be produced within the local community. During the childhood of many people living today, an orange was a once-a-year Christmas treat.

To a great extent improved methods of marketing goods have brought about improvement in our standard of living. Marketing costs may seem high; yet how often do you think families in Vermont could eat pineapple if they had to go to Hawaii for it? And how many people in Minnesota or Michigan could drive cars if they had to travel to Texas or Oklahoma for gas and oil? As you can see, our system of marketing enables consumers to have many goods they could not afford to buy otherwise.

BUILDING YOUR VOCABULARY

Copy the five sentences below, completing each one by replacing the question mark with the appropriate term from the column at the left.

functions of marketing
marketing
middleman
retailer
wholesaler

1. The process of getting goods from producers to consumers is ? .
2. A retailer is sometimes called a ? .
3. A business enterprise that sells directly to consumers is a ? .
4. A merchant who buys goods in large quantities and resells them in smaller lots is a ? .
5. Tasks that middlemen perform in the process of moving goods from the original producer to the point of final sale are ? .

CHECKING YOUR READING

1. Explain why marketing is a part of production.
2. What is the simplest form of marketing?
3. What kind of business enterprise markets most of the consumer goods and services sold in the United States? Give examples. From whom do these merchants usually obtain their merchandise?
4. Most goods are marketed in one of three ways. What are they?
5. What determines how a particular product is marketed?
6. On the average, how much of every dollar that is spent for consumer goods represents the cost of marketing the goods?
7. Why is the cost of marketing food higher than the average cost of marketing for all consumer goods?
8. What determines the cost of marketing a particular item?
9. Name five functions of marketing.
10. What are some reasons for packaging goods?
11. What does the "processing of goods" mean? Give examples of how processing may increase sales of a product.
12. Why is it often necessary to store finished goods?
13. Why do business enterprises advertise?
14. Give some examples of how businesses try to make it convenient for consumers to buy their goods.
15. How is marketing related to our standard of living?

SHARING YOUR OPINION AND EXPERIENCE

1. Explain why the process of marketing is sometimes called distribution.
2. Why do you think retailers and wholesalers are called middlemen?
3. What reasons can you give for the fact that the marketing costs for food have been rising at a faster rate than for most other products?
4. Self-service markets are one example of how businessmen have attempted to reduce marketing costs. Explain.
5. What kinds of goods are commonly sold in your community by door-to-door salesmen? Why are these articles sold in this way?
6. Look up the word "vend" in your dictionary. Then tell why we call machines that dispense goods and services "vending machines."

PROJECTS AND PROBLEMS

1. Give six examples of goods that producers sell directly to consumers in your community.
2. Make a list of ten articles found in your home that you probably could not have if you had to buy them directly from the original producer. After each one explain why it would have been difficult to obtain.
3. On a form similar to that shown on page 23 list ten business enterprises in your community. Following each one place a check mark ($\surd$) in the appropriate column to indicate whether the business makes goods, markets goods, or does both. If it markets goods, indicate whether it is a wholesale or retail enterprise.

Name of Business	Makes Goods	Markets Goods	
		Wholesaler	Retailer
Example: Sardi's Bakery	√		√

4. Write the following items in the left-hand column of a form like that shown: desk lamp, orange juice, potato chips, facial tissue, coal, hosiery. After each one place a check mark (√) in the appropriate column or columns to indicate which of the five functions usually are performed in marketing the item.

Item	Processing	Packaging	Transporting	Storing	Advertising

5. On the left half of a sheet of paper indicate which of the five functions of marketing you would perform for yourself if you purchased apples at a roadside stand. On the right side of the same sheet list the marketing functions that would not be performed at all.

CHALLENGE PROBLEMS

1. The following article appeared recently in newspapers around the country. Read it carefully, then answer the questions below.

'MIDDLE' GAIN

Washington, D.C. Americans spent some $62 billion for groceries last year—not counting imports and seafoods. Farmers got $21 billion. And $41 billion went to the "middleman" for freezing, canning, transporting, packaging, and selling.

Ten years ago farmers got $20 billion—and the middleman got only $28 billion.

▪ *a.* Approximately what percent of the $62 billion spent for food went to the farmers who produced it? ▪ *b.* About what percent did the middleman get? ▪ *c.* Can the money the middleman got be considered as marketing costs? ▪ *d.* According to the article, what marketing functions did the middleman perform? ▪ *e.* How much did Americans spend for groceries ten years earlier? ▪ *f.* What percent of that amount did the middleman get? ▪ *g.* On the basis of this report, did the percent of the food dollar that went to pay marketing costs increase, decrease, or remain the same over the ten-year period?

2. Some businesses that sell directly to the consumer are known as "discount" stores. People who buy in these stores say they pay "wholesale" prices because the work of the retailer is eliminated. Do these stores actually reduce the cost of marketing the goods they sell? If so, how do they do it? Is it possible that it might cost more in the long run to buy from one of these stores? Why?

CONTENTS OF UNIT 2

Unit 2 / Business and Our Economic System

PART 4 WHY AN ECONOMIC SYSTEM?

PICK up any newspaper today, and you are almost certain to find something in it about our nation's economic system or economy. Why is that such an important topic? Because it concerns us all. How well we live depends on how well our economic system is working. Then is it just another name for business as some people seem to think? No. Business operates within our economic system. Business is a necessary part of it, but only a part nevertheless. Who or what else do you think our economy includes? What is its purpose? How would you describe the role of business?

WHAT IS AN ECONOMIC SYSTEM?

You cannot point to an economic system and say, "There it is." An ***economic system*** is simply the arrangements a nation makes for using its productive resources. A *resource,* as you may know, is a means of doing something. Money is a resource, because it is a means of buying goods or services. Your school is a resource, because it is a means of educating the young people in your community. ***Productive resources*** are the means of producing goods and services. They include natural resources, or the things nature provides. They include labor, or those who do the work. And they include capital, or the man-made things used in production, like tools, machinery, and buildings. The term, productive resources, then, is just another name for the factors of production.

Productive Resources Are Limited

In every nation, ours included, productive resources are limited. Each nation has only so much in the way of natural resources, only so many workers, and only so much capital. This means that the

Courtesy Cities Service Company

amount of goods and services any nation can produce is also limited.

Although resources can be used in different ways, no resource can be used in more than one way at a time. Land can be used to grow food; or it can be the site for an airport, an office building, a park, or a missile launching base. Workers can be employed to make guns, assemble automobiles, or build highways and schools. Factories may be used to produce consumer goods, like TV sets and refrigerators. They may be used to turn out producer goods, such as drill presses or delivery trucks. Or they may be used to produce military equipment, such as rifles and fighter planes.

But land used for growing food cannot also be occupied by an airport or office building. Workers producing guns are not available for assembling automobiles. When the productive resources of a nation are being fully used, therefore, it cannot produce more of anything without producing less of something else. During World War II, as your parents may recall, the production of consumer goods was sharply reduced to free resources needed for the production of war goods.

Courtesy Alberta Government Photograph

Natural resources are limited. Here strip mining has helped to make coal mining more productive and economical.

Human Wants Are Unlimited

In contrast to productive resources, human wants are endless. Even though a person may have all he wants of a few items, the person who has everything he wants is rare. Take yourself as an example. Is there ever a time when you do not want something? No sooner are some wants satisfied than new ones take their place. Many goods that are commonplace today—like automatic washers, food freezers, and air-conditioners—were not available a generation ago. Certain wants—like our desire for food and clothing—can never be fully satisfied. They return again and again. Finally, human wants are without limit because they multiply as the population grows.

Nations Must Economize

Since even the richest nations do not have enough resources to produce everything wanted, all nations must economize. To *economize* with something means to get as much from its use as possible. It is like your not having enough money to buy everything you would like to have. You have to decide which goods and services you will buy. And if you are wise, you try to choose those that will give you the most satisfaction. You may even decide to do entirely without some things in order to have others.

Nations must make similar choices. They must decide how to obtain the greatest possible benefit from their limited resources. This is the function of an economic system.

WHAT DECISIONS ARE MADE THROUGH AN ECONOMIC SYSTEM?

Although different kinds of economic systems are

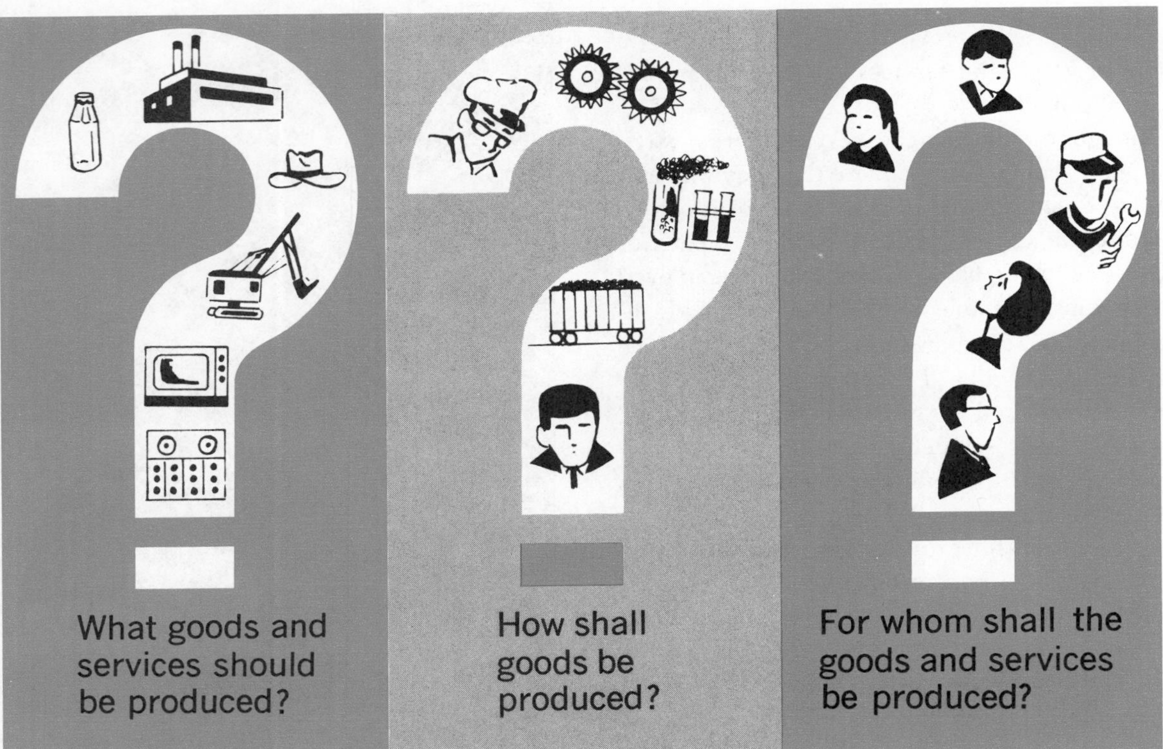
What goods and services should be produced?
How shall goods be produced?
For whom shall the goods and services be produced?

used throughout the world, the decisions made through them are the same. They are:

1. What Goods and Services Shall Be Produced? Because there is a limit to what can be produced, it is important that resources be used for the goods and services wanted most. What these are is one of the decisions a nation makes through its economic system. Should productive resources be used to make automobiles? washing machines? record players? If so, how many of these things should be made? How much of its resources should a nation use for the production of consumer goods? how much for producer goods?

2. How Shall Goods and Services Be Produced? As you learned in Part 2, production is the result of combining labor with natural resources and capital. In almost every kind of production, however, these resources can be combined in more than one way. A producer might use a great deal of capital and only a small amount of labor or the reverse combination—a great deal of labor and little capital.

For example, let us say that your family plans to build a new house. The first step would be to dig an excavation. This could be done by several men working with hand shovels, or by one man operating a power shovel. The second method would use less labor than the first, but more capital. Machinery —in this case a power shovel—would be substituted for some of the labor.

The fewer resources a nation uses in producing any one item, the more goods and services it can produce. Determining the most efficient method of producing goods is one of the tasks of an economic system.

3. How Shall Goods and Services Be Divided? Finally, every nation must decide how the things produced shall be shared. Who will get the cars, the washing machines, and the record players? Who will be left out if there are not enough of these to go around? How many of them will go to the owners of business enterprises? how many to the workers?

These, then, are the decisions every nation, rich and poor alike, must reach through its economic system: what kinds of goods and services to produce and how many? how will these goods and services be produced? and who shall have the goods and services produced?

HOW ARE DECISIONS MADE IN THE UNITED STATES?

Where economic systems differ from one another is in the way choices are made. In some countries the government makes most of or all the decisions. In others the people themselves decide—as consumers, as workers, or as owners of business enterprises. This is the way the majority of decisions are made in the United States.

Consumers Determine What Shall Be Produced

As you have already learned, production takes place in response to demand. In other words, the buying decisions of consumers, business enterprises, and government determine what and how much is produced. Normally most of the goods and services produced in the United States are bought by consumers. Except in wartime, therefore, the question of what to produce is decided mainly on the basis of consumer demand. ***Consumer demand*** refers to the buying done by individuals and families.

Your Purchases Are Economic Votes. For consumers in the United States every day is election day. Each time you make a purchase, it is almost as if you mark a ballot indicating that you favor the production of the good or service you buy. These *economic votes* tell producers what kinds of goods and services and how many of them consumers want. Business responds by producing those things most in demand. In this way consumers influence how the nation's productive resources are used.

Suppose, for example, that Fred Heinz decides to produce and market a waterless window cleaner that he has invented, called ALL-WEATHER CLEANER. He rents an empty garage not far from his home and installs the equipment needed to make the cleaner. For a start Fred orders enough materials to produce about 10,000 cans of cleaner and hires two people to help him. By advertising in the newspaper and over the radio, he tries to create a demand for his product. As part of his sales effort, he distributes free samples. If consumer demand for the cleaner is high enough to cover the cost of its production, more will be produced. And as long as the cleaner continues to be produced, some of the nation's limited resources will be used in its production. Consumer demand for ALL-WEATHER CLEANER will determine how much of our resources will be used in its production.

If consumer demand for the cleaner is too low to cover the cost of producing it, however, its production will be discontinued. Then the workers, materials, and capital no longer needed can be used for the production of other goods.

Consumers Influence the Production of Capital Goods. Capital, or producer goods, are produced in response to the buying decisions of business enterprises. The kinds and amounts of capital goods needed depend on the kinds and amounts of consumer goods demanded. As consumers decide to buy or not to buy ALL-WEATHER CLEANER, for example, they determine how much machinery and other equipment are needed to produce the cleaner.

Business Decides How Goods Are Produced

In the United States business is the major producer of goods and services. This means that business is responsible for using resources efficiently so that as much production as possible results from their use. In most cases, to dig an excavation with hand shovels would be a waste of labor. Using a power shovel instead would free some workers for other kinds of production. Usually the most efficient combination of resources is also the least costly. Because business gains by keeping production costs low, every enterprise strives to combine resources efficiently.

Income Determines How Goods and Services Are Divided

In Part 2 you learned that the results of production are shared through income. How many goods and services a person can buy depends on how much he earns. The question to be decided by the economic system then is: how much should each worker's income be? In general, the amount of a person's income depends on (1) the kind of work he does; (2) the demand for that kind of work; and (3) the number of persons who can perform the same work.

Today scientists and engineers are paid high salaries because they are few in number compared to the demand for their services. The demand for unskilled workers, on the other hand, is small compared to their numbers; therefore, they are paid less. Scientists and engineers, with their greater incomes, can buy more goods and services than unskilled workers.

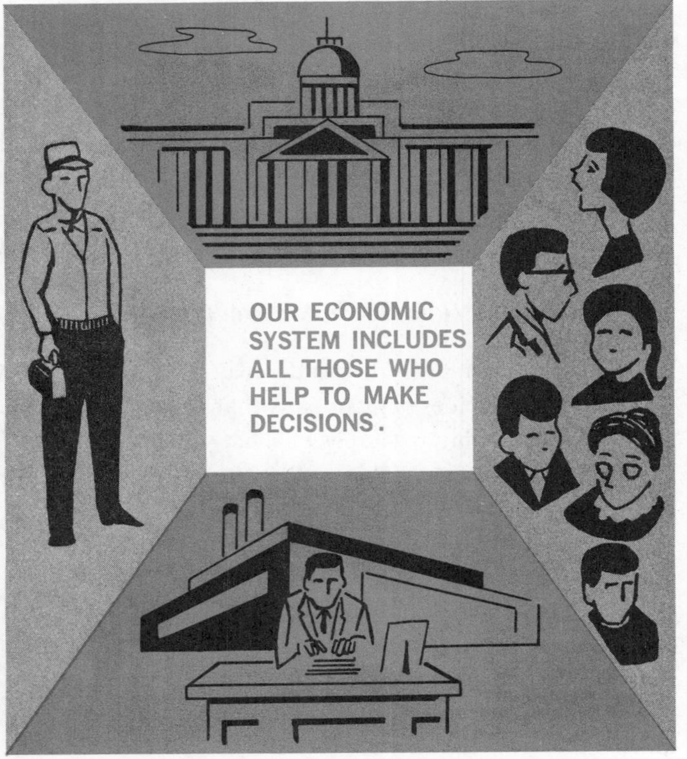

OUR ECONOMIC SYSTEM INCLUDES ALL THOSE WHO HELP TO MAKE DECISIONS.

Economic systems get their names from the way in which the basic decisions are made. A system in which the government makes most of or all the decisions is called a ***planned economy.*** A system like ours, in which individuals and business enterprises are allowed to make their own choices, is called ***free enterprise.*** Under free enterprise consumers are free to save their money or spend it, and to spend it how and where they please. Workers are free to choose their own jobs and to change jobs if they wish. Anyone who has the money to do so can start a business of his own. For the most part, owners of business enterprises are free to decide what to produce and what price to charge for it.

There are some exceptions, of course. The government does not permit the sale of items that might be harmful. Some kinds of business are restricted to conserve productive resources. In certain cases prices are regulated. In other words, even in the United States, some decisions are made by government as you will learn in Part 7. Actually no nation relies entirely on any one method of making economic choices. It is more a matter of which method is used most. The majority of decisions are made by the people individually in our country; but because some are made jointly through government, our economic system is sometimes described as a *mixed economy* or *modified free enterprise.*

Our Economy Is Many Sided

Since an economic system consists of all those responsible for making the necessary decisions, the economy of the United States includes its 9 million business and farm enterprises, its more than 192 million consumers, its 75 million workers, and Federal, state, and local governments.

BUILDING YOUR VOCABULARY

List the figures 1 through 5 on a sheet of paper, numbering down. Read the five statements given below at the right; then, for each statement, select from the column at the left the term that best matches it in meaning. Write this term next to the appropriate number.

consumer demand
economic system
free enterprise
planned economy
productive resources

1. The arrangements a country makes for using its productive resources
2. The means of production; also called the factors of production
3. The buying done by individuals and families
4. A system in which the government makes most economic decisions
5. A system in which individuals and businesses make their own economic decisions

CHECKING YOUR READING

1. Explain the statement that "in every nation productive resources are limited."
2. If a nation's productive resources are being fully used, how can it produce more of a particular item, such as cars or refrigerators?
3. Why must all nations economize?
4. What three basic decisions are made through an economic system?
5. What are some of the questions that must be answered in determining what goods and services will be produced?
6. Explain how productive resources usually can be combined in different ways.
7. How do economic systems differ from one another?
8. How are most economic decisions made in the United States?
9. In this country, who decides what and how much is produced?
10. Explain why every day is election day for consumers in the United States.
11. How do consumers influence the production of capital goods?
12. Who decides how goods are produced in this country?
13. What determines how many goods and services a person can buy?
14. What three things generally determine the amount of a person's income?
15. Why is our economic system sometimes called a mixed economy?

SHARING YOUR OPINION AND EXPERIENCE

1. Does the amount a nation can produce depend entirely on the quantity of its productive resources? Why?
2. Can a nation's productive resources be increased? Explain.
3. Explain the fact that people's wants are satisfied better today than they were formerly.
4. How does the businessman gain by using productive resources efficiently?
5. Do you believe it would be desirable to have most economic decisions made by government? Why?

6. Are you a qualified economic voter? Explain what you think the essential qualifications are.
7. Give an example of a country with a "planned economy."
8. What are the advantages of a free enterprise system to you as an individual?
9. What does it mean to "modify" something?

PROJECTS AND PROBLEMS

1. One reason nations must economize is that natural resources are limited. Few exist in great quantities in any one location. List as many natural resources as you can that are abundant in the state where you live.
2. With your parents' help, make a list of items the typical family wants today that would not have been included in such a want list when your parents were your age. Limit your list to ten items.
3. List five different economic votes you have cast during the past week.
4. On the left half of a sheet of paper, copy the following list of events: water shortage, school dance, population increase, Christmas parade, football game, exploration of outer space, longer paid vacations for workers, a world war, newspaper strike, political campaign. After each one explain briefly how it would affect the operation of our economic system.
5. Facts stated in numbers are called *statistics*. Statistics are often presented in tables. The table below, for example, gives statistics about the gross national product (GNP) of eight countries in a recent year. Using these statistics, answer the questions following the table. Write your answers on a separate sheet of paper.

GROSS NATIONAL PRODUCT FOR EIGHT COUNTRIES

Country	*Gross National Product*	
	Total (billion dollars)	*Per Capita (dollars)*
Federal Republic of Germany	**69**	**1,296**
France	**58**	**1,268**
Ghana	**2**	**225**
Italy	**32**	**645**
Japan	**39**	**416**
Sweden	**12**	**1,631**
United Kingdom	**71**	**1,345**
United States	**505**	**2,817**

▪ *a.* Which of the countries listed had a total gross national product closest to that of the United States? ▪ *b.* How did the gross national product of the Federal Republic of Germany compare with that of the United Kingdom? ▪ *c.* Which country had the smallest gross national product? What reason can you give for its GNP being small? ▪ *d.* The GNP of the United States was approximately how many times the GNP of France? ▪ *e.* What does "per capita" mean? ▪ *f.* Which country had the largest GNP per capita? ▪ *g.* Which country had the second largest GNP per capita? ▪ *h.* Can you always tell from a nation's total GNP whether its GNP per capita is high or low compared to other countries? ▪ *i.* From the information given in the table, which country would you assume had the higher standard of living—France or Sweden? ▪ *j.* Of the countries listed, which would you assume had the highest standard of living? ▪ *k.* In addition to its GNP per capita, what other important factor determines a country's standard of living?

6. Statistical tables are used when it is important that the figures given be fairly exact. When figures are to be compared, however, a graph is sometimes more helpful. The graph you see below is called a *bar graph.* It shows the amount of capital goods provided by different industries for each worker directly engaged in production. Because the bars extend across rather than up and down, it is called a *horizontal* bar graph. The bottom line on the graph is called the base line or horizontal axis. Along this line you will find the dollar amounts. Each division represents $5,000. The upright line on the left side is the vertical axis. Along this line you will find the names of the different industries for which figures are given. By noting the lengths of the bars, you can compare the amount of capital used by one industry with the amount used by another. You can tell almost at a glance, for example, that the chemical industry uses approximately twice the amount of capital per worker as the paper industry.

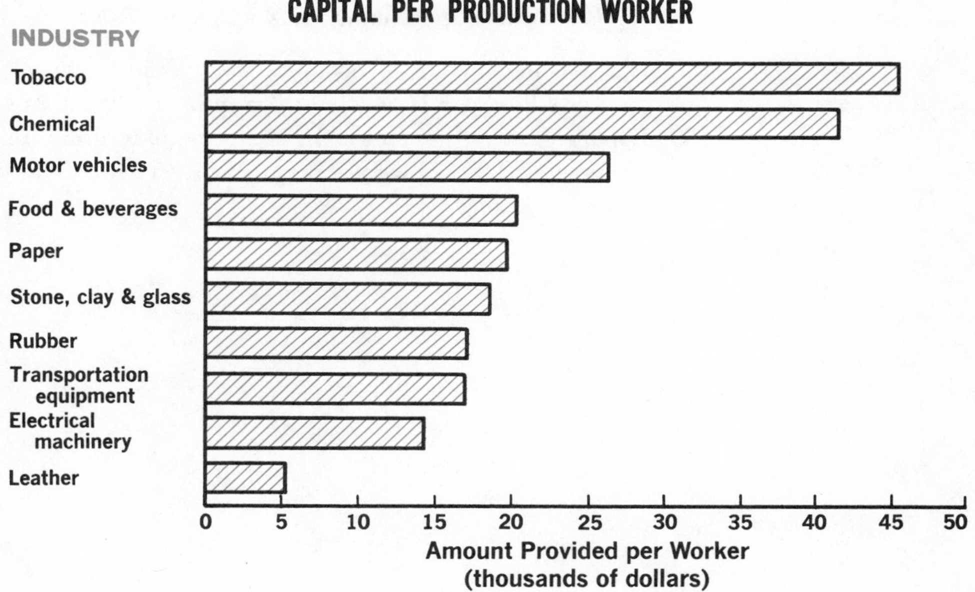

■ *a.* Approximately how much capital (to the nearest $5,000) was provided per worker in each of the following industries: tobacco, motor vehicles, rubber, leather? ■ *b.* Approximately how many times more capital does the rubber industry provide per worker than the leather industry? ■ *c.* The amount of capital per worker in the motor-vehicle industry is approximately what fraction of that for the tobacco industry? ■ *d.* In what two industries was the capital per worker most nearly identical?

7. Bring to class three or four items from recent newspapers or magazines that pertain to our economic system. If they do not mention our economic system specifically, explain why you think they pertain to it.

CHALLENGE PROBLEMS

1. In an economic system where individuals are free to make their own decisions, the ability to distinguish between fact and opinion is important. A fact is an actual truth. An opinion is simply a belief or viewpoint about a person or thing that is open to question. Your opinions, as a rule, are formed by your experiences. Which of the following statements would you say are fact and which are opinion? Be prepared to defend your answers.

   ■ *a.* Some farm enterprises do not engage in food production. ■ *b.* People were better off when families were self-sufficient. ■ *c.* If middlemen were eliminated, the cost of marketing goods would be reduced. ■ *d.* Goods sold door to door cost more than those bought in a retail store. ■ *e.* It is the consumer who pays the cost of advertising. ■ *f.* Some nations have a greater quantity of productive resources than other nations. ■ g. In a planned economy resources are used more efficiently than in a free enterprise system. ■ *h.* The use of machines in production tends to reduce the number of workers needed.

2. Is a person's income always directly related to the value society receives from the work he does? How would you measure "value to society"?
3. Explain how two school-equipment manufacturers might combine productive resources in different ways as they make such items as the desks, chairs, and tables in your classroom.

PART 5 CHARACTERISTICS OF OUR FREE ENTERPRISE SYSTEM

IT is easy to see how a planned economy works. A committee appointed by the government decides what is to be produced and how it is to be produced. Resources are then assigned to the production of these goods and services. Producers simply carry out the orders of the planning committee. The mystery is how an economic system in which everyone helps to make the decisions can work at all. What assurance is there that anyone will produce the goods and services wanted? What is to prevent owners of business enterprises from turning out poor quality goods and charging far more than they are worth?

Yet our economic system not only works, it operates with amazing efficiency. Without prodding, people start enterprises of their own at the rate of about half a million each year. In general, the goods and services wanted are available at reasonable prices when and where they are wanted. And if there is anything mysterious about it, it is only the fact that the forces responsible for the system's operation are unseen. These unseen forces are essential characteristics of a free enterprise system. One of them is freedom, or the right of individuals to make their own economic choices. What do you think the others might be?

THE MEANS OF PRODUCTION ARE PRIVATELY OWNED

One distinguishing mark of a free enterprise system is that it permits individuals to own property of almost any kind. Anything owned by an individual is ***private property.*** Your clothes, books, records, and anything else that belongs to you are your private property. In some countries personal belongings of this kind are all that individuals may own. Other forms of property, like natural resources

Courtesy Mac Brown

and capital goods, belong to the government. Under such a system no one could operate his own enterprise unless the government rented him the land, buildings, and necessary equipment. This gives the government control over what is produced. In fact, a government can control production pretty well just by owning the natural resources of a country and the essential industries like steel, transportation, communications, and electric power.

In the United States not only capital goods, like factories and machinery, but even such resources as land, forests, coal, and natural gas may be privately owned. More than that, the owner of property has the right to use it in just about any way he pleases. He may put it to work earning an income. He may lease or sell it to others, or he can give it away. These property rights are protected by law. They enable anyone wanting to go into business for himself to do so, provided he has the money. As a result, the business enterprises that produce 90 percent of our goods and services are privately owned. This is why our economy is sometimes called a ***private enterprise*** system.

PROFIT IS NECESSARY FOR FREE ENTERPRISE

The right of private property makes it possible for individuals to go into business. Profit provides a reason for doing so. ***Profit*** is the difference between what a business earns and what it costs that business to operate.

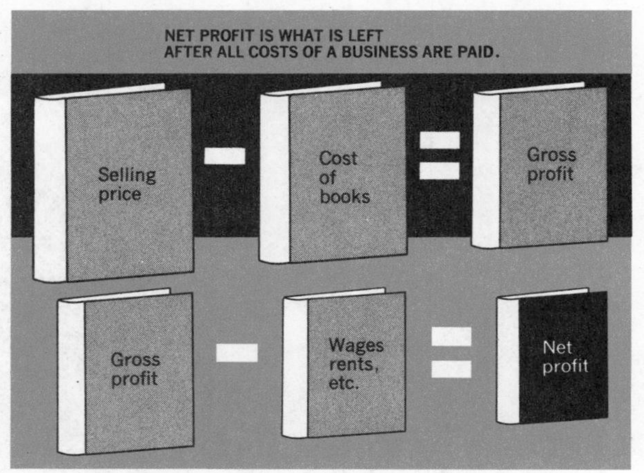

Suppose, for example, that you owned a retail bookstore. You buy books from several publishers at wholesale prices, and you sell them at retail prices. Let us say that the dictionaries you sell for $5 cost you $4.10; the cookbooks you sell for $3.95 cost you $3.25, and so on. The difference between what the books cost you and what you get for them is *gross profit.* But the books are only one of your costs. In addition you would have to pay the rent for the store, the wages of employees, and the bills for heat, light, and advertising. Your true, or *net profit,* is what remains after all costs are paid. Something else to be considered in estimating the amount of your profit is your own wages or salary. A profitable business is one that returns to its owner *more* than he could earn by working for someone else.

What Profits Do

Of all the characteristics of a free enterprise system, profit is probably the least understood. Yet profits perform important functions that benefit everyone in some way.

Profits Encourage Risk Taking. Although free enterprise gives individuals the right to go into business, it does not guarantee the success of any enterprise. Persons who go into business do so at their own risk. The owner of a new business cannot be certain that anyone will buy what he plans to sell. Even for the owner of an established enterprise there is always the possibility that consumers will switch their demand to a new product.

If a business fails, its owner may lose all or part of the money he has put into it. He also will be out the money he might have earned working for someone else. If people are to take this risk, they must be encouraged by the hope of some reward for success. In a free enterprise system, profit is the reward for risk taking.

Profits Direct Production. Profits also help to determine how materials, labor, and capital are used. In order to make a profit, a business must produce a good or service that consumers are willing to buy. Thus, the desire for profits forces business to produce those things most in demand. If consumers lose interest in a product and no longer purchase it, the resources used in its production are soon shifted to new or more profitable uses.

COMPETITION REGULATES FREE ENTERPRISE

When people are free to choose their own lines of business, some make identical choices. This naturally leads to ***competition.*** You know what competition is, of course. The boys in your school compete with one another for positions on the football and basketball teams. Your teams in turn compete with teams from other schools. The object of each team is to outdo its rivals.

Enterprises producing similar goods or services for the same customers also try to outdo one another in some way. One way is to sell at a lower price. This is known as *price competition.* The producer who charges more than his competitors may find himself at a disadvantage. This kind of competition benefits consumers by holding prices down.

Producers also engage in *product competition;* that is, each producer tries to make his product different or in some way better than competing products. This kind of rivalry encourages producers to improve their products and to develop new ones. For the consumer, of course, this means not only better goods and services but a greater variety as well.

Sometimes competition is only a matter of advertising or sales promotion. The trading stamps so popular in many places today are an example of this kind of competition. Producers may also offer buyers extra services like credit and delivery.

Competition Promotes Efficiency

Just as profit helps to determine what is produced, competition among producers determines how goods and services are produced. Price competition, you see, is not restricted to consumer goods. It also regulates the prices of raw materials, labor, and capital goods. In most cases a producer has to pay as much as his competitors for these things. This two-sided competition forces business firms to produce efficiently. The more efficient a producer is, the less he needs to charge for his goods or services to make a profit.

The inefficient producer, on the other hand, cannot charge higher prices than his efficient competitors without losing customers. Neither can he pay less for workers and materials. He must either improve his production methods or go out of business. Thus, efficient production benefits the nation by conserving productive resources.

Competition Varies

Most producers operate under competition but not always the same kind or amount. Some firms compete only with other firms that make or sell identical products. Others compete in addition with producers of substitute goods or services. Movie theaters compete with other movie theaters; but they also compete with television, skating rinks, bowling alleys, sporting events, and other forms of entertainment. Railroads compete with airlines, bus lines, and trucking companies. Plastics compete with metals, and steel competes with aluminum.

A few types of business, on the other hand, are protected from competition by the government. In return for this protection their prices are also regulated by the government. More will be said about this in Part 7.

IT IS AN INTERDEPENDENT SYSTEM

Freedom, private property, profit, and competition are the forces that enable a free enterprise system to operate. Any economic system in which workers, business firms, and regions specialize, however, has another characteristic. It is ***interdependence.***

The advantage of specialization is that it enables us to produce more than we could otherwise. Goods are produced faster when each worker does the kind of work he can do best. No time is lost changing from one job to another. Furthermore, performing the same task over and over again increases a worker's skill. But specialization also makes us interdependent. Workers in the city depend on farmers for food and other agricultural products. Farmers depend on city workers to produce the machinery, furniture, cars, and clothes they need. Business enterprises not only depend on one another, but they also depend on consumers to buy what has been produced. Consumers depend on business for goods and services; and workers depend on business for jobs. One region of the country depends on other regions for goods that it cannot produce or cannot produce efficiently.

Because of this interdependence, what happens in one part of the economic system may affect other parts or even the entire system. A strike among steel workers, for example, could halt the production of automobiles, household appliances, and dozens of other products made of steel, leaving hundreds of workers without jobs and incomes. In time the jobs and incomes of other workers would also be affected.

The stores in this shopping center offer many similar goods. They must therefore compete for the customers' business not only pricewise but also qualitywise.

Courtesy Sears, Roebuck and Co.

BUSINESS HAS UPS AND DOWNS

No economic system works perfectly all the time under all circumstances, and ours is no exception. Business activity does not remain at a constant level. Instead it moves up and down something like this. In other words total income, production,

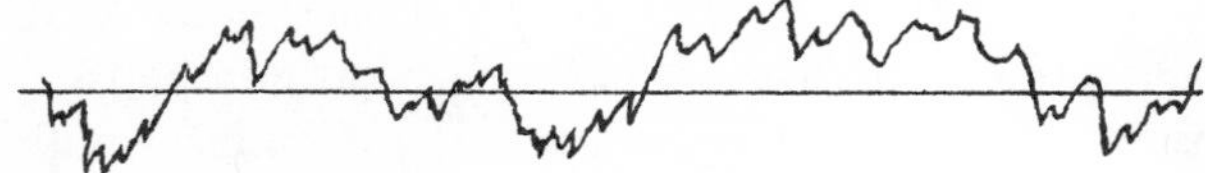

and employment rise and fall. These changes do not follow any regular pattern. An upswing or downswing may be long or short as shown by the illustration. It may occur in only one kind of production, like construction or manufacturing. Or it may involve all kinds. Because of the interdependent nature of our economy, however, a change in any direction tends to spread.

Suppose, for example, that the demand for new automobiles slows down for some reason. The production of automobiles will then be reduced. Some automobile workers might be laid off. Or they might work fewer hours. In either case they would have less income to spend than before. They would spend only for things they had to have, like food and clothing. They would put off buying things like new refrigerators, stoves, and TV sets. Production of these things would then slow down. More workers might lose their jobs and all or part of their incomes. Total spending would again be reduced. The merchants with whom these workers traded would then find their incomes dropping, and they would spend less. Thus, total spending, production, and income would continue to go

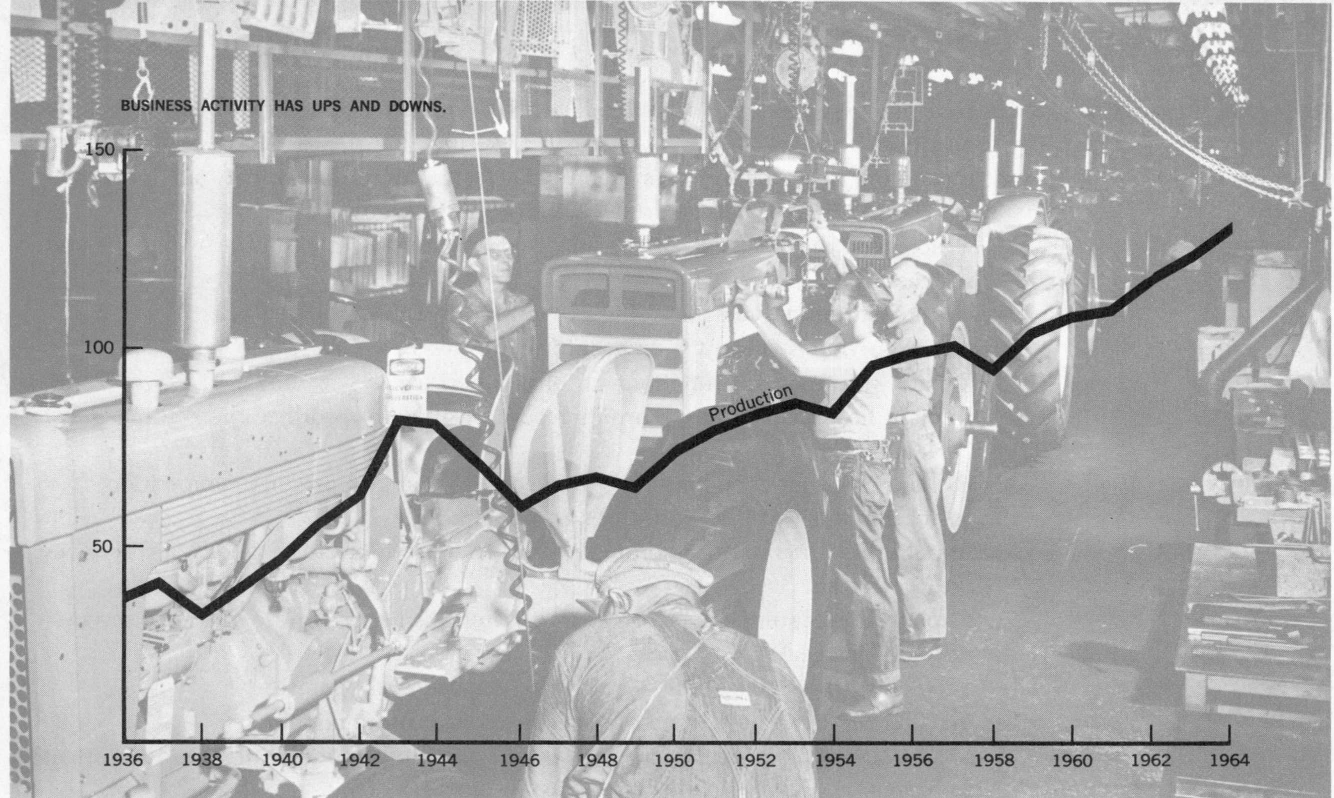

Ewing Galloway

down and down. A slump in business activity is called a ***recession.*** But when a recession is widespread and long lasting, it is called a ***depression.***

A rise in business activity can also spread. An increase in the demand for goods and services can push production and incomes to higher and higher levels. A period when business activity is rising is called ***prosperity.***

There is no simple explanation of why these changes in business activity occur. But they have been a part of our economy from the beginning. Not to include them among its characteristics would create a false impression of our economic system.

BUILDING YOUR VOCABULARY

Copy the eight sentences below, completing each one by replacing the question mark with the appropriate term from the column at the left.

competition
depression
interdependence
private enterprise
private property
profit
prosperity
recession

1. Anything owned by an individual is ? .
2. An economy in which the majority of businesses are privately owned is a ? system.
3. The difference between what a business earns and what it costs that business to operate is ? .
4. Rivalry between two or more businesses is ? .
5. Specialization among workers, business firms, or regions results in ? .
6. A slump in business activity is a ? .
7. A widespread and long-lasting slump in business activity is a ? .
8. A period when business activity is rising is ? .

CHECKING YOUR READING

1. In a planned economy, who decides what will be produced and how it will be produced?
2. Under our free enterprise system, what kinds of property may an individual own? What may a person do with the property he owns?
3. Who owns the business enterprises that produce 90 percent of our goods and services?
4. Explain the difference between gross profit and net profit.
5. Describe what is meant by a profitable business.
6. What two important functions do profits perform?
7. Explain how the desire for profits forces business to produce those things most in demand.
8. Explain the difference between price competition and product competition.
9. In what other ways do businesses compete?
10. Explain how competition among producers determines how goods and services are produced.
11. Explain how competition may exist among businesses whose goods or services are not identical.
12. What four forces enable a free enterprise system to operate?
13. What is the main advantage of specialization in production?
14. Why does an upswing or a downswing in one kind of production tend to spread to others?

SHARING YOUR OPINION AND EXPERIENCE

1. What is the meaning of the statement that "property rights are protected by law"?
2. A profitable business is one that returns to its owner *more* than he could earn by working for someone else. According to this definition, many businesses operating today would not be considered profitable. Explain why you think their owners continue to run them.
3. Do you believe that profits should be limited in some way? Why or why not?
4. Why is our economy sometimes described as a "profit and loss" system?
5. Many businesses lose money and are forced to close every year. Who is affected by these failures? How are they affected?
6. It has been said that, when business produces as great a variety of goods and services as we have in the United States, all producers compete for a share of the consumer's dollar. Explain.
7. One characteristic of our free enterprise system is that it permits individuals to own property of almost any kind. What forms of property in the United States may *not* be privately owned?

PROJECTS AND PROBLEMS

1. Bill Washington's father operates a small shoe store. He employs one salesperson to help him. On a separate sheet of paper list the costs that Mr. Washington has in addition to the cost of the shoes themselves. Limit your list to eight items.

2. On a separate sheet of paper list eight pairs of different though related products that compete with each other; *example: butter and margarine.*
3. Sometimes advertising campaigns are so successful that all products of a particular kind become known by the name of one brand of the product. For example, many people call all transparent tape Scotch Tape, which is a particular brand of this kind of tape. Make a list of other products that are incorrectly identified in this way.
4. Product competition often is reflected in the advertisements of competing firms. Make a careful study of television, radio, newspaper, and magazine advertisements, and then list at least five advertising slogans that emphasize new or improved features of a product; *example: "Buy Double X gasoline with the new, improved formula."*
5. In an interdependent economic system, what happens in one industry may affect many businesses in other industries. List six types of businesses that would be greatly affected if aluminum producers suddenly went out of business; *example: manufacturers of cookware.*
6. A frequently used term in business is *percent.* For example, on page 36 of this book it says "the business enterprises that produce 90 percent of our goods and services are privately owned." The term *percent,* you will remember, means *per* 100 or *parts* of 100. In other words, 90 percent means 90 out of 100, or $\frac{90}{100}$. Thus, the statement in the text means that privately owned business enterprises produce $90 worth of goods and services out of every $100 worth produced.

   Another way of writing percent, of course, is with the symbol %; that is, 90 percent may also be written 90%. Or a percent value may be expressed as a decimal in which case 90 percent would be written .90. To change a percent value to a decimal, you simply move the decimal point two places to the left and drop the % sign. To change a decimal to a percent value, you do just the opposite. Move the decimal point two places to the right and add the percent sign. For example:

   .15 = 15% .007 = .7% 3 = 300% .4 = 40% 1.35 = 135% .015 = 1.5%

   Increase your skill in changing decimals to percent values by writing each of the following as a percent.

(*a*) **.05**	(*b*) **.09**	(*c*) **.013**	(*d*) **.352**	(*e*) **.6**	(*f*) **.1**
(*g*) **2**	(*h*) **9**	(*i*) **4.62**	(*j*) **1.25**	(*k*) **.0175**	(*l*) **.0003**

7. To know the amount of profit a business earns is meaningless unless you also know the size of the business. What amounts to a big profit for a barbershop would be a very small profit for an automobile manufacturer. For this reason profit is often stated as a percent. For example, net profit may be expressed as a percent of sales. To find what percent one number is of another, you divide. To find what percent profit is of sales, you divide the amount of sales into the amount of net profit.

▪ *a.* A manufacturing firm recently reported a net profit of $2,304,000 based on sales of $53,691,000. To the nearest whole percent, what was the firm's profit stated as a percent of sales? ▪ *b.* To tell how well a particular firm is doing, you compare its percent of profit with that for other firms of the same kind. If the average profit for all manufacturing firms of this kind is 3 percent, how well did this company do?

CHALLENGE PROBLEMS

1. Tables may be used to present statistics that compare one period of time with another. For example, the table below gives economic statistics for the United States for the 30-year period from 1930 to 1960. Study the table and answer the questions that follow it.

ECONOMIC STATISTICS FOR THE UNITED STATES—1930–1960

	1930	*1940*	*1950*	*1960*
Population	**123,188,000**	**132,122,000**	**151,683,000**	**179,323,175**
Gross national product	**$91,100,000,000**	**$100,600,000,000**	**$284,600,000,000**	**$502,600,000,000**
Size of labor force	**50,080,000**	**56,180,000**	**64,749,000**	**73,126,000**
Number of unemployed	**4,340,000**	**8,120,000**	**3,350,000**	**3,931,000**
Income per person (after taxes)	**$604**	**$576**	**$1,369**	**$1,947**
Spending by Federal government	**$ 3,440,269,000**	**$ 9,062,032,000**	**$ 39,617,003,000**	**$ 76,539,000,000**

▪ *a.* What was the increase in population between 1930 and 1960? ▪ *b.* During which 10-year period did the gross national product increase most? ▪ *c.* During which 10-year period did spending by the Federal government increase most? ▪ *d.* Government spending in 1950 was approximately how many times as great as it was in 1940? ▪ *e.* During what year was the number of workers without jobs the highest? ▪ *f.* During which period did personal income after taxes drop? ▪ *g.* What rose sharply during the same period in which personal income dropped? Explain what you think the relationship might be between these two facts. ▪ *h.* During what year was the proportion of the population in the labor force greatest?

2. If profit is the reward for risk taking, profit expectations should be highest when risk is greatest. List five types of business in which risks (and profit expectations) are greater than those in most businesses.

PART 6
HOW BUSINESS ENTERPRISES ARE ORGANIZED

AS you already know, the economic system of the United States includes business enterprises of all sizes. They range from the one-man firm that occupies no more space than a hole in the wall to giant automobile factories, steel plants, and oil refineries. Whether a business is large or small, however, it must follow some plan of organization. The organization of a business involves such matters as *who owns it? who makes the decisions?* and *who gets the profits?* Since no one type of organization is best for every kind of enterprise, four different plans are used. How many of them do you know? How might the size of a business influence the way it is organized?

WHAT DETERMINES THE SIZE OF A BUSINESS?

In general, the size of a business is determined by the kind of goods or services it produces. Some goods can be produced most efficiently in large quantities. This is known as ***mass production.*** Because of mass production automobiles are turned out at prices low enough so that most consumers can buy them. But mass production—whether of automobiles, washing machines, or television sets—involves the use of complicated machinery, which may cost thousands or even millions of dollars. Only a big business can raise the funds needed to purchase such machinery.

When goods are produced on a large scale, the market for them must, of course, be equally large. Automobiles, petroleum products, paper, steel, and household appliances are sold nationwide. Businesses like repair shops, barbershops, and hardware stores, on the other hand, depend mostly on the local community for customers. They need be only big enough to meet the demand for their goods and services.

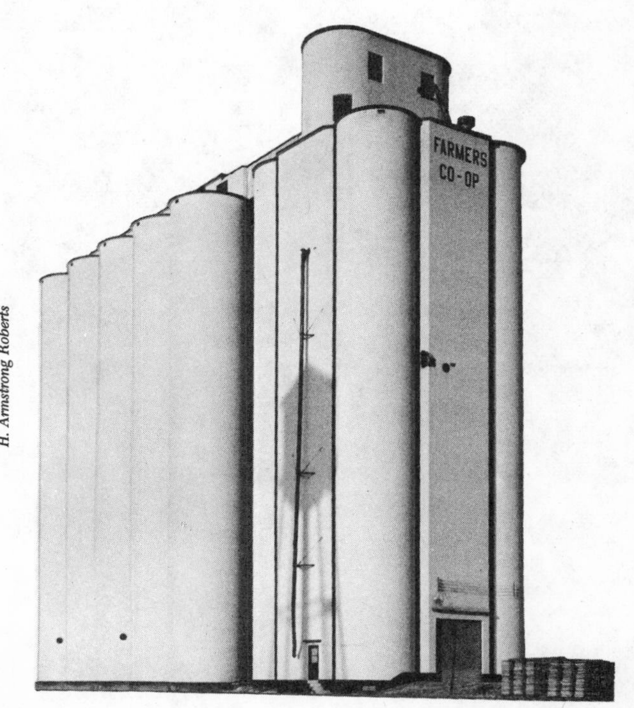

H. Armstrong Roberts

To a considerable extent, the size of a business also determines the way it is organized. Most businesses are individual proprietorships; some are partnerships; some are corporations; and a few are cooperatives.

MOST BUSINESSES ARE INDIVIDUAL PROPRIETORSHIPS

In spite of the growth in big business during the last one hundred years, opportunities for an individual to go into business for himself are as numerous as ever. One person in business for himself is an ***individual proprietorship.*** Individual proprietorships are most common among retail stores and service enterprises such as repair shops, barbershops and beauty shops, and laundry and dry-cleaning establishments. Most farms are individual proprietorships. In fact, the majority of enterprises in this country are the one-owner type.

Advantages of a One-Owner Business

Mary Davies is the owner of an individual proprietorship called Mary's Card and Gift Shop. Ask Mary the advantages of this form of organization and here is what she will tell you. An individual proprietorship is easy to start and suited to enterprises that require only small amounts of money capital. It gives the person with ideas and ability a chance to be his own boss. This is extremely important in a free enterprise system. As sole owner of Mary's Card and Gift Shop, Miss Davies makes all decisions and is entitled to all profits. She may sell out or quit at any time.

Disadvantages of a One-Owner Business

Miss Davies can also tell you some of the drawbacks of an individual proprietorship. Its success depends on the business judgment of its owner. Many small enterprises of this kind fail because their owners do not know how to run a business.

This attractive gift shop is operated as a sole proprietorship.

Courtesy Mary Davies

Another common reason for failure is too little money capital. A single owner may not have the money to keep an enterprise operating when business is poor. As the owner of an individual proprietorship, Miss Davies takes all risks. If the shop should fail, she is responsible for all its debts. If necessary, her personal property—such as her home, car, and savings—can be claimed in payment for these debts. This is known as *unlimited liability.*

A PARTNERSHIP HAS TWO OR MORE OWNERS

Across the street from Mary's Card and Gift Shop is Krause and Daily Clothiers, a business organized as a partnership. A ***partnership*** is much like an individual proprietorship except that it has two or more owners.

A partnership may be formed by verbal agreement, but it is more businesslike if the agreement is in writing. When Ben Krause and Sam Daily first decided to go into business together, they consulted a lawyer. The lawyer helped them draw up a written agreement called *articles of copartnership.* This agreement stated how much money each partner was to provide; what the responsibilities of each would be; and how the profits were to be divided.

ARTICLES OF COPARTNERSHIP

a. *Date*	This agreement made and entered into this (current) day of (current month & year)19--, between Benjamin Krause and Samuel Daily of Centerville, U.S.A.
b. *Identity of partners*	Witnesseth:
1. *Nature of the business*	**One.** The parties Benjamin Krause and Samuel Daily agree to become partners in the operation of a clothing store
2. *Name and location of firm*	**Two.** The business of the partnership shall be conducted under the firm name of Krause and Daily Clothiers on Main Street in Centerville, U.S.A.
3. *Duration of partnership*	**Three.** The partnership shall begin on date this agreement is executed and shall continue for a term of five years.
4. *Investment of partners*	**Four.** Benjamin Krause shall contribute to the capital of the partnership the sum of thirty thousand dollars ($30,000) and Samuel Daily the sum of fifteen thousand dollars ($15,000). These contributions shall be without interest.
5. *Sharing of profits and losses*	**Five.** All profits resulting from the business shall be divided in proportion to their investments; Krause, two-thirds , and Daily, one-third. All losses incurred by the business shall be borne by them in similar ratio.
6. *Accounts of business*	**Six.** Proper books of account shall be kept of all transactions relating to the business of the partnership. At the end of each calendar year, a full inventory shall be prepared; a statement of the business made; the books closed; and the account of each partner credited or debited, as the case may be, with his proportionate share of the net profit or the net loss. A statement of the business may be made at such other time as the partners agree on.
7. *Partners' drawings*	**Seven.** Each partner may draw from the business, for his own use, a sum not to exceed $400 a month, to be withdrawn at such times as he may choose.
8. *Duties of partners*	**Eight.** During the continuance of this partnership, each partner agrees to devote his entire time and attention to the business and to engage in no other business enterprise without the written consent of the other. Benjamin Krause is to be in charge of accounting operations and Samuel Daily is to be in charge of buying and selling operations.
9. *Restraints on partners*	**Nine.** Neither party shall, without the written consent of the other, become surety or bondsman for anyone.
10. *Termination of partnership*	**Ten.** At the termination of this partnership, a full inventory and balance sheet shall be prepared; the debts of the business shall be discharged; and all property then remaining shall be divided between the partners in the ratio that each partner's capital account bears to the total at the time of the termination of the partnership.

In witness whereof, the parties have hereunto set their hands and seals the day and year first above written.

In the presence of James Lamb — Benjamin Krause (seal)
Hugh Benson — Samuel Daily (seal)

Articles of copartnership

Krause, on the other hand, is an expert accountant. He keeps all records, makes up the payroll, and looks after the many details of running the store. Together they do very well.

Disadvantages of a Partnership

As Mr. Krause and Mr. Daily would be quick to point out, a partnership also has disadvantages. Should the business fail, each partner can be held personally responsible for all unpaid debts, if the other cannot pay his share. In other words, each partner has *unlimited liability,* the same as if he were the sole owner. Furthermore, unless the rights of each owner are limited by the partnership agreement, either partner may act on behalf of the enterprise. If all partners possess sound judgment, this may not be serious. But an unwise decision on the part of one owner could work a hardship on the other. For these reasons, say Mr. Krause and Mr. Daily, it is most important for anyone considering a partnership business to choose his partners carefully.

Although there is no limit to the number of partners a business may have, too many could be a disadvantage. Yet one of the most famous partnerships of all time, the brokerage firm of Merrill Lynch, Pierce, Fenner and Beane, had 112 partners. This firm now operates as a corporation under the name of Merrill Lynch, Pierce, Fenner and Smith.

A CORPORATION IS OWNED BY ITS STOCKHOLDERS

Few individuals or even partnerships could raise the money needed to start an airline, a chain of grocery stores, or a steel plant. For a business requiring a great deal of money capital, the ideal plan of organization is the ***corporation.*** A corporation may have any number of owners. General Motors, the largest manufacturing enterprise in the United States, has more than a million. The Centerville Brick and Tile Company has 300. They became owners by purchasing stock in the enterprise. They are its ***stockholders.*** In the United States 20 million people are part owners, or stockholders, in business enterprises.

Mr. Carpenter, president of the Centerville Brick and Tile Company, likes to tell how it was started. The idea of constructing a brick plant began with a group of contractors and building-supply dealers in Centerville and neighboring towns. They found that to acquire the land; build the buildings; buy the kilns, shale planer, grinding equipment, and other things needed would cost around $2,500,000. Each of the men was willing to provide part of the money; but all of them together did not have $2,500,000. The group then decided to form a corporation and raise the money by selling shares of stock.

The plan for incorporating was drawn up with the aid of a lawyer and sent to the proper state official with a request for a charter. A corporation must be chartered by the state in which it is located.* The charter specifies what types of business the corporation may engage in and how many shares of stock it can issue. It was agreed that ownership of the Brick and Tile Company would be divided into 250,000 shares to be sold at $10 a share. The members of the organizing group bought over half the shares. Mr. Carpenter bought 2,500 shares for which he paid $25,000. Thus, he owned one percent of the corporation. The remaining shares of stock were sold to local businessmen who saw the value of having a large, new industry in the community.

How Is a Corporation Managed?

One way a corporation differs from both individual proprietorships and partnerships is in its management. In any kind of business important decisions have to be made daily. Someone must decide how many goods are to be produced and how they are to be produced. Someone must decide what quantity of raw materials to order. Someone must decide when, where, and how much to advertise. Someone must hire and supervise workers. In every firm the person or persons who make these decisions and provide the leadership are its ***management.***

The owners of individual proprietorships and partnerships usually manage their own enterprises. But in a corporation every stockholder is a part owner, and one corporation may have hundreds or thousands of stockholders. In addition, each stockholder is free to sell some of or all his stock at any time. This means that the ownership of a corporation may change frequently. In most cases, therefore, it would be impractical for all owners of a corporation to participate directly in its management. Instead they meet once a year to vote on matters of general policy and to elect a board of directors to represent them. Each stockholder is

* Some banks obtain their charters from the Federal government.

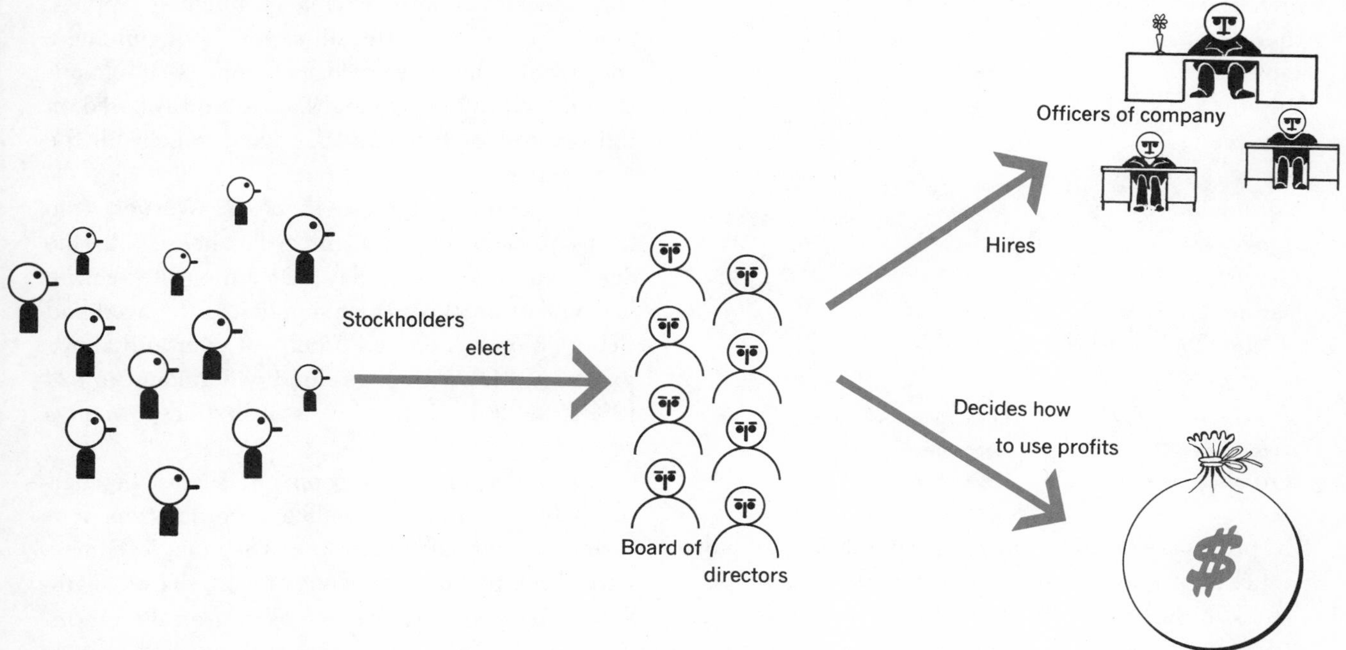

allowed as many votes as he owns shares of stock. Mr. Carpenter, with his 2,500 shares in the Centerville Brick and Tile Company, is entitled to 2,500 votes.

The board of directors appoints officers—a president, vice-president, secretary, etc.—to manage the business. The management is then responsible to the board of directors. It is not necessary for an officer of a corporation to be a stockholder. Neither is it necessary for a stockholder to vote or to take an active interest in the business.

How Are Corporation Profits Divided?

The board of directors of a corporation also decides how the profits shall be used. Last year the Centerville Brick and Tile Company earned a profit of $300,000. More than half of this amount went for Federal and state income taxes. The board voted to distribute $87,500 of the remaining profits to the stockholders. This amounted to 35 cents a share. A payment of this kind is called a ***dividend.*** For his 2,500 shares Mr. Carpenter received dividends for a total amount of $875 for the year.

The Centerville Brick and Tile Company, like most corporations, does not distribute all its profits after taxes to its stockholders. Some are kept to help replace worn-out equipment or to improve the business in other ways. Last year, for example, a portion of the profits was used to buy an additional shovel and dragline.

A Corporation Has Advantages and Disadvantages

The chief advantage of a corporation, of course, is that it provides a way to raise large amounts of money capital. Another advantage is that the owners' responsibilities are limited if the business fails; that is, they can lose only the money they paid for their stock. No claim can be made on their personal property. In other words, the owners of a corporation have *limited liability.* It is for this reason that small firms sometimes organize as corporations.

The main disadvantage of the corporation is that

CORPORATIONS ARE RESPONSIBLE FOR THE LARGEST SHARE OF PRODUCTION, EVEN THOUGH THEY ARE NOT SO NUMEROUS AS INDIVIDUAL PROPRIETORSHIPS.

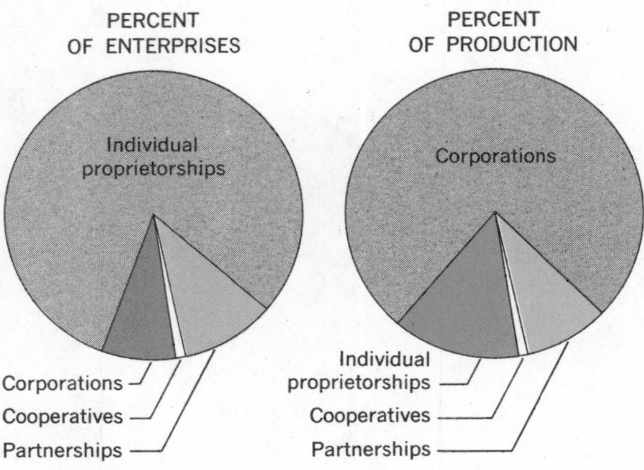

its profits are taxed twice. The corporation must pay a tax on profits before they are divided among the stockholders. Then the stockholders are required to pay a tax again on the share of the profits they receive as dividends.

COOPERATIVES ARE OWNED BY THEIR CUSTOMERS

A very small number of businesses in the United States are organized as cooperatives. A ***cooperative*** is an enterprise owned by its customers. The Seed and Feed Co-op is such an enterprise. Like the Centerville Brick and Tile Company, the Seed and Feed Co-op has many owners. All are farmers who live in the area around Centerville. This business, however, was not organized to make a profit by selling goods to others. Its purpose is to save the owners money on the things they buy. The Seed and Feed Co-op carries such items as fertilizer, seed, stock feed, farm machinery, building supplies, and insect sprays. After all expenses of running a cooperative have been paid, any money that remains is refunded to the owners. This refund is based on the amount of business they have done with the cooperative.

For example, suppose that Mr. Warner, who farms just outside of Centerville, belongs to the Seed and Feed Co-op. Say that during the year he has bought $800 worth of supplies. If the Seed and Feed Co-op has earned 3 percent over and above expenses, Mr. Warner's refund will amount to $24 (3% × $800 = $24). This is called a *patronage refund.*

Like a corporation, a cooperative must be chartered by the state. And, like a corporation, it is formed by the sale of stock. Anyone may become a part owner by purchasing one or more shares. Shareholders in a cooperative, however, are called *members.* Usually the membership is made up of a group of people with the same needs and interests. They elect a board of directors, which in turn appoints a manager. But unlike stockholders in a corporation, each member has only one vote regardless of the number of shares he owns.

Cooperatives are organized for many purposes: to provide insurance protection, medical care, electric power, and to lend money. Food stores, bookstores, apartment buildings, housing developments, service stations, and restaurants are examples of cooperative businesses. Not all businesses that operate as cooperatives, however, call themselves cooperatives. In some parts of Europe cooperative enterprises are numerous. The fact that there are so few of them in the United States could mean that people feel the prices charged by profit-making enterprises are not unreasonable.

BUILDING YOUR VOCABULARY

List the figures 1 to 8 on a sheet of paper, numbering down. Read the eight statements given below at the right; then, for each statement, select from the column at the left the term that best matches it in meaning. Write this term next to the appropriate number.

cooperative	1. The manufacture of goods in very large quantities
corporation	2. A one-owner business
dividend	3. A business in which two or more owners share both the profits and risks
individual proprietorship	4. A business organization in which the liability of the owners is limited
management	5. The owners of a corporation
mass production	6. A share of corporation profits paid to the owners of the corporation
partnership	7. The person or persons in a business who make major decisions and provide the leadership
stockholders	8. A business enterprise owned by its customers

CHECKING YOUR READING

1. What usually determines the size of a business?
2. What are four types of business organization in this country? Which type is the most numerous? Which type is used least?
3. Among what kinds of businesses are individual proprietorships most common?
4. What are the main advantages of an individual proprietorship?
5. Name three disadvantages of an individual proprietorship.
6. What does "unlimited liability" mean?
7. What is the chief difference between an individual proprietorship and a partnership?
8. What are some of the advantages of a partnership over an individual proprietorship?
9. Why is it so important to choose partners carefully before forming a partnership?
10. What type of organization is best for a business that requires large amounts of money capital?
11. Who manages a corporation? How are they selected?
12. Explain how corporation profits are divided.
13. If a corporation fails, how much can each owner lose? How does this differ from an individual proprietorship? a partnership?
14. In what way does the purpose of a cooperative differ from that of other types of businesses?
15. How do the members of a cooperative share in its earnings?
16. In what ways is a cooperative like a corporation? In what important way does it differ from a corporation?

SHARING YOUR OPINION AND EXPERIENCE

1. Why is it possible for a big business to produce some goods more cheaply than a small business could produce them?
2. Most professional people, such as lawyers, dentists, architects, and physicians, do business as individual proprietorships or partnerships. Why do you suppose they use these types of organization?
3. According to the partnership agreement of Krause and Daily Clothiers, Mr. Krause's share of the profits or losses of their business is two-thirds; and Mr. Daily's share is one-third. Why do you think they are divided this way?
4. Sometimes a member of a partnership may transfer ownership of such property as his home and car to his wife or relatives. What might he hope to accomplish by such a step?
5. When you buy something from a business, does it make any difference to you if it is an individual proprietorship, a partnership, or a corporation? Would it make any difference if you were thinking about lending money to the business? Why?
6. Although there are many more individual proprietorships than corporations in the United States, corporations do a greater amount of business. Can you explain why?

PROJECTS AND PROBLEMS

1. List six kinds of goods or services that are not mass-produced. Following each explain briefly why. (*Example: shoe repairing*)
2. List the names of ten businesses in your community in the left-hand column of a form similar to the one shown below. Following each one, indicate the kind of business it is and how it is organized; that is, as an individual proprietorship, a partnership, a corporation, or a cooperative.

Name of Business	Kind of Business	Type of Organization
Example: *Davis and Engles*	*Department store*	*Corporation*

3. The following table shows the number and the total sales of businesses operating as individual proprietorships, partnerships, and corporations during a recent year.

NUMBER AND SALES OF DIFFERENT TYPES OF BUSINESS ORGANIZATIONS DURING A RECENT YEAR

Type of Organization	*Number of Businesses (thousands)*	*Sales (millions)*
Individual proprietorships	**9,090**	**$171,257**
Partnerships	**941**	**72,771**
Corporations	**1,141**	**763,337**

Source: National Industrial Conference Board

■ *a.* Which type of organization was used by the largest number of businesses? ■ *b.* For which of the three types of organization were sales the greatest? ■ *c.* How many more corporations than partnerships were there? ■ *d.* The number of individual proprietorships was approximately how many times as great as the number of corporations? ■ *e.* Corporations had approximately how many times the sales of the individual proprietorships and the partnerships combined? ■ *f.* Approximately what percent of the total number of businesses was made up of corporations? ■ *g.* Approximately what percent of the total sales did the corporations make?

4. The change in the number of business establishments in the United States for a recent 5-year period is given in the following table.

CHANGES IN THE NUMBER OF BUSINESS ESTABLISHMENTS DURING A RECENT FIVE-YEAR PERIOD

Year	*Firms in Operation (thousands)*	*New Businesses (thousands)*	*Discontinued Businesses (thousands)*
1st	4,533	397	347
2d	4,583	422	346
3d	4,658	438	384
4th	4,713	431	389
5th	4,755	430	387

Source: The National Industrial Conference Board

■ *a.* How many new business establishments were started during the first year shown in the table? the fourth year? the fifth year? ■ *b.* How many firms were in operation during the third year? the second year? the first year? ■ *c.* What was the total number of new business establishments started during the 5-year period? ■ *d.* What was the total number discontinued during the same period? ■ *e.* What was the average number of new businesses started yearly during the 5 years? ■ *f.* What was the average number discontinued yearly? ■ *g.* How many more new businesses were started during the fourth year than were discontinued?

5. After paying all its expenses, the Seed and Feed Co-op had enough money left over to pay a patronage refund of $2\frac{1}{2}$ cents on each dollar spent by its members during the year. Fred Brown had purchased $725 worth of supplies and new farm machinery worth $1,815. What was the amount of Mr. Brown's refund check?

6. If there is a consumer cooperative in your community, have a committee interview the manager or one of the officers to find out some of the problems connected with this type of business organization. The committee will report to the class. If possible, the manager or an officer of the cooperative might be invited to talk to the class.

7. If you know anyone in your school or community who is a member of a Junior-Achievement company, invite him to talk to your class about the work and purpose of the Junior-Achievement program.

CHALLENGE PROBLEMS

1. When the contractors and building-supply dealers of Centerville started the brick plant, why do you think the organizing group bought more than half the shares of stock?
2. There are additional advantages and disadvantages of the corporation that were not mentioned in this book. See how many more of each you can find through additional reading or by talking with your parents or friends.
3. In what way does a community benefit from having a new industry?
4. The Seed and Feed Co-op in Centerville is a producer cooperative rather than a consumer cooperative. Explain.
5. Find out how cooperatives are taxed compared to other kinds of businesses. Some people feel that cooperatives do not pay their fair share of taxes. Explain why you agree or disagree.

PART 7 THE ROLE OF GOVERNMENT

THE role of government varies from one economic system to another. It is much smaller in a free enterprise system than in a planned economy. Yet even in the United States, government owns about 100,000 enterprises; produces close to 10 percent of our gross national product; buys about 20 percent of all goods and services produced; and employs about one out of eight of the nation's workers.

Some people mistakenly believe that in a free enterprise system government and business are opposing forces. The truth is that like all parts of the economy, government and business are interdependent. Business depends on government to uphold the foundations of our free enterprise system—the right of individuals to conduct their own business affairs, to own property, and to go into business. Government, in turn, depends on business to supply it with goods and services. In fact, the two are so interdependent that almost any action by government has some effect on business. That is why you cannot talk about business for very long without mentioning government.

What are some of the economic activities of government? How do they affect business?

WHAT IS GOVERNMENT?

Government in this country is made up of representatives chosen to do the things that we, the people, want to do for ourselves as a group. In other words, government in the United States is a tool of the people, and not the other way around as in some countries. Because this is a large country, government is organized on three levels—local, state, and national. These separate governing units vary in size and purpose much like business organizations. A local government—such as a county, township, village, or city—serves the needs

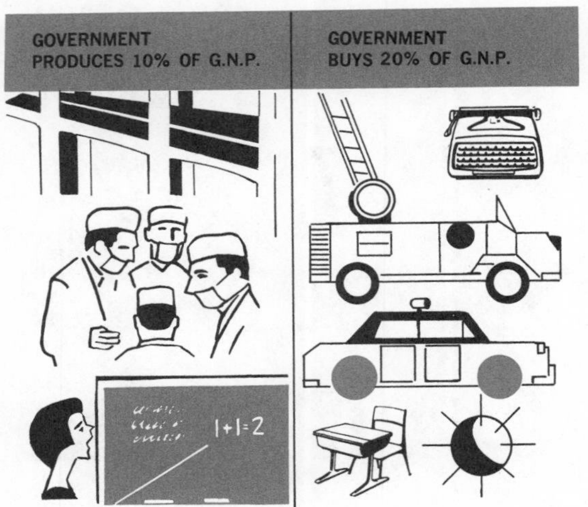
GOVERNMENT
PRODUCES 10% OF G.N.P.
GOVERNMENT
BUYS 20% OF G.N.P.
1+1=2

of the immediate community. A state government deals with matters of concern to all people living within its borders. The activities of our national government (also called Federal government) extend throughout the entire land. Yet they are closely linked to those of local and state governments, just as the work of big business firms is related to the work of smaller ones.

WHAT ARE THE ECONOMIC FUNCTIONS OF GOVERNMENT?

Simply stated, government's responsibility in our economic system is to make it possible for the system to function efficiently. A complete list of the ways in which government carries out its responsibility would more than fill a book this size. Those described in this part are but a few examples. Throughout the remainder of this book, however, the relationship between government and business is discussed many times.

Government Provides Essential Public Services

Under free enterprise, privately owned businesses operated for profit produce goods and services in response to demand. Demand is measured by what people buy. What they buy and how much they buy depends on their incomes. But long ago the people of this country decided that certain services should be available to all persons, regardless of their ability to pay for them. Instead of buying them individually, therefore, the people provide them for themselves through government.

Your local government operates the public school system in your community; paves and maintains the streets; and provides police and fire protection, garbage collection, libraries, parks, and playgrounds. State governments patrol the highways; help to finance state colleges and universities; build roads and bridges; and provide parks, hospitals, courts, and prisons. The Federal government maintains an army, navy, and air force to protect you from possible attack by other nations; constructs dams to prevent floods, to supply water for irrigation, and to produce electric power; and works in other ways to conserve land and other natural resources.

In some cases local, state, and Federal governments cooperate in providing services. State governments, for example, share with local governments the cost of operating public school systems. They also cooperate with the Federal government in constructing and maintaining highways.

An important point to keep in mind about most of these services that we buy and consume jointly is that privately owned enterprises still help to produce them. For example, if your local government decides a new school is needed, private business firms will construct it. The materials used to build highways, the cars used to patrol them, and the books, desks, and typewriters used in your school are all bought from private enterprises.

Government Owns Some Enterprises

Compared to most other countries, there are very few government-owned enterprises in the United States—less than 1 percent of the total. The majority of these provide services of the type just described. Over half of them are school systems. Most cities operate their own water companies and some provide gas and electric power as well. Local governments own and operate airports, and sometimes city transportation systems. One enterprise familiar to all is the post office, which employs ½ million workers and is operated by the Federal government.

Government Regulates Private Enterprise

Millions of workers depend on business for their jobs and incomes. Twenty million people own shares of stock in corporations. And 198 million consumers depend on business for goods and services. In one way or another, the manner in which business is conducted affects us all. To make certain that business operates for everyone's benefit, government regulates it in a number of ways. Following are a few examples.

For the protection of workers there are laws requiring the use of safety devices, establishing minimum wage rates, and prohibiting the employment of children. For the protection of both consumers and businessmen, there are standards of weight and measurement. A foot has to be 12 inches, a pound is always 16 ounces, and a gallon is never more or less than 4 quarts. For the protection of the public, theaters and other public buildings must have fire escapes; restaurants, barbershops and beauty parlors must operate under sanitary conditions; and goods that might be harmful, such as fireworks, are not allowed to be sold.

Local governments have zoning laws restricting the location of business enterprises. These prevent anyone from establishing a business in an area zoned for residences. State governments require doctors, lawyers, teachers, beauticians, and plumbers to be licensed.

Government Enforces Competition

As you learned in Part 5, free enterprise works best when there is competition among producers. Competition holds prices as well as profits down and forces business to produce efficiently. A business that has no competition whatsoever would have a monopoly. In all but a few types of business, monopolies are prohibited by law.

Monopoly is the ability to control the supply and price of a good or service. If there were only one producer of shoes, he could charge any price he pleased. He might even decide not to make as many shoes as people wanted. Then, because people would pay almost any price to get shoes, he could charge more for each pair than if he made enough for everyone.

The fact that a firm is the only producer of a good or service, however, does not give it a monopoly. It might still have to compete with producers of substitute products. In the case of shoes, consumers would have no choice but to buy them or go without. On the other hand, several firms acting together might create a monopoly. Suppose, for example, that only a few firms made all bicycles in this country. Suppose further that

Costly projects such as this bridge are frequently financed jointly by the Federal, state, and local governments.

Photo Joe Ruskin

Courtesy City of Chicago, Dept. of Weights and Measures

A Department of Weights and Measures inspector is checking the gauge on a fuel oil delivery truck to ensure accurate measurement.

these firms agreed to charge the same price, one high enough so that even the least efficient producer could make a profit. They might also try to keep out new producers by controlling the materials needed to make bicycles. This would be a violation of the law.

Legal Monopolies Are Regulated. Although the public benefits from competition generally, there are exceptions. If two or more telephone companies served your community, you might have to buy service from each one to call all your friends. If two companies supplied gas to the same community, both would have to install mains under the streets. Since they would need identical equipment, the cost of supplying gas to that community might be doubled.

Whenever an essential service can be produced more efficiently by one business than by competing enterprises, the government does one of two things: (1) it either operates the enterprise itself; or (2) it allows a privately owned enterprise to operate without competition. When a private enterprise is given the exclusive right to sell its services within a given territory, however, the government controls the prices it may charge.

A private enterprise of this type is called a ***public utility.*** In addition to telephone, gas, and transportation companies, public utilities include electric, water, and telegraph companies.

Government Helps Business

Although you hear a great deal about how government regulates business, you hear very little about the many ways in which government helps business. The forecasts of the United States Weather Bureau, which most of us take for granted, are of vital importance to many businesses. American firms that do business in other countries depend on the United States Department of Commerce for information concerning the trade policies of those countries. Federal and state governments cooperate in maintaining experiment stations where farmers can learn the latest facts about controlling insects and diseases that attack plants or animals; about processing and marketing farm products; or about fertilizing soil.

Government also gives various kinds of financial assistance to private enterprises. Assistance of this type is called a ***subsidy.*** A subsidy may be a direct payment of money, a reduction in taxes, or a gift of property. At present, the Federal government makes direct payments to farmers, to airlines, and to numerous other types of business. Late in the nineteenth century more than 130,000,000 acres of land were given to the railroads. Just think how much rail transportation was helped along by this gift. In an effort to attract new industries, state or local governments may excuse them from paying taxes for a period of time. Or they may offer them land or buildings at a price far below their true value.

Usually subsidies are intended to encourage certain kinds of production. Since we have a surplus of certain farm products, however, some farm subsidies are intended to reduce the production of those products.

Government Works to Prevent Depressions

Every so often in our free enterprise system, business activity slumps. There is a drop in production, in spending, in employment, and in income. A severe slump, you remember, is a depression. For a long time people thought that nothing could be done about depressions. Then in the 1930's the United States, along with other countries throughout the world, had its worst depression. Production of manufactured goods fell almost 50 percent. At one point nearly 13 million workers were without jobs. People began to demand that the government do something.

One of the things the government did at that time was to construct highways, bridges, parks, dams, and post offices. Construction projects of this kind are called ***public works.*** This spending by government helped to make up for the lack of spending by consumers and business. It provided jobs and income for people made jobless by the depression. These people were then able to buy food, clothing, shelter, and other things they needed. Their spending meant jobs and income for other people.

In spite of this and other attempts on the part of government to restore business activity to a normal level, recovery was gradual. Nevertheless, it convinced people that something could be done when depression threatened. Today it is expected that government will act to correct a slowdown in business activity before the depression stage is reached.

The Federal government accepted responsibility for preventing depressions with passage of the Employment Act of 1946. This Act states that it is the responsibility of the Federal government to promote employment and production. It does not state what course of action the government is to take. But it does provide for the appointment of a Council of Economic Advisers to make recommendations to the President when action is needed.

WHAT SHOULD THE ROLE OF GOVERNMENT BE?

The role of government in our economic system is one of the most debated topics of our time. Almost everyone considers it not only desirable but proper for government to provide such services as national defense, police protection, mail delivery, and public education. Many, on the other hand, are opposed to the government's selling electric power or operating other public utilities. This type of production, they say, puts government into competition with privately owned enterprises. Nearly everyone agrees that there must be some regulation of business by government. Yet there is no agreement about what kinds of regulation are needed or how much. Some say there is already too much; others say there is not enough. Human nature being what it is, people are inclined to applaud government actions that protect them and to criticize those that restrict them.

This is not to say that every action on the part of government is wise. In a democracy the government acts in response to the demands of the people, and people sometimes make mistakes. Before long you, too, will be helping to decide what part government should play in our economic system. This is one more reason why it is important for you to learn as much as possible about business and the economic system within which it operates.

BUILDING YOUR VOCABULARY

On a separate sheet of paper, write each of the terms listed in the left-hand column below. Read the three definitions to the right of each term. After each term, copy the definition that best describes it.

1. ***monopoly***
   - *a.* A business that is the only producer of a good or service
   - *b.* The ability to control the supply and price of a good or service
   - *c.* An agreement among several businesses to produce the same good or service
2. ***public utility***
   - *a.* A business that produces an essential service
   - *b.* A government-owned enterprise
   - *c.* A private enterprise that provides a service so essential that its prices are regulated by the government
3. ***public works***
   - *a.* Services provided by the government, such as street lighting, rubbish disposal, and snow removal
   - *b.* Construction projects, such as highways, bridges, and parks undertaken by the government
   - *c.* Spending by the government during a recession
4. ***subsidy***
   - *a.* Payments to farmers to make up for the lack of spending by consumers and business
   - *b.* A tax on new business enterprises
   - *c.* Financial assistance given by the government to a private enterprise

CHECKING YOUR READING

1. What percent of our gross national product is produced by government? What percent of all that is produced does government buy?
2. Explain how government and business are interdependent.
3. Name the three levels of government in the United States.
4. What is the responsibility of government in our economic system?
5. Name some services that are provided by government rather than by privately owned business. Why does government provide these services?
6. Explain how privately owned businesses help to produce services provided by government.

7. Approximately what percent of all enterprises in the United States are government owned?
8. More than half of the government-owned enterprises in the United States are of one kind. What kind are they? What are some of the other enterprises that our governments operate?
9. What are some of the ways government regulates business?
10. Explain why a firm that is the only producer of a good or service does not necessarily have a monopoly.
11. Why would a monopoly be against the public interest if it were not regulated?
12. Give examples of cases in which it might be better for a single company to supply a good or service rather than to have two or more firms competing to supply it. Why is this so?
13. How are consumers protected when a business is given the right to operate as a monopoly?
14. Describe several ways in which government helps business.
15. Give evidence to support the statement that government subsidies are not new.
16. In what way has the Federal government accepted responsibility for preventing depressions?
17. Who is responsible for the decisions of government in the United States?

SHARING YOUR OPINION AND EXPERIENCE

1. Fred Miller works for the telephone company and lives with his family on a quiet residential street in Freeport. Fred's hobby is woodworking, and he has become quite expert at making novelty furniture items. Several friends have suggested that Fred quit his job and convert his basement workshop into a small factory to make novelties for sale. Fred likes the idea and discussed it recently with one of his neighbors. The neighbor told Fred that it would be illegal to set up such a business in his basement.

   ▪ *a.* What laws or ordinances might Fred violate if he did set up the business? ▪ *b.* Since Fred owns his home, would you say that laws of this kind interfere with his property rights? ▪ *c.* How can a law that would keep Fred from using part of his home for a business be justified in a free enterprise system?

2. Why are government-owned enterprises sometimes called "public" enterprises?
3. Would you be opposed to government-owned enterprises producing goods for sale? Give reasons.
4. Do you think it is desirable for the Federal government to join local and state governments in helping to pay the costs of public schools? Give reasons for your answer.
5. Do you believe business gains or loses as a result of government regulation? Why?
6. What are antitrust laws?
7. What is a legal monopoly?

8. Do you feel that government has too much to say about the operation of private enterprises? Why?

PROJECTS AND PROBLEMS

1. Make a list of twelve services (not public utilities) that the people in your community provide for themselves through government. After each service, indicate whether it is provided by your local, state, or Federal government. If two or more levels of government are involved, include both or all three.
2. Divide a sheet of paper into three columns. In the first column, list the names of public utilities that operate in your community. In the second column, indicate the type of service each one provides. In the third column, indicate whether it is a government-owned or a private enterprise.
3. List at least six laws in effect where you live that affect business but are designed for your protection. After each law, indicate whether you think it is necessary or whether you believe you and your friends could get along just as well without it.
4. Read the newspaper item reprinted below and answer the questions following it.

SUBSIDIES AFFECT ALL, CONGRESS UNIT SAYS

Washington, D.C. Federal subsidies have expanded "to the point where few segments of our economy are completely unaffected by them," a congressional committee said Sunday.

Commenting on an 80-page report on "subsidy and subsidy-like programs," Sen. Paul H. Douglas, committee chairman, said that the report was a first step in determining the extent and impact of federal aid, direct and indirect, on the nation's economy.

According to the report, "there has been a fairly steady increase" in total direct subsidies, from $1,900,000,000 in 1951 to $7,460,000,000 in 1960.

Annual farm subsidies rose from $905,000,000 to $3,568,000,000 between 1951 and 1960. Business concerns got subsidies that grew from $809,000,000 in 1951 to $1,352,000,000 in 1960. Labor also received subsidies, growing from $197,000,000 in 1951 to $327,000,000 in 1960.

In some cases, the report said, it was difficult to identify who benefitted from federal subsidies. "The school lunch program subsidizes the farmer by helping reduce farm surpluses, but also subsidizes the students who receive the food and their parents. The second-class postage rates far from cover the costs of carrying the magazines and newspapers within this class but the benefit is shared by publishers, advertisers, and readers.

▪ *a.* Which level of government does the article pertain to? ▪ *b.* How much did total direct subsidies increase from 1951 to 1960? ▪ *c.* Name at least four groups that benefit from subsidies according to the article. ▪ *d.* Which group mentioned received the greatest increase in subsidies between 1951 and 1960? ▪ *e.* Which group received the smallest increase? ▪ *f*. In what ways do consumers benefit from subsidies?

5. With the help of your teacher, parents, or friends, make a list of buildings, roads, parks, and the like in your community that were constructed under a program of public works.
6. Appoint a committee to find out the various zoning classifications for property in your community. Instruct the committee to include in its report the procedures that must be followed in order to have a zone changed from one classification to another.
7. If there is a chamber of commerce in your community, have one of its representatives speak to your class about what is done to encourage new businesses to locate in your area.

CHALLENGE PROBLEMS

1. How do you explain the fact that government regulation of business has increased rather than decreased over the years? Does your answer suggest any guides for your own conduct or your own obligations in a free society?
2. As the United States and other nations move forward in the exploration of space, there undoubtedly will be many arguments about whether private business should be allowed to own and operate space stations, communications devices, and the like. Already this question has been raised about certain communications satellites. Do you think private enterprises should be allowed to use outer space to earn a profit? Why?
3. Make a list of private businesses in your community that have received or are now receiving a kind of government financial assistance that could be called a subsidy. Indicate in each case whether you think the subsidy is justified. You may get help in gathering the information by talking with your parents, your teachers, and other adults that you know.

PART 8 THE NATURE AND FUNCTION OF MONEY

AMONG man's most useful discoveries are fire, the wheel, and money. Money is so important in an economic system like ours that it is sometimes called a *money economy*. The surprising thing is that although everyone uses money, most people know very little about it. Many people, for example, confuse money with wealth. But only goods are ***wealth.*** They may be producer or consumer goods; they may be man-made or natural, such as land, coal, forests, oil, and water. A nation's wealth is measured by its stock of natural resources and whatever man-made goods are in existence at any time. A person's wealth consists of everything he owns. Money is simply a means of obtaining wealth. It is a tool, and like any other tool, it sometimes fails to work properly.

Now what about you? You help money do its work. Yet how much do you really know about it except that it is needed to buy things? What jobs does money perform in our economic system? What is money in the United States? What is "sound money"?

WHAT IS MONEY?

Money is anything generally accepted in payment for goods, services, or debts. All sorts of things have served as money at different times and in different parts of the world. Brick tea, fishhooks, gun powder, cattle, woodpecker scalps, feathers, and cowrie shells are only a few examples. In ancient Rome soldiers were given salt as part payment for their services. This was called a "salt ration," or salarium, in Latin. Do you see why a person's income is sometimes called a *salary*? In Colonial Virginia tobacco leaves were used for money while farther up the coast it was grain, fish, or furs. In Britain it was bars of iron; in Russia, compressed cheese. During and immediately following World War II, American servicemen stationed overseas used cigarettes and chocolate bars for money.

Money of this kind is called *commodity money*. A *commodity* is simply a good that can be transported or carried. To be money, however, it must be generally accepted, within a given area, as payment for goods, services, or debts. In other words, it is *acceptability* that determines whether something is or is not money. The first white settlers on this continent accepted wampum from the Indians because the Indians would accept it from them in trade for other things.

What Do We Use for Money?

The basic unit of the money system in the United States is the dollar. The coins and paper bills that you ordinarily think of as money are called *currency dollars* or ***currency.*** Actually, however, the most popular form of money in this country is checks.

A ***check*** is an order to a bank to pay a stated sum of money to another person or business. Following is an illustration of a check written by Norman Gross ordering the Gulf State Bank to pay $15.78 to the Olson Hardware Company. Anyone who writes a check, of course, must have money in the bank to pay it.

Checks are money because they are widely accepted in payment for goods, services, and debts. Business firms pay their workers with checks. Families pay their household bills with checks. Our governments pay for almost everything by check. In fact, it is estimated that over 6 billion dollars' worth of goods and services are exchanged in the United States daily, and that approximately 98 percent of this amount is paid for with checks. Money in the form of checks is sometimes called *checkbook dollars* or *checkbook money*.

WHAT DOES MONEY DO?

In times past when people had no money, they simply traded goods for other goods. A man who had more grain than he needed exchanged his surplus for fish or something else he lacked. Trading goods for goods is ***barter.*** Barter is still practiced to some extent today; for example, trading an old car as partial payment on a new one is common practice.

Because the use of commodity money also involves trading goods for goods, people often confuse it with barter. The difference is that in one case a single commodity is used in every kind of exchange. With barter, people traded any commodity they were willing to give up in exchange for another.

Barter, however, has certain drawbacks that the

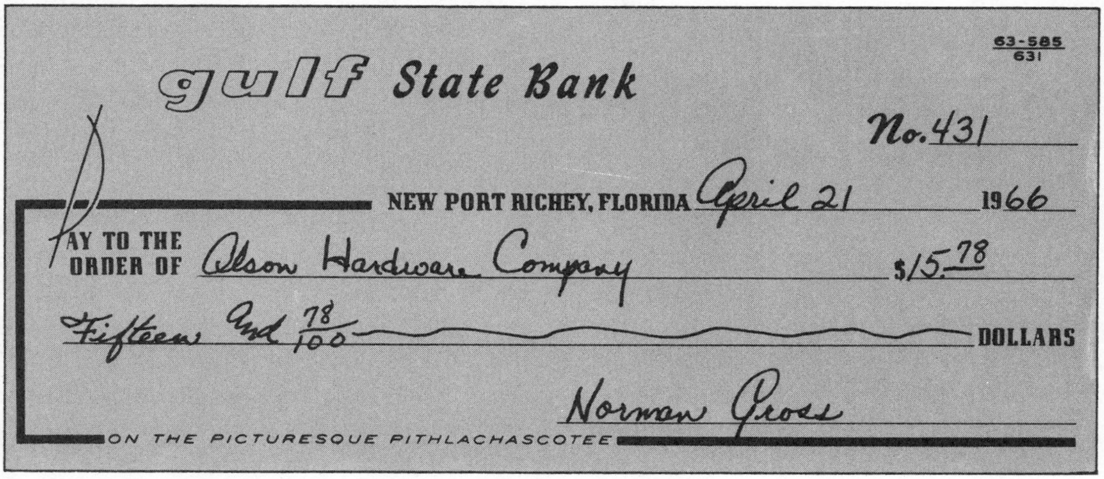

Gulf State Bank 63-585/631
No. 431
NEW PORT RICHEY, FLORIDA April 21 1966
PAY TO THE ORDER OF Olson Hardware Company $15.78
Fifteen and 78/100 DOLLARS
Norman Gross
ON THE PICTURESQUE PITHLACHASCOTEE

use of money overcomes. For one thing, it is not always easy to work out a trade. Before an exchange can take place, each person must want what the other has. Suppose that you needed shoes, and the only thing you had to offer in exchange for them was a camera. You would probably have no trouble finding people who wanted a camera. But what if none of them had a pair of shoes your size? Someone with shoes your size, on the other hand, might be unwilling to trade them for a camera. It was probably this kind of difficulty that led to the use of money in the first place.

Money Is a Medium of Exchange

Nevertheless, as long as people produced most of their own goods and services, they could get along with barter. Few things had to be bought, and these usually could be obtained in exchange for eggs, or meat, or cloth. The self-sufficient household always had something to trade. In fact, many families managed with practically no money at all.

By contrast, workers who specialize in the production of one good or service are extremely dependent on money. The man who installs car windows, or pilots an airplane, or specializes in any other way must have some means of trading his services for food, clothing, shelter, and the many other things he needs. Money is the only possible means. The money he receives in exchange for his work can be exchanged in turn for the goods and services he wants. Because money enables people to exchange their goods or services for the goods and services of others, it is a MEDIUM OF EXCHANGE.

Money Is a Standard of Value

In every exchange, value is an important factor. The *value* of a good or service is its worth in terms of other goods and services. With barter there is no simple way of deciding how much one thing is worth compared with another. Even if you found someone willing to trade you shoes for a camera, it might be difficult to work out a fair exchange. In spite of your thinking the camera was worth two pairs of shoes, the other person might insist on trading for only one pair.

The use of money makes it possible to put prices on goods and services. A ***price*** is the value of anything expressed in money terms. When goods and services have prices, their values can be compared easily. If the price of a camera is $26 and the price of a pair of shoes is $13, you know at once the camera is worth two pairs of shoes.

The amount a worker earns is the price of his labor. If he earns $2.25 an hour, one hour's work entitles him to $2.25 worth of groceries, or clothes, or gasoline, or whatever goods and services he wants. Because money measures the exchange values of all goods and services, it is a STANDARD OF VALUE.

Money Is a Store of Value

Today a worker who receives money in exchange for his services does not have to spend it all immediately. If he wishes, he can save part of it for future use. In other words, he may store part of the value of his work. If he were paid in goods or services, on the other hand, he would find it difficult to save much. Some goods would spoil before they could be used, and services could not be saved at all.

But the money in use today is simply a claim to goods and services. It can be presented whenever the goods or services are wanted—at once, a little at a time, or years from now. Because the value of money can be stored, it is a STORE OF VALUE.

WHAT IS MONEY WORTH?

In the past things used for money had value of their own in addition to their exchange value. Salt was valuable because it was the only way to preserve meat. Beads were worn for adornment; furs kept out the cold; food satisfied hunger; and coins were made of precious metals.

MONEY MAKES IT POSSIBLE TO COMPARE THE VALUES OF DIFFERENT GOODS AND SERVICES.

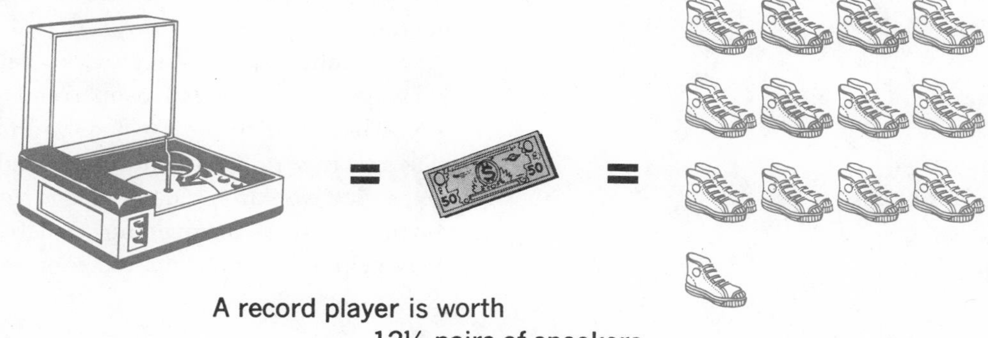

A record player is worth 12½ pairs of sneakers

Today money by itself has little value. A dollar bill is only paper; the metal in a half-dollar is worth much less than 50 cents. Money is just a convenience. Its only *real* value is its purchasing power. Money's *purchasing power,* of course, is what it will buy.

From now on whenever you see the word "real" used in connection with money, remember that it refers to purchasing power. The terms *real income* or *real wages,* for example, do not mean dollars-and-cents earnings. They refer to the purchasing power of income or wages—the amount that can be bought with the money earned.

Does the Real Value of Money Change?

In one way money never changes. Five pennies always equal a nickel; 2 nickels, a dime; 5 nickels, a quarter; 2 quarters, a half-dollar; 2 half-dollars, a dollar; and so on. A dollar always buys a dollar's worth of goods and services. But the amount that a dollar will buy may change from time to time. The reason is that the prices of goods and services change. If prices rise, money buys less; if prices fall, money buys more. In other words, the real value, or purchasing power, of money varies with prices.

An increase or a decrease in the price of just one good or service does not affect the value of money. In a business system that produces as many things as ours, prices of individual goods and services are changing constantly. While some are going up, others are going down. It is only when the prices of most goods and services move up or down that the purchasing power of money changes. A general increase in prices is ***inflation.*** A general decrease in prices is ***deflation.***

Effects of Inflation. Suppose that you had $2, and someone stole 16 cents of it from you. Your buying power would be reduced by 16 cents as a result. Inflation is like a thief. It does not rob you of your money, but it does steal part of its purchasing power. A general price increase of 8 percent would reduce the purchasing power of $2 by 16 cents. In other words, your $2 would buy only as much as $1.84 would have bought before. Between 1940 and 1951 that is what happened in the United States. Prices rose an average of 8 percent a year.

A person whose income is rising along with other prices may not notice the harmful effects of inflation. For those whose incomes rise slowly, if at all, a loss in the purchasing power of money can spell tragedy. Furthermore, money of changing value does not function well as a store of value.

Suppose you saved your money for some future use, like a college education or a trip. If prices rose in the meantime, your money would be worth less than when you put it away. You might not have enough to carry out your plans.

THE AMOUNT A DOLLAR CAN BUY VARIES FROM TIME TO TIME.

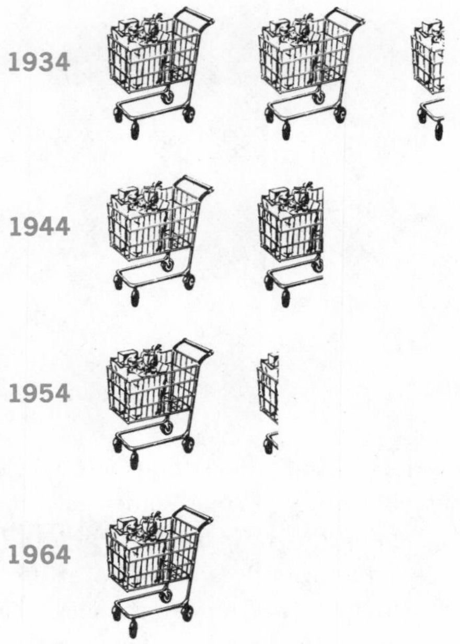

Effects of Deflation. Deflation, of course, has effects just the opposite to those of inflation. A decrease in prices gives money more purchasing power. This might cause you to assume that everyone would benefit from deflation, but that is not true. One important thing to remember is that income is also a price. The money a worker earns is the price paid for his services. When other prices fall, the incomes of many workers also fall. Although a dollar may buy more, with fewer dollars to spend these workers are no better off than before.

People who own property are especially hard hit by deflation, since the value of their property is reduced. Furthermore, if they are still paying for the property, their payments are not likely to change. Should their incomes go down, they may even lose the property because they are unable to meet the payments.

An additional harmful effect of deflation is that when prices begin to fall, people tend to put off buying. They wait to see if prices will fall still more. The result is a decrease in total spending followed by a decrease in production and income and a further decrease in spending. Deflation, therefore, may help to bring about a recession.

BUSINESS DEPENDS ON A SOUND MONEY SYSTEM

Our business system works best when the purchasing power of money remains fairly stable. Money that holds its value is *sound money*. In an effort to keep our money sound, the Federal government attempts to control inflation as well as to prevent depressions. One job of the President's Council of Economic Advisers is to keep constant watch over prices and wages. If there is a marked change either up or down, the government is expected to take steps to correct it.

Only the Federal government is authorized to coin or print money. Money made by anyone else is *counterfeit*. The special type of paper as well as special inks and secret printing processes used make our paper money difficult to copy. In addition the United States Secret Service was organized to track down counterfeiters. It is estimated that less than one-thousandth of 1 percent of the money in circulation today is counterfeit.

BUILDING YOUR VOCABULARY

Copy the eight sentences given below and on page 67, completing each one by replacing the question mark with the appropriate term from the column at the left.

barter	1. A nation's natural resources and man-made goods make up its ? .
check	2. Anything generally accepted in payment for goods, services, or debts is ? .

currency
deflation
inflation
money
price
wealth

3. An order to a bank to pay a stated sum of money to another person or business is a ? .
4. The coins and paper bills used as a means of payment are ? .
5. The value of anything expressed in money terms is its ? .
6. A general increase in prices is ? .
7. Trading goods for goods is ? .
8. A general decrease in prices is ? .

CHECKING YOUR READING

1. Explain how money is related to wealth.
2. What is commodity money?
3. What is the test that determines whether something is or is not money?
4. What is the basic unit of our money system?
5. What is the most popular form of money in the United States?
6. How does the use of commodity money differ from barter?
7. What are some of the disadvantages of barter?
8. Why is money so important when workers specialize?
9. Explain how money is used as a medium of exchange; as a standard of value; as a store of value.
10. What determines the real value of money?
11. Explain how inflation is like a thief.
12. Who are the people most hurt by inflation?
13. Why doesn't everyone benefit during a period of falling prices?
14. What is sound money? Who is responsible for keeping our money sound?
15. Who makes and issues our currency and coins?
16. How is our money protected against counterfeiting?

SHARING YOUR OPINION AND EXPERIENCE

1. Why do you suppose tobacco leaves were used for money in Colonial Virginia while furs were used for the same purpose in Northern colonies?
2. Why do you think checks are the most popular form of money in this country today?
3. Acceptability determines whether something is or is not money. What are some of the factors that make a particular item acceptable as money?
4. It has been said that mass production would be impossible if we had no uniform type of money in this country. Explain why this is true.
5. It costs approximately the same to print a twenty-dollar bill as it does to print a five-dollar bill. Why is one worth four times as much as the other?
6. What does the term "legal tender" mean?
7. During the past thirty years Mr. Green's wages have increased from $60 a week to $120 a week, which represents an increase of 100 percent. Mr. Green says, however, that his real wages have increased only 50 percent. Explain how both these statements can be true.
8. Why must the government be extremely careful to protect our money against counterfeiting?

PROJECTS AND PROBLEMS

1. As the use of money increased, people soon realized that, in addition to being valuable, the things used for money had to have certain other characteristics: be durable; be acceptable to everyone; be divisible; be portable (easy to carry); and be stable in value. Five items that have been used for money in the past are diamonds, rice, furs, fish, and iron. Using a form similar to that shown below, list these items in the left-hand column. Following each one, write *yes* or *no* in each of the other columns to indicate whether it did or did not have that characteristic.

CHARACTERISTICS OF GOOD MONEY

ITEM	Durable	Acceptable	Divisible	Portable	Stable
Example: Diamonds	*yes*	*yes*	*no*	*yes*	*yes*

2. The trading of an old car as partial payment on a new one is one example of how barter is practiced even today. List five other examples of barter that might take place today. You may get help from your parents or by looking at the classified ads in a newspaper.
3. The following table shows the average retail prices of selected foods for the two years indicated. Study the table carefully and answer the questions below it.

AVERAGE RETAIL PRICES OF SELECTED FOODS IN 1958 AND 1963

Food Item	*1958 Price (per pound)*	*1963 Price (per pound)*
Bacon	**$ .74**	**$ .66**
Bread	**.19**	**.22**
Cheese	**.58**	**.36**
Coffee	**.91**	**.69**
Potatoes	**.06**	**.06**
Round steak	**1.04**	**1.09**
Tomatoes	**.32**	**.38**

▪ *a.* How many items increased in price between 1958 and 1963? ▪ *b.* How many items decreased in price during the five-year period? ▪ *c.* Which item cost the same in 1963 as in 1958? ▪ *d.* Which item increased most in price from 1958 to 1963? ▪ *e.* Which item decreased most in price during the five-year period? ▪ *f.* Was the cost of all items listed more or less in 1963 than in 1958?

4. In Problem 7 of Part 5 you learned that the amount of profit a company makes has greater meaning when it is expressed as a percent of some other amount, such as sales. Similarly, a price increase or decrease is more meaningful when expressed as a percent of what the price was before the change; that is, the percent of increase or decrease is a better measure of price changes than the amount of increase or decrease.

Since you already know how to find what percent one number is of another, it will be easy for you to find percent increases or decreases in prices. First, you must find the amount of increase or decrease by subtracting the smaller of the two numbers from the larger one. Then divide your answer by the price of the item during the earlier period. For example, if the price of bacon decreased from 74 cents a pound in 1958 to 66 cents a pound in 1963, the amount of decrease was 8 cents (.74 − .66 = .08). The percent of decrease was 11 percent (.08 ÷ .74 = .11).

On a separate sheet of paper draw a form similar to the one below and copy on it the items and prices from the table in Problem 3 on page 68.

Food	1958 Price	1963 Price	Amount of Increase or Decrease	Percent of Increase or Decrease

■ *a.* Find the amount of increase or decrease in the price of each item and write it in the appropriate column. Indicate increases by a + sign and decreases by a − sign. Write a 0 (zero) in the space if there was no change in price. ■ *b.* To the nearest whole percent, find the percent of increase or decrease in the price of each item. Write your answers in the right-hand column. Again indicate increases with a + and decreases with a −. ■ *c.* Which food item had the greatest percent increase in price between 1958 and 1963? ■ *d.* Did the same one have the greatest amount of increase during this period? ■ *e.* Which food item had the greatest percent decrease in price? ■ *f.* Was it also the one that had the greatest amount of decrease?

5. Bring to class some article that you own and are willing to trade. Try to trade it for an item someone else has. Count the number of times you try but are unable to make a trade. List the reasons why each attempt was unsuccessful.
6. As a committee project, prepare an exhibit of old coins and paper money. Students who have coin collections should help with the exhibit.

CHALLENGE PROBLEMS

1. What is a consumer price index? What, if anything, does it have to do with the real value of money?
2. In a period of inflation would you rather be a person who had borrowed money or one who had loaned it? Why? Which would you rather be during a period of deflation? Why?
3. Who would be hurt least during a period of deflation, a teacher or a factory worker? Why?

CONTENTS OF UNIT 3

Unit 3 / You as a Consumer

PART 9
THE ROLE OF THE CONSUMER IN A FREE ENTERPRISE SYSTEM

Courtesy A & P Food Stores

YOU may not think of yourself as an important economic force, but you are. You are a consumer; and business owes its existence to the fact that consumers never run out of wants. If anything, the more they have the more they seem to want. No longer content to settle for just the necessities—food, clothing, and shelter—consumers today want comfort, pleasure, and goods that save time and energy—air-conditioned houses, stereo phonographs, and dishwashers. By continually developing new products, business itself often creates wants that did not exist before. And sometimes the satisfaction of one want makes for additional wants. When you buy a phonograph, you want records. When you have a car, you also need oil and gasoline. Each year finds thousands of newlyweds needing places in which to live, pans to cook in, furniture, linens, and a host of other items. Each day 11,000 new births increase the numbers to be clothed and fed. In no time at all these infants are adding to the demand for buggies, high chairs, toys, vitamins, music lessons, and dental care.

The purpose of business in our economic system is to produce the goods and services that consumers want. How well does business fulfill its purpose? In what ways does consumer spending affect business?

HOW CONSUMER SPENDING AFFECTS BUSINESS

Nowhere in the world do consumers occupy a position of greater influence than in the United States. The way they spend their money determines what goods and services are produced. Where they spend money determines, to a large extent, which enterprises succeed and which fail. How much they spend determines total production. No wonder it is said "The consumer is king!" in a free enterprise system.

Consumer Spending Determines What Is Produced

Most goods and services in this country are produced in response to consumer demand. Consumer demand is simply all our individual spending decisions added together. When you purchase one good or service rather than another, you tell producers the kinds of goods and services you want. This is sometimes called *economic* or *dollar voting*. If you do not want a product, you vote against it by not buying it. A few years ago, for example, consumers began to turn their backs on the large cars then being produced in the United States. Their purchases indicated a preference for the small cars made in Europe instead. Each year sales of foreign cars in this country rose until American manufacturers began to feel the competition. As a result, American manufacturers started producing the compact cars consumers wanted.

Because some consumers have more money to spend than others, they are able to cast more dollar votes. Every vote counts, nevertheless. As a teenager, you belong to one of the most influential consumer groups of all. It is estimated that young people, 13 to 19 years of age, spend nearly $14 billion annually in addition to what their parents spend for them. They buy most of the used cars, small radios, and phonograph records. They take about one-fourth of the snapshots, and in a recent year spent over $300,000,000 on grooming aids and cosmetics alone. They also influence many of the buying decisions of their parents.

These buying decisions help to determine what goods and services are produced just as certainly as those of other consumers. As a consumer in a free enterprise system, therefore, you share the responsibility for deciding how our productive resources are used.

Consumer Spending Determines the Fate of Business Enterprises

Whether a business enterprise is large or small; whether it produces directly for consumers or for other producers, its success depends on the buying decisions of consumers. Obviously, an enterprise producing consumer goods or services not in demand must produce something else or go out of business. But even if a business sells only to other producers, its fate rests with consumers. Unless a sufficient number of consumers buy a good or service, the enterprises that supply the materials or equipment used in its production cannot make a profit.

Consumer demand, of course, is subject to change. Goods wanted today may not be wanted tomorrow. As consumer spending shifts from one good or service to another, some businesses grow; others may shrink or quit altogether. The rising demand for automobiles at the beginning of this century marked the end of the buggy industry. The popularity of television forced some movie theaters to close. If a business enterprise is to survive, it must produce or help to produce something consumers want at a price they are willing to pay.

Consumer Spending Determines How Much Is Produced

In the long run the amount of goods and services bought determines the amount produced. Whenever business finds that it is producing more than it is able to sell, production is slowed down. If buyers want more than is being produced, an effort is made to speed up production. In other words, total production varies with total spending. They go up and down together.

In addition to consumers the major spenders in our economic system are business and government, as you know. Business and government together, however, buy only about one-third of all that is produced. Normally consumers buy the remaining two-thirds. Furthermore, the spending decisions of business are based on consumer spending. Business enterprises will build factories and buy materials and machines for producing goods and services only if consumer spending is at a high level. If consumer spending slows down, business spending will usually slow down. Consumer spending, therefore, affects the production of both producer and consumer goods. Thus, total production depends heavily on consumer spending.

WHY CONSUMER SPENDING IS WATCHED

Most of the money consumers spend is income earned by them or by some other family member by helping to produce a good or service. Whenever total production is reduced, of course, there is less income for workers to divide and to spend. This means that fewer consumer goods will be bought. Then production, income, and spending will fall even more. If this slowdown continued to spread, there could be a recession. For this reason, the President's Council of Economic Advisers watch total spending closely. They pay particular attention to consumer spending because this makes up the largest part of the total and because it affects business spending.

Consumer purchases are of two kinds. One kind consists of ***nondurable goods.*** These are things like food, clothing, gasoline, soap, and cosmetics that are used up within a fairly short time. The other kind is ***durable goods,*** products that last a long time—usually three or more years. Automobiles, furniture, television sets, and washing machines are examples of durable goods. If people are uncertain about their jobs and incomes, or if they think prices are too high, they will put off buying certain kinds of goods. They will spend money only for things they consider essential. For example, they will usually spend less for clothes. They will postpone building or buying a new house; and they will put off buying new cars and other durable goods.

The Council of Economic Advisers, therefore, keep an eye on such things as the amount bought at department stores; the number of new houses under construction; and how many new cars and other durable goods consumers are buying. Any slowdown in consumer spending is likely to show up first in sales of these items. During the great depression of the '30s purchases of nondurable goods fell 15 percent, a sizable amount. Purchases of durable goods, on the other hand, fell 50 percent. During the mild recession that occurred in 1957–58, consumer spending for nondurables fell only 2 percent, while spending for durable goods fell 10 percent. At that time leaders in business and government appealed to consumers to buy all they could to stimulate production. This is just one more indication of how important consumer spending really is.

Can There Be Too Much Spending? Sometimes consumers, business, and government try to buy goods and services faster than the rate at which they can be produced. When this happens, prices in general rise; and we have inflation. Some of the causes of inflation will be explained more fully in Part 46.

IS A CONSUMER-DIRECTED ECONOMY DESIRABLE?

Our economic system is sometimes criticized on the grounds that when consumers direct production, resources are not always used wisely. One critic has said that the share of our productive resources used for yachts and sports cars is too great. The amount going into schools, hospitals, and slum clearance, on the other hand, he says is too small. Another claims that "American consumers buy gadgets rather than books." A third argues that in a free enterprise system producers must guess what consumers are likely to buy. If they guess wrong and consumers fail to buy what has been produced, the resources used in its production are wasted.

To a certain extent, these critics may be right. It is true that business does produce many items of questionable value, such as zany greeting cards, useless souvenirs, and silly wigs; and consumers buy them. But these items represent only a tiny fraction of total production. It is also true that producers guess wrong occasionally about what consumers will buy. Today, however, efforts are being made to avoid waste of this kind. Business enterprises, institutions such as universities, and some departments of the Federal government are constantly collecting information about what consumers want both at the present time and in the future.

Right or not, these criticisms of our economic system overlook one very important point. Americans prize freedom. One of their freedoms is the right to make up their own minds whether to save or spend their money. And if they spend it, it is their right to decide what and where to buy. This includes the right to buy foolish frills. The price we pay for this freedom is the risk that some small portion of our resources may be wasted. There is no proof that resources are used any more wisely in countries where government makes the decisions.

HOW WELL DOES BUSINESS SATISFY CONSUMER WANTS?

The purpose of business in our economic system is to produce the goods and services that consumers want. The satisfaction of consumer wants is called *consumption*. ***Consumption*** is the opposite of production—it is the using up of goods and services. Our standard of living depends on our consumption of goods and services. Or putting it another way, our living standard depends on how well business satisfies our wants.

Living standards in the United States are among the highest in the world. As a nation we consume more goods and services and a greater variety of them than any other nation. This is so because we produce more than other nations. With scarcely more than 6 percent of the world's population, the United States produces more than one-third of the

Courtesy Record & Music Center

These teenagers have budgeted for fun and are now buying a few of their favorite records.

world's goods and services. It turns out almost one-half of the world's manufactured goods. Moreover, our standard of living has been rising steadily. The average citizen lives better today than even the rich did at the turn of the century. This rise in our standard of living is the result of *economic growth.*

Economic growth is an increase in a nation's gross national product, or the total amount produced. To raise its standard of living, a nation's total production must increase at a faster rate than its population. During the past century, total production of goods and services in the United States nearly doubled every 20 years. The population increased only $2\frac{1}{2}$ times during that same 100 years. In 1900 the production of goods and services amounted to $1,048 worth for each person. In 1964 it amounted to $3,243 worth for each person.

Increased Production Has Changed Consumption

The rise in our standard of living is not just a matter of the quantity of goods consumed. It is noticeable in the kinds of things consumed. Over the last fifty years there has been a rapid increase in the consumption of durable goods. Today consumers spend approximately 14 percent of their incomes for such durable goods as automatic washers and dryers, television sets, food freezers, power lawn mowers, dishwashers, and automobiles. The demand for services such as medical care, haircuts, dry cleaning, and transportation has also grown. At present approximately 40 percent of consumer spending is for services.

Finally, the gain in living standards is reflected in increased leisure. Business not only produces more goods today than ever before, it is producing them in less time. In 1850 workers spent an average of 70 hours a week at their jobs. Today the average workweek is about 40 hours. As the length of the workweek has become shorter, the working consumer has more time in which to enjoy himself. This has led to an increase in the consumption of leisure goods and services—outboard motors, camping equipment, barbecues, patio furniture, and travel.

BUSINESS MUST CONTINUE TO GROW

Even today some consumers in the United States are poorly fed, poorly clothed, and poorly housed. But on the whole business has fulfilled its purpose very well. By 1975, however, the number of consumers in the United States is expected to be well over 200 million. Business must continue to increase its production of goods and services if it is to satisfy the wants of that many consumers. Otherwise our present standard of living cannot be maintained.

BUILDING YOUR VOCABULARY

On a separate sheet of paper, write each of the terms listed in the left-hand column below and on page 77. Read the three definitions to the right of each term. After each term, copy the definition that best describes it.

1. *consumption*
- *a.* The making of goods and services
- *b.* The using up of goods and services
- *c.* The spending of money

2. *durable goods*
- *a.* Products that usually last three years or more
- *b.* Products that are used up within a short time
- *c.* Products that are used in the manufacture of other goods

3. ***economic growth***
   a. An increase in the number of consumers in a nation
   b. A rise in a nation's standard of living
   c. An increase in a nation's gross national product

4. ***nondurable goods***
   a. Products such as automobiles, television sets, and furniture
   b. Products that last at least three years
   c. Products that are used up within a short time

CHECKING YOUR READING

1. Explain why you and other students like you are an important economic force.
2. How does business itself create new consumer wants?
3. What is consumer demand?
4. How do you tell producers which goods and services you want? How do you let them know which goods and services you do not want?
5. Why are some consumers able to cast more economic votes than others?
6. In what way do you share the responsibility for deciding how our productive resources will be used?
7. Explain how consumers affect the fate of a business that sells only to other producers.
8. What happens to business enterprises when consumer spending shifts from one good or service to another?
9. In the long run, what determines the amount of goods and services produced?
10. In addition to consumers, who are the major spenders in our economic system?
11. What fraction of all that is produced in this country do consumers buy?
12. Explain why the spending decisions of business are based on consumer spending.
13. Why does the President's Council of Economic Advisers watch total spending closely?
14. A slowdown in consumer spending is likely to show up in sales of what kinds of items?
15. What efforts have been made in recent years to help avoid the waste that results when businesses make wrong guesses about what consumers will buy?
16. Why do most Americans prefer a consumer-directed economy?
17. Why are the people of the United States able to consume more goods and services than the people of any other nation?
18. What does a nation have to do in order to raise its standard of living?
19. Describe some of the noticeable changes that have taken place as our standard of living has increased.
20. Why is it important for business to continue to grow?

SHARING YOUR OPINION AND EXPERIENCE

1. What are necessities? Would you consider an automobile a necessity? Did your grandparents?
2. What are luxuries? Do you think the definition of luxuries might change as a nation's standard of living rises?

3. A well-known manufacturer of clothing for young women watches very carefully all census reports and estimates of future population figures. Why?
4. Sometimes a consumer may want a good or service and have enough money to buy it, yet not buy it. Why?
5. In 1964 the Congress of the United States voted a sizable reduction in Federal income taxes. What consumer action was expected to follow the tax cut?
6. Do you believe you should have the right to buy foolish frills if you have the money and want to spend it that way? Why?
7. We consume many things collectively through government, such as schools, parks, playgrounds, and libraries. Do these make up part of our standard of living? Explain.
8. The economic system of the United States is sometimes called a "market system." In what way do you think this name fits our type of economy?
9. What is market research?

PROJECTS AND PROBLEMS

1. Divide a sheet of paper in half lengthwise. On the left side list six to ten items you have purchased or might purchase that would create additional wants. Following each item, list on the right-hand side the items you would need or want as a result of buying it.

Article	Additional Wants
Example: Bicycle	*Tires, tubes, wire basket, bike light, speedometer, repair service, paint*

2. The way you spend your money helps to determine what goods and services are produced. Make a list of all your purchases during the past two weeks to show the kinds of goods and services you voted for. Be sure to include the money you spent for bus fare, dry cleaning, haircuts, and the like.
3. Classify the following items as either durable or nondurable goods: clothes dryer, pair of shoes, radio, breakfast cereal, vacuum cleaner, electric range, sweater, shampoo, wristwatch. Use a form similar to the one below.

Durable Goods	Nondurable Goods
	Example: Wooden pencil

4. The graph shown on page 79 is known as a *curve* or *broken-line* graph because it consists of a series of lines drawn from one point to another, sometimes in different directions. This type of graph is used to show changes of a particular kind that have taken place over a period of time. The one here, for example, shows changes in the production, or output, of consumer durable goods during a 32-month period. The units of quantity are shown along the vertical axis (upright

line at left). In this graph the numbers given indicate percents. The units of time (years, in this case) are shown along the horizontal axis (bottom line). Each small division represents one month. The upright lines running all the way to the top of the graph indicate the beginning of the year.

Output for each of the 32 months is compared with the average output during 1947 to 1949. This is called the *base period.* To read a broken-line graph, you compare the distance from each point to the horizontal axis. For example, in January of the first year, output of consumer durables was approximately 131 percent of output during the base period. Read the graph and answer the questions following it.

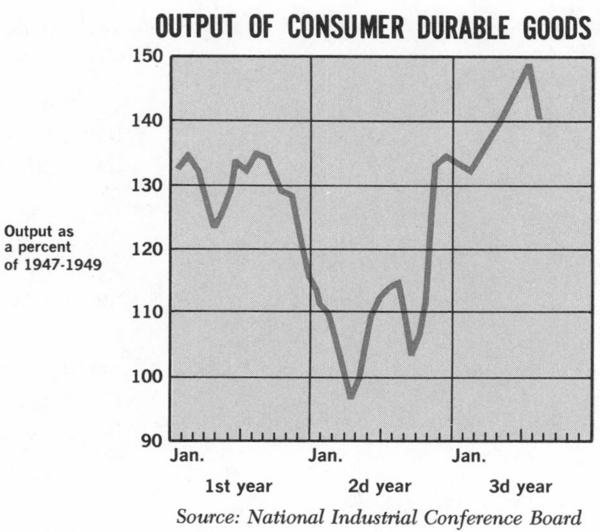

Source: National Industrial Conference Board

▪ *a.* During which of the three years was production of consumer durable goods lowest? ▪ *b.* Approximately what was the percent of decrease in production from the high point of the first year to the low point on the graph? ▪ *c.* Judging from the information given for the first eight months of the third year, would you estimate that output during the third year might be greater or less than for the first year? ▪ *d.* From what you learned about consumer spending in this part, what might have taken place during part of the first and much of the second year?

CHALLENGE PROBLEMS

1. Do you think that the amount of our nation's resources being used for schools is too small? Defend your position.
2. The United States is the richest nation in the world, and its standard of living has been rising steadily. Why then do we still have consumers who are poorly fed, poorly clothed, and poorly housed?

PART 10 PROBLEMS OF THE CONSUMER

ONCE upon a time, as you may remember, there was a king named Midas who wished that everything he touched would turn to gold. Hardly had his wish come true, however, than he regretted having made it. When first his glasses, then his food, and finally his daughter turned to gold, he realized how foolish he had been.

This tale simply proves that even kings have problems, including King Consumer. Day after day finds him surrounded by goods and services all of which seem to be saying, "Buy me!" They stare out at him from shop windows; they peer up at him from magazine and newspaper advertisements; they beckon to him from radio and TV commercials. But since he has only so much money to exchange for them, he must pick and choose. And, like King Midas, he does not always know what he wants or want what he gets. Because of foolish choices, he sometimes fails to make the most of his opportunities to achieve a high standard of living.

Why is it so difficult for consumers to make wise choices? How do a consumer's choices affect his standard of living?

Eastern Photo Service

WHAT ARE THE CONSUMER'S PROBLEMS?

Consumers in the United States may well be the envy of consumers elsewhere for reasons you already know. Nevertheless they do have problems. One of their big problems is that of deciding how to spend their money. Actually it is an economic problem. Most of us simply do not have enough money to satisfy all our wants. We are continually having to decide which ones to satisfy. This is sometimes very hard to do.

Consumers Have Many Choices

Imagine that you are very hungry and standing by a table heaped with all your favorite foods. In your hand you hold a ticket that entitles you to eat a certain number of them—say two or maybe three. If you take the pizza and the banana cake, then you cannot have the chili and lemon pie, or the hamburger and French fries, or the ice cream, or the chocolate eclair. It is difficult to make up your mind.

Having to choose between two or more desirable things is rarely easy, and the more choices we have, the harder it is. Our business system produces not only an abundance of goods and services, but a great variety of them. In addition, because of competition among producers, there are many brands of almost all of them. Take a simple thing like soap.

When the pioneer housewife needed soap, she got out her big iron kettle and made it. This soap was used for everything—the family wash, dishes, hands, face, bath, and hair. Today's homemaker may choose between soap or a detergent for the laundry. Moreover, she can select from a dozen or more brands of either one. Special products for washing dishes are just as numerous. Soaps for bathing include a kind that floats, a kind that rids the skin of germs, a kind that prevents odors, and a kind that comes in colors to match your bathroom. Shampoos come in cream or liquid; for dry, normal, or oily hair; and packaged in tubes, jars, bottles, or plastic containers. As someone once remarked, "It was easier for great grandmother to make a kettleful of soap than for today's housewife to decide which kinds to buy." Although this statement may be somewhat exaggerated, it serves to emphasize what a wide range of choices today's consumers have.

Consumers Lack Buying Skill

Back in the days when people made almost everything for themselves, a knowledge of how to buy was not important. Today, however, we purchase 90 percent or more of the many things we consume. How much we get for our money depends on our skill as buyers. Indeed, buying skill is so important a part of spending wisely that business firms hire specialists to do their buying. Yet the average family today buys a greater variety of items than most businesses and has little knowledge to guide it.

Consumers' efforts to spend their money wisely often fail because of their inability to judge quality. With so many goods and services for sale, it is hard to know which is best. Those who try to judge the quality of goods by their appearance often find that appearance can be deceptive. A used car may shine like new, but the motor may be worn out. A fresh coat of paint may cover up some very serious defects in a house. Packaged products are sometimes impossible to inspect before purchasing. Others like fountain pens, cars, and refrigerators are mechanical in construction and operation. Even if all their separate parts were visible, few consumers would be able to judge the quality of such products.

Lacking other means for judging quality, consumers sometimes use price as a guide. But prices for the same goods may vary from one store to another. Also, one article may be higher priced than another because of differences in style. White sidewall tires, for example, cost more than plain ones of the same quality because they are more costly to produce and not because they will wear longer. Consumers who use price as a guide to quality encourage producers to charge more for their goods and services than they are worth.

WHAT INFLUENCES CONSUMER CHOICE?

Some consumers work very hard at spending their money wisely. They try to choose from all goods and services available those that will give the most satisfaction. Others buy whatever happens to strike their fancy at the moment; that is, they buy

Photo courtesy B. Franklin

There are many ways consumers can be influenced to buy; one way is through fashion shows.

on ***impulse.*** But whether a consumer plans his purchases or buys on impulse, his decisions are bound to be influenced in some way by one or more of the following factors: income, personal values, fashion, desire to impress others, custom and habit, and advertising. Do you recognize any that play a part in your own spending decisions?

Income Influences Consumer Choice

How much does it cost? Isn't that one of the first things you want to know about anything you think of buying? If the price of a good or service is high compared to the amount you have to spend, you are not likely to buy it. In other words, income, or the amount of money available for spending, has an important bearing on consumer choices.

It stands to reason that the more money people have to spend, the more goods and services they can buy. Not quite so easy to see, perhaps, is the fact that what kinds of goods and services people buy also depends on how much they have to spend. Most of us try to satisfy our essential wants first. A student with a small allowance will spend most of it for necessities like bus fare to and from school, lunches, and school supplies. The smaller a student's allowance, therefore, the less choice he has in how he will spend it. The larger his allowance, the more extras he can buy like entertainment, snacks, grooming aids, or magazines. The same is true of families. The lower a family's income, the higher the portion spent for necessities such as food, clothing, and shelter. As family income rises, there is a tendency to buy more expensive kinds of food, clothing, and shelter. Money also becomes available for such things as recreation, travel, education, and jewelry. Usually the percent of income saved also increases.

The buying of goods and services other than necessities is called ***discretionary spending.*** It is in their discretionary spending that consumers have the widest choice.

Personal Values Influence Consumer Choice

The fact that families have identical incomes does not mean that they spend them in the same way. Although each of us has unlimited wants, we do not want exactly the same things. One person finds satisfaction in books or music, while another prefers to water-ski. One family likes to travel; another enjoys a beautifully furnished home. The family to whom a car is important may buy a new one every year. The family that drives the same car year after year may save its money for the children's college education instead. Our values, or what we consider important, are almost always reflected in the choices we make as consumers.

Fashion Influences Consumer Choice

Next to income, fashion probably influences consumer choice more than any other single factor. Everyone has it! Everyone is wearing it! Everyone is doing it! How often do you justify your spending on those grounds? Fashion dictates clothing styles, hairdos, colors, and leisure-time activities. And teen-agers are not its only followers, by any means.

Fashions come and go. A fad starts with a few students in school, then spreads as one after another adopts it. Just when it seems to be at its height, something new appears to take its place. Keeping up with fashion often leads to waste or unwise choices. Clothing may be discarded before it is worn out because it is no longer in style. Cars are sometimes traded in when still like new because they are not the latest model. People even dress in ways that are unbecoming to them rather than be different.

The Desire to Impress Others Influences Consumer Choice

Just as some people want to "follow the crowd," some want to stand out from the crowd. They buy to impress others. This is known as ***conspicuous consumption.*** Young people often attempt to impress others by being among the first to buy anything new or novel. Older people buy things that are considered marks of success, like furs, fancy cars, swimming pools, or boats. This is not to say that everyone who buys furs, an expensive car, a swimming pool, or a boat is looking for attention. It is only to say that the desire to impress others often leads people to buy these things, even though they cannot afford them.

Custom and Habit Influence Consumer Choice

When a couple becomes engaged, it is customary for the man to give the girl a diamond ring. In many colleges and high schools members of graduating classes wear caps and gowns. Custom and tradition play a bigger part in consumer choice than most of us realize. These are but two examples. It may be a family custom, a religious custom, a community custom, or a national custom. When faced with a choice, some people simply find it easier to do the customary thing than to make their own spending decisions.

At other times consumers often buy things as a matter of habit. They get in the habit of using the same brand of a product, eating at the same restaurant, shopping at the same store. They continue to do so without considering what other choices they have.

Advertising Influences Consumer Choice

Few goods are made to order today as they were at one time. Instead producers offer the kinds of goods and services they think people want. Then they must try to persuade consumers to buy what has been produced; therefore they advertise. They advertise in newspapers and magazines, on television and radio, by mail, or on billboards. A producer may even hire a skywriter to trace the name of his product high in the air. But no matter what form advertising takes, its purpose is to attract

Courtesy Gare Jewelers

Because of established customs, many couples feel that an engagement is incomplete without a ring.

Courtesy Michigan Consolidated Gas Company

Advertising has been effective in promoting the popularity of winter sports, which are a form of discretionary spending.

attention and create a demand for the good or service advertised.

Advertisers know well the factors that influence consumers' choices, and they use this knowledge to advantage. They appeal to our desire to be like everyone else—"Join the crowd and start wearing Snappy Sneakers." Some appeal to our desire to impress others—"Drive the car preferred by men of distinction." Some attempt to establish brand loyalty, so that consumers will get into the habit of buying that brand—"Always ask for Grandma's cookies." Many ads are designed to appeal to our pride or hidden fears. "Your family deserves the best!" or "If he doesn't ask for a second date, your breath may be the reason." This is known as ***emotional advertising.***

Another type of ad is the ***testimonial.*** In this type well-known persons—such as movie actors, professional athletes, or radio and television stars—are shown using a product. This is supposed to make you want it.

Few people escape the influence of advertising completely, nor should they want to. If used intelligently, good ads can help you spend your money wisely. It is largely through advertising that consumers learn of the choices available to them. Advertising is a harmful influence only when it misrepresents or when it persuades people to make unwise choices.

IT PAYS TO BE AN EFFICIENT CONSUMER

A consumer's buying decisions are important because they help to determine how the nation's productive resources are used. They also determine, to a great extent, the consumer's own standard of living. It is not at all unusual for families with identical incomes to have vastly different standards of living. This is because standards of living depend not only on the amount but also on the kinds of goods and services consumed. It is actually possible for people to improve their standards of living by becoming efficient consumers. An efficient consumer makes intelligent choices, plans his spending, and buys wisely. Much of this book is devoted to helping you become an efficient consumer.

BUILDING YOUR VOCABULARY

List the figures 1 to 5 on a sheet of paper, numbering down. Read the five statements given below at the right; then, for each statement, select from the column at the left the term that best matches it in meaning. Write this term next to the appropriate number.

conspicuous consumption
discretionary spending
emotional advertising
impulse buying
testimonial advertising

1. Spending without thought or plan
2. Buying goods and services from choice rather than necessity
3. The buying of goods for the purpose of impressing others
4. A way of promoting the sale of a product by appealing to the consumer's pride or fears
5. A recommendation for a product by persons who supposedly use it

CHECKING YOUR READING

1. What is one of the big problems for consumers in the United States? What factors tend to make the problem difficult?
2. What determines how much consumers get for the money they spend?
3. Why do consumers often fail in their efforts to spend their money wisely?
4. Is the price of a product a reliable guide in judging its quality? Why?
5. Explain how income, or the amount of money available for spending, influences the kinds of goods and services people buy.
6. What usually happens to the percent of income saved as a family's income rises?
7. Why do families with identical incomes not spend their money in the same way? Give examples.
8. Next to income, what factor probably influences consumer choice more than any other?
9. Explain how keeping up with fashion may lead to waste or unwise choices.
10. What is likely to happen when people buy goods just for the sake of impressing others?
11. How do custom and habit influence consumer choice?
12. Why do producers advertise?
13. How can advertisements help you spend your money wisely?
14. When is advertising harmful?
15. How does a person gain by becoming an efficient consumer? Describe what is meant by an "efficient consumer."

SHARING YOUR OPINION AND EXPERIENCE

1. Who has more problems as a consumer—a person who has a very large income or one who has a small income? Explain your answer.
2. What do you consider to be your biggest problem as a consumer?

3. Do you think people can learn to buy wisely?
4. Does the fact that you make wise or unwise choices as a consumer affect only you, or are others affected as well? Explain. What does your answer suggest about your responsibilities as a consumer?
5. How does the consumer benefit when there are many different brands of a particular product? Is it ever to his disadvantage to have many different brands?
6. How might the consumer's inability to judge quality make competition less effective?
7. As consumers we often imitate our friends and neighbors by spending money as they do. Is imitation ever a good thing? Give examples.
8. Some people say that changes in fashion tend to waste the consumer's money. Do you agree or disagree? Give reasons to support your position.
9. The statement is sometimes made that American automobile and appliance manufacturers follow a policy of "planned obsolescence." What does this statement mean?
10. Do you think the great amount of advertising done by business helps the consumer? If so, how?
11. Who pays the cost of advertising?
12. It has been said that consumers determine the type of advertising that producers use. Explain.

PROJECTS AND PROBLEMS

1. List several purchases you made recently that you now think were foolish or unwise. Explain what influenced you to make each purchase.
2. The table below shows how much of their incomes, after taxes, consumers spent for six items during three different years. Amounts shown are to the nearest one-tenth of a cent. In 1940, for example, consumers spent 26.7 cents out of every dollar of income for food and beverages. Test your ability to read the table by answering the questions following it.

THE CONSUMER DOLLAR

Item	*Cents per Dollar of After-Tax Income*		
	1940	*1950*	*1960*
Food and beverages	**26.7**	**26.6**	**22.8**
Housing	**12.2**	**10.2**	**12.0**
Clothing and shoes	**9.7**	**9.4**	**8.0**
Furniture and household equipment	**5.1**	**6.7**	**5.3**
Recreation	**2.2**	**1.9**	**1.7**
Personal service	**2.0**	**1.9**	**1.6**

▪ *a.* For which items did consumers spend a smaller percent of their incomes in both 1950 and 1960 than in 1940? ▪ *b.* For which item did they spend a larger percent in both 1950 and 1960 than in 1940? ▪ *c.* For which item did consumers spend less of their incomes in 1950 than in 1960? ▪ *d.* Approximately how many cents out of every dollar of income did consumers spend for food, clothing, and housing combined in 1940? in 1950? in 1960? ▪ *e.* The percent spent for food in 1960 was approximately how many times the percent spent for recreation? ▪ *f.* The number of cents per dollar spent on most items was less in 1960 than it was in 1940. Was this because prices were lower in 1960? If not, what other explanation can you give? ▪ *g.* The table does not list all items consumers buy. What one big item of expense has been omitted?

3. List five purchases that you or members of your family made recently in which the choices were influenced by fashion.
4. Many advertisements are designed to appeal to such human feelings as pride and fear. Others appeal to our desire for comfort, convenience, and conformity. Following are some headlines that have appeared in newspaper and magazine advertisements. Copy the headlines on a form similar to that shown below, and indicate by a check mark the appeal in each case.

Headline	Appeals to				
	Fear	Pride	Comfort	Convenience	Conformity
Example: It's easy to get into.				√	

▪ *a.* Do as "The Casuals" do. ▪ *b.* You don't have to search for frozen food in this freezer. ▪ *c.* In style! In step! ▪ *d.* Your morning is as good as your mattress. ▪ *e.* How can you live without this kind of car? ▪ *f.* How much is an eye worth? ▪ *g.* Science promises you new beauty. ▪ *h.* Are your child's "shots" up to date? ▪ *i.* How slender you were in the glow of the fire. ▪ *j.* Shoes that are kind to your feet.

5. As you read the name of each of the products listed below, write down the first brand name that comes to mind.

Soap	Chewing gum	Chocolate bar
Toothpaste	Bicycle	Shampoo

▪ *a.* For which items did the majority of the class name the same brand? ▪ *b.* How do you account for this result? ▪ *c.* Where did you learn about the brand names you listed?

6. Bring to class copies of two or three ads that really make you want to buy what is advertised. Explain why each ad appeals to you and causes you to want the product.

CHALLENGE PROBLEMS

1. A well-known advertising executive has urged consumers to boycott products they believe are "dishonestly advertised." He added that "when you suffer in silence, the good advertiser is confused and misled by your silence."

   ▪ *a.* What does "boycott" mean? ▪ *b.* What do you suppose he meant by "dishonestly advertised"? ▪ *c.* Do you agree or disagree with the advice? Why? ▪ *d.* Is there anything else you can do to discourage advertisements that are "dishonest" or in poor taste?

2. The following article appeared recently in newspapers throughout the country. Read it carefully, then answer the questions below.

REDS FAVOR ADVERTISING

Moscow.—Does the Soviet Union's planned economy need advertising? An emphatic "Yes" has appeared in *Izvestia*, the government newspaper.

Reporting on its own survey of advertising needs and facilities, the paper called for a system of billboards, posters, and other promotion methods to help the consumer make up his mind.

Izvestia said the growing consumer choice in the Soviet Union pointed to a need for a government-run advertising agency that would employ "not only artists and designers but market-research economists who would study the ebb and flow of demand, its prospects, its characteristics, its geography."

▪ *a.* According to the article, what purpose can advertising serve in a country that has a planned economy? ▪ *b.* What means of advertising did the article suggest be used in the Soviet Union? Do we use these same means in the United States? ▪ *c.* What development in the Soviet Union led to a need for advertising? ▪ *d.* Who would own and control the advertising agency? ▪ *e.* What did the article suggest that market-research economists do? ▪ *f.* Who makes studies of this kind in the United States and why?

PART 11 PLANNING YOUR SPENDING

THINK of all the people you know. Aren't there some who always get things done and still have time left over for fun? Can you also think of a few who never seem to accomplish anything worthwhile? Jim Cooper is like that where money is concerned. His allowance slips through his fingers like water through a sieve. Yet Jim never has much of anything to show for the money he spends.

Money is like time. Most of us never seem to have enough of it. Not long ago people from all parts of the nation were asked, "Next to world peace, what one thing do you want most for your family?" The majority answered, "More money." Yet these people had incomes ranging from $2,500 to $25,000 a year!

This seems to prove that money problems are not always a matter of "too little" money, even though there are many who would like to think so. They often result from a failure to manage money wisely. In other words, it is not only the amount of money you have that counts, but also how you use it.

WHAT IS WISE MONEY MANAGEMENT?

Unfortunately, many people confuse wise money management with penny-pinching. They call it being thrifty. But ***thrift*** does not mean hanging on to every possible cent. It means making the best use of anything that is limited in supply whether it be time, energy, or money. Saving a part of each allowance or paycheck is a good habit. The person who tries to save all his money, however, is no more sensible than the one who spends all of his.

Money is simply a medium of exchange. Your money is your claim to a share of the goods and services that have been produced. It is a means of satisfying your wants. When you do not have enough money to satisfy all your wants, you have

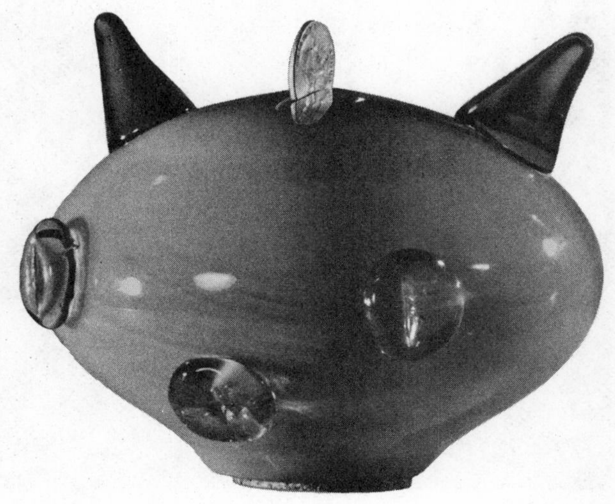

to ***economize.*** You have to make choices. Wise money management consists of making the right choices. It means using money in such a way as to obtain the greatest possible amount of satisfaction in return.

Spending Should Be Planned

The only sure way of getting the utmost satisfaction in return for your money is to plan your spending. A plan for spending is a ***budget.*** A budget is not a device for taking the fun out of life, as you might think from the way some people talk. It is simply a businesslike way of handling money. Successful business firms, governments, churches, clubs, and schools all budget.

There is nothing magic about a budget, to be sure. It will not put more money into your pocket. But if given a fair chance, it will help you to avoid financial difficulties resulting from poor management. Like the architect's blueprint, the dressmaker's pattern, and the traveler's map, a budget is a guide. It directs your spending. Like time, money has a way of just disappearing unless it is guided in the direction you want it to go.

A Budget Helps You to Live Within Your Income. Have you ever run out of money before it was time for your next allowance? Perhaps you had to stay at home while your friends went to that special movie you wanted to see. Or maybe you had to borrow bus fare or lunch money from your parents until "payday." Then you had even less to spend the following week because you had to repay the loan. After an experience of that kind it takes careful planning to keep from getting further into debt. Some people spend a lifetime dodging bill collectors and worrying over unpaid debts.

A budget helps you fit your spending to your income. When you plan your spending, you know how much money is needed for essentials like bus fare, lunches, and school supplies. And you know how much you can afford for snacks, fun, gifts, and hobbies. You can really enjoy these pleasures when you know that they have not been bought at the expense of needed items.

A Budget Helps You to Make Wise Choices. How many times have you spent money for one thing and then wished later you had kept it for something else? Well, no amount of wishing will give you everything you want. Budget or not, you still have to make choices. The only difference is that when you plan your spending, you stand

At home, the family gets together to plan the budget. In business, the top executives meet for the same purpose.

Ewing Galloway

a better chance of making the right choices.

There is a rule for making wise choices called the *principle of real cost.* Every choice involves a sacrifice. In order to have one thing, you have to give up another. The ***real cost*** of any choice is what you give up. Suppose, for example, that you have 35 cents left from your allowance this week. You can buy the latest issue of your favorite magazine, or you can join your friends for a malt after school. If you choose the malt, its real cost is the magazine; and vice versa. If you choose the magazine, its real cost is the malt. It is up to you to decide which will give you the most satisfaction. Planning your spending forces you to weigh the cost of your choices before you make them.

A Budget Forces You to Look Ahead. One of the difficult things about managing money is that expenses vary from week to week or month to month. Some, like music lessons, club dues, and church contributions occur regularly, while others occur only occasionally. These occasional expenses are often too large to be taken care of with one week's allowance. An example might be the school supplies you buy mostly at the beginning of each semester. The yearbook is another. To be sure of having enough money for these things when the time comes to buy them, you must set aside a little each week. Unless spending is planned, however, you are apt to satisfy only your present wants and ignore the future.

WHAT ARE THE CHARACTERISTICS OF A GOOD BUDGET?

All budgets have two things in common. They include (1) an ***estimate*** of income and (2) an estimate of expenses. This is true whether the budget is to be used by a business, a family, a club, or an individual. In addition, a good budget has three other important characteristics.

1. It includes a goal.
2. It is tailor-made.
3. It provides for systematic savings.

A Good Budget Has a Goal

The purpose of a budget, remember, is to help you get the things you want. This means that before you can budget, you have to decide what you do want. You have to face the fact that you cannot have everything you daydream about—at least not all at once. You will have to settle for one or a few things at a time. Otherwise, you would not need to budget. Once you have decided what you want, getting it becomes your goal. To reach it, you plan your spending so that some portion of your money is set aside for that purpose.

Some people find that it helps to make a written list of their wants in order of their preference. Such a list might look like this:

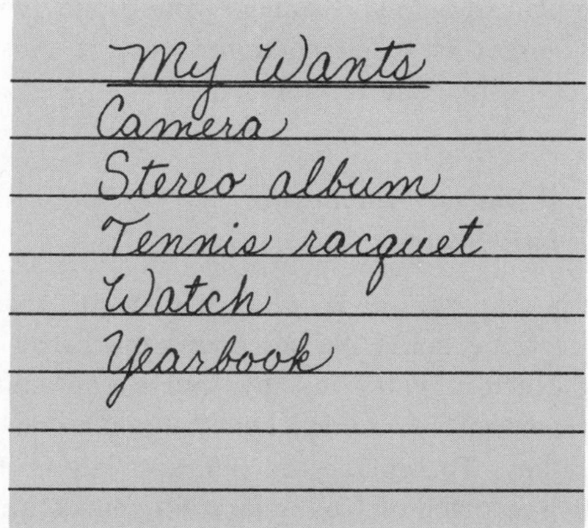

My Wants
Camera
Stereo album
Tennis racquet
Watch
Yearbook

The advantage of a written list is that it enables you to compare your wants from the standpoint of how important each one really is to you. Another advantage of a list is that you can refer to it from time to time. Some wants are lasting; others become less important as time goes on. You may find your order of preference changing. You may want to add or subtract items. Unless an item continues to hold top place on your want list, it may not give you as much satisfaction as something else. Even though your goal may change before you reach it, it is the heart of your budget. Budgeting without a goal would be like taking a trip without a destination.

You might never get anywhere. When you succeed in reaching one of your goals, you are ready to start working toward another.

A Good Budget Is Tailor-Made

Do you know what a tailor-made suit or dress is? It is one cut to the exact measurements of the person who is to wear it. Tailor-made clothes usually fit better than ready-made ones. This is also true of budgets. Just as no two people are exactly the same size and shape, no two have exactly the same values. Since people's values determine their goals, a spending plan that works well for one individual or family might not work at all for another. That is why you cannot rely on a ready-made plan to help you manage your money wisely. If a budget is to succeed for you, it must be designed especially for you.

A Good Budget Provides for Systematic Savings

Nothing can ruin a spending plan faster than an unexpected expense. No one knows this better than Patty Horton. Patty lost her purse containing a small amount of money, her ball-point pen, and locker key. To replace the pen and key cost her $1.99, the price of Cokes for two weeks, and an evening at the skating rink. Compared to adult misfortunes, such as illness, accidents, or losing a job, Patty's troubles may seem minor. For both teen-agers and adults, however, the best safeguard against unexpected expenses is a savings fund. Some people call them "rainy day" funds as if their only purpose was to tide you over bad times. But the unexpected can also be good fortune. It might be a chance to take a trip or to buy something you've been wanting at a special price. Joe Rivera's habit of saving part of each allowance enabled him to take advantage of just such an opportunity.

Joe played the drums in the high school band, using a set that belonged to the school. As you might guess, he hoped to someday have drums of his own. Then when he least expected it, he was offered a good set of secondhand drums at a fair price. Had he not had the money to buy them, Joe would have been bitterly disappointed.

You cannot predict good fortune or bad. But you can be financially prepared for either one if your budget includes a definite amount to be saved regularly.

NOW IS THE TIME TO BEGIN

The ability to manage money wisely is not something people are born with. Neither is it acquired with age. The ability to manage money is developed through practice. If you think that what you do with your money now does not matter, you are mistaken.

You will have more to spend when you are older, of course. But you will also be expected to pay for more things. If you cannot handle your present allowance or earnings successfully, you probably will do no better with your income later on. Habits formed in youth become firmly fixed as you grow older. You can get ready for the big job of spending your future income by learning to manage the money you have today, regardless of the amount. This is one case where experience really is the best teacher.

FAMILY BUDGETS REQUIRE COOPERATION

The rules for managing money wisely are the same for families as for individuals. Both must live within their incomes; they must apply the real cost principle to their choices; they must get ready to meet large occasional expenses; and they must prepare for emergencies by saving regularly. What complicates a family budget is the fact that it must meet the needs of a group rather than those of only one person. How a family uses its income affects every

A few coins saved each day can help buy extra vacation fun.

H. Armstrong Roberts

member. And how each member handles money affects the whole family. When you fail to live within your allowance, for example, you make it harder for your family to live within its income. Every extra cent you get means that much less money for something that the whole family might enjoy.

In many homes today budgeting is a cooperative affair. Every member of the family who is old enough participates. Together they decide how they can make the best use of the family's income. The advantages of having children share the responsibility for managing the family's finances are: (1) They learn some of the problems of maintaining a home. (2) They learn why money is not always available for the things they want. (3) They learn to manage their own money better by taking part in budgeting and buying with their parents.

Some mothers and fathers, on the other hand, feel they are sparing their children when they do not burden them with money matters. Others hesitate for fear their personal affairs will be discussed outside the family. But whether or not you help plan your family's spending, you can still practice wise management with your own money. The next part outlines the steps for you to follow.

BUILDING YOUR VOCABULARY

On a separate sheet of paper, write each of the terms listed in the left-hand column below and on page 94. Read the three definitions to the right of each term. After each term, copy the definition that best matches it in meaning.

1. budget
- *a.* A statement of income
- *b.* A record of money spent
- *c.* A plan for spending and saving

2. *economize*
a. To use money or some other resource to the best advantage
b. To plan the spending of money
c. To manage on as little money as possible

3. *estimate*
a. A record of income and expenses
b. A reasonably accurate guess
c. A budget based on past spending

4. *real cost*
a. The price of an article before sales tax is added
b. The price of an article including all taxes and selling expenses
c. The price of an article in terms of other goods or services the buyer might have bought

5. *thrift*
a. Efficient use of anything limited in supply
b. The habit of saving all or most of one's allowance
c. The practice of recording how money is spent

CHECKING YOUR READING

1. In what way is money like time?
2. What is wise money management?
3. In what way is a budget like a road map?
4. How can a budget help you get greater enjoyment from your spending?
5. Why is making choices so difficult?
6. How can a budget help you make wise choices?
7. Why do you need to look ahead in planning your spending?
8. What two things do all budgets have in common?
9. What are three characteristics of a good budget?
10. What are the advantages of making a written list of your wants?
11. Why do you need a goal when you make a budget?
12. Why should a budget be tailor-made?
13. Why should a budget include provision for saving?
14. How does a person learn to manage his money wisely?
15. Why is it important that you learn to manage money wisely while you are young?
16. Why is budgeting for a family more difficult than budgeting for an individual?
17. What are the advantages of having children share responsibility for managing the family's finances?

SHARING YOUR OPINION AND EXPERIENCE

1. It is generally considered wise to be thrifty, but unwise to be a miser. What is a miser? How does a thrifty person differ from a miser?
2. What should determine the size of a high school student's allowance?
3. It has been said that "the person who is careless in the use of what he buys is a poor money manager." Do you agree or disagree? Why?
4. Does the use of a budget guarantee wise choices? Why or why not?

5. How far ahead should a high school student be expected to plan the use of his money?
6. At what age do you think children should be brought into the family conference on money management?
7. Is it just as important to have definite goals in planning the use of your time as it is in planning the spending of your money? Explain.
8. "A good budget provides for systematic savings." What does "systematic" mean?
9. Give examples from your own experience of how a "rainy day" fund served as a "sunny day" fund.
10. If everyone spent money only for the things he absolutely had to have and saved the rest by hiding it under the mattress or placing it in a strongbox, how would business be affected?

PROJECTS AND PROBLEMS

1. Following is a list of items for which young people between twelve and eighteen spend their money.

Books and magazines
Bus fare or carfare
Candy
Church contributions
Club dues
Cosmetics
Dates
Gifts for others
Gum
Haircuts
Hobbies (camera, collections, models, etc.)
Ice cream
Jewelry
Lunches
Movies
Phonograph records
Savings
School events (plays, games, etc.)
School supplies
Soft drinks
Sports equipment
Student annual

Copy the list on a form similar to the one illustrated below.

Item	Spend Money for Each Week	Spend Money for Now and Then	Never Buy	Others Buy for Me
Example: × *Snacks*	√			

▪ *a.* Following each item, place a check mark in the appropriate column to indicate whether you purchase the item each week, now and then, or never. Also indicate by check marks which items your parents or others buy for you.
▪ *b.* Place a check mark in front of each item you consider a necessary expense.
▪ *c.* Place an "X" in front of each item for which you think you spend too much money.

2. In Part 10 you learned that each person and family has certain needs which should be taken care of first. After that the consumer is free to exercise his choice. In order to make wise choices, you must decide what you want. Divide

a separate sheet of paper into two columns, one headed "Needs," the other "Wants." Under "Needs" list the items you checked as necessary expenses for problem 1 as well as any other needs for which you are expected to provide that are not listed. Under "Wants" list the five or six things you would most like to have, that you might possibly buy for yourself by saving a little money each week. Circle the item you would choose as your goal for the budget you will be asked to make in Part 12. A month from now check to see what changes you would make in your list of "Wants."

3. The first step in making a budget is to find out how you are spending your money now. On a form similar to the one below, keep a record of your income and expenses for a week. Record the dates you receive money, where you get it, and the amounts. Write down every day the items for which you spend money and the amount you spend for each. Enter amounts saved in the right-hand column, but circle these amounts.

Date	Money Received	Amount		Date	Money Spent	Amount	
3/10/6–	*Example: Allowance*	2	25	*3/11/6–*	*Example: Bus fare*		*20*

4. According to some authorities, wise money management includes planning for a satisfactory income as well as planning for spending. List as many ways as you can think of that persons your age may earn extra money in their spare time. Place check marks after those that are especially suitable for boys and an "X" after each one especially suitable for girls. Make no marks after those that are equally suitable for both boys and girls.
5. When young people begin to earn money through part-time jobs, some people feel they should give up their regular allowances. Others feel they should continue to receive their allowances and use their own earnings for extras. Select a group to take part in a panel discussion on this subject or make it a topic for debate.
6. Choose four or more of your classmates and prepare and present a skit using a family conference on money management as the theme.

CHALLENGE PROBLEMS

1. Benjamin Franklin once said, "The use of money is all the advantage there is in having it." Explain what you think he meant by this statement.
2. People's values influence the way they spend their money. What determines the values a person has? To what extent should a person continue to examine and change his values?
3. It has been said that imagination and humor can be important aids in planning a budget. Give examples to illustrate how each might help you with your money-management problems.
4. How do you benefit today from the fact that others have saved in the past?

PART 12 MAKING AND KEEPING A BUDGET

OLAF JOHANNSEN managed his money as well as most boys his age. At least he made it last from one week to the next. Yet Olaf was dissatisfied because he never seemed to get any of the important things he wanted—like a certain record album that cost $4.98. Although Olaf was far from convinced that budgeting would enable him to buy the album, he decided to give it a try. After all, what could he lose? Olaf 's experiences are retold here merely to show how a person goes about making and keeping a budget.

BUDGETING INVOLVES THREE BASIC STEPS

As stated in Part 11, a spending plan must be designed to fit the income, expenses, and goals of the one who is to use it. Your budget would probably differ from Olaf Johannsen's in several ways. Everyone who budgets, however, follows pretty much the same procedures. They are:

1. Estimate income.
2. Plan how income is to be used.
3. Put your plan into action.

A spending plan must be based on some definite period of time, of course. As a rule, the length of the period is determined by how often you receive your allowance or pay. Olaf Johannsen decided to budget by the week because he received his money weekly.

Estimate Your Income

Estimating your income, the first step in budgeting, is the easiest. At least it is easy for people like Olaf who can count on a regular amount each week or month. Olaf receives a weekly allowance of $4

Monkmeyer Press Photo Service

from his parents and earns an additional $3 each week taking care of a neighbor's yard. His estimate of income for one week looked like this:

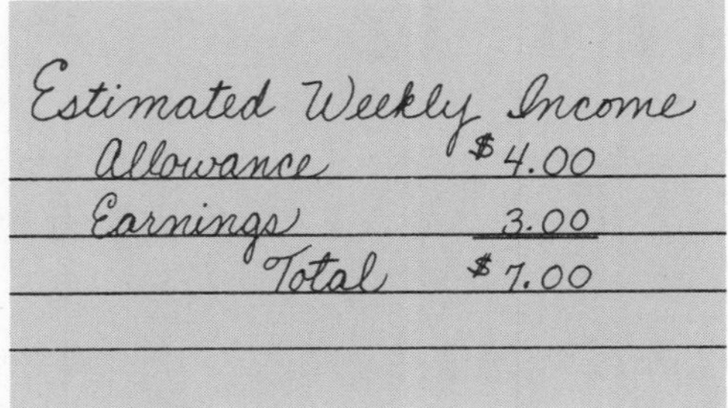

Estimated Weekly Income

Allowance	$4.00
Earnings	3.00
Total	$7.00

In estimating his income, Olaf decided not to include money received as gifts. Neither did he include extra amounts he sometimes earned washing the neighbor's car. Anything other than his regular allowance and earnings would go toward the record album.

If your income varies from one week to the next, that does not mean you cannot budget. You will simply have to figure on an average amount. Just remember that it is better to underestimate your income than to overestimate it. Otherwise, you may find that you do not have enough money to carry out your plan.

Plan the Use of Your Income

The hardest part of budgeting is planning how you will use your money. What makes it hard is that you can usually think of more ways to use money than your supply will cover. On the other hand, planning the use of your money is the most rewarding part of budgeting. These are the plans that are going to help you reach your goal.

People budget for one reason—to improve the way they spend their money. To do this, you have to know how you spend your money now. Big items and those that occur regularly are fairly easy to remember. For example, Olaf Johannsen had no difficulty remembering his bus fare to and from school and lunches on school days. He also remembered his church contribution and haircuts. But he had no idea how much he spent for such things as entertainment, snacks, hobbies, gifts, and school supplies. Rather than guess he did what many people do who are budgeting for the first time. He kept a record of his expenditures for a few weeks. An ***expenditure*** is an amount that has actually been spent. Olaf recorded his expenditures in a small notebook that he carried in his pocket. His record looked something like this:

Monday, Nov. 1	
Bus fare	$.20
Lunch	.30
Candy bar	.10
Notebook	.10
Tuesday, Nov. 2	
Bus fare	.20
Lunch	.30
Coke	.10
Popcorn	.15
Magazine	.35
Wednesday, Nov. 3	
Bus fare	.20
Lunch	.30
Film for camera	.35
Ice cream cone	.10
Ink	.15

Olaf's expenditure record revealed a few surprises; for example, he discovered that he was spending between $1.50 and $2 a week on snacks without realizing it. Twice he had paid fines for not returning his library books on time. The amounts were not large, to be sure. Nevertheless, Olaf felt the money could have been put to a better use, like helping him get the album he wanted. By the time he was ready to plan his future spending, he had decided that some of his old habits needed changing.

Begin with Fixed Expenses. In planning his future spending, Olaf began with his ***fixed expenses.*** These are expenses that are difficult to change. Olaf's fixed expenses consisted of bus fare to and from school, lunch on school days, his weekly church pledge, school supplies, and haircuts.

Managing money would be easier, of course, if all expenses were the same each week like the first three items on Olaf's list. Some, however, like his school supplies, vary. There were weeks when he bought none. At other times he bought quite a few. Altogether he estimated that he spent about $10 for school supplies during the year, not counting books. Olaf then divided the $10 by 40, the number of weeks school was in session, and put down 25 cents a week for school supplies. His haircuts cost $1.50 every other week. In estimating his weekly expenses, therefore, he put down 75 cents for haircuts.

Looking ahead, Olaf realized that in 12 more weeks he would have to pay for the yearbook he had ordered. The cost was $4.80. Dividing that by 12, he found that he would need to set aside 40 cents a week for this expense. For the present he considered that one of his fixed expenses.

Plan Discretionary Spending. By estimating his fixed expenses first, Olaf knew exactly how much money he had left to spend as he pleased. Now he had to stop and ask himself what he wanted his money to do for him. What goal or goals was he going to set for himself? His chief goal at the moment, of course, was the record album. Since this was his first attempt at budgeting, Olaf was wise to choose a goal that he could reach in a fairly short time. As he gained experience, he would be able to make long-range plans. Olaf also decided to protect his plan against an unforeseen expense by starting a savings fund and adding a definite amount to it each week.

What a Finished Plan Looks Like. When Olaf had finished estimating his future expenses, his plan looked like this:

Estimate of Weekly Expenses	
Bus fare	$1.00
Lunches	1.50
Church	.50
Haircut	.75
School supplies	.25
Fun	1.40
Savings	.50
Album	.70
Yearbook	.40
Total	$7.00

Notice that Olaf grouped some of his expenses. For example, snacks, magazines, entertainment, hobbies, and other recreation activities were lumped together under "Fun."

Olaf's first estimates of planned expenses did not fit his income exactly as you might think from the illustration. Like most people, he found it necessary to make a few adjustments. He also felt a little disappointed that he could set aside only 70 cents each week toward the record album. This meant that it would be seven weeks before he had enough to buy it. Without a spending plan, however, he might never get it.

Put Your Plan into Action

The success of any budget depends on how close actual expenditures come to the amounts planned for them. After planning how he would use his money, therefore, Olaf Johannsen continued to keep a record of his expenditures. Whenever he spent any money, he wrote down the amount and what it was for in the notebook he carried. In addition, Olaf worked out a system for recording his income, his budget estimates, and his actual expenditures on the same sheet. Every day or two he took a few minutes to transfer the items in his notebook to this sheet. He called it a COMBINED

INCOME AND EXPENSE RECORD. You will find it illustrated below.

You will notice that the groups into which Olaf divided his spending appear as column headings under "How I Used My Money." In the column marked "Other," he recorded expenditures that did not fall into one of the special groups. On November 25, for example, he entered the 15 cents spent for shoelaces in this column. The cost of his haircuts and his church contribution were also recorded there.

Just below each group heading, he wrote the amount estimated for that group. This enabled him to tell almost at a glance how well he was following his plan. The amount under savings included both his yearbook and record-album funds in addition to his regular savings.

Olaf left space on the extreme right of his record to explain payments that were not perfectly clear. Amounts shown under "Other" were usually explained, and sometimes money that had been spent for "Fun," as the magazine he bought on November 24. He always made note of sums spent for snacks, because this was an expense he intended to control. The small check marks indicate to which items his explanations refer.

By studying this record, you will see that Olaf wrote the date in the first column. The month he indicated only at the beginning of each week or when the month changed. He recorded his income in the "Money Received" column. In the "Money Spent or Saved" column, he entered the total of each day's expenditures and savings. The totals of the five columns under "How I Used My Money" should equal the total of the "Money Spent or Saved" column. You can check this on Olaf's record, if you like. The difference between the totals of the "Money Received" and the "Money Spent or Saved" columns should equal the cash on hand. Olaf could check on this at any time, but he entered it in his record only once each week. In the illustration the cash on hand is shown as the ***Balance.*** Any balance

Olaf Johannsen

COMBINED INCOME AND EXPENSE RECORD FOR THE PERIOD BEGINNING Nov. 24, ENDING Nov. 30

DATE	MONEY RECEIVED		MONEY SPENT OR SAVED	HOW I USED MY MONEY					EXPLANATION
				Savings	Bus Fare and Lunches	School Supplies	Fun	Other	
				EST. $1.60	EST. $2.50	EST. $.25	EST. $1.40	EST. $1.25	
Nov. 24	Balance	15							
24	Allowance	4 00	1 85	1 00	50		35		Magazine
25			65		50			15	Shoelaces
26			65		50	05	10		Coke
27			50		50				
28	Earnings	3 00	1 05		50	10	45		
29			75	60			15		Caramel corn
30			50					50	Church
	Totals	7 15	5 95	1 60	2 50	15	1 05	65	
	Balance		1 20						
		7 15	7 15						
Dec. 1	Balance	1 20							

was then carried over to the following week as money received.

GIVE YOUR BUDGET A FAIR TRIAL

You cannot judge your spending plan on the basis of only one or two weeks. Total expenditures for one group seldom come to exactly the amount planned each week. Sometimes they will be more; sometimes less. Only by averaging your expenditures over a period of time can you tell how accurately you have estimated.

Suppose, after a fair trial, you find that one group of expenditures still exceeds the amount planned. Then either you have underestimated this group, or you are spending carelessly. On the other hand, should one group be consistently under your estimate, you have probably allowed too much for it. Your record of expenditures will show you where your budget needs to be adjusted. You may have to experiment for several weeks before you get your plan operating properly.

A budget is not a hard-and-fast rule for spending. Always think of your budget as a ***flexible*** plan that can be changed to meet changing conditions. Every budget has to be revised occasionally. Your wants will change from time to time. Your income may go up or down. The cost of the things you buy may increase. Whenever your plan is not meeting your needs, the time has come to ***revise*** it.

WHY KEEP RECORDS?

The most disagreeable part of budgeting to some people is the record keeping. It is important to understand, however, that the expenditure record is not the budget. Your budget is the plan you make for spending your money. An expenditure record is nothing more than a device for checking on how well you are carrying out your plan. The thing that really counts is how you use the record. Knowing where your money has gone is of little value unless the knowledge serves as a basis for improving your spending.

It is even possible to budget without keeping records. Some people use a set of envelopes, one for

This young man realizes that his budget will have to be changed considerably now that he wants to buy a car to replace his motor scooter.

each kind of expenditure. When they receive their allowance or pay, they put in each envelope the amount their plan calls for. Sometimes small jars, boxes, or cans are used in place of envelopes. A system of this kind, of course, makes it awkward to carry money with you. It would seem less trouble and certainly more business-like to keep a simple record. The combined income and expense record Olaf uses requires only a few minutes' work each day. Yet it tells him everything that he needs to know.

Your group headings for such a record might not be the same as Olaf's. The student who buys some of his own clothing, for example, would need a column for that. Remember, though, that too many groups of expenditures can make your record difficult to handle.

Wise money management, after all, is really an attitude toward money. Once you have developed this attitude, you may no longer need to write down each expenditure. In the long run your success in budgeting will depend on your ability to make wise choices and your ability to make and carry out a plan.

BUILDING YOUR VOCABULARY

Copy the five sentences below, completing each one by replacing the question mark with the appropriate term from the column at the left.

balance
expenditure
fixed expenses
flexible
revise

1. An amount of money that has actually been spent ? .
2. A budget that can be changed to meet changing conditions is ? .
3. Costs that are necessary and difficult to change are ? .
4. Whenever a budget is not meeting your needs, you should change or ? it.
5. The difference between "Money Received" and "Money Spent or Saved" is the cash on hand or ? .

CHECKING YOUR READING

1. Name three steps that are generally followed in making and keeping a budget.
2. What usually determines the length of the period covered by a budget?
3. What is the first thing you should do in making a budget?
4. If you do not have a regular income, how do you go about estimating what your income will be?
5. Why is it better to underestimate your income than to overestimate it?
6. What is the most difficult part of budgeting? Why is it difficult?
7. For what one reason do people budget?
8. Which types of expenditures usually are easiest to remember?
9. Why should fixed expenses be estimated first in making up a budget?
10. Why is it important to continue to keep a record of actual expenditures even after budget estimates have been made?
11. Why is a week or two not long enough to judge how well a budget is working?
12. Why does every budget have to be revised occasionally?
13. Explain how it may be possible to budget without keeping records.
14. Why should you avoid dividing your expenditures into too many groups?
15. In the long run, what determines your success in budgeting?

SHARING YOUR OPINION AND EXPERIENCE

1. Does the fact that you plan your spending mean that you will have to buy less than you could buy otherwise? Explain.
2. Some people believe that in planning the use of your income you should list savings first. Do you agree or disagree? Why?
3. Would it have been less important for Olaf to budget if his income had been $14 a week instead of only $7? Explain.
4. What does the expression "balancing the budget" mean?
5. Some people maintain that a written record of expenditures should contain only the big items. Do you agree or disagree? Why?
6. What is meant by a one-sided budget or spending plan?
7. Should all boys consider haircuts a fixed expense? Why?
8. Olaf could have accumulated the money for his record album in less time had he set aside 25 cents instead of 50 cents each week for his regular savings fund or if he had decided to put money in the savings fund only when he wanted to give up part of his fun money. Do you think either course would have been advisable? Why?
9. What will Olaf do with the $1.20 he had left over at the end of his first week of keeping a combined income and expense record?
10. Why does your attitude toward budgeting make a difference in whether your budget is successful or not?

PROJECTS AND PROBLEMS

1. On the left half of a sheet of paper list the major fixed expenses you would expect most students your age to have. On the right half of the same sheet list some of the flexible expenses (those variable in amount but still certain to occur) that most students have. Use a form similar to the following.

Fixed Expenses	Flexible Expenses
Example: School lunches	*Example: Snacks*

2. Bill Anderson, who is a sophomore in high school, receives a weekly allowance of $2 and earns $6.50 working part time. In spite of the fact that his total weekly income is $8.50, he always seems to be short of money. When a friend suggested that he budget, Bill decided to give it a try. He wrote down his income and made an estimate of his expenses for the coming week. His first attempt at a budget is shown on page 104. As you can see, the total of his expenses was greater than his income; and he had allowed nothing for savings.

   Copy Bill's budget in the first two columns of a form similar to the one shown. In the right-hand column show how you think Bill should revise his spending plan in order to make the best use of his income. Be prepared to explain each change you make in Bill's budget.

Income		*Estimated Expenses*	
Allowance	**$2.00**	**Savings**	**$0.00**
Earnings	**6.50**	**Bus fare**	**.75**
Total	**$8.50**	**Ball games**	**.75**
		Cokes	**.50**
		Dates	**3.00**
		Lunches	**2.25**
		Movies	**.75**
		School supplies	**.25**
		Miscellaneous	**2.00**
		Total	**$10.25**

Income			Estimated Expenses			Revised Estimates		

3. Write the following group headings across the top of a sheet of paper: Savings, Clothing, Lunches, School Supplies, Fun, and Other. Using the record of income and expenses you kept for problem 3, on page 96 of Part 11, list each expenditure under the appropriate heading. Total the amount spent for each group. For example, if you spent 40 cents for notebook paper and 25 cents for pencils, the total spent for school supplies would be 65 cents.
4. The chart you prepared in problem 3 shows how you spent your money last week. On a form similar to the one below, prepare an estimate of your income and expenses for next week.

HOW I PLAN TO USE MY MONEY NEXT WEEK					
Estimated Income			Estimated Expenses		

5. If you are not using the Student Activity Guide, rule a combined income and expense record similar to the one illustrated on page 100. Use only as many columns under "How I Used My Money" as you need, and use whatever column headings fit the way you spend your money. Include on your record the amounts estimated in problem 4. Keep a record of your income and expenses for the next two weeks, and see how well you can follow the budget you have made.

CHALLENGE PROBLEMS

1. One family of four with a monthly after-tax income of $500 planned its spending as follows:

Clothing	$ 65
Food	125
Operating expenses	45
Savings	110
Shelter	80
Advancement	75
	$500

▪ *a.* What items do you think would be included under "Operating Expenses"? ▪ *b.* What do you suppose the item "Advancement" includes? ▪ *c.* Do you think this is a realistic spending plan? Why? ▪ *d.* What changes would you make in the budget? ▪ *e.* Why is it important for people to plan their spending on the basis of their after-tax income?

2. Budgets of businesses, charitable organizations, clubs, governments, and other organizations are similar in some ways to personal or family budgets. In other respects they may be quite different. Study a recent copy of the budget of the Federal government (you may find one in a newspaper or news magazine on file in your school library). Then answer the following questions.

▪ *a.* What were the major items listed in the budget? ▪ *b.* Give examples of some of the expenditures that might fall under each of the major items in the budget. ▪ *c.* Was the total of proposed expenditures less than, the same as, or greater than estimated income? Was this the answer you expected? ▪ *d.* Are the principles of budgeting the same for governments as for individuals? If not, how do they differ and why?

PART 13 THE ART OF SPENDING

SPENDING is an art. It is the art of changing money into goods and services. Some call it *buymanship;* others, *buying skill* or *know-how.* But whatever you call it, it is a skill worth developing. Haven't you ever noticed how some people seem to get more in exchange for the same amount of money than others? Not only that, they do it with less effort. These people know and practice the art of spending. They have buying skill.

Perhaps your parents still make the decisions about your major items of expense, such as food and clothing. Your own money may be used only for small purchases. Even so you want to get just as much for your money as you can. Moreover, just as your income will increase, so will your buying responsibilities. Buying skill, like any other skill, takes time to acquire.

How does buying skill affect a person's or family's standard of living? How might a consumer's lack of buying skill work against competition? How would you describe an efficient shopper?

WHY IS BUYING SKILL IMPORTANT?

Budgeting is only the first step in managing money wisely. Buying skill is the second. The purpose of planning your spending is to make certain you get *what* you want for your money. *How much* you get depends on how good a shopper you are. You may follow your budget faithfully yet waste some of your money needlessly through careless buying habits.

Buying skill cannot increase the amount of money you have to spend any more than a budget can increase it. Buying skill can, however, increase your ***purchasing power*** or the amount your money will buy. Suppose, for example, that by shopping carefully you saved 5 cents out of every dollar. In

Courtesy A T & T Photo Service

time these savings would enable you to buy additional things, goods you would not be able to buy otherwise. It would be the same as if you received a 5 percent increase in your allowance or pay. In other words, you would be extending your own purchasing power through efficient shopping. Any increase in purchasing power, of course, makes possible a higher standard of living.

Getting all the value you can for your money is important for another reason. Consumers who are particular about what they buy and how much they pay for it encourage producers to turn out good quality products at low prices. Competition cannot do its job well when consumers pay more than necessary for poor quality goods or services.

WHAT IS BUYING SKILL?

Shopping requires more than money. It also takes time and energy. Buying skill is nothing more than common-sense practices that make wise use of all three. What are some things you might do to save time and energy as well as money when you go shopping? The first one is to plan beforehand. Planning seems to be the key to success in many of our activities, doesn't it? It not only seems that way, it is a fact. Whether you are giving a party, taking a trip, or exchanging your money for goods or services, the results depend largely on the planning you do beforehand. In other words, efficient shopping begins at home.

An important part of this planning, of course, is budgeting or deciding how to spend your money. In addition, it should include most or all of the following.

Decide What to Buy

It may seem unbelievable that anyone would go shopping without having decided what he was going to buy; but it happens over and over again. Charlie Barnes is the perfect example. Charlie saw a tie he liked in the window of a men's store. So he marched right in and bought it without a second thought. Imagine his disappointment when he got home to find that the tie did not go with his suit.

When you make a budget, you decide in a general way how you will spend your money. Suppose, for example, that you have $25 a month to spend. Out of this you are expected to buy most of your own clothes. Let us say you decide to budget half of it, or $12.50 for clothes. Before spending your $12.50, however, you should know exactly what your clothing needs are. Here is the way Jean de Fraine went about it.

Like Charlie Barnes, Jean was responsible for buying her clothes. But before going shopping, Jean took an ***inventory*** of her wardrobe to see what clothes she already had. On the basis of this inventory she decided that her next purchase should be a blouse. Since the blouse was for school, she felt a simple style would be best. A white or plain color would go with all her skirts. Five dollars was the most she could pay.

This kind of systematic planning should not be limited to buying clothes. Food shopping is easiest for the housewife who plans her meals in advance. Likewise, a family will achieve better results in furnishing its home if it begins with an overall plan. Then each new purchase can be chosen to fit into the plan.

Decide What Quality to Buy

A rule among smart shoppers is "Buy on the basis of intended use." What does this mean? It means that the way an article is to be used should determine your choice. Take an ordinary item like pencils. Pencils usually carry a number, ranging from 1 to 4. The lower the number, the softer the lead. Soft lead makes a blacker mark than hard lead. The number to buy depends on how you intend to use the pencil.

The way an article is to be used also determines the quality you need. When Kathy Burgess needed a costume for the school play, her mother bought the least expensive material she could find for the purpose, knowing that the costume would be worn only a few times. When buying material for Kathy's school clothes, however, Mrs. Burgess is careful to choose a kind that will wear well.

Price, as you already know, is not always a reliable guide to quality. Nevertheless, goods of high quality generally do cost more than similar goods of lower quality. You would expect a garden hose ***guaranteed*** to last ten years to cost more than one guaranteed for only five. Suppose the better hose cost $6.57 compared to $4.77 for the other. Anyone needing a garden hose would get more for his money by taking the higher-priced one.

When buying goods intended to last a long time, it is wise to get the best quality you can afford. Sometimes, however, to buy the best quality might be a waste of money. Dan Bolsted, who is 15, needs a new suit of clothes that he will wear only for special occasions. No suit on the market will last Dan any longer than it will take him to outgrow it. For his purpose Dan does not need the best quality. Buying for intended use is one of the best ways to make your shopping dollars go further. Deciding in advance what quality you need also saves time.

Decide Where to Buy

Some stores carry a large selection of merchandise. Others offer buyers little choice. In some a well-trained staff of clerks is on hand to serve you. In others you wait on yourself. The point to keep in mind is that marketing services cost money. This cost must be included in the prices charged for merchandise. Usually goods are least expensive where a minimum of service is provided. Where you buy, therefore, may make a difference in whether or not you make the best use of your money.

Choosing the right place to shop is like choosing the right quality. The decision has to be made on the basis of each individual's requirements. Mrs. Kennedy, a busy housewife with three small children, finds it convenient to shop by telephone, to charge goods, and to have them delivered. The merchants who provide her with these services charge higher prices for the same goods than those who do business on a cash-and-carry basis. But to Mrs. Kennedy the extra service is worth the extra cost.

Mrs. Flannery prefers to shop in person, so that she can make her own selections. For most of her purchases she pays cash and, except in the case of unusually large or bulky items, carries them home herself. If Mrs. Flannery traded at stores where prices included the costs of credit and delivery, she would be wasting part of her money. She would be paying for services that she did not use.

Where you buy is important not only from the standpoint of how much you get for your money, but it is also important to our business system as a whole. Remember that every time you make a purchase, you are encouraging the merchant who serves you to stay in business. If he is a reliable merchant, then you are encouraging good business practices. On the other hand, when you buy from ***unethical*** dealers, you are approving their way of doing business.

Decide When to Buy

Did you know that in some places haircuts cost more on Saturdays than on other days of the week? This is because barbershops are busiest on Saturdays. If you can get your haircut earlier in the week, you will not only save time and money, you may get a better haircut.

Timing your buying to avoid rush hours can work to your advantage in several ways. Clerks are able to give you better service when they are not being hurried by a line of waiting customers. When stores are crowded, you too are apt to feel rushed.

You may get more for your money in a self-service clothing store, but it takes time, energy, and real buying skill.

Courtesy Robert Hall

You may not always take the time to examine merchandise carefully, to ask questions, and to make up your mind leisurely. In such a situation, you can easily make a wrong decision.

Seasonal goods, like fresh fruits and vegetables, are cheapest when they are most plentiful. Prices of this year's models of automobiles and household appliances are reduced just before and after the new models are introduced. Clothing prices are lowest at the end of the season. You may be able to get a much better buy on a winter coat in February than in October, although you will not have so large a selection from which to choose. In picking the time to buy, you have to decide which is more important to you—price or selection.

Watch for Sales

Real bargains can sometimes be had by shopping at sales. Many stores have regularly scheduled sales to encourage buying during slack periods. January white-goods sales, July shoe sales, and August furniture sales are examples. Most stores also have clearance sales to get rid of seasonal goods and make room for new merchandise. Right after Christmas, for example, tree ornaments, gift wrappings, and greeting cards can often be bought at greatly reduced prices.

Some retailers, however, have endless fire or closing-out sales that are not sales at all. Others do not reduce the price of their regular stock but bring in merchandise especially for the sale. If you are able to judge the quality of merchandise, you can sometimes profit by shopping at sales. Just beware of any store that has one sale after another.

One danger of buying at sales is that because of low prices you may be tempted to buy things for which you have little use. Regardless of its price, nothing is really a bargain unless you need it.

Make Good Use of Advertising

When a TV show you are watching is interrupted for a "few words from the sponsor," is that when you go fix yourself a snack? Sometimes advertising is a real nuisance, to be sure. But aren't there even more times when you depend on it for information about new products, the latest styles, or what's showing at the movies? Good shoppers also study ads to find out where the things they want may be purchased and what they cost. The more you know about the things you are going to buy, the more likely you are to make the right choices. You can often learn the features of different brands through advertisements. Advertisements that tell you what you want to know about a product are called ***informative*** advertisements. Unfortunately, all advertising is not of this type. Sometimes you have to be pretty alert to distinguish between the advertiser's fanciful claims and the facts. Even so, it would be foolish to ignore advertising completely just because some is exaggerated or in poor taste.

As an aid in planning your buying, perhaps no advertisements are more helpful than those in your newspaper. They not only inform you about what is for sale in local markets, they often enable you to compare prices without leaving home.

Make a Shopping List

Of all things a person might do before leaving home to shop, making a list of the items he plans to buy seems the most obvious. A list is a great time-saver because it helps to organize a shopping trip. It prevents your forgetting things. But more than that, the fact that you have made a list indicates that you know what you want. Yet nearly two-thirds of the nation's shoppers never carry a list. They make most of their purchases on impulse. As a result they often buy more than they should or pay more than they should. Even worse, they are often disappointed with their purchases.

Shopping List
Notebook and paper
Dark green knee socks
Silk head scarf
Ball-point pen
Record (1 from top-10-list)
Gift for Mary Jane – costume jewelry

Use the Telephone

How many times have you darted from one store to another looking for something you wanted? Telephoning to find out which stores handle what you want can save time as well as steps. A few telephone calls may also enable you to compare prices without going directly to the stores.

BUILDING YOUR VOCABULARY

Copy the six sentences below and on page 111, completing each one by replacing the question mark with the appropriate term from the column at the left.

guarantee
informative
inventory
purchasing power
seasonal
unethical

1. The amount money will buy is its ? .
2. An itemized list of property or possessions is an ? .
3. A promise that a product is as represented or will perform in a certain way is a ? .
4. A dealer who has no regard for good business practices is ? .
5. Goods that are more plentiful during certain times of the year than at other times are ? .

6. Advertisements that tell you what you want to know about a product are ? .

CHECKING YOUR READING

1. Why is buying skill just as important as budgeting?
2. Explain how buying skill can increase your purchasing power.
3. How is business competition affected when consumers are efficient shoppers?
4. What is buying skill?
5. What is the first thing you should do if you want to be a skillful shopper?
6. How can taking an inventory of your wardrobe before going shopping increase the satisfaction you get from your clothing purchases?
7. What guide should you follow in deciding what quality article to buy?
8. When is it wise to buy the best quality you can afford? When might it be unwise?
9. Why is it important to plan where you will shop?
10. Explain why your decisions about where you buy are important to our business system.
11. What are the advantages of timing your shopping so as to avoid rush hours?
12. What are the advantages of seasonal buying? What are the disadvantages?
13. Can a person ever save by buying at sales? Explain.
14. What are some things you should be cautious about in connection with sales?
15. Why do wise buyers study advertisements before they go shopping?
16. What type of advertising is probably most useful from the standpoint of planning your shopping?
17. What are the advantages of making a shopping list before you go shopping?
18. In what ways can the use of the telephone make you a more efficient shopper?

SHARING YOUR OPINION AND EXPERIENCE

1. Why is buying skill more important today than it once was?
2. Explain the meaning of the old saying, "A penny saved is a penny earned."
3. What are some things other than a difference in quality that might make one article cost more than a similar one?
4. Do you have any special methods of judging the quality of the things you buy? If so, what are they?
5. Explain how an article of poor quality may actually be more expensive than a similar one of better quality even though the poor quality article costs less.
6. What is your definition of a bargain?
7. How does the amount and variety of stock a merchant carries affect his operating costs?
8. From the standpoint of personal satisfaction, what were the best and the worst buys you ever made? What made the difference between the two?
9. Give some examples from your own experience of how you saved money by timing your buying.

10. In Part 11, you learned about the importance of making wise choices. How does choice making differ from actual shopping?

PROJECTS AND PROBLEMS

1. Some goods are in greater supply and some are in greater demand at certain times of the year than at others. Using a form similar to that shown below, copy in the left-hand column the following items: sweet corn, Christmas cards, air-conditioner, men's straw hats, lawn mower, swimsuit, a rental vacation cottage in Florida, a rental vacation cottage in Minnesota, snow skis, a winter coat. After each item indicate when it is most plentiful and when the demand for it is greatest. If there is little change in the supply of an item throughout the year, write the word "constant" in the "Supply" column. In the last two columns indicate when the price of each item is lowest and when it is highest.

Item	In Greatest Supply	In Greatest Demand	When Cheapest	When Most Expensive
Example: Snow shovel	*Nov.–Dec.*	*Dec.–Feb.*	*Apr.–June*	*Nov.–Feb.*

All items you listed in your table are seasonal in nature. But some are lowest in price when in season; others are highest in price when in season.

▪ *a.* When they are highest in price, which is greater—the demand for them or the supply of them? ▪ *b.* When they are lowest in price, which is greater—the demand or the supply? ▪ *c.* What generally happens when the demand for an item increases but the supply of it does not? ▪ *d.* What generally happens when the demand for an item decreases while the supply remains unchanged?

2. Some stores hire a staff of well-trained salespersons to serve you, while others let you "serve yourself." List four types of stores in which you would prefer to serve yourself and four in which you would prefer to have trained salesclerks serve you. Give your reasons in each case.
3. Sometimes it is wise to buy the best quality item available even though the price is high. In other cases, a medium quality item is the most economical buy. Indicate for each of the following items whether you would buy a good quality or a medium quality. Give reasons for your answers.

   ▪ *a.* shoes for a two-year-old child ▪ *b.* bicycle ▪ *c.* portable typewriter ▪ *d.* Halloween costume ▪ *e.* pair of summer shoes ▪ *f.* tennis racquet for a beginner ▪ *g.* billfold ▪ *h.* binder for your loose-leaf note paper.

4. List four items you plan to buy in the near future. Describe what purpose you expect each article to serve. For example, if you plan to buy a shirt or blouse, do you want it for school, for dress, or both? List the special features you want the article to have, such as long sleeves, short sleeves, washability, and the like. Estimate the cost of each item and the places where you might purchase it.

5. The following statements have appeared in newspaper advertisements. On the left half of a sheet of paper, copy each statement that you think is helpful to the consumer. On the right half of the sheet, copy each statement that you think has little or no meaning.

▪ *a.* 100% wool ▪ *b.* All parts guaranteed 30 days ▪ *c.* Made to sell for $40 ▪ *d.* Double your money back if you are not satisfied ▪ *e.* You get more miles per gallon ▪ *f.* The best buy of the year ▪ *g.* Jumbo pound ▪ *h.* Offers you substantial savings ▪ *i.* Grade A ▪ *j.* All-steel construction ▪ *k.* Hand tailored ▪ *l.* 25 cents off ▪ *m.* Sanforized ▪ *n.* Giant half-gallon

6. Sometimes style is more important to a consumer than quality. List four items for which you consider style or looks so important that you would be willing to pay extra for them. White sidewall tires might be an example.
7. In the left-hand column of a form similar to the one shown below, list the names of five stores in your community. For each store listed, answer questions *a–d.* Answer questions *a* and *b* by writing "Yes" or "No" in columns *a* and *b.* Answer question *c* by writing "Higher," "Lower," or "Same" in column *c.* Answer question *d* by writing the special services offered by each store in column *d.*

▪ *a.* Does it carry a large selection of merchandise? ▪ *b.* Does it employ an adequate sales staff? ▪ *c.* Are the prices higher, lower, or the same as those charged by other stores for merchandise of the same quality? ▪ *d.* What other services does it offer—credit, delivery, phone orders, mail orders, etc.?

Name of Store	a	b	c	d
Example: Wright Drug Co.	*Yes*	*Yes*	*Same*	*credit, free delivery, 24-hour service*

8. Select a newspaper or magazine advertisement that you think is helpful to consumers. List the ways in which the ad is helpful. Select another ad that you think is not helpful to consumers and tell why it is not.

CHALLENGE PROBLEMS

1. Many businesses offer "free" trading stamps that customers may save and exchange for valuable merchandise. Are these stamps really free? If not, who pays for them? Under what circumstances would you consider it wise to buy where you receive the stamps?
2. Roy Adams bought a new pair of trousers that were guaranteed to last for three months. The first time Roy wore them, however, he fell and ripped the trousers. Could he return them and get his money back or receive a new pair of pants at no cost? Why? Do you think this is a fair way to handle such a situation?

3. Read the newspaper article reprinted below and answer the questions that follow it.

COUNCIL STUDIES NEW CURBS ON 'FIRE' SALES

Centerville.—Legislation tightening regulation of "fire" and "going out of business" sales was introduced in the city council Friday. The ordinance was backed by the local Better Business Bureau.

"The new legislation is designed primarily to establish stricter control over goods sold and frequency of the sales," a member of the council said. Under the measure, merchants would be prohibited from increasing inventories above average during the 90-day period before applying to the city for a sale license.

This restriction is intended to protect the public from businessmen who load up with cheap, shoddy merchandise in anticipation of a sale and then "push it off" on customers at supposed bargain prices, which in reality carry big profit margins. Sales at the same location would be limited to one a year.

▪ *a.* Why do you suppose "fire" and "going out of business" sales were mentioned together in this article? ▪ *b.* What is an ordinance? How is it created? ▪ *c.* What is a Better Business Bureau? Why do you suppose the bureau in Centerville favored the new ordinance? ▪ *d.* Why are some businesses able to "push off" cheap merchandise at a high profit during a sale? What would be your best protection against such practices? ▪ *e.* Do you believe a city should require a business to buy a special license before it can have a sale? Be prepared to defend your point of view. ▪ *f.* Do you think a business should be permitted to have more than one sale a year? Give your reasons.

4. An old rule of retailing is known as *caveat emptor*. What does the term mean? What precautions does the rule suggest you take when you go shopping? What responsibility does the seller have to the customer?

PART 14 GETTING YOUR MONEY'S WORTH

HOW often in your life have you expressed dissatisfaction with a purchase by saying, "I didn't get my money's worth"? What does "not getting your money's worth" mean? Does it mean that something you bought failed to measure up to your expectations? Either it wore out before you thought it should; or it was not suitable for your purpose; or it did not perform as you thought it would. In one way or another it just was not worth the price you paid for it.

Spending money today is easy. Getting your money's worth is becoming more difficult all the time. There are so many goods to choose from, and so much is claimed for all of them. Are such products as soap, gasoline, and toothpaste really improved by adding hard-to-pronounce ingredients like hexachlorophene, tetraethyl lead, and stannous fluoride? Is buying and trying the only way a consumer has of judging a good or service? Is getting your money's worth today all a matter of luck? Not by any means. In addition to advance planning, buying skill includes practices that, when followed, help consumers to get their money's worth. What are some of these practices?

TAKE ADVANTAGE OF BUYING GUIDES

"It's all very well to talk about saving time and money by planning your shopping in advance," said Mike Holmes, "but it isn't always easy to carry out your plans after you're in the store." Mike had set off with $4 to buy a pair of jeans. He found jeans for that price at two stores. How could he tell which was the better buy? One article is said to be a better buy than another when it offers more quality or quantity for the price charged.

Mike's problem is a common one. When faced with two or more possibilities, it often is hard to

Courtesy E. I. Dupont de Nemours and Co., Inc.

know which is best. At a time like that good shoppers depend on buying guides. A *buying guide* is just a way of getting information about a product.

Labels Are a Guide to Quality

One of the first things a good shopper looks for on a product is a label. A ***label*** is a message about the product. It may be a tag, a carton, a wrapper, or a seal. If it is a good label, it provides the information you need to judge the product. In general, a good label should answer the following questions: 1. What will the product do? (performance); 2. What is it made of? (composition); 3. How is it made? (construction); 4. How should it be cared for? (maintenance); 5. How should it be used? (purpose); 6. Who made it? (the name and address of the manufacturer or distributor). Such labels are called *informative* or ***descriptive labels*** because they describe or inform you about the product.

Take that pair of jeans Mike Holmes wanted to buy. If you were Mike, what are some of the important facts you would want to know about a pair of jeans? Well, no matter how well a garment is made, unless it fits, it is not of much use to you, is it? You would choose your correct size to begin with, of course; but jeans have to be washed, and if they shrink as much as 5 percent, they will be a whole size smaller. To be sure that will not happen to jeans you buy, you will want to know if they are Sanforized. The term "Sanforized" on any garment is your guarantee that the garment will shrink no more than 1 percent.

Denim, the material from which jeans are made, varies in weight from 6 ounces to 14 ounces per square yard. The 6-ounce weight is very light and does not wear well, while 13- or 14-ounce denims are the heavy qualities used in men's work clothes. Assume that you decide a medium weight of 10 or 11 ounces is about right for you. Do you think you could judge the weight of the material just by looking at it or feeling it? Neither could you tell whether the jeans would shrink after they were washed. On

A Cone Fabric with RETENTO finish

SANFORIZED

Residual shrinkage not over 1%

LITTLE OR NO IRONING REQUIRED

CARE INSTRUCTIONS

This fabric is WASHABLE by AUTOMATIC WASHING MACHINE, by hand or may be sent to your laundry. Deep shades or reds should be washed separately for first few launderings to remove excessive dye.

- Retains Color and hand after repeated washings
- Dries quickly
- Use any all-fabric or oxygen type powdered bleach

®CONE MILLS INC.
New York 18, N. Y.

Tag printed in U.S.A. C-300-5

An informative label

the other hand, if these facts are clearly stated on a label attached to the garment, you would know exactly what you were getting. When faced with a choice, you would have a basis for comparison.

Labels Enable You to Buy on the Basis of Intended Use

Labels not only help you to judge quality, they help you buy the product best suited to your purpose. Gretel Meyer's mother sent her to the store for a can of peaches she planned to use in a salad. Mrs. Meyer's main concern was the appearance of the peaches. To make certain Gretel brought home the right kind, Mrs. Meyer said she wanted large halves of Cling peaches. She needed at least five. Cling peaches are the smooth, glossy, firm variety. Since Gretel could not see inside the cans of peaches, she had only the information on their labels to guide her in her selection. Part of the label from the can she bought is pictured on page 117. Do you see how it helped her make the right choice?

Food Products Are Sometimes Graded. The quality of some food products is indicated by a ***grade label.*** Canned fruits and vegetables, for example, come in three grades: Grade A, Grade B, and Grade C. Grade A may also be called "Fancy"; Grade B, "Choice"; and Grade C, "Standard." The quality of beef is indicated by the terms "Prime," "Choice," "Good," "Standard," "Commercial." Grades for veal and lamb are similar. These grades

Courtesy California Packing Corporation

have been established by the United States Department of Agriculture.

The difference between a descriptive label and a grade label is that the descriptive label *itemizes* the information. The grade label *summarizes* it. Grade labels enable you to make a quick comparison. Producers who use grade labels usually combine them with descriptive labels.

The important thing to know about food grades is that they are not a measure of food value. Meat grades indicate only such characteristics as tenderness, juiciness, and flavor. Low grades take longer to cook; high grades cost more to buy. All grades provide the same amount of nourishment. Canned fruits and vegetables are graded on the basis of their size, color, and degree of ripeness. All grades are equally wholesome. The grade to buy depends on how the product is to be used. When appearance is the important factor, as in Gretel's case, the highest grade is the right choice for those who can afford it. Had Gretel's mother planned to cut up or mash the peaches, a lower grade would have served her purpose. And it should cost less.

Are Labels Dependable? Unfortunately all labels are not helpful any more than all advertising is helpful. Some carry phrases like "Quality Controlled" or "None Finer" that sound impressive but do not mean anything. The absence of a good informative label is no indication that a product is inferior. You would think, though, that the producer of a really good article would want buyers to know how good it is. On the other hand, the best label in the world will not do you any good unless you understand what it says. To be a good shopper, you must know how to read labels.

You may not always be able to find all information you want on a label. The information that is there, however, must be accurate. Federal and state laws prohibit mislabeling. If a product does not live up to the facts stated on the label, then you have just cause for returning it.

Examine Goods Whenever Possible

Examining goods is perhaps the oldest of all methods for judging their quality. It was common practice for the Colonial housewife to bite the nutmeg offered for sale by a traveling peddler. Only in this way could she tell before she bought it if it was genuine or made of wood.

Even though the number of consumer goods that can be inspected is decreasing, inspection is still a valuable guide in many cases. When buying fresh fruits and vegetables, a careful examination may be the only way to determine their freshness, to detect decayed spots, and to judge their all-round quality.

In other cases inspection may be used together with other guides. When buying a dress, you may not be able to identify the material from which it is made. Neither can you tell whether it will fade or shrink. You have to depend on labels for this information. You can, however, inspect the fit, the quality of the stitching, the depth of the hem, and the width of the seams. Careful inspection is especially important when you are buying merchandise that is on sale at reduced prices. Very often such merchandise cannot be returned.

Obtain Expert Opinions

With a little effort you can soon learn what to look for in goods you buy frequently. But where the important features of a product are hidden, or when buying something you know little about, it is wise to seek the opinion of an expert. Who would know better than your dentist whether you should use an electric toothbrush and what kind? Fewer used-car purchases would end in disappointment if more buyers consulted a good automobile mechanic before closing the deal. A repairman who services more than one brand of an appliance knows the strong and weak points of each brand. There are also testing agencies that report on the quality of a vast assortment of products. These agencies are described in Part 38.

TAKE TIME TO COMPARE PRICES

Have you ever bought something and discovered later you could have bought it at a lower price somewhere else? Even though it was your own fault for not taking time to shop around, you felt a little cheated, didn't you? Price competition among retailers today is lively. Many have adopted as their slogan, "We will not be undersold." Usually, therefore, it is advisable to shop more than one store. Almost everyone does this when buying a big item like a car, a stove, or a refrigerator on which the amount saved may be considerable. But shopping where prices are lowest for things you buy everyday can quickly add up to big savings too.

This is not to say you should always shop around for the lowest price. You have to consider the gasoline or bus fare or time consumed in the process. An important part of buying skill is knowing when to shop around as well as when not to.

Buy the Most Economical Size

Today almost all packaged goods come in more than one size. A good shopper is careful to choose the size that offers him the most for his money. If milk is 21 cents a quart and 36 cents a half gallon, the larger size represents a saving of more than 14

Ewing Galloway

Consumers must choose their purchases carefully. Here the salesman is answering some important questions about the engine.

percent. Goods are frequently cheaper in large sizes than in small ones. Nevertheless, there are exceptions. Sometimes the small sizes offer as much or more for the money. The only way to make certain is to figure the cost for each unit of weight or measure. When comparing prices of different brands, don't be fooled by their apparent sizes. Packages may be the same in size yet differ in weight.

Even though goods may be cheaper in large sizes than in small ones, it is never ***economical*** to buy more than you can use. Suppose you bought a half gallon of milk because it cost less than buying it a quart at a time. If it spoiled before you used it all, what would you save?

ONLY BY FIGURING THE UNIT COST CAN YOU DETERMINE WHICH IS THE BETTER BUY.

15 cents an ounce

17 cents an ounce

MAKE IT EASY FOR SALESCLERKS TO HELP YOU

A good salesclerk who knows his merchandise can be a big help when you go shopping. Whether he is or not often depends on you. The consumer who is reasonable in his demands and approaches salespeople in a courteous and businesslike manner will usually receive the same kind of treatment in return.

The salesclerk can be of most help to you if you follow these steps:

1. Know what you want.
2. Describe what you want in a brief and accurate manner.
3. Indicate frankly at the beginning the price range in which you are interested.
4. Ask intelligent questions.
5. Expect intelligent and accurate answers to your questions.

REMEMBER WHO PAYS FOR MARKETING

As you already know, the cost of marketing goods is finally paid by the consumers who buy them. Yet it is often the consumers themselves who needlessly add to marketing costs.

Goods that are soiled or damaged by careless customers frequently result in heavy losses to retailers. To pay for these losses, retailers must charge higher prices for other goods. Returning goods also creates an extra expense for the seller. There may be just cause for taking merchandise back occasionally. But very often it is returned because the buyer did not make his selection carefully in the first place. Failure to pay bills on time is another way consumers add to the merchant's operating costs. Unfortunately, these increased costs must be paid by both those who are responsible for them and by those who are not.

YOUR PURCHASES DESERVE GOOD CARE

Any gains you may make by careful planning and buying are quickly lost if you do not use and care for your purchases properly. Too many quick stops and starts will shorten the life of automobile tires. Dust or a poor needle can soon ruin your phonograph records. Failure to have wool clothing cleaned before storing it for the summer is an invitation to moths. Anything that cuts down on the amount of service or enjoyment a purchase can provide reduces your standard of living.

BUILDING YOUR VOCABULARY

On a separate sheet of paper, write each of the terms listed in the left-hand column below. Read the three definitions to the right of each term. After each term, copy the definition that best matches it in meaning.

1. ***descriptive label***
   - *a.* A statement found on a product that itemizes important information about the product
   - *b.* A tag carrying a message about the product to which it is attached
   - *c.* A statement carried on a product that promises the product will perform in a certain way

2. ***economical***
   - *a.* The largest size in which a particular product is packaged
   - *b.* The saving of money or other resource
   - *c.* Avoiding waste or extravagance in using money or other resources

3. ***grade label***
   - *a.* A label describing the materials from which a product is made
   - *b.* A label found on some food products indicating the amount of nourishment in the product
   - *c.* A label indicating the quality of the product that bears it

4. ***label***
   - *a.* The brand name placed on a product by the manufacturer or seller
   - *b.* A tag, carton, wrapper, or seal that carries a message about the product to which it is attached
   - *c.* A tag attached to a product indicating its price

CHECKING YOUR READING

1. Why is it becoming more difficult all the time to get your money's worth?
2. When is one article considered to be a better buy than another?
3. What purpose does a good label serve? What are some of the things a good label should tell you about a product?
4. Why is it more important for packaged items to be well labeled than for other kinds of goods?
5. If food grades are not a measure of food values, what should determine the grade to buy?
6. To what extent can you depend on labels to give you the information you want about the products you buy?
7. How reliable is the information you find on labels?
8. What is perhaps the oldest method for judging the quality of goods?
9. Give examples of some articles for which inspection is the best way to judge quality.
10. How can you determine quality when you buy something you know little about?
11. Why is it usually advisable to shop more than one store before you buy?
12. Does shopping around to compare prices, quality, and quantity always pay? Give examples of when it does and when it does not.

13. Explain why it may sometimes be unwise to buy in large sizes even though the goods are cheaper than when purchased in small quantities.
14. What can you do to get the most help from salesclerks?
15. What are some ways that consumers increase marketing costs needlessly? How does this affect other consumers?
16. Why is the way you use and care for your purchases an important factor in getting your money's worth?

SHARING YOUR OPINION AND EXPERIENCE

1. For what kinds of products do you rely on labels in your buying?
2. In a recent test in a Philadelphia department store, identical jeans were offered for sale—with and without labels. The labeled jeans outsold the unlabeled ones 13 to 1. Since there was no difference between the two sets of jeans, how do you explain the fact that most buyers preferred the labeled ones?
3. Of all the ways suggested for determining the quality of goods, which one do you think is most helpful? Why?
4. What advantage, if any, is there in buying well-known brand names of merchandise?
5. Should you examine goods carefully even when you buy them from a reputable store? Why or why not?
6. Give an example from your own experience of how shopping around to compare prices saved you money on a purchase.
7. What do people mean when they give as a reason for not buying a good or service that "the price is too high"?
8. If only one store in your community carries a particular article that you want, how could you compare its price with another seller's price?
9. Why are producers sometimes able to sell their goods for less in large quantities than in small ones?
10. What do you consider the most important characteristics of a good salesperson?
11. Mr. and Mrs. Whitsell are very loyal to their local merchants. Even when they know they might be able to buy some items for less in the next town or by mail order, they purchase everything they can at stores in their own town. They claim that their town cannot progress if its citizens spend their money elsewhere. The Cranstons take a different view, however. They feel they need to look out for themselves first. They buy wherever they can get the best bargains. Which family do you think is right? Why?

PROJECTS AND PROBLEMS

1. A good label provides information that helps the consumer judge the product. Not all information appearing on labels is equally helpful, however. In the left-hand column of a form similar to that shown on page 122, copy the following statements taken from labels. Rate each statement as "very helpful," "somewhat helpful," or "not helpful" by placing a check mark in the appropriate column.

Statement	Very Helpful	Somewhat Helpful	Not Helpful
Example: None finer			√

▪ *a.* Wash and wear ▪ *b.* 50% wool, 50% Dacron ▪ *c.* Genuine antique ▪ *d.* Waterproof ▪ *e.* Dry-clean only ▪ *f.* Extra long life ▪ *g.* Colorfast ▪ *h.* Easy to install ▪ *i.* Delicious ▪ *j.* Two-ply yarn ▪ *k.* Recommended by manufacturers ▪ *l.* Resists tarnishing

2. The quality of many goods can be determined by careful examination. List five items whose quality you feel can be adequately judged by inspection.
3. The quality of some merchandise is difficult to determine even after close inspection. List five articles whose quality is difficult to judge in this way.
4. Imagine that you are planning to buy each of the items listed below. For each one, indicate the method or methods you would use to determine its quality and tell what you could learn about the product by that method. Copy the items on a form similar to the one below.

Product	Labels	Salesclerks	Inspection	Experts
Example: Sweater	*Size, material, proper care*	*Opinion on looks and fit, how it launders, style*	*Fit, weave, buttons, and buttonholes*	*Wearing qualities*

▪ *a.* winter coat ▪ *b.* shoes ▪ *c.* frozen food ▪ *d.* automobile ▪ *e.* automatic washer ▪ *f.* shoe polish

5. The following article appeared recently in newspapers throughout the country. Read it carefully and answer the questions that follow it.

MAKERS OF SUNGLASSES BOOST THEIR SALES BY FOCUSING ON FASHION

New York. "Sunglasses give women a pretense of elegance. I envision the average well-dressed woman as having at least four pairs in her sunglass wardrobe." This pronouncement, from a leading authority on fashion, points up one of the main reasons why sunglass sales have been soaring in the past few years.

Dark glasses, an expert believes, add a note of romantic intrigue to everyday life. "They provide sanctuary," he says, "and in a sense are like the Greek masks of comedy and tragedy that can be used to conceal one's feelings."

Teen-agers, of both sexes, make up one of the fastest growing markets for sunglasses, makers say. "Our market surveys show teen-agers equate sunglasses with popularity," says the sales vice-president of a leading producer of the glasses.

▪ *a.* What new appeal are the manufacturers of sunglasses using to sell their product? ▪ *b.* What is the relationship, if any, between being in fashion and being well dressed? ▪ *c.* Do you think a person needs several pairs of sunglasses to be well dressed? Why or why not? ▪ *d.* What is a market survey? What purpose does it serve? ▪ *e.* Do people buy sunglasses for reasons other than those mentioned in the article? If so, what are some of them? ▪ *f.* What would you consider most important in getting your money's worth in a pair of sunglasses?

6. Sometimes the value you get for your money depends on how well you can distinguish opinion from fact. Which of the following statements do you think are opinions and which are facts? Give reasons for your answers.

   ▪ *a.* Skillful buyers are born, not made. ▪ *b.* An article that is guaranteed is better than one that carries no guarantee. ▪ *c.* Most advertisements are designed to mislead the consumer. ▪ *d.* It is often difficult for the average shopper to judge the quality of items such as furniture and household appliances. ▪ *e.* Low-quality merchandise may sometimes be a better buy than similar merchandise of a higher grade. ▪ *f.* Stores usually try to have their best selections of merchandise during peak selling periods. ▪ *g.* Prices for perishable goods are usually lowest at the peak of the season.

7. As was pointed out in the text, goods are frequently cheaper when purchased in large quantities than in small ones. Shop a store in your neighborhood for the following items: shampoo, milk, candy bar, theme paper, cereal. Compare prices of the large and small sizes for the same brand of each item. Put the information on a form similar to the one shown here.

Brand of Item	Quantity in Large Size	Price of Large Size	Quantity in Small Size	Price of Small Size	Cheaper Size
Example: Crest toothpaste	*6¾ oz.*	*.44*	*5 oz.*	*.38*	*large*

   ▪ *a.* Is the small size of any of the above items a better buy than the large size? ▪ *b.* If not, have you found any instances where the small size of a product offered more for the money than the larger size of the same brand? Explain.

8. Bring to class examples of good labels and poor ones. Be prepared to explain why you think each is either good or poor.

CHALLENGE PROBLEMS

1. What is the purpose of such publications as *Consumers Bulletin* and *Consumer Reports*? What information do they provide? How should they be used?
2. Emmerson's Market had been doing a modest business for many years as a small, neighborhood grocery. Recently a large food chain opened a new supermarket across the street. Since the supermarket has a greater variety of goods at lower prices, sales at Emmerson's Market are slowly dwindling. Who benefits from a situation of this kind? Who is hurt by it? Where would you shop if you lived in this neighborhood? Why? Should a chain store be permitted to drive a small store out of business? Defend your position.

CONTENTS OF UNIT 4

Unit 4 / Making Effective Use of Credit

PART 15 THE ROLE OF CREDIT IN OUR ECONOMIC SYSTEM

Courtesy The Durst Organization

ONE of the unique features of our business system is that it operates to a large extent on promises, called *credit.* Business firms sell to consumers on credit and buy from other businesses on credit. The construction of schools, hospitals, and highways is also financed with credit. The word "credit" comes from the Latin *credere* which means "to trust." The widespread use of credit in the United States is evidence of the trust that its people have in one another.

Credit, like money, is a tool that helps our economic system work more efficiently than it might otherwise. Credit stimulates production. It is not a mere coincidence that production in this country and the use of credit have risen together. On the other hand, if used carelessly, credit can be harmful. Too much credit has brought financial ruin to both individuals and businesses.

Who uses credit? How does credit affect spending? Do you think an economic system like ours could operate without credit?

WHAT IS CREDIT?

Suppose you buy a pair of shoes, but instead of paying for them you tell the salesclerk to "charge them." He has you sign the sales slip, and you leave with the shoes. In exchange for the shoes, the store accepts your promise that you will pay for them later. In other words, you obtain the shoes on credit. ***Credit,*** then, is a means of obtaining something of value in exchange for a promise to pay at some future time. The thing of value may be goods, such as shoes. It may be a service like medical care. Or it may be money.

In every credit transaction there are two parties: (1) the ***creditor*** who supplies the goods, services, or money; and (2) the ***debtor*** who promises to pay for the goods, services, or money at some future time. Until the promise has been fulfilled, the amount owed is a ***debt.***

All Credit Is a Form of Borrowing

Anyone who obtains credit is using someone else's money. Until the debt is paid, the creditor cannot use his money in any other way that might benefit him. Thus, all credit is a form of borrowing, even though it is used to obtain goods or services rather than money. The one who supplies goods, services, or money on credit is a *lender.* The one who owes for goods, services, or money is a *borrower.*

WHO USES CREDIT?

Credit substitutes for money as a medium of exchange. As you might expect, therefore, it is used by those who do the spending in our economic system. This means consumers, business firms, and state, local, and Federal governments. Credit enables each of these groups to time their spending by providing purchasing power when it can be used to the best advantage.

Consumers Use Credit

Credit used by individuals and families for personal reasons is ***consumer credit.*** Not so many years ago the use of credit by consumers was frowned upon. In Colonial times people were imprisoned for failure to pay their debts. This created a fear of indebtedness that lasted long after this form of punishment became illegal. Today the use of consumer credit is so widespread that people often joke about cash going out of style. One of the main reasons for this change is that people are much more dependent on money now than they were formerly. The early farm families that produced most of what they consumed had little need to borrow or to buy on credit. If they wanted a house, they built one, using whatever materials were at hand. If they needed furniture, they made it. Their incomes were both meager and uncertain. Their ability to pay a debt was just as uncertain.

Today production is a matter of specialization, and goods and services are exchanged for money. Most families can count on a certain amount of income regularly and can safely carry a limited amount of debt. With credit, consumers can "buy now and pay later," as the ads say. In other words, by using future purchasing power consumers can obtain goods and services when they need them most.

For example, young families with growing children have the greatest need for houses. But if such a family has an annual income of only $5,000, it would take it a long time to save and pay cash for a house costing $12,500. By then its housing needs would probably change. With credit, however, it can buy a $12,500 house and live in it while paying for it.

Businesses Use Credit

If it were not for credit, many business enterprises operating today could never have been started. The one thing needed to get a business of any kind going is money—money to acquire capital goods, money to hire workers, money to buy materials to get into production. Seldom does one individual have enough money of his own to make a new business go. He has to depend on other people's money to help him. One way of obtaining the needed funds is to form a partnership. Another is to organize a corporation and sell shares of stock. A third is to borrow the money and repay it with future earnings. That is the way many new enterprises are financed.

It is not just new businesses that use credit, however. Old, established firms also borrow, including big and wealthy ones. Credit used by business firms is called ***producer credit.*** Producer credit is used for two reasons: to cover the costs of production and to increase production.

To Cover the Costs of Production. As you know, money to pay the costs of production comes from the sale of the goods and services produced. Between the time goods go into production and the time they are sold, however, producers have many expenses to pay. Among others, there are the wages of workers; the cost of materials; charges for telephone and electric service; and rent. As a rule, credit used to cover production costs is needed for only a short time—one to six months. For that reason it is called *short-term credit.*

Business firms often obtain short-term credit from other business firms; that is, they charge their materials and supplies just as consumers charge their purchases at retail stores. Sometimes, however, they borrow the money they need from a bank. Short-term credit helps a retailer obtain the extra merchandise he needs during peak selling periods like Christmas and Easter.

Farmers especially have need of short-term credit. Although their expenses continue the year round, they must wait for their incomes until their crops have been harvested and sold. Should they run short of money before then, short-term credit enables them to buy such things as feed, seed, fertilizer, and gasoline.

To Increase Production. Another reason business firms and farmers use credit is to increase production. A dairy farmer might borrow to buy more cows. A manufacturer might borrow to buy new machinery, or to enlarge his present plant, or to build a new one. The cows, the machinery, and the plant are all *capital goods,* which is the name for goods used in the production of other goods. By adding to their supply of capital goods, the farmer and the manufacturer will be able to produce more. By producing more, they expect to increase their profits. These additional profits will enable them to repay their loans.

Any purchase of capital goods is called an ***investment.*** Credit used for this purpose is called *investment credit.* A business firm may obtain investment credit from a bank or other financial institution. A large corporation, however, needing a vast sum of money for a long time may obtain it by selling bonds. A ***bond*** is a printed promise to pay a cer-

Ewing Galloway

This farmer is getting a short-term loan at the bank to help pay his expenses until his crops are harvested.

tain amount at some future date. Those who buy corporation bonds are lending their money to the corporation that issues them. Bonds usually are issued for ten or more years.

Since capital goods are a productive resource, investment credit helps to increase the nation's productive resources. Any increase in productive resources, of course, increases our ability to produce.

Governments Use Credit

Governments, like consumers and business enterprises, also use credit and for some of the same reasons. Even a government may run short of money to pay its ordinary operating expenses. This is most likely to happen during recessions when employment and income are down. Then tax collections usually shrink too. The Federal government may even borrow in order to step up its spending during a recession. As you learned in Part 7, this is to make up for the slowdown in spending by consumers and business. Governments, like anyone else, sometimes incur unusual expenses too large to be met out of current income. The Federal government, for example, has borrowed heavily to pay the enormous cost of fighting wars.

State and local governments use credit mostly to finance the construction of durable capital goods: schools, highways, parks, and hospitals. To collect enough taxes to pay for these projects during construction would require a huge tax increase that might work a hardship on many taxpayers. Instead, governments borrow to pay for improvements of this kind and use a portion of each year's taxes to pay off the debt. In this way the cost is spread over several years.

Like corporations, when a government wants to borrow money for any length of time, it issues bonds. Those who buy the bonds are lending their money to the government. The bonds are paid off at some future time with tax money.

CREDIT AFFECTS TOTAL SPENDING

Credit provides purchasing power. Total spending, therefore, includes credit buying as well as cash buying. For example, if Mr. McGrath borrowed $2,500 and bought a car, total spending would increase by $2,500. Similarly, a loan to a business firm would enable the business to increase its spending; and a loan to a government would enable that government to increase its spending. The total amount bought on credit by all consumers, businesses, and government adds to total spending.

While some consumers, business firms, and governments are going into debt, of course, others are paying off their debts. Those paying off debts spend less than they would otherwise. Suppose, for example, that Mr. McGrath makes payments of $100 a month on his loan. This would leave him $100 less to spend each month until the loan is repaid. During that time, therefore, there would be a $100 decrease in total spending each month. But Mr. McGrath is just one consumer. Total spending would also be decreased by the total amount other consumers, business firms, and governments were paying on their debts.

Local school districts raise money to build schools by borrowing from the public.

Eligible for Investment by Savings Banks and Trust Funds in New York State
Interest Exempt from all present Federal and New York State Income Taxes

NEW ISSUE

Standard & Poor's: A
Moody's: A

$1,590,100

Union Free School District No. 2

Town of Poughkeepsie

Dutchess County, New York

3.25% Unlimited Tax

General Obligation Bonds

Dated March 1, 1965 Due November 1, 1965-94

Principal and interest (November 1, 1965 and semi-annually thereafter) payable in New York City or Poughkeepsie. Coupon $5,000 Bonds (one $100 Bond) fully registerable.

This School District (population 10,000) is located on the Hudson River just south of the City of Poughkeepsie. I.B.M. is the District's largest employer and taxpayer. Dutchess County (Moody's Aa) is responsible for the full collection of school taxes.

Amount	*Due*	*Yield or Price*
$50,100	1965	2.20%
55,000	1966	2.40
55,000	1967	2.55
55,000	1968	2.65
60,000	1969	2.75
60,000	1970	2.80
60,000	1971	2.85
60,000	1972	2.90
120,000	1973-74	2.95
185,000	1975-77	3.00
130,000	1978-79	3.05
130,000	1980-81	3.10
130,000	1982-83	3.15
100,000	1984-85	3.20
140,000	1986-89	100
40,000	1990	3.30
80,000	1991-92	3.35
80,000	1993-94	3.40

Circular on request

Roosevelt & Cross Incorporated   **Blair & Co., Granbery, Marache** Incorporated

Wood, Struthers & Co., Inc.   **R. D. White & Company**

As long as the additional spending of all new borrowers equals the decreased spending of all those paying off debts, total spending remains unchanged. But if borrowing takes place at a faster rate than repayment of debts, total spending increases. As you already know, total spending determines total production. An increase or decrease in total spending will cause production to rise or fall. Because total spending includes credit purchases, an increase or decrease in the use of credit can also cause production to rise or fall.

CREDIT MAKES SAVINGS AVAILABLE FOR SPENDING.

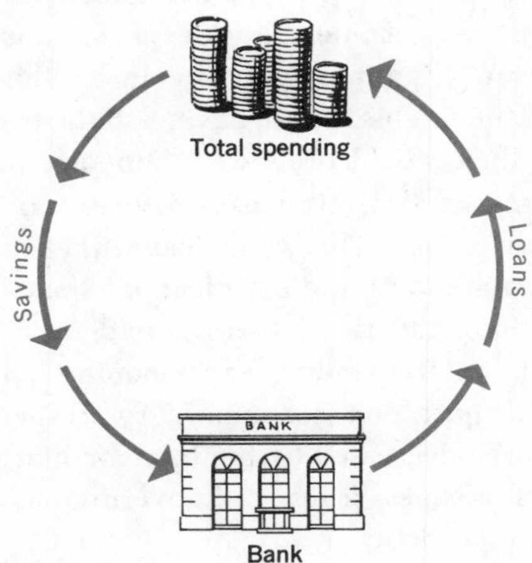

CREDIT MAKES SAVINGS AVAILABLE FOR SPENDING

Just as consumers sometimes want to spend more than their incomes, they sometimes want to spend less. In other words, they want to save part of their present earnings for future use. As a group, consumers do tend to spend less than they earn. Their combined savings amount to billions of dollars. If this money were just stored away somewhere, its purchasing power would be lost. Every dollar saved would decrease total spending just that much more; but because of credit, this does not happen.

What does happen is that banks and other financial institutions where people keep their savings lend this money to others. It may be used to build homes, churches, stores, factories, highways, or any number of other things. In some cases people lend their savings directly to business by purchasing bonds. Either way, the money continues to do its work of encouraging production and providing jobs and income for workers. This is perhaps the most important function of credit.

BUILDING YOUR VOCABULARY

List the figures 1 to 8 on a sheet of paper, numbering down. Read the eight statements given below at the right; then, for each statement, select from the column at the left the term that best matches it in meaning. Write this term next to the appropriate number.

bond	1. A means of obtaining something of value in exchange for a promise to pay at a future time
consumer credit	2. One who supplies goods, services, or money on credit
credit	3. One who owes for goods, services, or money obtained on credit
creditor	4. An amount owed by one person or business to another
debt	5. Credit used by individuals and families for personal reasons
debtor	6. Credit used by business firms
investment	7. An exchange of money for capital goods
producer credit	8. A printed promise to pay a certain sum at a future date

CHECKING YOUR READING

1. What did the term "credit" mean in its original Latin form? Does that meaning still apply today?
2. Who are the two parties to every credit transaction?
3. Explain why all credit is a form of borrowing.
4. Who uses credit in our economic system?
5. Why do people use credit more today than in former times?
6. Explain why credit may be especially valuable to a young family with small children.
7. For what purpose does a new business use credit?
8. What is short-term credit? For what purpose is it usually used?
9. What is investment credit? How is it used?
10. Explain how corporations use bonds to borrow money.
11. Why do governments use credit?
12. What is the advantage of using credit to finance the construction of such durable capital goods as schools, highways, and parks?
13. What effect does borrowing have on spending?
14. What effect does the repayment of debts have on spending?
15. Under what circumstance may the combination of borrowing and the repayment of debts increase total spending? Under what circumstance may it decrease total spending?
16. What effect does an increase or a decrease in total spending have on total production?
17. As a group, do consumers tend to spend more or less than they earn?
18. Explain how credit makes savings available for spending.

SHARING YOUR OPINION AND EXPERIENCE

1. What arguments can you give to support the idea that people should not be imprisoned for failure to pay their debts? What punishment, if any, do you think people should receive when they do not pay their debts?
2. If businesses did not sell goods or services on credit, what effect would it have on the amount of coins and paper money that would be needed?
3. What is the meaning of the statement, "When you buy on credit, you are mortgaging your future"?
4. How does a corporation bond differ from a share of stock in a corporation?
5. From whom do governments borrow?
6. What are municipal bonds? Why are some wealthy persons eager to buy them?
7. The Harry Whittakers charge all their purchases at the Miller Department Store and pay their bill at the end of each month. Does this increase total spending more than if they paid cash for their purchases? Explain.

PROJECTS AND PROBLEMS

1. The term "consumer credit outstanding" means the total amount of debt consumers owe at any one time. The graph below shows changes in consumer credit outstanding in the United States each year from 1940 to 1964. Study the graph and answer the questions following it.

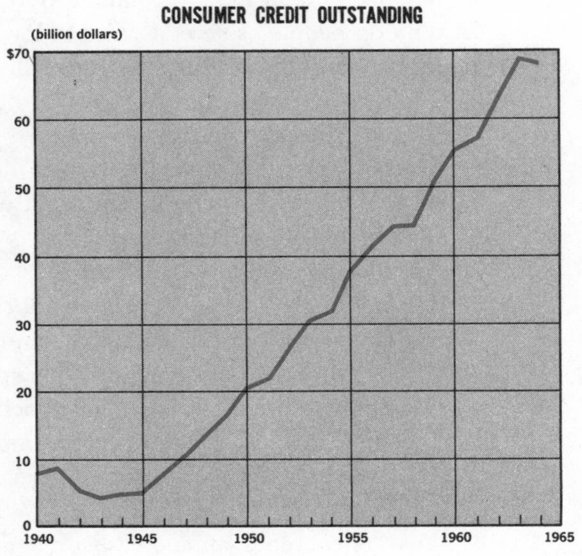

Source: National Industrial Conference Board

▪ *a.* What kind of graph is it? ▪ *b.* How many dollars of debt does each division along the vertical axis represent? ▪ *c.* Approximately how much did consumers owe in 1940? 1945? 1950? 1955? 1960? 1964? ▪ *d.* During what 4-year period was consumer debt lowest? ▪ *e.* What took place during this period to cause a decrease in the use of consumer credit? ▪ *f.* Approximately 28 percent of the consumer credit outstanding in 1950 was used to purchase automobiles. About how much did consumers owe for automobiles in 1950? ▪ *g.* What was the approximate percent of increase in credit outstanding from 1945 to 1950? (Instructions for finding percent increases and decreases can be found on page 69.)

2. List all reasons why you think a business gains an advantage by extending credit to its customers.
3. Divide a sheet of paper into three columns lengthwise. In the left-hand column list five businesses that sell goods or services on credit. In the center column, list five that sell for cash only. In each case try to choose different types of businesses. In the right-hand column, explain why you think the second group does not extend credit.

Businesses That Sell on Credit	Businesses That Sell for Cash Only	Reasons Why Businesses Sell for Cash Only
Example: Marsh's Clothing Store	*Root Beer Stand*	*Most sales are too small in amount to justify use of credit.*

4. In Part 4 you learned about a horizontal bar graph. The graph below is called a *vertical bar graph* because the bars go up and down rather than across the page. This graph shows the total debt of the Federal government for the years listed along the horizontal axis. The amount of the debt is shown along the vertical axis at the left. Study the graph and answer the questions following it.

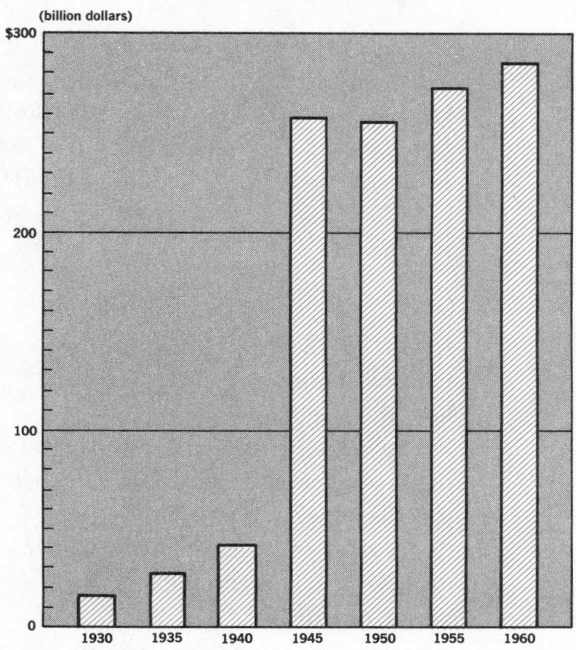

Source: Federal Reserve Bulletin

▪ *a.* How much money does each small division along the vertical axis represent? ▪ *b.* Approximately how much (to the nearest $5 billion) did the Federal government owe in 1930? 1940? 1945? 1960? ▪ *c.* During which 5-year period did the debt increase most? ▪ *d.* What do you think accounted for the very large increase in Federal debt during the period referred to in (*c*) above. ▪ *e.* During which 5-year period did the debt decrease? ▪ *f.* The amount of debt in 1945 was approximately how many times that for 1940?

5. The total amount owed by both consumers and privately owned business enterprises is known as *private debt.* The total owed by all levels of government—Federal, state, and local—is known as *public debt.* Public and private debt together make up total debt. The table on page 134 shows total debt for the years listed. It also shows how much of the debt for each year was public and how much was private. By studying the table, answer the questions following it.

TOTAL DEBT IN THE UNITED STATES
(billions of dollars)

Type of Debt	*1929*	*1938*	*1945*	*1954*	*1963*
Public	**$ 34.7**	**$ 67.0**	**$309.2**	**$332.3**	**$ 434.5**
Private	**179.3**	**136.6**	**154.1**	**381.8**	**825.9**
Total	**$214.0**	**$203.6**	**$463.3**	**$714.1**	**$1,260.4**

▪ *a.* In which year was the total of public and private debt lowest? ▪ *b.* In which year was the public debt lowest? ▪ *c.* When was the private debt lowest? ▪ *d.* Which type of debt increased most between 1929 and 1963? ▪ *e.* Which type increased most between 1938 and 1945? ▪ *f.* What was the percent of increase in public debt between 1945 and 1963? ▪ *g.* What was the percent of increase in private debt during the same period? ▪ *h.* Approximately what percent of total debt in 1929 was public? ▪ *i.* Approximately what percent of total debt in 1963 was public?

CHALLENGE PROBLEMS

1. In No. 1 of the Projects and Problems section, you were asked (question "*e*") what took place during the 4-year period when consumer credit was lowest. Explain how this event affected the use of consumer credit.
2. Study the table used in No. 5 of the Projects and Problems section, and you will notice that private debt decreased between 1929 and 1938. How do you explain this decrease?
3. Again refer to the table used in No. 5 of the Projects and Problems section. As a percent of total debt, which type of debt increased the most from 1929 to 1963, public or private?
4. The fact that consumers as a group spend less than they earn has had an important effect on the growth of our economy. Explain.

PART 16 KINDS OF CONSUMER CREDIT

IN the preceding part you learned that as people's dependence on money grew, the use of consumer credit grew. This growth has been helped along by two factors. One is that the number and kinds of goods and services that can be obtained on credit have been increasing steadily. At one time about the only thing families bought on credit was groceries. If they wanted a new chair for the living room, or a suit of clothes, they had to pay cash. Today you can buy almost anything on credit—cameras, pets, an education. You can also dine out, take a trip, or stay in hotels. In fact, many families now buy almost everything on credit except groceries. Moreover, consumers are not only encouraged to use credit, but new credit plans are being devised all the time that make it easier and easier for them to do so.

Why do you think sellers encourage consumers to use credit? What are some different kinds of consumer credit plans?

WHAT CONSUMER CREDIT INCLUDES

Consumers, like producers, use both long-term and short-term credit. For consumers long-term credit serves a special purpose since it is used to finance the purchase of homes. This use of credit is discussed in Part 29. The name "consumer credit" usually refers to short-term agreements, covering periods of one month to three years. The remainder of this unit is about that kind of credit.

When credit is used to acquire goods, either durable or nondurable, it is called *sales* or *purchase credit.* When used to purchase services such as gas, electricity, medical care, or transportation, it is called *service credit.* When used to obtain money, it is called *loan credit.* In general, however, there are only two kinds of consumer credit—installment and noninstallment. It is *noninstallment credit* when

Courtesy of companies shown

the debt is to be paid in full with one payment. It is ***installment credit*** when the debt is paid in two or more payments.

To describe in detail all credit plans in use today would be impossible. It is also unnecessary since their differences are slight, and all are patterned in some way after one of the major plans explained below.

CHARGE ACCOUNTS

The oldest form of sales or purchase credit for consumers is probably the ***charge account.*** It has even been called the granddaddy of consumer credit. Other names for this type of credit are *open-book credit,* the *open charge account,* or *30-day account.* An open account is one that can be added to at any time. But payment of the full amount owed for goods or services is expected at regular intervals—usually monthly or every 30 days. In other words, charge accounts are noninstallment credit. Countless families are using charge-account credit when they pay monthly for gas or electricity used during the previous month.

Retail stores, among the first to offer consumer charge accounts, have been joined in recent years by many other types of business. Most oil companies, for example, issue credit cards entitling their owners to charge gasoline and other items at the company's service stations throughout the country. Hotel chains, car-rental agencies, and many other businesses issue similar credit cards. Today it is even possible for consumers to buy on credit from a variety of businesses with a single charge account. Some plans of this type are limited to local businesses. Others extend to businesses throughout the United States as well as in other countries. With a charge account of this kind, you can travel almost anywhere with scarcely more than a few dollars in your pocket. Transportation, meals, lodging, car rentals, and even theater tickets can be charged and paid for later.

Charge accounts, once the most-used type of consumer credit, have dwindled in importance as new credit plans have been developed. Today charge accounts make up less than one-tenth of consumers' total use of credit.

INSTALLMENT CREDIT

The most-used type of consumer credit today is installment sales or purchase credit. Some people call it "buying on time." Installment credit differs from an open or 30-day charge account in several ways. The principal one, of course, is in the way payment is made. When using an open charge account, the consumer pays nothing at the time of sale. It is assumed, however, that the account will be paid in full each month. When goods are bought on installment credit, the buyer is often asked to make a partial payment at the time of purchase. This is called a ***down payment.*** The balance is then paid with a series of regular payments.

Another difference between installment credit and charge-account credit is in their cost to the consumer. Seldom is a direct charge made for the privilege of using an open charge account. Instead the cost of providing the service is spread over all merchandise sold. Cash and credit buyers pay the same prices. The installment buyer, on the other hand, must pay for the privilege of extending his payments over a period of time. The charge made for installment credit is called a *carrying charge,* a *finance charge,* or a *credit service charge.*

A third difference is that an open charge account is a continual agreement between a buyer and a seller. As long as the amount owed is paid when due, the buyer can go on charging additional purchases. An installment-credit agreement generally covers the sale of specific merchandise, usually items involving a large expenditure of money. For example, two-thirds of all new car purchases are financed with installment credit. Household appliances and furniture are other goods commonly sold on installments.

A fourth difference between installment credit and an ordinary charge account is that the install-

Many businessmen enjoy the convenience of using a credit card to pay their plane fare. On a few short-run flights within the United States, the transaction can be completed during the flight.

Courtesy Eastern Airlines

ment buyer must sign a formal agreement known as an ***installment contract.*** The contract covers all terms of the purchase, including how much is to be paid, when and how payments are to be made, and what will happen if payments are missed. A contract of this kind is illustrated on page 138. Open charge accounts involve no signed promises on the part of the buyer.

Installment-purchase credit has one other feature that distinguishes it from charge-account credit. When goods are purchased on an open charge account, ownership of the goods passes from the seller to the buyer immediately. In other words, if you bought a camera on an open charge account, the camera would be yours at the time of delivery. In the case of an installment purchase, however, the seller usually retains ownership of the goods until all payments have been made. According to the terms of most installment contracts, the seller has the right to reclaim the goods if the buyer does not keep his part of the agreement.

OTHER TYPES OF SALES CREDIT

In addition to open-charge and installment credit, sellers offer any number of other credit plans that are a combination of both types. One is the three-pay, or 90-day, account. Another is the revolving charge account.

Three-Pay, or 90-Day, Account

Under the 90-day plan, sometimes called a budget account, consumers may charge a large purchase in the same manner as on a regular charge account. Instead of paying the full amount all at once, however, they pay one-third of the original debt each month for three months. Suppose, for example, that you bought a winter coat costing $60, using a three-pay account. Each month for three months you would pay $20, or one-third of the original debt.

At least that is one way the plan works. Each seller makes his own rules. Some limit the three-pay

CONDITIONAL SALES CONTRACT

Date February 13, 19-- Buyers' Name Maurice Crandall

To Ray G. Schmidt (Seller) Residence Address 1202 Maple Drive

843 Elm Street (Street)

Palo Alto, California (City, State) Palo Alto, California (City, State)

I (meaning the undersigned buyer or buyers, jointly and severally) hereby buy from you the following goods.

Article	Model No.	Serial No.
Stereo-HiFi	Premier 63	P81-73021

Use This Schedule If Monthly Payments Are Unequal

$__ on __ 19__ (ten blank lines)

Cash price	$ 229.95
Sales tax	$ 6.90
Credit service charge	$ 6.00
Total purchase price	$ 242.85
Down payment (a) Cash $ 42.85	
(b) Allowance for trade-in $ none	$ 42.85
Balance	$ 200.00

which is payable in installments of $ 20 on the 10th day of each month, commencing on April 10, 19--.

Title to goods purchased under this contract is retained by you until payment of full purchase price. I agree to keep the goods safely and free from all other liens and at the above address unless you consent in writing to their removal.

The full balance shall become due on default, together with a 15% attorney's fee if then placed with an attorney for collection. In case of default, you shall also have the right to retake the goods wherever located, hold and dispose of them and collect expenses, and I shall have the right to redeem the goods or require their sale at public auction, all as provided by the law of the State of California.

This is our entire agreement, subject to any written guarantee or service contract duly delivered by you and cannot be changed orally. If I shall be given written notice that you have assigned this contract, you shall continue responsible for all of your obligations, but your assignee's rights shall be independent of my claims against you.

THIS IS A CONDITIONAL SALES CONTRACT

Ray G. Schmidt — Accepted: Seller's Signature Maurice Crandall — Buyer's Signature

I have received an executed copy of this contract. No other extension of credit exists, or is to be made, in connection with this purchase.

By J. C. R. Supt. — Title Maurice Crandall — Buyer's Signature

A conditional sales contract

privilege to the purchase of items costing over a certain amount. Others permit it to be used only for certain kinds of items. Some merchants charge customers nothing extra for the privilege of stretching out their payments. Others charge a percent of the unpaid balance, usually 1 to $1\frac{1}{2}$ percent a month. Still others charge a fixed amount depending on the unpaid balance. One store, for instance, charges 20 cents on balances of $10 to $15.

Three-pay plans are popular with department and clothing stores. They enable consumers to spread the cost of major purchases over a longer time than is possible with a regular charge account.

Revolving Charge Accounts

Revolving credit plans are offered under a variety of names, but all operate in much the same way. As with a regular charge account, new purchases may be added to a revolving account without making new credit arrangements. Unlike a regular charge account, however, payment may be made in installments.

The amount a customer can owe at any one time on a revolving account is limited. The limit in each case is determined by how much the customer earns and what other expenses he has. Once the amount charged reaches the limit set, no more can be charged until a payment has been made.

As an example, suppose you have a revolving charge account with a credit limit of $100. You can charge one item costing $100 or any number of items as long as the total does not exceed $100. Now suppose you owe $100 on your account and you make a payment of $15. You may then charge another $15 worth of purchases.

For this type of credit you pay 1 to $1\frac{1}{2}$ percent of the balance owing each month. In other words, if your unpaid balance at the end of one month is $65 and the service charge is $1\frac{1}{2}$ percent, your cost for credit that month would be 98 cents ($.015 \times \$65 = \$.975$).

In some cases customers using revolving credit plans are required to pay a definite amount monthly, such as $10, $15, or $20. In other cases the required payment depends on the balance owed. At one store, for example, if the balance owing is $75 or less, the payment required that month is $7.50. If the unpaid balance is more than $75 but not more than $100, the required payment is $10. Some stores have no planned schedule of payments. A customer may carry up to the maximum balance indefinitely as long as he continues to pay the credit service charge.

Teen-age Accounts. More and more stores today are extending credit privileges to teen-agers. These accounts are usually some form of revolving credit with payments tailored to fit the teen-ager's earnings or allowance. Usually, though not always, a teen-ager must have the permission of his parents to open such an account. Another frequent requirement is that the teen-ager's parents have a charge account at the same store.

LOAN CREDIT

Since loans are the subject of Part 20, little needs to be said about them here. Like purchase credit, loan credit may be either installment or noninstallment credit. A noninstallment loan, called a ***single-payment loan*** is repaid in a lump sum, usually 30, 60, or 90 days after it is made. An installment loan is repaid by weekly or monthly payments, the same as an installment purchase. The majority of consumer loans are of this type.

Some banks also offer a revolving type of loan credit similar to the revolving credit plans offered by retailers. One bank calls its plan a *check-credit account.* It works like this. When applying for a loan, the borrower states how much he can repay monthly. He is then allowed a maximum credit of twelve times that amount. For example, if he can pay $25 a month, his maximum credit is $300. Instead of giving him that amount of money, however, the bank gives him a supply of checks. He is free to use these for any purpose he wishes—to pay bills, to buy things, to travel—as long as he does not go over his $300 limit. In other words, he draws on his credit simply by writing checks.

Each time a payment is made to reduce the loan, the amount of credit available for use increases by the same amount. The borrower is charged only for the amount of money he actually uses. For example, if he writes checks totaling only $65 during one month, he pays only for the use of $65. In addition most banks also charge a fixed amount each month for the service, usually about 50 cents. The borrower must pay this whether he uses his credit during the month or not.

BUILDING YOUR VOCABULARY

On a separate sheet of paper, write each of the terms listed in the left-hand column below and on page 140. Read the three definitions to the right of each term. After each term, copy the definition that best matches it in meaning.

1. charge account

a. A credit plan that entitles consumers to charge purchases at a number of stores
b. A credit plan that permits customers of oil companies to charge gasoline and oil
c. A credit plan that permits the user to charge any number of purchases and pay for them monthly

2. down payment

a. An amount paid on an installment purchase at the time of purchase
b. The amount a customer is charged for using installment credit
c. The amount of the unpaid balance on an installment purchase

3. ***installment contract***
   - *a.* A formal agreement covering the sale of items involving a large expenditure of money
   - *b.* A formal agreement signed by the person who obtains an installment loan
   - *c.* A formal agreement covering the purchase of goods bought on installment credit

4. ***installment credit***
   - *a.* A type of credit used by low-income families
   - *b.* A type of credit that provides for repaying the amount owed in two or more payments
   - *c.* A type of credit that limits the consumer to the purchase of one item at a time

5. ***single-payment loan***
   - *a.* A loan that is repaid in a lump sum
   - *b.* A loan that is repaid within 30 days
   - *c.* A loan that the borrower obtains from a bank

CHECKING YOUR READING

1. What are some factors that have contributed to the growth of consumer credit?
2. What type of agreements does the term "consumer credit" usually refer to?
3. How does sales credit differ from service credit? from loan credit?
4. Generally speaking, there are only two kinds of consumer credit. What are they?
5. Describe the characteristics of an open charge account.
6. Name some types of businesses that encourage their customers to use charge accounts.
7. Do charge accounts make up a large part of consumers' total use of credit? Explain.
8. What is the most-used type of consumer credit today?
9. Name five ways in which installment credit differs from an open charge account.
10. How does a business usually cover the cost of providing open charge-account credit?
11. Who pays the cost of providing installment credit? What is this charge called?
12. Give examples of items that are often financed with installment credit.
13. How does the three-pay account differ from a regular charge account?
14. Explain how a revolving charge account works.
15. What are the two types of loan credit? Which type is most used?
16. Explain how a revolving-loan credit plan operates.

SHARING YOUR OPINION AND EXPERIENCE

1. If you owned a retail store, would you sell for credit? Why or why not?
2. Do you think there should be a difference in the amount of credit that a store extends to different customers?
3. Do you think that cash customers should have to pay the same prices for goods as charge-account customers? If not, how would you handle it so that charge customers paid more?

4. Why should a consumer have to pay for the privilege of using installment credit?
5. Why do you think sellers retain the ownership to goods sold on installment credit?
6. Some revolving credit plans permit a customer to carry up to the maximum balance indefinitely as long as he continues to pay the credit service charge. Can you think of reasons why this may not be a good idea from the standpoint of the customer?
7. Do you think teen-agers should have credit accounts of any kind? Why?
8. Installment credit was developed originally to expand the market for durable goods. Explain.

PROJECTS AND PROBLEMS

1. List five kinds of service credit that your family or other families in your community use.
2. The table below shows total consumer credit outstanding each year from 1956 through 1962. It also shows how much of the total each year was installment credit and how much was noninstallment credit. Finally, it shows how much of the noninstallment credit was in the form of single-payment loans, how much was charge-account credit, and how much was service credit. Study the table and answer the questions following it.

CONSUMER CREDIT OUTSTANDING, YEAR END 1956–1962
(in billions of dollars)

	1956	*1957*	*1958*	*1959*	*1960*	*1961*	*1962*
Total	42.3	45.0	45.1	51.5	56.0	57.7	63.5
Installment	31.7	33.9	33.6	39.2	42.8	43.5	48.2
Noninstallment	10.6	11.1	11.5	12.3	13.2	14.2	15.2
Single-payment loans	3.3	3.4	3.6	4.1	4.5	5.1	5.6
Charge accounts	5.0	5.1	5.1	5.1	5.3	5.3	5.6
Service credit	2.4	2.6	2.8	3.1	3.4	3.7	4.0

Note: Parts may not add to totals due to rounding. *Source: Federal Reserve Board*

▪ *a.* What was the total amount of consumer credit outstanding in 1956? Write your answer in the usual way, using a dollar sign and zeros. ▪ *b.* What was the total amount of consumer credit outstanding in 1962? ▪ *c.* How much did total consumer debt increase from 1956 to 1962? ▪ *d.* Which type of credit increased most from 1956 to 1962, installment or noninstallment? ▪ *e.* Which of the three forms of noninstallment credit contributed most to the increase in that type of credit? ▪ *f.* Approximately what percent of total consumer credit outstanding in 1956 was charge-account credit? ▪ *g.* Approximately what percent of total consumer credit outstanding in 1962 was charge-account credit? ▪ *h.* In terms of consumers' total use of credit, have charge accounts increased or decreased in importance? ▪ *i.* Do your answers to (*g*) and (*h*) agree with what the text says about charge accounts?

3. You have already learned how to read two kinds of graphs—bar graphs and line graphs. You see below another kind, a *circle graph.* It is sometimes called a *pie chart.* It is used to compare single items within a group with the entire group. For example, in the graph below, the circle represents total installment credit outstanding in a recent year. Each division within the circle represents one use of installment credit. When the information is presented in this way, you can see almost at a glance how each use compares with the total. Study the graph and answer the questions following it.

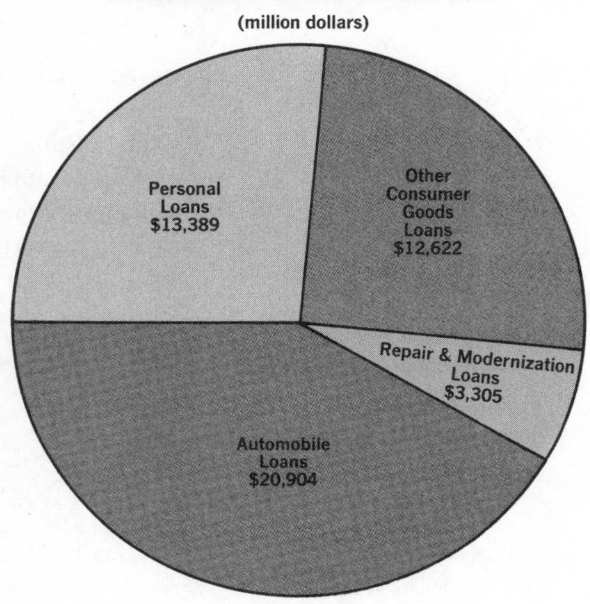

▪ *a.* What was the total amount of consumer credit outstanding for the year shown by the graph? ▪ *b.* Which use of installment credit made up the largest part of the total? ▪ *c.* What percent of the credit outstanding was used for personal loans? ▪ *d.* What percent of the total credit was used to repair and modernize homes? ▪ *e.* What percent of the installment credit was used to purchase consumer goods other than automobiles? ▪ *f.* Automobile loans accounted for approximately how many times as much installment credit as repair and modernization loans? ▪ *g.* When automobiles and other durable goods are purchased on installments, why are these purchases referred to as "automobile loans" and "consumer-goods loans"?

4. Construct a circle graph similar to the one shown above. In place of the dollar amounts, show what percent of the total each use of installment credit represents.
5. The following is an item that appeared in newspapers throughout the nation a few years back. Read it carefully. Then answer the questions at the end.

DEBT TOTAL SOARS BUT WEALTH CLIMBS FASTER

New York. Debt totals, both public and private, are soaring to new highs in America this year. But comfort can be found in a report that the nation's tangible wealth is increasing much faster than its debts. It is estimated that the total of public and private debt owed by the American people will pass the 700 billion dollar mark by the end of the year. This will be 294 billion more than we owed at the end of World War II.

What we own, however—land, buildings, equipment, stocks of goods, and other tangible wealth—has increased by 844 billion dollars since the end of the war. It is estimated that by the end of this year these will be worth nearly $1\frac{1}{2}$ trillion dollars—a sum too big for many of us to grasp. At the end of 1945 our debts were nearly three-fourths as big as our total wealth. Now the debts are only about half as big.

▪ *a.* What is public debt? ▪ *b.* What is private debt? ▪ *c.* What is increasing at a faster rate than debt? ▪ *d.* Approximately what was the total of public and private debt at the end of World War II? ▪ *e.* How does the article describe "tangible wealth"? ▪ *f.* How much more did tangible wealth increase than debt since the war?

CHALLENGE PROBLEMS

1. It was once the practice among businesses to send statements or bills at the end of the month to all their credit customers. Now many business firms divide their customers alphabetically, according to the first letters of their last names. Each group is assigned a certain day of the month on which statements are sent to persons in that group. Thus bills are sent throughout the month rather than just at one time. What is this system of billing called? Why do businesses use it? From the standpoint of the customers, does this method have any advantages?
2. Charge accounts are used by more people today than ever before. Yet they make up less than one-tenth of consumers' total use of credit. How can both statements be true?
3. Why are most consumer loans installment loans?
4. According to the table used in No. 2 of the Projects and Problems section, total consumer credit outstanding increased the least in 1958 and 1961. What business conditions existed during those years that might have caused this?
5. One important reason for the increased use of consumer credit has not been mentioned. What is it?

PART 17 ESTABLISHING YOUR CREDIT

CONSUMERS are fairly well divided in their attitudes toward using credit. Half, or slightly more than half, use credit regularly. This means that nearly half of the families in the United States still prefer the cash method of doing business. How do you explain the fact that some people are willing to use credit while others are not? What kind of consumers do you think use credit the most? the rich? the poor? the young? the old? the in-between? Why?

WHY DO CONSUMERS USE CREDIT?

The use of consumer credit is growing all the time. According to one retail mail-order firm, eight out of ten items bought by its customers are now purchased on credit. This can mean only one thing: the number of consumers who use credit is growing all the time. It includes people in all income groups, of every age (except the very young), married and single, working at every kind of job, and living in all types of communities. The majority of them, however, are middle-income families earning from $5,000 to $10,000 a year. Most of them are under 45. Some of them use credit even though they have the money to pay cash. The question is why?

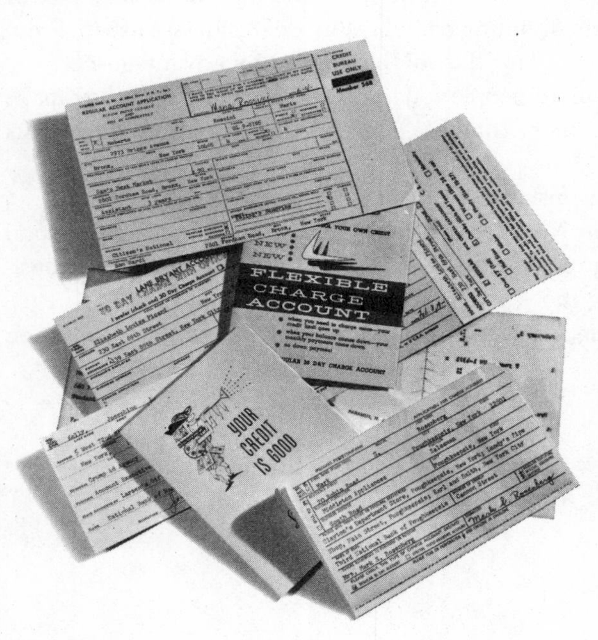

Credit Is a Convenience

One of the main advantages of credit is its convenience. Paying for a number of purchases at one time is easier than paying for each one separately. It does away with the need to carry large amounts of cash with you when you go shopping. It also simplifies shopping by telephone. It is because of its convenience that many consumers use credit even though they could pay cash.

Credit Gives You the Immediate Use of Goods

Probably the number one reason people use credit is to obtain expensive durable goods sooner than if they saved first to buy them. Because of efficient production methods, prices of such things as automobiles, television sets, clothes dryers, and refrigerators are within the reach of many consumers. Even so the price of any one of these items may be more than the average family can pay all at once. By using credit, it is possible to have the use of goods like these while paying for them.

Credit Can Improve One's Standard of Living

Money just seems to burn a hole in some people's pockets. They dribble it away on gadgets and knickknacks of little value. The surprising thing is that even people who do not have the willpower to save usually manage somehow to meet the payments on their credit purchases. Consumers like these can raise their standard of living by obligating themselves to pay for worthwhile items on credit. Indeed, if it were not for credit, some consumers might never have a car, a television set, or very much of anything in the way of long-lasting durable goods.

The Use of Credit May Save Money

In some cases the use of credit may actually save money. One family used credit to take advantage of a special sale on carpeting which it planned to buy soon anyway. Another paid for a washing machine with money that would otherwise have been spent having clothes done at the laundry.

Credit Customers May Receive Better Service

Not everyone would agree that credit customers receive better service than cash customers. Nevertheless, it is one of the reasons people often give for using credit. They claim that credit purchases are more easily returned than cash purchases if found unsatisfactory. Whether or not this is true, credit customers do enjoy some special privileges. Frequently advance notice of sales is sent to credit customers before the sale is announced to the public. This gives the charge customer an opportunity to make his selection before the goods have been picked over.

The Wise Use of Credit Establishes Your Credit Rating

Although we frequently speak of merchants granting or giving credit, this is not an accurate description. Credit is like a reputation. You establish your own. Just as your reputation is based on past deeds, your ability to obtain credit depends largely on how responsibly you have used it in the past. This determines your ***credit rating.*** If you always pay

OF ALL STORES, DEPARTMENT STORES SELL THE LARGEST PORTION OF GOODS ON CREDIT.

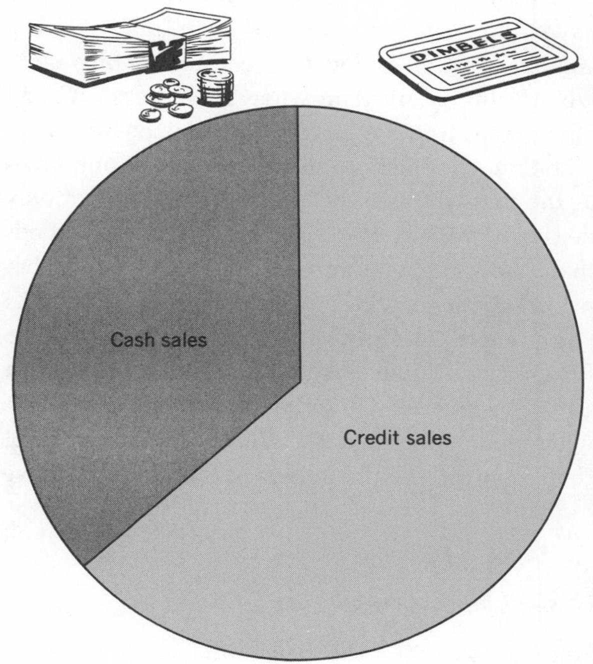

cash, how could anyone tell whether you would pay your debts promptly?

Should the time ever come when you need credit, you might want it in a hurry. Credit can be obtained with greater speed if you have already established yourself as a good credit risk.

WHY DO SOME CONSUMERS AVOID USING CREDIT?

It is pretty difficult these days not to use credit in some form. Most people pay for their daily newspaper by the week or month rather than on each delivery. They also pay for metered services like gas and electricity by the month. Therefore it might be hard to find many consumers who could honestly say they never use credit. But it is possible to find any number who still pay cash for practically everything. And they too have their reasons.

Credit Is a Temptation to Overbuy

One reason retailers sell on credit is because they have found that it increases their sales. This is another way of saying that consumers buy more when using credit than when paying cash. Credit encourages impulse buying. The person who pays cash is not so likely to make unplanned purchases as the one who merely says "Charge it." Not only do those who buy on credit tend to buy more goods than they might otherwise, they also buy higher priced goods. A difference in price never seems so large when you do not have to pay it until some future time. If one jacket costs $12.95 and another $16.95, you are likely to buy the higher priced one when you can charge it. Cash buyers have to limit their spending to the amount of money they have on hand.

Credit Uses Up Purchasing Power

Some people mistakenly believe that credit increases their purchasing power. All credit really does is to make it possible for people to use some of their future purchasing power in advance. But this is not a free privilege. Credit is a service; and like any other service, it costs money. In some cases, mainly charge accounts, the cost of providing credit is spread over all goods and services sold. For most types of credit, however, consumers pay a direct charge. Sometimes having the immediate use of an item may justify the extra cost of buying it on credit. On the other hand, credit charges can eat up part of a family's income, leaving less to spend for other goods and services. In the long run consumers who pay cash are able to buy more goods with a given amount of income than those who do their buying on credit.

As an example, one family found that over a ten-year period it had paid $400 in credit costs to buy $2,400 worth of appliances. Another was even more shocked to discover that, in nine years of credit buying, $7,000 of its income had gone for finance charges.

Credit Is Habit Forming

The fact that credit uses up future purchasing power is something too many consumers overlook. More than one family has found to its dismay that a good-sized portion of each paycheck is needed to pay for past purchases. The only way it can satisfy its present wants is to continue using credit. In no time at all credit becomes a habit that is very hard to break.

Credit Ties You Down

Another reason merchants encourage the use of credit is because it keeps customers coming back. Once people get into the credit habit, they can shop only at stores that will extend them credit. Cash buyers, on the other hand, are free to shop for price and quality rather than credit. They stand a better chance of getting exactly what they want at the best price.

SHOULD YOU USE CREDIT?

From the standpoint of getting your money's worth, perhaps a pay-as-you-go system is best. This also saves having to worry about unpaid bills. If you are the type of person who cannot resist the temptation to overbuy, you probably should pay cash for most things. The ability to follow a spending plan is doubly important when you use credit. As you may have noticed, however, the disadvantages of credit lie in the way it is used. Whether you use it sparingly or often, therefore, you should learn to use it carefully and wisely.

YOU HAVE TO ESTABLISH YOUR CREDIT

Of course, no one can just walk into a store, make a purchase, and say "Charge it." Neither can anyone obtain a loan without first establishing his credit. Most businesses require persons wanting credit to fill out an application form. In many cases, the applicant is also interviewed in person. Both the written application and the interview are the usual means of finding out if a person is a good credit risk.

What Is the Basis of Credit?

In deciding whether or not to extend credit, reliable merchants and loan agencies are guided by three things—the borrower's character, capacity, and capital. These are the three "C's" of credit.

Character refers to a person's reputation for honesty and dependability in paying debts. This is the most important factor in determining whether or not someone is a good credit risk. You probably would not hesitate to lend a quarter to one of your schoolmates who is reliable in money matters. You might not be so willing to do the same for one who is careless about paying his debts. The same principle is followed in business. The privilege of using credit is extended to consumers and producers who have a reputation for paying their bills promptly.

Capacity is the ability to pay a debt. A borrower may be honest and willing to pay a debt but lack the ability to pay it. An important measure of capacity is income or the amount a borrower earns. But there are some other factors that may affect his ability to pay a debt. One is the number of debts he already owes. Another is how much it costs him to live. Can you think of others?

ROGERS PEET COMPANY — APPLICATION FOR CHARGE ACCOUNT

MR. ☑ MRS. ☐ MISS. ☐ FIRST NAME (Please Print): RICHARD — INITIAL: C. — LAST NAME: LANG

☑ BILL TO ☐

RESIDENCE STREET: 3100 Q Street N.W. — CITY: Washington — STATE: D.C.

BUSINESS CONNECTION: Helm Stationery Co. — POSITION: Salesman

BUSINESS ADDRESS: 1406 F Street N.W. — CITY: Washington — STATE: D.C.

PLEASE GIVE THREE STORE OR PERSONAL REFERENCES: John Murphy, 3512 Alton Place N.W., Wertheimer's Dept. Store, Lane's Specialty Store

NAME OF BANK: National Mechanics Bank — ADDRESS OR BRANCH: Broadway & F Street, Washington, D.C.

☑ REGULAR CHECKING ☐ SPECIAL CHECKING ☐ SAVINGS

OTHERS AUTHORIZED TO PURCHASE ON ACCOUNT: my wife, Cora Lang

PLEASE CHECK THE TYPE OF CHARGE ACCOUNT DESIRED: ☑ REGULAR 30 DAY ACCOUNT ☐ SPECIAL THREE-PAYMENT ACCOUNT

SIGNATURE: Richard C. Lang

PLEASE TEAR ON PERFORATION ↓ AND ENCLOSE IN ENVELOPE

Application for a charge account

Courtesy Rogers Peet and Company

Courtesy Oregon Association of Credit Management, Inc.

This credit bureau keeps files on users of credit in the area. A businessman will frequently need this information before he extends credit to a new applicant.

Capital, when used in connection with the granting of credit, means wealth or what a borrower owns. In the case of a consumer, capital would include such things as a home, furniture, an automobile, insurance, jewelry, a savings account, stocks, and bonds. Ownership of such things shows that a person manages his money wisely and that he saves part of his income. A person who has nothing to show for the money he has earned in the past is probably a careless spender. Also if anything should happen to a borrower or his income, his possessions can be used to pay his debts.

Notice the credit-application form on page 147. Do you see any questions that are related to the three "C's" of credit? If a person who applies for credit is using credit for the first time, the information he provides about himself is checked carefully. If he has used credit before, however, the only investigation necessary may be to check with the local credit bureau.

What Is a Credit Bureau?

In a town of any size, it is a gigantic task to investigate the credit of hundreds, sometimes even thousands, of individuals. For that reason many cities have agencies called ***credit bureaus.*** Each bureau keeps on file the credit records of persons who live in its area. These records contain information supplied by business firms that extend credit. This information is available to all business firms who belong to the bureau. The consumer who fails to pay his bills at one store usually finds that he cannot obtain credit at another. Credit bureaus also exchange information with one another. When a person moves from one city to another, his credit rating follows him.

BUILDING YOUR VOCABULARY

Copy the five sentences given below, completing each one by replacing the question mark with the appropriate term from the column at the left.

capacity
capital
character
credit bureau
credit rating

1. The way in which a person has used credit in the past determines his ? .
2. The reputation a person has for honesty and dependability in paying his debts is his ? .
3. The ability to pay a debt is known as ? .
4. What a person owns in the way of property, a car, jewelry, furniture, etc., is wealth or ? .
5. An agency through which business firms exchange information about their credit customers is a ? .

CHECKING YOUR READING

1. Approximately what fraction of the consumers in the United States uses credit regularly?
2. In what income group is the majority of families who use credit?
3. What are six advantages of using credit?
4. Explain how the use of credit is a convenience.
5. What is probably the chief reason why people use credit?
6. Explain how some consumers can raise their standard of living by using credit.
7. How can the use of credit save money?
8. What are some of the special benefits that credit customers enjoy?
9. How does a person establish his credit rating?
10. It is difficult not to use some form of credit today. Explain.
11. What are some of the disadvantages of using credit?
12. Explain how the use of credit may cause consumers to spend more than they would otherwise.
13. If credit does not increase purchasing power, what does it do?
14. Why are consumers who pay cash able to buy more in the long run than those who buy on credit?
15. In what way is credit habit forming?
16. Explain how the credit habit may tie consumers down.
17. What three things are considered in determining whether or not a person is a good credit risk? Explain them.
18. Explain the services of a credit bureau.

SHARING YOUR OPINION AND EXPERIENCE

1. What kind of person is most likely to use credit wisely?
2. Warren Spears claims that only families earning $10,000 or more a year should be allowed to use credit. He feels that credit is a luxury only those with higher-than-average incomes can afford. Do you agree or disagree? Why?

3. Clarence Goodman insists that if consumer credit were abolished, both consumers and business would benefit. Consumers would benefit because goods and services would cost less. Business would benefit because more goods and services could be sold if prices were lower. Do you agree with Clarence? Give reasons for your answer.
4. Should a person buy on credit just to establish a credit rating even though he has the money to pay cash?
5. Does the fact that a person is short of money and uses credit mean that he has not managed his money wisely? Explain.
6. A credit bureau serves as a protection for business firms, but it also protects buyers. In what way?
7. Why is character more important than capacity or capital in determining whether someone is a good credit risk?
8. If character is so important, why do lenders bother to investigate a borrower's ability to pay a debt?
9. If one person's annual income is $6,000 and another's is $11,000, is the person with the higher income a better credit risk? Why?
10. Bill Krinsky is business manager for the school yearbook. Normally, all orders must be accompanied by a payment of $3, the cost of the yearbook. Several students have asked Bill to take their orders and let them pay later. Explain what you would do if you were Bill.

PROJECTS AND PROBLEMS

1. One disadvantage of using credit is that finance charges use up purchasing power and leave less to spend for other goods and services. Study the following table and figure how much purchasing power a consumer will lose if he buys on credit each of the articles listed.

Article	*Credit Terms*			*Total Credit Price*	*Cash Price*	*Purchasing Power Lost to Credit Charges*
	Down Payment	*No. of Payments*	*Amount of Each Payment*			
a. **Desk**	**$14.00**	**15**	**$5.00**	?	**$ 79.00**	?
b. **Typewriter**	**29.95**	**16**	**7.00**	?	**129.95**	?
c. **Camera**	**5.00**	**8**	**6.25**	?	**49.50**	?
d. **Refrigerator**	**25.00**	**20**	**8.47**	?	**179.00**	?
e. **Bicycle**	**10.00**	**9**	**3.75**	?	**39.95**	?

2. Which of the following items of information would be important in deciding whether to grant credit to someone? Be prepared to give reasons for each choice.

   ▪ *a.* Home address ▪ *b.* place of birth ▪ *c.* employer ▪ *d.* college attended ▪ *e.* monthly income ▪ *f.* church membership ▪ *g.* children's names ▪ *h.* color of eyes and hair ▪ *i.* former address ▪ *j.* wife's earnings

3. Mr. and Mrs. Edwards live in Brynwood, a small town near a medium-sized city.

Mr. Edwards works in the city and drives the 10 miles to and from his job each day. Their car is now 4 years old, and he would like to trade it in on a new one. A local dealer has offered to sell him a new car for his old one and $1,800 in cash. Mr. Edwards does not have that much money, but he can buy the car on installments by paying a credit charge of $216 over a 2-year period. Mrs. Edwards thinks it would be better to keep the old car until they have saved enough money to pay cash for a new one.

Divide a sheet of paper into two columns. In the left-hand column list the advantages of buying the car on credit now. In the right-hand column, list the disadvantages. Then decide whether you favor Mr. Edwards' plan or Mrs. Edwards' plan. Or suggest what you think might be a better plan under the circumstances.

4. A. J. Atkins operates a clothing store in a small college town. Most of his customers are young men who attend the college. Mr. Atkins has always operated on a cash basis but is considering the possibility of extending credit to customers who want it. List all arguments you know for and against extending credit in this case.
5. Many persons are alarmed by the amount of consumer debt in the United States and the fact that it is rising. True, total consumer debt has increased year after year, but so have the incomes of the people who owe the debts. One way to judge the size of consumer debt is to compare it with disposable personal income. *Disposable personal income* is the total amount of income consumers have for spending after payment of taxes. The table below compares changes in total consumer debt and disposable personal income from 1950 to 1964. In 1950, for example, disposable personal income was $207.7 billion. Consumer debt, on the other hand, was $21.5 billion, or slightly more than 10 percent of disposable personal income. Study the table and answer the questions following it.

CONSUMER DEBT AND DISPOSABLE PERSONAL INCOME 1950–1964

Year	*Consumer Debt (in billions of dollars)*	*Disposable Personal Income (in billions of dollars)*
1950	**21.5**	**207.7**
1951	**22.7**	**227.5**
1952	**27.5**	**238.7**
1953	**31.4**	**252.5**
1954	**32.5**	**256.9**
1955	**38.8**	**274.4**
1956	**42.3**	**292.9**
1957	**45.0**	**308.8**
1958	**45.1**	**317.9**
1959	**51.5**	**337.1**
1960	**56.0**	**349.4**
1961	**57.7**	**363.6**
1962	**63.5**	**384.4**
1963	**69.9**	**402.4**
1964	**68.9**	**418.7**

■ *a.* Was there any year in which consumer debt was less than the previous year? if so, which year or years? ■ *b.* Was there any year in which disposable personal income was less than the previous year? which year or years? ■ *c.* Which year was the increase in consumer debt smallest? ■ *d.* Which year was the increase in disposable personal income smallest? ■ *e.* Which year did consumer debt increase the most? ■ *f.* Which year did disposable personal income increase the most? ■ *g.* What percent of disposable personal income was total consumer debt in 1964? ■ *h.* Was there any year in which consumer debt was less than 10 percent of disposable personal income?* if so, which year? ■ *i.* In which year was debt the largest in relation to income?* ■ *j.* What was the percent of increase in consumer debt from 1950 to 1964? ■ *k.* What was the percent of increase in disposable income from 1950 to 1964? ■ *l.* Would you say that consumer debt has been rising at a faster or slower rate than disposable personal income?

* Try to answer without figuring the percents for each year.

CHALLENGE PROBLEMS

The following article appeared recently in a well-known newspaper. Read it and answer the questions below.

WILD SPENDING PUTS DENTIST IN FINANCIAL HOLE

Centerville. Dr. M., a dentist, recently plunked down $3,535 of borrowed money for a shiny new red sedan bristling with extras, a gift for his son in college. Not too unusual—except that creditors had already whisked away most of the dentist's possessions and were clamoring for nearly $100,000 he still owes them. "The boy wanted it," says the 44-year-old Dr. M. "I know I can't afford that car, but it makes a good front," he said.

The average bill-paying citizen may find it hard to believe a sane man could land himself in Dr. M's predicament. Actually, the dentist has plenty of company in his troubles. He is simply an extreme representative of a fairly sizable body of Americans. Last year petitions for voluntary bankruptcy by such people rose to a record 128,000 from 122,000 the previous year. Installment debt reached a record level, too.

■ *a.* What does being in a "financial hole" mean? ■ *b.* What is unusual about Dr. M. using credit to buy a car? ■ *c.* Who took away the dentist's possessions? ■ *d.* What right did they have to take them? ■ *e.* What did Dr. M. mean when he said ". . . it makes a good front"? ■ *f.* What is buying for this reason called? ■ *g.* Is Dr. M. typical of most American consumers? ■ *h.* What is a petition for voluntary bankruptcy? ■ *i.* How do you suppose Dr. M. was able to buy the car on credit when he already owed so much money?

PART 18 USING YOUR CREDIT

SOONER or later most consumers find a reason for using credit. A student may need a loan to finance his education. A family may decide to buy a house. A man might have a chance to take over a business. Or the old refrigerator might give out while dad and mom are still paying for having Junior's teeth straightened. No one ever knows when an emergency or an opportunity will force him into using credit. But if that should happen, it's a mighty secure feeling to know your credit is good. The nice part about it is that you can use your credit and still keep it good if you use it wisely.

The consumer who uses credit wisely does four things. (1) He uses the right kind of credit for his purpose. (2) He shops for credit just as he shops for the other things he buys. (3) He takes on no more debt than he can carry safely. (4) He pays his debts promptly.

What difference does it make what kind of credit a person uses as long as he pays his bills? How much debt can a consumer afford? Why should anyone shop for credit?

USE THE RIGHT KIND OF CREDIT

Most of the things you will buy in the years ahead can be divided into three groups. Some items you will buy often, like food, household supplies, gasoline, grooming aids, and newspapers. Others you will buy seldom, like furniture and carpets, automobiles, television sets, and work-saving appliances like washers and dryers. In between will be the things you will buy only occasionally. These might include major clothing items—such as coats and suits—and home furnishings—such as draperies, bedspreads, blankets, and lamps.

That, more or less, is the way it is with credit too. There is a kind for everyday; a kind for special

Courtesy Socony Mobil Oil Company, Inc.

occasions; and a kind for everything in between. To use credit wisely you must know the difference.

Charge Accounts Are for Everyday Purchases

An open, or 30-day, charge account is simply a convenience. It is the one kind of credit for which no separate charge is made. It is the only type of credit to use for those purchases that you will make almost daily. If financed in any other way, except cash, these items may be consumed long before they are paid for. In addition, when credit is extended beyond 30 days, it begins to cost money. And who wants to pay for the privilege of buying on credit things like toothpaste and socks? That would just be adding unnecessarily to your cost of living. Because purchases charged on an open account have to be paid for in full each month, it is almost like paying cash.

Installment-Purchase Credit Is for Special Purchases

The main advantage of installment credit is that it gives you an extended time in which to pay for your purchases. This makes it an ideal form of credit for those long-lasting durable goods that you will buy only now and then. In fact, it was developed for just that purpose. Installment-purchase credit is a wonderful invention when properly used. What is and what is not proper use, however, is something each consumer has to decide for himself. Following are some questions designed to help you make a wise decision.

Is It Worth the Extra Cost? Installment credit costs money. Sometimes it's worth it; and sometimes it is not. For example, Mrs. Healy, the mother of two teen-aged daughters wants to buy a sewing machine so she can make their clothes herself. If she buys the machine on installments, it will cost $20 more than if she saved and paid cash. By having the machine at once, Mrs. Healy thinks she can save that much and maybe more. For this reason she feels that the use of installment credit is worth what it will cost. She might not feel the same way if the item she wanted were something else.

Before you decide definitely to buy anything on installments, find out how much more it will cost than if you paid cash. Then ask yourself if the article is really so necessary, so useful, or so timesaving that it is worth the extra cost of buying it on credit.

Does the Article Cost Enough to Use Installment Credit? Buying on time becomes such a habit with some people that they use installment credit for items that could be paid for with current income. One family paid $1.50 extra to buy a toaster, costing $14.50, on installments; $2.50 extra to buy a $20 radio; and $4 for the privilege of taking 8 months to pay for a $39.95 vacuum cleaner. In each case, using credit increased the cost of the items more than 10 percent. The total cost for credit on all three items came to $8, more than half the price of the toaster. Yet to pay cash for any one of these items would have meant saving for only a short period of time at the most. Using expensive credit for inexpensive items is a waste of money.

Is the Article Needed? It is sometimes hard to say whether or not an item is really needed. It is even harder if the item can be obtained on credit. A man may need a car to drive back and forth to work. But if he is buying it on credit, he can usually think of many arguments for buying a high-powered, high-priced one when a medium-priced one would serve his purpose just as well. Installment-purchase credit, like other types of credit, is an invitation to buy things, not because we need them, but because we want them—or because other people have them.

There is no denying that a refrigerator is needed to preserve food. But when it comes to boats, jewelry, furs, and other out-and-out luxuries that people buy on installments, that is a different matter. This is not to suggest that there is anything wrong with buying such things if you can afford them. One of the most important facts to learn about credit,

Consumers use installment credit to buy expensive durable goods, such as TV sets, so that they can enjoy their use while paying for them.

Monkmeyer Press Photo Service

however, is that each person has only a limited amount. To use it unnecessarily reduces the amount available should a real need for credit arise. Besides, anyone who really wants a boat or fur ought to be willing to save for it by denying himself other less important things. He will have to do that anyway in order to pay for it if he does buy it on credit.

Can I Meet the Payments? It is almost unbelievable how many people go into debt with no plan for getting out of it. Before you agree to buy anything on installments, check your budget to make sure of your ability to meet the payments. Then test your ability to pay for the item. Try saving an amount equal to the payments for a couple of months to see if you can spare that much from your income. You may decide to continue saving until you have enough to pay cash.

Have I Read the Installment Contract Carefully? Installment buying, as you know, involves a written contract. This is a legal document. Once it is signed, you can be held to it by law. Before you sign such a contract, therefore, read it carefully to make certain you know what you are signing. Much of the contract may be in very small print. The smaller the print, the more reason there is for reading it. Following are some points to check:

1. Does the contract state when and where each payment is made?
2. What does it say will happen if you fail to make a payment on time?
3. Are charges itemized, so that you know how much you are paying for merchandise and how much you are paying for credit?
4. Can you get a refund if you pay the entire debt before it is due?

Examine the contract illustrated on page 138 to see how well it covers the above points. If there is anything in a contract you do not understand, ask to have it explained to you before signing. Under no circumstances should you sign a contract that has not been completely filled in.

Revolving Credit Is Not for Everyday Use

What about financing those in-between items that

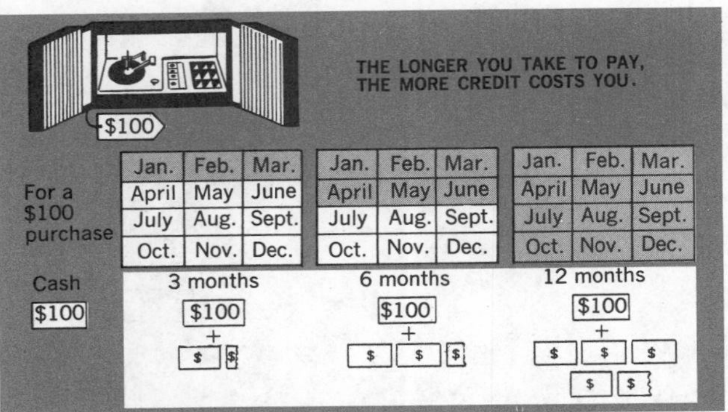

cost more than you can manage out of one paycheck but not enough to use regular installment credit? That's the time, and the only time, when you might consider using either a three-pay or a revolving charge account. In most cases you pay extra for their use. For that reason you should be just as careful about using accounts of this kind as you are about using installment credit. Actually that is what revolving charge accounts are—a kind of continuous-payment installment credit. They may be fine for items you need two, three, or even four months to pay for. But many people make the mistake of using them for everything and paying extra to do so month after month after month.

Growing in popularity is a credit plan that may be used as either an open account or a revolving charge account. In other words, you have a choice. You may pay the full amount owing at the end of the month. Or you may make a partial payment plus a service charge on the amount left unpaid. This enables you to avoid paying credit charges on small purchases. On the other hand, it also gives you extra time to pay for major items. But it is up to you, and not the store, to decide when it is worthwhile to stretch out your payments. An account of this type is often called an ***option account.***

PAY NO MORE FOR CREDIT THAN NECESSARY

Credit is a service that is bought and sold. What few consumers seem to realize, however, is that the cost of credit varies. They may shop for hours, even days, comparing the prices of merchandise yet never bother to ask how much the finance charge is. All they want to know is the size of the payments.

Where credit is concerned, time is money. The longer you take to repay a debt, the more the credit costs you. The smaller the payments, the longer the debt has to run. So do not be misled by the "Nothing down—months to pay" advertising appeals. The easier the ***credit terms,*** the more costly the credit.

When you buy anything on installments, make as large a down payment as you can and pay the balance as quickly as you can. One way to do this is to limit your use of this type of credit to one thing at a time. Suppose, for example, that a family budgets $20 a month for furniture and household equipment and $40 a month for car payments. It could use the entire $60 monthly to buy furniture one year, then use both allowances for a car the next two years. The total cost for credit would be less than if payments for both the furniture and car were extended over three years.

HOW MUCH DEBT CAN YOU AFFORD?

Credit involves risk for the borrower as well as the lender. The person who fails to pay his debts for any reason stands to lose a great deal. His creditor may ***repossess*** the item for which payment is overdue. That means he takes possession of the goods again. The seller has a legal right to do this since, in most cases, the goods belong to him until paid for. In addition to losing the goods, the debtor may have to pay what it costs the creditor to repossess them. If the goods are resold for less than the amount of the debt, he is still responsible for the difference. Sometimes a creditor will take legal action to have the amount owed him deducted from the debtor's wages. Many employers consider this a nuisance and will discharge workers rather than be bothered.

Before using credit of any kind, you should be fully aware of all risks involved. How certain is your future income? Do you have savings you could draw on in an emergency? How much do you already owe? The more debt you assume, of course, the greater the risk. Unfortunately, some sellers make it so easy to obtain credit that many consumers get into financial difficulties by taking on more debt than they can handle.

Authorities are not agreed about how much debt consumers can safely carry. Some say 10 percent of their annual ***after-tax income,*** which means the amount they actually have left for spending after paying their taxes. This does not include what is owed on homes. There are those who will argue that 10 percent is too high and those who claim it is too low. The truth is that it is impossible to make a rule that applies to everyone, because so many factors must be considered. A childless couple living in a two-room apartment can handle more debt than a couple with a large house and five children, even if their incomes are equal.

In the long run each consumer must set his own credit limit. Regardless of what that limit may be, however, the consumer who stretches his credit to the breaking point risks losing it altogether. It is always a good idea to keep some credit in reserve.

WHAT IF YOU CANNOT PAY?

The way you meet your credit obligations becomes a matter of record. When you are unable to pay a debt, get in touch with your creditor before payment is due and explain your difficulty. Reliable merchants and lenders will almost always try to help a debtor work out a solution to his credit problem. Sometimes it is possible to refinance the balance due. To ***refinance*** a debt means to arrange for smaller payments over a longer period of time. This will increase the cost of the credit, but it will prevent the loss of your purchases and save you embarrassment. Most important of all, it will protect your good credit rating.

BUILDING YOUR VOCABULARY

List the figures 1 to 5 on a sheet of paper, numbering down. Read the five statements given below at the right; then, for each statement, select from the column at the left the term that best matches it in meaning. Write this term next to the appropriate number.

after-tax income
credit terms
option account
refinance
repossess

1. A credit plan that may be used as either an open account or a revolving charge account
2. To take back goods sold on credit if the buyer fails to make payments when due
3. The amount of earnings a worker has for spending
4. To arrange repayment of a debt, so that payments are smaller than they were originally
5. The details covering an installment purchase, such as the down payment, number and size of payments, and service charge

CHECKING YOUR READING

1. What four things does the consumer who uses credit wisely do?
2. Most things that people buy can be divided into three groups according to how often they are purchased. Explain and give examples.

3. What is the best type of credit to use for things purchased often and consumed within a short time? Why?
4. What is the main advantage of installment credit?
5. For what purpose should installment credit be used?
6. What five questions should a consumer ask himself before using installment credit?
7. Why should inexpensive items not be purchased on the installment plan?
8. Why should a consumer not use installment credit to buy articles he does not really need?
9. How can a person test his ability to pay for an item before buying it on credit?
10. What points should you check before signing an installment contract?
11. What should a person do if he does not understand certain parts of an installment contract?
12. When should a person consider using a revolving charge account?
13. Why should consumers shop for credit just as they shop for merchandise?
14. Explain the statement that "where credit is concerned, time is money."
15. What may a person lose in addition to the merchandise if he fails to keep up the payments on an installment purchase?
16. Why is it difficult to say how much debt consumers can safely carry?
17. What should a person do if he is unable to pay a debt on schedule?
18. What advantages might there be in refinancing a debt?

SHARING YOUR OPINION AND EXPERIENCE

1. What is a charge-plate? How is it used?
2. Why is it usually unwise to buy on credit such items that will be consumed before they are paid for?
3. Should the use of installment credit be limited to the purchase of durable goods only? Why?
4. What is the difference between a need and a want? Is it possible that one person's want might be another person's need? Explain.
5. Why should a person refuse to sign an installment contract that has not been completely filled in?
6. One company advertised recently: "Spend 21 delightful days in Scandinavia! Only $107.50 down, $86.30 a month." Do you think it is wise to use credit to pay for a vacation?
7. What is a *lay-away* plan? How does it differ from buying on the installment plan?
8. How can a family determine its own credit limit?
9. Fred Lang was issued a credit card by one of the big oil companies. The card entitled him to charge purchases at any one of the company's service stations throughout the United States. Unfortunately, Fred lost the card. What should he do? Why?

PROJECTS AND PROBLEMS

1. Every business that grants credit to its customers has its own way of handling credit sales. The major steps in making a charge purchase, however, are similar in most businesses. When a customer makes a purchase on an open charge account, a salesclerk makes a record of the sale on a form called a *sales ticket.* Two or more copies of the ticket are made, and the customer is asked to sign the form. If the goods are to be delivered, some businesses do not require the customer's signature. One copy of the ticket is given to the customer, and the store keeps all remaining copies. An illustration of a completed sales ticket is shown below. Study it and answer the questions to the left of it.

■ *a.* What did the customer buy? ■ *b.* Who was charged for the purchase? ■ *c.* To whom was the merchandise delivered? ■ *d.* What was the total amount of the sale? ■ *e.* Is the purchaser's signature on the form? ■ *f.* Who is the creditor? ■ g. Who is the debtor? ■ *h.* What was the date of the sale? ■ *i.* For what was the customer charged in addition to the merchandise?

CASHIER'S STAMP | TOTAL SALE
102176-48
HS | SOLD BY 148 | DATE 7/10/66 | THE DAYTON COMPANY

DEPT.	QUAN.	ARTICLE	
31	1	wrap dress	5 98
	1	cotton suit dress	17 95
APPLIED CREDIT NO.- SPECIAL ORDER NO., ETC.		GIFT WRAP / CARD — Sales Tax	1 20
		TOTAL	25 13

CHARGE TO: FIRST MIDDLE LAST — Mrs. Allen Douglas
NO. STREET — 45 Alexander Street
CITY STATE — Centerville 102176-48
SERVICE MGR. AUTHORIZATION | PURCHASER Mary Douglas
FILL THIS SECTION IN IF CHARGE AND SEND TO ADDRESSES ARE DIFFERENT
SEND TO
M
ADDRESS
SOLD BY | DATE / | HOW SOLD | CHGE. AUTH. OR AMT. RECD.
SOLD BY | DATE / | HOW SOLD | PROMISED DATE
SEND TO: Mrs. Allen Douglas
NO. STREET — 45 Alexander Street
CITY STATE — Centerville
APT. ROOM | INSTRUCTIONS
THE DAYTON COMPANY
CENTERVILLE 102176-48
ENCLOSE IN WHITE ORIGINAL SALESCHECK ENVELOPE

A charge-account sales ticket

2. Whether a person buys on credit or pays cash, he sometimes has to return goods. When merchandise that has been purchased on credit is returned, a record of the return is made on a form known as a *credit ticket* or *credit memorandum.* A credit ticket is handled in the same way as a sales ticket. The customer gets one copy, and the business keeps the other copies. The ticket shows the amount of credit the customer is to receive for the returned merchandise. This means that the price of the returned goods is to be subtracted from what the customer owes the store. An example of a credit ticket is shown on page 160. Answer the questions next to it.

▪ *a.* What was returned for credit? ▪ *b.* What was the price of the returned article? ▪ *c.* Whose account was credited for the returned merchandise? ▪ *d.* What was the total amount of the credit? ▪ *e.* Who received the returned article at the store? ▪ *f.* Who else signed the credit ticket?

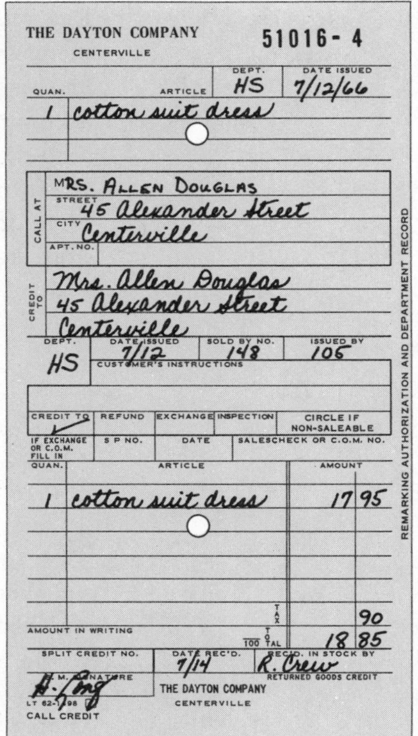

THE DAYTON COMPANY 51016-4
CENTERVILLE

QUAN.	ARTICLE	DEPT.	DATE ISSUED
1	cotton suit dress	HS	7/12/66

CALL AT: MRS. ALLEN DOUGLAS
STREET 45 Alexander Street
CITY Centerville
APT. NO.

CREDIT TO: Mrs. Allen Douglas
45 Alexander Street
Centerville

DEPT.	DATE ISSUED	SOLD BY NO.	ISSUED BY
HS	7/12	148	106

CUSTOMER'S INSTRUCTIONS

CREDIT TO ✓ | REFUND | EXCHANGE | INSPECTION | CIRCLE IF NON-SALEABLE

IF EXCHANGE OR C.O.M. FILL IN | S P NO. | DATE | SALESCHECK OR C.O.M. NO.

QUAN.	ARTICLE	AMOUNT
1	cotton suit dress	17 95
	TAX	90
	TOTAL	18 85

AMOUNT IN WRITING

SPLIT CREDIT NO. | DATE REC'D. 7/14 | REC'D. IN STOCK BY R. Crew

M. SIGNATURE [illegible] | RETURNED GOODS CREDIT
THE DAYTON COMPANY
CENTERVILLE
LT 62-[illegible]98
CALL CREDIT

REMARKING AUTHORIZATION AND DEPARTMENT RECORD

A credit ticket

3. Customers who buy on open account usually receive a monthly statement from each business with which they have an account. Such a statement contains a record of all purchases, returns, and payments for the month. Some statements identify purchases by name, while others list only the amount of each purchase. When purchases are not identified, copies of all sales tickets are usually enclosed with the statement. These sales tickets are to be used to check the accuracy of the store's statement. Study the statement shown on page 161 and answer the following questions.

▪ *a.* Who is expected to pay the amount shown in the statement? ▪ *b.* During what period were the purchases made? ▪ *c.* When should the amount shown on the statement be paid? ▪ *d.* What is the amount to be paid? ▪ *e.* How much did the customer owe for the period just before this one? ▪ *f.* Did the customer pay all he owed the previous month? ▪ *g.* How many purchases did the customer make during the month?

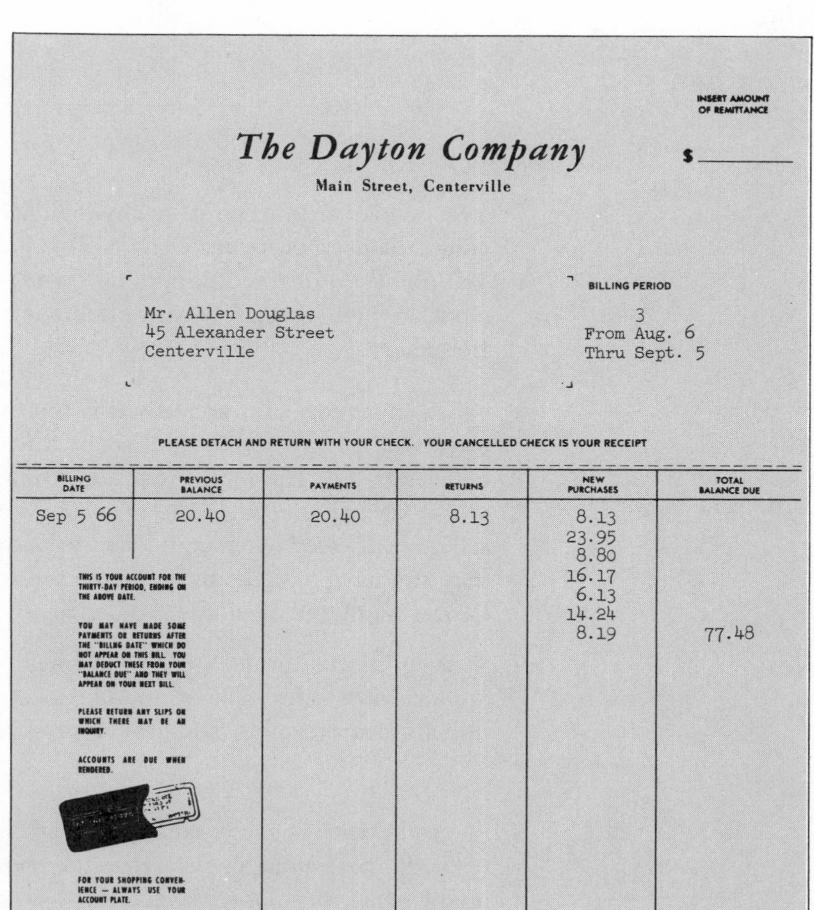

INSERT AMOUNT OF REMITTANCE

$ ________

The Dayton Company

Main Street, Centerville

Mr. Allen Douglas
45 Alexander Street
Centerville

BILLING PERIOD
3
From Aug. 6
Thru Sept. 5

PLEASE DETACH AND RETURN WITH YOUR CHECK. YOUR CANCELLED CHECK IS YOUR RECEIPT

BILLING DATE	PREVIOUS BALANCE	PAYMENTS	RETURNS	NEW PURCHASES	TOTAL BALANCE DUE
Sep 5 66	20.40	20.40	8.13	8.13	
				23.95	
				8.80	
				16.17	
				6.13	
				14.24	
				8.19	77.48

THIS IS YOUR ACCOUNT FOR THE THIRTY-DAY PERIOD, ENDING ON THE ABOVE DATE.

YOU MAY HAVE MADE SOME PAYMENTS OR RETURNS AFTER THE "BILLNG DATE" WHICH DO NOT APPEAR ON THIS BILL. YOU MAY DEDUCT THESE FROM YOUR "BALANCE DUE" AND THEY WILL APPEAR ON YOUR NEXT BILL.

PLEASE RETURN ANY SLIPS ON WHICH THERE MAY BE AN INQUIRY.

ACCOUNTS ARE DUE WHEN RENDERED.

FOR YOUR SHOPPING CONVENIENCE — ALWAYS USE YOUR ACCOUNT PLATE.

A statement

4. Study the installment sales contract on page 138 and answer the following questions:

   ▪ *a.* Who is the buyer? ▪ *b.* Who is the seller? ▪ *c.* How much is the buyer paying for the use of credit? ▪ *d.* How much are his monthly payments? ▪ *e.* How much was the down payment? ▪ *f.* What will happen if the buyer does not make his payment? ▪ *g.* Under what conditions may the article be moved from the address shown on the contract? ▪ *h.* May the contract be changed by oral agreement? ▪ *i.* Who is the legal owner of the article until the final payment has been made?

5. Copy the following list of goods and services in the left-hand column of a form similar to the one shown on page 162: automobile, clothes, color TV set, electric toaster, electricity, ice-cream cone, living-room sofa, medical services, milk, newspaper, textbook, washing machine. After each item, place a check mark in the appropriate column to indicate whether a family is more likely to pay cash for it, buy

Article	Pay Cash	Buy on Open Charge Account	Buy on Installment Plan
Example: Pencil	√		

it on open charge account, or buy it on the installment plan. Be prepared to give your reasons in every case.

6. The ability to distinguish opinion from fact may help you to make wise use of credit. Which of the following statements do you think are opinions and which are facts?

   ▪ *a.* Using credit adds unnecessarily to the cost of living. ▪ *b.* Almost all families use credit in some form. ▪ *c.* Usually it is not wise to buy expensive luxury items on credit. ▪ *d.* The most important thing to look for in an installment contract is the size of the payments. ▪ *e.* Sam Kerr bought a food freezer, which the seller repossessed when Sam failed to make his payments. It is possible that Sam may still have to make payments to the seller. ▪ *f.* Refinancing a debt is so embarrassing that it should be avoided at all costs.

7. As a committee project, collect forms used in connection with credit, such as applications, sales tickets, credit tickets, statements, and so on. Prepare a bulletin-board exhibit, using these forms.

CHALLENGE PROBLEMS

1. "A credit ticket or memorandum should be kept in a safe place until it is no longer needed." Do you agree with this statement? Why? How does one know when a credit ticket is no longer needed?
2. What precaution should you take when you pay a debt with cash?
3. A man who was in financial difficulty because he had used credit too freely blamed his creditors for his troubles. "They made buying on credit too easy for me," he said. Do you think a person who overbuys on credit is justified in blaming those who extend him the credit? Explain.
4. Because installment credit has helped to expand the market for durable goods, such things as automobiles, washing machines, outboard motors, and television sets cost less than they would otherwise. Explain.
5. Frank Morris says that, when he buys durable goods such as automobiles and household appliances, he prefers to use installment credit and extend the payments as long as possible. He maintains that, since prices in general tend to rise over a period of time, money gradually loses value. The money with which he pays off his debts will, therefore, be worth less than the money he would have spent had he paid cash. What does Mr. Morris mean? Do you agree or disagree? Why?
6. How can the careless use of credit reduce a family's real income?

PART 19
THE COST OF USING CREDIT

ALMOST everyone who uses credit expects to pay for it, but hardly anyone seems to know exactly how much he pays. Even those who think they know usually estimate the cost to be one-half or one-third of what it actually is. This is not really as odd as it might sound. Credit, you see, doesn't always carry a price tag like shoes, or bread, or phonograph records. And when it does, the stated price may not be the true price. Consumers who want to know the true price usually have to figure it out for themselves, and not very many know how.

To use credit wisely, you must know how much it costs. Otherwise, you cannot compare credit charges; and you may pay more than you have to. In fact, unless you know what you pay for credit, you have no basis for deciding whether it is worth the price.

What determines the cost of credit? Why do credit charges vary? Why do some consumers have to pay more for credit than others?

WHAT DETERMINES THE PRICE OF CREDIT?

The price of credit, like the price of almost any other good or service, depends on the costs of providing it. If you buy a phonograph record, the price you pay must cover the seller's costs of doing business plus a fair profit. When you use credit, the price you pay has to cover the lender's costs plus a fair profit. The reason credit charges vary is because some lenders have higher costs than others. In general, however, all lenders have the same three kinds of costs: interest, operating expenses, and risk.

Interest

Money has many uses. Anyone who extends credit

H. Armstrong Roberts

cannot use his money in some other way until the debt is paid. He, therefore, has a right to charge for its use. This charge is called ***interest.*** Interest is usually expressed as a percent, such as 4 percent or 6 percent. This is the ***interest rate.*** An interest rate of 4 percent means that for every dollar owed, the borrower must pay 4 cents. Unless stated otherwise, interest is usually quoted as an annual charge. A rate of 4 percent would mean a charge of 4 cents for each dollar owed for a year.

Interest is a price. Like other prices it may vary from time to time. One factor that affects interest rates is competition. Sometimes the demand for credit is greater than the amount of money available for lending. Then borrowers compete with one another to obtain credit. This tends to push up the interest rate. At other times the amount of money available for lending is greater than the amount wanted. Then lenders compete with one another for business. This tends to force down the interest rate.

Operating Expenses

Business enterprises that extend credit have some of the same operating expenses as other businesses. They must pay rent. They also pay for heat, light, telephone service, and equipment. And they must pay their workers.

In addition, lenders have the expense of investigating credit applicants to find out if they are good risks. Collection is another big item of cost for lenders. Collection includes sending notices when payments are due and keeping a record of payments made. The more payments there are to collect, the greater the cost. When you pay a debt in a lump sum, the cost of collecting occurs only once. When you pay a debt in installments, the cost of collecting occurs as many times as there are payments. For a debt paid in 12 installments, the cost of collecting occurs 12 times. That is why installment credit always costs more than single-payment loans and charge accounts. When borrowers fail to pay their debts on time, of course collection costs increase.

The cost of investigating a borrower's credit and the cost of collection do not vary much regardless of the amount of credit involved. In other words, it costs no more to investigate a borrower wanting $500 worth of credit than to investigate one wanting $100 worth. Similarly, the cost of collection is no different whether payments are $20 or $50. Only the number of payments makes a difference. But see what happens when investigation and collection costs are added to $500 worth of credit and when they are added to $100 worth. Suppose that investigating the borrower and recording payments costs a lender $15 when a debt is paid in 12 installments. On $500 worth of credit this amounts to 3 percent. On $100 worth of credit it is 15 percent.

Risk

Extending credit always involves a ***risk*** for the lender since he can never be certain the debt will be paid. When a lender is unable to collect a debt, he takes a loss. Losses from unpaid debts are an added cost of doing business. Needless to say, such losses are highest among lenders who assume the greatest risk. Lenders who deal only with people who are known to pay their debts promptly have few losses. The more risk a lender is willing to assume, the more he must charge.

As you can see, it pays to have a good credit rating. But to make it pay, you have to deal with lenders who specialize in good risks.

HOW TO COMPARE CREDIT COSTS

There are two ways of comparing credit charges. One way, and the simplest way, is in terms of their dollar cost. The other way is on the basis of their percent cost. Some lenders state their charges in dollars and cents; others state their charges

There are times when the expense of using credit is justified. An emergency trip, for example, cannot be delayed until the money is saved.

Courtesy Trans World Airlines

as percents. Regardless of how a charge is stated, however, it may or may not tell the true cost of the credit. In figuring the true cost of credit, the two most important factors are the amount of money involved and the length of time you use it.

Finding the Dollar Cost

Finding the dollar cost of a loan is simple. You merely deduct the amount of money you receive from the amount you pay back. The difference is the dollar cost of the loan. For example, suppose you could borrow $75 and repay it in 20 months at $5.06 a month. The dollar cost of such a loan would be $26.20

$5.06	(monthly payments)
×20	(number of payments)
$101.20	(total paid to lender)
−75.00	(received from lender)
$26.20	(dollar cost)

Finding the dollar cost of installment-purchase credit is a little more complicated. This is because it involves two kinds of shopping. First you have to shop for the *lowest* cash price for which the item you plan to buy can be bought. The reason is that some sellers claim they do not charge for installment credit. What they do is to charge higher cash prices than other sellers to make it appear as if there were no credit charge. A little shopping will usually uncover this fact. Second, you have to shop for the best credit price. The difference between the lowest cash price and the credit price is the true dollar cost of using installment credit.

For example, suppose you want to buy a portable stereo phonograph. At a store that sells only for cash, the price is $125. At another store you can buy the phonograph on installments for $14.00 down and $10.50 a month for 12 months—a total of $140.

Down payment	$14.00
Monthly payments (12 × $10.50)	126.00
Total credit price	$140.00

The dollar cost of credit in this case would be $15:

Total credit price	$140.00
Lowest cash price	125.00
Dollar cost	$15.00

Finding the Percent Cost of Credit

Dollar cost is an ideal way to compare credit charges when (1) charges are for loans or purchases of the same amount; (2) the balance to be paid in each case is the same; and (3) payment is to be completed within the same length of time. But suppose you want to compare credit charges when credit terms differ in some way, as they often do. Say, for example, that a down payment is required in one case but not in another. Or you have 10 months to repay in one case and 12 in another. Then you need to find the percent cost in each case to make a fair comparison. Even though credit charges include more than interest, the percent cost of credit is often called the "true interest" rate. *True interest* usually means the percent cost for a year.

For a Single-Payment Loan for One Year. Finding the percent cost of a single-payment loan is easy. You divide the dollar cost for a year by the amount you obtain from the lender. For example, suppose you borrow $200 for one year. At the end of that time you pay the lender $212. The dollar cost of the loan is $12, the difference between the amount you receive and the amount you pay. To find the percent cost, you divide the $12 (the dollar cost) by $200 (the amount you receive). The percent cost is 6 percent ($12 ÷ $200 = .06).

For Less Than One Year. The only thing wrong with the above example is that single-payment loans to individuals seldom run for as long as a year. As a rule, such loans are limited to 3 months, or 90 days. In figuring interest, a month (or 30 days) is $\frac{1}{12}$ of a year; three months is $\frac{3}{12}$, or $\frac{1}{4}$, and so on. To find the percent cost of credit when a debt runs for less than one year, you first divide the dollar cost by the amount borrowed. This gives you the rate for whatever length of time the loan is to run. Then you multiply by the necessary amount to find the annual rate. If the loan is to run 6 months or half a year, you multiply by two. If it is to run 4 months or $\frac{1}{3}$ of a year, you multiply by three, and so on.

For example, suppose you borrowed $200 for 3 months, or 90 days, at a dollar cost of $3. To find the true annual rate, first divide the dollar cost ($3) by the amount you actually receive ($200).

$3 ÷ $200 = .015

Since 90 days is only $\frac{1}{4}$ of a year, you multiply by 4 to find the annual rate, which is 6 percent.

4 × .015 = .06

For More Than One Year. If a debt is for more than a year, you reduce the percent rate by dividing. For example, if you borrowed $1,000 for 2 years at a dollar cost of $100, you would divide the rate by 2 to find the true annual rate.

$100 ÷ $1,000 = .10 (rate for 2 years)
.10 ÷ 2 = .05 (annual rate)

When Interest Is Discounted. For single-payment loans, banks usually use the ***discount*** method of charging interest. This means that the interest is deducted from the amount borrowed when the loan is made. For example, say you borrow $200 for a year at a dollar cost of $12. The bank will take out the $12 in advance and give you only $188. But you will have to pay back $200. A charge of $12 for a $200 loan appears to be a rate of 6 percent. Since you have the use of only $188, however, the true rate is slightly more than that. You can prove this for yourself by dividing the $12 by $188.

When Debt Is Paid in Installments. Finding the percent cost of credit is most difficult when the debt is repaid in installments. Usually you can estimate it closely enough by remembering one fact. The true annual rate for installment credit is approximately double what it appears to be. The reason is that a portion of the debt is repaid each month or week; therefore, you do not have the use of the full amount of money for the entire time. Instead you have, on the average, only about half of the original amount.

For example, suppose you did buy a phonograph on installments and paid a dollar cost of $15 for credit. The lowest cash price, you remember, was $125. Payments were $10.50 for 12 months. In this case the percent cost of credit appears to be 12 percent ($15 ÷ $125 = .12). Since the amount you owe will decrease with each payment, however, you have the entire $125 for only one month. After your first payment you have only $114.50; after the second payment, only $104, and so on. The last month you have only $10.50. In other words, your average debt for the 12 months is about $62.50, or half the original amount. This means that the true annual rate is 24 percent, or twice what it appears to be.

When You Know the Monthly Rate. One more fact you will want to remember is that when a credit charge is stated as a monthly rate, you multiply by 12 to find the true annual rate. A typical charge for revolving credit plans, for example, is 1½ percent a month on the unpaid balance. This is a true annual rate of 18 percent (12 × .015 = .18). A monthly rate of 2½ percent is an annual rate of 30 percent, and so on.

KNOW WHAT YOU'RE BUYING

Shopping for the best buy in credit takes time and effort, but it can save you a lot of money. To compare credit charges fairly, however, you must consider what they include. Some sellers add a fee for insurance to protect themselves in case goods are damaged before payment is completed. This is often the case when the purchase is an automobile. Frequently there is a charge for insurance that will pay off the debt in case the borrower dies. Some lenders even charge for health and accident insurance. You may or may not want these extras. But if you do want them, you will have to pay extra for them.

BUILDING YOUR VOCABULARY

On a separate sheet of paper, write each of the terms listed in the left-hand column below. Read the three definitions to the right of each term. After each term, copy the definition that best matches it in meaning.

1. ***discount***
   a. Interest added to the amount borrowed at the time a loan is repaid
   b. Interest deducted from the amount borrowed at the time a loan is made
   c. Interest charged at the rate of 6 percent

2. ***interest***
   a. A charge made for the use of money
   b. A charge made for a credit investigation
   c. A charge made for collecting a debt

3. ***interest rate***
   a. Interest expressed in dollars and cents
   b. Interest expressed as a percent of the amount borrowed
   c. Interest expressed as an annual charge

4. ***risk***
   a. A loss resulting from unpaid debts
   b. A loss that occurs when credit is extended
   c. The possibility of a loss

CHECKING YOUR READING

1. Why do so few people really know how much they pay for credit?
2. Why is it important to know how much you will have to pay for credit?
3. Why do credit charges vary from one lender to another?
4. What three kinds of costs do all lenders have?
5. Why does a lender have a right to charge for the use of his money?
6. Why do interest rates vary from time to time?
7. Why does installment credit always cost more than single-payment loans and charge accounts?
8. Explain why investigation and collection costs usually are a higher percent of a small loan than they are of a large loan.
9. How are credit charges affected by the risk the lender takes?
10. What are two ways of comparing credit charges?
11. What two important factors must be considered in figuring the true cost of credit?
12. Explain how the dollar cost of a loan is determined.
13. How do you find the true dollar cost of installment-purchase credit?
14. When is dollar cost an ideal way to compare credit charges?
15. When should you find percent cost in order to make a fair comparison of credit charges?
16. How do you find the percent cost of a single-payment loan for one year?
17. Explain why the true annual percent cost of installment credit is approximately double what it appears to be.
18. If a credit charge is stated as a monthly rate, how do you find the true annual rate?
19. What must you take into consideration to make a fair comparison of credit charges?

SHARING YOUR OPINION AND EXPERIENCE

1. Even though an individual has a good credit rating, he might have to pay a rate of 6 percent for a loan. A business, however, might be able to borrow at the rate of 4 percent. Why would a lender be willing to extend credit to a business at a lower rate?
2. Would it be wise for a person with a steady income and a good credit rating to borrow from a lender who specializes in loans of $300 or less to persons with uncertain incomes? Why or why not?
3. How does the interest rate a consumer has to pay for a loan compare with the interest rate he is paid on his savings account? What is the reason for the difference?
4. Why is the amount of money available for lending sometimes greater than at other times?
5. Why do you suppose some lenders state their credit charges as monthly rates rather than as annual rates?
6. What factors determine how high an interest rate a particular borrower may have to pay?

7. If interest rates are affected by competition, how can one lender stay in business when his rates are twice as high as those of another lender?
8. Why would a seller insure an article that he sold on installment credit?
9. Should a young person pay for his college education with an installment loan if there is no other way to finance it? Or should he work a few years following graduation from high school in order to earn the money he needs?

PROJECTS AND PROBLEMS

1. Jane Wong shopped carefully for a formal to wear to the Senior Prom. The cash price of the one she liked best was $49.95, but Jane was not prepared to pay that much for a dress. The salesclerk said she could buy it on the installment plan by paying $9.95 down and three monthly payments of $14 each. What would the dollar cost of credit be if Jane paid for the dress in installments?
2. Harry Levinson is interested in buying a home movie projector. If he pays cash, he can buy the projector he wants for $139.95. Or he can buy it on credit for $19.95 down and $10.60 a month for twelve months. What would the dollar cost of using credit be? What does the percent cost of credit appear to be? What is the true annual rate?
3. John Wright needs $150 to pay the balance owing on a hospital bill. He shopped for a loan and found these choices: (*a*) he could borrow the $150 and repay the full amount plus $4.50 in interest at the end of six months; (*b*) he could borrow $150 and repay a total of $168 at the end of a year; (*c*) he could borrow the money at a monthly rate of 1½ percent on the unpaid balance. Which of the three choices offers the lowest annual rate? Explain your answer by showing what the rate would be in each case.
4. Dick Swanson borrowed $160 for 120 days, at which time he paid the lender a total of $171.20. What annual rate did he pay?
5. A lending agency advertised loans up to a limit of $600 on the following terms:

12 Months		*20 Months*	
Cash You Get	*Monthly Payments*	*Cash You Get*	*Monthly Payments*
$100	$10	$100	$ 7.00
150	15	250	17.50
250	25	430	30.10
400	40	600	42.00

▪ *a.* What is the dollar cost of a $250 loan to be repaid in 12 months? ▪ *b.* What is the apparent rate for a $250 loan repaid in 12 months? ▪ *c.* Since the loan would be repaid in installments, what is the true annual rate? ▪ *d.* Is the annual rate the same for all amounts to be repaid in 12 installments? ▪ *e.* What is the true annual rate on a $600 loan to be repaid in 20 months? ▪ *f.* Is the annual rate the same for all amounts listed under the heading, "20 months"?

6. Mr. Welch applied for a loan of $500 for 30 days. The lender deducted $10 for interest and gave Mr. Welch $490 in exchange for his promise to repay $500 at the end of the 30 days. What rate of interest did Mr. Welch pay? (Figure to the nearest one-half of 1 percent.)
7. The following item appeared recently in most of the nation's newspapers.

ADVISORY COUNCIL PROPOSES STEPS TO PREVENT DISGUISED CREDIT COSTS

Washington. The President's Consumer Advisory Council has recommended a number of steps to ensure that consumers know the real cost of borrowing. The Council proposed the elimination of what it considers loopholes in the laws against misrepresenting the cost of credit.

The Council supports the "truth in lending" bill. That bill would require lenders to disclose to borrowers in advance the true annual rate charged for credit. The Council pointed out that one federal agency ruled recently that it is a deceptive practice to charge the advertised interest rate on the whole amount of a loan while the loan is being repaid gradually.

■ *a.* What is meant by "disguised credit costs"? ■ *b.* What are "loopholes" in laws? ■ *c.* What is the purpose of the "truth in lending" bill? ■ *d.* Whose point of view does the Advisory Council represent? ■ *e.* Whom does the Council advise? ■ *f.* What is the practice to which the Council is objecting? ■ *g.* How do you think lenders might react to the Council's recommendation?

CHALLENGE PROBLEMS

1. One lender advertises rates as follows: $2\frac{1}{2}$ percent per month on the unpaid balance up to $300 and $1\frac{1}{2}$ percent per month on the remaining unpaid balance. Why do you suppose this lender charges a higher rate of interest on the first $300?
2. As was pointed out in the text, the amount of money available for lending is one factor that affects interest rates. Is the amount available likely to be greater during periods of prosperity or during periods of recession? During which of these periods is the demand for credit likely to be greatest?
3. The biggest users of installment credit are middle-income families with children. How do you account for the fact that these families use this type of credit to a greater extent than either low-income or high-income families?

PART 20 BORROWING MONEY

FIFTY years ago the consumer who needed a loan was to be pitied. Unless fortunate enough to have a friend or relative willing to lend him money, he was forced to deal with an illegal lender. This was usually a ruthless individual who hung around outside factories and other places of work. He specialized in making loans to workers who ran short of money between paydays. The charge for such loans was so high that borrowers found it difficult to free themselves of debt. In fact, they usually found it difficult to get out of sight of the lender who was always waiting for them on paydays to collect.

Today there is no need for consumers to suffer such abuses. There are several reputable sources from which they may obtain loans. True, not all are open to everyone. But unless a consumer is an extremely poor credit risk, he should be able to find one from which he can borrow. What are some sources of consumer loans? How would you define a consumer loan? What do you think is the chief reason consumers borrow?

WHAT IS A CONSUMER LOAN?

In Part 15 you learned that all credit is a form of borrowing since the debtor owes the creditor money. The term "borrowing" as used in this part, however, refers only to loan credit; that is, the borrower obtains cash in exchange for a promise to repay cash. The discussion is further limited to borrowing by consumers for periods of 1 to 36 months. It does not apply to home loans, which are explained in Part 9 and which may run as long as 30 years. Another name for the kind of short-term consumer loan that is discussed in this part is ***personal loan.***

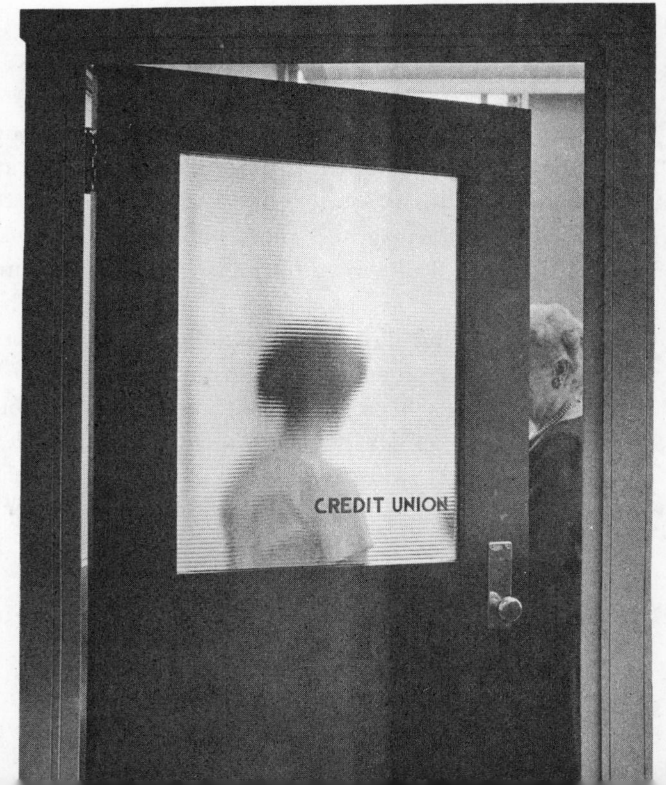

A list of reasons why consumers borrow would include almost everything you could think of. They borrow to buy expensive durable goods like cars, furniture, and home appliances when the cost of borrowing is less than the cost of installment-purchase credit. They also borrow to pay taxes; to take trips; to pay medical, dental, and hospital bills; to finance moving expenses; to pay for education; and to help friends and relatives in need. But the leading reason consumers borrow is one you might never guess. It is to "consolidate debts." To consolidate debts means to combine several debts into one. When a consumer has more debts than he can handle at one time, he may borrow enough money to pay them all. Instead of several debts, he then has only one.

The advantage of consolidating debts is that it gives the borrower a longer time to pay the total amount owed. His loan payment, therefore, is smaller than the total payments on his separate debts. Most important of all, he is able to preserve his good credit rating which might be lost if he fell behind on his other debt payments. In some cases, however, borrowing to consolidate debts is so costly that the consumer would be wise to ask his creditors for an extension of time.

MONEY IS BORROWED

FROM

TO PAY

HOW DO CONSUMERS OBTAIN LOANS?

As you will soon learn, there are differences among lenders; and one of these differences is in the way they make loans. Most lenders ask a borrower to sign a ***promissory note,*** commonly called a *note.* This is simply a written promise that the amount borrowed will be repaid on a certain date. The borrower who signs the note is the ***maker.*** A note signed by George Curtin is illustrated on page 173.

A person with a good credit rating may be able to borrow on his signature alone. This is called a ***signature*** or ***character loan*** because the borrower's character is the important factor in the lender's decision to make the loan. He has only the borrower's promise that the money will be repaid. In some instances, the lender may require the signature of a second person on the note. Anyone who signs a note in addition to the borrower is called a *cosigner.* A cosigner is responsible for paying the debt should the borrower fail to do so.

A borrower may be asked to furnish *security* that will guarantee repayment of his loan. Security may be property, such as an automobile, furniture, stocks and bonds, or jewelry. If the loan is not paid, the lender has the right to sell the property in order to collect his money. Anything used as security for a loan is called ***collateral.*** A loan backed by security is called a *secured loan.*

Another method of securing a loan is to have a friend or relative of the borrower endorse the note. As *endorser* this person becomes responsible for payment of the loan if the borrower fails to pay. The difference between a cosigner and an endorser is that a cosigner shares the responsibility for payment of a loan. An endorser becomes responsible only after the lender has used all other means of collecting payment and failed.

If a borrower has nothing of sufficient value to offer as security, he may be asked to sign a wage-assignment agreement. This gives the lender the right to take a portion of the borrower's wages if he fails to pay the loan when due.

If you hit a financial snag today, you would probably ask your parents or a friend to help you out. But in future years should you ever need to borrow, you will want to go about it in a more businesslike manner. Different types of lenders specialize in different types of loans for different types of borrowers. Some ask for security; others make mostly character or signature loans. Some will lend for very short periods; others will not. Some will make a loan almost immediately; others want time to investigate the borrower. Some will not make loans for less than $50; others discourage borrowers who want less than $100.

Unfortunately, consumers are often in a hurry when they want to borrow. They do not always take time to find out about all possibilities for obtaining a loan. The best time to find out about loan sources is before you need to borrow. This may save precious time as well as needless expense.

Banks

At one time banks made loans only to business firms. Today they are the leading source of consumer loans. Although banks prefer secured loans, they also make signature or character loans. Either kind may be repaid in installments or in one lump sum. The smallest amount most banks will lend is $100.

Because banks lend other people's money, their credit requirements are very strict. Not everyone is able to meet them. For those who do, however, banks are one of the least expensive sources of personal loans. Their charges are regulated by law and vary according to the type of loan and the method of repayment. Single-payment loans, for example, cost less than installment loans. A secured loan should cost less than an unsecured one since it involves less risk. The true annual rate for a bank loan may be as low as 6 percent or as high as 18 percent. A typical rate is about 12 percent.

Small-Loan Companies

Because consumer loans are small in amount compared to those made to business, they are often called *small loans.* Businesses that specialize in making such loans are known as *small-loan companies.* Other names for them are *personal finance companies* or *consumer finance companies.* These companies are licensed to operate in all but about two states under laws regulating the size of loans

A promissory note

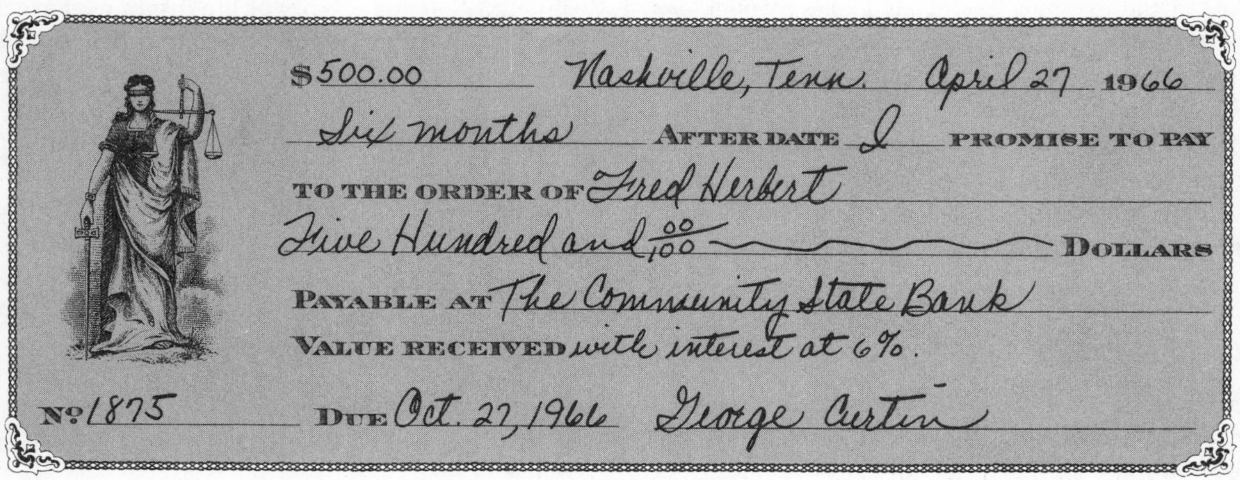
$500.00 Nashville, Tenn. April 27 1966
Six months AFTER DATE I PROMISE TO PAY
TO THE ORDER OF Fred Herbert
Five Hundred and 00/100 DOLLARS
PAYABLE AT The Community State Bank
VALUE RECEIVED with interest at 6%.
No. 1875 DUE Oct. 27, 1966 George Curtin

and the rates charged. Regulations vary from one state to another. In California a consumer may borrow up to $5,000; in New York the limit is $800. Half or more of the loans made by small-loan companies are signature or character loans. Practically all are repaid in installments.

Depending on state laws, the rates charged by small-loan companies range from 1½ percent to 3½ percent a month on the unpaid balance. As a rule, the smaller the amount owing, the higher the rate. In one state, for example, small-loan companies may charge 3 percent a month on amounts up to $150 and 2 percent on amounts between $150 and $300. As you learned in the previous part, a rate of 3 percent a month is 36 percent a year ($.03 \times 12 = .36$). This, however, is a true rate. In other words, the borrower is charged only on the amount he owes each month and not on the total amount borrowed.

Nevertheless, the cost of borrowing from a small-loan company is high compared to borrowing from a bank. One reason is that small-loan companies are more willing to lend small amounts. The average loan made by a small-loan company is around $400. The average consumer loan made by banks is about $600. Collection and investigation costs, you recall, do not change with the size of the loan. The smaller the loan, therefore, the higher the charge must be in proportion. Since a lender sets his rates according to the average size of his loans, a small-loan company has to charge more than a bank.

Another reason small-loan companies charge more than banks is that they are not so strict in their credit requirements. In other words, the loan companies assume a greater risk than banks by lending to persons who may not qualify for a bank loan.

Credit Unions

A third source of consumer loans is a credit union. A ***credit union*** is a business organized as a cooperative that provides its members a means of saving as well as borrowing. Members save by purchasing shares usually costing $5 each. These savings provide the funds from which loans are made. A credit union lends only to its members. As with other cooperative organizations the members of a credit union are people with a common interest. They may be employees of the same firm, or members of the same lodge, church, or labor union.

Although the average credit-union loan is around $400, a member may borrow as little as $20. The maximum rate credit unions are permitted to charge for loans is 1 percent a month on the unpaid balance. Some charge as little as ½ percent a month. This is sometimes less than a borrower pays for a bank loan. For those who qualify for membership, a credit union may be the best loan source. Credit unions are able to charge such low rates because (1) they lend only to members and rarely have to investigate loan applicants; (2) much of their work is done by members on a volunteer basis; (3) office space is sometimes provided free of charge by the businesses for which the members work; (4) like all true cooperatives, credit unions are nonprofit organizations.

Life Insurance

Another possible source of loans is a life insurance policy. When you study insurance in Unit 7, you will learn that some types of life insurance have a cash or loan value. Anyone who owns this type of insurance may borrow up to the amount of the cash value. The rate charged for such a loan is usually 5 or 6 percent a year. On G.I. insurance* it is only 4 percent.

Insurance loans have three advantages: (1) they are easy to obtain; (2) they cost less than almost any other type of loan available to consumers; (3) the borrower may take as long as he wants to repay the loan. On the other hand, there are two big disadvantages to borrowing on life insurance: (1)

*Insurance provided by the Federal government to members of the Armed Forces.

because the borrower is not obligated to repay the loan, he may let it run indefinitely. This increases the dollar cost of the loan, as he must continue to pay interest as long as he has the money. If the interest is not paid when due, it is added to the amount of the loan. (2) The value of the insurance is reduced by the amount of the loan. For example, if a man died leaving an unpaid loan of $100 on a $1,000 policy, his family would receive only $900.

Anyone who borrows on his life insurance should repay the loan as quickly as possible. This not only reduces the cost of the loan but assures full protection for dependents.

DEAL ONLY WITH LICENSED LENDERS

Borrowing is no disgrace. Anyone may find himself facing a financial emergency through no fault of his own. If money is urgently needed, he may even be willing to pay 30 percent or more for its use. The fact that most consumer loans are used to pay off accumulated debts, however, suggests that many people are using credit carelessly. Businessmen borrow only when it is to their advantage to do so. Wise consumers follow the same rule. In addition they deal only with licensed lenders.

Unlicensed or illegal lenders still manage to operate in places that do not have effective small-loan laws. They are called *loan sharks* because once they get hold of a borrower, they rarely let go. These lenders are not interested in the repayment of a loan but in keeping the borrower in debt. Most of them refuse to accept any payment except the full amount, and all of them charge enormously high rates—240 to 1,200 percent a year. They find their customers among those who are ignorant of, or unable to borrow from, reputable sources.

If you cannot obtain a loan from a reputable source, then you probably should not borrow. When a licensed lender turns down a request for a loan, it usually means the applicant has already stretched his credit to the breaking point. By keeping him from going further into debt, the lender is doing him a favor.

BUILDING YOUR VOCABULARY

List the figures 1 to 6 on a sheet of paper, numbering down. Read the six statements given below at the right; then, for each statement, select from the column at the left the term that best matches it in meaning. Write this term next to the appropriate number.

collateral	1. A loan made to an individual for a period of three years or less
credit union	2. A written promise to repay a loan by a certain date
maker	3. The person who signs a note to borrow money
personal loan	4. A loan backed only by the borrower's promise to pay
promissory note	5. Property used as security for a loan
signature loan (*character loan*)	6. A cooperative organized to make loans to its members

CHECKING YOUR READING

1. How has consumer borrowing changed within the last 50 years?
2. In what way does loan credit differ from other types of credit?
3. What is the leading reason consumers borrow today? Explain. What is the chief advantage of borrowing for this reason?

4. Why is an unsecured loan often called a character loan?
5. What responsibility does the cosigner of a note have?
6. What is the purpose of requiring security for a loan?
7. If a borrower has no property, in what two ways may he furnish security for a loan?
8. Explain the difference between a cosigner and an endorser of a note.
9. What right does a wage-assignment agreement give to a lender?
10. What are the four leading sources of consumer loans today?
11. Why are the credit requirements of banks very strict?
12. Why should a secured loan cost less than an unsecured one?
13. What is a small-loan company?
14. Why do small-loan companies usually charge more for loans than banks do?
15. One purpose of a credit union is to lend money to its members. What other service does it provide?
16. Give several reasons why credit unions are able to charge low interest rates.
17. What are some of the advantages of insurance loans? What are the chief disadvantages?
18. When do wise consumers borrow?
19. Where do loan sharks operate? Who borrows from them?

SHARING YOUR OPINION AND EXPERIENCE

1. Benjamin Franklin once said, "He who goes a borrowing goes a sorrowing." What do you think he meant? Do you agree or disagree with his view?
2. The money that banks lend belongs to their depositors. Where do small-loan companies get the money they lend?
3. What are some of the factors that determine how much a person can safely borrow?
4. Most states have small-loan laws. Are they for the benefit of the borrower or the lender? Explain.
5. What is a pawnshop? How does one get a pawnshop loan? How important is a good credit rating in obtaining such a loan?
6. Some loan agencies insist that a borrower set up a budget before they will lend him money. Why?
7. John Luzak went to his bank to borrow money, but the loan officer advised against it. Should John follow the bank's advice or go elsewhere for a loan?
8. Many people who could join credit unions prefer not to use their services. Can you think of any reasons why?
9. Lending agencies lose very little money as a result of unpaid loans. How do you explain this fact?
10. What effect does a person's credit rating have on his ability to get an insurance loan?

PROJECTS AND PROBLEMS

1. Study the promissory note illustrated on page 173 and answer the following questions:

   ▪ *a.* When was the note signed? ▪ *b.* What was the amount of the loan? ▪ *c.* When did the borrower promise to repay the loan? ▪ *d.* What rate of interest did he promise to pay? ▪ *e.* Who was the maker of the note? ▪ *f.* Who was the lender? ▪ *g.* For how long a time was the money borrowed? ▪ *h.* Was there a cosigner of the note?

2. The following table shows the amount of consumer installment loans held by three types of lending agencies from 1956 through 1963. Study the table and answer the questions that follow it.

INSTALLMENT LOANS HELD BY THREE LENDING AGENCIES 1956–1963
(in billions of dollars)

End of Year	*Banks*	*Credit Unions*	*Consumer Finance Companies*
1956	**$11.8**	**$2.0**	**$2.9**
1957	**12.9**	**2.4**	**3.1**
1958	**12.8**	**2.7**	**3.1**
1959	**15.2**	**3.3**	**3.3**
1960	**16.7**	**3.9**	**3.7**
1961	**17.0**	**4.3**	**3.8**
1962	**19.0**	**4.9**	**4.1**
1963	**21.6**	**5.6**	**4.6**

Source: Federal Reserve Bulletin

▪ *a.* From which of the three lenders did consumers borrow most in 1956? in 1963? ▪ *b.* In 1956 the amount that consumers borrowed from banks was approximately how many times the amount borrowed from credit unions? ▪ *c.* The amount they borrowed from banks in 1963 was about how many times the amount borrowed from credit unions? ▪ *d.* What is another name for consumer finance companies? ▪ *e.* Did consumers borrow more from credit unions or from consumer finance companies in 1956? How much more? ▪ *f.* From which of these two lenders did they borrow more in 1963? How much more? ▪ *g.* What was the percent of increase (to the nearest whole percent) from 1956 to 1963 in the amount consumers borrowed from banks? ▪ *h.* What was the percent of increase in the amount borrowed from credit unions? ▪ *i.* What was the percent of increase in the amount borrowed from consumer finance companies?

3. Each of the following statements identifies one of the four consumer-loan sources discussed in this part—banks, small-loan companies, credit unions, and life insurance. On a separate sheet of paper, list from the top down the letters (*a*) through (*n*). After each letter write the name of the loan source that each statement represents. Use your textbook for information if necessary.

▪ *a*. Charges are less than those of almost any other loan source. ▪ *b*. Practically all loans are repaid in installments. ▪ *c*. Organized by people with a common interest. ▪ *d*. The borrower may take as long as he wishes to repay. ▪ *e*. Decreases financial protection of dependents. ▪ *f*. Lends only to members. ▪ *g*. Charges the highest rate of the four sources. ▪ *h*. Charges from 5 to 6 percent a year. ▪ *i*. The leading source of consumer loans. ▪ *j*. Nonprofit organization. ▪ *k*. Rates of interest usually vary from 1½ to 3½ percent a month. ▪ *l*. Not everyone is able to meet the credit requirements. ▪ *m*. A cooperative enterprise. ▪ *n*. Rates usually vary from ½ to 1 percent a month.

4. Assume that it costs a lending agency $25 to make a credit investigation and collect a loan that is repaid in twelve installments. This is true regardless of the amount borrowed. What percent of the loan would this cost be for each of the following?

a. $50 loan	*c*. $200 loan	*e*. $800 loan
b. $100 loan	*d*. $400 loan	*f*. $1,000 loan

5. Along the vertical axis of the bar graph shown below, you see five purposes for which consumers borrow. For each purpose there are two bars on the graph. One bar shows the percent of all loans made by small-loan companies for that purpose in 1960. The other bar shows the percent of all loans made by small-loan companies for the same purpose in 1948. The two blocks at the right of the graph are a key to the year each bar represents. For example, in 1960, 40 percent of all loans made by small-loan companies were used to consolidate debts. In 1948, about 27.8 percent of all loans were obtained for this purpose. Study the graph and answer the questions on page 179.

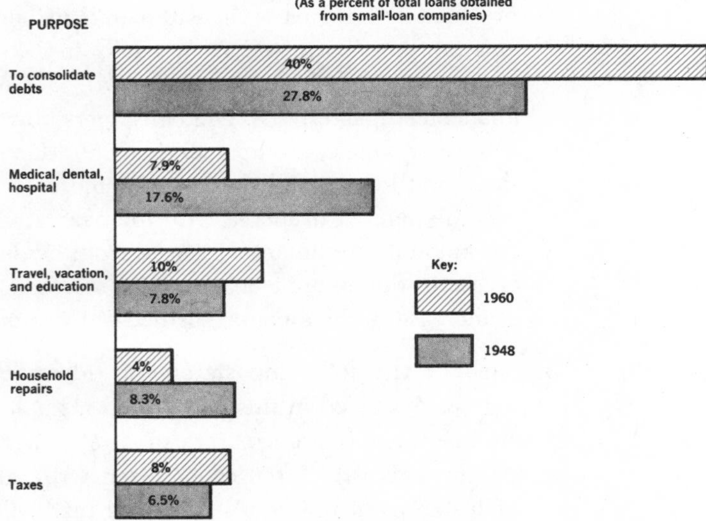

■ *a.* What percent of all loans made by small-loan companies in 1960 was for the purpose of paying taxes? ■ *b.* What percent of all loans made in 1948 was obtained to pay medical, dental, or hospital expenses? ■ *c.* For what purpose was the largest percent of loans used in 1960? ■ *d.* Does your answer to (*c*) agree with what you learned from reading the text? ■ *e.* As a percent of total loans, which purposes for borrowing increased from 1948 to 1960? ■ *f.* Which one increased the most? ■ *g.* As a percent of total loans, which purposes for borrowing decreased from 1948 to 1960? ■ *h.* Which decreased the most? ■ *i.* The percent of loans obtained to consolidate debts in 1960 was how many times greater than the percent obtained for the next leading purpose in 1960? ■ *j.* Stated as a percent, approximately how many more loans were obtained to consolidate debts in 1948 than were obtained for the next leading purpose that year?

CHALLENGE PROBLEMS

1. If a loan is not repaid, the lender has a right to sell collateral in order to collect his money. Suppose the collateral is sold for more money than is due on the loan. Who gets the extra amount? If the collateral is sold for less than the amount due, does the borrower still have to pay the remainder?
2. Explain the difference between an installment contract and a promissory note.
3. It has been said that "Most pawnshop loans are not really loans at all." Explain.
4. What is a remedial-loan society? What conditions led to the organization of these societies? Ask your teacher for help in finding this information.
5. According to the graph used for No. 5 of the Projects and Problems Section, the percent of loans obtained to pay medical expenses decreased between 1948 and 1960. How do you explain this decrease?
6. Why do you think borrowing to pay taxes increased between 1948 and 1960?
7. In 1960 40 percent of all loans made by small-loan companies were obtained to consolidate debts. Does that mean that 40 percent of all money borrowed from small-loan companies was for the purpose of consolidating debts? Explain.

CONTENTS OF UNIT 5

Unit 5 / Using the Services of Banks

PART 21 HOW BANKS SERVE YOU AND YOUR COMMUNITY

Courtesy The Chase Manhattan Bank

THE business system of the United States includes about 14,000 enterprises called commercial banks. A commercial bank is the kind most of us know best. It is found in almost every community. And wherever it is found, it is the center of the business life of that community. Without banks, other business enterprises would find it difficult to operate. But banks are also important to individuals.

Why are banks important to the business life of a community? Why do you think commercial banks are sometimes called "full-service" banks? For what purposes do individuals use banks?

WHAT IS A BANK?

A *bank* is a business enterprise that deals in money and credit. Some people think that because the word "national" or "state" appears in the names of banks they are owned by the government. But this is not so. A bank is a private corporation whose owners, or stockholders, often live in the community served by the bank.

Like all corporations a bank must obtain a charter before it can do business. A charter will be granted only if a bank is needed in the locality for which it is planned. The charter may be obtained from either the Federal or the state government. The word "national" in the name of a bank tells you that it operates under a Federal charter; otherwise it is a state bank. About two-thirds of the banks in this country are state banks.

WHAT SERVICES DO COMMERCIAL BANKS PROVIDE?

A bank is a service enterprise. One commercial bank in a large midwestern city advertises that it serves its customers in fifty ways. These services range from simple things like maintaining an information desk to complex things like financing the importing and exporting of goods. The same number and kinds of services may not be available at every bank, to be sure. But almost all banks offer the following three important services:

1. They accept and safeguard money deposited with them.
2. They transfer money payments made by check.
3. They make loans to individuals, businesses, and governments.

Banks Accept Deposits

How often have you heard or read about people whose money has been lost, stolen, or destroyed by fire? Tragedies like these can be prevented by keeping money in a bank. Money left with a bank for safekeeping is a ***deposit.*** When you put your money in a bank, you are a ***depositor.*** This does not mean that somewhere in the bank a package of money is stored away with your name on it. It simply means that the bank owes you a sum of money equal to the amount you deposited. In other words, your deposit is a debt of the bank. If you deposit $50, the bank owes you $50.

In order to know how much money each customer has on deposit, a bank keeps a careful record of deposits and withdrawals. A ***withdrawal*** is the opposite of a deposit. It occurs when money is taken out, or withdrawn, from the bank. A bank's record of a customer's deposits and withdrawals is an ***account.*** If you are a depositor at a bank, you have an account with the bank.

Together the 14,000 commercial banks in this country hold about $300 billion of money belonging to individuals, business enterprises, government bodies, clubs, schools, churches, and other organizations. These deposits include both savings and checking accounts.

Savings Accounts Are Time Deposits. Martin Martinez, a junior in high school, works part-time to earn money for college. Each week Martin deposits his paycheck in a savings account at the bank. There his money is not only safe, it earns interest.

Notice that Martin, like most people, keeps in his savings account money that he does not plan to spend soon. This is the purpose of a savings account. A bank even has the legal right to require 30 to 60 days' notice before funds may be withdrawn from a savings account. This right, however, is seldom exercised. Nevertheless, it explains why savings accounts are called ***time deposits.***

Checking Accounts Are Demand Deposits. Like a savings account, a checking account provides protection against the loss or theft of money. It also offers the convenience of paying by check. Checks cannot be written on funds deposited in a savings account.

Because money you deposit in a checking account may be withdrawn any time you want it, checking accounts are called ***demand deposits.*** Banks are not allowed to pay interest on demand deposits. For that reason people deposit in checking accounts money that they plan to spend in the near future.

Most Bank Deposits Are Insured. Before the 1930's people who kept their money in a bank did so at their own risk. Even during prosperous times some banks failed; in 1928, for example, nearly 500 banks closed. During depressions, of course, failures among banks multiplied. In some cases depositors recovered only a fraction of their money; and in some, they lost it all. Since 1934, when the Federal government organized the Federal Deposit Insurance Corporation, this risk has been largely eliminated.

Through the FDIC, as it is called, individual deposits are insured up to $20,000. Anyone who has more than $20,000 can insure it fully by having accounts in more than one bank. At least 98 percent of the nation's commercial banks carry this insurance.

Banks Transfer Checkbook Money

Like currency (coins and paper bills), demand

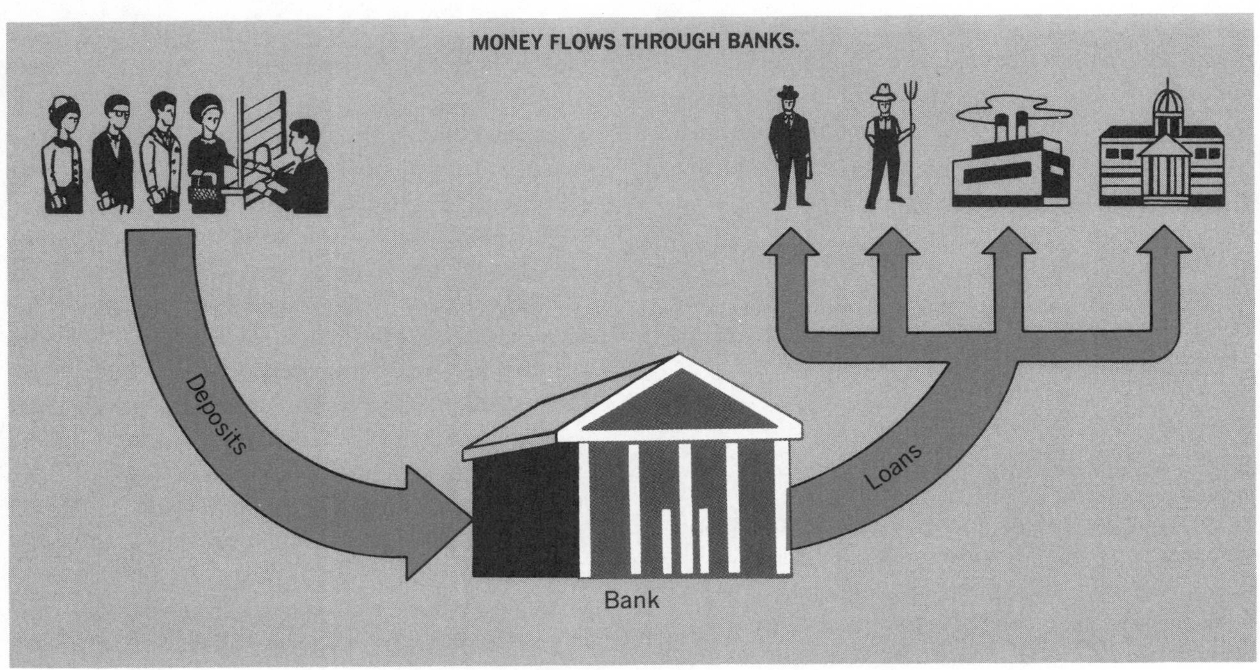
MONEY FLOWS THROUGH BANKS.
Deposits
Loans
Bank

deposits circulate. Ownership of these deposits is transferred from one person or business to another by means of checks. Each day approximately $18 billion in checkbook money changes hands in the United States. A single bank may handle thousands of checks that its depositors have written or received. Each bank must make payment for checks drawn on funds deposited with it; and each bank must collect payment for checks drawn on funds deposited with other banks. It makes no difference how far away the other bank may be. Handling checks is a big part of a bank's work, whether done by hand or by machine.

Banks Lend Money

A bank must always keep enough cash on hand to pay its withdrawals. But it is unlikely that all depositors of a bank would demand their money at the same time. In fact, while some are making withdrawals, others are making deposits. Over the long run these deposits and withdrawals tend to balance each other. Normally, therefore, a bank can take care of its withdrawals with new deposits. This means that the amount of cash a bank needs to keep on hand may be only a small portion of its total deposits. If a bank were to keep all cash deposited by its customers, the nation's total purchasing power would be reduced. Funds that a bank does not need immediately are used instead to make loans. In this way money that might otherwise be idle is kept in circulation. You might say that banks serve as middlemen between those who want to save and those who want to borrow.

Lending money is one of the chief functions of a commercial bank. Loans are made to individuals, to farmers, to businesses, and to the government. As you learned in your study of credit, these loans are important to the operation of our business system. Consider, for example, what happens when a bank lends money to finance the building of a house. Money goes to pay the contractor. He uses it to pay for building materials and the wages of his workers. They spend it at the grocery, the department store, and the filling station. Borrowed money has helped to create jobs for millions of workers.

Other Services Provided by Banks

Although the major services of banks are those just described, most banks do provide other services. One is the renting of safe-deposit boxes. *Safe-deposit boxes* are used to store articles of value other than money, such as important papers, jewelry, stocks, and bonds.

Many banks also provide trust services. A ***trust*** is a fund of money or property that a bank manages for someone else. It may be property belonging to an individual or a corporation. As an example, suppose a man had money, stocks and bonds, or other property of considerable value. And suppose his children were too young or too inexperienced to handle this property wisely. He could make arrangements with a bank to manage it for them in the event of his death; that is, he would leave the management of his property to someone he trusts. This service explains why the names of some banks include the words "Trust Company."

HOW DO BANKS EARN THEIR MONEY?

Like any other business enterprise, a bank is organized to earn a profit for its owners. Yet in some cases banks charge less for their services than it costs to provide them. Customers with large deposits in their checking accounts may not pay anything for this service. Even those with small sums on deposit are not always charged enough to cover the full cost of handling their accounts. Banks are paid rent for the use of safe-deposit boxes and fees for handling trusts. The major source of income for banks, however, is interest on loans.

ARE THERE OTHER KINDS OF BANKS?

In addition to commercial banks, there are banks that accept only time deposits. These *mutual savings banks,* as they are called, are found in but one-third

This young couple has probably obtained a loan from a bank to finance the building of their home.

Monkmeyer Press Photo Service

Courtesy Manufacturers Hanover Trust Co.

Valuables of all kinds may be kept in safe-deposit boxes.

of the states. Savings-and-loan associations also accept time deposits and make loans. Some also provide safe-deposit service. Nevertheless, savings-and-loan associations are not banks in the true sense, even though their services are much like those of savings banks. The chief difference lies in the way they are organized and in the regulations governing their operation.

Another kind of financial institution, called an investment bank, is not really a bank at all. An *investment bank* is a wholesaler of stocks and bonds. Its job is to assist corporations and governmental units in obtaining money capital for long-term use. Like a wholesaler of goods, an investment bank buys newly issued stocks and bonds in large lots and resells them in smaller lots. Money obtained in this way is used to finance the building of factories, refineries, and other projects for private enterprises, as well as roads, sewers, and public facilities of all kinds.

There is one more type of bank that you should know about, however, even though you are not likely to use it personally. That is the Federal Reserve bank.

WHAT IS A FEDERAL RESERVE BANK?

Federal Reserve banks were created by the Federal Reserve Act passed by Congress in 1913. Under this act the nation was divided into twelve districts, known as Federal Reserve districts. In each district there is a Federal Reserve bank and one or more branch Federal Reserve banks. Together these banks make up the Federal Reserve system.

Each of the twelve main Federal Reserve banks is a corporation. Its stockholders, or owners, are commercial banks in the district served by the Federal Reserve bank. These stockholder banks are called *member banks*. All national banks must be members of the Federal Reserve system. State banks may belong, but they are not required to do so.

What a Federal Reserve Bank Does

A Federal Reserve bank does not provide service to the general public. It is a bank for banks; that is, it provides the same services for its members that those banks provide for their customers. Among the services Federal Reserve banks provide are these:

THE FEDERAL RESERVE SYSTEM

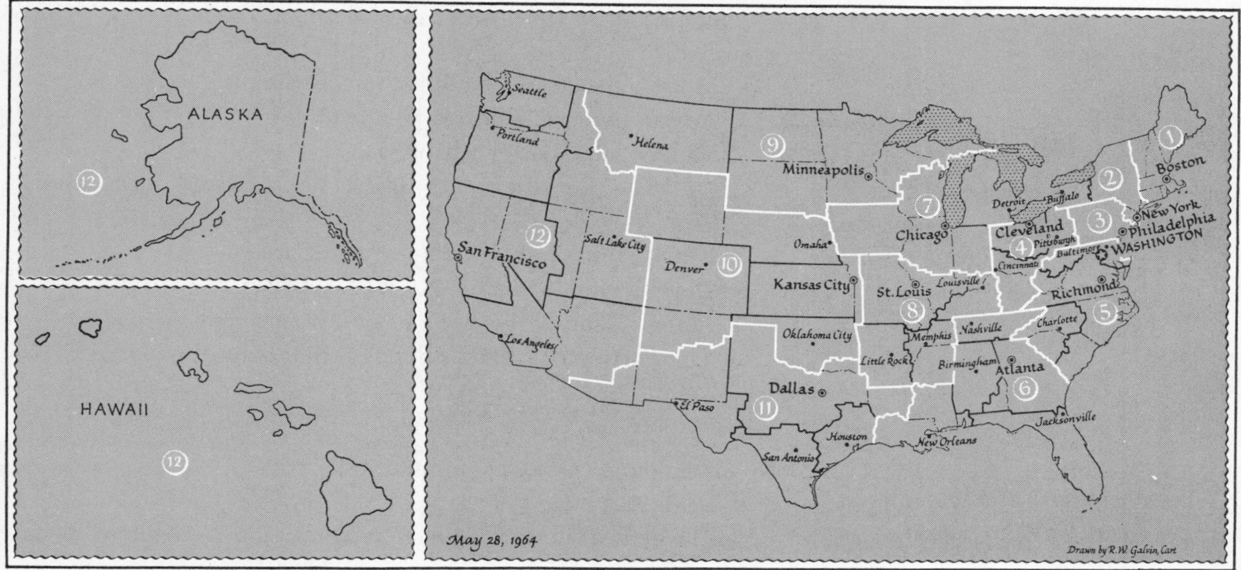

Legend: ═ Boundaries of Federal Reserve Districts —— Boundaries of Federal Reserve Branch Territories
✪ Board of Governors of the Federal Reserve System ◉ Federal Reserve Bank Cities • Federal Reserve Branch Cities

Courtesy Federal Reserve System

1. They accept deposits from member banks.
2. They make loans to member banks.
3. They assist member banks in transferring money payments by check.
4. They act as bankers for the Federal government.

The purpose of the Federal Reserve system is to regulate banking for the protection of the public. To cite one example of its regulation, all member banks are required to carry deposit insurance with the Federal Deposit Insurance Corporation.

To cite another example, each Federal Reserve bank indirectly controls how much money its member banks can lend. A Federal Reserve bank cannot order a member bank to stop making loans. What it does is to require banks to keep a certain percent of their deposits as *reserves*. ***Reserves*** are that portion of a bank's deposits that cannot be loaned. Suppose a bank is required to keep reserves of 15 percent. That means that for every $100 the bank owes in demand deposits it must keep $15 of reserves. These reserves are deposited with the Federal Reserve bank. Banks keep in their own vaults only enough cash to meet their depositors' demands for currency.

Although only about half of the nation's banks are Federal Reserve members, nearly 86 percent of the nation's demand deposits are in member banks. This is because the largest banks in the country are members of the Federal Reserve. Nonmember banks are among the smallest.

BUILDING YOUR VOCABULARY

Copy the eight sentences given below, completing each one by replacing the question mark with the appropriate term from the column at the left.

account	1. Money placed in a bank for safekeeping is a ? .
demand deposits	2. Anyone who puts money in a bank is a ? .
deposit	3. Money taken out of a bank is a ? .
depositor	4. A bank's record of a customer's deposits and withdrawals is his ? .
reserves	5. Deposits made in a savings account are ? .
time deposits	6. Deposits made in a checking account are ? .
trust	7. Money or property that a bank manages for others is a ? .
withdrawal	8. The portion of a bank's deposits that cannot be loaned are ? .

CHECKING YOUR READING

1. What kind of bank is found in most communities?
2. Who owns the banks in this country?
3. How can you tell whether a bank is chartered by the Federal or a state government?
4. Name three important services that almost all banks offer.
5. What are two important differences between savings accounts and checking accounts?
6. How are a bank's depositors protected against loss of their money?
7. Explain how demand deposits are transferred from one person to another.
8. Why does a bank usually keep only a small part of its total deposits in cash?
9. What does a bank do with the funds it does not need immediately?
10. What are safe-deposit boxes?
11. How do banks earn their money?
12. How do savings banks differ from commercial banks?
13. What service does an investment bank perform?
14. How many Federal Reserve banks are there?
15. Who owns the Federal Reserve banks?
16. What banks are members of the Federal Reserve system?
17. Who are the customers of a Federal Reserve bank?
18. What major services do Federal Reserve banks provide?
19. What is the purpose of the Federal Reserve system?
20. How does a Federal Reserve bank control the amount of money its member banks can lend?

SHARING YOUR OPINION AND EXPERIENCE

1. Why is a bank a good place to go for financial advice?
2. Why do banks seldom exercise their right to require 30 to 60 days' notice before funds are withdrawn from a savings account? Under what conditions might a bank find it necessary to exercise this right?

3. If banks kept on hand all cash their customers deposited, what effect would it have on the production of goods and services?
4. Frequently the earnings of a child actor or entertainer are placed in trust with a bank. Do you think this is a good idea? Why?
5. Although about 98 percent of the nation's commercial banks carry insurance with the FDIC, only about half of all money on deposit is insured. How do you account for this fact?
6. Commercial banks have been called "the department stores of banking." Explain.
7. In what ways does a person render a service to others by depositing his money in a bank?

PROJECTS AND PROBLEMS

1. Some banks claim to offer as many as fifty services to their customers. Several of the ways in which they serve are discussed in this part. List five services not mentioned in the text that a bank in your community provides.
2. People use safe-deposit boxes to store many articles of value. List ten items (other than those mentioned in the text) that people might keep in these boxes.
3. Demand deposits and time deposits held by all United States banks in the years 1956 through 1963 are shown in the table below. Study the table and answer the questions following it.

BANK DEPOSITS, 1956–1963
(in billions of dollars)

End of Year	*Demand Deposits*	*Time Deposits*
1956	**$129.0**	**$80.9**
1957	**127.9**	**88.1**
1958	**134.4**	**97.5**
1959	**136.7**	**101.1**
1960	**139.4**	**108.0**
1961	**147.9**	**120.8**
1962	**148.2**	**139.0**
1963	**147.3**	**155.5**

Source: Federal Reserve Bulletin

▪ *a.* How much did demand deposits increase from 1956 to 1963? ▪ *b.* How much did time deposits increase during the same period? ▪ *c.* What was the total of all deposits in 1956? ▪ *d.* Approximately what percent of total deposits in 1956 were time deposits? ▪ *e.* What was the total of all deposits in 1963? ▪ *f.* Approximately what percent of total deposits in 1963 were time deposits? ▪ *g.* Was there any year in which demand deposits were less than in the previous year? If so, in which year or years? ▪ *h.* During which year did time deposits increase most? ▪ *i.* In terms of total deposits, did time deposits increase or decrease in importance during the eight years?

4. Describe one or more banking services that each of the following might use:

■ *a.* A high school student who is planning to attend college ■ *b.* The owner of a retail clothing store ■ *c.* A girl who has her first job and is just starting out on her own ■ *d.* A family preparing for a vacation trip around the United States ■ *e.* A woman who owns jewelry, stocks, and bonds ■ *f.* A child who inherits a large sum of money ■ g. A young couple planning to buy a home. ■ Use a form similar to the one illustrated below.

Person Using the Service	Banking Services Used
(a) High school student	

5. The twelve Federal Reserve districts are identified by number. On page 187 there is a map showing the location of the main Federal Reserve bank for each district as well as the locations of branch banks. For example, the main Federal Reserve bank for District 10 is located in Kansas City. Using this map, do the following: (*a*) List by district number the cities in which main offices of Federal Reserve banks are located; (*b*) List twelve cities where there are branch Federal Reserve banks. Place a check mark opposite the number of the Federal Reserve district in which you live.
6. The article reprinted below appeared in the Centerville newspaper in late summer of a recent year. Read the article and answer the questions following it.

CITY BANKS RAISE PRIME INTEREST RATE

Centerville, U.S.A. Centerville's two banks today raised their prime lending rate from $4\frac{1}{2}$ to 5 percent.

The prime rate is the interest that banks charge their biggest borrowers with the best credit ratings. Rates for all other borrowers are scaled upward from the prime rate.

The prime rate was last increased in May from 4 percent to $4\frac{1}{2}$ percent. The latest increase makes the rate the highest in 28 years.

The increase was made because of the demand for loans. John Murray, president of Centerville National Bank, said the demand has been greater in this area than elsewhere.

Although loans of the nation's banks are equal to 51 percent of deposits, in Centerville the loan-deposit ratio is almost 60 percent, Murray said.

Although money is still available for lending, banks are rationing nonproductive loans, he said. Banks also are discouraging long-term loans.

Gordon Moore, president of the Midland State Bank of Centerville, said demand for loans is heavy in all types of business, but especially heavy at this time of year for crop marketing purposes. Moore cautioned that if the business boom continues, money available for lending will get scarcer and interest rates could rise again.

■ *a.* What is the lowest rate now charged for loans by Centerville banks? ■ *b.* Are all loans by Centerville's banks made at the same rate? ■ *c.* How much higher is the prime rate now than it was before the increase in May? ■ *d.* Is the prime rate charged by Centerville banks now higher than ever before? ■ *e.* Why was the prime rate raised? ■ *f.* What portion of their deposits have the Centerville banks loaned? ■ *g.* Have the Centerville banks loaned more or less of their deposits than the average for all the nation's banks? ■ *h.* In what type of business is the demand for loans greatest in Centerville? ■ *i.* At the time this article appeared, was the nation in a period of recession or prosperity? ■ *j.* What could cause interest rates to rise again?

CHALLENGE PROBLEMS

1. Most banks now carry deposit insurance with the FDIC. In what other ways do banks protect the money of their depositors?
2. Who pays for deposit insurance?
3. Fewer banks have failed since the FDIC was organized than before. How do you think the FDIC might have influenced this change?
4. Why do you suppose banks are not allowed to pay interest on demand deposits?
5. From 1956 to 1963, time deposits in the nation's banks almost doubled. What might have been happening to income during this period to cause the increase?
6. When a commercial bank makes a loan to one of its depositors, it usually does not give the borrower cash. Instead it creates a demand deposit for the borrower. Explain.

PART 22 OPENING A CHECKING ACCOUNT

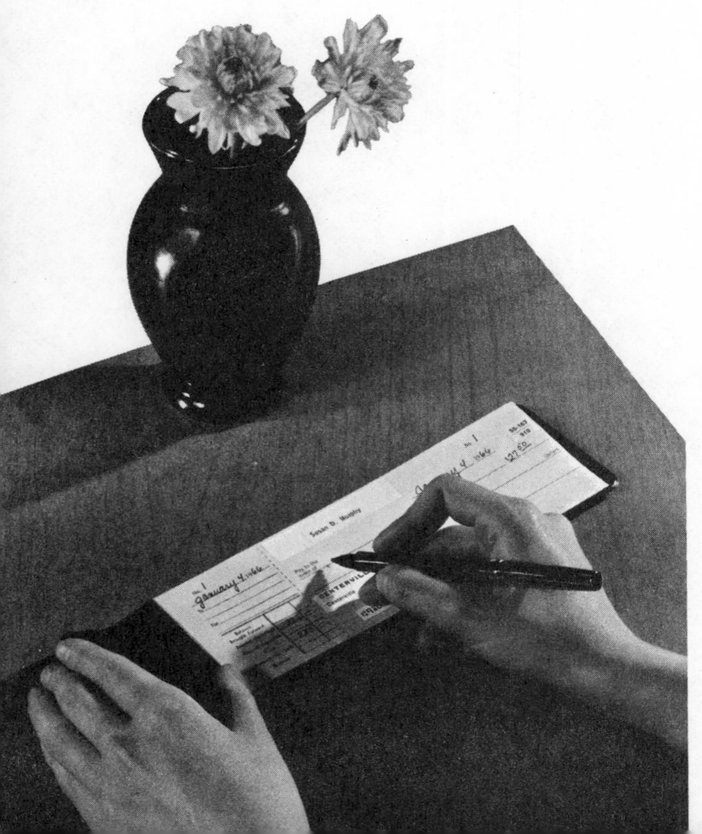

MONEY has two forms, as you already know. One form is currency or cash, consisting of coins and paper bills; the other is checks. Checks, of course, are simply a means of spending money deposited in banks. The cash that people carry in their pockets and purses is sometimes called *pocketbook money*. Demand deposits, or the money people have in their checking accounts, are called *deposit* or *checkbook money*.

These two kinds of money—pocketbook money and checkbook money—are interchangeable; that is, one may be exchanged for the other at any time. You may trade currency for a demand deposit simply by depositing the currency in a checking account. Or if you have a checking account, you can write a check against your account and withdraw currency.

Today there are over 53 million checking accounts in the United States. Why do you think so many people and organizations prefer to keep some of their money in the form of demand deposits?

WHY HAVE A CHECKING ACCOUNT?

One important reason for having a checking account, of course, is safety. Cash can be lost or stolen. With a checking account your money is protected against both risks. If a check is lost or stolen, you may ask the bank not to pay it.

Keeping most of your money in a checking account also reduces the temptation to buy on impulse. You are more likely to think twice about a purchase if you have to write a check in payment than if you can just reach in your pocket for cash.

Another reason for the popularity of checking accounts is their convenience. A check can be written for any amount as long as there is money on deposit to cover it. And since checks can be sent safely by mail, you can pay bills without ever leaving home.

Checks also provide proof of payment. When a check that you have written has been paid by the bank, it is returned to you. This is a legal receipt. Finally, if properly used, a checking account provides a record of expenditures. In short, a checking account helps you to handle your money in a businesslike way. Once you have a checking account, you may wonder how you ever got along without one.

HOW MUCH DOES A CHECKING ACCOUNT COST?

Cashing the average check may involve as many as 28 different operations and the work of many people. Most of these activities the depositor never sees. Nevertheless, handling checks is a big item of expense for banks. Most of them, therefore, charge a fee for checking-account service. This fee is called a ***service charge.*** Service charges are not the same for all banks throughout the country, but usually they are similar among banks within the same area.

The cost of a checking account also varies with the type of account a depositor has. Most banks have two types—regular and special.

Regular Checking Accounts

With a regular checking account, the service charge is based mainly on the balance in the account. The ***balance*** is the amount on deposit at any time. The balance, of course, changes with each deposit and withdrawal.

The income of a bank, you remember, comes mostly from using the funds deposited with it to make loans. The more money a depositor keeps in his account, the more income the bank receives from its use. If a depositor keeps enough money in his account to pay the cost of handling it, he does not have to pay a service charge. If an account earns less than the cost of handling it, the depositor is charged the difference.

Some banks use the minimum monthly balance in figuring charges. The minimum balance is the smallest amount on deposit at any time during the month. Others base their charges on the average monthly balance. The average balance is found by adding the balances for each day during the month and dividing by the number of days.

Following is the schedule of service charges used by one bank:

EARNINGS:	Each account will earn 25 cents a month for each $100 of minimum balance.
ACTIVITY COSTS:	Checks paid against the account, each 5 cents
	Maintenance charge, $1.00 (This charge is made only for months during which deposits are made or checks drawn.)
	NO CHARGE FOR DEPOSITED ITEMS

As an example of how service charges would be computed according to this schedule, suppose you had a regular checking account at this bank. During one month your lowest, or minimum, balance was $237, and the bank paid 15 checks for you.

At 25 cents per $100 of balance, your minimum balance of $237 would earn 50 cents. At 5 cents each, your 15 checks would cost 75 cents. The cost of maintenance would be $1, the same as for all accounts with deposits or withdrawals during the month. Based on the above schedule, therefore, your service charge for the month would be $1.25.

For example:

15 checks paid @ 5 cents each	$ .75
Maintenance charge	1.00
Total activity cost	$1.75
Less account earnings	.50
Service charge	$1.25

Special Checking Accounts

Most banks also offer special checking accounts with

such names as "Dime-a-Time," "Pay-As-You-Go," and "Economy Account." These are for people who write only a few checks during a month and do not carry a large enough balance to have a regular account. Usually no minimum balance is required. The depositor must keep only enough money in his account to cover the checks he writes plus a small amount to pay the cost of handling each check. A typical charge is 10 cents for each check paid by the bank. Some banks charge an additional 25 to 50 cents a month for maintenance.

HOW DO YOU OPEN A CHECKING ACCOUNT?

Opening a checking account at a commercial bank is really quite easy. Just walk in and ask anyone working in the bank for the person in charge of new accounts. Because a bank must be certain that its customers are people of good character, you will probably be asked to furnish proof of your identity. One of the best ways to identify yourself is to have a friend known at the bank introduce you. Otherwise, the names of two or three ***references*** are usually required. These references should be people, other than relatives, who know you personally. They may be close friends, neighbors, your employer, or others with whom you work.

The bank's service charges and the different types of checking accounts will be explained. If you are in doubt about whether a regular or special account is more suited to your needs, the banker will advise you.

You Will Fill Out a Signature Card

When you deposit money in a bank, the bank becomes responsible for its safety. To guard against anyone else's withdrawing money from your account, you will be asked to fill out a ***signature card.*** This card, showing your signature exactly as you will sign it on your checks, is kept on file at the bank. It enables the bank to identify your checks. Only those checks on which the signature matches that on the card will be paid.

The following illustration shows Susan Murphy's signature card. Notice that Susan signed her name "Susan D. Murphy." If she should forget and sign a check just "Susan Murphy" without the "D," the bank has the right to refuse payment.

If a bank pays a check on which the depositor's signature was written by someone else, the bank must accept the loss. The money cannot be taken from the depositor's account.

You May Have a Joint Account

Your first account will probably be an individual account; that is, only you will be able to write checks against it. A checking account used by two or more persons is a ***joint account.*** Husbands and wives frequently have accounts of this kind. Both sign the signature card, and both may write checks against the account. One advantage of the joint account is that it makes for a larger balance than if the same amount of money were divided between two separate accounts.

Your Account May Be Given a Number

Many banks, particularly large ones, assign numbers to checking accounts to make identification easier.

Courtesy The Chase Manhattan Bank

REGULAR CHECKING ACCOUNT

PLEASE TYPE OR PRINT

CARD NUMBER O F

ACCOUNT NUMBER 12-34-567

AUTHORIZED SIGNATURE CARD OF SUSAN D. MURPHY

NO. OF SIGNATURES REQUIRED

CHECKS	NOTES
1	1

NAME (PLEASE TYPE)	TITLE	SPECIMEN SIGNATURE
SUSAN D. MURPHY		Susan D. Murphy

WHENEVER AN ITEM PAYABLE AT ONE OFFICE OF THIS BANK IS CREDITED AT ANOTHER OFFICE THEREOF, SUCH CREDIT MAY BE CANCELLED IF THE ITEM IS NOT GOOD WHEN PRESENTED AT THE OFFICE WHERE IT IS PAYABLE. THE AMOUNT OF ANY ITEM PAYABLE AT ANOTHER BANK AND CREDITED AT ANY OFFICE OF THIS BANK MAY BE CHARGED BACK UNLESS THE ITEM, AND/OR ANY INSTRUMENT RECEIVED IN PAYMENT THEREOF, BE HONORED IN DUE COURSE. THE WORD "OFFICE" IN THIS PARAGRAPH IS INTENDED TO COVER THE HEAD OFFICE AND ALL BRANCHES OF THIS BANK.

RULE OUT SPACES NOT USED AND STATE ON REVERSE SIDE THE NUMBER OF SIGNATURES AUTHORIZED TO

CENTERVILLE NATIONAL BANK

COR. 4 REV. 8-61

IMPORTANT—SEE REVERSE SIDE OF THIS CARD

A signature card

This number will appear on your signature card. You will use it in making deposits and withdrawals.

HOW DO YOU MAKE A DEPOSIT?

After the bank has accepted you as a customer and your signature card has been filled out, you will make a deposit. To deposit either cash or checks, you fill out a printed form called a ***deposit slip.*** This form will vary slightly from one bank to another. You will find one illustrated below. It provides places for the depositor to write in his own name and account number. The depositor, in this case, is Susan D. Murphy whose account number is 12-34-567. The illustration on page 196 is a *personalized* deposit slip; that is, the name of the depositor is printed right on it as is his account number. This is the set of seven figures you see on the bottom line of the slip. It is 28-11-384. On both slips the depositor writes in the date, the items to be deposited, and the total amount of the deposit. Both the deposit slip and deposit are then given to the bank clerk, or ***teller.***

Items to be deposited are classified in three ways: CURRENCY, COIN (or SILVER), and CHECKS. You will notice that the deposit slip on page 196 uses the term CASH in place of CURRENCY and COIN. The deposit slip shown below shows a total deposit of $285, consisting of $14 in currency or paper bills, $6.38 in coins, and three checks.

Checks Are Listed by Bank Numbers

Notice that each check to be deposited is listed separately by the number of the bank on which it was drawn. This number, which appears in the upper right-hand corner of the check, looks like this:

$$\frac{82-33}{1021}$$

Only the number above the line is written on the deposit slip. The first part of the number designates the city or state in which the bank is located. The number 82 shown here, for example, is for the state of Colorado. The second part of the number is that of the individual bank. The number 33 belongs to the First National Bank of Greeley, Greeley, Colorado. If a city is large enough to be assigned a number of its own, banks in that city do not use the state number.

The number below the line is a Federal Reserve bank number used in sorting checks. This will be explained in a later part.

A deposit slip

DEPOSIT TICKET

NAME Susan D. Murphy

DATE January 3 1966

Use reverse side for listing more than three checks, insert total in space provided.

Centerville National Bank

Centerville, U.S.A.

ACCOUNT NUMBER 12-34-567

DELUXE CHECK PRINTERS 500-B

CURRENCY		14	00
COIN		6	38
CHECKS LIST SINGLY	55-167	185	37
	61-13	30	10
	55-94	49	15
	Total from reverse side.		
SUB TOTAL			
LESS CASH RECEIVED			
NET DEPOSIT		285	00

All items credited subject to final payment and subject to the terms and conditions of depositor's signature card.

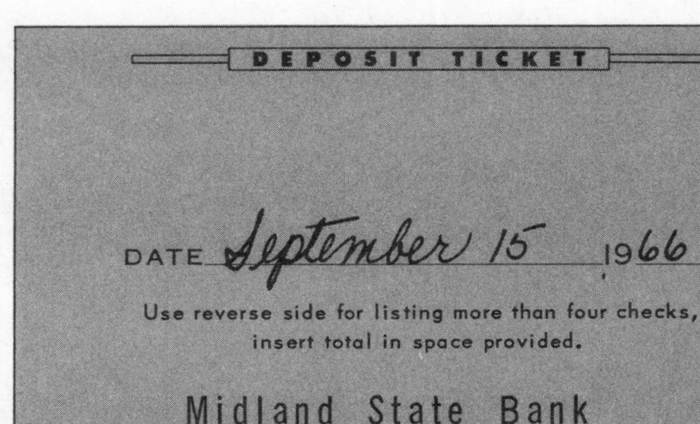

DEPOSIT TICKET

CASH		25	00
CHECKS LIST SINGLY • BE SURE EACH ITEM IS ENDORSED	14-9	18	75
	84-387	26	02
	73-14	4	95
	73-61	11	57
	Total from reverse side		
SUB TOTAL		86	29
LESS CASH RECEIVED			
NET DEPOSIT		86	29

All items credited subject to final payment and subject to the terms and conditions of depositor's signature card.

DATE September 15 1966

Use reverse side for listing more than four checks, insert total in space provided.

HENRY WHITE

Midland State Bank

Centerville, U.S.A.

28‥11‥384‥

DELUXE CHECK PRINTERS 500-B

A personalized deposit slip

Deposits May Be Mailed or Made After Hours

If you are unable to go to the bank, you may mail in your deposit. Most banks provide special deposit slips and mailing envelopes for this purpose. Such deposits should never include cash unless sent by registered mail. Workers sometimes arrange to have their paychecks sent directly to their banks for deposit in their accounts.

Most banks also have night depositories for those who want to make deposits after banking hours. There is an illustration of a night depository on page 197.

THE BANK WILL ISSUE A RECEIPT FOR YOUR DEPOSIT

Money that you deposit in a bank, remember, becomes a debt of the bank. For each deposit accepted, therefore, the bank issues a receipt. Some banks use a printed receipt on which the amount deposited and the date are recorded by

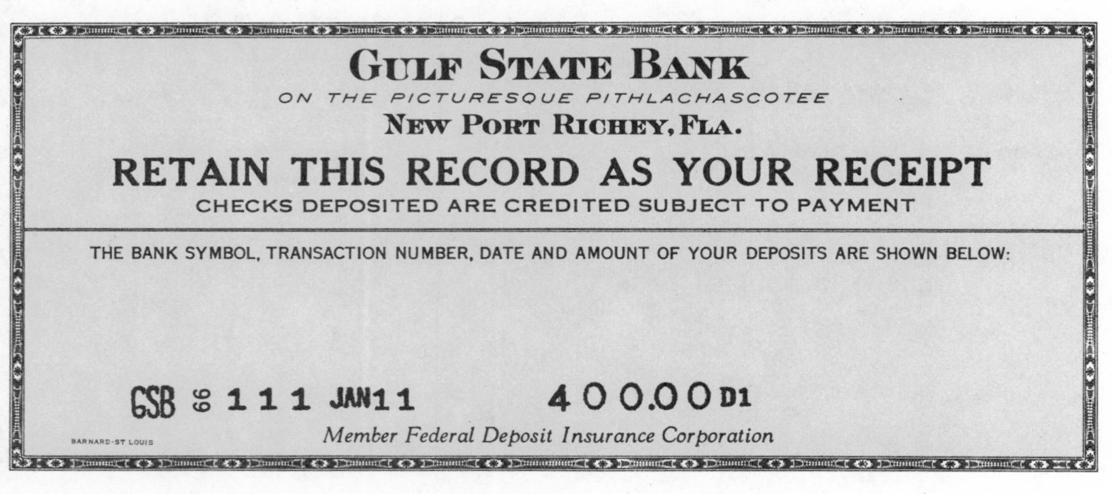

GULF STATE BANK

ON THE PICTURESQUE PITHLACHASCOTEE

NEW PORT RICHEY, FLA.

RETAIN THIS RECORD AS YOUR RECEIPT

CHECKS DEPOSITED ARE CREDITED SUBJECT TO PAYMENT

THE BANK SYMBOL, TRANSACTION NUMBER, DATE AND AMOUNT OF YOUR DEPOSITS ARE SHOWN BELOW:

GSB 66 111 JAN11 400.00 D1

BARNARD-ST LOUIS

Member Federal Deposit Insurance Corporation

A deposit receipt

machine. A receipt of this kind is illustrated on page 196.

Some banks have depositors make out two deposit slips. The teller keeps one and receipts the other. The receipted one is returned to the depositor as evidence of the deposit. And some banks provide each customer with a small book, called a ***passbook,*** in which the teller records each deposit. This record is the depositor's receipt. If a depositor does not have his passbook with him, he can make out two deposit slips as described above. Later he can have the amount recorded in his passbook by presenting it together with the receipted deposit slip. Any type of receipt should be kept by the depositor until he receives his monthly statement from the bank. Statements are explained in Part 24.

YOU WILL RECEIVE A CHECKBOOK

At the time you open a checking account, or within a few days afterwards, you will get a ***checkbook,*** containing printed forms to be used in writing checks. In some cases these are furnished by the bank without charge. More and more banks, however, are encouraging the use of personalized checks that carry the name, address, and account number of the depositor. The cost of these is deducted from the depositor's account.

Courtesy the Mosler Safe Company

A bank customer is making a late deposit in the night depository. Note that the bank's name is on the bag. Only the bank whose name appears on the bag has the key to open the bag.

In the next part you will learn how to use your checkbook properly.

BUILDING YOUR VOCABULARY

Copy the nine sentences below and on page 198, completing each one by replacing the question mark with the appropriate term from the column at the left.

balance
checkbook
deposit slip
joint account
passbook
references
service charge
signature card

1. A fee paid to a bank for checking-account service is a ? .
2. The amount on deposit in a bank account at a given time is the ? .
3. Friends or acquaintances who can furnish information about your identity and character are ? .
4. The bank's record of the way a customer signs his checks is a ? .
5. A checking account used by two or more persons is a ? .
6. A form on which a depositor lists the items to be credited to his account is a ? .

teller

7. A bank clerk who accepts deposits and handles withdrawals is a ?
8. A book used for recording deposits that serves as the depositor's receipt is a ?
9. A bound set of printed forms used in writing checks is a ?

CHECKING YOUR READING

1. Explain the difference between pocketbook money and checkbook money.
2. Name five advantages of a checking account.
3. Why do most banks charge a fee for checking accounts?
4. What two types of checking accounts do most banks offer?
5. What usually determines the amount of the service charge for a regular checking account?
6. Explain the difference between the minimum monthly balance and the average monthly balance in a checking account.
7. When is it better to use a special checking account instead of a regular account?
8. What is the first step in opening a checking account?
9. What is the purpose of a signature card?
10. Who must take the loss if a bank pays a check on which the depositor's signature was written by someone else?
11. Who signs the signature card for a joint account?
12. How should checks be listed on a deposit slip?
13. Describe two ways that deposits may be made after banking hours.
14. Give three examples of how banks issue receipts for deposits.
15. How long should a deposit receipt be kept?
16. What are personalized checks?

SHARING YOUR OPINION AND EXPERIENCE

1. Why must a bank be careful in accepting depositors?
2. Why do you think service charges are not the same for all banks throughout the country?
3. Checks of the Miller Electric Company must be signed by both Jerome Miller, vice-president, and Harlan Robbins, treasurer. Why would a business firm require the signatures of two persons on its checks?
4. What is a forged check? How does a bank guard against such checks?
5. Why do banks want currency and checks listed separately on the deposit slip?
6. Why should cash not be included when deposits are sent to the bank by ordinary mail?
7. Many deposit slips contain the statement, "All items credited subject to final payment." What does this statement mean?
8. To open a checking account at the Centerville National Bank, a person must be 18 or older. Why do you think the bank has this rule?

PROJECTS AND PROBLEMS

1. Study the deposit slip shown on page 195. How many different kinds of information does it contain? List them.
2. You have the following items to deposit in your checking account:

   ▪ *a.* $23 in bills ▪ *b.* $4.39 in coins ▪ *c.* Checks as follows: $21.75 on the Second National Bank of Minneapolis (Bank No. 17-18); $13.61 on the First National Bank of Auburn, Alabama (Bank No. 61-519); $32.50 on the Union County Trust Company of Elizabeth, New Jersey (Bank No. 55-101). ▪ Prepare a deposit slip showing how these items should be listed.
3. Jerry Goodman had the following items to deposit in the checking account of the Young Men's Shop:

   ▪ *a.* $289 in bills ▪ *b.* $67.42 in coins ▪ *c.* Checks as follows: $7.22 on the First National Bank, Greeley, Colorado (Bank No. 82-33); $24.18 on the Lincoln National Bank and Trust Company, Syracuse, New York (Bank No. 50-46); $18.50 on the Bank of Virginia, Richmond (Bank No. 68-677); $42.35 on the First National Bank and Trust Company, Lexington, Kentucky (Bank No. 73-2); $162 on the First National Bank of Boston, Massachusetts (Bank No. 5-39). ▪ Prepare the deposit slip for Jerry.
4. Frank Haynes has a checking account in the Merchants and Farmers Bank, which uses the following schedule of service charges:

SCHEDULE OF MONTHLY SERVICE COST

Minimum Balance	*Number of Checks Allowed*	*Maintenance Cost*
From 1 cent to $100	**5**	**$1.00**
From $100 to $200	**10**	**None**
From $200 to $300	**15**	**None**
	Each Additional Check 5 Cents	

Accounts having minimum balance in excess of $300 will be subject to similar charges, but additional credit of 5 checks will be allowed for each additional $100 minimum balance over $300.

An examination of Frank's account provided the following information:

Month	*Minimum Balance*	*Number of Checks Written*
January	**$75**	**8**
February	**118**	**11**
March	**234**	**9**
April	**198**	**15**
May	**325**	**18**
June	**413**	**20**

What was Frank's service charge for each of the months shown?

5. Instead of stating service charges in the manner shown on page 199, some banks use a table such as the one below. The table provides a simplified method of computing most charges.

SERVICE-CHARGE SCHEDULE

		Average Monthly Balances									
Number of Checks	*Under $100*	*$100 to $199*	*$200 to $299*	*$300 to $399*	*$400 to $499*	*$500 to $599*	*$600 to $699*	*$700 to $799*	*$800 to $899*	*$900 to $999*	*Number of Checks*
0	.70	.60	.50	.40	.30	.20	.10	.00			**0**
1	.75	.65	.55	.45	.35	.25	.15	.05			**1**
2	.80	.70	.60	.50	.40	.30	.20	.10	.00		**2**
3	.85	.75	.65	.55	.45	.35	.25	.15	.05		**3**
4	.90	.80	.70	.60	.50	.40	.30	.20	.10	.00	**4**
5	.95	.85	.75	.65	.55	.45	.35	.25	.15	.05	**5**
6	1.00	.90	.80	.70	.60	.50	.40	.30	.20	.10	**6**
7	1.05	.95	.85	.75	.65	.55	.45	.35	.25	.15	**7**
8	1.10	1.00	.90	.80	.70	.60	.50	.40	.30	.20	**8**
9	1.15	1.05	.95	.85	.75	.65	.55	.45	.35	.25	**9**
10	1.20	1.10	1.00	.90	.80	.70	.60	.50	.40	.30	**10**
11	1.25	1.15	1.05	.95	.85	.75	.65	.55	.45	.35	**11**
12	1.30	1.20	1.10	1.00	.90	.80	.70	.60	.50	.40	**12**
13	1.35	1.25	1.15	1.05	.95	.85	.75	.65	.55	.45	**13**
14	1.40	1.30	1.20	1.10	1.00	.90	.80	.70	.60	.50	**14**
15	1.45	1.35	1.25	1.15	1.05	.95	.85	.75	.65	.55	**15**
16	1.50	1.40	1.30	1.20	1.10	1.00	.90	.80	.70	.60	**16**
17	1.55	1.45	1.35	1.25	1.15	1.05	.95	.85	.75	.65	**17**
18	1.60	1.50	1.40	1.30	1.20	1.10	1.00	.90	.80	.70	**18**
19	1.65	1.55	1.45	1.35	1.25	1.15	1.05	.95	.85	.75	**19**
20	1.70	1.60	1.50	1.40	1.30	1.20	1.10	1.00	.90	.80	**20**

(Additional checks subject to an extension of this schedule)

Note: Accounts having average balances in excess of one thousand dollars and accounts with unusually large deposit activity will be fully analyzed. Service charges shown in shaded area are waived.

Use the table to figure the monthly service charge for each of the following:

Name of Depositor	*Average Monthly Balance*	*Number of Checks Written*
Frances Bishop	**$375**	**11**
John Erickson	**90**	**8**
Samuel Goldberg	**940**	**20**
L. J. Mitchell	**480**	**17**
Gene C. Harper	**625**	**5**

6. Demand deposits do not earn interest. Instead checking-account depositors usually receive credit for maintaining balances above a certain amount. In the illustration on page 193, for example, accounts earn a credit of 25 cents a month for each $100 of minimum balance. If this were an interest payment, what would the annual rate of interest be?
7. Most banks charge a fee for checking-account services because of the work and expense involved in handling these accounts. List five of the activities that are required in handling a checking account. (You may get help from your parents or from someone you know who works in a bank.)

CHALLENGE PROBLEMS

1. Harry Kramer has a checking account in a bank with a service-charge schedule identical to the one on page 193. Harry usually writes 20 to 30 checks a month and has a low minimum balance in his account. But, in addition, he has $800 in a savings account which pays 3 percent interest. Would it be better for Harry to deposit this money in his checking account in order to maintain a bigger balance? Explain.
2. The bank that uses the service-charge schedule shown in problem 5 of the Projects and Problems section also offers special checking-account service. Depositors with special checking accounts are charged 10 cents for each check paid by the bank. No minimum balance is required. Under what circumstances would a depositor be wise to use a special checking account?

PART 23 MAKING AND RECEIVING PAYMENTS BY CHECK

ALTHOUGH banks provide printed forms for checks, there is no law requiring the use of these forms. All a bank needs to pay money from a regular checking account is a written order from the depositor. This could be a letter. Or you could write a check on a plain piece of paper. Checks have been written on practically everything—paper bags, matchbook covers, even wood shingles. Except in case of an emergency, however, it is wise to use the forms provided by your bank. These are printed on special paper that makes it easy to detect erasures.

It is also important to learn to write checks properly. Every day banks receive checks that are not filled out completely or correctly. What is the correct way to write a check? Why must you endorse checks made out to you? How do you endorse a check?

Monkmeyer Press Photo Service

A CHECKBOOK HAS TWO PARTS

Even though checkbooks differ in some ways, they all contain the same two things—blank checks and some provision for recording deposits and withdrawals. In one type of checkbook a ***check stub*** is attached to each check by a perforated line. These stubs are used for record keeping. A check with stub attached is illustrated on page 203. Another type of checkbook record is the ruled form on page 204.

The check stub or other record form is an important part of your checkbook. By filling it in properly each time you write a check or make a deposit, you always know exactly how much money you have in your account. This will save you the embarrassment of overdrawing your account. To ***overdraw*** your account means to write a check for more than you have on deposit. Writing a worthless check intentionally is a criminal offense.

Enter Each Deposit on the Checkbook Record

The first thing to do after receiving your checkbook is to enter the amount of the deposit with which you opened your account. The illustration on this page shows the first stub in Susan Murphy's checkbook. Susan opened her account with $285. She entered this amount on the line next to "Amount Deposited." She also wrote $285 on the line following "Total" since that was the balance, or total amount, she had in her checking account at that time. Each time you make a deposit, of course, the amount should be entered on the checkbook record and added to your balance.

PREPARE THE CHECK RECORD FIRST

Before you write a check, it is advisable to fill out the stub or other record; otherwise, you may forget to do so. The illustration below shows Susan Murphy's first check, which was made out to her dentist, Dr. Leonard Brett. As you can see, the check stub, at the left of the illustration, gives the same information as that written on the check.

The number of the check appears on the first line of the stub. The date on which the check is written appears on the second line. The name of the person to whom the check is written goes on the third line following the word "To." What the check was for is shown on the fifth line following the word "For."

Susan carefully subtracted the amount of the check, $27.50, from her total balance. The balance of $257.50 was the amount left in her account against which she could still write checks. She wrote this amount on the line following Balance Brought Forward on the second stub in her checkbook.

After a check has been written and removed from the checkbook, the depositor has a record of his transactions on the stubs that remain. Occasionally you may find it necessary to use a check other than one from your regular checkbook. Whenever this happens, it is important that a record of the check be made in your checkbook as soon as possible. The best way is to record the information about the check on a stub, then destroy the check attached to the stub. This applies only to users of regular checking accounts. Persons with special accounts must use the check forms provided by the bank.

HOW ARE CHECKS WRITTEN?

After you have filled out the stub or other record in your checkbook, you are ready to write your check. For your own protection, checks should be written in ink since those written in pencil can be altered easily. Or they may be written on the typewriter and then signed in ink. If you make a

A check with its stub correctly filled in

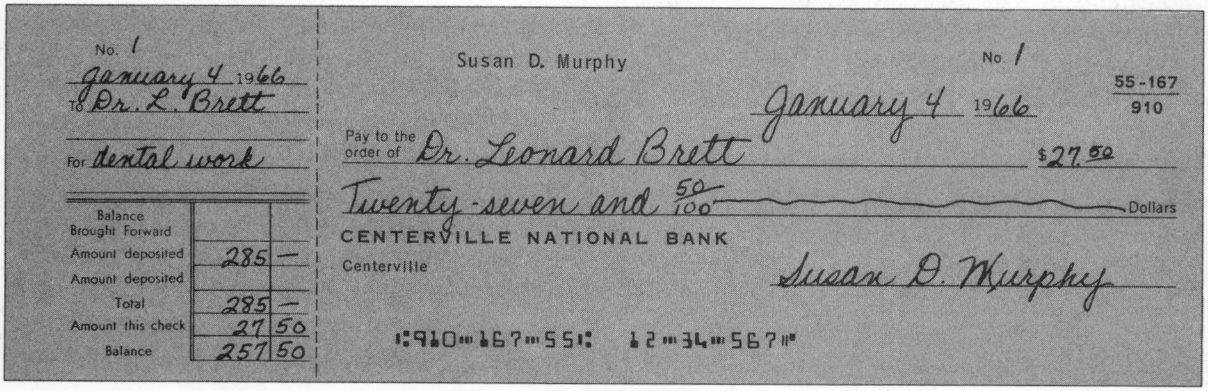

No. 1
January 4 1966
To Dr. L. Brett
For dental work

Balance Brought Forward		
Amount deposited	285	—
Amount deposited		
Total	285	—
Amount this check	27	50
Balance	257	50

Susan D. Murphy
No. 1
55-167
910
January 4 1966
Pay to the order of Dr. Leonard Brett $27.50
Twenty-seven and 50/100 Dollars
CENTERVILLE NATIONAL BANK
Centerville
Susan D. Murphy
⑆910⑉167⑉55⑆ 12⑉34⑉567⑈

CHECK NO.	DATE	CHECK ISSUED TO	AMOUNT OF CHECK		✓	DATE OF DEP.	AMOUNT OF DEPOSIT		BALANCE	
						1/3	285	00	285	00
1	1/4	Dr. Leonard Brett	27	50					257	50

A ruled checkbook record

mistake in writing a check, write a new one. As a rule spoiled checks should be destroyed, but there is an exception. Depositors using special accounts often pay for their checks in advance. The usual charge is $2 for a book of 20 checks. In that case, a spoiled check should be returned to the bank either for credit or for a new check.

There are six separate items to be written on the face of each check: the number, the date, the payee's name, the amount in figures, the amount spelled out, and the signature.

The Check Number

Each check should be numbered in the space provided. Numbering makes it easy to sort your checks after they have been returned to you by the bank. It also provides a means of identifying lost or stolen checks. The usual procedure is to number them consecutively. The number on the check and stub or other record should agree.

The Date

The date includes the month, the day, and the year on which the check is written. Some people have the mistaken idea that banks will not honor checks dated on Sundays. The truth is that checks written on Sunday are just as good as checks written on any other day of the week.

The Payee's Name

The person or business to whom a check is written is the ***payee.*** Dr. Leonard Brett was the payee on Susan's first check. She wrote his name on the line beginning "Pay to the order of."

When a person presents a check for payment, he may be asked for identification. If his name is spelled differently on the check than on his identification, he may have trouble cashing it. It is important, therefore, to spell the payee's name correctly.

If you want to withdraw cash from your checking account, you may write in your own name as the payee. Or you may make the check payable to "Cash." A check made payable to "Cash," however, can be cashed by anyone. If it is lost, whoever finds it may cash it. For that reason make a check to "Cash" only after you are inside the bank, and cash it immediately.

The Amount

You will note in the illustration on page 203 that the amount of the check appears twice, once in figures and once in words. The purpose of stating the amount twice is to make sure that it is stated correctly. If the amount shown in figures is not the same as the amount in words, the bank pays the amount written in words. It may refuse to honor

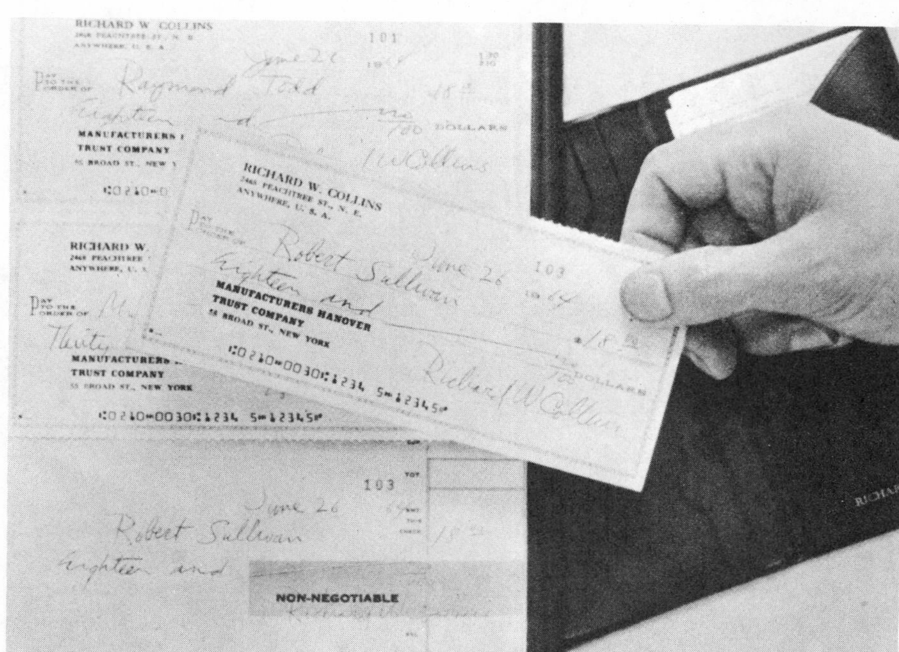

Many banks now make it easy for the depositor to keep a check record by having a carbon copy for each check. This carbon remains in the checkbook as a permanent record.

Courtesy Manufacturers Hanover Trust Company

a check if the difference between the two amounts is great.

The amount in figures should be written as close to the dollar sign as possible. This is to keep anyone from increasing the amount by putting figures in front of those already there. For the same reason, the amount in words should be written as far to the left as possible. Then no one can raise the amount by writing a word before it. Fill in any unused space between the written amount and the word "Dollars" with a wavy line.

Notice how Susan wrote the amount, with the cents smaller than the dollar amount. This makes it easier to read the check and is a further protection against anyone changing the amount. Also notice that where the dollar amount is in words, the cents appear as a fraction of a dollar. In this case, the fraction is $\frac{50}{100}$. If the check is for less than $1, write the word "only" preceding the amount and follow the amount with the word "cents." Then draw a line through the word "Dollars." You will find an illustration of this on page 206.

The number of checks a depositor writes is an important factor in determining the service charge on his account. For that reason the habit of writing checks for small amounts can be costly. Nevertheless, when sending payments by mail, it is advisable to use a check for amounts over 50 cents.

The Signature

The last part of a check to be written is the signature. The person who signs a check is known as the ***drawer.*** When signing checks be careful to write your name in the same way you wrote it on your signature card. Never sign a check that has not been filled in. If the check were lost, anyone finding it could make it payable to himself. Since the signature on the check would be genuine, the bank would pay it, if the balance in your account would cover it.

STOPPING PAYMENT ON A CHECK

Suppose that someone to whom you give a check loses it. Or suppose a check that you write is stolen. You can ask the bank not to honor the check

No. 2
January 11 1966
To Alice Cary Gifts
For gift wrap

Balance Brought Forward	257	50
Amount deposited		
Amount deposited		
Total	257	50
Amount this check		85
Balance	256	65

Susan D. Murphy

No. 2

January 11 1966

55-167
910

Pay to the order of Alice Cary Gifts $85 cents

Only eighty-five cents ~~Dollars~~

CENTERVILLE NATIONAL BANK
Centerville

Susan D. Murphy

⑆910⑈167⑈55⑆ 12⑈34⑈567⑈

A check for less than one dollar

when it is presented for payment. This is known as *stopping payment on a check.*

The customary practice is to fill out a stop-payment request form at the bank. Such a form is illustrated below. The bank will need to know the number of the check, its date, the name of the payee, and the amount of the check. Banks usually charge a fee for this service.

If you cannot go to the bank, you may order payment of a check stopped by letter or telephone. When such a request is made by telephone, however, it should be confirmed immediately by letter.

CHECKS YOU RECEIVE HAVE TO BE ENDORSED

In the years ahead you will not only write checks, you will receive them; that is, you will be the payee instead of the drawer. It is just as important to handle properly checks made out to you as it is to write your own checks correctly.

A check gives the payee the right to collect a certain amount of the money that the drawer has on deposit at the bank. To collect the money, however, the payee must first endorse the check. You ***endorse*** a check by signing your name on the back of it. The payee's signature on the back of a check is an *endorsement.* The person who endorses a check is the *endorser.*

After a check has been endorsed, you can do one of the following things with it:

1. You may cash it.
2. You may deposit it in the bank.
3. You may transfer it to another person or business.

CENTERVILLE NATIONAL BANK
CENTERVILLE

STOP PAYMENT ORDER

[✓] Head Office
[ ] ________ Branch

BANK COPY

Please accept the following stop payment which becomes effective only if the check has not already been paid.

Date October 11, 1966

ACCOUNT NUMBER	DRAWER'S NAME (PLEASE PRINT CLEARLY OR TYPE)	CHECK DATED	CHECK NUMBER	AMOUNT
12 34 567	Susan D. Murphy	Oct. 10, 1966	10	$35.67

This check has not been paid as shown by the latest statement rendered to me. Should I issue a new check in place of this check, I shall use a different date and number.

PAYEE Rite-Fit Dress Shop

As provided by law, this stop payment order is effective for only six months after receipt, unless renewed in writing by the undersigned.

Miss Susan D. Murphy
25 Elm Street
Centerville

CHECK ONE
[X] REGULAR CHECKING
[ ] SPECIAL CHECKING
[ ] EMPLOYEE CHECKING
[ ] PERSONAL MONEY ORDER
[ ] CHRISTMAS CLUB

CHECK ONE
[X] ORIGINAL STOP PAYMENT
[ ] RENEWAL
[ ] CONFIRMATION OF STOP PAYMENT

SIG-SP-8 REV. 11-64

Please sign this Stop Payment Order and return to us. Retain the attached copy for your records.

Susan D. Murphy
CUSTOMER'S OFFICIAL SIGNATURE

Courtesy The Chase Manhattan Bank

A stop-payment order

George Mallory

A blank endorsement

Pay to the order of
Felix Kramer
George Mallory

A full endorsement

For Deposit Only
George Mallory

A restricted endorsement

Your endorsement is proof that you have received payment for the check or that you have transferred ownership of the check to someone else.

A check may be endorsed many times. For example, you may endorse a check made payable to you and give it to another person. He, in turn, may endorse it and give it to a third person, and so on. Each person who becomes owner of the check by having it endorsed and transferred to him must sign his name on the back before he cashes it or gives it to someone else.

Each Endorser Assumes a Responsibility

Anyone who endorses a check assumes responsibility for payment of the check. Suppose that you endorse a check made payable to you and cash it at the bank. If the person who wrote the check does not have enough money in his account to pay it, you will have to refund the money the bank gave you for it. If you endorse the check and give it to another person and it turns out that the check is no good, you will have to pay him the amount of the check. Each endorser is responsible only to those who receive the check after him.

Where and How Should Checks Be Endorsed?

Although a check may be endorsed anywhere on the back, it is customary to sign at the left end of the check. It is easier for the bank if all checks are endorsed in the same place.

Endorse a check in exactly the same way as your name is written on the face of the check. If you receive a check on which your name is misspelled, first sign your name as it is written on the check and then write it correctly. For your own protection, endorsements should be written in ink, the same as checks.

The three principal kinds of endorsements are:

1. Blank endorsement
2. Full endorsement
3. Restrictive endorsement

Blank Endorsement. The most common and easiest way to endorse a check is to write just your name. This is known as an ***endorsement in blank*** or a ***blank endorsement.*** A blank endorsement should be used only when you are at the bank to cash or deposit a check. The reason is that a check endorsed in blank may be cashed by anyone who gains possession of it. In other words, if you lost the check, anyone who found it could cash it.

Full Endorsement. A ***full endorsement*** is one in which the endorser indicates to whom payment is to be made. For example, in the illustration at the center, above, the endorsement reads "Pay to the order of Felix Kramer" and is signed by George Mallory. This means that Mr. Mallory wants the check paid to Mr. Kramer. By endorsing the check in this manner, Mr. Mallory has made certain that no one except Mr. Kramer will be able to cash it.

Restrictive Endorsement. A ***restrictive endorsement*** limits the use of a check by stating the intentions of the endorser. For example, suppose you have a check that you wish to deposit by mail. If you endorse the check by signing only your name on the back and the check is lost or stolen, anyone will be able to cash it. But if the words, "For Deposit Only," are written above your signature, the check can be credited only to your account at the bank. When checks are endorsed in this way, they are of no value to anyone else. If you changed your mind about depositing it, even you could not cash it.

DEPOSIT OR CASH CHECKS PROMPTLY

Checks that you receive should be presented for payment as soon as possible. Legally, a check is good in most states for six years. A check held too long, however, becomes "stale." If it is not presented within a reasonable period of time, the bank may refuse to accept it without the approval of the person who wrote it.

BUILDING YOUR VOCABULARY

On a separate sheet of paper, write each of the terms listed in the left-hand column below and on page 209. Read the three definitions to the right of each term. After each term, copy the definition that best describes it.

1. ***blank endorsement*** *(endorsement in blank)*
   a. An endorsement that permits a check to be cashed by anyone
   b. An endorsement that permits a check to be cashed only by the payee
   c. An endorsement that permits a check to be cashed by anyone named by the payee

2. ***check stub***
   a. The place on a check where the depositor signs his name
   b. A form on which the depositor keeps a record of his checking-account transactions
   c. The part of a check on which the depositor writes his endorsement

3. ***drawer***
   a. The person who signs a check
   b. The person who writes his name on the back of a check
   c. The person who cashes a check

4. ***endorse***
   a. To sign one's name on the back of a check
   b. To sign one's name on a signature card
   c. To sign one's name on the face of a check

5. ***full endorsement***
   a. An endorsement that indicates when the check should be cashed
   b. An endorsement that indicates to whom the check is transferred
   c. An endorsement that indicates the bank where the check must be cashed

6. *overdraw*
   a. To write a check on a bank where you do not have an account
   b. To write a check for more than enough to pay a bill
   c. To write a check for more than you have on deposit

7. *payee*
   a. The person who has possession of a check
   b. The person who writes a check
   c. The person to whom a check is written

8. *restrictive endorsement*
   a. An endorsement that makes it impossible for anyone to cash a check
   b. An endorsement that limits the use of a check by stating the endorser's intentions
   c. An endorsement used only when checks are mailed to the bank

CHECKING YOUR READING

1. Why should you use the check forms provided by the bank except in case of an emergency?
2. What is the purpose of the check stub or checkbook record? When should it be filled out?
3. Why should checks be written in ink?
4. What should you do with a check if you make a mistake in writing it?
5. Why should all checks be numbered?
6. What date should be used when writing a check?
7. Why is it important that the payee's name be spelled correctly on a check?
8. When is the only time a check should be made payable to cash? Why is it unwise to write a check to cash at any other time?
9. The amount of a check appears in two different places. How is it written each time? If the two amounts do not agree, which one does the bank pay?
10. Describe how the amounts on a check are written so that they will be difficult to alter.
11. How should you sign a check, and when?
12. How do you stop payment on a check? Under what circumstances would you stop payment?
13. What three things may you do with a check after you have endorsed it?
14. What does your endorsement of a check prove?
15. In what way are you responsible for a check that you endorse?
16. Where should a check be endorsed?
17. How should you endorse a check if your name is misspelled on the face of the check?
18. When should a blank endorsement be used? Why?
19. What is the advantage of a full endorsement?
20. Give an example of a restrictive endorsement. Why is it used?

SHARING YOUR OPINION AND EXPERIENCE

1. What does postdating a check mean? Why is it a poor practice?
2. What is a counter check? How does it differ from a regular check?
3. John Rothberg did not subtract the amount of each check he wrote from the balance shown on his check stubs. Instead, he took time only every few weeks to bring his checkbook record up to date. Do you think this was a good idea? Why or why not?
4. Who may cash a check that is made payable to "Bearer"? In what way, if any, does it differ from a check made payable to "Cash"?
5. Should two people who have a joint checking account use one checkbook or two? Explain.
6. Some banks charge a special fee each time a depositor overdraws his account. Why do you suppose they make such a charge?
7. Many checks carry the words, "Void after 60 days." What does this mean?
8. Why should the endorser of a check have to assume responsibility for payment of the check when he transfers it to someone else?
9. Why is it just as important to endorse checks in ink as it is to write them in ink?
10. Mr. King bought the paint and other supplies he needed for painting his house from the Craftsmen Wallpaper and Paint Store. He wrote a check for $76.07 in payment. Before placing the check in the drawer of the cash register, Mr. Earl, manager of the paint store, used a rubber stamp to print the following on the back of the check.

Why did Mr. Earl do this immediately after accepting the check since he did not intend to deposit it until later?

PROJECTS AND PROBLEMS

1. Study the check and stub shown on page 211. On a separate sheet of paper, write your answers to the questions following it.

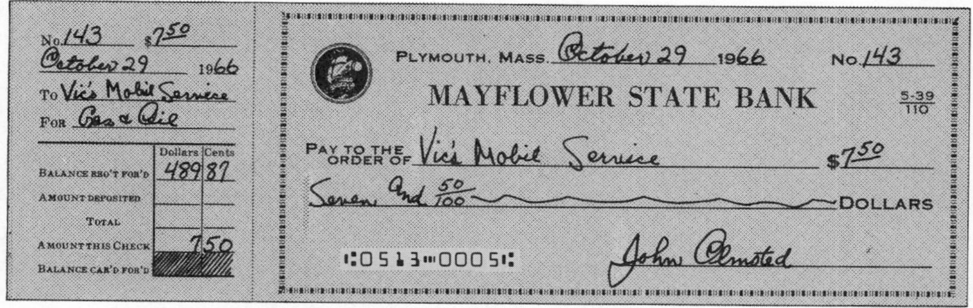

No. 143 $7.50
October 29 1966
To Vic's Mobil Service
For Gas & Oil

	Dollars	Cents
Balance Bro't For'd	489	87
Amount Deposited		
Total		
Amount This Check	7	50
Balance Car'd For'd		

Plymouth, Mass. October 29 1966 No. 143

MAYFLOWER STATE BANK $\frac{5-39}{110}$

Pay to the order of Vic's Mobil Service $7.50

Seven and 50/100 Dollars

⑆0513⑈0005⑆ John Olmsted

▪ *a.* On what bank is the check drawn? ▪ *b.* What is the number of the check? ▪ *c.* What is the number of the bank on which it is drawn? ▪ *d.* Who is the drawer? ▪ *e.* Who is the payee? ▪ *f.* What was the check given in payment for? ▪ *g.* After writing the check, how much did the person who wrote it have left in his checking account?

2. Write the following checks, filling in the stubs first in each case. If you are not using the *Student Activity Guide,* rule forms similar to the one on page 203. The balance in your checking account before writing the first check was $79.25. Use the current date.

   ▪ *a.* Check No. 23 to Miller's Department Store, for raincoat, $7.95 ▪ *b.* Check No. 24 to House of Music, for record album, $3.98 ▪ *c.* Enter deposit of $56.41 on stub for Check No. 25 ▪ *d.* Check No. 25 to Ray's Photo Shop, for portraits, $13.80 ▪ *e.* Check No. 26 to Home Shop, for gift for Mother, $16.50

3. Assume that you have a checking account with a balance on deposit of $372.85. Figure the balance to be carried forward after each of the following transactions:

   ▪ *a.* Check No. 273 to Valley Power Company for $18.73 ▪ *b.* Check No. 274 to National Insurance Company for $12.85 ▪ *c.* Deposit of $272.19 ▪ *d.* Check No. 275 to J. L. Thompson, dentist for $4 ▪ *e.* Deposit of $18.58 ▪ *f.* Check No. 276 to United Fund for $15.

4. On September 1, Howard Compton had a balance of $432.33 in his checking account. During the month he made two deposits of $221.57 each. He wrote checks for $18.75, $9.27, $24.50, $106.05, $45.91, $6.87, $2.98, $84.25, and $175. What was his balance at the end of the month?

5. Assume that you have three checks made payable to you. On the back of three forms resembling checks, write endorsements to illustrate:

   ▪ *a.* blank endorsement ▪ *b.* full endorsement to J. M. McGrath ▪ *c.* restrictive endorsement for deposit in State Planters Bank of Commerce.

6. Robert L. Smyth received a check with his name written Robert L. Smith. On a piece of paper about the size of a check, write a blank endorsement the way Mr. Smyth should do it.
7. Write the proper endorsements for each of the following situations:

   ▪ *a.* Fred Tipton sent his young son to deposit a check in the First National Bank. He wished to protect himself in case the check is lost. ▪ *b.* R. D. Sexton endorsed a check and gave it to Buford Nelson. The endorsement was made so that no one but Mr. Nelson could cash the check. ▪ *c.* Frances Hale endorsed a check and cashed it in person at the bank.

8. Have each student in the class whose parents have checking accounts bring a printed check form to class. Compare the forms used by the different banks. What differences do you find?

CHALLENGE PROBLEMS

1. Printed check forms have the words, "Pay to the order of," preceding the space for the payee's name. What does this mean? Why would it not be just as good to use the words, "Pay to"?
2. What is a check protector? Who uses it and why?
3. One bank charges its customers $3 for each returned check. What is a returned check? Why do you suppose the bank charges such a large fee for it?
4. Bill Ryan wrote a check for $27.50 to George Anderson. Mr. Anderson endorsed the check and gave it to Mary Higgins. Miss Higgins endorsed it to Albert Thomas, and he endorsed it and gave it to Charles Weber. Mr. Ryan did not have enough money in the bank to pay the check.

   ▪ *a.* Who is responsible for paying Mr. Weber the $27.50? ▪ *b.* To whom is Miss Higgins responsible for the amount of the check? ▪ *c.* If Miss Higgins has to pay, can she claim an equal amount from anyone else? If so, from whom? ▪ *d.* If Mr. Ryan is never able to make payment but all endorsers are, who will lose the $27.50?

5. One winter the Abernathys, who lived in Michigan, decided to go to Florida for two months. There they rented a cottage for which they paid $375. The man who owned the cottage accepted Mr. Abernathy's personal check in payment for the rent. But when Mr. Abernathy tried to cash a check for $50 at the local bank, he was refused. Why do you think the cottage owner was willing to take a check for such a large amount and yet the bank refused a much smaller one?

PART 24 WHAT HAPPENS TO THE CHECKS YOU WRITE?

MORE than 30 million checks are deposited in, or cashed at, banks daily. Each of these checks must be sent to the bank on which it was drawn and payment collected. The process of collecting payment for checks is called ***clearing.*** Because banks use an efficient clearing system, checks travel about the nation with such speed that $18 billion of checkbook or deposit money changes hands each day. Moving that much money around the country is a big job. Yet the amazing thing is that it is done without actual cash being sent from one place to another.

What does a bank do with checks drawn on it after the checks have been paid? How is it possible to pay for and collect checks without transferring any cash?

HOW ARE CHECKS CLEARED?

On the basis of information found on checks, portions of demand deposits are constantly moving from one bank to another. If a person deposits in his account a check written by another depositor of the same bank, the deposit is transferred easily. The bank simply deducts the amount of the check from the drawer's account and adds it to the payee's account. For example, Susan Murphy works for a firm that has its checking account at the Centerville National Bank where Susan also banks. Each payday when Susan deposits her check in the bank, all the bank does is to deduct the amount from the firm's account and add it to Susan's.

Between Banks in the Same City

When a check is drawn on one bank and deposited or cashed at another bank in the same city, the procedure is slightly more complicated. Suppose

Eastern Photo Service

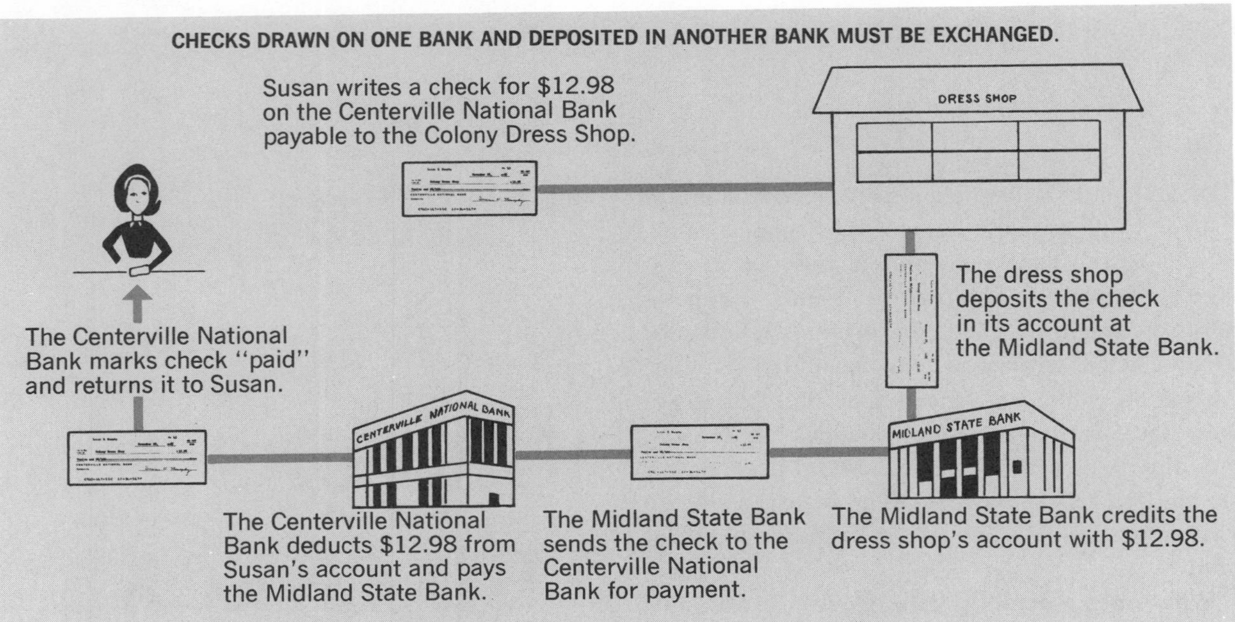
CHECKS DRAWN ON ONE BANK AND DEPOSITED IN ANOTHER BANK MUST BE EXCHANGED.
Susan writes a check for $12.98 on the Centerville National Bank payable to the Colony Dress Shop.
DRESS SHOP
The dress shop deposits the check in its account at the Midland State Bank.
The Centerville National Bank marks check "paid" and returns it to Susan.
CENTERVILLE NATIONAL BANK
MIDLAND STATE BANK
The Centerville National Bank deducts $12.98 from Susan's account and pays the Midland State Bank.
The Midland State Bank sends the check to the Centerville National Bank for payment.
The Midland State Bank credits the dress shop's account with $12.98.

that Susan Murphy wrote a check for $12.98 on the Centerville National Bank and made it payable to the Colony Dress Shop. The Colony Dress Shop deposits the check in its account at the Midland State Bank of Centerville. The Midland State Bank credits the Colony Dress Shop's account with $12.98 and sends the check to the Centerville National Bank for payment. When the Centerville National Bank receives the check, it pays the Midland State Bank $12.98 and deducts that amount from Susan's account.

When there are only a few banks in a city, they usually clear checks directly with one another; that is, they exchange checks daily and settle any difference between the amounts paid. For example, in Centerville there are only two banks, the Centerville National Bank and the Midland State Bank. Suppose that in the course of a day the Centerville National Bank pays 123 checks drawn on the Midland State Bank; the Midland State Bank pays 137 checks drawn on the Centerville National Bank. At a certain time every day, the banks exchange checks, so that each receives the checks drawn on it.

Now suppose that the 123 checks which the Centerville National Bank paid for the Midland State Bank totaled $2,759. The 137 checks paid by the Midland State Bank for the Centerville National Bank totaled $3,253. The Centerville National Bank would then give the Midland State Bank a check for the difference of $494.

If there are more than two banks in a town, each bank exchanges checks with every other bank and settles the difference between the total amounts of the checks paid.

Between Banks in a Large City

The more banks there are in a community, the more complicated the process of exchanging checks becomes. In a large city where there are many banks, therefore, checks are cleared through a central clearing agency, called a ***clearinghouse.*** The clearinghouse then sorts the checks and returns them to the banks on which they were drawn.

Each bank keeps a sum of money on deposit with the clearinghouse. The clearinghouse credits each bank's account with the total of all checks paid for other banks. It also deducts from each bank's account the total of all checks paid for that bank by other banks.

Between Banks in Different Cities

Checks paid by a bank in one city for a bank located in another city are usually cleared through a Federal Reserve bank. To see how this is done, suppose that Susan Murphy orders Christmas cards by mail from a company in New York. The card firm deposits Susan's check in the First National City Bank in New York. The First National City Bank then sends the check, together with other out-of-town checks, to the Federal Reserve Bank of New York.

Banks that are members of the Federal Reserve system, you remember, are required to keep a certain percent of their deposits as reserves. Each bank keeps its reserves in a checking account at the Federal Reserve bank in its district. This is known as its *reserve account.*

When the Federal Reserve Bank of New York receives the checks, including Susan's, from the First National City Bank, it credits the reserve account of that bank for the total amount of the checks. Susan's check is then sent for collection to the Federal Reserve bank in the ninth district. This is the district in which the Centerville National Bank is located. The sorting clerk in New York found this out from the number below the line in the upper right-hand corner of Susan's check.

The number above the line, you recall, identifies the bank on which the check is drawn. The number below the line is a routing symbol. The number below the line on Susan's check is 910. The first digit is the number of the Federal Reserve district to which the check should be sent for collection. In the case of the tenth, eleventh, and twelfth districts, there is a four-digit number below the line. A number of this kind is shown on page 195. When a routing symbol contains four digits, the first two identify the district.

The digit following the district number indicates to which Federal Reserve bank in that district the check should be sent. The 1 on Susan's check means the check should be cleared through the main Federal Reserve bank in the ninth district, and not a branch bank. The last number indicates how many days it will be before the bank that cashed the check will receive credit for it. A zero means the bank will receive credit immediately.

WHEN BANKS IN DIFFERENT CITIES ARE INVOLVED, THE FEDERAL RESERVE BANKS ACT AS THE CLEARING HOUSES.
Susan mails check for $10 to Card Company in New York,
which deposits the check in its account at
First National City Bank of New York, which credits Card Company's account with $10,
CARD COMPANY
FIRST NATIONAL CITY BANK of NEW YORK
then sends the check to
FEDERAL RESERVE BANK of NEW YORK
Federal Reserve Bank of New York, which credits the account of the First National City Bank of New York with $10,
then sends the check to
FEDERAL RESERVE BANK of MINNEAPOLIS
Federal Reserve Bank of Minneapolis, which deducts $10 from the reserve account of the Centerville National Bank,
then sends the check to
CENTERVILLE NATIONAL BANK
Centerville National Bank, which deducts the amount from Susan's account,
then sends the cancelled check back to her.

When the ninth district Federal Reserve bank, which is in Minneapolis, receives Susan's check and the others, it deducts the total amount from the Centerville National Bank's reserve account. Then

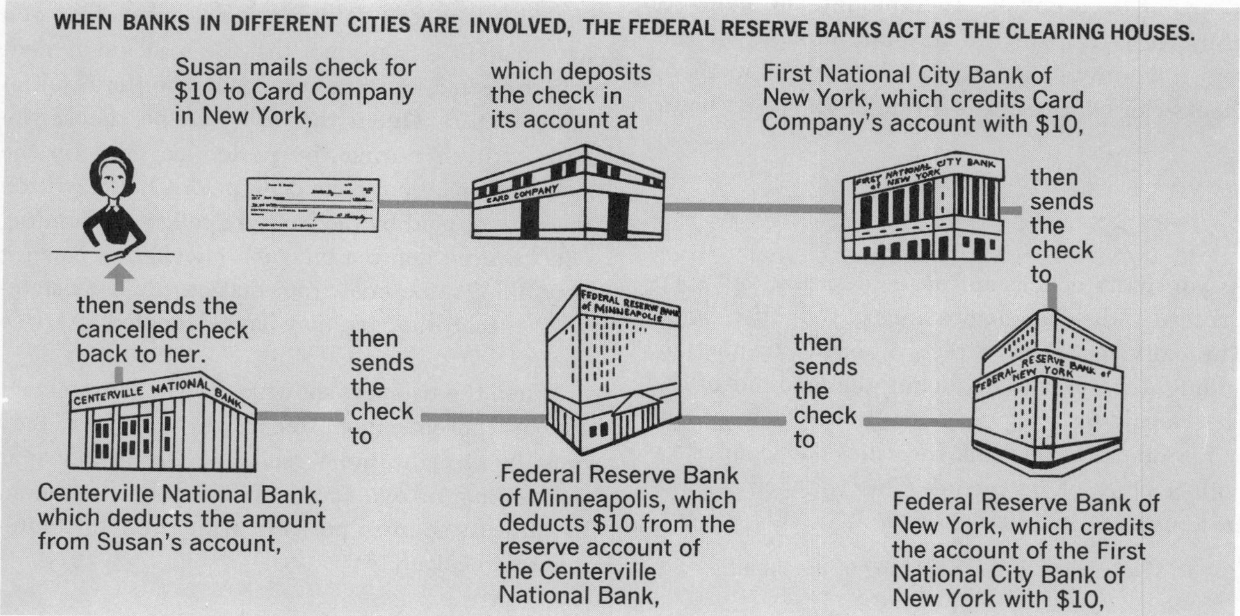

the checks are returned to the Centerville National Bank. The Centerville National Bank deducts the amount of Susan's check from her account and the amounts of the other checks from the accounts of the depositors who wrote them.

The final step in the clearing operation takes place in Washington, D. C. At the office of an institution called the Interdistrict Settlement Fund, balances are shifted from one Federal Reserve district to another. There the accounts between the New York and Minneapolis Federal Reserve banks are settled.

MACHINES ARE TAKING OVER THE JOB OF CHECK HANDLING

Each year the number of checks written in the United States increases by a billion. To speed up the handling of checks, more and more banks are installing machines to do the job. This is possible because of the coded message that is printed in magnetic ink across the bottom of every check. A machine reads this message and routes each check to its proper destination. As it reads, the machine puts in motion a printer that makes a complete record of each check—the amount, the bank on which it is drawn, the account number of the person who wrote it, and so forth. By this method, checks can be sorted at the rate of 72,000 an hour.

YOUR CHECKS COME BACK TO YOU

As you write checks and make deposits, you keep a record of the changing balance in your checkbook. The bank also keeps a record of your balance by adding deposits and deducting the amounts of the checks paid for you.

Periodically the bank furnishes each depositor with a copy of its record. This is called a ***bank statement.*** It includes:

1. The balance at the beginning of the month
2. The deposits made during the month
3. Deductions for checks paid by the bank during the month
4. The service charge, if any
5. The balance on deposit at the end of the month

With his statement the depositor receives all checks the bank has paid for him during the month. These are called ***canceled checks.***

Susan Murphy's bank statement for March, illustrated on page 217, shows that her balance at the beginning of the month was $248.46. She made two deposits: one on March 1 for $85 and one on March 15 for $70. The bank paid a total of 14 checks for Susan during March. The item followed by the letter "s" is a service charge. The service charge on Susan Murphy's checking account for the period shown on the bank statement was $1.05. Her bank balance at the end of the month, according to the bank's records, was $278.14.

Your Records May Not Agree With the Bank's

More often than not, the final balance shown on your bank statement will differ from that on your checkbook record. This does not mean that you have made a mistake, nor that the bank's statement is incorrect. The difference could be the result of other factors. One is that some of the checks you have written during the period covered by the statement may not have been paid. Checks written but not yet paid by the bank are called ***outstanding checks.*** Another reason your checkbook balance may differ sometimes from that on the bank statement is that the bank may have deducted a service charge.

When the balances shown on the bank statement and on the checkbook record do not agree, they must be brought into agreement. This is known as *reconciling,* or *balancing,* your account. It should be done as soon as possible after the bank statement is received.

STATEMENT OF ACCOUNT WITH

CENTERVILLE NATIONAL BANK

CENTERVILLE, U.S.A.

PERIOD ENDING 3-28-66

ACCOUNT NUMBER 12-34-567

Susan D. Murphy
25 Elm Street
Centerville

May we help you today?

CHECKS - LISTED IN ORDER OF PAYMENT - READ ACROSS			DEPOSITS	DATE	NEW BALANCE
					248 46
			85.00	3 1	333 46
13.12				3 1	320 34
10.24				3 4	310 10
4.64				3 6	305 46
8.25				3 9	297 21
12.00				3 10	285 21
2.75				3 12	282 46
5.98				3 14	276 48
			70.00	3 15	346 48
1.05	S			3 15	345 43
14.60				3 16	330 83
9.82				3 18	321 01
17.65				3 19	303 36
3.00				3 21	300 36
7.22		5.00		3 26	288 14
10.00				3 28	278 14

PLEASE ADVISE US OF ANY CHANGE IN ADDRESS

EXPLANATION OF SYMBOLS
R REVERSING ENTRY
M MISCELLANEOUS ENTRY
S SERVICE CHARGE
O.D. OVERDRAFT
L LISTED CHECKS

PLEASE EXAMINE AT ONCE. REPORT ANY ALTERATIONS, FORGERIES, OR OTHER IRREGULARITIES DIRECTLY TO THE CUSTOMER AUDITOR. IF NOTHING IS REPORTED WITHIN THIRTY (30) DAYS, THIS STATEMENT WILL BE CONSIDERED CORRECT.

A monthly bank statement

How to Balance Your Account

The usual method of reconciling, or balancing, involves the following steps.

1. Subtract from your checkbook balance any service charges shown on the bank statement.

2. Add to your statement balance any deposits made after the date of the statement.

3. Sort your checks by number to see if all those you have written have been returned. Add the amounts of all outstanding checks and subtract the total from the final balance shown on the bank statement.

With these adjustments your checkbook balance and your statement balance should agree. If not, compare the amount of each check with the entry in your checkbook record. If they are the same in every case, then check the arithmetic on your check stubs. If you find any errors, correct the checkbook balance. If you find an error in the statement, report it to the bank immediately.

On the backs of most bank statements a printed form is provided for use in balancing. After receiving the statement shown above, Susan Murphy used the form on the back to balance her account. This is illustrated on page 218.

On the last day of the period covered by the statement, Susan's checkbook balance was $252.91 From this amount she deducted the service charge of $1.05. This made her checkbook balance $251.86. According to the statement, Susan's balance at the end of the month was $278.14. She entered this amount on the line provided. Following "Total (1 and 2)," she again wrote the statement balance, $278.14. Had Susan made a deposit that did not

THIS FORM IS PROVIDED TO HELP YOU BALANCE YOUR ACCOUNT

Checks Outstanding – Not Charged to Account

No.	$	
63	15	58
71	10	70
TOTAL	$ 26	28

Month March 1966

1 Bank Balance Shown on this Statement $ 278.14

2 ADD + Deposits Not Credited in this Statement (if any) $

TOTAL (1 and 2) + $ 278.14

SUBTRACT Checks Outstanding $ 26.28

BALANCE $ 251.86

Should agree with your check book balance after deducting service charge (if any) shown on this statement for previous month.

A reconcilement of account

appear on the statement, she would have added this to the statement balance. But since the statement included all her deposits, Susan left this space blank on the form. Then she sorted her canceled checks and found that checks numbered 63 and 71 had not yet been paid by the bank. She listed these in the proper place on the form. The two checks totaled $26.28. She wrote this amount on the line following "Checks Outstanding" and subtracted it from the statement balance, which gave her an adjusted balance of $251.86. This brought the two balances into agreement.

PROTECT YOUR CANCELED CHECKS

Remember your canceled checks are valuable receipts. They should be kept in a safe place, the same as other types of receipts, for at least six years. Any checks you wish to destroy should be burned. Otherwise they might fall into the hands of someone who could use them to copy your signature.

BUILDING YOUR VOCABULARY

On a separate sheet of paper, write each of the terms listed in the left-hand column below and on page 219. Read the three definitions to the right of each term. After each term, copy the definition that best describes it.

1. ***bank statement***
   - *a.* A report made by a commercial bank to a Federal Reserve bank
   - *b.* A report made by a bank to a depositor showing the depositor's checking-account transactions
   - *c.* A report made by a bank to its owners showing the bank's financial condition

2. ***canceled checks***
   - *a.* Checks written but not yet paid by the bank
   - *b.* Checks that have been returned to a bank by the Federal Reserve bank
   - *c.* Checks that have been paid by the bank

3. ***clearing***
   - *a.* The process of collecting payment for checks
   - *b.* The process of transferring canceled checks from one bank to another
   - *c.* The process of recording checking-account deposits and withdrawals

4. ***clearinghouse***
   a. An agency that collects payment of checks for a number of banks
   b. An agency that serves as a bank for commercial banks
   c. An agency that sorts checks by Federal Reserve number

5. ***outstanding checks***
   a. Checks paid by the bank and returned to the drawer
   b. Checks paid by the bank but not yet returned to the drawer
   c. Checks written but not yet paid by the bank

CHECKING YOUR READING

1. Explain how the money is transferred when a person deposits in his account a check written by another depositor in the same bank.
2. Describe how checks are cleared in small communities where there is no clearinghouse.
3. How does a clearinghouse serve banks in a large city?
4. Explain how checks paid by a bank in one city for a bank in another city are usually cleared.
5. What is a reserve account? In what kind of bank is it kept?
6. What is the purpose of a check-routing symbol? Where is it located on a check?
7. What is the Interdistrict Settlement Fund and what does it do?
8. The use of checks is increasing at the rate of about a billion a year. How are banks able to handle such a large number of checks?
9. Name five kinds of information included on a bank statement.
10. What are two reasons why the balance shown on your bank statement may differ from that on your checkbook record?
11. What does reconciling your bank account mean?
12. Describe the steps to follow in reconciling your account.
13. What should you do if you find an error in your bank statement?
14. What should you do with your canceled checks? Why?
15. Why should you burn any checks you wish to destroy?

SHARING YOUR OPINION AND EXPERIENCE

1. David Austin opened a checking account at the Midland State Bank by depositting a check drawn on an out-of-town bank. The official who accepted the deposit requested that David not write any checks for two or three days. Why would a bank make such a request?
2. Why do you think banks send statements to their depositors?
3. Why should a depositor bother to keep his own check record if the bank sends him a detailed statement each month?
4. Mr. Hart keeps all his canceled checks except those made out to "Cash." Why do you think it might be unnecessary to keep checks made out to "Cash"?
5. A canceled check is evidence that payment has been made, but a check stub is not. Explain.

6. When Mr. Lindholm received his bank statement, he noticed that the amount in the "Balance" column was shown in red for two days. Why do you think the bank printed the amount in red for those days?
7. Why should a checking account be reconciled as soon as possible after the bank statement is received?
8. One day while shopping, Mrs. Wallace ran short of cash. She asked to cash a check at the Baker Co., one of the city's large department stores. Since she had a charge account at the store, Mrs. Wallace had no difficulty having a check cashed; however, she was requested to make the check payable to "Cash" rather than to the Baker Co. Why do you think the store wanted the check made to cash?

PROJECTS AND PROBLEMS

1. Grace Bradshaw has a checking account in the Augusta County Bank in Greenville. She wrote a check for $20 payable to Betty's Beauty Salon. The beauty salon deposited the check in the First Merchants Bank of Greenville. Draw a diagram similar to that shown on page 214, tracing the movement of this check from the time Grace wrote it until it was returned to her.
2. The following are routing numbers that appeared on checks received by Graham's Nursery: 213, 611, 510, 110, 723, 1211.

   For each check, indicate the following:

   ▪ *a.* The number of the Federal Reserve district to which the check should be sent for collection ▪ *b.* The location (city) of the Federal Reserve bank to which the check should be sent (Refer to the map of the Federal Reserve system on page 187.) ▪ *c.* The number of days before the bank that cashed the check will receive credit for it.

Use a form similar to the one shown below:

Check Routing Number	Federal Reserve District Number	Location of Federal Reserve Bank	Number of Days Before Bank Will Receive Credit
Example: 810	8	*St. Louis*	*None (will receive credit immediately)*

3. Henry Clark's November bank statement showed a balance of $216.27. His checkbook balance was $162.52. Checks No. 15 for $17.32, No. 17 for $24.89, and No. 19 for $12.79 were outstanding. The bank statement showed a service charge of $1.25.

   Using the procedure outlined on the form that Susan Murphy's bank supplied (page 218), prepare a reconcilement of account for Mr. Clark.
4. When Mark Bagley received his monthly statement from the bank, he prepared a reconcilement of account, using the same method as Henry Clark (problem 3). Still Mr. Bagley's checkbook balance and statement balance did not agree. List five reasons why this might have happened.

5. On August 16 the Centerville National Bank paid checks amounting to $4,362.18 drawn on the Midland State Bank. On the same day the Midland State Bank paid $3,782.93 for checks drawn on the Centerville National Bank.

▪ *a.* Which bank received money from the other at the end of the day? ▪ *b.* How much money did that bank receive?

6. On February 12 the Federal Reserve Bank of Dallas cleared checks totaling $2,375.61 drawn on the Lone Star Bank. That same day the Federal Reserve Bank collected for the Lone Star Bank checks totaling $2,741.84 that were drawn on other banks. The following day the checks drawn on the Lone Star Bank totaled $3,742.17. The checks drawn on other banks and collected for the Lone Star Bank totaled $3,585.94.

▪ *a.* Did the reserve account of the Lone Star Bank increase or decrease on February 12? ▪ *b.* What was the amount of the change on February 12? ▪ *c.* Did the Lone Star's reserve account increase or decrease on February 13? ▪ *d.* What was the amount of the change on February 13? ▪ *e.* At the end of the two-day period was the reserve account of Lone Star Bank greater or less than it was at the end of business on February 11? ▪ *f.* What was the amount of increase or decrease for the two-day period?

7. Examine a copy of a bank statement used by a bank in your community. How is it different from the statement illustrated on page 217. What, if anything, is printed on the back of it?

CHALLENGE PROBLEMS

1. When Susan Murphy deposited her paycheck in the Centerville National Bank, the bank simply traded one debt for another. Explain.
2. When depositors make withdrawals from their checking accounts, do they usually withdraw currency?
3. If a bank's depositors make more withdrawals than deposits over a period of time, what happens to the bank's reserves?
4. It has been said that improvements in methods of collecting and clearing checks have promoted the growth of checking accounts. Explain why this is true.

PART 25 OTHER METHODS OF MAKING MONEY PAYMENTS

MONEY circulates. It keeps changing hands as consumers, business enterprises, and governments spend it for goods and services. Each year the amount of money that is circulated by means of checks grows larger. In a few kinds of business transactions, however, personal checks are not acceptable as payment. This is sometimes true when a very large sum is involved. Or it might happen when the person to whom payment is owed does not know the writer of the check. Then, too, there are some people even today who do not have checking accounts. They may be young persons who are not yet earning a regular income. Or they may be persons living in meager circumstances who have little occasion to write checks. Nevertheless, payment in cash is neither wise nor convenient in all situations. Obviously there are times when other methods of transferring money are needed. And fortunately, there are other methods that are just as safe to use as ordinary checks.

What are some ways of making money payments in addition to cash and ordinary checks? What factors would determine which one to use in each case?

SPECIAL CHECKS ARE FOR TRANSFERRING LARGE SUMS

When a sizable amount of money is to be transferred, some kind of check is usually the best method. If an ordinary personal check is not acceptable, either a certified check or a cashier's check is the appropriate choice.

What Is a Certified Check?

A ***certified check*** is a personal check for which payment is guaranteed by the bank. The use of a

Courtesy American Express Company

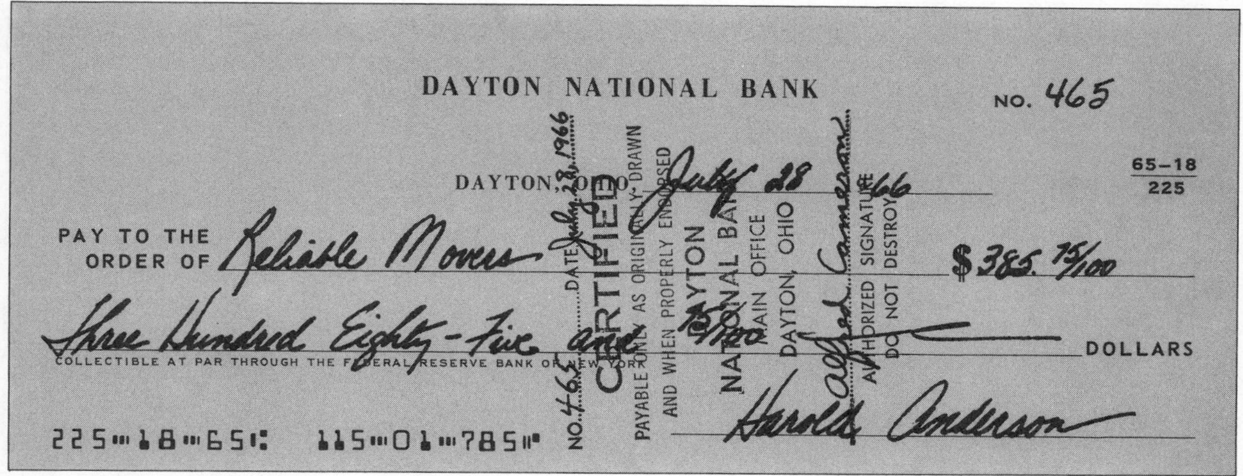
DAYTON NATIONAL BANK NO. 465

DAYTON, OHIO July 28 1966 65–18/225

PAY TO THE ORDER OF Reliable Movers $385.75/100

Three Hundred Eighty-Five and 75/100 DOLLARS

COLLECTIBLE AT PAR THROUGH THE FEDERAL RESERVE BANK OF NEW YORK

Harold Anderson

NO. 465 DATE July 28, 1966

CERTIFIED

PAYABLE ONLY AS ORIGINALLY DRAWN AND WHEN PROPERLY ENDORSED

DAYTON NATIONAL BANK MAIN OFFICE DAYTON, OHIO

AUTHORIZED SIGNATURE

DO NOT DESTROY

A certified check

certified check is often required in transactions involving the sale of real estate. As a rule, long-distance movers also request their customers to pay with a certified check. This was the case when the Anderson family moved from Dayton, Ohio, to Harrisburg, Pennsylvania.

As soon as the van had been loaded and weighed, the Andersons were told what the exact amount of the moving bill would be. The movers then asked Mr. Anderson to have a certified check for that amount ready when the family's household goods were delivered in Harrisburg. Mr. Anderson went to his bank and made out a check in the usual manner, then asked one of the bank officers to certify it. After making certain that Mr. Anderson had enough money on deposit to cover the check, the officer deducted the amount of the check from Mr. Anderson's account. This money then became the property of the bank until the check was presented for payment.

The bank officer stamped the word "Certified" and the name of the bank across the face of the check. Then he signed his name. In certifying a check the bank promises to pay it when properly endorsed. When a certified check is canceled, it is returned to the depositor with the other checks he has written.

If a certified check is not used, it should be returned to the bank. This is the only way the money that has been set aside to pay the check can be reclaimed.

What Is a Cashier's Check?

If Mr. Anderson had not had a checking account, he could have paid his moving bill with a cashier's check. A ***cashier's check*** is one that the bank draws on its own funds. It is usually signed by the cashier of the bank, which explains how the check got its name. Banks often use cashier's checks to pay their own bills.

It is not necessary to have an account with the bank in order to use a cashier's check. Anyone can buy a check of this kind simply by paying the amount of the check plus a service fee. Another name for a cashier's check is *treasurer's check.*

MONEY ORDERS ARE BEST FOR TRANSFERRING SMALL SUMS

Money payments often travel long distances. To send actual cash through the mail is unsafe, as you know. But suppose a person does not have a checking

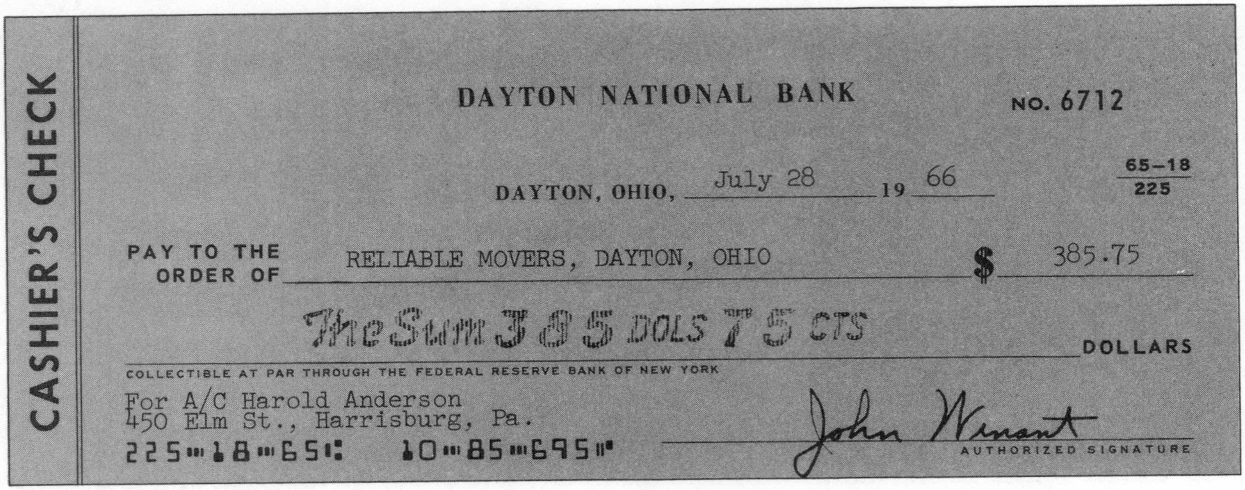

CASHIER'S CHECK

DAYTON NATIONAL BANK

NO. 6712

DAYTON, OHIO, July 28 19 66

65–18
225

PAY TO THE ORDER OF RELIABLE MOVERS, DAYTON, OHIO $ 385.75

The Sum 3 8 5 DOLS 7 5 CTS DOLLARS

COLLECTIBLE AT PAR THROUGH THE FEDERAL RESERVE BANK OF NEW YORK

For A/C Harold Anderson
450 Elm St., Harrisburg, Pa.

225⑈18⑈651⑆ 10⑈85⑈695⑈

John Winant
AUTHORIZED SIGNATURE

A cashier's check

account. Or suppose the one who is to receive the money is in a place where it would be difficult to cash a check. Unless the amount of money to be transferred is fairly large, the wise thing to do is to send a ***money order.*** Money orders are sold by most post offices, banks, telegraph companies, and express companies. Since they are made payable to a specific person, they are of no value to anyone else if lost.

Postal Money Orders

The postal money order is the type most commonly used. It is issued by one post office directing another post office to pay money to a specified business or person, or "to his order" (another person named by him).

George Hunt sent a roll of camera film to the Flash Photo Company for developing and printing together with a postal money order for $4.75 to cover the cost. The money order is illustrated on page 225. George bought the money order at the post office by paying $4.75 plus a fee. The fee varies according to the amount of money being sent. In George's case, the fee was 20 cents.

As you can see, a postal money-order form has three parts. The first part is the money order itself. The second is the purchaser's receipt. The third is the post office record. George told the postal clerk the amount he wished to send, and the clerk wrote this amount, $4.75, on each part. Following the words, "NOT VALID FOR MORE THAN," he stamped "TEN." This is done to make it difficult for anyone to increase the amount. Each part was also stamped with the date.

The clerk then detached the post office record part of the form and gave the other two parts to George. George wrote "Flash Photo Company" on the line beginning with "Pay to" and his own name and address on the next three lines. Before mailing the money order, George tore off the purchaser's receipt. He wrote the name and address of the Flash Photo Company on the back of his receipt, which he will keep in a safe place. If a money order is lost, the purchaser can obtain a duplicate by presenting his receipt at the post office where it was purchased.

A postal money order, like a check, must be endorsed by the payee. It may then be cashed at a post office or bank, or it may be transferred to a second person or firm. Ownership of a money order, however, may be transferred only once. The person or firm to whom it is endorsed must present it either to the post office or to the bank for payment.

One hundred dollars is the largest amount for

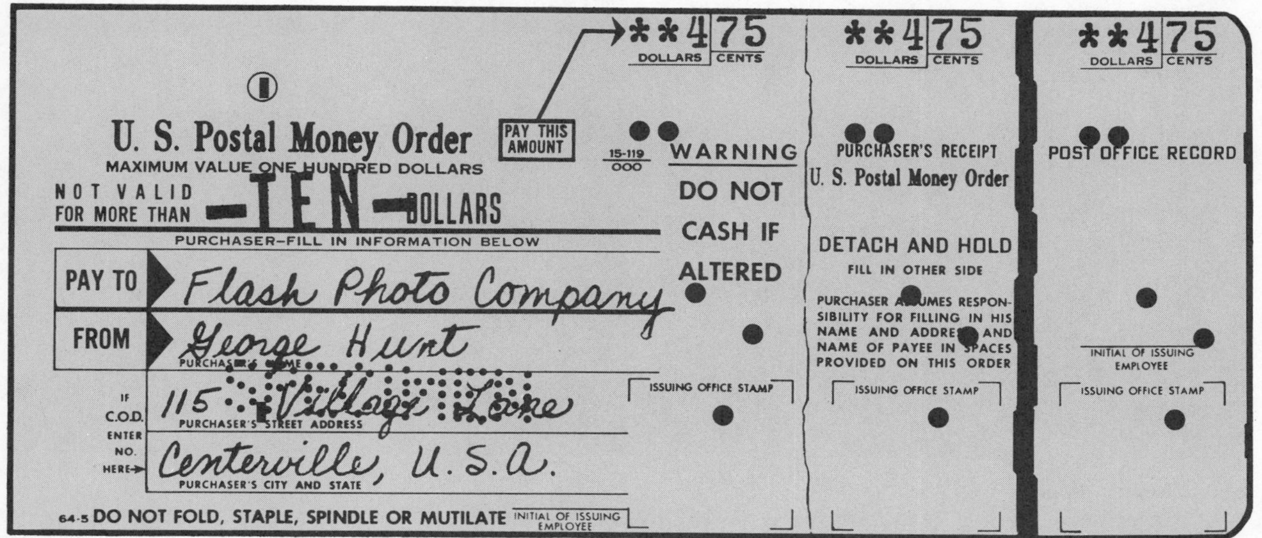

**4 75
DOLLARS CENTS

U. S. Postal Money Order
MAXIMUM VALUE ONE HUNDRED DOLLARS
NOT VALID FOR MORE THAN —TEN— DOLLARS
PAY THIS AMOUNT
15-119
000
WARNING
DO NOT CASH IF ALTERED
PURCHASER—FILL IN INFORMATION BELOW
PAY TO Flash Photo Company
FROM George Hunt
PURCHASER'S NAME
IF C.O.D. ENTER NO. HERE
115 Village Lane
PURCHASER'S STREET ADDRESS
Centerville, U.S.A.
PURCHASER'S CITY AND STATE
ISSUING OFFICE STAMP
64-5 DO NOT FOLD, STAPLE, SPINDLE OR MUTILATE
INITIAL OF ISSUING EMPLOYEE

**4 75
DOLLARS CENTS
PURCHASER'S RECEIPT
U. S. Postal Money Order
DETACH AND HOLD
FILL IN OTHER SIDE
PURCHASER ASSUMES RESPONSIBILITY FOR FILLING IN HIS NAME AND ADDRESS AND NAME OF PAYEE IN SPACES PROVIDED ON THIS ORDER
ISSUING OFFICE STAMP

**4 75
DOLLARS CENTS
POST OFFICE RECORD
INITIAL OF ISSUING EMPLOYEE
ISSUING OFFICE STAMP

A complete United States postal money order showing the detached post office record

Courtesy U.S. Post Office Department

which a single postal money order is issued. Anyone wishing to send more than that may purchase two or more orders. Or he may use some other method of making payment.

Bank Money Orders

Bank money orders are similar to postal money orders except that they are obtainable at a bank and in amounts up to $500. Suppose that instead of a postal money order George Hunt had purchased a bank money order with which to pay the Flash Photo Company. He would give the bank clerk the amount of the money order plus the service charge. The clerk would then stamp the amount on the money-order form and give it to George. He would fill in the rest of the information needed, such as the date, the name of the payee (Flash Photo Company), and his own name and address. The finished money order would have looked like the one illustrated on page 226.

The bank money-order form now in general use is made out in *triplicate;* that is, an original and two carbon copies. The original is sent to the payee. The second copy is the purchaser's receipt. The third copy is retained by the bank. When a bank money order has been paid, it is returned to the bank that issued it, where it is kept on file.

American Express Money Orders

Money orders may also be purchased from any American Express Company office or authorized agents, such as Western Union telegraph offices or the REA Express. Many supermarkets, department stores, and other retail establishments also sell American Express money orders.

Express money orders are similar to postal money orders and cost about the same. As with postal money orders, there is a limit of $100 on a single American Express money order. The buyer pays the amount he wishes to send, plus the service fee, and receives the money order and a receipt.

TELEGRAPHIC MONEY ORDERS SAVE TIME

The quickest way to send money from one point to another is by telegraphic money order. A ***telegraphic money order*** is a message from one telegraph office to another requesting that money be paid to a certain business or individual. This type of money

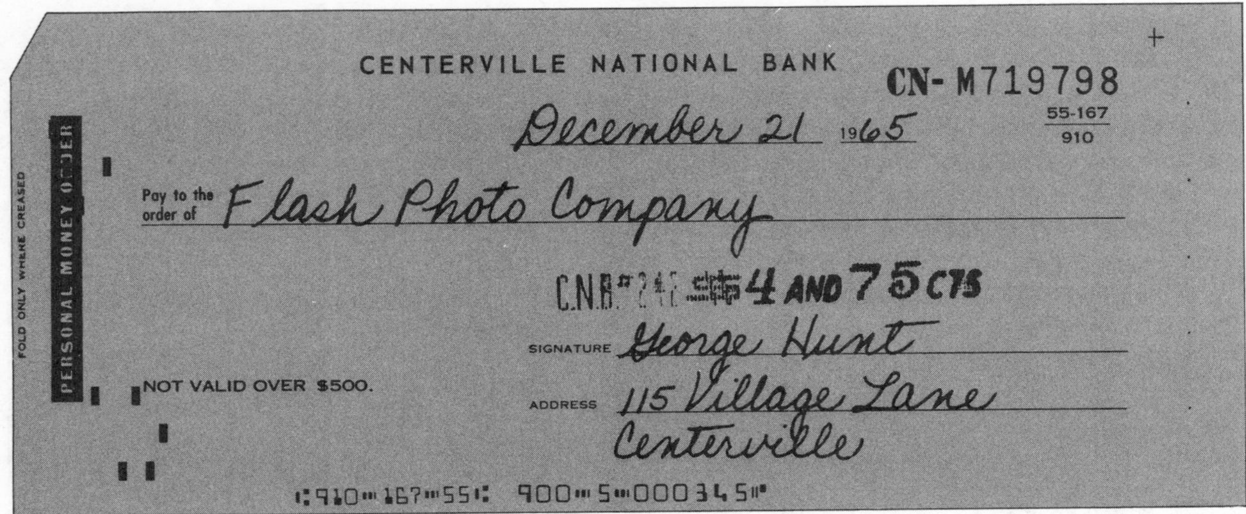

CENTERVILLE NATIONAL BANK CN-M719798

December 21 1965

55-167
910

PERSONAL MONEY ORDER

FOLD ONLY WHERE CREASED

Pay to the order of Flash Photo Company

C.N.B.#2 $4 AND 75 CTS

SIGNATURE George Hunt

NOT VALID OVER $500.

ADDRESS 115 Village Lane
Centerville

⑆910⑈167⑈55⑆ 900⑈5⑈0003451⑈

Courtesy The Chase Manhattan Bank

A bank money order

order should not be confused with express money orders, which are also sold by telegraph offices. Any amount can be sent by telegraphic money order.

Suppose that Mr. Crowley, who lives in Springfield, Illinois, wanted to send $150 to his son, Bruce, who is attending college in Berkeley, California. Bruce needed the money urgently. Mr. Crowley went to the nearest telegraph office and filled out a money-order form. He gave the form, together with the money to be sent, to the telegraph clerk who gave Mr. Crowley a receipt. The clerk then sent a message to the telegraph office in Berkeley ordering that office to pay $150 to Bruce Crowley. Bruce received the money in a very short while after the message was sent.

To be certain that no one but his son would be paid the money, Mr. Crowley supplied information for a question that only his son could answer. This is called a *test question.* You will notice in the illustration on page 227 that space is provided for the information at the bottom of the form. Mr. Crowley's question was "What is the name of Grandmother Crowley's cat?" The answer was "Samantha." Before the telegraph office in Berkeley paid the money to Bruce, he had to answer the question correctly. When sending a telegraphic money order, you may include a test question or not, as you wish.

An American Express money order

Courtesy American Express Company

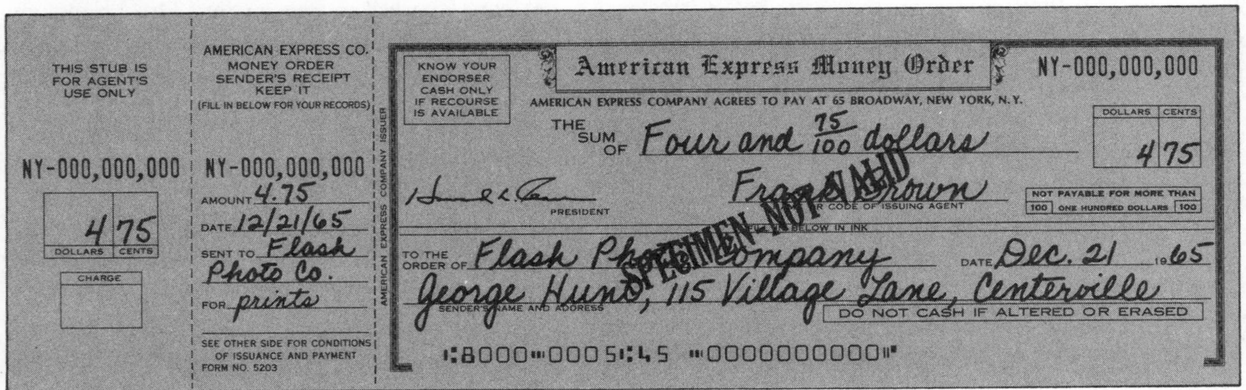

THIS STUB IS FOR AGENT'S USE ONLY

NY-000,000,000

4 75
DOLLARS CENTS

CHARGE

AMERICAN EXPRESS CO. MONEY ORDER SENDER'S RECEIPT KEEP IT

(FILL IN BELOW FOR YOUR RECORDS)

NY-000,000,000

AMOUNT 4.75

DATE 12/21/65

SENT TO Flash Photo Co.

FOR prints

SEE OTHER SIDE FOR CONDITIONS OF ISSUANCE AND PAYMENT FORM NO. 5203

AMERICAN EXPRESS COMPANY ISSUER

KNOW YOUR ENDORSER CASH ONLY IF RECOURSE IS AVAILABLE

American Express Money Order NY-000,000,000

AMERICAN EXPRESS COMPANY AGREES TO PAY AT 65 BROADWAY, NEW YORK, N.Y.

THE SUM OF Four and 75/100 dollars

DOLLARS CENTS 4 75

PRESIDENT

Frank Brown

SPECIMEN NOT VALID

NOT PAYABLE FOR MORE THAN 100 ONE HUNDRED DOLLARS 100

TO THE ORDER OF Flash Photo Company DATE Dec. 21 1965

George Hunt, 115 Village Lane, Centerville

SENDER'S NAME AND ADDRESS

DO NOT CASH IF ALTERED OR ERASED

⑆8000⑈0005⑆45 ⑈0000000000⑈

YOU CAN SEND A MESSAGE WITH YOUR MONEY *Only* A FEW CENTS MORE

WESTERN UNION TELEGRAPHIC MONEY ORDER

WU72 (R5-62)

THE FASTEST AND SAFEST WAY TO SEND OR RECEIVE MONEY

W. P. MARSHALL, PRESIDENT

Send the following Money Order subject to conditions below and on back hereof, which are hereby agreed to:

ACCTG. INFM.	CHECK	OFFICE	DATE AND FILING TIME

SENDING DATA

$ AMT. | $ CHGS. | TOLLS | ¢ TAX | TOTAL

DO NOT WRITE ABOVE THIS LINE

PAY AMOUNT: ONE HUNDRED FIFTY (PRINT AMOUNT DOLLARS) DOLLARS AND NO (FIGURES) CENTS (SHOW CAU OR VIG AS APPROPRIATE)

TO: BRUCE CROWLEY (PLEASE PRINT. IF WOMAN, GIVE MRS. OR MISS) (CARE OF OR APT. NO.)

ADDRESS: 500 VERNON STREET (STREET AND NUMBER) BERKELEY, CALIFORNIA (CITY AND STATE)

SENDER'S NAME: HOWARD CROWLEY

DELIVER THE FOLLOWING MESSAGE WITH THE MONEY:

Unless signed below the Telegraph Company is directed to pay this money order at my risk to such person as its paying agent believes to be the above named payee, personal identification being waived. Foreign money orders excepted.

Howard Crowley (SENDER'S FULL NAME)

85 Lincoln Drive, Springfield, Ill. (SENDER'S ADDRESS) 232-6291 (TELEPHONE NUMBER)

Information for test question: Grandmother Crowley's cat named Samantha

Application for a telegraphic money order

Courtesy Western Union

As you might expect, this method of transferring money is more expensive than any of the others. But when speed is important, the saving in time may be worth the extra cost. No extra charge is made for including a test question. Had Mr. Crowley sent a message with the money order, however, there would have been an additional charge for that. Overnight telegraphic money-order service is also available at a lower cost than regular service. Had Mr. Crowley used overnight service, Bruce would have received the money the following morning instead of the same day.

TRAVELER'S CHECKS ARE FOR THOSE ON THE GO

It may be fairly easy to cash checks close to home where you are known or can be identified easily. But when traveling in another part of the country where you are a stranger, you may have difficulty getting others to accept your personal check. Carrying large amounts of cash around with you, however, is risky. What you should have is a money substitute that will be readily accepted by others, but which can be replaced if lost or stolen.

Courtesy Western Union

THIS ORDER MAY BE CASHED BY ANYONE TO WHOM THE PAYEE IS KNOWN

WESTERN UNION MONEY ORDER 1-2/210

ISSUED AT Berkeley, California (CITY AND STATE) May 5, 1966 (DATE)

When Countersigned at Point of Issue Pay to Bruce Crowley OR ORDER

THE SUM OF One Hundred Fifty and no/100 DOLLARS $ 150.00

SPECIMEN

TELEGRAPHED FROM Springfield, Illinois (ORIGINATING POINT) May 6, 1966 (DATE) NUMBER ZW36931

THE CHASE MANHATTAN BANK
EIGHTEEN PINE STREET,
NEW YORK, N. Y.

COUNTERSIGNED

MONEY ORDER AGENT

THE WESTERN UNION TELEGRAPH COMPANY

TREASURER

⑆0210⑉0002⑆ 910⑉3⑉000049⑈

A telegraphic money order

KEEP UNUSED CHEQUES FOR FUTURE TRIPS
AND UNEXPECTED EXPENSES
Good Until Used No Time Limit
U.S. DOLLAR TRAVELERS CHEQUE
WHEN COUNTERSIGNED BELOW WITH THIS SIGNATURE
DA28·531·824
John Traveler
BEFORE CASHING WRITE HERE CITY AND DATE
19
American Express Company
AT 65 BROADWAY, NEW YORK, N.Y.
$20.00
Pay this Cheque to the Order of
IN UNITED STATES
TWENTY DOLLARS
IN ALL OTHER COUNTRIES
COUNTERSIGN HERE IN PRESENCE OF PERSON CASHING
PRESIDENT

Courtesy American Express Company

An American Express Traveler's Cheque

Such a substitute is a ***traveler's check*** shown above.

Traveler's checks can be purchased from a bank, an express company, a telegraph office, and at some of the larger railroad and bus company offices. They are issued in amounts of $10, $20, $50, and $100. If you are on a trip where you will be paying out money in many small amounts, it is advisable to buy checks in the smaller denominations. If you expect to make any payments for large amounts, carry some $50 or $100 checks.

At the time of purchase, the buyer signs each traveler's check in the presence of the agent issuing it. When a check is cashed, it is signed again in the presence of the person cashing it. This person compares the two signatures to see that they are identical. Traveler's checks will be accepted almost anywhere in the world.

The most valuable thing about a traveler's check is that if it is lost or stolen before it is signed the second time, its face value will be refunded to the owner. When you buy a book of these checks, you should keep a record of each check by denomination and serial number. Whenever a check is cashed, make a note on your record of the date and of the person or business who cashed it. In case of loss or theft, notify the agency that issued the checks. Your record will make it possible to supply the agency with the serial numbers of the missing checks.

As one company that issues traveler's checks advertises, "Never carry more cash than you can afford to lose."

BUILDING YOUR VOCABULARY

Copy the five sentences below, completing each one by replacing the question mark with the appropriate term from the column at the left.

cashier's check
certified check
money order
telegraphic money order
traveler's check

1. A means of making money payments that may be purchased at post offices or banks is a ? .
2. A check that must be signed in the presence of the person who cashes it is a ? .
3. A check that a bank draws on its own funds is a ? .
4. A personal check for which payment is guaranteed by the bank is a ? .
5. The quickest way to send money from one place to another is by ? .

CHECKING YOUR READING

1. Why are personal checks sometimes not acceptable as payment in business transactions?
2. When is it best to use either a certified check or a cashier's check in making a money payment?
3. How does a person obtain a certified check?
4. What should one do with a certified check that is not used? Why?
5. Is it necessary to have an account at a bank in order to get a cashier's check? Explain.
6. How does a cashier's check differ from a certified check?
7. When would a person send a money order instead of a personal check?
8. How does a person obtain a postal money order?
9. Why should the purchaser of a postal money order keep his receipt?
10. How many times may ownership of a postal money order be transferred?
11. What is one important difference between a postal money order and a bank money order?
12. In what ways are express money orders like postal money orders?
13. What is the purpose of the test question that is sometimes sent with a telegraphic money order?
14. In what two ways does a telegraphic money order differ from other money orders?
15. Why are traveler's checks better than personal checks when you are away from home?
16. How does the person who accepts a traveler's check in payment for goods or services identify the person who presents it?
17. What is the most valuable feature of traveler's checks?
18. Which means of making money payments discussed in this part are available at banks?

SHARING YOUR OPINION AND EXPERIENCE

1. Why do you think a certified check or a cashier's check is often required in the purchase of real estate?
2. Would it be safe to accept a certified check from a stranger? Explain.
3. Suppose you were in a strange city and telephoned your father to send you $75. Would it be better for him to send a money order or a personal check? Why?
4. When might a person buy a bank money order instead of a postal money order?
5. Mr. Holman sent a telegraphic money order to his son in Texas. The son received the money a few minutes after it was sent. The money did not travel over the wire, of course. What did take place?
6. With every book of traveler's checks there is a form on which the purchaser can list the serial numbers of his checks. Printed on this form is this statement: "Detach . . . carry separate from wallet." Why do you think this is a good suggestion?

PROJECTS AND PROBLEMS

1. Study the illustration of the postal money order on page 225, and answer the following questions:

   ▪ *a.* Who is the payee? ▪ *b.* Who purchased the money order? ▪ *c.* Where does the purchaser live? ▪ *d.* How much money will the payee receive? ▪ *e.* Who is responsible for writing in the name of the payee?

2. Which of the methods of making payments discussed in this part might be used to advantage in each of the following situations?

   ▪ *a.* To send payment through the mail for an expensive diamond ring you want shipped immediately ▪ *b.* To send a small amount of money to a friend who is visiting in a strange city ▪ *c.* To send $175 through the mail if you did not have a checking account ▪ *d.* To pay for meals and lodging while on a vacation trip ▪ *e.* To be sure a payment arrives in a distant city the same day it is sent ▪ *f.* To send $10 through the mail after 6 p.m. if you did not have a checking account ▪ g. To send $1,500 through the mail if you did not have a checking account

3. List the name of the place (or places, if there is more than one) in your community where you may obtain each of the following:

   ▪ *a.* postal money order ▪ *b.* bank money order ▪ *c.* certified check ▪ *d.* telegraphic money order ▪ *e.* express money order ▪ *f.* cashier's check ▪ g. traveler's check.

4. The table below shows the fees charged for postal money orders.

Amount of Order	*Fee*
$ 0.01 to $ 10.00	$0.20
10.01 to 50.00	0.30
50.01 to 100.00	0.35

What fee would you have to pay for each of the following money orders?

▪ *a.* $4.76 ▪ *b.* $13.85 ▪ *c.* $92.70 ▪ *d.* $27.42 ▪ *e.* $50.00 ▪ *f.* $7.22 ▪ *g.* $82.20 ▪ *h.* $10.00 ▪ *i.* $7.01

5. What would be the total fee for all money orders listed in problem 4?
6. How much money would a person need to buy all money orders listed in problem 4?
7. The following item is part of an article that appeared in a well-known news magazine. Read the item, then answer the questions that follow it.

USE OF TRAVELER'S CHECKS GROWS

New York. The sale of traveler's checks has grown from zero in 1891, when the American Express Company devised them, to $8.3 billion this year. Approximately 40,000 banks, travel agents, and other businesses around the world sell American Express traveler's checks today. In addition, at least five large banks also issue and sell their own traveler's checks.

Those who sell traveler's checks estimate that they have tapped only 25 percent of the travel market. In the future, they will aim for new sales further down the economic ladder and for greater sales in foreign countries.

The average traveler's check does not return to the issuing company for up to two months. The amount of checks that have not been returned for payment is highest in midsummer when travel is at a peak. It is lowest in early winter when travel is at a low point.

▪ *a.* When were traveler's checks first used? ▪ *b.* What company first issued them? ▪ *c.* How many different kinds of traveler's checks are there today? ▪ *d.* According to the estimates, what percent of the people who travel now use these checks? ▪ *e.* How do the companies that sell traveler's checks expect to increase their sales in the future? ▪ *f.* What does "further down the economic ladder" mean? ▪ *g.* How long does it take the average traveler's check to return to the issuing company? ▪ *h.* When is the amount of traveler's checks that have not been returned for payment highest? When is it lowest?

CHALLENGE PROBLEMS

1. The cashier's check illustrated on page 224 has the words "collectible at par" printed on it. What does this expression mean?
2. What is a bank draft? How does it differ from a cashier's check?
3. Special money orders may be used to send money to foreign countries. Where do you think you could find out about obtaining one of these money orders?
4. When people travel in foreign countries, they sometimes take with them a *letter of credit.* What is a letter of credit and how is it used?

CONTENTS OF UNIT 6

Unit 6 / Building Financial Security

PART 26 SAVING AND INVESTING

IN the course of a lifetime most people earn a small fortune. If you work for 40 years and your average pay is $100 a week, your total earnings will be $208,000. How much of this you will still have at the end of the 40 years, however, will depend on your ability to save. Saving, like spending, has to be planned. One of the characteristics of a good budget, remember, is that it provides for systematic saving.

Saving is the storing up of purchasing power. You save by not spending all your income or allowance on goods and services to be consumed. In other words, you keep some money, or purchasing power, in reserve. For as long as you keep it, this reserve is *savings.*

How does saving benefit an individual or a family personally? Should everyone save the same amount? If spending encourages production and creates jobs, does saving hold down total production?

Ewing Galloway

WHY SAVE?

People have different motives for saving. Some save simply because having money gives them more pleasure than spending it. Most savers, however, have a definite purpose in mind. For many it is a short-term goal. They are accumulating the funds needed to buy something they want fairly soon. It may be Christmas presents, a vacation, an air-conditioner, or the down payment on a house. Others have long-term goals, like a college education, retirement, or a business of their own. And some save for security or peace of mind; that is, they're safeguarding their plans for the future by building a reserve fund. This is a fund that will enable them to weather misfortune or to take advantage of opportunities, as the case may be. Perhaps you remember the boy who got a bargain on a set of secondhand drums because he had made a habit of saving a part of his weekly allowance. Then there was the man who was offered a better position in another city. His savings made it possible for him to move his family and accept the position.

Saving offers many rewards. Those who save not only have the satisfaction of seeing their dreams come true, but also avoid having to pay credit charges. Besides that, having money in reserve is like having a big umbrella for rainy days. You may never have to use it, but it is wonderful to have in case you need it. Best of all, if wisely invested, savings can provide extra income. More will be said about this later.

HOW MUCH SHOULD YOU SAVE?

Although authorities recommend that people save at least 10 percent of their incomes, there is no rule that can apply to everyone. The amount anyone can save depends on both his income and financial responsibilities. A large family with a low income might find it difficult to save anything at all. On the other hand, an unmarried man who is working and is responsible only for himself probably could save a large portion of his income.

Incomes and responsibilities change from time to time. And as they change, the percent of income that can be saved also changes. Newlyweds should find it easier to save before children arrive than afterward. As family responsibilities increase, the percent of income saved may have to be decreased. When children marry and leave home, the percent of income saved can again be increased. Unfortunately, many people fail to save enough when they are in a position to save the most.

SUCCESSFUL SAVERS FOLLOW THESE RULES

Saving is easy for some people; hard work for others. Those who do not save usually give as a reason that they do not earn enough. As has been pointed out, the ability to save does depend to a large extent on income. In general the more people earn, the more they save. Nevertheless, people whose incomes are so low that they cannot save at all are few in number. Most people can save some money without too great a sacrifice. But it takes willpower. To save you have to deny yourself the satisfaction of some present want. In other words, you have to make a choice.

The secret of successful saving is found in these five simple rules:

1. Decide How Much to Save. The best idea is to start small. One reason many people fail to carry through with their saving plans is that they try to save too much. Then they run short of money between paydays and have to dip into their savings. After this happens a few times, they become discouraged and give up trying to save altogether.

2. Save Regularly. Each time you receive your allowance or other income, pay your savings first. In the beginning this is more important than the amount saved. The reason is that, if done regularly, saving soon becomes a habit. And it is surprising how quickly even small sums add up. Just 20 cents a week will provide a fund of $10.40 in a year. And how many times during a year do you have use for an extra five or ten dollars?

3. Save for Something. Only misers save just to accumulate money. To save successfully most people need a definite goal. The principle of real cost

"REAL COST" APPLIES TO SAVINGS, TOO.

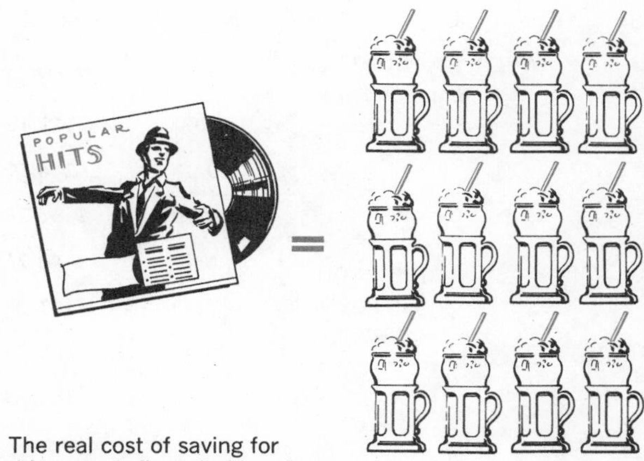

The real cost of saving for this record album is 12 sodas.

applies to saving the same as it does to any other choice. The real cost of saving, of course, is the thing you would most likely buy if you spent the money instead. Choose for your goal, therefore, something more important to you than anything you could buy right now. Then keep reminding yourself that you are saving for a record album, or a used car, or whatever it is. This way you will find as much satisfaction in saving as you do in spending. Unless you are an experienced saver, it is advisable to choose a goal you can reach in a fairly short time.

4. Put Savings to Work. Savings kept in a box under the bed or in a jar on the shelf are idle. They are not circulating and doing the work money is supposed to do. If all savings were just stored away until needed, total production would fall. Savings deposited in a bank, on the other hand, are put to work by the bank. As you learned from your study of credit, they are loaned to people who want to build houses or buy cars and other durable goods. They are also loaned to businessmen who want to buy or build machines, factories, stores, office buildings, and other capital goods. Thus, money saved and deposited in a bank is spent by others.

In return for the use of their depositors' money, banks pay interest. Dan Marty has a savings account with a bank where the interest rate on time deposits is $3\frac{3}{4}$ percent. This means that for every dollar he has on deposit for a year the bank pays him $3\frac{3}{4}$ cents. In other words, his savings earn an income. Putting savings to work earning income is called ***investing.***

5. Start Saving as Early in Life as Possible. Invested savings grow. The younger you are when you start saving and investing, the more opportunity your money has to earn and grow. Dan Marty's case is a good example. Dan deposits $5 each week in his savings account. In a year he will have saved $260. During that time his money will have earned $4.78 interest. The bank will pay the inter-

		1 Year	*3 Years*	*5 Years*	*10 Years*
WHEN YOU DEPOSIT WEEKLY	$ 1.00	$ 52.72	$164.70	$ 285.38	$ 629.63
	2.00	105.80	329.83	571.27	1,259.94
	3.00	158.80	494.90	857.04	1,890.09
	4.00	211.75	659.89	1,142.89	2,520.26
	5.00	264.78	824.96	1,428.59	3,150.43
WHEN YOU DEPOSIT SEMIMONTHLY	$ 2.00	$ 48.67	$152.08	$ 263.50	$ 581.39
	3.00	73.20	228.36	395.53	872.41
	4.00	97.69	304.57	527.49	1,163.38
	5.00	122.19	380.84	659.50	1,454.44
	10.00	244.50	761.80	1,319.21	2,909.22
WHEN YOU DEPOSIT MONTHLY	$ 3.00	$ 36.39	$114.08	$ 197.77	$ 436.42
	4.00	48.71	152.28	263.89	582.22
	5.00	61.07	190.58	330.12	728.11
	10.00	122.35	381.35	660.47	1,456.61
	15.00	183.63	572.22	990.91	2,185.23

All tables include interest at 3¾% per year compounded quarterly.

est by adding it to the principal in Dan's account. The ***principal*** is the amount of money that has been invested. In Dan's case, the principal would be $260. With the addition of interest, his total savings will be $264.78. If left in his account, the interest on his savings will also earn interest. When interest is paid on both the principal and interest already earned, it is called ***compound interest.***

Now suppose Dan continues to deposit $5 a week in his savings account. In five years he will have saved $1,300. If the bank continues to pay $3\frac{3}{4}$ percent interest during that time, and he leaves the interest in his account, he will have $1,428.59. In other words, his savings will have earned $118.59.

At only 2 percent interest compounded yearly, a given amount of money will double in about 35 years. At 4 percent, it will double in half that time.

SAVINGS MAY BE INVESTED IN SEVERAL WAYS

A savings account is only one way to invest savings. Another way is to purchase bonds issued by a government or a corporation. Some people invest their savings in a home or other forms of real estate. Some buy business enterprises and become their owners. Others become part owners of business enterprises by purchasing shares of stock in corporations. You may remember that the Centerville Brick and Tile Company was formed with money its stockholders invested in shares. Approximately 80 percent of the families in the United States are investing at least a part of their savings in life insurance. Each of these different ways of putting money to work is an *investment.*

In Part 15 you learned that the purchase of capital goods is called an investment. Capital goods, as you know, are tools, factories, machines, or any product used in production. Production, of course, results in income; so do invested savings. Now you see why the term "investment" fits in both cases.

THE NATURE OF INVESTMENTS VARIES

Investments differ in important ways. Some are suitable for long-term goals but not for short ones. Some require a big outlay of money all at one time.

Ewing Galloway

Saving can be fun when the goal is a vacation trip for the whole family.

Others provide an opportunity for the small investor. With some investments you can get your money back almost any time you want it. With others you might have to wait or lose part of the money you had invested. When money can be obtained from an investment quickly and without loss, the investment is said to be ***liquid.***

There are investments that you not only know will pay a return, you also know how much the return will be. And there are investments that guarantee nothing in the way of a return. The ***return*** is the income from an investment. If a person keeps his savings in a bank that pays 4 percent interest, the rate of return on his invested savings is 4 percent.

Why Are Some Investments Called Risky?

Another way investments differ is in the degree and kind of risk involved. One of the important things to understand about investments, however, is why some are considered risky and others safe. An investment is called "safe" if its dollar value remains constant. If its dollar value is subject to change—moves either up or down—it is termed "risky." It is risky because, if its value falls, it will be worth less than you paid for it.

An investment, you see, is something you buy. You exchange your savings for a bank deposit, property, a bond, or a share of stock. If you buy a so-called safe investment, you know that, when you want your money back, you will get a certain number of dollars. But suppose you buy an investment that changes in value. At the very time you want your money back, it may be worth less than you paid for it. In fact, the investment may never again be worth as much as you paid for it. This is the risk people take when they buy this type of investment. Why would anyone take such a chance when there are safer investments? Because in time an investment that changes in value may be worth a great deal more than was paid for it. In short, where there is risk, there is also the possibility of considerable gain.

Nevertheless, don't be fooled by the fact that some investments are called safe. There is even a risk with these investments. But it is a risk of a different kind as you will learn in the next part.

INVESTMENTS SHOULD BE CHOSEN WITH CARE

An investment that is ideal for one person might not suit another at all. The reason is that people with money to invest also differ. They differ in such important ways as age, income, financial responsibilities, and the amount available for investing. These are all factors to be taken into consideration when choosing an investment.

Naturally, the less money a person has to invest, the less risk he can afford to take. That is why your first investments should be those that provide the greatest safety for your money. Someone who already has one or more safe investments might be willing to risk some money in the hope of making a gain. If he should lose part or all of the money in one investment, he would still have the others. Furthermore, a person who is making his first investment, or saving for a short-term goal, is wise to choose a liquid investment. In other words, whether an investment is a wise or an unwise choice depends on the circumstances of the investor. The ***investor,*** of course, is the person who does the investing.

BUILDING YOUR VOCABULARY

List the figures 1 to 7 on a sheet of paper, numbering down. Read the seven statements given below at the right; then, for each statement, select from the column at the left the term that best matches it in meaning. Write this term next to the appropriate number.

compound interest	1. The storing up of purchasing power
investing	2. Putting savings to work to earn an income
investor	3. Interest paid on both principal and previously earned interest
liquid	4. Easily turned into cash without loss
principal	5. The interest or other income received from an investment
return	6. One who puts his savings to work
saving	7. A sum of money that has been invested

CHECKING YOUR READING

1. Why do most people save?
2. Give examples of how saving may give a person peace of mind.
3. What are some rewards of saving?
4. What two factors determine how much a person can save?
5. Why is it wise for a young couple to start saving as soon as they are married?
6. How does saving involve making a choice?
7. Give five rules for developing a successful savings plan.
8. Why is it wise to save only a small amount when you begin a savings program?
9. Why is it important to save regularly?
10. What is the real cost of saving?
11. Explain how savings deposited in a bank are put to work.
12. How does investing money help the investor?
13. Why is it wise to begin saving as early in life as possible?
14. Explain how compound interest helps savings grow.
15. What are some ways, other than savings accounts, in which people may invest their savings?
16. What are some important ways in which investments differ?
17. When is an investment considered to be "safe"?
18. What is a "risky" investment?
19. Why are some people willing to buy risky investments?
20. Why should your first investments be those that provide the greatest safety for your money?
21. What determines whether a particular investment is wise or unwise?

SHARING YOUR OPINION AND EXPERIENCE

1. In what way is saving similar to buying on installments?
2. Authorities recommend that people save 10 percent of their incomes. Is 10 percent of your allowance and other income a reasonable amount for you to save? Why or why not?

3. Jerry Calhoun says that he does not save regularly because the amount he can afford to save is too small. Is this a good reason? Explain.
4. How do you help other people by investing your savings?
5. What is the relationship of wise money management to a savings program?
6. Why is it important for a person to have some liquid investments?
7. Explain how the money people have saved and invested in the past has helped our economy grow.
8. Would you expect the return to be higher on a safe investment or on a risky investment? Explain.
9. Savings hidden in a jar are idle and cannot do the work money should do. Can you think of any other reasons why savings should not be kept in a jar?

PROJECTS AND PROBLEMS

1. To save successfully, most people need a purpose for saving. List as many reasons as you can think of why a young person your age might want to save.
2. If a person saves regularly, even small amounts quickly add up to a surprising sum. How much would you accumulate in just one year if you saved the following amounts?

   ▪ *a.* $0.50 a week ▪ *b.* $2.50 a month ▪ *c.* $5.00 a week ▪ *d.* $10.00 twice monthly ▪ *e.* $15.00 a month ▪ *f.* $0.15 a day

3. At least seven different ways of investing money were mentioned in this part. List these ways in the order in which you would choose them if you were beginning a savings program. Number your first choice 1, the second 2, and so on. Place a check mark before each investment that you consider to be liquid.
4. On page 236 there is a table showing how different amounts saved regularly will grow when deposited in a savings account at $3\frac{3}{4}$% interest compounded quarterly. For example, if a person deposited $1 every week, he would have $285.38 at the end of 5 years. After 10 years, he would have $629.63. Use the table to answer the following questions.

   ▪ *a.* If a person deposited $3 monthly, how much money would he have in his savings account at the end of 5 years? ▪ *b.* How much would he have deposited? ▪ *c.* How much interest would his savings have earned? ▪ *d.* If he continued depositing $3 monthly, how much would he have in his savings account at the end of 10 years? ▪ *e.* How much of the money in his account after 10 years would be earned interest?

5. Using the table on page 236 determine how much a person's total accumulated savings would be if he made regular deposits as follows:

   ▪ *a.* $3 a week for 3 years ▪ *b.* $2 twice a month for 1 year ▪ *c.* $4 monthly for 1 year ▪ *d.* $5 monthly for 10 years ▪ *e.* $10 monthly for 5 years

6. In each case in problem 5, how much of the total amount accumulated would be interest?
7. Using the table on page 236 determine how often and about how much you would have to deposit in a savings account at $3\frac{3}{4}$% interest to accumulate the following sums. Select the amount that would bring you closest to your goal.

   ▪ *a.* \$100 in 1 year ▪ *b.* \$750 in 3 years ▪ *c.* \$1,000 in 5 years ▪ *d.* \$2,000 in 10 years ▪ *e.* the largest amount shown on the table in 10 years

8. Some of the following investments are generally considered safe, and others are considered risky. On the left half of a sheet of paper, list those that you think are safe. On the right half of the same sheet, list those you think are risky.

   ▪ *a.* home ▪ *b.* bank savings account ▪ *c.* corporation bonds ▪ *d.* land ▪ *e.* government bonds ▪ *f.* loan to an acquaintance ▪ *g.* insurance ▪ *h.* shares of stock

9. One reason some people save is to buy Christmas gifts for their families and friends. Many banks encourage this kind of saving by inviting their customers to deposit money regularly in Christmas Club accounts. Some time before Christmas each year the accumulated savings are returned to the depositors.

   The following article about Christmas Club savings appeared in the Centerville paper in November of a recent year. Read the article and answer the questions that follow it.

CHRISTMAS SAVINGS MELON IS $6,700,000

Centerville.—Christmas savings-club checks amounting to an estimated \$6,700,000 are being paid out to some 64,000 accounts in the Centerville area this week. This figure represents a slight drop from last year, when \$6,737,492 was paid out to 76,300 accounts.

The flood of money, saved over a 50-week period, is released annually into the economy just prior to the Christmas shopping season. The benefits to the economy are shown in a survey of the savers made by the Christmas Club Corporation. The survey shows that 38.1 percent of the money will actually be used for Christmas purchases, 31 percent for savings and investment, 12.5 percent for taxes, and the remainder for miscellaneous purposes.

Nationwide the Associated Press reported that 14,750,000 Christmas Club members saved \$1,774,172,000 this year. The money is being distributed by 9,900 banks and savings-and-loan institutions throughout the country. The total compares with savings of \$1,659,430,000 last year.

▪ *a.* Were the Christmas Club savings in the Centerville area for the year reported greater or less than for the previous year? by how much? ▪ *b.* Was the number of Christmas Club accounts up or down over the year before? by how many? ▪ *c.* What percent of the money saved will actually be used for Christmas purchases? ▪ *d.* What percent will be kept as savings? ▪ *e.* For what other major purpose will the money be used? ▪ *f.* What is the percent remaining to be used for miscellaneous purposes? ▪ g. How many people throughout the country saved money in Christmas Clubs during the year? ▪ *h.* How much did they save all together? ▪ *i.* Nationally, what was the average amount saved per account?

CHALLENGE PROBLEMS

1. Refer to your answers for problem 4 of the Projects and Problems section. Is the amount of interest earned by saving $3 monthly for 10 years (*e*) exactly twice the amount earned in 5 years (*c*)? If not, explain why.
2. According to the table on page 236, if a person saved $10 monthly for 10 years, he would have $1,456.61 including interest earned. Saving the same amount monthly, how long would it take to accumulate $1,456.61 if his savings earned no interest?
3. The newspaper article reprinted for problem 9 of the Projects and Problems section mentions the "benefits" of the Christmas Club savings to the economy. In what way or ways would the economy benefit from this money?
4. Many authorities say that one characteristic of a good investment is that it pays a reasonable return. What is a reasonable return?
5. It has been said that there is no such thing as a perfect investment. Explain why.

PART 27 SAVINGS ACCOUNTS AND SAVINGS BONDS

DAY after day people go without things they would like to have in order to save money. Then they risk losing their savings by investing them unwisely. The interesting fact about investment losses, however, is that they most often occur because people attempt to get rich too fast.

The purpose of saving and investing is to build financial security; and, as when building anything else, it is important to start with a good foundation. The best foundation is safe investments. Two such investments are savings accounts and United States savings bonds. These are called fixed-dollar investments.

What is a fixed-dollar investment? Why should investments of this kind be bought before other kinds? What is the risk with fixed-dollar investments?

EVERYONE SHOULD HAVE A SAVINGS ACCOUNT

Although both investors and investments differ, there is one investment that everyone should have. It is a savings account. A savings account is opened in much the same way as a checking account. You may have an account in just your own name; or you may have a joint account with one or more other persons. Joint accounts are often used by a husband and wife or a parent and child. Procedures for putting money in and taking it out are simple.

A Savings Account Is a Convenient Way to Invest

Since several types of institutions accept savings deposits, one of them is sure to be available to everyone with savings to invest. In addition to commercial banks, there are mutual savings banks that accept only time deposits. Another type of savings

Courtesy of banks shown

institution is the savings-and-loan association. In all, there are more than 7,000 of these associations throughout the United States. Credit unions also provide an opportunity to invest in a savings account.

Like banks, both savings-and-loan associations and credit unions are chartered by either the Federal or a state government. In other ways they differ from banks. Those who invest their savings in a savings-and-loan association or credit union, for example, are usually called *members* rather than *depositors*. This is because they do not exchange their money for a deposit as would be the case if they invested in a bank savings account. They exchange their money for shares in the savings-and-loan association or credit union. In other words, they buy shares in a business with their savings. The business of a savings-and-loan association is to lend money to citizens within the community for the purpose of buying, building, or remodeling homes. A credit union, you recall, is a cooperative organized to make loans to its members.

Most banks and savings-and-loan associations have "save-by-mail" plans. These enable a person to open and add to a savings account without going any farther than the mailbox. Many business firms have payroll savings plans. Under this plan a worker can arrange to have a certain amount withheld from his paycheck and deposited in a savings account for him. If requested to do so, commercial banks will usually transfer a definite sum each month from a depositor's checking account to his savings account. Plans of this kind make saving and investing almost automatic.

Just as credit unions make it possible for some people to save where they work, school banks provide a way for students like you to save where they learn. More than 12,000 of the nation's schools are helping students to acquire the savings habit by operating banks in cooperation with a local bank. Until recently, the Federal government operated through its post offices a savings-account system called *postal savings*. Years ago when people had less confidence in banks than they do today, postal-savings accounts were very popular.

A Savings Account Is a Safe Investment

Generally speaking, your money is safe in a savings account. In fact its safety may be guaranteed. As you know, deposits in most banks are insured up to $20,000 through the Federal Deposit Insurance

Courtesy Muir & Co.

Many employees find it convenient to save each payday.

Corporation. All Federal savings-and-loan associations carry a similar kind of insurance.

Although money invested in credit-union shares is not insured, these organizations have a good safety record. Moreover, in many instances, their loans are insured. In other words, if a member fails to repay money borrowed, the loss is covered by insurance. This is a protection for savers since it is their money that is loaned. Nevertheless, it would be unwise to trust your savings to an institution that provided no insurance without first finding out how well it is managed.

A Savings Account Provides for the Investment of Small Amounts

Naturally, the amount a person is able to save at one time limits his choice of an investment. Some investments call for a large expenditure of money. A savings account, on the other hand, is one investment within reach of everyone who can save anything at all. At most banks and savings-and-loan associations a savings account can be opened with only $1. In some cases, a school savings account may be started with as little as 5 cents. Membership in a credit union usually costs $5, the price of one share. Although there may be exceptions, most savings institutions will accept additions of almost any amount. Postal savings is one of the exceptions. The minimum deposit that will be accepted is $5.

A Savings Account Is a Liquid Investment

Money deposited in a savings account can usually be withdrawn at any time without loss to the investor. Some savings institutions have a rule that notice must be given 30 to 90 days before funds are to be withdrawn; however, this rule is seldom enforced. For this reason a savings account is the ideal way to invest funds being accumulated for a special purpose, such as a car, vacation, college, or the down payment on a house. It is also the best place to keep funds that might be needed in an emergency. Authorities on financial matters say that everyone should have a reserve of from three to six months' income.

Savings Accounts Earn a Reasonable Return

The return on savings accounts varies from one region to another and with different types of savings institutions. It may be as little as $2\frac{1}{2}$ percent or as much as 6 percent. It depends on where you live and what type of savings institution you choose. In any case, you could not find an investment that is as safe, as liquid, and as convenient that pays more.

Commercial banks call their payments to savers *interest.* Savings-and-loan associations and credit unions call such payments *dividends.* Some mutual savings banks use one term and some the other. There is also a difference in how often interest or dividends are paid. Some institutions pay ***quarterly,*** or every 3 months. Some pay ***semiannually,*** or every 6 months. And some pay only once a year. From the standpoint of the investor, the more often interest or dividends are paid, the better, since that money then goes to work immediately to earn more money.

UNITED STATES SAVINGS BONDS ARE A WISE INVESTMENT FOR MANY

In Part 15 you learned that governments, like individuals and business enterprises, often need to borrow. One of the ways they borrow is by issuing bonds. A bond, you remember, is a printed promise to pay a certain sum on a definite future date. Thousands of people invest their savings by purchasing government bonds. In other words, they lend their savings to the government that issues the bonds.

At almost any time there are hundreds of different state and local government bonds that can be

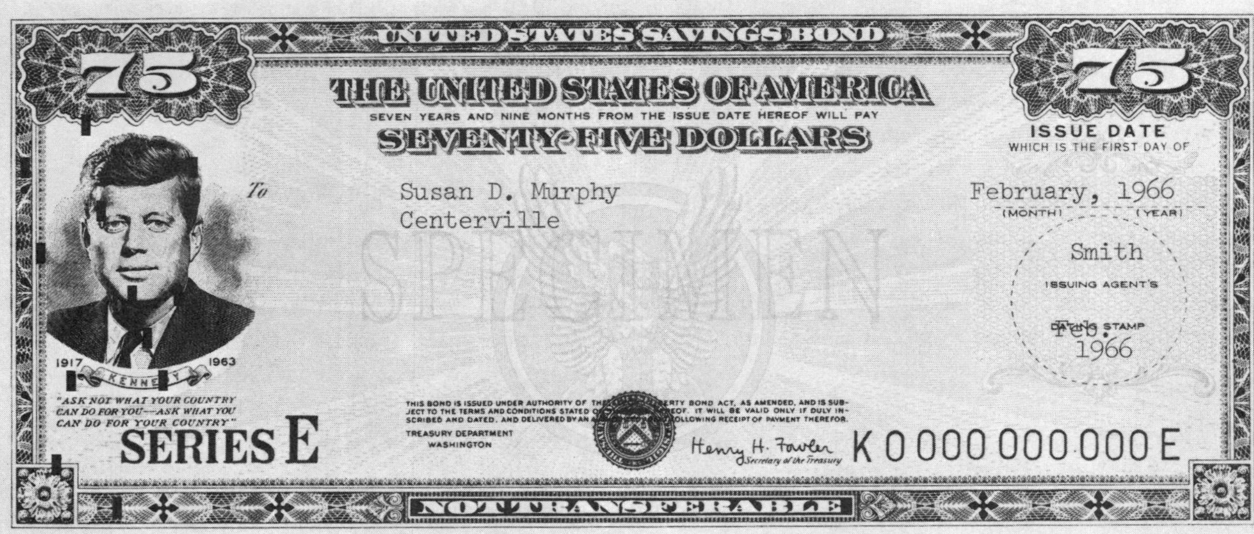

A United States Series E savings bond

purchased and dozens of different United States government bonds. The one most likely to be bought by the beginning or small investor, however, is United States savings bonds, Series E. These can be obtained from banks or directly from the Treasury Department in Washington, D.C.

How Much Do Series E Bonds Cost?

The purchase price of a Series E bond is three-fourths of its face value; that is, you pay $18.75 for a $25 bond, $37.50 for a $50 bond, and so on, as shown by the following table.

Purchase Price	*Face Value*
$ 18.75	$ 25
37.50	50
56.25	75
75.00	100
150.00	200
375.00	500
750.00	1,000

Not everyone, of course, is able to save $18.75, the price of the smallest Series E bond, at one time. Many companies help their employees buy Series E bonds by deducting a regular sum from each paycheck. When the amount of an employee's deductions is sufficient to purchase a bond, one is bought for him. And, of course, money needed to buy larger investments can always be accumulated in a savings account.

How Much Do Series E Bonds Earn?

The date on which the face value of a bond is to be repaid is its ***maturity date.*** If you hold a Series E bond until maturity, you will receive its full face value. The difference between the amount you pay for such a bond and the amount you receive for it is the interest you earn.

In recent years, the return on other types of savings has been rising. For that reason, the interest rate paid on Series E bonds has also been raised from time to time. This is done by shortening the time between purchase and maturity. When first introduced, Series E bonds matured in 10 years. Later the maturity time was changed to 9 years and 8 months, then 8 years and 11 months, then 7 years and 9 months. This last change resulted in a return of $3\frac{3}{4}$ percent.

The interest rate paid on Series E bonds, however, is an average rate. The first year they earn only 1.7 percent; the second year 2.7 percent; the third year 3 percent and so on. You receive the full $3\frac{3}{4}$ percent interest only if you hold your bonds until maturity. If a bond is cashed before that time, the rate of return will be somewhat less. An unusual feature of Series E bonds is that they continue to pay interest even if held after maturity.

Why Series E Bonds Are a Good Investment

Backed by the United States government, Series E savings bonds are as safe as any investment you can make. The name of the owner of each bond is kept on record. In case a bond is lost or stolen, it can be replaced. For an investment offering such a high degree of safety, $3\frac{3}{4}$ percent interest is a good return.

Series E bonds are also a liquid investment. The investor may cash in a bond and obtain his money any time after two months following the date of purchase. To cash, or ***redeem,*** a bond, you merely take it to a bank and fill out the request-for-payment form that is found on the back of the bond.

For someone who already has a savings account and who plans to hold his bonds until maturity, Series E bonds are a good investment. Money that is being saved for a short-term goal or that might be needed in an emergency should be kept in the savings account. In this way the investor protects himself against having to cash his Series E bonds before they mature.

SAVINGS ACCOUNTS AND SAVINGS BONDS ARE FIXED-DOLLAR INVESTMENTS

The dollar value of savings accounts and savings bonds is something you can count on. In other words, any time you want to exchange either investment for cash, you know exactly how many dollars you will receive. Because their dollar value is fixed, as it were, investments of this kind are called ***fixed-dollar investments.***

If fixed-dollar investments are chosen with care, chances of losing any of the money invested are slight. The uncertainty is whether the dollars you get back will be worth more or less than those you invested. They will be worth more if prices are lower than when you made the investment, because they will buy more. But they will be worth less if prices are higher than when you made the investment, because the dollars you get back will buy less. The risk with fixed-dollar investments, then, is that the money invested may lose some of its purchasing power. How investors guard against this risk is explained in the next part.

BUILDING YOUR VOCABULARY

On a separate sheet of paper, write each of the terms listed in the left-hand column below and on page 248. Read the three definitions to the right of each term. After each term, copy the definition that best describes it.

1. ***fixed-dollar investments***
   - *a.* Investments that are available only in standard amounts such as $5, $10, or $25
   - *b.* Investments that do not increase or decrease in dollar value
   - *c.* Investments that protect against inflation

2. ***maturity date***
   - *a.* The date on which the interest on a bond is paid
   - *b.* The first date on which a Series E bond may be cashed

c. The date on which the face value of a bond is to be repaid

3. ***quarterly***
   a. Every four months
   b. Every three months
   c. Every six months

4. ***redeem***
   a. To exchange for cash
   b. To replace a bond
   c. To determine the cash value

5. ***semiannually***
   a. Twice a year
   b. Once a year
   c. Once every two years

CHECKING YOUR READING

1. What is the most frequent cause of investment losses?
2. What is the best foundation for a good investment program?
3. What is one investment that everyone should have?
4. Name four kinds of financial institutions that accept savings deposits.
5. How does an investment in a savings-and-loan association or a credit union differ from an investment in a bank savings account?
6. Explain how many savings institutions make saving and investing almost automatic.
7. How do some schools help students acquire the savings habit?
8. What makes a savings account a safe investment?
9. Why is a savings account a good investment for anyone who can save only a small amount at a time?
10. Why is a savings account a good way to invest funds being accumulated for a special purpose or a possible emergency?
11. How much reserve for emergencies do financial authorities think a person should have?
12. Why is the return on a savings account considered reasonable?
13. Why is it to the advantage of the investor when interest is paid quarterly rather than semiannually?
14. Why do governments issue bonds?
15. What determines the amount of interest paid on Series E savings bonds?
16. What determines the rate of interest on Series E bonds?
17. Under what circumstances would an investor receive less than the full interest rate on a Series E bond?
18. Why are Series E bonds considered a good investment?
19. Are Series E bonds a wise investment choice for everyone? Explain.
20. What is the risk with fixed-dollar investments?

SHARING YOUR OPINION AND EXPERIENCE

1. Why do you suppose many teen-agers have joint savings accounts with their parents rather than accounts in their names only?
2. Most savings institutions provide passbooks to persons who open savings accounts. These passbooks are used for recording deposits, withdrawals, and interest or dividend payments. Why should a depositor guard his passbook as valuable property?
3. Banks that sponsor school savings programs usually do not make a profit on them. Why do you think these banks continue to cooperate with schools on savings programs?
4. Why do savings-and-loan associations pay dividends rather than interest?
5. What factors determine how large a reserve fund a person should have?
6. In some cities savings institutions compete for business by offering premiums to persons who open accounts with them. What is a premium?
7. Why does the government raise the interest rate on Series E bonds when other savings institutions raise the rates they pay on savings?
8. Why is the interest rate on Series E bonds less during the first years they are held than it is later on?
9. Before the Federal Deposit Insurance Corporation was organized, people often had greater faith in postal-savings accounts than they did in bank savings accounts. Since neither type of account was insured, why do you suppose this was true?

PROJECTS AND PROBLEMS

1. The following table shows how much money individual savers had in four types of investments in the years shown. Study the table and answer the questions that follow it.

HOLDINGS OF INDIVIDUALS IN FOUR TYPES OF INVESTMENTS—1956–1964
(in millions of dollars)

	Amount of Savings Invested in			
End of Year	*Commercial Bank Savings Accounts*	*Mutual Savings Bank Savings Accounts*	*Savings-and-Loan Association Shares*	*U.S. Savings Bonds*
1956	**50,577**	**30,000**	**37,148**	**50,100**
1957	**56,139**	**31,662**	**41,912**	**48,200**
1958	**63,166**	**34,006**	**47,976**	**47,700**
1959	**65,884**	**34,947**	**54,583**	**45,900**
1960	**71,380**	**36,318**	**62,142**	**45,700**
1961	**82,145**	**38,420**	**70,885**	**46,500**
1962	**97,440**	**41,478**	**80,422**	**46,900**
1963	**110,794**	**44,467**	**91,308**	**48,000**
1964	**125,600**	**49,000**	**101,847**	**49,000**

Source: National Industrial Conference Board

▪ *a.* In which type of investment did savers have the most money in 1956? ▪ *b.* In which type of investment did they have the second largest amount in 1956? ▪ *c.* Which type of investment held the greatest amount of savings in 1964? ▪ *d.* Which type of investment held the second largest amount of savings in 1964? ▪ *e.* In which of the four types of investments did the amount of savings increase during each successive year shown? ▪ *f.* In which type of investment was the amount of savings less in 1964 than it was in 1956? How much less was it? ▪ *g.* Which type of investment showed the greatest percent of increase from 1956 to 1964? What was the approximate percent of increase? ▪ *h.* How much money did savers have in all four types of investments in 1956? ▪ *i.* How much was their total investment in the four types in 1964?

2. The following information was taken from a savings-account passbook issued by a commercial bank. Read it carefully, and answer the questions that follow it.

   1. **DEPOSITS.** ▪ Deposits of one dollar and upwards to any amount will be received.

   2. **PASSBOOK.** ▪ Every person depositing shall be furnished a passbook, in which the deposits and payments shall be entered as soon as they are made. The bank will endeavor to prevent fraud on its depositors, yet all payments made by the bank to any person producing the passbook shall be valid as against the depositor. Should the passbook be lost, destroyed, or fraudulently obtained from the depositor, immediate written notice must be given to the officers of the bank.

   3. **INTEREST.** ▪ Interest is compounded quarterly and will be credited by March 31, June 30, September 30, and December 31 of each year. Interest is computed from the first of each month to the end of the quarter. Deposits made during the first ten days of each month are treated as though deposited on the first day of the month. Withdrawals may be made the last three days of the quarter without loss of interest.

   4. **MINORS.** ▪ Deposits made personally by any minor on his or her account shall be repaid in the same manner as if he or she were of full age.

   ▪ *a.* What is the minimum amount the bank will accept in a single deposit? ▪ *b.* When are deposits and payments entered in the passbook? ▪ *c.* If a passbook is lost and an unauthorized person uses it to withdraw savings, who loses the money? ▪ *d.* What should the depositor do if his passbook is lost or stolen? ▪ *e.* How often is interest paid? ▪ *f.* When would money deposited on May 8 begin to earn interest? ▪ *g.* When would money deposited on July 12 begin to earn interest? ▪ *h.* If the depositor withdrew $200 on March 27, would he lose interest on that amount for the entire 3 months? ▪ *i.* May a 15-year-old person withdraw money from his savings account without the signature of his parent?

3. The line graph on page 251 shows the percent of individuals' total savings invested in savings accounts each year from 1946 to 1963. For example, toward the end of 1947 about 20 percent of their total savings was in savings accounts. Study the graph and answer the questions relating to it.

   ▪ *a.* Approximately what percent of individuals' savings was in savings accounts at the beginning of 1947? at midyear in 1949? at midyear in 1953? at the beginning of 1957? at the end of 1957? ▪ *b.* In which year did individuals deposit the

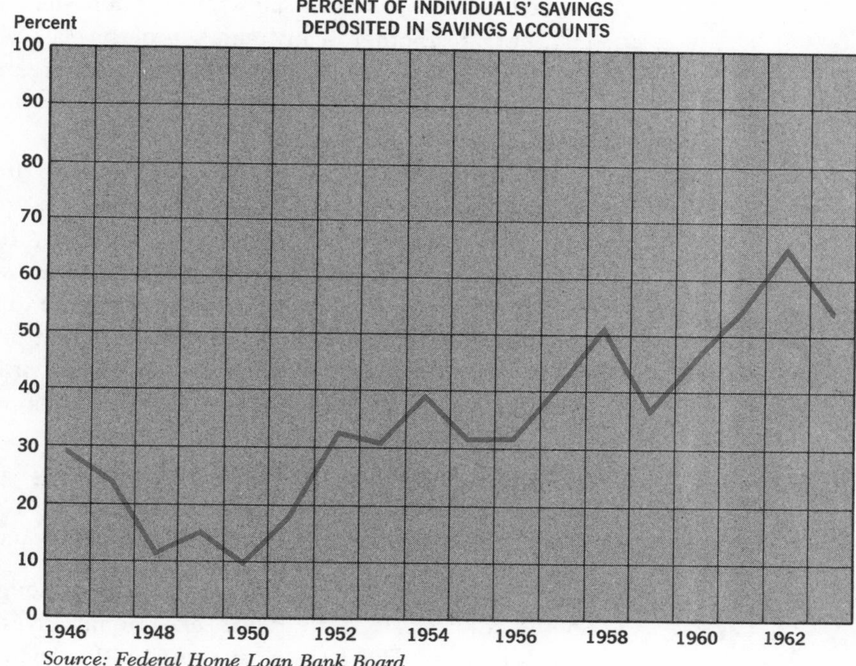

Source: Federal Home Loan Bank Board

smallest percent of their savings in savings accounts? ▪ *c.* In which year did individuals invest the largest percent of their savings in savings accounts? ▪ *d.* In which years did the percent of savings invested in savings accounts decrease from the preceding year? ▪ *e.* In general, did the percent of savings invested in savings accounts tend to increase or decrease during the period shown?

4. George Chandler needed $300 to pay a bill due on May 31. He had $800 in a savings account at the Citizens Savings Bank where the interest rate on time deposits was 4 percent per year. If he withdrew the money before June 30, he would lose the interest on the $300 for an entire quarter. So instead of withdrawing the money from his account, he obtained a savings-account loan of $300 at a cost of 4 percent per year. George left his passbook at the bank as security for the loan. At the end of the month, the bank credited his savings account with the interest his $800 had earned. Then the bank deducted the $300 he had borrowed plus the interest owing on the loan from the balance in his savings account and returned the passbook to George.

▪ *a.* How much interest would George have to pay on the $300 for one month? ▪ *b.* How much interest would he have lost by withdrawing the money from his savings account? ▪ *c.* How much did he save by borrowing the money? ▪ *d.* How much did the bank deduct from his savings account on June 30? ▪ *e.* What was the balance in George's account after the loan and interest had been deducted?

5. Procedures for making savings-account deposits and withdrawals vary from one institution to another. If any members of the class have savings accounts, ask them to explain the way deposits and withdrawals are made at their banks.

CHALLENGE PROBLEMS

1. Since savings institutions have to pay interest on time deposits, why do they compete with one another for new depositors?
2. In addition to regular savings accounts, many banks sell savings certificates. These are available in different denominations, such as $100, $250, $500, or $1,000. Persons who buy such certificates agree to keep them a certain length of time after the date of purchase—usually a year or longer. The reason they buy them is that banks pay a somewhat higher rate of interest on savings certificates than they pay on regular savings accounts. Explain why you think this is the case.
3. Why does the return paid on savings accounts vary from one region to another?
4. Why do you suppose the return paid on savings accounts varies from one type of savings institution to another?
5. Refer to the table used in No. 1 of the Projects and Problems section.

   ▪ *a.* How do you account for the fact that although total savings by individuals increased from 1956 to 1964, the amount invested in United States savings bonds decreased? ▪ *b.* In most communities savings-and-loan associations pay a slightly higher interest rate on time deposits than commercial banks. Then why do you suppose more savings are deposited in commercial banks than with savings-and-loan associations? ▪ *c.* How do you explain the fact that mutual savings banks held the smallest amount of individual savings during most of the period shown in the table?

PART 28 INVESTING IN CORPORATE SECURITIES

EVERY business, large or small, has two major problems. One is to produce goods and services efficiently. The other is to raise the money capital needed for production. As you know, the least costly way to produce many goods and services is on a large scale. This usually requires equipment that is both complex and expensive. That is why businesses like public utilities, automobile manufacturers, and airlines are organized as corporations.

A corporation, you recall, is a type of business organization that provides a way to raise large amounts of money capital. A corporation may obtain money capital in two ways. One is by selling stock; the other is by selling bonds. Another name for stocks and bonds is ***securities.*** By investing in stocks and bonds, millions of Americans jointly provide the money needed for production.

How do stocks differ from bonds? What are the advantages and disadvantages of stocks and bonds as an investment? Does a person have to be rich to make such investments?

WHAT ARE STOCKS?

A newly formed corporation obtains the funds it needs by selling stock. Stock is issued in units, called *shares.* A person who buys one or more shares of stock in a corporation becomes a part owner, or stockholder. He receives a printed form, called a ***stock certificate,*** which shows the number of shares he owns. Today more than 20,000,000 people own stock in corporations. Some corporations have only a few stockholders; others have millions.

If a corporation is successful, its stockholders are entitled to a portion of its profits. In case you have forgotten, a stockholder's share of profits is called a *dividend.* How much a corporation pays in divi-

Courtesy The Dreyfus Fund Inc.

LESS THAN 100 SHARES

COMMON STOCK
PAR VALUE $5. PER SHARE

G00-000

10

INCORPORATED UNDER THE LAWS OF THE STATE OF DELAWARE

GENERAL MOTORS CORPORATION

THIS CERTIFICATE IS TRANSFERABLE IN NEW YORK, CHICAGO, DETROIT, WILMINGTON, DEL. TORONTO OR MONTREAL

This is to Certify that RICHARD ROE

is the owner of ★ ★ ★ ★ TEN ★ ★ ★ ★ fully paid and non-assessable shares OF THE PAR VALUE OF $5 EACH OF THE COMMON STOCK OF GENERAL MOTORS CORPORATION (HEREINAFTER CALLED THE "CORPORATION") transferable in person or by duly authorized attorney upon surrender of this Certificate properly endorsed. A statement of the rights, privileges, preferences, restrictions and voting powers of the several classes of stock of the Corporation is printed on the reverse side hereof, and this Certificate and the shares represented hereby are subject to all the terms, conditions and limitations of the Certificate of Incorporation and all Amendments thereto and Supplements thereof (copies whereof are on file with the Transfer Agent). This Certificate is not valid until countersigned by a Transfer Clerk and registered by the Registrar.

Witness the signatures of its duly authorized officers MARCH 3, 1955.

SECRETARY PRESIDENT

REGISTERED: THE CHASE NATIONAL BANK OF THE CITY OF NEW YORK REGISTRAR

AUTHORIZED OFFICER

COUNTERSIGNED: GENERAL MOTORS CORPORATION

TRANSFER CLERK

SPECIMEN

A common stock certificate

Courtesy General Motors Corp.

dends depends on its earnings. These may vary from year to year. A business that has a poor year may not pay any dividends at all.

If a corporation fails, its stockholders must bear the losses. Each stockholder's loss, however, is limited to the money he has invested in the stock. No claim can be made on his personal property.

Some corporations issue two kinds of stock: ***common*** and ***preferred.*** Preferred stock is so named because dividends are paid on that kind of stock before they are paid on common stock. This does not mean that dividends on preferred stock are certain. It simply means that when dividends are paid, preferred stockholders have the first claim on them.

On the other hand, the dividend on preferred stock is usually limited to a definite amount, such as $4 or $5 a year. If the corporation is highly successful, owners of common stock can expect an increase in dividends. But the preferred stockholder receives no more than the fixed amount.

If a corporation issues only one kind of stock, it is common.

WHAT ARE BONDS?

When an established corporation needs money with which to expand, it may issue additional shares of stock. Or it may borrow the needed funds by issuing bonds. Bonds issued by a corporation are called ***corporate bonds.*** A bond is like a promissory note. It states that the borrower will pay the ***bondholder*** (the person who buys the bond) the face value of the bond on a certain date. For the use of the money the corporation promises to pay a fixed rate of interest, such as 4 percent or 5 percent a year. A bond, then, is evidence of a debt. Persons who buy bonds lend money to the corporation. They are creditors and not owners.

As creditors of the corporation, bondholders must be paid their interest before dividends are paid to stockholders. Also, if a corporation fails or goes out of business, the bondholders are paid before the stockholders.

Corporate bonds usually have a face value of $1,000, but some have been issued for $500 and some for as little as $100. Interest is figured on the face value. For example, a 4 percent bond with a face value of $1,000 earns $40 interest each year. The interest rate on a bond depends on two factors: (1) interest rates in general when the bond is issued; and (2) the credit rating of the corporation issuing the bond. Like consumers, corporations with good credit ratings can borrow at low interest rates. This is because there is less risk for the lender.

As a rule, interest is paid on corporate bonds every six months. With Series E bonds, you remember, interest is paid only when the bonds are cashed.

HOW DO CORPORATE SECURITIES RATE AS INVESTMENTS?

Stocks and bonds cannot be turned into cash so easily as savings accounts or Series E bonds. The owner of a corporate bond must wait until his bond has matured to get his money back. Otherwise, he must sell it. Stocks, whether preferred or common, can be exchanged for cash only by selling them.

Unlike savings accounts and Series E bonds, the dollar value of stocks and bonds is subject to change. The dollar value of any investment, remember, is the amount of money its owner would receive if he exchanged it for cash. The dollar value of corporate securities, then, is the price they can be sold for.

When first issued, stocks and bonds are sold at an established price. Once sold, however, their prices do not remain fixed. If resold, they may bring more or less than was paid for them originally. How much they bring depends on what others are willing to pay for them. This is known as their ***market value.***

Prices of common stocks fluctuate most of all. They may rise or fall sharply from one day to the next. They may even change several times within the course of a day.

WHY INVEST IN COMMON STOCKS?

People differ in their attitudes toward common stocks. Some will not buy them because their dollar value changes. They fear that a drop in price might result in a loss of money. Other people buy common stocks because their dollar value does change. They see an opportunity for gain if the price of their stock goes up. For example, if a man buys stock at $37 a share and sells it later for $49, he makes a profit of $12 a share. A profit of this kind is called a ***capital gain.***

There is something to be said for both views. Certainly common stocks are not a good way to invest short-term savings or money that might be needed in a hurry. If it became necessary to sell when prices were down, some money might be lost. For a long-term investment, however, common stocks may be a wise choice. The reason is that they provide protection against inflation. Inflation, as you know, is a general increase in prices. When inflation occurs, money loses some of its purchasing power; that is, it takes more money to buy the same quantity of goods and services.

Usually, when prices in general are rising, prices of good common stocks also rise. Or putting it another way, their dollar value increases. If prices rise, then an investment in common stock may be worth more dollars than the investor paid for it.

Although prices can go down as well as up, it is a fact that over the long run they tend to rise. Normally the rise is so gradual that losses in purchasing power are scarcely noticeable from one year to the next. But when you compare prices over a period

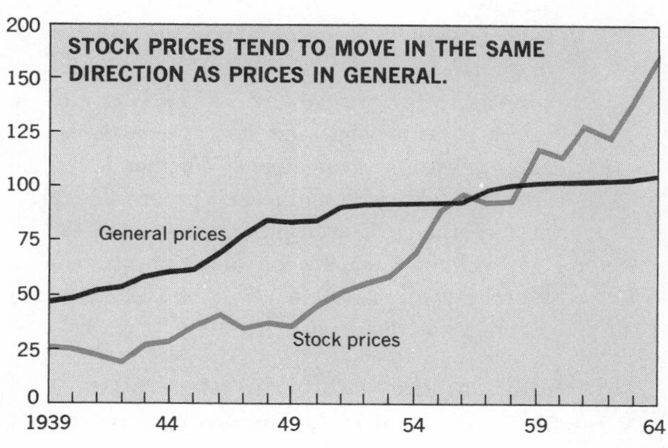

of time, you can almost always see a difference. In 1964, for example, a little more than $1.07 was needed to buy what a dollar bought in 1959.

When people make long-term investments, therefore, they often buy common stocks. The dollars they get back later will not buy more than any other dollars, but they may get extra dollars. These extra dollars can make up for any loss in purchasing power resulting from higher prices.

WHO SHOULD INVEST IN CORPORATE SECURITIES?

There was a time when only people of great wealth bought corporate securities. But this is no longer true. Half the nation's stockholders have annual incomes of $8,600 or less. Eighteen percent of those who own stocks earn less than $5,000 a year. Anyone who has a systematic plan for spending and saving can look forward to being a part owner in our business system. For as little as $40 every three months, stocks can be purchased on the installment plan. Some corporations sell their stock to their employees through a system of payroll deductions.

Nevertheless, before anyone considers investing in corporate securities, he should do the following:

1. Buy enough life insurance to provide adequate protection for dependents.
2. Build an adequate cash reserve in savings accounts or government bonds that can be used in case of an emergency. This will protect the investor from having to sell his securities at a loss in order to obtain funds.
3. Investigate before investing. In the long run the safety of both bonds and stocks depends on the corporation that issues them. Whether it will be able to pay its debts and make a profit will depend on its earnings. Does it produce a good or service that will be in demand for some time to come? Is it under good management? What is its record of earnings and dividends?

In addition, the careful investor attempts to spread his risks; that is, he divides his investment dollars among different industries. One year, for example, he might invest in a food company; the next year in a transportation industry; the third year, in a chemical firm; and so on. If chosen wisely, all his investments might pay a good return. Should one turn out poorly, however, he might gain enough from the others to cover the loss.

HOW ARE SECURITIES BOUGHT AND SOLD?

Stocks and bonds are not marketed in quite the same way as goods and services. When securities are first issued, their sale is handled by an investment bank. You may remember reading about this in Part 21. After that they are simply transferred from one owner to another. A corporation obtains the money capital it needs from the original sale of its stocks and bonds. The extent to which its securities are traded afterwards does not affect the financing of the corporation.

Before you can buy stocks or bonds, you must find someone who owns them and is willing to sell. Before you can sell them, you must find a buyer. In either case, you deal with an ***investment broker*** whose job it is to handle the purchase or sale for you. For this service you pay a fee.

Brokers have two methods of buying and selling securities. One is to trade with one another through central agencies known as ***stock exchanges.*** There are fifteen of these in the United States, but the largest is the New York Stock Exchange. Before a corporation's securities can be traded through an exchange, however, they must be listed by that exchange. Stocks and bonds not listed by any exchange are sold "over-the-counter." This simply means that brokers deal with one another directly rather than through an exchange.

Not even an investment broker can predict with certainty whether a stock will increase in value in years to come. But he can provide information about corporations in which you might want to invest. He can also help you to choose the type of investment that is best for you.

WHAT ARE INVESTMENT COMPANIES?

Inexperienced investors, persons who invest in small amounts, and persons who lack time to manage their investments often buy shares of investment companies. An *investment company* is a corporation whose business is that of investing in securities. You buy its shares just as you buy stock in any other company. The investment company then invests its stockholders' money in the securities of many different enterprises. This makes it possible for the small investor to spread his risks. A further advantage is that investment-company funds are managed by trained and experienced investors.

The shares of some investment companies are limited in number like those of other corporations. The only way you can buy shares in companies of this kind is to find someone who has shares he wants to sell. The stock of such companies may be listed by an exchange or sold "over-the-counter." Many investment companies, however, continue to issue new shares of stock whenever there is a buyer for them. Shares of stock in these companies are called *mutual funds*. These shares are not traded. Instead the company agrees to take them back at any time and pay their owner whatever they are worth at that time.

Eastern Photo Service

Customers in this broker's office are eagerly watching the board to see the latest prices of stocks traded on the New York Stock Exchange.

Some investment companies have done very well; others not so well. Before buying shares in one, therefore, it is important to investigate it thoroughly, just as you would any other company before investing in it.

BUILDING YOUR VOCABULARY

Copy the ten sentences given below, completing each one by replacing the question mark with the appropriate term from the column at the left.

bondholder
capital gain
common stock
corporate bonds
investment broker
market value
preferred stock
securities
stock certificate
stock exchanges

1. Another name for stocks and bonds is ? .
2. A printed form representing ownership of stock in a corporation is a ? .
3. Stock that has first claim on dividends is ? .
4. Stock that has no preference over other stock is ? .
5. An investor becomes a creditor of a corporation by buying ? .
6. A person who owns a bond is a ? .
7. The price that securities will bring at any given time is their ? .
8. If an investor sells stock for more than he paid for it, the profit is a ? .
9. An individual investor buys or sells securities through his ? .
10. Central agencies through which securities may be traded are ? .

CHECKING YOUR READING

1. In what two ways may a corporation obtain money capital?
2. What determines how much a corporation pays in dividends?
3. If a corporation fails, who bears the loss? How is each one's loss limited?
4. With respect to dividends, how does preferred stock differ from common stock?
5. In what way is a corporate bond like a promissory note?
6. How does a bondholder's relationship to a corporation differ from that of a stockholder?
7. What two factors usually determine the rate of interest paid on corporate bonds?
8. Why can a corporation with a good credit rating borrow money at low interest rates?
9. Why are stocks and bonds not as liquid as savings accounts or Series E bonds?
10. What determines the market value of corporate securities?
11. Which type of corporate security fluctuates most in price?
12. Why are common stocks not a good way to invest short-term savings?
13. Explain how common stocks provide protection against inflation.
14. What three steps should anyone take before investing in corporate securities?
15. What should you find out about a corporation before investing in it?
16. Give an example of how a person who buys stocks can spread his risks.
17. How are corporate securities bought and sold?
18. Why might a small investor prefer to buy mutual funds rather than to buy securities outright?

SHARING YOUR OPINION AND EXPERIENCE

1. Banks sometimes invest their depositors' money in corporate bonds, but they are not permitted to buy common stocks. Do you think this is a wise policy? Explain.
2. Corporate bonds usually pay a higher rate of interest than Series E bonds. Can you think of any reasons why this is true?
3. Investors sometimes buy common stock even when they know that little or no dividends will be paid on it. What reasons can you give for buying such stock?
4. Why are corporate bonds considered a safer investment than stocks?
5. When does a person become an investor in a corporation?
6. Reference was made in this part to short-term and long-term investments. What do you think is the difference between the two? Why would a person choose one kind of investment for the short term and another for the long term?
7. Some very successful large corporations have only a few stockholders. Why do you suppose more people have not bought stock in these companies?
8. Why do you think corporate bonds are usually more stable in price than common stocks?

PROJECTS AND PROBLEMS

1. Herbert Bell owns 60 shares of preferred stock in the Harris Manufacturing Company. The dividend on the stock is $4 a year and is paid quarterly. These dividends have been paid every quarter for 30 years.

▪ *a.* How much does Mr. Bell receive in dividends each quarter? ▪ *b.* What is his monthly income from these dividends? ▪ *c.* What is his annual income from dividends? ▪ *d.* If he had owned the stock for the past 30 years, what total amount would he have received in dividends?

2. One way experienced investors judge the value of a stock is to compare its price with the company's earnings per share. As an example, suppose the price of one company's stock is $30 a share. The company's net profit per share of stock for the year amounts to $2. Then the stock is selling for 15 times earnings. This is figured by dividing the price of the stock by the earnings per share: $30 (price) ÷ $2 (earnings) = 15. This is known as the *price-earnings ratio.*

   In general, a price equal to 10 times earnings is considered low. A price of 20 times earnings is considered high. Listed below are recent prices and earnings of six corporations. What is the price-earnings ratio in each case? Round off to the nearest whole number.

	Name of Company	*Price of Stock per Share*	*Earnings per Share*
▪ *a.*	**National Insurance Company**	**$54**	**$2.00**
▪ *b.*	**Central Tile Company**	**40**	**2.75**
▪ *c.*	**Steele Brothers, Inc.**	**19**	**2.10**
▪ *d.*	**Builders, Inc.**	**42**	**2.65**
▪ *e.*	**Kansas Industries**	**43**	**4.25**
▪ *f.*	**Swift Air Lines**	**60**	**4.00**

3. The following article appeared recently in the nation's newspapers. Read the article and answer the questions that follow it.

TOP-QUALITY STOCKS HEDGE AGAINST INFLATION

New York.—Have stock prices and dividends increased in periods of inflation during the past century and thus helped protect an investor's nest egg against increasing living costs? If so, how often have they increased and how much protection have they given an investor?

Some of the answers are surprising to many people. Since 1871 stock prices have usually risen when the cost of living has increased. In the great majority of cases, increases in stock prices matched or bettered increases in the cost of living. Also, in the vast majority of periods since 1871, dividends have increased as living costs increased.

What happened to stock prices during the periods of deflation since 1871? They went down only 19 percent of the time over long periods of deflation. Also, the widespread fear that dividends evaporate or are sharply reduced during deflation has no basis in history. In four-fifths of the long-term deflation spans since 1871, dividends actually increased.

▪ *a.* What does "hedge against inflation" mean? ▪ *b.* Since 1871 what has usually happened to the price of stocks as living costs have increased? ▪ *c.* Did the stock prices generally increase as much as the cost of living? ▪ *d.* Did the dividends paid on stock usually increase, decrease, or remain the same as living costs increased? ▪ *e.* During periods of deflation, what happens to prices in general? ▪ *f.* Have stock prices always shown a steady decrease during long periods of deflation? ▪ g. Were dividend payments usually reduced during long-term deflation periods? ▪ *h.* What actually happened to dividend payments during these periods? ▪ *i.* Was an investor more likely to gain or to lose by holding stocks during long periods of deflation?

4. The rate of return on corporate securities is often called the *yield.* The yield on either a share of stock or a bond is found by dividing the amount of the return by the price paid for the stock or bond. The return on a bond, of course, is the interest paid on it. The *amount* of interest always remains the same. For example, on a bond with a face value of $1,000 that pays 5 percent interest, the return will always be $50 a year. The market price of such a bond, however, may change. If you bought the bond for $950, the yield would be almost 5.3 percent.

   $50 (amount of return) ÷ $950 (price paid) = .053 or 5.3 percent (yield)

   On the other hand, if you paid $1,050 for the bond, the yield would be less than 5 percent.

   Figure the rate of return, or yield (to the nearest one-tenth percent), on each of the following bond investments.

Face Value of Bond	*Interest Rate on the Bond*	*Price Paid for the Bond*
▪ *a.* $1,000	4 %	$ 950
▪ *b.* $1,000	4¼%	$1,075
▪ *c.* $1,000	4½%	$ 975
▪ *d.* $ 500	5 %	$ 470
▪ *e.* $ 500	5 %	$ 525
▪ *f.* $1,000	3½%	$ 940

5. The return on stocks is the amount received in dividends. If the annual dividend on a stock were $2 and the purchase price were $56, the yield would be 3.6 percent.

   $2 (amount of return) ÷ $56 (price paid) = .036 or 3.6 percent (yield)

   As in the case of bonds, what happens to the price of a stock during the time an investor owns it does not affect its yield. Only an increase or a decrease in the amount of the dividend would affect the yield; and unlike bonds the amount of return on stocks can and often does change. For example, Harvey Kahn bought some stock in the Smith Transport Company for which he paid $72 a share. During the first five years he owned the stock, he received dividends in the amounts shown on page 261. Figure the yield on Mr. Kahn's stock for each of the years shown.

Year	*Annual Dividend per Share*
1	$2.88
2	3.24
3	2.52
4	2.74
5	3.02

6. Assume that your main reason for buying stocks is to obtain a high rate of return. List the following stocks in the order in which you would buy them.

Name of Stock	*Current Market Price*	*Current Annual Dividend*
Phillips Coal	$192	$5.38
Holiday House Furniture	47	1.55
Hampton Manufacturing	84	2.52
Florida Utilities	19	0.75
Glen Cove Insurance	54	1.00

CHALLENGE PROBLEMS

1. In the past many corporations have encouraged small investors to buy their stock. Recently, however, some companies have tried to buy back their stock from holders who have only a few shares. What reasons do you think these corporations have for wanting to "buy out" their small stockholders?
2. Some investors buy only "blue-chip" stocks. What are blue-chip stocks?
3. One investment broker commented recently that "more people should be investing and fewer should be speculating." What is the difference between investing in stocks and speculating in them?
4. You have learned in this part about the market value of stocks. What is *par value?* What relationship does it have to market value?
5. When the market value of its stock increases considerably, the directors of a corporation sometimes decide to "split" the stock. What does this mean?
6. In No. 2 of the Projects and Problems section, you learned how to compute the price-earnings ratio of a stock. The price-earnings ratio of a stock is said to reflect the opinions of other investors regarding that stock. Explain.

PART 29 INVESTING IN A HOME

MANY people believe there is no better way to invest savings than in real estate. ***Real estate*** is property of a permanent nature—land, houses, and buildings. Some people buy property of this kind for the income they expect to receive by renting it to others. Some buy with the hope of making a profit by reselling it later for more than they paid. For most people, however, investing in real estate means buying a home of their own.

In 1950, 42 percent of the families in the United States were homeowners. In 1958, it was 56 percent; in 1964, 60 percent. The possibility that you will someday buy a home, therefore, is growing all the time. Does that mean home ownership is a wise investment for everyone? What risks does it usually involve?

Ewing Galloway

WHAT KIND OF INVESTMENT IS A HOME?

A home is not an investment in the usual sense. It pays neither dividends nor interest. Yet it does have some of the same characteristics as an investment in common stocks. When a person buys stocks, he acquires a share of a business enterprise. When a family buys a home, it acquires a share of the community in which it lives. And like stocks, a home can be exchanged for cash in the event it becomes necessary.

Home ownership even involves the same risk as an investment in stocks; that is, the dollar value of a home, like the dollar value of stocks, may rise or fall. Usually it rises during periods of prosperity when prices in general are rising. And it falls during recessions when prices in general are most likely to fall. History shows, however, that prices rise more often than they fall. Any decrease in property values caused by falling prices, therefore, probably would be temporary.

IS HOME OWNERSHIP A WISE INVESTMENT FOR EVERYONE?

In addition to food and clothing, one thing all of us need is shelter—a place to live. But that is not the same as saying that everyone should buy a home of his own. Home ownership has advantages, to be sure; but so does renting.

Why Buy?

The favorite, and probably oldest, argument for home ownership is that when you buy a home, you have something of value to show for the money spent. People who rent, so the argument goes, have nothing but rent receipts. This is not the only reason people buy homes, however.

Home ownership provides a feeling of security. You don't have to worry about being asked to move. Because it is your property, you can decorate, landscape, or remodel in any way you wish. Sometimes you can have a better home for less money when you buy than when you rent. Owning your home improves your credit rating. Most important of all, perhaps, is that a home is a protection against inflation. When prices in general are rising, prices of real estate also rise.

For families with children, who plan to locate permanently in a community, home ownership is a good investment. In fact, for most families with school-age children, home ownership should come ahead of investing in corporate securities.

Why Rent?

Turn around all those arguments for home ownership, and you will have most of the reasons why more than one-third of the nation's householders prefer to rent.

Although home ownership may provide greater security than renting, it also ties a family down. Families that rent are free to move whenever it is necessary or to their advantage to do so. Having to sell a house when property values are down could result in a financial loss. When you rent, it is the landlord who takes all risks. The landlord is also responsible for painting, decorating, and making major repairs.

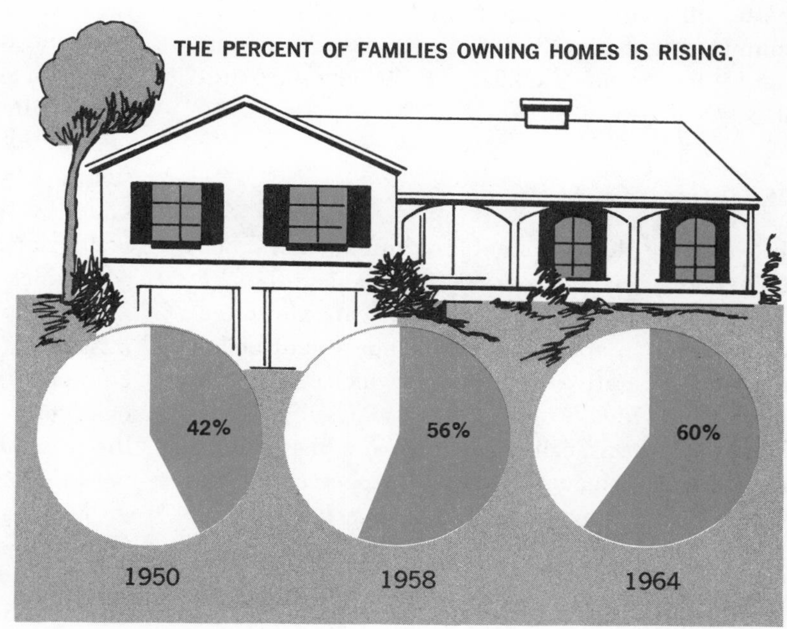

Courtesy The Consolidated Edison Company of New York, Inc.

These attractive apartments are cooperatively owned by their tenants.

As you can see, home ownership is not advisable for everyone. Unmarried persons, families who move often, and anyone who does not want the responsibilities that go with owning a home may be better off renting. A family that is new in a community might also find it an advantage to rent until it has become familiar with its new surroundings.

What Is a Home?

In weighing the arguments for and against home ownership, it is necessary to realize that "home" does not always mean "house." It can, and often does, mean an apartment. Some apartment buildings are cooperative enterprises in which each apartment is individually owned. It is also possible to buy homes on wheels, called *mobile homes,* that can be moved long distances. Each year 13 percent of the nation's new single-family dwellings are mobile homes. Thus, many people are enjoying some of the advantages of home ownership while escaping certain of its disadvantages.

MOST HOMES ARE BOUGHT ON CREDIT

A home is the biggest single purchase most families ever make. Few buyers have enough savings to pay cash. Most of them have only enough for a down payment; then they borrow the balance. The home is security for the loan. If the borrower fails to pay, the lender can take over the property. A loan secured by property is called a *mortgage loan,* or simply a ***mortgage.*** Mortgage loans may be obtained from commercial banks, savings banks, savings-and-loan associations, and some insurance companies.

Most mortgage loans are repaid in fixed monthly installments over a period of years—10, 15, or 20. Some may run as long as 25 or 30 years. A portion of each monthly payment goes toward paying off the ***principal,*** or amount borrowed. The remainder pays the interest due on the loan each month. This is shown in the payment schedule illustrated on page 266. Notice that in this case, the interest payment at the beginning is greater than the payment on the principal. Since interest is figured only on the balance owed, however, the interest cost decreases with each payment. The amount applied to the principal, on the other hand, increases. When the last payment is made, the house belongs to the buyer free and clear.

HOW MUCH SHOULD YOU PAY FOR A HOUSE?

Because a home is paid for over a long period of time, people may be tempted to buy houses costing more than they can afford. There is an age-old rule that says that the price of a home should not be more than $2\frac{1}{2}$ times the buyer's annual income. This gives families a general idea of what they can pay. But it is not a completely reliable guide, because the amount a buyer pays for a home is only part of the cost of owning it. The best way for anyone to figure out whether or not he can afford a particular house is to estimate the total monthly cost of owning it. Then he should compare this amount with what his budget allows for housing.

Estimate the Costs of Home Ownership

For most home buyers, the biggest monthly cost is the mortgage-loan payment. The size of the monthly payment, of course, depends on three things: (1) the amount of the loan; (2) the length of time it is to run; and (3) the interest rate. For example, a loan of $12,000 at $5\frac{1}{2}$ percent to be paid in 20 years would cost $82.55 monthly.

One cost that no homeowner can escape is the payment of property taxes, which continue to be an expense even after a house is paid for. Taxes on property vary from one community to another. Even within the same community, they may change from one year to the next; therefore, no one can tell exactly what the taxes on a particular house will be in a few years. Nevertheless, anyone planning to buy a house should know the amount of the present taxes. In most communities property taxes are paid only once or twice a year. To estimate their cost per month, the annual cost must be divided by 12.

Another item of expense is insurance that pro-

Courtesy Mobile Homes Manufacturers Association

For the family that expects to move frequently, a mobile home may be the answer.

LOAN AMORTIZATION SCHEDULE

Payment Number	*Payments On*		*Total Payment*	*Balance of Loan*
	Interest	*Principal*		
1	$55.00	$27.55	$82.55	$11,972.45
2	54.87	27.68	82.55	11,944.77
3	54.75	27.80	82.55	11,916.97
4	54.62	27.93	82.55	11,889.04
5	54.49	28.06	82.55	11,860.98
6	54.36	28.19	82.55	11,832.79
7	54.23	28.32	82.55	11,804.47
8	54.10	28.45	82.55	11,776.02
9	53.97	28.58	82.55	11,747.44
10	53.84	28.71	82.55	11,718.73
11	53.71	28.84	82.55	11,689.89
12	53.58	28.97	82.55	11,660.92
235	2.23	80.32	82.55	405.56
236	1.86	80.69	82.55	324.87
237	1.49	81.06	82.55	243.81
238	1.12	81.43	82.55	162.38
239	.74	81.81	82.55	80.57
240	.37	80.57	80.94	00

This amortization schedule is for a $12,000 loan at 5.5% that requires 240 payments spread over 20 years.

tects the homeowner against loss from fire, windstorm, and other hazards. In fact, no lending agency would agree to finance the purchase of a home that was not insured. Insurance for homeowners is covered in Part 32.

One of the most important costs of home ownership is upkeep. Keeping a home in good repair will protect its value. How much this costs will depend to some extent on the age of the property. A new home might require very little in the way of upkeep. As time goes on, however, the need for painting, decorating, and repairs usually increases. The average annual cost for upkeep is generally about 2 percent of the value of the house. For a $15,000 house, this would be $300 a year, or $25 a month.

Compare With Budget Allowance

Suppose that Jean and Harry Frazer want to buy a house. They have $3,000 for a down payment, and they now spend $125 monthly for rent. The price of the house they want to buy is $15,000. This means they will have to borrow $12,000.

Taxes on the house are $270 a year. They obtained this information from the present owner. By inquiring of an insurance company, they learned that insurance on the house would cost $60 a year. The market value of the house was $15,000 so they estimated 2 percent of that amount, or $300, for upkeep each year. The total for these three items came to $52.50 monthly.

Taxes ($270 ÷ 12)	**$22.50**
Insurance ($60 ÷ 12)	**5.00**
Upkeep ($300 ÷ 12)	**25.00**
	$52.50

This leaves the Frazers only $72.50 for a loan payment:

$125 (housing allowance) − $52.50 = $72.50

To stay within their budget, the Frazers will have to obtain a 25-year loan at 5½ percent. Even then their monthly loan payments would be $73.80. If they are unable to arrange for such a loan, they have two choices. They can wait until they have the money for a larger down payment. Or they can look for a less expensive house.

IT PAYS TO SHOP CAREFULLY

Shopping carefully for a home not only assures satisfaction for the buyer. It is wise from an investment standpoint. A house that is poorly constructed or badly located will lose value quickly. Before agreeing to buy any house, it is wise to make certain it is worth the price asked. One way to do this is by comparing it with the prices of similar houses on the market. Another way is to have an appraisal made. An ***appraisal*** is an estimate of the value of a piece of property by someone qualified to judge its value. Lending agencies always have property appraised before they agree to make a loan on it. Sometimes the amount an agency is willing to lend is a clue to the value of the property. For example, suppose the maximum loan a lender will make on a house is 80 percent of its value. This means that if he would lend $12,000 on a house, he considers it to be worth at least $15,000.

Shopping Includes Shopping for a Mortgage

When you have found the house that best meets your needs, the next step is to finance its purchase. The difference between the price of the house and the down payment will be the amount you must borrow; of course, the less you have to borrow, the lower your interest cost will be. Nevertheless, you should not use all your savings for a down payment. Some funds should be held in reserve for use in an emergency. In addition, cash will be needed to pay moving costs and to buy new furnishings and equipment. There are also expenses a home buyer must pay called ***closing costs.*** These include the fee charged by the lender for making the mortgage loan, the appraisal fee, the fee for recording the mortgage, and certain other costs connected with the purchase of a home.

One thing you learned from your study of credit is that credit costs vary from one lending agency to another. Shopping for the best mortgage-loan terms, therefore, can result in big savings. A difference of only 1/2 percent in the interest rate may seem small. But in 20 years' time, a difference of 1/2 percent on a loan of $12,000 would amount to $822.

In the long run, however, faster repayment of a loan can save more than a lower interest rate. At 6 percent, interest charges on a $12,000 loan for 20 years would total $8,633.16. At 5½ percent, interest charges on the same amount for 25 years would be $9,807.60. Of course, the less time a borrower has in which to repay a loan, the larger his payments will be.

Because most buyers are limited in the amount they can pay monthly, it is advisable to obtain a mortgage that provides a *prepayment privilege.* This permits the borrower to make extra payments on the principal that will result in a saving of interest. You will understand this more clearly by working No. 5 of the Projects and Problems section for this part.

BUILDING YOUR VOCABULARY

On a separate sheet of paper, write each of the terms listed in the left-hand column below. Read the three definitions to the right of each term. After each term, copy the definition that best describes it.

1. ***appraisal***
   a. An estimate of the taxes on a piece of property
   b. An estimate of the value of property
   c. An investigation of the credit rating of a home buyer

2. ***closing costs***
   a. Fees and other expenses that a home buyer must pay at the start, in addition to the down payment
   b. The costs of moving furniture and other possessions into a new home
   c. The final payment to be made on a mortgage

3. ***mortgage***
   a. A loan obtained from a commercial bank or savings-and-loan association
   b. A loan secured by property
   c. A loan repaid in fixed monthly installments over 25 years

4. ***principal***
   a. The amount of a loan
   b. The amount of interest paid on a loan
   c. The balance due on a loan

5. ***real estate***
   a. Property of a permanent nature, such as land and buildings
   b. Property that is rented to produce income
   c. Property used as security for a loan

CHECKING YOUR READING

1. What are some of the reasons why people buy real estate?
2. In what ways can an investment in a home be compared to an investment in stocks?
3. What are some of the reasons why people buy homes of their own?
4. Why is it sometimes better to rent rather than buy a home?
5. Explain why buying a "home" does not always mean buying a "house."
6. How do most buyers arrange to pay for their homes?
7. From what sources may mortgage loans be obtained?
8. How are most mortgage loans repaid?
9. Why does the interest cost decrease with each payment made on a mortgage loan?
10. What general guide can a family use in estimating the amount it can safely pay for a home?
11. What is the best way for a family to tell whether or not it can afford a particular house?
12. What is the biggest monthly cost for most home buyers?
13. What three factors determine the size of the monthly payment on a mortgage?
14. What are some other costs that homeowners have?

15. How can a buyer find out whether or not a house is worth the price asked for it?
16. Why should a family not use all its savings for a down payment on a house?
17. Why should a buyer shop for a mortgage?
18. Explain why a home buyer should look for a mortgage with a prepayment privilege.

SHARING YOUR OPINION AND EXPERIENCE

1. According to one point of view, "A family that owns its home is more likely to take an active interest in community affairs than one that rents." Do you agree or disagree? Why?
2. Part of a home buyer's monthly costs is usually considered a savings rather than an expense. Which part?
3. As you learned in this part, taxes are one cost of owning a home. Is this cost more likely to increase or decrease over a period of time? Why?
4. Why are lending agencies unwilling to finance a home that is not insured?
5. The Hamptons bought a house 10 miles from where Mr. Hampton works. Do you think his transportation costs should be included as an expense in owning the home?
6. According to some estimates, it costs almost half as much to live in a house after it is completely paid for as it cost while mortgage payments were being made. What expenses continue even after the mortgage is paid off?
7. Why might one family be able to pay more for a house than another, even though their incomes are the same?
8. Some agencies that make mortgage loans take care of paying the taxes and insurance on the property. The buyer then pays these to the agency monthly together with the payment on his mortgage. Why would a lending agency want to handle the payments this way? Do you think it is a good arrangement for the buyer? Why?
9. Some authorities say that one cost of owning a home is *depreciation*. What is depreciation?
10. Do people who rent avoid the cost of taxes, insurance, and upkeep on the houses or apartments they occupy? Why or why not?

PROJECTS AND PROBLEMS

1. According to many authorities the most important single consideration in buying a home is its location. List the factors that should be considered in deciding whether or not a house is in a good location.
2. On the left half of a sheet of paper list the advantages of owning a home. On the right half of the sheet list the advantages of renting.
3. As you learned in this part, the average annual cost for upkeep of a house is about 2 percent of its value. How much should be budgeted *monthly* for the upkeep of houses costing the following amounts?

▪ *a.* \$10,000 ▪ *b.* \$12,500 ▪ *c.* \$17,500 ▪ *d.* \$24,000 ▪ *e.* \$13,200 ▪ *f.* \$16,200

4. If a family should spend no more than $2\frac{1}{2}$ times its annual income for a home, what is the greatest amount that families with the following incomes should spend for a home?

▪ *a.* $8,400 a year ▪ *b.* $5,200 a year ▪ *c.* $7,224 a year ▪ *d.* $530 a month ▪ *e.* $478 a month ▪ *f.* $910 a month ▪ *g.* $94 a week ▪ *h.* $125 a week ▪ *i.* $175 a week

5. You read on page 267 that a mortgage prepayment privilege permits a homeowner to reduce his interest costs by making extra payments on the principal of his loan. The amount of interest that will be saved with each extra payment can be determined from the loan-payment schedule. Portions of such a schedule for a $12,000 loan at $5\frac{1}{2}$ percent for 20 years are shown on page 266. As the schedule shows, the monthly payments for interest and reduction of the principal are $82.55. Suppose, however, that when the homeowner makes payment No. 1, he wants to make an extra payment on the principal. He can do this by paying the amount of principal shown for payment No. 2 ($27.68). This means that he would pay a total of $110.23 ($82.55 + $27.68). In this way he would save the interest charge of $54.87 shown for payment No. 2. The following month he would be ready to make payment No. 3.

   Using the schedule on page 266 figure how much a homeowner could save in each case by making an extra principal payment along with the following regular payments.

▪ *a.* Payment No. 4 ▪ *b.* Payment No. 6 ▪ *c.* Payment No. 9 ▪ *d.* Payment No. 11 ▪ *e.* Payment No. 235 ▪ *f.* Payment No. 238

6. The table below shows the percent of families in various income groups that owned their homes in 1949 and in 1962. Study the table and answer the questions that follow.

HOME OWNERSHIP OF NONFARM FAMILIES

Money Income of Family Head	*Percent of Families That Owned Their Homes*	
	1962	*1949*
Under $1,000	**35**	**46**
$ 1,000 to $ 2,000	**42**	**34**
2,000 to 3,000	**45**	**43**
3,000 to 4,000	**45**	**49**
4,000 to 5,000	**42**	**58**
5,000 to 6,000	**51**	**63**
6,000 to 7,500	**71**	**63**
7,500 to 10,000	**66**	**73**
10,000 and over	**75**	**73**

Source: National Industrial Conference Board

■ *a.* In which income group did the largest percent of families own their homes in 1962? ■ *b.* In which group(s) did the largest percent own their homes in 1949? ■ *c.* In which income group did the smallest percent of families own their homes in 1949? ■ *d.* In which group did the smallest percent own their homes in 1962? ■ *e.* In which income groups was the percent who owned their homes smaller in 1962 than in 1949? ■ *f.* In which groups was the percent who owned their homes larger in 1962 than in 1949? ■ *g.* In which income groups did fewer than half the families own their homes in 1962?

CHALLENGE PROBLEMS

1. Why is the family who owns its home protected against inflation better than the family who rents?
2. The amount of taxes on a house is not based on the actual value of the property, but on its assessed value. What is assessed value?
3. Why is it wise to consult a lawyer when buying a home?
4. According to the table used for No. 6 of the Projects and Problems Section, the percent of homeowners with incomes of less than $1,000 was greater in 1949 than in 1962. How would you explain this fact?
5. In estimating the costs of home ownership, some people include the interest that could have been earned had they invested their money in some other way. Explain.

CONTENTS OF UNIT 7

Unit 7 / Buying Protection Through Insurance

PART 30 SHARING ECONOMIC LOSSES THROUGH INSURANCE

EACH minute of the day or night everyone faces the possibility of a financial loss. A home and all its contents may be destroyed by fire, damaged by lightning, or demolished by a tornado. Personal belongings may be stolen. A car may be damaged in an accident; or it may cause injury to people and property. Income may be lost as the result of death, disability, or unemployment of the family wage earner. The chance that money losses of this kind may occur is called an ***economic risk.***

Savings, of course, provide one way to take care of money losses. But savings is not the answer to large losses. The best way to guard against large losses is through insurance.

Why is insurance a better protection against large financial losses than savings? What types of losses can be insured?

WHAT IS INSURANCE?

Insurance is simply a way of sharing economic losses. Take, for example, Bob Crockett and five of his friends who formed a dance band, called "The Downbeats." Each member of the band owns a valuable instrument; Bob's clarinet alone cost $200. If an instrument were stolen or damaged, it would be a serious financial loss for its owner.

Suppose, however, that each member of the band agrees to pay $2 a month into a fund. Then, if an instrument were stolen or damaged, the loss would be paid for with money from the fund. Under this plan, each boy would lose a small amount, but none a great deal. In other words, they would share the loss. This is the principle behind all insurance. Persons facing the same risk pay regularly into a fund to take care of whatever losses might occur among them.

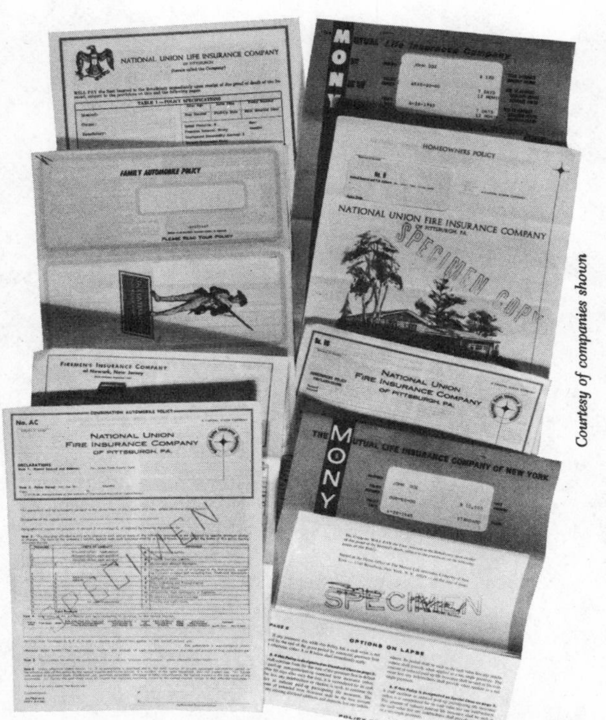

Courtesy of companies shown

Risks Must Be Widespread

From an insurance standpoint, an informal agreement like that made by the "Downbeats" has two major weaknesses. One weakness is that not enough people are sharing the risk. With only six boys in the band, it will take a long time to build a fund large enough to pay for just one instrument. Meanwhile, if a loss occurs, it would be only partly covered. To cover the loss of just one instrument a year, each boy would have to pay in twice the present amount.

Another weakness of the plan is that all instruments might be stolen or damaged at the same time. The boys rehearse together in the Crocketts' garage and sometimes leave their instruments there between rehearsals. They also travel together in a station wagon when they play at a dance. Suppose a thief broke into the garage one night and made off with all the instruments? Or what if the garage caught fire, or all instruments were damaged in an accident on the way to or from a dance? To cover the entire loss, each boy would have to contribute to the fund an amount equal to his loss. This would be the same as if he had carried no insurance and paid for his own loss.

To provide adequate protection, the cost of insurance must therefore be spread among many people, only a few of whom are likely to have actual losses.

INSURANCE IS BIG BUSINESS

Providing insurance protection is the business of more than 5,750 enterprises in the United States called *insurance companies.* Among them are some of the nation's biggest corporations. Some companies sell all kinds of insurance; some sell only one kind. Altogether they employ close to $1\frac{1}{4}$ million people.

When you buy insurance, you enter into a written agreement with the insurance company. This agreement is called a ***policy.*** The person who buys insurance is called the ***policyholder.*** According to their agreement, the insurance company promises to pay the policyholder if he has certain types of losses. In other words, the insurance company assumes a particular kind of risk for the policyholder. For this protection, the policyholder agrees to make regular payments to the insurance company. Each payment is called a ***premium.*** The premiums paid by all policyholders provide the funds with which to pay those who have losses. Thus, a loss that might result in great financial hardship for one person or one family is shared by many people.

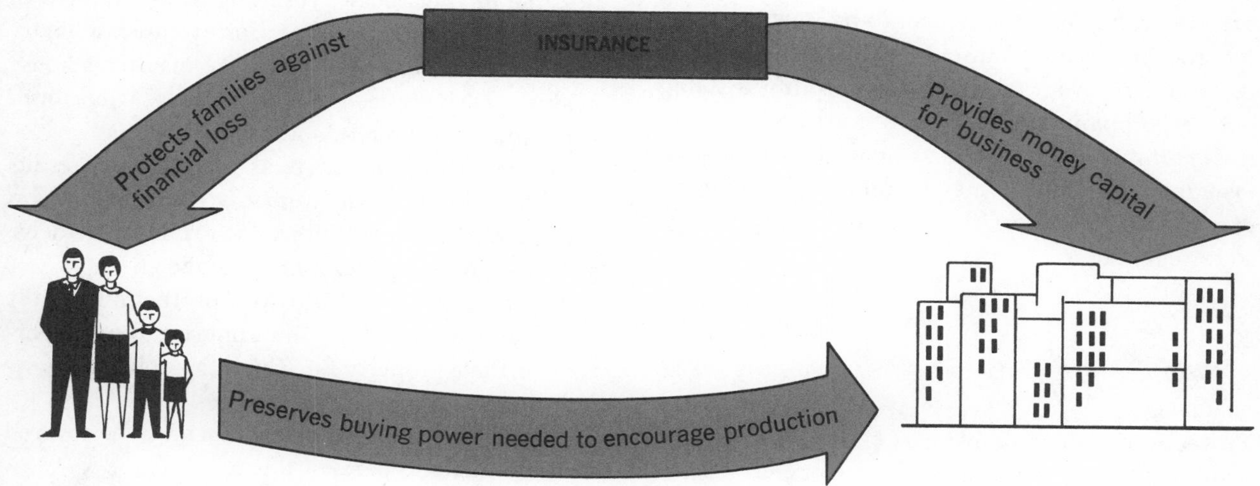

The insurance agent can give valuable advice on the type of policy to buy.

H. Armstrong Roberts

Because most insurance companies operate on a large scale, they provide a way for a large number of people to share their risks and losses. Since only a portion of these people will actually have losses, premiums are small compared to the amount of protection provided in exchange.

Insurance Companies Are Regulated by Law

Insurance companies, like banks, are the guardians of other people's money. Like banks, therefore, they are closely regulated. Each state has laws governing the operation of insurance companies within the state. In order to do business within a state, both a company and its agents must be licensed. An *insurance agent* is a man or woman who sells insurance. A company may be refused a license, or it may lose its license, if it does not comply with state regulations.

WHAT RISKS MAY BE INSURED?

Protection against almost any kind of loss can be provided through insurance. A singer may insure his voice. An artist may insure his hands. A dancer may insure his legs. A businessman can insure his place of business. He can also insure against a loss of profits during an interruption in business following a fire or other damaging accident. A farmer can insure his crops against hail damage and his livestock against accidental death or theft.

Most kinds of insurance, however, can be divided into three broad groups: property, personal, and liability.

Property insurance provides protection against possible financial losses resulting from damages to the policyholder's property. For example, a homeowner buys property insurance to insure his house against such perils as fire and lightning, windstorm, explosion, riot, aircraft, and vandalism.

Personal insurance protects against losses resulting from illness, bodily injury, or death. Common examples of personal insurance are life, accident, sickness, and hospitalization insurance.

Liability insurance provides protection against financial losses resulting from injuries to other persons or their property for which the policyholder is held responsible.

These different types of insurance will be covered in the remaining parts of this unit.

WHO MAY BUY INSURANCE?

A person may buy insurance only if he has an ***insurable interest*** in the person or property insured. An insurable interest is a money interest. In other words, no one can insure another person's life unless he would suffer a money loss should that person die. Neither can anyone insure property unless he would suffer a money loss if it were destroyed or damaged.

Every person has an insurable interest in his own life, health, and safety. A wife has an insurable interest in the life of her husband; and children, in the lives of their parents. Business partners may insure each other's lives. Because the success of a business depends greatly on its management, a corporation may insure the lives of persons in management positions.

The person who holds a mortgage on someone else's property has an insurable interest in the property. Usually, he will require the owner to carry insurance on it. Suppose, however, that a homeowner insures his house against fire and later sells it without canceling his fire insurance policy. If the house were damaged as the result of a fire, he could not collect for the damages, because he would suffer no money loss.

WHAT DETERMINES THE COST OF INSURANCE?

The main factor affecting the cost of any kind of insurance is the amount of risk involved. The more risk an insurance company assumes for a policyholder, the higher will be the premium. Risk is measured in terms of probable losses. An insurance company has to collect enough money from all its policyholders to pay whatever actual losses some of them will have. In deciding how much each policyholder must pay, therefore, a company begins by estimating its probable losses. It does this by studying its record of past losses. From their records, for example, insurance companies can tell how many of their policyholders will *probably* die each year; how many will *probably* be hospitalized and

Courtesy Skokie Police Department

In an automobile accident such as this one, it is important that the car owner have liability insurance.

be unable to work; and how many homes will *probably* catch fire and what the average loss will *probably* be. Thus, a company can figure about how much it will have to pay in losses during a year and what premiums it must charge.

Another factor that affects the price of insurance is the company's operating costs. Like other businesses, insurance companies have such expenses as employees' salaries, office space, supplies, and equipment. Premiums must be high enough to cover these costs as well as all losses.

The third factor affecting the cost of insurance is the earnings insurance companies receive from their investments. Although insurance companies must keep money available to pay losses, the money collected in premiums is never idle. It is invested. A large amount of it is invested in both corporate and government securities. A big portion is invested in mortgages, and some is invested in loans to policyholders. The earnings from these investments help to keep down the cost of insurance.

INSURANCE HELPS OUR BUSINESS SYSTEM

It might be said that insurance does three jobs. First, it protects the standard of living of individuals and families by guarding them against financial loss and reduced buying power. During a recent year, for example, $11 billion was paid out in life insurance benefits alone. ***Benefits*** are what a policyholder is entitled to if a loss occurs. Benefits may include more than just the payment of a sum of money. One benefit of automobile insurance may be that the insurance company will defend the policyholder in court if he is sued following an accident.

Second, by preserving buying power, insurance helps to prevent a decrease in production. As you know, a drop in spending for any reason usually causes a slowdown in production.

Third, the dollars spent for insurance provide some of the money capital needed by business. Investments of life insurance companies alone total nearly $150 billion. These investments have helped to start new businesses, enlarge old ones, and create additional jobs.

FEWER ECONOMIC LOSSES MEAN ECONOMIC GAIN

In an economic system that operates on money, there is bound to be some risk of financial loss. Actual losses, however, can be reduced. Recent studies show, for example, that seven out of ten automobile accidents are the result of traffic violations. In fact most losses are the result of carelessness or neglect. If you ignore sound health practices, you increase your chances of becoming ill. The homeowner who permits rubbish to accumulate in his garage or attic increases the chances of a fire. The person who is careless about locking his car increases the chances of its being stolen.

On the other hand, some automobile owners have driven for twenty-five years or more without an accident. Is this because they were luckier than other drivers? Not usually. It is because they obeyed the rules of safety by keeping their equipment in good condition and observing traffic regulations. Likewise owners of factories and stores prevent fire and loss of life by installing sprinkler systems. Schools stage regular fire drills so that students will know what to do in case of an emergency. Cities and states spend millions of dollars to provide safe and sanitary conditions for their citizens.

Any reduction in economic losses will result in some economic gain. For one thing, insurance would cost less. To take one example, it has been estimated that, if all drivers would exercise a little more care in observing traffic regulations, automobile insurance premiums could be reduced an average of $15 a year. The other goods and services you buy would also cost less. Insurance, you see, is one of the costs of doing business. Like other costs, it must be included in the prices we pay for goods and services. A decrease in economic losses, therefore, could mean an increase in our standard of living. Most important of all, it would mean less human suffering and less waste of economic resources.

BUILDING YOUR VOCABULARY

List the figures 1 to 7 on a sheet of paper, numbering down. Read the seven statements given below at the right; then, for each statement, select from the column at the left the term that best matches it in meaning. Write this term next to the appropriate number.

benefits	1. The possibility of a money loss
economic risk	2. A written agreement between an insurance company and a policyholder
insurable interest	3. A way of sharing economic losses
insurance	4. A payment for insurance protection
policy	5. A person for whom an insurance company assumes a risk
policyholder	6. A money interest in property or in a person's life
premium	7. Money or services a policyholder receives when a loss occurs

CHECKING YOUR READING

1. Name some of the economic risks that people face every day.
2. What does "sharing economic losses" mean?
3. Explain how insurance helps people to share economic losses.
4. How can an insurance company afford to provide protection to a policyholder that is many times greater than the premium he pays?
5. Why are insurance companies closely regulated by law?
6. Give examples of different kinds of risks that may be covered by insurance.
7. What kind of protection does property insurance provide?
8. What protection is provided by personal insurance?
9. What kinds of losses are covered by liability insurance?
10. Who may insure a person's life or a piece of property?
11. How does an insurance company determine what premiums it must charge policyholders?
12. What does an insurance company do with the money it receives as premiums? How does this affect the cost of insurance?
13. Name three important ways in which insurance helps our business system.
14. How does insurance protect the standard of living of individuals and families?
15. What are some ways in which economic risks can be reduced?
16. Explain how a reduction in economic losses results in economic gain.

SHARING YOUR OPINION AND EXPERIENCE

1. What is the difference between an economic risk and an economic loss?
2. Why do insurance companies collect premium payments in advance?
3. Why does a businessman have an insurable interest in the life of his partner?
4. Would you prefer to buy insurance from a company that has only a few policyholders or from one that has many? Why?
5. Why do insurance companies spend money to teach people how to reduce accidents?

6. Many companies now sell "trip insurance" which insures a person's life while he travels from one place to another. Would you expect the premiums on such insurance to be high or low? Why?
7. Why would a professional piano player wish to insure his hands?
8. If a person 21 years old and another 45 years old each bought a $10,000 life insurance policy, which one would have to pay the higher premium? Explain why.

PROJECTS AND PROBLEMS

1. Economic losses resulting from traffic accidents totaled $9 billion in a recent year. There were approximately 190 million people in the United States in the same year. If the cost of these accidents had been divided equally among all the people, how much (to the nearest dollar) would each person have had to pay?
2. There are 750 homes in the town of Rosedale. Records for the past 15 years show that fires in Rosedale caused approximately $33,750 worth of damage to homes each year. The homeowners were granted permission by the state to organize an insurance company to protect themselves against fire losses.

   ▪ *a.* How much would each homeowner have to pay annually to the fund just to cover expected losses? ▪ *b.* A fire at the home of Mr. Craft, a member of the group, caused damages amounting to $1,845. How much did Mr. Craft save by belonging to the insurance group?

3. As you learned in Part 16, a circle graph is used to compare single items within a group with the entire group. Often the size of each item is expressed as a percent of the entire group. In that case, the total space within the circle represents 100 percent. In the graph below, the circle represents 100 percent of the investments of life insurance companies in the United States during a recent year. Each division within the circle represents the percent of funds that these companies had in one type of investment. Study the graph and answer the questions that follow it.

HOW FUNDS OF LIFE INSURANCE COMPANIES WERE INVESTED IN A RECENT YEAR

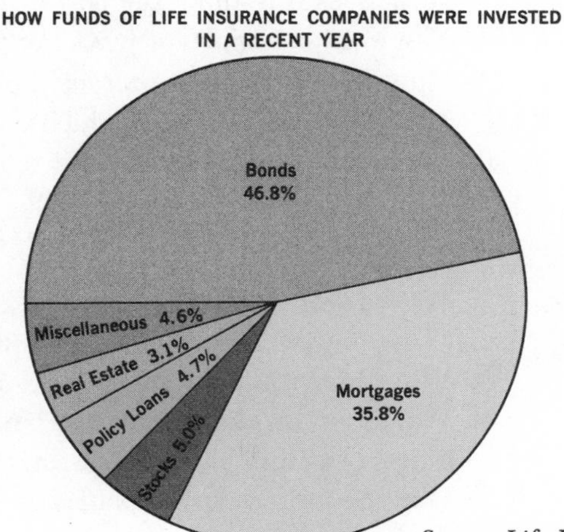

Source: Life Insurance Fact Book, 1965

▪ *a.* In what type of investment did life insurance companies have the largest percent of their funds? ▪ *b.* In what type of investment did they have the second largest percent of their money? ▪ *c.* What was the total percent of funds in these two types of investments? ▪ *d.* How did the percent of funds invested in stocks compare with the investment in policy loans? ▪ *e.* Approximately how many times as much money was invested in mortgages as in real estate? ▪ *f.* Approximately how many times as much money was invested in bonds and mortgages as in all other types of investments combined?

4. Each year accidents occurring at places of work result in large economic losses. These losses include medical expenses, lost wages, damage to equipment and materials, production delays, and other related costs. The table below shows the amount of such losses for eight different years. Study the table and answer the questions that follow it.

ECONOMIC LOSSES FROM WORK ACCIDENTS IN THE UNITED STATES

Year	*Amount of Loss (billion dollars)*
1943	$2.4
1946	2.4
1949	2.6
1952	2.9
1955	3.5
1958	3.9
1961	4.6
1964	5.2

Source: Insurance Facts, 1965

▪ *a.* In which year(s) was the economic loss from work accidents least? ▪ *b.* In which year was the loss greatest? ▪ *c.* During which three-year period did the amount of the losses increase most? ▪ *d.* How much greater was the amount of the loss in 1964 than it was in 1943? ▪ *e.* What was the percent of increase in losses between 1943 and 1964? ▪ *f.* Based on your study of this table, what would you say has been the general trend in economic losses resulting from work accidents? ▪ *g.* Would you expect the losses in 1974 to be more or less than $5,200,000,000? Why?

5. As almost everyone knows, the general standard of living in the United States has risen over the years. One of the important ways in which it has improved is that people have greater financial security than they had formerly. Proof of this is seen in the fact that nearly every year sales of insurance increase. The bar graph on page 282 shows the amount of new life insurance Americans bought each year from 1944 to 1964. Study the graph and answer the questions that follow it.

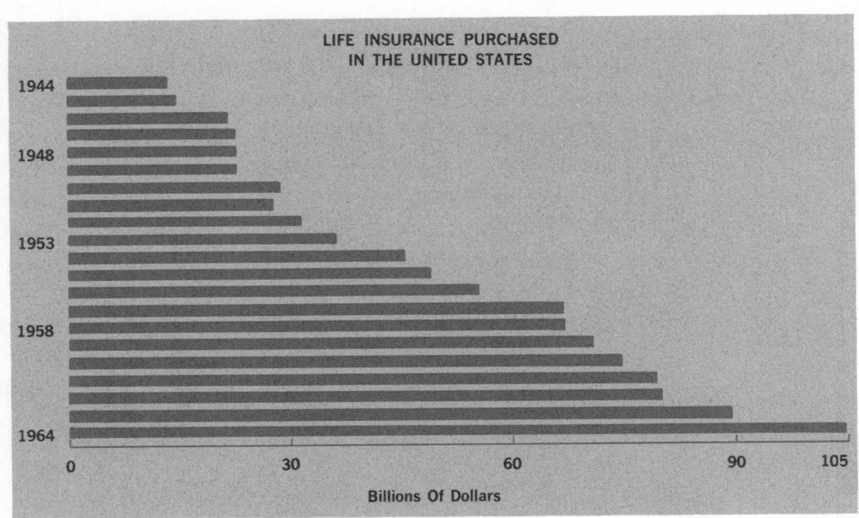

Source: *Life Insurance Fact Book, 1965*

▪ *a.* What was the approximate amount of life insurance purchased in 1944? in 1954? in 1964? ▪ *b.* In which year(s) did people buy less life insurance than in the preceding year? What do you think may have caused this? ▪ *c.* In what year did the amount of new life insurance purchased increase most over the preceding year? ▪ *d.* Approximately how many times as much insurance was purchased in 1954 as in 1944? ▪ *e.* The amount of new life insurance purchased in 1964 was approximately how many times the amount purchased in 1954?

CHALLENGE PROBLEMS

1. As indicated by the circle graph in Projects and Problems No. 3, life insurance companies invest a large part of their funds in bonds and mortgages. Why do you suppose they put so much more money into these two types of investments than they put into stocks?
2. The table in Projects and Problems No. 4 shows the amount by which economic losses resulting from work accidents increased from 1943 to 1964. One possible reason for the increase is a greater number of accidents. What else might have caused the amount of loss to increase?
3. One type of loss resulting from work accidents is production delays. Why would a delay in production result in an economic loss?

PART 31
AUTOMOBILE INSURANCE

NEXT to a home, an automobile is usually the most valuable single item a family owns. It is also one of the most dangerous. Today there are close to 80 million motor vehicles on our streets and highways. And they cause nearly 14 million accidents annually. This means that about one out of every six cars runs into something or somebody each year. The outcome may be nothing more than a dented fender. Or it may be permanent injury or loss of life for one or more persons. In any case the driver who is judged at fault is responsible for payment of losses. A request for payment of losses is called a ***claim.*** Claims arising from a serious accident may amount to hundreds or even thousands of dollars. The only way most people can protect themselves against the risks that go with owning an automobile is to buy insurance. The insurance company then assumes responsibility for settling claims resulting from accidents.

What kinds of protection do automobile owners need most? Why do some drivers have to pay more for insurance than others?

HOW DOES INSURANCE PROTECT THE AUTOMOBILE OWNER?

An automobile owner may incur financial loss in a number of ways. His car may injure pedestrians or persons riding in another car or damage property belonging to others. He or other persons riding in *his* car may be injured. His car may be damaged in some way, or it may be stolen. He or members of his family might be injured by an uninsured driver.

To guard against all these risks, the automobile owner needs several types of insurance. But he need not buy each one separately, because all types can be obtained in one policy. On page 285 is an illustration of an automobile policy showing the types of protection bought by Mr. Andrew Harrison.

Courtesy State of New York Department of Public Works

When a person has insurance protection against a certain type of risk, he is said to be *covered* against that risk. The insurance protection is called ***coverage.*** An explanation of the major types of coverage available to car owners follows.

Automobile Liability Insurance

One type of insurance no automobile owner can afford to be without is liability. In a few states it is required by law. *Automobile liability insurance* is designed to protect against losses arising from injury to other persons or damage to property belonging to others. It includes two types of coverage—*bodily injury liability* and *property damage liability*.

Bodily Injury Liability Insurance. As its name tells you, ***bodily injury liability insurance*** protects the automobile owner against financial losses resulting from injuries to pedestrians, to persons riding in other cars, or to guests in his car. Bodily injury coverage is usually stated in two figures. You will notice in Mr. Harrison's policy, illustrated on page 285, that he carries \$50,000–\$100,000 of bodily injury insurance. This means that the insurance company will pay up to \$50,000 for injuries suffered by one person in an accident; but no more than \$100,000 will be paid for a single accident.

The minimum amount of bodily injury insurance an automobile owner may buy is \$5,000–\$10,000, but this does not provide enough protection. Since the amounts awarded by the courts to accident victims have been rising, most drivers want more than the minimum protection; and additional coverage costs very little more. For example, Mr. Harrison pays \$63 a year for coverage of \$50,000–\$100,000. This is only \$15 more than he would have to pay for \$10,000–\$20,000 coverage. In other words, by paying a 30 percent higher premium, he gets five times as much protection.

Property Damage Liability Insurance. Almost every accident causes damage to someone's property. ***Property damage liability insurance*** protects the automobile owner from losses resulting from damage to the property of others. In most cases the property damaged is another car; but it may be buildings, trees, telephone poles, light posts, or fences. The only property not covered by property damage insurance is the policyholder's own car.

Property damage insurance is usually purchased in units of \$5,000. In a few states, however, it may be

Courtesy State Farm Insurance

Here an insurance adjuster is checking the damage and needed repairs on a policyholder's car.

The Ætna Casualty and Surety Company
Hartford 15, Connecticut

This Declarations page, with "Policy Provisions—Section 1," completes the below numbered "FAMILY AUTOMOBILE POLICY"

DECLARATIONS Policy Form 13119 Policy No. VF283162

1. Named Insured and Address (No.—Street—Town—County—State)

ANDREW HARRISON
45 SYCAMORE DRIVE
CENTERVILLE, U. S. A.

The owned automobile will be principally garaged in the town designated in item 1, unless otherwise stated herein:

2. Policy Period: From 6/30/66 To 6/30/67
12:01 A.M., standard time at the above address.

3. **The insurance afforded is only with respect to such of the following coverages as are indicated by specific premium charge or charges. The limit of the Company's liability against each such coverage shall be as stated herein, subject to all the terms of this policy having reference thereto.**

Coverages	Limits of Liability	H.O. Use	Premiums Car 1	Premiums Car 2
PART I				
A. Bodily Injury Liability	50 thousand dollars each person; 100 thousand dollars each occurrence		$ 63.00	$
B. Property Damage Liability	5 thousand dollars each occurrence		$ 31.00	$
PART II				
C. Medical Payments	1,000 dollars each person		$ 8.00	$
PART III				
D. (1) Comprehensive	Actual Cash Value unless otherwise stated herein $		$ 17.00	$
(2) Personal Effects	$100			
E. Collision	Actual Cash Value less Car 1 $ 100 Car 2 $ deductible		$ 70.00	$
F. Towing and Labor Costs	$ per disablement		$	$
PART IV				
G. Family Protection	10 thousand dollars each person; 20 thousand dollars each accident		$ 5.00	$
Endorsements (Attached on reverse side)				
	Total Premium $		194.00	

4. Description of owned automobile or trailer:

	Class,	Year,	Trade Name,	Body Type,	Identification No.,	Model	Symbol	Purchase Date	New Used
Car 1	2	1966	Chevrolet	4-door Sedan	742W18712	BelAir	J	11/65	N
Car 2									

5. (a) The total number of private passenger, farm and utility automobiles owned on the effective date of this policy by the named Insured does not exceed the number of such automobiles described in item 4, unless otherwise stated herein:
   (b) The named Insured does not own any trailer on the effective date of this policy unless otherwise stated herein: (required only if Coverage D or E is afforded)

6. During the past three years no insurer has cancelled insurance, issued to the named Insured, similar to that afforded hereunder, unless otherwise stated herein:

7. Any loss under Part III is payable as interest may appear to the named Insured and: (If automobile is encumbered show name and address of lien-holder and due date of final payment)

Schedule of Installment Payments (Not Applicable in Texas)	Payment Due Mo. Day Yr.	Bodily Injury Car 1	Bodily Injury Car 2	Property Damage Car 1	Property Damage Car 2	Physical Damage Car 1	Physical Damage Car 2	Amount of Payment

("FA" Form)
(13120-B) 2-63

Countersigned by C R Brown

Courtesy The Aetna Casualty and Surety Company

Application for an automobile insurance policy

purchased in units of $1,000. You will notice that Mr. Harrison carries $5,000 of protection.

Medical Payments Insurance

Anyone who carries bodily injury insurance may also obtain ***medical payments insurance*** for only a small additional premium. Medical payments insurance pays for medical expenses resulting from injuries from automobile accidents. But it differs from bodily injury insurance in two important ways. One is that medical payments insurance covers injuries to the automobile owner and members of his family as well as guests riding in his car. Bodily injury insurance applies only to persons outside the policyholder's family. The second difference is that medical payments insurance pays expenses resulting from injuries regardless of who is responsible for the accident. Bodily injury coverage pays for losses only when the policyholder is judged to blame for the accident.

Medical payments insurance is bought in units of $500. As you can see, Mr. Harrison has medical payments coverage of $1,000. This means that $1,000 is the most the insurance company will pay to any one person in any one accident.

Collision Insurance

Property damage liability insurance pays for damages to automobiles belonging to others. To protect himself against losses resulting from damage to his own car, the automobile owner must carry ***collision insurance.*** This type of insurance pays for damage to the insured's car resulting from collision or upset regardless of who is responsible. Because minor accidents are so numerous, the cost of complete collision coverage is high. Most people, therefore, buy *deductible* collision insurance. This means that the policyholder agrees to pay part of the damages himself.

For example, suppose you bought $50 deductible collision insurance. If your car is damaged to the extent of $140, you would have to pay $50 of the cost to repair it. The insurance company would pay the remaining $90. If the loss amounted to $50 or less, you would pay the total cost. Collision insurance is also available with $100, $150, or $250 deductible provisions. The table below shows a comparison of the rates Mr. Harrison would have to pay for each type.

Amount of Coverage	*Annual Cost*
$ 50 deductible	$99
100 deductible	70
150 deductible	56
250 deductible	42

Comprehensive Physical Damage Insurance

Protection against damages to the policyholder's car that are not covered by collision insurance is provided by ***comprehensive physical damage insurance.*** This coverage, known simply as *comprehensive,* pays for losses resulting from fire, theft, and glass breakage. Fire is not a common cause of damage, but thousands of cars are stolen annually. Comprehensive coverage also pays for losses caused by hail, windstorm, vandalism, explosion, and falling objects such as tree branches. Its cost is quite low when you consider the number of risks it covers.

Uninsured Motorists Coverage

Sometimes people are unable to collect for injuries caused by other motorists. They might be victims of a hit-and-run driver or accidents caused by persons who have no insurance and no money to pay for the losses. In cases of this kind the automobile owner is protected by ***uninsured motorists coverage.*** Another name for this type of insurance is *family protection coverage.*

The difference between uninsured motorists coverage and medical payments insurance is this. Medical payments insurance only takes care of actual expenses incurred as the result of injuries. It does not pay for such things as income lost because of inability to work following an accident. Neither does it pay for suffering endured by the injured or for permanent disfigurement resulting from an injury. But uninsured motorists coverage does. It pays all losses in connection with injuries, the same as if the driver who was responsible had carried insurance.

WHAT DETERMINES THE COST OF AUTOMOBILE INSURANCE?

When the price of anything is based on some other amount, it is often called a *rate*. The price of borrowing money, for example, is an interest rate. Since the price of insurance is based on the amount of coverage provided, insurance prices are also called rates. The cost of automobile insurance, like the cost of other kinds of insurance, depends on the amount of risk the insurance company assumes. Insurance companies, therefore, set their rates so that those who have the most losses pay the highest premiums. In addition, automobile insurance rates are regulated by the commissioner of insurance in each state. It is his job to see that rates charged by insurance companies are no higher than necessary to pay for the risk.

Some factors that help to determine the amount of risk are explained in the following paragraphs.

The Value of the Car

It stands to reason that an expensive make of car would cost more to repair or to replace than a lower priced one. On the other hand, cars do decrease in value as they are used. When a policyholder suffers a total loss of his automobile, the amount he is paid depends on the value of his car at the time of the loss. Rates for collision and comprehensive coverage, therefore, vary with the make, model, and age of the car.

Classification of Drivers

In an effort to establish fair rates, automobile insurance companies divide their policyholders into classes. They then assign a rate to each class. One of the ways policyholders are classified is according to the ages of those driving the car. If one driver

Courtesy Aetna Life Affiliated Companies

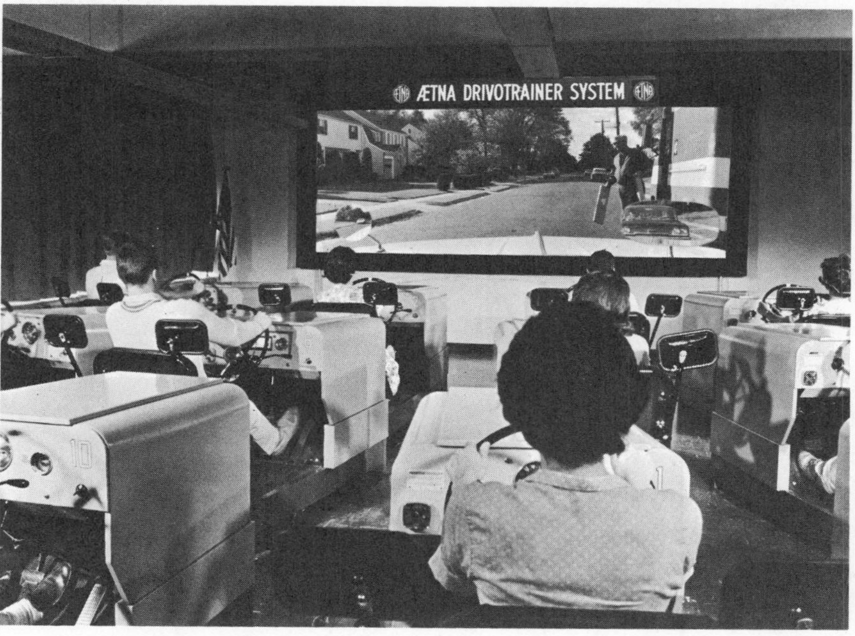

Driver-training classes in high schools help to reduce careless driving and accidents.

is under 25 and unmarried, for example, the policyholder has to pay a higher premium than if all drivers are over 25. Some insurance companies, however, give a discount if a young driver has successfully completed a driver-training course.

Policyholders are also classified according to how their cars are used and the number of miles they are driven. Premiums are lower on cars that are used mainly for pleasure than on those used for business. In some cases, if a car is driven less than 7,500 miles annually, its owner pays a lower premium than he would pay if his total mileage were more.

Where the Policyholder Lives

Not only are automobile insurance rates different in different states, but they vary within a state. They are usually higher in cities where traffic is heavy than in small towns or rural areas where traffic is light. They are higher in regions where roads are often covered with snow and ice than in areas where roads are dry. They are highest in communities where the amounts awarded by the courts to accident victims are highest.

Driving Record of Policyholder

Sometimes a person may be such a poor risk that no company will sell him insurance at regular rates. He may have a bad accident record; or he may have been convicted of drunken driving or some other major traffic violation. To obtain insurance he will have to pay more than the regular premium rate. How much more will depend on how bad his driving record is.

IT PAYS TO KNOW WHAT PROTECTION YOU HAVE

If people shopped as carefully for car insurance as they do for cars, they could save themselves much grief. Many drivers discover too late that they do not have the protection they thought they had. For example, when a car is bought on credit, the lending agency often arranges for the insurance. The cost of the insurance is included in the buyer's monthly payment. Since the lender is concerned mainly with protecting himself from loss, the policy he obtains may provide only collision and comprehensive coverage. It may not include any liability protection for the owner.

Even people who arrange for their own insurance do not always know what it covers. Policyholders with children of driving age sometimes think that their insurance covers the children if they are driving a car owned by someone else. This may or may not be the case.

The time for an automobile owner to find out what protection he actually has is before he has an accident, not afterwards.

Today all states have what are known as *financial responsibility laws*. According to these laws, if an automobile owner is involved in an accident resulting in bodily injury or property damage, he must show proof of his ability to pay for the losses. Otherwise, he loses his right to drive. This is true whether or not he is responsible for the accident. The purpose of these laws is to protect the public from drivers who are unable to pay for damages or injuries they might cause.

BUILDING YOUR VOCABULARY

List the figures 1 to 8 on a sheet of paper, numbering down. Read the eight statements given below at the right; then, for each statement, select from the column at the left the term that best matches it in meaning. Write this term next to the appropriate number.

bodily injury liability insurance
claim
collision insurance
comprehensive physical damage insurance
coverage
medical payments insurance
property damage liability insurance
uninsured motorists coverage

1. Pays medical expenses for persons injured while riding in the policyholder's car regardless of who is responsible for the accident
2. Pays for damages caused by the policyholder's car to any type of property belonging to others
3. Protects against financial losses resulting from injuries to pedestrians, to persons riding in other cars, or to guests in the policyholder's car
4. Pays for all losses resulting from injuries caused by other drivers for which the policyholder is unable to collect
5. Any type of insurance protection
6. Protects against losses resulting from damage to the policyholder's car regardless of who is responsible
7. A request for payment of losses
8. Pays for damages to the policyholder's car that are not covered by collision insurance

CHECKING YOUR READING

1. What responsibility does the insurance company assume when a person buys automobile insurance?
2. What are some of the risks automobile owners face?
3. Which type of automobile insurance is most important to the car owner? Why?
4. What two types of coverage does automobile liability insurance include?
5. Bodily injury coverage is often stated in two figures, such as \$20,000–\$40,000. Explain the meaning of these two figures.
6. Why is the minimum amount of bodily injury insurance usually not enough?
7. What property is not covered by property damage liability insurance?
8. How does medical payments insurance differ from bodily injury liability insurance?
9. Collision and property damage liability insurance differ in two ways. What are they?
10. What responsibility does the car owner assume when he buys deductible collision insurance?
11. What types of losses are covered by comprehensive physical damage insurance?
12. What is the difference between uninsured motorists coverage and medical payments insurance?

13. How does the amount of risk an automobile insurance company assumes affect the cost of insurance?
14. Why do insurance rates vary with the make, model, and age of the car?
15. How do automobile insurance companies classify their policyholders?
16. Why do the rates for automobile insurance vary within a state?
17. Why is it important to shop carefully for car insurance?
18. What are financial responsibility laws, and what is their purpose?

SHARING YOUR OPINION AND EXPERIENCE

1. Would automobile insurance still be needed if every driver observed all traffic regulations? Why?
2. Why do you suppose automobile insurance rates are higher for an unmarried person under 25 than for a married person under 25?
3. Why do you think some states require automobile owners to carry automobile liability insurance?
4. Why do you think property damage coverage of $5,000 is usually enough, while bodily injury coverage of $5,000–$10,000 is considered too little?
5. What reasons can you give for the increase in insurance rates when a car is used for business purposes?
6. Why would an insurance company be willing to give a discount to a young driver who has successfully completed a driver-training course?
7. Insurance companies usually advise policyholders not to admit responsibility for any accidents in which they are involved. Why do the companies make this request?
8. It has been said that "traffic accidents increase our cost of living." Explain.
9. Why do you think $150 deductible collision insurance would cost Mr. Harrison only about half of what he would have to pay for $50 deductible coverage?
10. In a recent year, more automobile insurance claims were paid in New York and in California than in any of the other states. What reasons can you give for this fact?

PROJECTS AND PROBLEMS

1. Prepare a table showing the types of automobile insurance coverage discussed in this part and the kinds of protection provided by each. Use a form similar to the one shown here.

Type of Coverage	Protection Provided

2. The graph on page 291 shows the dollar cost of economic losses resulting from traffic accidents each year for a period of 26 years. Each upright line represents the end of a year. During the year ending December 31, 1939, for example, losses were approximately $1.85 billion. By the end of 1941, the losses had increased to about $2.2 billion a year. Study the graph and answer the questions that follow it.

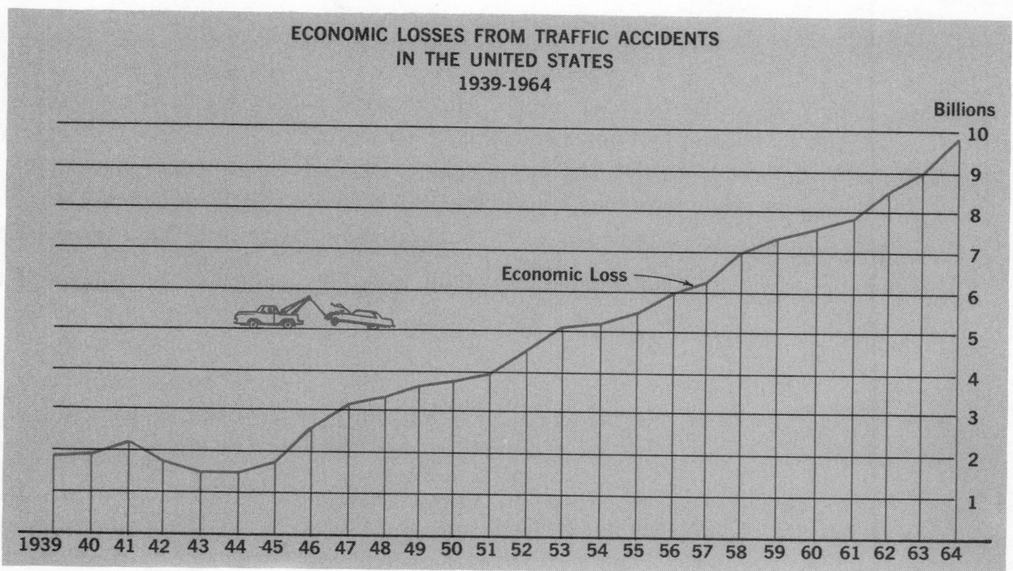

Source: *Insurance Facts, 1965*

▪ *a.* In which year was the dollar cost of traffic accidents greatest? What amount did total losses reach that year? ▪ *b.* In which year(s) was the amount of loss from accidents lowest? What was the approximate amount of loss? ▪ *c.* How much did the cost of traffic accidents increase in the 14-year period beginning with 1951 and including 1964? ▪ *d.* During which one-year period(s) did losses from traffic accidents increase the most? What was the approximate amount of increase during the period(s)? ▪ *e.* During which period did losses from traffic accidents decrease? ▪ *f.* The cost of accidents in 1958 was approximately how many times the cost in 1948? ▪ g. What was the approximate percent of increase in the cost of accidents during the 26 years shown on the graph?

3. Study Mr. Harrison's insurance policy illustrated on page 285 and answer the following questions.

▪ *a.* What is the total yearly cost of Mr. Harrison's automobile insurance? ▪ *b.* What types of coverage does Mr. Harrison have? ▪ *c.* How much does Mr. Harrison pay each year for collision insurance? ▪ *d.* How many cars does Mr. Harrison have insured? ▪ *e.* On what date does the insurance coverage begin? On what date does it end? ▪ *f.* Suppose that Mr. Harrison's car struck a tree following a blowout and that the repairs cost $275. How much of the damage would the insurance company pay?

4. Mr. Auman's automobile insurance includes $10,000–$20,000 bodily injury liability, $5,000 property damage liability, $100 deductible collision, comprehensive, and medical payments coverage. As the result of an accident in which Mr. Auman was at fault, three passengers of another car were injured. Through court action Mr. Auman was required to pay $12,000; $6,500; and $2,100 respectively to the three injured persons.

▪ *a.* Under which type of coverage was Mr. Auman protected for these losses? ▪ *b.* How much of the amount paid to the three injured persons was not covered by insurance? ▪ *c.* Mr. Auman also had to pay $875 for damages to the other car. Under which type of coverage was he protected against this loss? ▪ *d.* Damage to Mr. Auman's car amounted to $625. How much of this amount was covered by insurance? ▪ *e.* What was the total amount the insurance company had to pay?

5. The following article appeared recently in the Centerville newspaper. Read it and answer the questions that follow.

HERE'S WHAT PUSHES AUTO RISK RATES UP

Have you ever wondered about what has sent your auto insurance costs spiraling over the past 10 years? The answer is an increase in the factors that make for accidents plus an increase in accident costs.

Here are some of the reasons why accidents are on the upswing. Miles of annual vehicle travel have increased 75 percent in the past 10 years. The number of registered vehicles is up 77 percent, and the number of licensed drivers up 51 percent.

In addition, the average rate of speed in highway travel has increased 10 percent over the last decade.

In addition to the increase of these "accident breeding" factors, the costs of parts and labor demanded after an accident are higher.

Personal injuries suffered in auto accidents also are more expensive than they were 10 years ago. Average per patient hospital costs, for example, have increased 167 percent. General medical care costs have increased 38 percent.

▪ *a.* According to the article, what two major factors account for the increasing cost of automobile insurance? ▪ *b.* What four reasons are given for the increase in number of auto accidents? ▪ *c.* Which increased most in the past 10 years—number of registered vehicles or vehicle travel? ▪ *d.* What two reasons are given for the increase in the cost of each accident? ▪ *e.* Why are personal injuries suffered in auto accidents more expensive than they were 10 years ago?

6. Most automobile insurance companies advise their policyholders what to do in case of an accident. The advice may be printed on the insurance policy itself, or it may appear in a special handbook given to all policyholders. Using information provided by your family's insurance company or by someone who knows what to do, make a list of the steps to follow when an accident occurs.

CHALLENGE PROBLEMS

1. Mr. Thornton bought a new car for $3,000. The first year he paid $85 for collision insurance. Today the market value of his car is only $1,500, but the annual cost of the collision insurance is $68. Since the car is worth only half its original value, why is the cost of collision insurance only 20 percent less than it was the first year?
2. Automobile insurance companies often want to know the occupation of each policyholder. Why do you think they are interested in this information?

PART 32 INSURANCE FOR THE PROPERTY OWNER

IN addition to an automobile, most people own other kinds of property worth insuring. It may be ***real property,*** such as a house, a garage, or a barn; or it may be ***personal property,*** such as furniture, books, clothing, jewelry, and pictures. The amount of money invested in both kinds of property may be large. If either one were destroyed, or even partly damaged, the loss could be great.

Common causes of property losses are fire and theft. But many other things can damage, destroy, or cause people to lose their property. And year by year the list of risks grows longer. Consequently, insurance policies are revised from time to time to cover new risks. Today a property owner can protect himself against almost every kind of loss; but only if he keeps his insurance up to date.

What are some ways a property owner might incur financial losses? How many insurance policies would he have to buy to insure himself against these different losses?

FIRE IS THE GREATEST RISK

The purpose of any type of insurance is to protect people against large financial losses. The greatest risk to property, other than automobiles, is fire. A home catches fire somewhere in the United States about every 24 seconds. This means that more than $1\frac{1}{4}$ million homes are damaged by fire annually. In a recent year the nation's fire losses, including buildings and their contents, totaled $1,405,558,000.

A homeowner may insure his house under one policy and his household goods and other personal property under another. Or he may insure both under one policy that includes several types of coverage. This combination policy, called a *homeowner's policy,* is explained later in this part.

In addition to the damage caused by the fire itself, fire insurance covers damages resulting from the following:

Courtesy New York City Fire Department

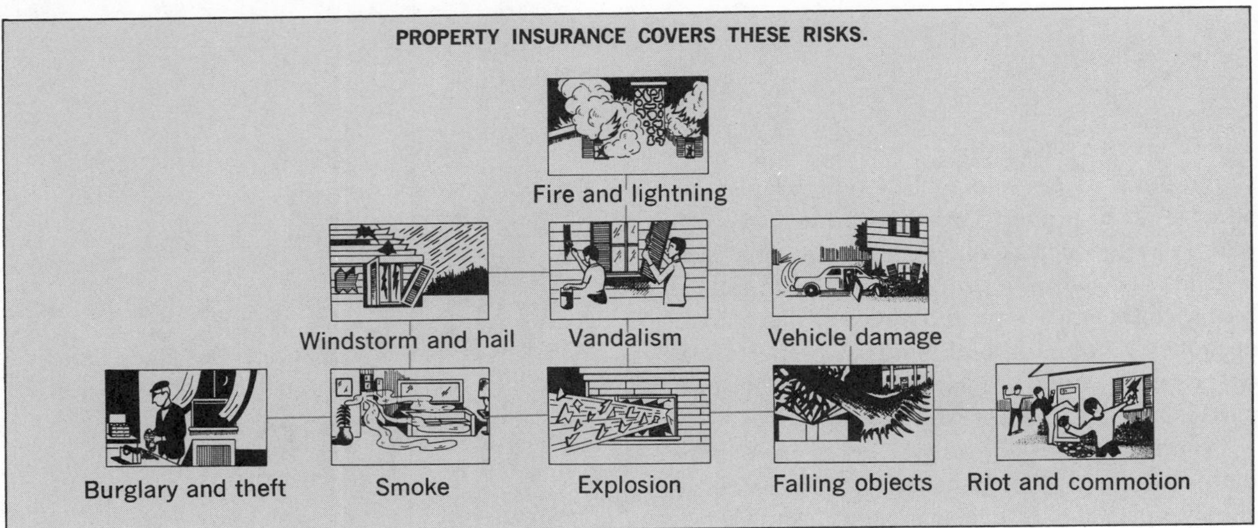

1. Smoke that accompanies the fire
2. Water or chemicals used in fighting the fire
3. Lightning, whether or not the lightning started a fire

EXTENDED COVERAGE MAY BE ADDED

Although fire is the property owner's greatest risk, serious losses do result from other causes. In some regions of the country hailstorms cause considerable property damage. In some, windstorms and tornadoes occur frequently during the summer months. Property may also be damaged by aircraft, vehicles, or explosion. Insurance that provides protection against this whole group of risks is called ***extended coverage.*** One type of loss this insurance does *not* cover is damage resulting from floods.

Extended coverage is sold in combination with fire insurance. It costs about the same as fire insurance.

WHAT DETERMINES THE COST OF FIRE INSURANCE?

As you have already learned, the cost of any kind of insurance is based on the degree of risk assumed by the insurance company. The greater the risk, the higher the premium must be. Premiums for extended coverage, for example, are highest in regions where windstorms and tornadoes are common. Following are some of the factors which affect the rates for fire insurance:

1. The Materials from Which the Building Is Made. Rates for brick or stone houses are lower than those for houses made entirely of wood. In some areas, houses with slate, tile, or composition-shingle roofs can be insured at a lower cost than those with wood-shingle roofs.

2. The Efficiency of the Local Fire Department. Communities are rated in ten different classes according to the protection they provide against fire. Those with excellent fire protection are given the highest rating. Fire insurance premiums in those communities are low. A community that has no organized fire-protection system is rated in the tenth class and has a high fire insurance rate.

3. The Location of the Property. If property is located where there is danger of fire from nearby buildings, the risk of fire is increased. In some communities the distance from a house to the nearest fire hydrant affects the rates charged.

4. The Period of Time Covered by the Policy. Rates are usually figured on each $100 of insurance protection. Suppose that the rate for fire and extended coverage on a certain house is 45 cents for $100 of protection for one year. If the owner buys

$10,000 of insurance, he pays $45 for one year's protection. His yearly cost would be less, however, if he paid for his insurance three or five years at a time.

As an example, for three years' protection paid in advance, one company charges 2.7 times the amount for one year. In other words, the $10,000 of insurance that costs $45 for one year would cost $121.50 if purchased for three years—a saving of $13.50. If taken for five years, $10,000 of protection could be bought for 4.4 times the cost for one year—or for a premium of $198. This represents a saving of $27.

THEFT INSURANCE IS THE MOST EXPENSIVE

Another risk to personal property is theft. As a rule, only items that can be carried easily are stolen. For that reason the amount of theft insurance needed is usually less than the amount of fire insurance carried on personal property.

The rates for theft insurance are high compared with the cost of other kinds of insurance. Before purchasing this protection, a person should consider whether his personal belongings are valuable enough to justify the expense.

MAJOR CAUSES OF FIRE

Causes of Ignition	*Claims*		*Property Loss*	
	Number	*Percent*	*In Dollars*	*Percent*
Matches and smoking	499,475	22.5%	$ 690,511,303	14.9%
Electricity and electrical equipment except lightning and static	459,718	20.7	1,547,432,643	33.5
Heat, flames, or sparks from sources other than defective heating units or welding torches	286,122	12.9	313,607,849	6.8
Lightning	268,655	12.1	247,442,068	5.4
Defective heating units—all fuels combined	226,571	10.2	514,746,384	11.1
Exposure	144,798	6.5	346,626,493	7.5
Defective or overheated chimneys, flues, etc.	77,620	3.5	143,460,974	3.1
Sparks from bonfires, rubbish, etc.	57,814	2.6	90,464,346	2.0
Known but not otherwise classified	56,493	2.5	160,011,101	3.5
Open lights	47,867	2.1	50,220,557	1.1
Spontaneous ignition	36,841	1.7	160,369,478	3.5
Incendiarism, vandalism, etc.	26,587	1.2	144,094,180	3.1
Welding torches	12,702	0.6	129,207,743	2.8
Friction and friction sparks	10,405	0.5	53,478,670	1.1
Backfire or hot exhaust from internal-combustion engines	5,208	0.2	12,435,977	0.3
Fireworks, firecrackers	2,898	0.1	5,287,329	0.1
Static electricity and static sparks	2,049	0.1	11,063,774	0.2
Total	2,221,823	100.0%	$4,620,460,869	100.0%

PROOF OF LOSS IS REQUIRED

When a loss from fire or theft is covered by insurance, the insurance company will pay up to the face value of the policy. Settlement is usually made on the replacement value of the property damaged or stolen, less depreciation. ***Depreciation*** is a decrease in the value of property as a result of age and use. Like automobiles, clothing and household furnishings depreciate in value with the passage of time. A chair that is ten years old may be worth only a fraction of what it cost when new. Possible exceptions are valuable antiques, which sometimes increase in value as time goes on.

Before a policyholder can collect for damages, he will be required to furnish proof of loss. If fire damages a building, the loss is not difficult to estimate. But when the contents of a home are destroyed by fire or stolen, the owner must have some means of determining the loss. The best means is a household inventory. A ***household inventory*** is an itemized list of personal property, showing the cost of each item and the date of its purchase. It should include furniture, books, pictures, art objects, silverware, appliances, jewelry, and clothing. A partial inventory of this kind is shown below.

Forms to be used in preparing a household inventory may be obtained from insurance companies. The completed inventory should then be kept in a safe-deposit box. As new items are purchased for the home, the list should be brought up-to-date. If a great many new things are added, the policyholder may want to increase the amount of his protection.

Some people photograph each room of their homes and keep the pictures in their safe-deposit boxes. In case of a fire or theft these pictures, like an inventory, will help them to remember items that are missing or were destroyed. The person who has neither pictures nor an inventory might fail to claim his entire loss.

PERSONAL LIABILITY INSURANCE PAYS FOR OTHER PEOPLE'S LOSSES

One type of insurance no property owner should be without is personal liability. ***Personal liability insurance*** protects the property owner against losses resulting from injuries to other persons or damage to another's property. For example, suppose a guest tripped over a toy left on the steps and was seriously injured. Or suppose that while a property owner is burning trash, the wind carries sparks to a nearby house. The house catches fire and is badly damaged. Claims for damages in cases of this kind are sometimes very high. In addition to damages, the property owner may have to pay legal fees and court costs as well. But if he has personal liability insurance, the insurance company will pay damages up to the limits stated in the policy. It will also pay the legal fees and court costs in case the policyholder is sued for damages.

Personal liability insurance even covers claims arising from accidents that occur away from the policyholder's property if he, a member of his family, or a family pet is responsible. For example, suppose

FURNITURE—LIVING ROOM	YEAR PURCHASED	ORIGINAL COST
sofa	1960	$299
2 end tables	1960	80
lounge chair	1961	165
floor lamp	1962	40

Davenport
Chairs
Tables
Lamps
Radio
TV Set
Magazine Rack
Hassocks
Pictures
Desk
Bookends
Andirons
Vases
Bookcases
Whatnot Shelves

FURNITURE—DINING ROOM	YEAR PURCHASED	ORIGINAL COST
dining table	1963	$175
6 dining chairs	1963	240
linen chest	1964	135
rug	1965	350

Table
Chairs
Buffet
Server
Drapes
Curtains
China Cabinet
Mirrors
Pictures
Candelabra
Fernery

A section of a household inventory

The deadly funnel of a tornado cutting a path through a section of Dallas. Property owners are wise to protect themselves against the possible losses caused by this type of disaster.

United Press International photo

the policyholder hit a golf ball that struck another golfer. Or suppose one of his children broke a neighbor's window while playing ball, or his dog bit the mailman. In each case, personal liability insurance would cover the damage.

SOME POLICIES PROVIDE SEVERAL TYPES OF COVERAGE

As mentioned earlier, it is possible to buy one insurance policy that combines several different types of protection. This policy, called a *homeowner's policy*, is available to persons who own and occupy one- or two-family residences. It includes fire and extended coverage insurance on both the home and its contents. It also pays extra living expenses if a family must vacate its home temporarily while repairs are being made. In addition, a homeowner's policy provides theft insurance, plus a limited amount of coverage on personal property not in the home when stolen or destroyed by fire.

Suppose, for example, a family spends its vacation at a lake cottage. While they are out fishing one day, the cottage catches fire or a thief breaks into it. Under a homeowner's policy, the insurance company would pay for the loss of personal property that the family had in the cottage.

Nevertheless, homeowners' policies do differ in the amounts and types of coverage provided. The one bought most often insures against 19 risks. One policy includes protection against more risks, and one insures against fewer risks. Naturally, the cost varies with the amount of protection provided. In any case, a homeowner's policy has two major advantages: (1) The policyholder pays only one premium rather than several; and (2) a homeowner's policy costs from 20 to 30 percent less than if a separate policy were bought for each type of coverage.

There is also a combination policy for persons who do not own their homes. It provides fire, extended coverage, and theft insurance on personal property. In addition, like all homeowners' policies, it provides personal liability coverage.

HOW MUCH INSURANCE DOES A PROPERTY OWNER NEED?

Regardless of how much insurance a property owner carries, the insurance company will pay no more than the total amount of his loss. Neither will the company pay more than the face value of the policy, even though the actual loss may exceed it. It is much more common for people to carry too little insurance than to carry too much, however. One reason is that people keep adding to their possessions without increasing their personal property coverage. Another reason is that they fail to take into consideration increases in the value of real property. As you learned in Part 29, when real estate prices rise, the dollar value of houses and other real property also rises. A house built twenty years ago might be worth twice as much today as it cost then. A survey in one state revealed that three-fourths of the homeowners did not carry enough insurance to cover even half the value of their homes.

The amount of property insurance a person needs depends on the replacement value of his property. Anyone who is uncertain of the replacement value of his home should have it appraised. If kept up to date, a household inventory makes it fairly easy to estimate the replacement value of personal property. The most difficult thing for the property owner to determine is how much personal liability coverage he needs. Usually, the more property he owns and the more income he receives, the more liability insurance he should carry.

Surprising as it may seem, many policyholders fail to collect for losses because they are unaware that their insurance covers those losses. And just as many try to collect for losses that their policies do not cover. Perhaps you can understand why the author of a book on insurance once remarked that the three most important sentences in his book were: "Read your policy. Read your policy. Read your policy."

BUILDING YOUR VOCABULARY

Copy the six sentences given below, completing each one by replacing the question mark with the appropriate term from the column at the left.

depreciation
extended coverage
household inventory
personal liability insurance
personal property
real property

1. Insurance that provides protection against losses due to hailstorms, tornadoes, and similar causes is ? .
2. Land and buildings are ? .
3. A decrease in the value of property resulting from age and use is ? .
4. Movable property, such as furniture, clothing, or books is ? .
5. Insurance that protects the property owner against claims resulting from injuries to others while on his property is ? .
6. A list of personal property contained in a home is a ? .

CHECKING YOUR READING

1. What is the greatest risk to real and personal property?
2. What losses, in addition to those caused by fire itself, are covered by fire insurance?
3. What protection is included in extended coverage?
4. What type of protection is *not* included in extended coverage?
5. What four factors affect the rates for fire insurance?

6. Explain how the location of property affects the rates charged for fire insurance.
7. How can a homeowner save by buying fire insurance for three or five years at a time?
8. Why is the amount of theft insurance a property owner needs usually less than the amount of fire insurance he should carry?
9. When property is stolen or destroyed by fire, on what basis is settlement made by the insurance company?
10. Why is it important to keep an inventory of personal property?
11. What information should be included in a household inventory?
12. What types of risks are covered by personal liability insurance?
13. What types of risks are covered by a homeowners policy?
14. What are the major advantages of a homeowner's policy?
15. Do property owners usually carry too much or too little property insurance? Why?
16. What determines the amount of property insurance a person needs?
17. Why is it important for the policyholder to read his policy?

SHARING YOUR OPINION AND EXPERIENCE

1. Why do you think the cost of fire insurance is higher in rural areas than in cities?
2. Next to fire insurance, what type of coverage is most needed by property owners in your community? Why?
3. Why do you think automobiles are insured separately rather than included in coverage carried on other property?
4. Why do you think the rates for theft insurance are high compared with the cost of other kinds of insurance?
5. Why might a single insurance company not wish to insure all houses in one city block?
6. Why is the cost per year less when property insurance is purchased for a five-year period rather than a one-year period?
7. Why do you suppose personal liability insurance does not cover injuries to the policyholder or to members of his family?
8. Most homeowners do not include the value of the land when they determine how much property insurance they need. Is this a wise decision? Why?

PROJECTS AND PROBLEMS

1. Divide a sheet of paper into two columns lengthwise and prepare a form similar to the one given below. At the top of the left-hand column, write "Real Property"; at the top of the other, write "Personal Property." Classify the following items by listing each one in whichever column it belongs: barn, car, garage, house, lamp, land, mirror, sofa, trees, typewriter.

Real Property	Personal Property
Example: fence	*Example: books*

2. The rate for fire insurance and extended coverage on Mr. Hilliard's house is $3.50 per $1,000 of protection for one year.

▪ *a.* If Mr. Hilliard insures his home for $15,000, what would the cost of insurance be for one year? ▪ *b.* Using the figure given as an example in the text, what would Mr. Hilliard's insurance cost if purchased for a 3-year period? ▪ *c.* If purchased for a 3-year period, what would Mr. Hilliard's insurance cost per year? ▪ *d.* How much less would Mr. Hilliard's insurance cost if purchased for a 3-year period rather than three 1-year periods? ▪ *e.* Using the figure given as an example in the text, what would Mr. Hilliard's insurance cost if purchased for a 5-year period? ▪ *f.* How much would Mr. Hilliard save each year if he bought his insurance for a 5-year period rather than for one year at a time? ▪ *g.* How much less would his insurance cost per year if purchased for a 5-year period rather than for a 3-year period?

3. Use the information in the table on page 295 to answer the following questions. ▪ *a.* How many fires resulted from the five leading causes? ▪ *b.* What percent of all fires resulted from the five leading causes? ▪ *c.* Which cause of fire resulted in the greatest amount of property loss? ▪ *d.* What was the total amount of property loss resulting from the five leading causes? ▪ *e.* What percent of the total dollar loss from all causes resulted from the five leading causes of fire?

4. The number of fires in the United States for each year from 1954 through 1964 is given in the table below.

NUMBER OF FIRES IN THE UNITED STATES 1954–1964

Year	*Number of Fires*	*Year*	*Number of Fires*
1954	845,116	1960	923,492
1955	822,392	1961	1,023,946
1956	865,561	1962	1,150,378
1957	847,396	1963	1,314,286
1958	846,097	1964	1,309,771
1959	906,135		

Source: Insurance Facts, 1965

Put the information from the table on a horizontal bar graph similar to the one on page 282. Use the base line, or horizontal axis, to represent the number of fires, making each division equal to 100,000. Use the side line, or vertical axis, to represent the years. Fill in the bars with black or colored pencil. When you have finished, answer the following questions by studying the table. Then check your graph to see if it provides the same answers.

▪ *a.* In which years was the number of fires less than the preceding year? ▪ *b.* In which year was the number of fires lowest? ▪ *c.* In which year did the number of fires increase the most over the preceding year? ▪ *d.* In which year did the number of fires decrease the most over the preceding year?

5. Economic losses from fires and injuries to others are often the result of carelessness on the part of property owners. Make a list of rules that, if followed, would help to prevent fire in the home. Make another list of things the property owner might do to prevent others from being injured while on his property.
6. Compare the house or building in which you live with another nearby for which you think the rate for fire insurance should be higher or lower. List all facts about the two properties that would make for different fire insurance rates.

CHALLENGE PROBLEMS

1. The greatest losses from fires occur during the months of December, January, February, and March. How would you explain this fact?
2. The present market value of Mr. Pedro's home is $17,000. He has it insured for $15,000 with one company and for $12,000 with another company. If the house should be destroyed by fire, what total amount could Mr. Pedro collect from the two companies?
3. Why should a person who owns property worth $50,000 carry more personal liability insurance than one who owns property worth only $15,000?

PART 33 LIFE INSURANCE—WHAT IT IS AND WHAT IT DOES

THE main purpose of life insurance is to make up for losses resulting from someone's death. Life insurance differs from other kinds of insurance in one important way. It does not protect against something that may or may not happen. It protects against something that is bound to happen eventually. The uncertainty is when.

Average length of life today is a little over 70 years. This means that many people live much longer than that. It also means that some die earlier. And when that happens, it may cause severe financial hardship for persons still living. Life insurance provides the only practical way to guard against this risk.

Is all life insurance the same? What determines its cost? Can anyone buy life insurance?

HOW DOES LIFE INSURANCE WORK?

When a person buys life insurance, he enters into an agreement with the insurance company. He agrees to pay a certain premium each year. In exchange, the company promises to pay a certain sum of money to the person or persons named by him if he should die during the period covered by the agreement. The amount to be paid by the insurance company is the *face value* of the policy. The entire amount may be paid at one time. Or the money may be paid in regular monthly installments. The person named to receive payment is the ***beneficiary.***

The amount of the premium depends on several factors. One is the age of the insured at the time he buys the insurance. As a rule, the older he is at the time of purchase, the higher will be the premiums. A second factor affecting the premium is the face value of the policy. As with all types of insurance, the more protection a person buys, the more he must pay for it. Finally, the amount of the premium depends on the type of policy purchased. Some types cost more than others, as you will learn.

Courtesy Northern Indiana Public Service Company

HOW IS LIFE INSURANCE OBTAINED?

If a person wants fire insurance on his house, the insurance company will want to know whether the house is made of brick or wood. This is one way the company determines how great a risk it is assuming. For the same reason, a person wanting life insurance is asked to fill out an application form giving information about his age, occupation, past illnesses, and present health. A form of this kind is illustrated on page 304. In addition, an applicant may be asked to undergo a physical examination at the insurance company's expense. These measures help to determine whether or not the applicant is a good risk. If his health is below average, he may have to pay a higher premium than he would otherwise. This might also be the case if his job is a dangerous one. Fewer than 3 percent of those who apply for life insurance today, however, are actually turned down.

Life Insurance May Be Temporary or Permanent

Although there are many different types of life insurance policies, there are really only two kinds of life insurance—term insurance and permanent insurance. Their names almost tell you one of the ways in which these two kinds of insurance differ. But there are other differences between them that are equally important.

TERM INSURANCE

Term insurance is nothing but insurance. Like automobile and property insurance, it provides only protection against loss. It is called ***term insurance*** because it is purchased for a limited period of time, such as 5, 10, or 20 years. If the policyholder dies during that period, the face value of the policy is paid to his beneficiary. If the policyholder is still living at the end of the term stated in the policy, the protection ends and the policy expires.

Some term policies are *renewable*. This means that the insured may continue to carry the insurance for one or more additional periods without another physical examination. Each time the policy is renewed, however, the premium increases. For example, a man 25 years of age can buy $10,000 of 5-year renewable term insurance from one company for an annual premium of $52.10. At age 30, if he renews the policy, he would have to pay an annual premium of $55.10. At age 50, his term insurance would cost him $154.30 a year; and at age 60, $345.50. At age 70, he could no longer obtain term insurance. But most term policies issued

SAVINGS COMPARISON OF FOUR TYPES OF LIFE INSURANCE

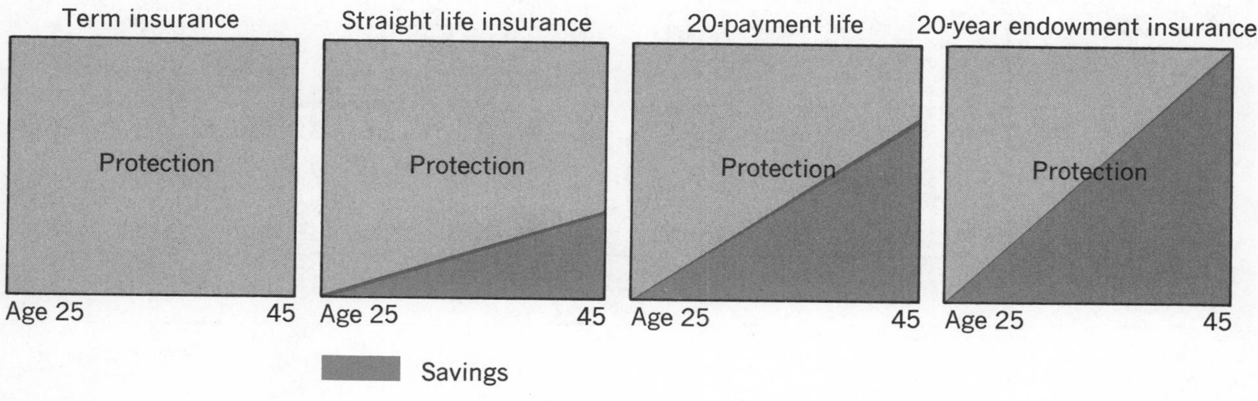

MUTUAL LIFE INSURANCE COMPANY
APPLICATION FOR INSURANCE

1. Full name of applicant USE BLACK INK ONLY
JOHN NORTON

2. A. Residence: Street
City or Town MONTCLAIR
County ESSEX State NEW JERSEY
B. Residence addresses (ST., CITY AND STATE) last three years
35 HILLSIDE DR. MONTCLAIR N.J.
C. Do you contemplate a change in residence or foreign travel? IF SO, GIVE DETAILS
NO

3. A. Occupation
ACCOUNTANT
B. Name of employer and business address
BROWN + WHITE 300 BROAD ST. NEWARK N.J.
C. Previous occupations in last five years
STUDENT + PRESENT POSITION
D. Have you any other occupations? IF SO, GIVE DETAILS
NONE
E. Do you contemplate any change in occupation? IF SO, GIVE DETAILS
NO

4. A. Have you ever piloted or have you any intention of piloting any type of aircraft? NO
B. Have you taken any aerial flights in the last 12 months other than as a passenger? NO
IF EITHER PART IS ANSWERED "YES" SUBMIT AVIATION SUPPLEMENT

5. Will insurance now being applied for replace insurance in this or any other company? IF SO, GIVE DETAILS
NO

6. Are you insured in this Company? NO

7. A. Is your life insured in any other company or companies? IF SO, GIVE FULL DETAILS BELOW

Names of Companies	Amounts	Kinds	Dates of Issue	Special Provisions: Waiver	Dis. Inc.	A.D.B.
X LIFE INS. CO.	5000	GROUP	1955			

B. What would be the amount of your disability income, if disabled? EXCLUSIVE OF INSURANCE IN THIS COMPANY
FROM 1. All life insurance policies $ per month
FROM 2. All accident and health policies $ per month

8. Date of Birth — Month: MAY — Day: 12 — Year: 1935 — Age last birthday: 30

9. Birthplace CITY, STATE DENVER, COLORADO

10. Are you CHECK ☐ Single ☑ Married ☐ Widowed ☐ Divorced

11. During the past five years have you had advice, attendance, or treatment by a physician or any other person? If so, give nature of ailment, duration, approximate date and names and addresses of physicians or other persons consulted.

LAST ANNUAL PHYSICAL EXAM. NOV. 12, 1959

12. A. Plan of insurance
STRAIGHT LIFE
CHECK PROVISIONS DESIRED
B. ☑ Waiver of Premiums C. ☐ Waiver of Premiums and Monthly Income D. ☑ Double Indemnity Benefit

13. Amount of insurance $ 5,000

14. Premiums payable in advance CHECK METHOD OF PAYMENT
☐ Annually ☐ Semiannually ☑ Quarterly ☐ Monthly

15. Beneficiary GIVEN NAME AND RELATIONSHIP
MARY NORTON, WIFE (if living) OTHERWISE, ANN NORTON, DAUGHTER

(Endowments are made payable to the insured at maturity unless otherwise requested.)

16. Which of the following rights do you reserve as to a change of beneficiary, any change being subject to the consent of the Company? STRIKE OUT ONE
A. The right to change and successively change to any beneficiary
~~B. No right to change except with the consent of all beneficiaries~~

17. Dividends to be: STRIKE OUT METHODS NOT DESIRED
~~A. Paid in cash~~
~~B. Applied in reduction of premium~~
~~C. Used to purchase paid-up additions~~
D. Left with the Company to accumulate at interest

18. Is the Automatic Premium Loan Provision requested? CHECK ☑ YES ☐ NO

19. Has the first premium on the insurance hereby applied for been paid? YES If so, state amount paid $ 27.60

I understand and agree that:

1. If the premium on the insurance herein applied for has been paid to the Company's agent, in exchange for the Company's signed advance premium receipt numbered the same as Part 1 hereof, the insurance as provided by the policy shall be effective from the date of Part 2 of this application PROVIDED the Company shall approve this application at its Home Office. If this application is not so approved, I will accept the return of the premium paid and surrender the advance premium receipt.

2. If the premium on the insurance herein applied for has not been paid, such insurance shall become effective on the date of issue stated in the policy PROVIDED the Company has approved this application at its Home Office, the premium has been paid, and the policy delivered to me while I am in good health.

I hereby declare that all the answers and statements herein contained are full, complete, and true, and have been correctly recorded.

Signed at Montclair (City), New Jersey (State)
and dated this 1 day of August, 1965
In My Presence Oscar Mills

Applicant John Norton
Address all mail to 35 Hillside Drive Montclair, N.J.

General Agent submitting application

Agent who actually solicited this application

Courtesy Institute of Life Insurance

An application for life insurance

today are also *convertible.* This means that they can be exchanged for another type of insurance without a physical examination.

PERMANENT INSURANCE

Permanent insurance differs from term insurance in three ways: (1) Permanent insurance provides lifetime protection. (2) Premiums for permanent insurance do not change regardless of how long a policy is in force. For example, suppose you purchased a permanent type of life insurance at age 17 on which the premium was $107.30 a year for $10,000 of protection. At age 60 your premium on that policy would still be $107.30 a year. If you were to take out a new policy at age 60, however, the premium would be about $528.30 a year. (3) Permanent forms of life insurance are a combination of savings and insurance. That is why insurance companies can provide permanent protection at the same cost to the policyholder year after year.

The person who buys term insurance, remember, pays only for protection. The person who buys permanent insurance, on the other hand, pays more at the start than he would have to pay for protection alone. This difference in premiums is placed in a fund that grows larger each year. The amount in the fund at any time is the ***cash value*** of the policy.

The longer a policyholder carries his insurance and the greater his cash value becomes, the less risk there is for the insurance company. To illustrate, if you take out a $10,000 policy, the insurance company immediately assumes a risk of $10,000. Now suppose that after five years, the policy has a cash value of $320. Since this is really your money, the company is then assuming a risk of only $9,680. After ten years, if the policy has a cash value of $930, the risk carried by the company drops to $9,070. Twenty years from now the policy might have a cash value of $2,190. In other words your premiums would be the same each year, but they would buy a smaller amount of protection. The growing cash value makes up the difference.

Permanent Insurance is Bought in Two Ways

Permanent insurance includes two types of policies. One is called *straight life;* the other, *limited payment life.* Both provide protection for an entire lifetime. The difference between these two types of policies is the length of time premiums are paid.

With ***straight life insurance*** the policyholder pays premiums for as long as he wants the protection. With a ***limited payment life*** policy, premiums are paid for a stated number of years. A 20-payment life policy, for example, means that the insured is required to pay premiums for only 20 years. Other limited payment policies are issued for 10, 15, 25, or 30 years, or to age 60 or 65. After the last premium is paid, the policy becomes paid up and remains in force for the remainder of the insured's life.

Since fewer premiums are paid for limited payment life, each premium has to be higher than is charged for the same amount of straight life insurance. Because the premiums are higher, limited payment life insurance builds cash values faster than straight life insurance.

WHAT IS ENDOWMENT INSURANCE?

In addition to term and permanent insurance, there is a type of insurance called *endowment.* ***Endowment insurance*** is actually an insured savings plan. The policyholder agrees to pay premiums for a definite period of time. At the end of that time, the cash value of the policy is equal to its face value. The policy is then said to mature, and the insurance expires. The policyholder may take the money in a lump sum or as a monthly income for a certain number of years or for life. The amount he would receive each month would depend on the amount of the policy and the length of time income was to be paid.

Should the policyholder die before completing payment for his endowment policy, the face amount is paid to his beneficiary. In other words, the insurance company completes the savings program for him.

Endowment policies are issued for almost any period of time, such as 10, 20, or 30 years. Or premiums may run until a certain age such as 60 or 65. The shorter the period, the higher the premium. In any case the premium for endowment insurance is higher than that for either straight life or limited payment life insurance. As a result endowment insurance builds cash values more rapidly, which is the main reason people buy this type of insurance. For example, a man might buy an endowment policy to save the money for a child's college education. If he dies before the policy matures, the insurance will provide the funds needed. Many people use endowment insurance as a means of setting aside part of their present earnings for use during their retirement years.

CASH VALUES MAKE LIFE INSURANCE AN INVESTMENT

In Part 26, life insurance was mentioned as one of the ways people invest their savings. A person is said to *invest* in life insurance when he buys permanent insurance. One reason is that he may exchange his policy for its cash value any time he wishes. In other words, the cash value of a policy is like money deposited in a savings account. It can be withdrawn at any time.

When a policyholder exchanges his policy for its cash value, of course he loses his insurance protection. The amount of money he will receive in exchange depends on two things: (1) the face value of the policy, and (2) how long the policy has been in force. A $10,000 policy would have a greater cash value than a $5,000 policy. Also the cash value of a policy increases each year. A policy that has been in force 15 years would have a greater cash value than one for the same amount that has been in force only 10 years. In any case the amount of a policy's cash value is guaranteed. Every permanent life insurance policy contains a table showing the cash value of the policy for each year it is in force. These amounts are fixed; that is, they neither increase nor decrease with changes in business conditions.

Courtesy Michigan Consolidated Gas Company

A paid-up endowment policy can provide the means for a college education.

Another reason life insurance is called an investment is because the money insurance companies hold for their policyholders actually is put to work. As you know, it is invested in corporate securities, in government bonds, in home mortgages, in shopping centers, and in office buildings. The return on these investments helps to keep down the cost of life insurance. The investments themselves provide money capital for production which in turn creates jobs and income.

Cash Values Have Other Uses

As you learned in your study of credit, a person may borrow part or all of the cash value of his life insurance policy. The policy, however, remains in force. If he dies before the loan is repaid, the amount of the loan is deducted from the face value of the policy. In other words, when he borrows, he gives up part of his protection. In addition, he has to pay interest for the use of the money. Since the money belongs to him, you may wonder why. The reason is that when life insurance premiums are figured, the company deducts the return it expects to receive on its investments. When a policyholder borrows the cash value of his policy, that money cannot be invested in any other way. The company must, therefore, charge him interest the same as it would if the money were loaned to someone else.

In time a person may outlive his need for insurance; but no one outlives his need for an income. If a person has permanent insurance which he feels he no longer needs, he can have the cash values paid to him as income. Many people do this when they reach retirement age. In fact insurance companies pay millions of dollars annually to the policyholders themselves. Such payments are called *living benefits*.

Other important uses of cash values are explained in Part 35.

BUILDING YOUR VOCABULARY

List the figures 1 to 6 on a sheet of paper, numbering down. Read the six statements given below at the right; then, for each statement, select from the column at the left the term that best matches it in meaning. Write this term next to the appropriate number.

beneficiary
cash value
endowment insurance
limited payment life insurance
straight life insurance
term insurance

1. Insurance that provides protection for a limited period of time
2. Permanent life insurance on which the policyholder pays premiums for as long as he wants the protection
3. The amount a policyholder can obtain in exchange for a permanent life insurance policy
4. Permanent life insurance that becomes fully paid up after a stated number of years
5. Insurance that pays the face amount to the policyholder himself if he is living when it matures
6. The person to whom an insurance policy is made payable

CHECKING YOUR READING

1. What is the main purpose of life insurance?
2. In what important way does life insurance differ from other kinds of insurance?
3. What is the face value of a life insurance policy?
4. What three factors affect the amount of the premium a person must pay for life insurance?
5. Why are medical examinations often required of persons applying for life insurance?
6. What are the two principal kinds of life insurance?
7. What is a renewable term insurance policy?
8. How is the premium affected each time a term insurance policy is renewed?
9. What is the advantage of a convertible term policy?
10. In what three ways does permanent life insurance differ from term insurance?
11. Explain why the risk for the insurance company lessens the longer a permanent life insurance policy remains in force.
12. What is the main difference between straight life and limited payment life insurance?
13. Explain how endowment insurance works.
14. What is one of the important purposes for which endowment insurance is used?
15. What type of life insurance is considered an investment and why?
16. What two factors determine the cash value of a permanent life insurance policy?
17. How can a policyholder find out what the cash value of his permanent life policy is?
18. When a person borrows from the cash value of his life insurance policy, what happens to his protection?
19. Why does a policyholder have to pay interest when he borrows the cash value of his policy, since the money really belongs to him?
20. Explain the term "living benefits" as it is used in this part.

SHARING YOUR OPINION AND EXPERIENCE

1. More people buy straight life insurance than any other kind. Why do you think this is so?
2. Many companies now offer life insurance to women at lower premiums than they charge for men. Why do you suppose they do this?
3. Why should the premium for a term policy that is renewable and convertible be higher than for one that is not?
4. What is the main advantage of term insurance over permanent insurance? What is its chief disadvantage?
5. It has been said that many of the people who need life insurance most cannot obtain it. Why do you think this might be so?
6. It is important for a wage earner to carry life insurance, but should his wife also have insurance? Why or why not?
7. Many people prefer to think of life insurance as "living insurance" rather than "death insurance." Explain.
8. Should an endowment insurance policy, intended for a child's education, be on the child's life or the father's life? Why?

PROJECTS AND PROBLEMS

1. Study the application for life insurance illustrated on page 304 and answer the following questions.

   ▪ *a.* What is the occupation of the applicant? ▪ *b.* Does the applicant have other life insurance? If so, how much? ▪ *c.* How old is the applicant? ▪ *d.* What type of policy is he applying for? ▪ *e.* Who is named as beneficiary of the policy? ▪ *f.* What amount of insurance is being applied for? ▪ *g.* May the applicant change the beneficiary of the policy? ▪ *h.* How often are premiums to be paid? ▪ *i.* What was the amount of the first premium?

2. In Part 30 you learned that a circle graph is used to compare single items within a group with the entire group. A rectangle, or *bar,* may be used in the same way. The bar graph below, for example, represents all (100%) life insurance in force in the United States in a recent year. Each section of the bar shows the percent of insurance represented by a particular type of policy.

   Study the graph and answer the questions relating to it.

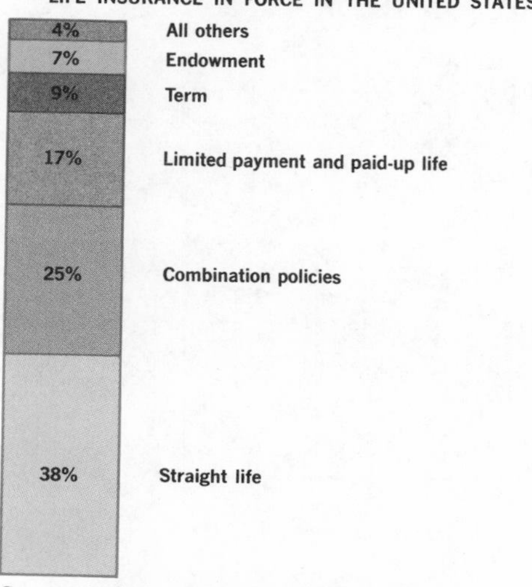

Source: Life Insurance Fact Book, 1964

   ▪ *a.* Which type of policy accounted for the largest percent of life insurance in force? ▪ *b.* What fraction of all insurance in force was in combination policies? ▪ *c.* What percent of all insurance was in the three leading types of policies? ▪ *d.* The percent of insurance in straight life policies was approximately how many times greater than that in term policies? ▪ *e.* The percent of insurance in straight life policies was approximately how many times greater than that in limited payment and paid-up life? ▪ *f.* According to the graph, straight life insurance accounted for 38 percent of all the life insurance in force. Does that mean that 38 percent of all life insurance policies that year were straight life insurance? Or does it mean that of the total amount of life insurance in force, 38 percent was in straight life policies?

3. During a recent year, life insurance companies in the United States paid a total of $10,028,200 in benefits to policyholders or their beneficiaries. Beneficiaries received 42 percent of the total benefits.

▪ *a.* How much money did the beneficiaries receive? ▪ *b.* What percent of the total payments did the policyholders themselves receive? ▪ *c.* How much money did the policyholders receive?

4. Sometimes graphs are used to show the relationship between two or more kinds of information. The following graph, for example, shows how the amount of life insurance per family in the United States changed as family income increased from 1950 to 1964. By looking at the graph you can see that the amount of life insurance per family in 1950 was $4,600. Disposable personal income per family was $4,100 that year. Following the graph are some questions for you to answer.

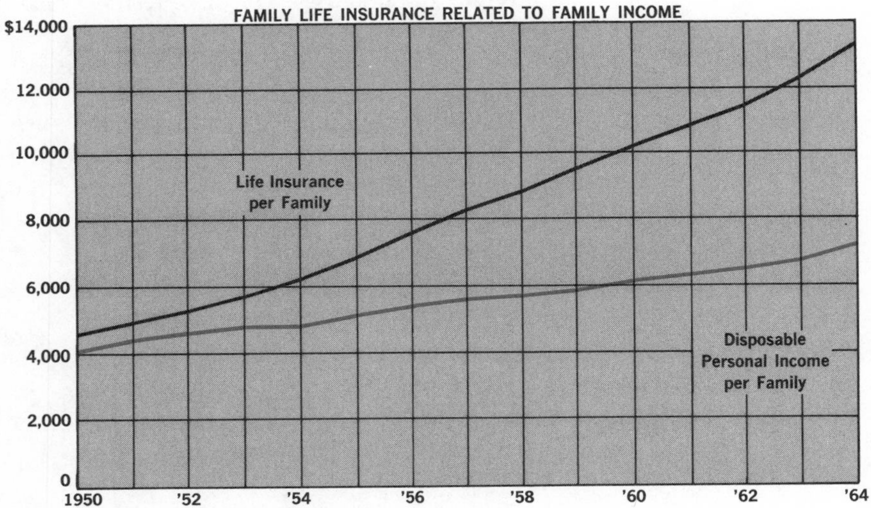

Source: *Life Insurance Fact Book, 1965*

▪ *a.* What is disposable personal income? ▪ *b.* Approximately how much was disposable personal income per family in 1964? ▪ *c.* Does this mean that every family in the United States had that amount of income in 1964? ▪ *d.* How much did disposable personal income per family increase between 1950 and 1964? ▪ *e.* Did the incomes of some families increase more than that amount? ▪ *f.* What was the amount of life insurance per family in 1964? ▪ g. Does the graph show that all families living in the United States owned life insurance in 1964? ▪ *h.* Approximately how much did the amount of life insurance per family increase between 1950 and 1964? ▪ *i.* In 1950, about how much difference was there between the amount of life insurance per family and disposable income per family? ▪ *j.* In 1964, about how much difference was there between the amount of life insurance per family and disposable income per family? ▪ *k.* Which increased more rapidly between 1950 and 1964—disposable personal income or life insurance per family? ▪ *l.* If the lines on the graph were perfectly straight, it would mean that the amount of increase in each case was the same each year. As you can see, however, neither line is perfectly straight. Lay a ruler, the edge of a piece of paper or of a card next to each line from one point to the other. Then notice how the lines rise more sharply at some points than at others. Which increased at a more even rate—life insurance per family or disposable income per family? ▪ *m.* Did the amount of life insurance per family increase more rapidly before or after 1956?

5. The figures in the table below show the number of life insurance policies in force in the United States in certain years.

Year	*Number of Policies in Force (millions)*
1920	68
1930	128
1940	137
1950	210
1960	308

Put the information from the table on a line graph similar to the one in the preceding problem. Use the base line to represent the years. Use the side line to represent the number of policies. Make each division equal to 50 million.

6. In your own words, explain briefly why each of the following statements is true:

▪ *a.* The older a person is when he buys life insurance, the higher the premium will be. ▪ *b.* Loss of income is one of the greatest risks a family faces. ▪ *c.* Term insurance costs less than other forms of life insurance. ▪ *d.* A policyholder cannot borrow money on a term insurance policy.

CHALLENGE PROBLEMS

1. What is "GI" insurance? Who carries it?
2. What is credit insurance? When is it usually purchased?
3. Is life insurance a liquid investment? Explain.
4. The graph in Projects and Problems No. 2 shows that 17 percent of all life insurance in force during a recent year was in limited payment or paid-up life policies. What is a paid-up policy?
5. The graph in Projects and Problems No. 4 shows that in general, as a family's income rises, a larger proportion of it is spent for life insurance. What do you know about the relationship between income and spending that helps to explain this fact?
6. During which 10-year period shown on the graph you prepared for Projects and Problems No. 5 did the number of life insurance policies in force increase the least? What reason can you give for the small increase during that period?

PART 34 PLANNING A LIFE INSURANCE PROGRAM

FINANCIAL losses resulting from death are not all of one kind. Some are immediate; others continue for a long time. Immediate losses almost always include funeral costs. In many cases they also include the cost of a serious illness and a long period of hospitalization preceding death. Another loss of an immediate nature is unpaid bills. In these days of easy credit it is common for a person to owe a number of debts which together may amount to a sizable sum. These may consist of charge accounts, payments due on installment purchases; taxes owing but not yet paid. Normally, these obligations would be met as they come due out of regular income. But if income ends with death, they must be met in some other way. Indeed, it is when death occurs during a person's earning years that the money loss is usually greatest. The income he would have earned is then lost permanently.

Who needs life insurance? Why has the need for life insurance grown? What determines the kind of life insurance to buy?

Courtesy Metropolitan Life Insurance Company

WHO NEEDS LIFE INSURANCE?

If a person has no one who depends on him for support and he has enough savings to pay his debts and final expenses, he could manage without life insurance. But when anyone provides support for others, the most important insurance for him to carry is life insurance. Life insurance enables a person with ***dependents*** (others who depend on him for support) to provide for them in case anything happens to him.

HOW MUCH INSURANCE IS ENOUGH?

The amount of life insurance a person needs depends on what the costs and losses would be following his death. If a child dies, the family suffers a deep personal loss. But the money loss is limited to immediate expenses. If the husband and father of a young family dies, on the other hand, the financial loss would include both immediate expenses and loss of income. The amount of life insurance he should have would depend on how much money his family would need to carry on without him. This will vary from one family to another. It will vary even among families with identical incomes.

It will vary with the age of dependents. In the case of children, the younger they are, the longer it will be before they are self-supporting. Suppose a man wants to provide income for his family until the youngest child is 18. If the child is 5, income must be provided for 13 years. If the child is already 10, only 8 years of income are needed. The age of the children also affects the wife's ability to earn an income. If they are very young, it may not be advisable for her to take a job outside the home for a few years.

The need for insurance protection will also depend on the amount a person owes, including such long-term debts as a mortgage on a home. And finally, the need for insurance protection will depend on what other means are available for meeting losses. Most people can count on social security to cover some losses. (Social security is explained in Part 37.) In addition, many people have savings they can draw on if necessary.

The difference between estimated losses and the means available for meeting them is the amount of life insurance needed.

Most Families Have Too Little Insurance

Each year the amount of life insurance in force in the United States increases. Nevertheless the average amount of protection carried per family is less than average family income for two years. One reason is that planning for death is a disagreeable task that people tend to put off. Another reason is that many people are ignorant of their need for insurance. When a person says, "I have $10,000 of life insurance," it sounds like a great deal. It is only when he takes time to figure how much his insurance has to cover that he realizes how little it is. Saddest of all, perhaps, is that many families fail to get all the protection they could in return for their insurance dollars because they buy the wrong kinds of insurance.

Courtesy Western Electric Company, Inc.

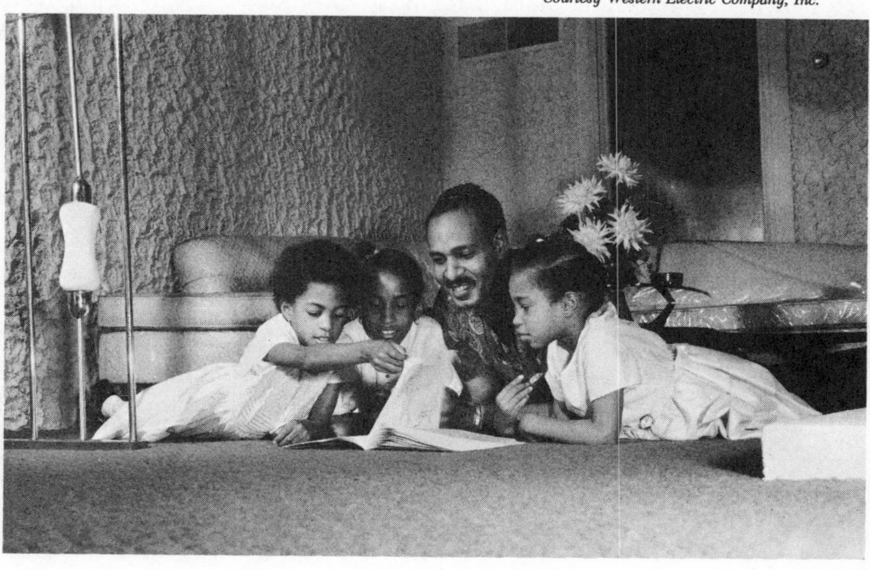

To provide for his family in the event of his death, a father of young children is wise to buy insurance protection.

PURPOSE DETERMINES THE TYPE OF INSURANCE TO BUY

As you have seen, life insurance needs differ. Some of them are temporary and some are permanent. When buying life insurance, therefore, the important thing is to choose the policy that matches the need best.

Term Insurance Takes Care of Temporary Needs

The least expensive form of life insurance is term. According to the table on page 315, a man age 30 can buy $15,000 of 5-year renewable and convertible term insurance for $120.75 a year. This is more than two and a half times the protection he could get for the same amount of money if he chose a straight life policy.

True, his term insurance provides protection for only a limited period of time. But it is also true that some of the biggest insurance needs exist for only a limited period of time. The largest one of all for a family is usually the need for income until the children are grown. This is not only a temporary need; it is a decreasing one. In other words, as time goes by, fewer years of income have to be provided.

A mortgage creates another temporary insurance need. Suppose, for example, a family takes out a $12,000 mortgage to finance the purchase of a home. As long as the chief wage earner lives, the family is fairly certain of its ability to pay off this debt. If he should die, however, the family might be unable to complete the payments on the house. A $12,000 term policy would pay off the mortgage if death prevented the head of the family from doing so. Here again the need for insurance is a decreasing one.

When people buy insurance to cover decreasing needs, they often buy what is called ***decreasing term insurance.*** This means that the amount of protection provided by the insurance gets smaller each year it is in force. Since the amount of insurance needed also decreases, decreasing term insurance serves the purpose well. It is even cheaper than regular term.

Permanent Insurance Is Bought for Lasting Protection

Although insurance needs may grow smaller in time, they do not disappear entirely. There are always final expenses and usually debts of some kind. Moreover even renewable term insurance expires eventually; and in most cases, a policyholder is still living when that time comes. It is because most policyholders outlive their term insurance that its cost is so low. Since term insurance has no cash

INSURANCE NEEDS CHANGE THROUGHOUT LIFE.

ANNUAL PREMIUM RATES FOR $1,000 INSURANCE FOR EACH OF FIVE TYPES OF LIFE INSURANCE POLICIES OFFERED BY ONE COMPANY

Taken at Age	*Five-Year Term (Renewable and Convertible)*	*Straight Life*	*Limited-Payment Life (Paid Up At Age 65)*	*Family Income (20-Year Period)*	*Endowment (at Age 65)*
15	$ 6.45	$13.75	$14.65	$17.45	$16.50
16	6.50	14.10	15.05	17.80	17.00
17	6.60	14.50	15.50	18.25	17.50
18	6.65	14.85	15.95	18.65	18.00
19	6.75	15.25	16.40	19.05	18.60
20	6.80	15.70	16.90	19.53	19.15
25	7.30	18.00	19.80	22.15	22.55
30	8.05	20.95	23.55	25.70	26.95
40	11.30	29.25	35.45	38.45	41.15
50	19.70	43.10	62.25	63.05	73.00

value, it provides no "living benefits" for the insured. Anyone who buys all his protection in the form of term insurance, therefore, will need to save and invest part of his income during his working years. Otherwise he faces retirement with neither protection nor savings.

Permanent insurance forces a person to save. At the same time, it provides protection for his dependents. Of the two types of permanent insurance, straight life is bought most often because of its lower premiums. Limited payment life is usually recommended for people who have a rather brief period of high earnings, such as professional athletes or actors. This serves a double purpose. It forces them to save when their earnings are highest. It enables them to finish paying for their insurance before their income drops.

YOU MAY BUY TWO KINDS OF INSURANCE IN ONE POLICY

Because most people need both temporary and permanent insurance, insurance companies offer them together in one policy. The most popular of these combination policies is called a ***family income policy.*** This is a straight life policy that provides both permanent protection and decreasing term insurance. The term portion of the policy provides the family of the insured with a monthly income if he dies within the term stated in the policy. The income is paid for the balance of the term. Suppose a man bought a 20-year family income policy and died 8 years later. His family would receive income for 12 years. If he died during the 15th year, the family would receive income for only 5 years. When the income stops, the straight life portion of the policy is payable immediately or it can be held for later use.

The typical family income policy provides an income of $10 a month for each $1,000 of straight life insurance. Thus, a $10,000 family income policy would provide a monthly income of $100 for the period stated in the policy, then $10,000 in cash or additional income.

INSURE THE MOST IMPORTANT NEED FIRST

From this discussion of life insurance one fact stands out. Life insurance needs change. They are usually small at first. Then with marriage and a

A limited-payment life insurance policy is often the best kind for a Big League baseball player.

H. Armstrong Roberts

family, financial responsibilities increase, especially for men. Later on responsibilities decrease. As a rule, earnings follow a similar pattern. Most men do not reach the peak of their earning power until middle age or later. Young people, therefore, can expect their earnings to rise.

For these reasons, few people buy their insurance protection all at once. They start small and add to it as their responsibilities and incomes increase. In other words, they have a long-range program or plan. A person who cannot afford all the insurance he needs is wise to cover the most important needs first.

As an example, take the man who is anxious to have his son go to college. An expensive endowment policy would provide the money in case anything happened to the father. But an even greater need from the boy's standpoint is money for food and clothing while he is still too young to provide for himself. If the father cannot buy enough insurance to provide both things, he should buy insurance to take care of his son's immediate needs.

PAYMENT OF PROCEEDS CARRIES OUT THE PURPOSE OF INSURANCE

The amount to be paid to the beneficiary of a life insurance policy is called the ***proceeds*** of the policy. When a person buys life insurance, he is asked how he wants the proceeds paid to his beneficiary. If his beneficiary is to receive all the money at once, this is called a ***lump-sum payment.*** Other methods of payment are called ***settlement options.***

Deciding how the proceeds of a policy are to be paid is just as important as choosing the right policy. If the beneficiary receives a lump-sum payment of the entire amount, there is a danger that the money may be lost in a poor investment or wasted through extravagance. On the other hand, when anyone dies, there is always a need for some cash.

The ideal arrangement is to have some of the proceeds paid in cash and the rest as income. All money left with the insurance company to be paid later to the beneficiary earns interest. Under a settlement option, therefore, the beneficiary receives more than the face value of the policy. The chart below shows the amounts paid on a $10,000 policy under each of four settlement options.

Even though a policy calls for a lump-sum payment of proceeds, the beneficiary may still choose a settlement option. If a policyholder selects a settlement option, however, it cannot be changed following his death unless the policy states that this may be done. The insurance company must distribute the proceeds according to the option chosen. For this reason, it is important for everyone who owns life insurance to review the settlement options from time to time. As family circumstances change, it may be advisable to have the proceeds paid in some other way.

PLANNING REQUIRES THE HELP OF A GOOD AGENT

Most people can determine their own insurance needs if they make the effort; that is, they can figure out how many dollars would be needed to pay for immediate losses. They could add to that how many dollars of income their dependents would need each month and for how many months. But not very many people would know how much insurance it would take to provide a certain number of dollars of income. As you have seen, some policies have extra value when paid in certain ways.

Helping people to work out the answers to their insurance problems is a job for an insurance agent. A good agent will advise which policy or policies are best for a particular purpose. He will not recommend a policy simply because he earns more for selling it than he would for selling some other kind. When choosing an agent, remember that, in order to help you, he will need a great deal of personal information—how much you earn, how much you spend, and how much you owe. He should be someone you can talk with easily and someone you can trust. It may be wise to talk with several agents before making your choice.

WHAT $10,000 WILL PROVIDE UNDER THE FOUR LIFE INSURANCE SETTLEMENT OPTIONS*

Option	*Settlement*
The Interest Option The money left at interest until the family asks for it	At 2½% guaranteed interest, $250 annually until money is withdrawn
The Amount Option A regular income of as much money as you want, paid until money and interest are used up	$100 a month for 9 years and 6 months $200 a month for 5 years and 5 months $250 a month for 3 years and 6 months
The Time Option A monthly income to last as many years as you want, paid until money and interest are used up	5 years' income of $179.10 a month or 10 years' income of $ 96.10 a month or 20 years' income of $ 55.10 a month
The Lifetime Income Option A regular income guaranteed for the person's lifetime	At age 55, $49.30 a month for life At age 60, $54.90 a month for life At age 65, $61.60 a month for life

* *Interest figured at a guaranteed rate of 2½%. Companies will pay higher interest than this as earned.*

BUILDING YOUR VOCABULARY

List the figures 1 to 6 on a sheet of paper, numbering down. Read the six statements given below at the right; then, for each statement, select from the column at the left the term that best matches it in meaning. Write this term next to the appropriate number.

decreasing term insurance
dependents
family income policy
lump-sum payment
proceeds
settlement options

1. Provides both straight life and decreasing term insurance protection
2. Different methods of paying life insurance benefits
3. The amount paid to the beneficiary of a life insurance policy
4. Persons who rely on someone else for support
5. The entire proceeds of a life insurance policy paid to the beneficiary at once
6. Provides a smaller amount of insurance protection each year it is in force

CHECKING YOUR READING

1. What are some of the financial losses that result from the death of a family wage earner?
2. Why is life insurance important for persons with dependents?
3. What determines the amount of life insurance a person needs?
4. What means other than life insurance might a family have for meeting losses resulting from death of the wage earner?
5. What are some of the reasons why most families have too little life insurance?
6. What is the least expensive form of life insurance?
7. What is usually the largest insurance need for a family?
8. When should a person buy term insurance?
9. What is the advantage of decreasing term insurance?
10. Why might a person buy permanent insurance rather than term insurance?
11. Which type of permanent insurance do most people buy?
12. Give examples of people for whom limited payment life insurance is recommended.
13. Explain how a family income policy is paid to the beneficiary.
14. Why do most people not buy all their life insurance at one time?
15. Give examples of how a person's life insurance needs change over a period of time.
16. What are some of the ways in which proceeds of life insurance are paid to the beneficiary?
17. What are two disadvantages of a lump-sum payment?
18. Explain why a beneficiary receives more than the face value of the policy under a settlement option.
19. Why should a policyholder review his settlement options from time to time?
20. What services does a good insurance agent perform for a policyholder?

SHARING YOUR OPINION AND EXPERIENCE

1. Why would a person buy life insurance even though he has no dependents and expects to have none in the future?
2. Why would a raise in pay for the head of a family increase his need for insurance?
3. Study the option chart on page 317. What is the difference between the amount option and the time option?
4. Betty Sibert is 22 years old, is single, and works as a stenographer. Her brother, Harold, is two years older than Betty, unmarried, and works for the telephone company. Betty recently bought a $5,000 endowment policy that will mature when she is 60. At the same time Harold bought a $10,000 straight life policy. Why do you think they chose different kinds of insurance? Do you think they made wise choices?
5. The Gradys have four children aged 6, 9, 13, and 15. They owe $10,000 on their home and $750 on their car. Mr. Grady has a $10,000 straight life policy and $3,000 additional insurance in a group plan where he works. He is considering purchasing a term policy to increase his protection. Do you think he is making a wise choice? If so, would you recommend that the policy be renewable, convertible, or both? Why?
6. Mr. Ziegler's life insurance proceeds are payable to his wife in one lump sum. Mr. Brady, on the other hand, has selected a settlement option so that his wife will receive $96.10 a month for 10 years after his death. Do you think Mr. Ziegler or Mr. Brady chose the better settlement plan? Why?

PROJECTS AND PROBLEMS

1. Prepare a table comparing the four basic types of life insurance—term, straight life, limited payment, and endowment. List the advantages and disadvantages of each. Give examples of persons who might buy each type. Use a form like this:

Type of Insurance	Advantages	Disadvantages	Examples of Who Might Buy

2. The chart on page 317 describes four settlement options from which a policyholder may choose if he does not want his insurance proceeds paid in a lump sum. Refer to the chart and indicate which option should be selected in each of the following cases.

   ▪ *a.* Mr. Levine has children who are 6, 8, and 11 years old. Should anything happen to him, he wants his life insurance to pay his wife a monthly income until the youngest child is 22. ▪ *b.* Mr. and Mrs. McGinty's children are grown and have families of their own. Mr. McGinty wants to be sure that if he should die his wife will have an income of $200 a month until his insurance and interest are used up. ▪ *c.* Mr. Beach has decided to use the cash value of his life insurance policies as retirement income. He wants the insurance company to pay him a regular monthly income for the remainder of his life. ▪ *d.* Mrs. Eckles is a commercial artist and plans to continue work until she is 65. Mr. Eckles feels that, if he should die before that time, his wife would not need the proceeds of his life insurance until she retires. He has requested the insurance company to keep the face amount of the policy until his wife is 65. In the meantime she would receive the interest earned on the money.

3. The table below shows the percent of family heads in different income groups who were covered by life insurance in a recent year. It also gives the average amount of insurance carried by the family heads in each group. Following the table are some questions for you to answer.

LIFE INSURANCE COVERAGE OF FAMILY HEADS IN DIFFERENT INCOME GROUPS

Annual Income of Family Head (dollars)	*Percent of Family Heads Insured*	*Average Amount of Insurance Carried (dollars)*
Under 3,000	71	3,783
3,000–4,999	87	6,000
5,000–8,999	96	11,616
9,000–14,999	95	22,042
15,000 or more	94	66,560

Source: Institute of Life Insurance

▪ *a.* Who is a family head? ▪ *b.* Which income group carried the largest average amount of insurance? ▪ *c.* In which income group was the largest percent of family heads insured? ▪ *d.* Did the average amount of insurance carried always increase as family income increased? ▪ *e.* Did the percent of family heads insured always increase as family income increased? ▪ *f.* Did some family heads with incomes of $9,000 to $14,999 carry more insurance than others? ▪ g. The life insurance protection of a family head earning $6,000 was equal to his income for approximately how many years? ▪ *h.* For all income brackets, what was the average percent of family heads insured? ▪ *i.* What was the average amount of insurance carried by all family heads during the year covered by the table?

Refer to the table of annual premium rates on page 315 for the information needed to work the following problems.

4. Mr. Conlin bought a $12,000 limited payment life policy (paid up at 65) at age 40.

▪ *a.* How much is the annual premium on his policy? ▪ *b.* What will be the total amount he will pay in premiums between the date he purchased the policy and the time it is paid up? ▪ *c.* If he had purchased the policy when he was 30, how much less would his annual premiums have been? ▪ *d.* What would the total cost of his policy have been had he bought it at age 30 and continued payments to age 65?

5. When he was 40, Mr. Joseph bought an $8,000 endowment policy which was to mature when he reached 65.

   ▪ *a.* How much is the annual premium on his policy? ▪ *b.* If Mr. Joseph continues his payments to age 65, how much will he have paid the insurance company? ▪ *c.* If he lives to age 65, will Mr. Joseph receive more or less than he paid the company in premiums? How much more or less?

6. Refer to the table of Annual Rates on page 315. Determine approximately how much insurance of each of the following types a man, age 30, could buy for an annual premium of $200.

   ▪ *a.* Five-year term (convertible and renewable) ▪ *b.* Straight life ▪ *c.* Limited payment life (paid up at age 65) ▪ *d.* Family income (20-year period) ▪ *e.* Endowment (at age 65)

CHALLENGE PROBLEMS

1. Some people say that an insurance agent should be chosen as carefully as a physician or a lawyer. Do you agree? Give reasons for your answer.
2. Jim Prentice insisted that anyone who invested in permanent life insurance was foolish. The reason he gave was that money gradually loses value over a period of time. Dollars invested in life insurance might be worth only half their present value when the policy is paid up. It is much wiser to invest in real estate or stocks because their values change as the value of the dollar changes. Do you agree? Why or why not?
3. In No. 2 of the Projects and Problems, the largest percent of family heads insured had incomes of $5,000–$8,999. Why was the percent smaller for those with lower incomes? for those with higher incomes?
4. In No. 5 of the Projects and Problems, you found that at age 65 Mr. Joseph would receive less from his endowment policy than he paid the company in premiums. Why do you suppose this is so?

PART 35 PAYING FOR LIFE INSURANCE

THE first rule in buying life insurance is to cover the most important needs first. The second is to check on prices and how much you get in return for your money. Some people are unaware that rates differ among insurance companies, even for the same type of policy. Some do not know that for a few extra dollars they can extend their protection or guard against losing it altogether. And some fail to realize that the way they pay for their life insurance affects its cost.

In addition to the insured's age and type of policy bought, what other factors affect the cost of life insurance? What are life insurance dividends? What happens if premiums are not paid on a policy?

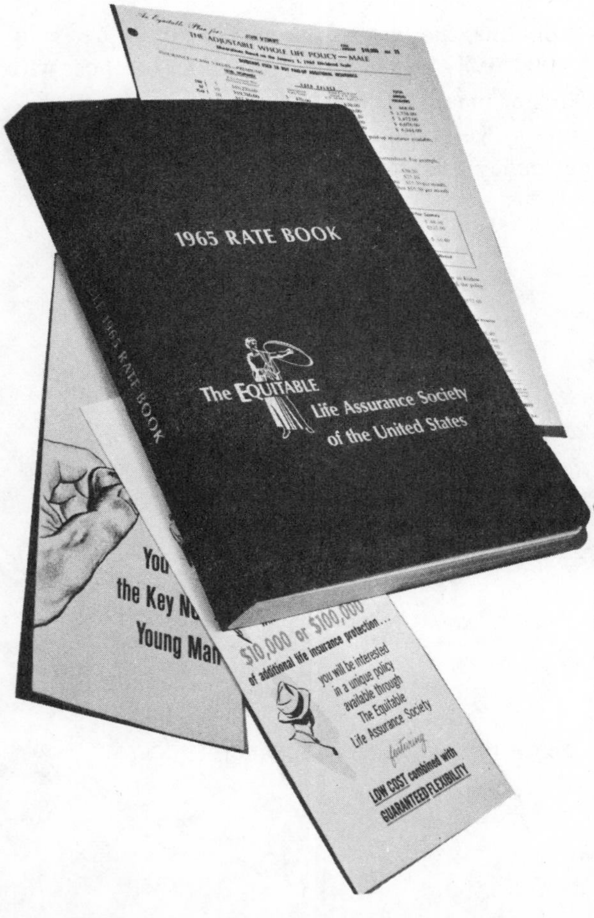

THE WAY LIFE INSURANCE IS BOUGHT AFFECTS ITS COST

American families buy more life insurance than the people of any other country in the world. This is another evidence of our high standard of living. One reason so many people are able to buy life insurance is that it is sold in three different ways—*ordinary, group,* and *industrial.* A person who is unable to obtain it by one method can usually do so by either or both of the other two. The way life insurance is bought, however, affects its cost.

Courtesy The Equitable Life Assurance Society of the United States

Ordinary Life Insurance

Ordinary life insurance is sold by agents on an individual basis in units of $1,000 or more. This is the oldest of the three ways in which life insurance is sold. Premiums are paid monthly, quarterly, semiannually, or annually. The policyholder himself chooses the payment schedule he prefers. He can change from one schedule to another simply by notifying the company. The less often you pay, the less your insurance will cost. The reason for the lower cost is that fewer payments mean less record keeping for the insurance company.

As an example of possible savings, suppose that the annual premium for an insurance policy is $100. If paid in semiannual installments, each payment would be $51. If paid in quarterly installments, each payment would be $26. Thus, it would be possible to save $4 by setting aside $\frac{1}{12}$ of the total payment each month and paying for your insurance just once a year.

Group Life Insurance

Group life insurance, as its name indicates, is a method of insuring a number of people under one policy. Many business firms provide group insurance for their employees. Usually the members of the group are not required to pass a physical examination. In most cases each member pays the same premium regardless of his age. Sometimes, however, different rates are established for different age groups. Where the group is made up of persons working for the same employer, the employer and employee often share the cost of the insurance. Some employers pay the entire cost.

Most group insurance is term insurance. Protection continues only as long as the person remains a member of the group. For example, if a person is insured under a group policy where he works and he leaves the company, his protection ends. But generally, he may exchange his group policy for a permanent type of individual policy.

When a person has a choice of whether or not to buy group insurance, it is nearly always to his advantage to take it. The cost is less than if the same amount of protection were bought through an individual policy. Furthermore, since no physical examination is required, group insurance enables some people to obtain life insurance who could not do so otherwise.

Industrial Life Insurance

Industrial life insurance, like ordinary life insurance, is sold on an individual basis. The difference is that premiums on industrial insurance are paid weekly or monthly and are collected in person by an agent of the insurance company. Premiums may be as small as 15 or 25 cents a week.

Although industrial insurance is available in amounts up to $2,000, it is usually purchased in amounts of $500 or less. As a rule, no physical examination is required; the applicant merely signs a statement that he is in good health. In most cases, industrial policies do not offer policyholders a choice of settlement options. The reason is that the amounts to be paid are too small to provide much in the way of a regular income.

Premiums for industrial insurance are high compared to those for ordinary life insurance. This is because the expense of collecting and recording payments for industrial insurance is higher. An industrial policy for $250 would cost a young person about as much as $1,000 of ordinary term insurance. Low-income families, however, are sometimes unable to save enough or to budget their earnings to meet even quarterly payments on life insurance. Industrial insurance may provide the only way for such families to obtain insurance protection.

DIVIDENDS MAY AFFECT THE COST OF INSURANCE

In comparing the rates charged for life insurance by different companies, people may be misled by the fact that dividends are paid on some insurance policies. Life insurance policies that pay dividends are called ***participating policies.*** Those that do not pay dividends are called ***nonparticipating policies.*** But dividends on a life insurance policy are not a share of the company's profits in the same way that dividends on common stock are a share of a corporation's profits. They are a refund of part of the premiums paid by the policyholder.

If a life insurance policy pays dividends, it is because the premiums charged for the insurance

A GROUP INSURANCE POLICY COVERS MANY PEOPLE.
Policy

amount to more than the company needs to cover its costs. Each year after all expenses of the company have been paid (including death losses, wages, and other operating expenses), the extra money collected in premiums is paid back to policyholders as dividends. In this way the insurance company is protected if its losses during the year are greater than expected.

When a person buys nonparticipating insurance, he knows what its exact cost will be because the rate is guaranteed for the life of the policy. When a person buys participating insurance, he knows only that the rate will not be more than a certain amount. The exact cost will depend on the amount of future dividends. It is not possible, therefore, to tell in advance whether a participating policy will cost more or less than a nonparticipating policy. In most cases any difference is likely to be small.

Dividends May Be Used in Four Ways

Dividends are paid on about two-thirds of the life insurance sold in the United States. Usually they are not paid until premiums on the policy are paid for the second year. But, like cash values, they increase with the life of the policy.

A policyholder may use the dividends in any one of four ways: (1) He may take them in cash. (2) He may use them to pay part of his next premium. (3) He may leave them with the insurance company where they will earn interest. (4) He may use them to buy more insurance. A $1,000 policy, for example, can become a $1,200 policy over a period of years if dividends are used to increase the amount of insurance. The decision as to how dividends shall be used is made by the policyholder.

POLICY PROVISIONS MAY INCREASE PREMIUMS

Every life insurance policy promises certain things in exchange for the payment of premiums. These promises are called ***provisions.*** Some provisions are found in all policies. The chief one is the company's promise to pay the face value of the policy to the beneficiary upon the death of the policyholder. Another provision is the policyholder's right to name his beneficiary.

Most policies also provide for a ***grace period.*** This is a period of time (usually 31 days) following the date for payment of premiums during which the policy will be kept in force. If the premium is not paid within this grace period, the policy may be canceled. To prevent the loss of his insurance protection, however, a person who has permanent insurance can have an *automatic loan provision* included in his policy. This gives the insurance company authority to pay the premium with a policy loan if it has not been paid within the grace period. The cash value of the policy, of course, must be enough to cover the premium.

There are other provisions that the policyholder may have included in a policy by paying an additional premium. For example, the right to renew a term policy is a provision for which the policyholder pays extra. So also is the right to convert a term policy to permanent insurance.

Another provision for which the policyholder pays an extra premium is called *disability waiver of premium*. This means that if a policyholder becomes permanently disabled, he will no longer have to pay the premiums on his insurance. It will continue in force as a paid-up policy. There is also a *disability income* provision which promises the policyholder a monthly income if he becomes disabled. This income may be $5 or $10 a month for every $1,000 of life insurance.

One provision almost everyone knows about is *double indemnity*. This is sometimes called the *accidental death benefit* provision. It promises to pay twice the face value of the policy if the insured dies as the result of an accident.

A policyholder may want some, all, or none of these provisions. The important point to keep in mind is that the more a policy promises, the more it will cost.

CASH VALUES CAN BE USED TO PAY FOR LIFE INSURANCE

For any one of several reasons, a person may decide to discontinue paying premiums on a permanent life policy. He may have bought it to meet a need that no longer exists. For example, a man might buy a policy to provide income for his children. After the children are grown, the policy is not as urgently needed as it once was. Or if a person's income drops after retirement, he may feel he cannot afford to pay the premiums on a policy. As stated earlier, a permanent life insurance policy can always be exchanged for its cash value. But the policyholder has another choice.

He may stop paying premiums yet keep his insurance protection by using the cash value of his policy to pay for it. If he wants protection for the

Courtesy General Electric Company

Having a paid-up life insurance policy adds peace of mind to retirement.

APPROXIMATE VALUES PER $1,000 OF INSURANCE FOR POLICIES ISSUED AT AGE 17

	Straight Life				20-Payment Life			
At End of Year	*Cash Value*	*Paid Up*	*Extended Term*		*Cash Value*	*Paid Up*		
			Yr.	*Days*			*Yr.*	*Days*
2	—	—	—	—	9	49	6	96
4	12	66	8	270	48	176	22	262
5	22	69	9	87	68	214	25	308
6	33	133	17	253	88	301	30	250
8	55	196	22	278	131	418	34	301
10	78	221	23	243	176	497	36	261
15	141	358	27	87	299	759	41	3
20	212	484	27	290	439	1,000	Paid up for life	

full amount of the policy, he exchanges the cash value for *extended term insurance.* This gives him protection equal to the face value of his policy but only for a limited time. It is the same as if he purchased term insurance. The length of time his protection will continue depends on the cash value of the policy and his age. The period is usually stated in the policy as a certain number of years and days. This is shown in the above table. For example, after premiums have been paid for 8 years, each $1,000 of straight life insurance bought at age 17 would provide extended term insurance for 22 years and 278 days. If the policyholder dies within that period, his beneficiary would receive the face value of the policy. If he is still living, the policy would have no further value.

Instead of extended term insurance, a person may exchange the cash value of a policy for a smaller paid-up policy. The amount of the paid-up policy is determined by the cash value and the number of years the policyholder is expected to live. You will notice in the table above that after 8 years, each $1,000 of straight life insurance bought at age 17 would provide a paid-up policy for $196. This is the amount his beneficiary would receive if the policyholder dies, regardless of when death occurs.

Whenever premium payments are stopped, the insurance company will continue the policy on an extended term basis unless the policyholder requests otherwise.

BUILDING YOUR VOCABULARY

Copy the seven sentences given below and on page 327, completing each one by replacing the question mark with the appropriate term from the column at the left.

grace period
group life insurance
industrial life insurance
nonparticipating policies
ordinary life insurance
participating policies
provisions

1. Insurance sold by agents on an individual basis in units of at least $1,000 is ? .
2. Insurance protection provided to a number of people under one policy is ? .
3. Insurance policies that pay dividends to the policyholders are ? .
4. A period following the date an insurance premium is due during which the premiums may be paid is a ? .

5. Insurance that is usually paid for in small weekly or monthly premiums is ? .
6. Promises made in an insurance policy are ? .
7. Insurance policies on which no dividends are paid are ? .

CHECKING YOUR READING

1. What are two rules to follow in buying life insurance?
2. In what three ways is life insurance sold?
3. What choices does the policyholder have in deciding how often he will pay premiums on ordinary life insurance?
4. How does the premium payment schedule the policyholder chooses affect the cost of his life insurance? Why?
5. For how long does a person's protection under a group policy continue?
6. When a person leaves a group that is insured under one policy, how can he continue his life insurance protection?
7. Why is it usually wise for a person to buy group insurance when he has the opportunity?
8. In what ways is industrial insurance like ordinary life insurance? In what ways is it different?
9. Why are premiums for industrial insurance high compared to those for ordinary life insurance?
10. Where do life insurance companies get the money to pay dividends to policyholders?
11. Why is it difficult to compare the costs of participating and nonparticipating policies?
12. In what four ways may a policyholder use his insurance dividends?
13. Name two provisions that are found in all life insurance policies.
14. What is the purpose of an automatic loan provision in an insurance policy?
15. What are some of the special provisions that a person may add to a life insurance policy by paying an extra premium?
16. Explain two ways in which a policyholder may use the cash value of his policy to extend his life insurance protection.

SHARING YOUR OPINION AND EXPERIENCE

1. Why is the amount of life insurance its people buy an indication of a country's standard of living?
2. Why do you suppose insurance companies usually do not require physical examinations of persons insured under a group policy?
3. Would you expect the premiums to be higher on participating policies or on nonparticipating policies? Why?
4. Why do you think so much of the life insurance sold in the United States is participating?
5. If you had a participating policy, what would you prefer to do with your dividends? Why?

6. Why do special provisions, such as the right to renew a term policy, increase the premiums on life insurance?
7. For whom would you recommend the double-indemnity provision in a life insurance policy?
8. Why would an insurance company want to keep a policy in force for 31 days even though the premium had not been paid?

PROJECTS AND PROBLEMS

1. The table below shows the amount of ordinary, group, and industrial life insurance in force in selected years between 1943 and 1963. Study the table and answer the questions that follow.

LIFE INSURANCE IN FORCE IN THE UNITED STATES (billion dollars)

Kind of Insurance	*Year*				
	1943	**1948**	**1953**	**1958**	**1963**
Ordinary	**$89.6**	**$131.2**	**$184.9**	**$287.8**	**$418.9**
Group	**22.4**	**37.1**	**72.2**	**144.6**	**228.5**
Industrial	**29.4**	**31.3**	**37.8**	**39.7**	**39.7**

Source: Life Insurance Fact Book, 1964

▪ *a.* What was the total amount of the three kinds of insurance outstanding in 1943? in 1963? ▪ *b.* The amount of ordinary insurance outstanding in 1943 was approximately how many times the amount of group insurance outstanding that year? ▪ *c.* In 1963, the amount of ordinary insurance outstanding was approximately how many times the amount of group insurance? ▪ *d.* During which five-year period was there the greatest increase in ordinary insurance? in group insurance? in industrial insurance? ▪ *e.* What was the approximate percent of increase between 1943 and 1963 in ordinary insurance? in group insurance? in industrial insurance? ▪ *f.* Which kind of insurance increased most in relative importance during the 20 years? Which decreased in importance?

2. The average size of insurance policies in force in the United States in certain years is shown in the table below. Use the information in the table to answer the questions that follow it.

SIZE OF THE AVERAGE INSURANCE POLICY IN THE UNITED STATES

Kind of Insurance	*Year*				
	1920	**1930**	**1940**	**1950**	**1960**
Ordinary	**$1,990**	**$2,460**	**$2,130**	**$2,320**	**$3,590**
Group	**960**	**1,700**	**1,700**	**2,480**	**4,030**
Industrial	**150**	**210**	**240**	**310**	**390**

Source: Life Insurance Fact Book, 1964

▪ *a.* For which of the three kinds of insurance was the average policy largest in 1920? in 1960? ▪ *b.* What happened to the size of the average ordinary life policy between 1930 and 1940? to the size of the average group policy? to the size of the average industrial policy? ▪ *c.* What reason can you give for the answers to question *b* above? ▪ *d.* What was the approximate percent of increase between 1940 and 1960 in the size of the average ordinary life policy? the average group policy? the average industrial policy? ▪ *e.* During which 10-year period did the size of the average group policy increase most?

Use the table of Approximate Values for Policies Issued at Age 17 on page 326 in computing the answers to problems 3, 4, and 5.

3. Fred Chen bought a $1,000 20-payment life policy at age 17. When he reached the age of 32, he could no longer pay the premiums.

   ▪ *a.* If he chose to exchange it for cash, how much could he get for his policy at that time? ▪ *b.* How much paid-up insurance would Mr. Chen have for the remainder of his life if he selected that option? ▪ *c.* To what age would he be insured for $1,000 even though he made no further payments?

4. Henry Orr bought a $5,000 straight life insurance policy at age 17.

   ▪ *a.* How much money could he borrow on the policy after paying premiums for 20 years? ▪ *b.* If he discontinued premium payments after 10 years, for what period of time into the future would he be insured for $5,000? ▪ *c.* Suppose Mr. Orr had bought a $10,000 policy and discontinued premium payments after 10 years. For what period of time into the future would he be insured for $10,000?

5. Roy Olson who is 17 years old bought a $1,000 straight life insurance policy. The annual premium is $19.30.

   ▪ *a.* In 5 years, how much will Roy have paid in premiums? in 10 years? in 15 years? ▪ *b.* After 5 years, what will be the cash value of his policy? after 10 years? after 15 years? ▪ *c.* How much did the cash value of Roy's insurance increase between the 5th and 10th years? between the 10th and 15th years? ▪ *d.* Was the increase more or less between the 10th and 15th years than between the 5th and 10th years?

CHALLENGE PROBLEMS

1. At the end of World War II industrial insurance represented 18 percent of all insurance outstanding. At the end of 1963 this kind of insurance represented only 5 percent of all life insurance outstanding. Why do you think industrial insurance declined so much in importance?
2. How do you explain the fact that the cash value of permanent life insurance increases at a more rapid rate as time goes by? (Refer to your answer to question *d* of No. 5 of the Projects and Problems.)
3. If group insurance is not available through a person's employer, how may he obtain it?

PART 36 INCOME INSURANCE

AS you learned in your study of life insurance, one of the greatest threats to financial security is loss of income. But death is only one of the things that can put a stop to income. Another is age. Today it is common practice among business firms to retire workers at a certain age, usually 65. Yet because people are living longer than ever before, a person who reaches 65 today may expect to live another 15 years or more. If people are to enjoy these added years, they must have enough income for their needs.

Another reason for loss of income is disability. In fact, disability of the family wage earner may result in a greater money loss than his death. It can keep him from earning an income while adding the cost of extra medical care to expenses. Finally, there is always a chance that a temporary period of unemployment will cause loss of income. During a business recession, many thousands of persons may be out of work temporarily. But even in prosperity, there is some unemployment.

How can workers protect themselves against loss of income? How might a loss of income among workers affect our economic system? What is social security?

Courtesy U.S. Department of Health, Education, and Welfare

WHAT PROTECTION IS THERE AGAINST LOSS OF INCOME?

One way a worker can guard against loss of income, of course, is to save. The person who saves and invests regularly when he is working will have funds for his old age or for an emergency. By investing part of his savings in life insurance, a worker can protect his family against complete loss of income in case he should die. If he buys a permanent form of insurance and lives to retirement age, he can have the cash value of the insurance paid to him as income. Or he can provide himself with a retirement income by purchasing annuities during his working years. An ***annuity,*** like a life insurance policy, is an agreement with an insurance company. Also like a life insurance policy, an annuity is usually purchased by the payment of premiums over a period of years. In exchange for the premiums, the insurance company agrees to pay a monthly income to the owner of the annuity when he reaches a certain age. The income may be guaranteed for the rest of his life or for a definite number of years. When a person has the cash value of a life insurance policy paid to him as income, he trades his insurance protection for an annuity.

Private pension plans are another source of retirement income. A ***pension*** is a regular payment of money to someone who has retired from active work. A *private* plan for providing income to such workers is one operated by an employer for the benefit of his employees. The employer may be a business enterprise, a school system, a unit of government, a church organization, a college, or university.

WHY DOES THE GOVERNMENT PROVIDE INCOME INSURANCE?

Unfortunately, most workers are not able to obtain enough income protection by their own efforts. A period of unemployment or disability can soon use up savings. Besides, many who saved for retirement in the past found their savings were not enough to take care of their needs. Their money had lost purchasing power as the result of inflation. Workers with large families, who need protection the most, often cannot afford much permanent insurance. They buy term insurance that will cover their needs at less cost but has no cash value that can be used as retirement income. For many such families, buying annuities is out of the question.

Because private pension plans are more common among large business firms than among small ones, fewer than half of those employed are covered by these plans. In addition, employees must meet certain requirements to qualify for retirement benefits. Under one company's plan, for example, an employee has to be 65 or over and must have worked for the company at least 15 consecutive years. Although pension plans differ, the average monthly income paid under such plans is less than one-third of the worker's monthly earnings before retirement.

For one reason or another, as you can see, workers find it difficult to provide themselves with adequate protection against loss of income. That is why the Congress of the United States passed the Social Security Act in 1935. Until 1965, when the Act was amended to include health insurance, social security was basically a system of income insurance. The insurance is intended to help make up for earnings lost because of retirement, death, disability, or temporary unemployment. To accomplish this purpose, the Social Security Act provides for two major income insurance plans. One is called ***old-age, survivors, and disability insurance.*** The other is ***unemployment insurance.*** The health insurance provision of the Act is explained in Part 37.

HOW DOES OLD-AGE, SURVIVORS, AND DISABILITY INSURANCE WORK?

Old-age, survivors, and disability insurance is operated entirely by the Federal government. It is financed by means of a tax on earnings, only half of which is paid by the worker. The other half is paid by his employer. The tax rate changes from time to time, as can be seen from the following table.

SOCIAL SECURITY TAX RATES

Years	*Employee*	*Employer*	*Total*	*Self-Employed*
1966	4.2 %	4.2 %	8.4%	6.15%
1967–68	4.4 %	4.4 %	8.8%	6.40%
1969–72	4.9 %	4.9 %	9.8%	7.10%
1973–75	5.4 %	5.4 %	10.8%	7.55%
1976–79	5.45%	5.45%	10.9%	7.60%
1980–86	5.55%	5.55%	11.1%	7.70%
1987 and after	5.65%	5.65%	11.3%	7.80%

In 1966, it was 8.4 percent of earnings. If a worker earned $100 a week that year, the amount to be paid for that worker each week was $8.40. The employer deducts half the amount of the tax from the worker's wages. The employer himself pays the remaining half. The rate for self-employed persons is slightly less than the combined rate for an employed worker and his employer. In 1966, for example, the rate for self-employed persons was 6.15 percent. Only a certain amount of earnings are taxed each year. Like the tax rate, this amount is subject to change. In 1966, it was $6,600. Workers with annual incomes of more than $6,600 did not pay tax on earnings above that amount.

Every three months, employers send the money collected from all their workers, together with their own share of the tax, to the United States Treasury Department. Self-employed persons, such as farmers, lawyers, or writers, pay their social security tax when they file their income tax returns. A part of all money collected in social security taxes is used to finance the health insurance provided under the Act. The remainder is placed in a fund from which old-age, survivors, and disability benefits are paid. Benefits become payable when a worker retires, becomes disabled, or dies. The amount of benefits paid depends on the worker's average earnings before retirement, disability, or death. Examples of monthly cash benefits are shown on page 333.

Today more than 90 percent of all workers are covered by old-age, survivors, and disability insurance. Each one is assigned a social security number and given a card bearing that number. The number identifies his account with the Federal Social Security Administration which keeps a record of each worker's earnings and the amount of tax paid for or by him. A worker's social security number remains the same throughout his entire lifetime, regardless of how many different positions he may hold. Anyone may obtain a report of his account record by writing to the Social Security Administration, Baltimore, Maryland 21203. It is advisable to do this about every three years.

What Benefits Does Social Security Provide?

Since 1937, when the Social Security Act first went into effect, benefits have been greatly increased. For example, the minimum monthly benefit for one person then was $10 compared to $44 in 1966. It is more than likely that there will be further increases in the future. According to the table, a worker whose average monthly earnings before retirement were $400 or more, is entitled to monthly benefits of $135.90. His wife is entitled to roughly half that amount, or $68. A wife who is also entitled to benefits based on her own earnings cannot receive two benefits. Instead she will be paid the larger of the two benefits.

If a worker is disabled for 12 months or more, so that he is prevented from earning a living, he is eligible for the same benefits as a retired worker. The benefits will be paid for as long as the disability lasts.

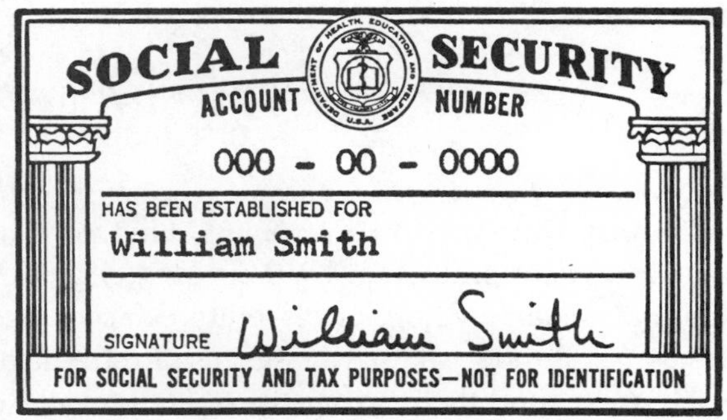

000-00-0000

[SOCIAL SECURITY ACCOUNT NUMBER]

William Smith
1234 Main Street
Baltimore, Maryland 21201

SIGNATURE William Smith

FOR SOCIAL SECURITY AND TAX PURPOSES—NOT FOR IDENTIFICATION

Upper and lower portion of social security card

EXAMPLES OF MONTHLY CASH BENEFIT PAYMENTS

Average Yearly Earnings after 1950	*$800 or Less*	*$1,800*	*$3,000*	*$3,600*	*$4,200*	*$4,800*
Retirement at 65	**$ 44.00**	**$ 78.20**	**$101.70**	**$112.40**	**$124.20**	**$135.90**
Retirement at 62	**35.20**	**62.60**	**81.40**	**90.00**	**99.40**	**108.80**
Wife's benefit at 65 or with child in her care	**22.00**	**39.10**	**50.90**	**56.20**	**62.10**	**68.00**
Wife's benefit at 62	**16.50**	**29.40**	**38.20**	**42.20**	**46.60**	**51.00**
One child of retired or disabled worker	**22.00**	**39.10**	**50.90**	**56.20**	**62.10**	**68.00**
Widow age 62 or over	**44.00**	**64.60**	**83.90**	**92.80**	**102.50**	**112.20**
Widow at 60, no child	**38.20**	**56.00**	**72.80**	**80.50**	**88.90**	**97.30**
Widow under 62 and 1 child	**66.00**	**117.40**	**152.60**	**168.60**	**186.40**	**204.00**
Widow under 62 and 2 children	**66.00**	**120.00**	**202.40**	**240.00**	**279.60**	**306.00**
One surviving child	**44.00**	**58.70**	**76.30**	**84.30**	**93.20**	**102.00**
Two surviving children	**66.00**	**117.40**	**152.60**	**168.60**	**186.40**	**204.00**
Maximum family payment	**66.00**	**120.00**	**202.40**	**240.00**	**280.80**	**309.20**
Lump-sum death payment	**132.00**	**234.60**	**255.00**	**255.00**	**255.00**	**255.00**

If a worker covered by social security should die, benefits are paid to his survivors. His *survivors* are those still living who depended on him for support. In addition, death benefits include a lump-sum payment to take care of immediate expenses.

What Factors Affect Payment of Benefits?

You will notice that retirement benefits shown in the table are based on retirement at age 65. Both men and women workers may retire any time after reaching age 62. Those who start drawing benefits before age 65, however, will receive less per month than if they waited until 65. At age 62, for example, a retired worker will receive only 80 percent of the amount he would be paid at age 65. Furthermore, if a worker chooses to retire before age 65 and take the smaller benefit, he no longer can qualify for the full benefit. He will continue to receive the reduced amount for as long as he lives.

Between the ages of 65 and 72, a worker is entitled to full retirement benefits only if his earned income is no more than $1,500 a year. ***Earned income*** means money received for work. It does not include income from investments. After age 72, a worker is entitled to full retirement benefits regardless of the amount he earns.

Children of a retired or disabled worker or a worker who has died are eligible for benefits until age 18. They may continue to draw benefits until age 22, however, if they are full-time students and unmarried. A worker's widow is eligible to receive full benefits if she is 62 or over or if she has children under 18. She may start drawing benefits as early as age 60, but she will be paid a smaller amount per month.

Benefits Must Be Claimed

Anyone who is entitled to receive retirement, survivors, or disability benefits must apply for them by filing a claim with the nearest social security office. Every major city and town has one. It is usually listed in the telephone directory under U.S. Gov-

ernment, Department of Health, Education, and Welfare. If there is no social security office where you live, the address of the nearest office may be obtained from your post office.

WHAT IS UNEMPLOYMENT INSURANCE?

Another part of the Social Security Act, called ***unemployment insurance,*** is designed to cover a temporary loss of income. It pays weekly benefits to workers who have lost their jobs through no fault of their own, but who are too young to retire. Unemployment insurance is operated jointly by the Federal and state governments; that is, each state runs its own plan which is subject to the provisions of the Social Security Act. Like old-age, survivors, and disability insurance, unemployment insurance is paid for by means of a tax. In all but two states, the employer pays the entire tax. Only businesses that employ 4 or more workers during 20 or more weeks of the year are required to pay an unemployment tax. The money collected in unemployment taxes is used to pay benefits to workers who are temporarily unemployed.

The amount a worker receives in jobless benefits depends on his past earnings, but the actual amount varies from state to state. On the average, benefits equal about half the worker's regular earnings. The number of weeks that benefits will be paid also varies. It may be as few as 13 or as many as 26. To qualify for benefits, a person must be physically able and willing to work. He must register for work at a public employment office and accept suitable employment when it is offered to him. And he must be unemployed for a period of from one to two weeks before he can begin to receive benefits. About two-thirds of the nation's workers are covered by unemployment insurance.

HOW SOCIAL SECURITY HELPS INDIVIDUALS AND THE NATION

Many people think that because they are covered by social security, they do not need to buy life insurance or to save and invest in other ways. The truth is that social security benefits alone will not provide sufficient income in most cases. Even in retirement, when people usually have fewer expenses than before, some other income is needed.

What social security can and does do is add to the protection individuals are able to provide for themselves. In other words, it takes individual savings and insurance plans plus social security benefits to give workers adequate protection against loss of income.

Social security performs another important function that few people realize. It helps to keep our economic system running efficiently. Production, remember, takes place as the result of spending. Loss of income means loss of purchasing power. A decrease in purchasing power means a decrease in spending and a decrease in production. Do you see what might happen if a large number of persons were without income because of retirement, unemployment, disability, or death of the family wage earner? Other workers might lose their jobs and incomes as the result of the slowdown in production. In time, this could lead to a recession. Social security benefits, however, supply purchasing power to persons who have lost all or part of their incomes. In that way they help to keep money circulating.

BUILDING YOUR VOCABULARY

On a separate sheet of paper, write each of the terms listed in the left-hand column below. Read the three definitions to the right of each term. After each term, copy the definition that best describes it.

1. ***annuity***
   - *a.* A special type of permanent life insurance purchased by payment of annual premiums
   - *b.* A plan by which employees of an insurance company share in the company's profits
   - *c.* A guaranteed retirement income purchased from an insurance company
2. ***earned income***
   - *a.* Money earned on investments
   - *b.* Money received for work
   - *c.* Money received in the form of social security benefits
3. ***old-age, survivors, and disability insurance***
   - *a.* A retirement plan operated by the Federal government for its employees
   - *b.* An insurance plan operated jointly by the Federal and state governments to cover temporary loss of income
   - *c.* An insurance plan operated by the Federal government that pays benefits when a worker retires, dies, or is disabled
4. ***pension***
   - *a.* A regular payment of money to a retired worker
   - *b.* Money paid to a worker who is temporarily unemployed
   - *c.* Money paid to the beneficiary of a life insurance policy
5. ***unemployment insurance***
   - *a.* An insurance plan operated jointly by the Federal and state governments that provides weekly benefits to workers temporarily out of work
   - *b.* An insurance plan operated jointly by the Federal and state governments that pays for retraining workers who have lost their jobs
   - *c.* An insurance plan operated by the Federal government that pays benefits to employees injured at work

CHECKING YOUR READING

1. Death of a wage earner results in loss of income. Name three other things that might result in loss of income.
2. Name several ways a worker may guard against the loss of income.
3. What is a private pension plan?
4. What are some of the reasons workers find it difficult to protect themselves against loss of income?
5. What two major income insurance plans are provided under the Social Security Act?
6. How is old-age, survivors, and disability insurance financed?
7. What factors determine the amount of retirement benefits a worker receives under social security?
8. At what age does a worker become eligible for retirement benefits?
9. At what age may a person receive full retirement benefits regardless of his earnings?
10. What should a person do in order to claim social security benefits to which he is entitled?
11. In what way does unemployment insurance protect workers?
12. Who pays the cost of unemployment insurance?
13. Under what conditions may a worker qualify for unemployment benefits?
14. Why should a person have insurance and savings if he is covered by social security?
15. How does social security help our economic system?

SHARING YOUR OPINION AND EXPERIENCE

1. Why do you suppose some employers set up private pension plans even though their employees are covered by social security?
2. Why do you think private pension plans are more common among large business firms than among small ones?
3. It has been said that insurance gives protection against dying too soon, but annuities provide protection against living too long. Explain.
4. Why do you suppose each person covered by social security is assigned an account number?
5. Why should a person obtain a report of his social security account record periodically?
6. A person between the age of 65 and 72 may receive full social security benefits only if he earns no more than $1,500 a year. What is the purpose of this ruling?
7. Regardless of how much income a person between 65 and 72 years of age receives from investments, he can still draw full social security benefits. Do you consider this fair or unfair. Why?
8. Why do you think unemployment insurance benefits are less than a person would earn if he were working?
9. Some authorities have called the Social Security Act the most important social law passed by Congress in this century. Why do you think the Act is considered so important?

PROJECTS AND PROBLEMS

1. At the end of a recent year, 6.6 million annuities were in force with life insurance companies in the United States. If kept in force until fully paid up, these annuities will provide a total annual income of $3,175,000,000.

   ▪ *a.* On the average, how much annual income (to the nearest dollar) will each annuity provide? ▪ *b.* What will be the average monthly income from each annuity? ▪ *c.* In the year in question, insurance companies were making payments on 23 percent of the annuities. How many annuities were providing income to their owners?

2. The illustration below shows the number of persons in the United States covered by private pension plans in the years 1940, 1950, and 1960.

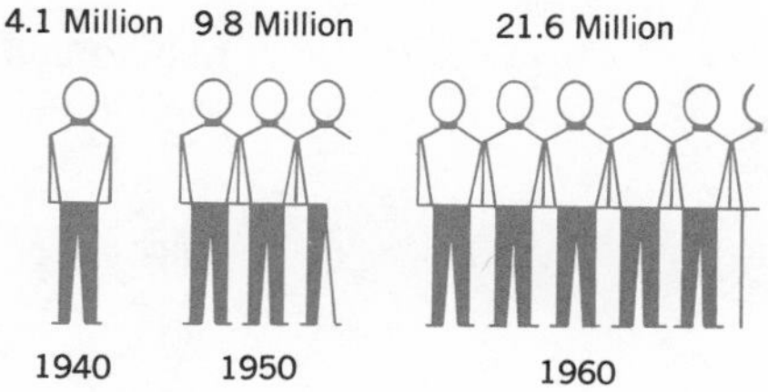

   ▪ *a.* How many more persons were covered by private pension plans in 1950 than in 1940? ▪ *b.* What was the average increase each year between 1950 and 1960 in the number of persons covered by private pension plans? ▪ *c.* The number of persons covered by private plans in 1960 was approximately how many times the number covered in 1940? ▪ *d.* Approximately 8 percent of the persons covered in 1960 were already receiving monthly retirement benefits. How many persons were receiving these monthly payments?

3. In 1965, the social security tax rate for employed persons was $7\frac{1}{4}$ percent of earnings. The rate for self-employed persons was 5.4 percent. That year, only the first $4,800 of earnings were taxed. In 1965, Mr. Gratz earned $450 a month in a job covered by social security.

   ▪ *a.* How much social security tax did Mr. Gratz pay as an employed worker in 1965? ▪ *b.* How much tax did his employer pay for Mr. Gratz in 1965? ▪ *c.* What was the total amount of tax credited to Mr. Gratz's account during the year? ▪ *d.* Had he been self-employed, how much social security tax would Mr. Gratz have had to pay in 1965?

4. In 1966, the social security tax rate for employed persons was raised to 8.4 percent of earnings. The rate for self-employed persons was 6.15 percent. That year the first $6,600 of earnings were taxed.

   ▪ *a.* Based on earnings of $450 a month, how much more did Mr. Gratz have to pay in social security taxes as an employed worker in 1966 than he paid in 1965? ▪ *b.* What was the approximate percent of increase in Mr. Gratz's social security tax in 1966? ▪ *c.* Had Mr. Gratz been self-employed, how much would his social security tax have increased in 1966? What was the percent of increase? ▪ *d.* Based on average monthly earnings of $450, a retired worker was entitled to benefits of $127 monthly in 1965. In 1966, the monthly benefit for such a worker rose to $135.90. What was the percent of increase in retirement benefits? ▪ *e.* Why do you think the tax increased by a greater percent than the retirement benefits?

5. The table below shows the number of persons receiving social security benefits at the end of each of the nine years listed. Amounts are in millions. According to the table, 9.1 million persons were receiving monthly benefits at the end of 1956. Following the table are some questions for you to answer.

OLD-AGE, SURVIVORS, AND DISABILITY INSURANCE

Year	*Number of Persons Receiving Monthly Benefits at Year End (in millions)*
1956	9.1
1957	11.1
1958	12.4
1959	13.7
1960	14.8
1961	16.5
1962	18.1
1963	19.0
1964	19.8

Source: Life Insurance Fact Book, 1965

▪ *a.* At the end of which year had the number of persons receiving monthly benefits increased most over the preceding year? ▪ *b.* What was the average increase each year between 1956 and 1964 in the number receiving monthly benefits? ▪ *c.* What was the percent of increase between 1956 and 1964 in the number receiving monthly benefits? ▪ *d.* In 1964 the population of the United States was approximately 192 million. What percent of all people in the country were receiving monthly benefits that year?

CHALLENGE PROBLEMS

1. Many employers now require their employees to retire at age 65. Do you think this is a good idea? Why?
2. Why do you think the social security tax rate changes from time to time?
3. The social security tax is compulsory for most workers. Why do you think this is so?

PART 37 HEALTH INSURANCE

ONE item that families find difficult to budget is health care. The reason is that the cost of health care cannot be estimated as accurately as other expenses. In a normal year, a family might spend between 5 and 6 percent of its income on doctors, dentists, hospitals, and other health needs. Another year, however, a serious illness or accident may push such expenses to twice that amount or more. In fact for some families the costs of a serious illness or injury may exceed the annual income. To protect themselves against the unexpected expense of a major illness or accident, three-fourths of the nation's population now carries some form of health insurance.

What types of losses can be covered by health insurance? What factors determine its cost?

HEALTH INSURANCE IS AVAILABLE IN FIVE FORMS

Health insurance provides protection against financial losses resulting from accident or illness. In general these losses are of two kinds. Expenses such as hospital bills, doctors' fees, drugs, and other medical costs are one kind. The other is the income that might be lost if a wage earner is injured or becomes ill. To provide protection against each type of expense, as well as loss of income, there are five forms of health insurance. They may be bought singly or in combination.

Hospital Expense Insurance

The biggest expense in connection with a serious illness or injury is apt to be hospital care. This explains why the most popular kind of health insurance is hospital expense insurance. If a policyholder is hospitalized, ***hospital expense insurance*** will pay part or all of his hospital costs.

H. Armstrong Roberts

Surgical Expense Insurance

If a policyholder undergoes an operation, part or all of the surgeon's fee will be paid by ***surgical expense insurance.*** Insurance policies of this kind usually list the operations covered, together with the maximum amount that will be paid for each.

General Medical Expense Insurance

Doctor bills for illnesses not requiring surgery are covered by ***general medical expense insurance.*** Some policies pay the doctor's bill only if the policyholder is a hospital patient. Others include payment for calls at the doctor's office, as well as calls the doctor makes to the policyholder's home.

Major Medical Expense Insurance

Unlike other forms of health insurance that pay for a particular kind of expense, ***major medical expense insurance*** provides protection against almost every type of expense. It covers hospital bills, physicians' and surgeons' fees, drugs, nursing care, and all kinds of treatment both in and out of a hospital. But its purpose is not to replace other forms of health insurance. It is designed to pay for treatment of a very serious injury or prolonged illness for which the costs may amount to thousands of dollars. In other words, its protection starts where the protection of other health insurance usually stops.

Major medical expense insurance is similar to deductible automobile collision insurance. The policyholder pays the first $100 to $1,000 of expense. The exact amount is stated in the policy. When expenses exceed the deductible amount, the insurance pays 75 or 80 percent of the remaining expenses up to a certain maximum. For example, one policy pays 80 percent of the costs of medical treatment over $300 and up to $7,500. Under this policy, if expenses of an illness came to $2,500, the policyholder's share would be $740.

Deductible amount	**$300**
20% of remaining $2,200	**440**
	$740

The insurance would cover the balance of expenses amounting to $1,760. Regardless of total costs, however, the insurance would not pay more than $7,500. The maximum paid by such policies varies. Some pay up to $25,000. Others are limited to $5,000.

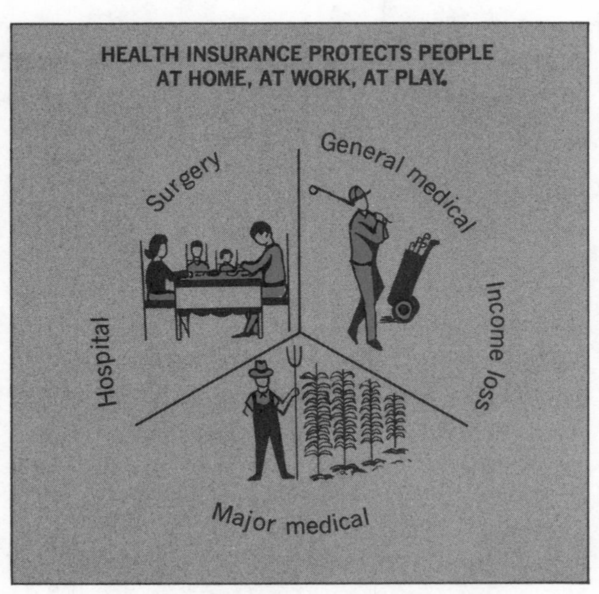

Loss of Income Insurance

As its name indicates, ***loss of income insurance*** helps to replace earnings lost as a result of illness or injury. This type of protection is also called *disability insurance.* Although no policy will pay benefits equal to earnings, some pay as much as 80 percent of regular income. Moreover, these payments are not subject to income tax.

HEALTH INSURANCE BENEFITS ARE OF TWO KINDS

One way in which health insurance plans differ is that some provide service benefits while others provide cash allowances. Under a service plan, the policyholder receives a certain amount of health care regardless of its cost. For example, if a person has hospital insurance that entitles him to service benefits, the policy states how many days of hospital care will be provided. The insurance pays the cost for that many days regardless of how much the hospital charges a day.

If a health insurance policy provides cash allowances, on the other hand, the policyholder is entitled to a certain number of dollars for any medical service he needs. Thus a policy of this kind might specify $20 a day for hospital care. If the actual cost of hospital care is more than that, the policyholder pays the difference.

Courtesy Kings County Research Laboratories, Inc.

Transfusions are sometimes needed during hospitalization. Here blood specimen is being placed in an AutoAnalyzer so that the blood type can be established.

WHAT DETERMINES THE COST OF HEALTH INSURANCE?

The cost of health insurance depends on three factors. One is the amount of protection the policy provides. A second is the way it is bought. The third is the age of the policyholder.

The Amount of Protection

The more protection a policy offers, the more it costs. For example, most insurance plans can be written to include a policyholder's dependents up to a certain age. Premiums for a family policy, however, are higher than for one that covers only the policyholder. A policy with a deductible feature should cost less than one without; and the higher the deductible amount, the less the policy should cost. Many policies contain "waiting period" clauses. A ***waiting period*** is the length of time the policy must be in force before the policyholder is entitled to benefits. The longer the waiting period in any type of policy, the less the premiums should be. Most policies contain a list of ***exclusions.*** These are the risks the policy does not cover. The more exclusions a policy contains, the less protection it affords and the less it should cost.

Method of Purchase

As with the other types of insurance, the most economical way to buy health insurance is with a group. The members of the insured group may be employees of the same business firm; or they may belong to the same lodge, labor union, or credit union. Premiums for group health insurance may be as much as one-third less than those for individual policies. One reason is that there are more people sharing the risk. In many cases, an employer shares the cost with his employees.

Age of Policyholder

Unlike life insurance, premiums for health insurance do not increase with each year of age. But until recently people could not obtain health insurance after reaching the age of 65. Today many private insuring organizations offer plans for those 65 or over. Premiums may be higher than those charged younger people, however; or benefits may be fewer.

SOCIAL SECURITY PROVIDES HEALTH INSURANCE FOR PERSONS OVER 65

Because many persons 65 and over are retired and living on small incomes, they cannot afford adequate health insurance coverage. It was for this reason that the Social Security Act was amended to include health insurance. The official name of this amendment is Hospital and Medical Care Insurance; but it is popularly known as "Medicare."

The insurance is of two types, both effective July 1, 1966. The first type pays a major portion of the cost of hospital care. Beginning in January, 1967, it will also cover nursing home care. The second type pays a major portion of doctor bills over $50 for treatment at home, in a hospital, or in a doctor's office.

To qualify for coverage under either plan, a person must be 65 or over. The hospital insurance covers all persons in that age group automatically whether or not they have ever worked under social security. And it covers them regardless of income. The doctor-bill insurance is voluntary; that is, persons who want it must apply for coverage. The cost to the individual is $3 a month—$6 for a man and wife.

This amendment to the Social Security Act will undoubtedly bring about some changes in the plans sold by private companies. In other words, policies issued by private companies to persons over 65 will be written to cover benefits not included in the government insurance.

THREE KINDS OF PRIVATE ORGANIZATIONS SELL HEALTH INSURANCE

Health insurance is available from three different types of private organizations. First, there are regular insurance companies. These offer hospital, surgical, and medical insurance. They also sell loss of income insurance. In most cases cash benefits are paid to the policyholder himself, and he pays his own bills. Insurance companies sell both group and individual policies.

The Blue Cross and the Blue Shield organizations represent the second type of insuring agency. These operate in most communities throughout the United States. ***Blue Cross*** is a hospital insurance plan sponsored by the hospitals of a community or state. ***Blue Shield*** is a medical and surgical insurance plan sponsored by the doctors of a county or state. Blue Cross and Blue Shield are both nonprofit corporations. Although they specialize in insuring groups, persons not eligible for group membership can usually obtain insurance on an individual basis. Most of these plans provide service rather than cash benefits. Payment is usually made directly to the hospital or doctor. Coverage under these plans varies.

The third type of nonprofit insuring organization operates like a cooperative enterprise. These organizations are called *independents.* Most of them employ their own doctors, and many have their own medical centers where patients go for treatment. A few have built their own hospitals. Independents have been organized by labor unions, corporations, doctors, and groups of citizens. Members pay an annual fee that entitles them to all services of the organization.

HOW TO BUY HEALTH INSURANCE

The rules for wise buying apply to health insurance just as surely as they do to anything else. The first step is to determine the kinds and amount of protection needed. The second step is to make certain that the policies bought meet those needs. Suppose a person lives in a community where the average cost of hospital care is $25 a day. A policy that pays $10 a day toward hospital expenses would

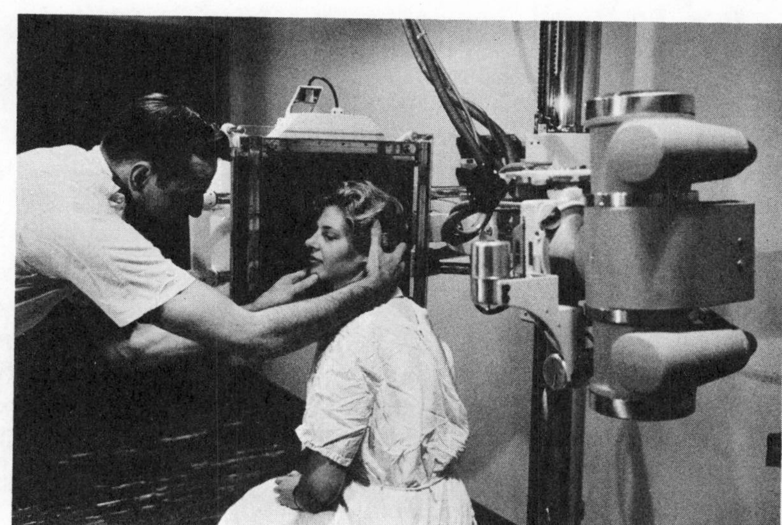

X-rays often are part of a thorough medical examination which is usually covered by health insurance.

Werner Wolf from Black Star

provide him little coverage. A person who travels to any extent needs insurance that provides coverage while he is away from home.

When you buy insurance, you are entering into a business agreement. Since you will get only what the policy says, it is important to read and understand its terms. Otherwise, you may fail to get the benefits you need most.

Buy From a Licensed Company

When you buy an individual health insurance policy, select your insurance company carefully. An insurance company that is licensed by the Insurance Department of your state is supervised by state authorities. If you buy health and accident insurance from one of these licensed firms, you have the assurance that the company has complied with state regulations designed to protect policyholders.

It is possible, however, for a company located in another state to do business by mail in your state without a license. Such companies are called *unlicensed companies.* Some of them have good reputations and give excellent service. Unfortunately, a few have aroused numerous complaints for failure to pay claims.

If a licensed company refuses to pay benefits to which a policyholder is entitled, he may take his case to his state insurance commissioner. If an unlicensed company refuses to pay a claim, it might be necessary to sue the company in its home state in order to collect. The Insurance Department of your state has no supervision over that company.

WHAT IS WORKMEN'S COMPENSATION INSURANCE?

The health insurance plans described so far in this part are sometimes called *voluntary* health insurance. Individuals and business firms are free to decide whether or not they wish to participate in such plans. There is also a type of health insurance plan that state governments require most employers to carry on their employees. It is called ***workmen's compensation insurance.***

Workmen's compensation insurance pays for injuries in the event an employee is hurt while on the job. It also pays a percent of his regular income while he is unable to work, as well as his medical and hospital expenses. If injury results in the death of a worker, his dependents are entitled to *compensation* for the loss. In all states the cost of workmen's compensation is paid entirely by employers. Benefits, however, vary widely from state to state.

BUILDING YOUR VOCABULARY

Copy the ten sentences given below, completing each one by replacing the question mark with the appropriate term from the column at the left.

- *Blue Cross*
- *Blue Shield*
- *exclusions*
- *general medical expense insurance*
- *hospital expense insurance*
- *loss of income insurance*
- *major medical expense insurance*
- *surgical expense insurance*
- *waiting period*
- *workmen's compensation insurance*

1. Insurance that pays all or part of the costs of hospitalization is ? .
2. Insurance that helps to replace earnings lost as a result of disability is ? .
3. To protect employees who may be injured on the job, most employers are required by law to carry ? .
4. Insurance that pays all or part of a doctor's fee for an operation is ? .
5. A nonprofit corporation that sponsors a hospital insurance plan is ? .
6. The length of time a policy must be in force before the policyholder may receive benefits is the ? .
7. Insurance that covers doctor bills for illnesses not requiring surgery is ? .
8. Risks not covered by a particular insurance policy are ? .
9. A nonprofit medical and surgical insurance plan sponsored by doctors is ? .
10. Insurance designed to pay expenses resulting from serious or prolonged illness is ? .

CHECKING YOUR READING

1. Why do families find it difficult to budget for health care?
2. What two kinds of financial losses may a family suffer because of accident or illness?
3. Why is hospital expense insurance the most popular kind of health insurance?
4. How does major medical expense insurance differ from other forms of health insurance?
5. Health insurance benefits are provided in two different forms. What are they?
6. What three factors determine the cost of health insurance?
7. Explain how the amount of protection offered by a policy affects its cost.
8. Why are premiums for group health insurance less than those for individual policies?
9. How does the age of the policyholder affect the cost of health insurance?
10. Why was the Social Security Act amended to include health insurance?
11. What two types of health insurance are provided under social security? What important difference is there in the operation of these two plans?
12. Name the three kinds of private organizations that sell health insurance.
13. Who sponsors Blue Cross insurance?
14. How does Blue Shield insurance differ from Blue Cross?
15. What are *independents?* Explain how they operate.
16. What rules should a person follow in buying health insurance?

17. Why should you purchase health insurance only from companies that are licensed by the state in which you live?
18. What benefits does a worker receive under workmen's compensation insurance?
19. Who pays the cost of workmen's compensation?

SHARING YOUR OPINION AND EXPERIENCE

1. If a person cannot afford the costs of complete medical insurance, which of the following alternatives is wiser? (*a*) Cover the everyday expenses, such as routine visits to the doctor's office and physical examinations; (*b*) insure against the big, unexpected losses. Give reasons for your answer.
2. Why do you think loss of income insurance is also called disability insurance?
3. Why is it not possible to buy loss of income insurance that will replace earnings completely?
4. Some health insurance policies cover only specific types of accidents or diseases. Do you consider a policy of this kind a good or a poor buy? Explain.
5. Do you think it is better to have a health insurance policy that provides service benefits or one that pays a cash allowance? Why?
6. Premiums for health insurance have increased considerably in recent years. What reasons can you give for the increase?
7. Should all health insurance plans be voluntary? Why?
8. What type of automobile insurance might be considered health insurance for the policyholder?

PROJECTS AND PROBLEMS

1. The amounts that Americans spent per person for various health purposes in 1948 and 1963 are shown in the table below. At the top of page 346 are some questions for you to answer.

PER CAPITA CONSUMER EXPENDITURES FOR HEALTH PURPOSES 1948 AND 1963

Purpose of Expenditure	*Amount*	
	1948	*1963*
Hospital services	**$11.63**	**$37.36**
Physicians' services	**17.15**	**34.21**
Drugs	**10.10**	**22.65**
Dentists' services	**6.20**	**12.57**
Eyeglasses and appliances	**2.97**	**7.54**
All other	**4.74**	**12.60**

Source: National Consumer Finance Association

▪ *a.* What was the total per capita expenditure for all health purposes in 1948? in 1963? ▪ *b.* What was the percent of increase (to the nearest whole percent) in health expenditures per person during the period from 1948 to 1963? ▪ *c.* Approximately what percent of the total expenditures was for hospital services in 1948? in 1963? ▪ *d.* Did the proportion spent for hospital services increase or decrease between 1948 and 1963? ▪ *e.* Did the proportion spent for physicians' services increase or decrease between 1948 and 1963?

2. In 1948, approximately 8 percent of the total consumer expenditures for all health purposes was paid by health insurance. In 1963, approximately 31 percent was paid by insurance. What was the average amount of health insurance benefit paid for each person in the United States in each of the two years? (Refer to your answer to question *a* of problem No. 1)
3. The graph below shows the percent of persons under 65 years of age and those 65 or older who had health insurance coverage in three different years. Study the graph and answer the questions that follow.

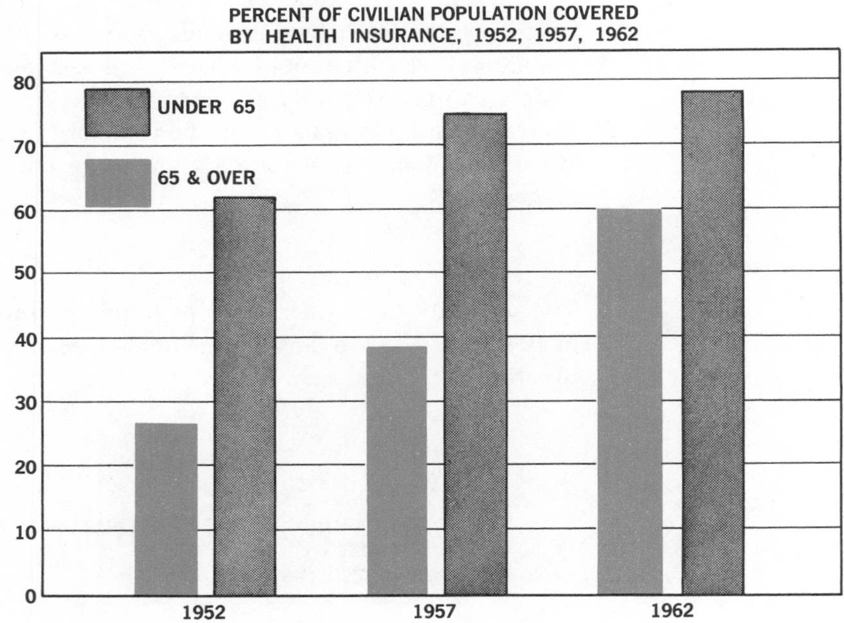

Source: Source Book of Health Insurance Data, 1963

▪ *a.* Approximately what percent of those persons under 65 years of age were covered by health insurance in 1952? in 1957? in 1962? ▪ *b.* Approximately what percent of those 65 or over were protected by health insurance in 1952? in 1957? in 1962? ▪ *c.* Between 1952 and 1962, did the percent of the population with health insurance coverage increase faster among persons under 65 or among those 65 and older? ▪ *d.* The title to the graph mentions "civilian population." Who makes up the civilian population? ▪ *e.* Does the fact that 60 percent of all persons 65 and over had health insurance in 1962 mean that all had adequate protection? ▪ *f.* Does the fact that nearly 80 percent of all persons under 65 had health insurance in 1962 mean that they had adequate protection? ▪ *g.* Is it possible that some persons over 65 had more health insurance coverage than those under 65?

4. The following article appeared recently in a well-known magazine. Read it and answer the questions that follow.

THE COST OF HEALTH CARE PROGRESS

The question has been asked, "How much are the people in the United States willing to spend on medical care?"

They put out nearly $24 billion a year now. This amounts to about 6 percent of their disposable income. Since World War II, medical care not only has been getting more expensive, it also has been absorbing a steadily increasing share of the people's income. In 1950, it took about 4½ percent of disposable income.

In the intervening years, medical science has made enormous strides. Life-saving techniques and operations unheard of 10 years ago are widely available today. Drugs and equipment are now available to beat defects and diseases that only a decade ago were almost always fatal.

Advances like these come at high cost. But there seems to be a growing response among the U.S. people to these strides. The idea is beginning to spread that if medicine can do so many new tricks, maybe it's worth paying more for it.

▪ *a.* When the article was written, how much were Americans paying each year for medical care? ▪ *b.* What percent of their disposable income were they paying for this care? ▪ *c.* What is disposable income? ▪ *d.* Does medical care now take a larger or a smaller percent of disposable income than it did in 1950? how much larger or smaller? ▪ *e.* Does the article say that every person in the United States spends the same percent of his disposable income on medical care? ▪ *f.* Does the article say what amount was spent on medical care in 1950? ▪ *g.* What happens to the cost of medical care as advancements are made in medical science? ▪ *h.* Do people appear willing to accept this fact?

CHALLENGE PROBLEMS

1. Most major medical expense policies have a coinsurance clause. What does this mean? Why do you suppose it is called coinsurance?
2. It has been said that a person's need for medical care is not related to his income. What do you think this statement means? Would the statement apply to other needs as well? Explain.
3. Why do you suppose hospitals are interested in sponsoring nonprofit insurance plans, such as Blue Cross?
4. The table in No. 1 of the Projects and Problems Section shows how much per capita expenditures for health purposes increased from 1948 to 1963. Why do you suppose the amount spent was so much greater in 1963 than in 1948?

CONTENTS OF UNIT 8

Unit 8 / Aids and Protection for the Consumer

PART 38 AGENCIES THAT SERVE AND PROTECT THE CONSUMER

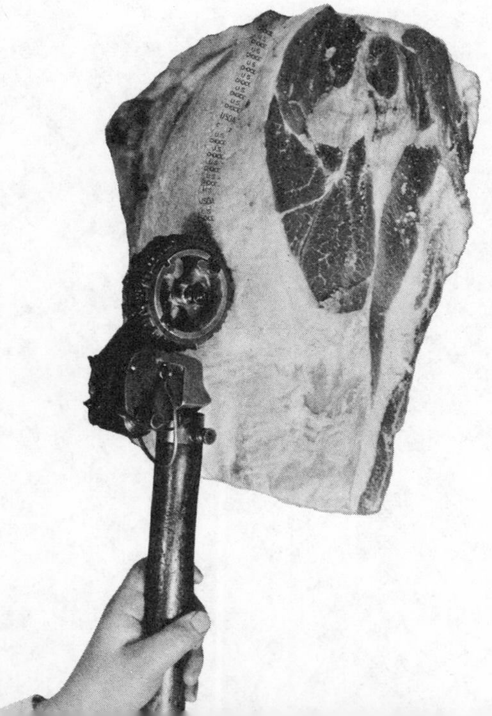

IN Part 14 you learned that getting your money's worth is not just a matter of luck. It is more often the result of finding out all you can about the things you buy. In other words, by studying labels, checking advertisements, and examining goods you have a basis for comparing quality and price.

Unfortunately, consumers are sometimes fooled into thinking they are getting their money's worth. A label may misrepresent a product. Advertising may be false or misleading. Foods may be unfit for consumption. A drug may be unsafe. The deception may not always be intentional. The number of producers who deceive buyers intentionally is small compared to the total number. But intentional or not, any kind of deception harms the consumer's pocketbook; and some kinds endanger his health and safety as well. It is not only consumers who are hurt by deception, either. Honest producers are at a disadvantage when they have to compete with inferior, worthless, or dishonestly labeled goods. For that reason there are agencies working full time to protect consumers against deception.

Who is mainly responsible for protecting consumers? In what ways are they protected? What can consumers do to gain the full benefit of this protection?

Courtesy U.S. Department of Agriculture

THE FEDERAL GOVERNMENT PROTECTS CONSUMERS

There are probably more agencies working to protect the consumer, directly or indirectly, than most people realize. Some agencies are ***private.*** But many of them are ***public*** which means they are government agencies. The major responsibility for protecting consumers lies with the Federal government. This is to be expected since the Federal government represents *all* the people, and everyone is a consumer. Because a list of Federal agencies involved in consumer protection is long, only a few can be described in this part.

The Food and Drug Administration

Of all Federal agencies working to protect the nation's consumers, none does more than the Food and Drug Administration. It is responsible for enforcing the Federal Food, Drug, and Cosmetic Act. The purpose of this Act is to make certain that foods, drugs, and cosmetics are pure and wholesome; are made under sanitary conditions; and are truthfully labeled. In other words, the Food and Drug Administration guards consumers against dangerous, impure, or dishonestly labeled foods, drugs, and cosmetics. These are the products for which consumers spend approximately one-fourth of their incomes.

The FDA's biggest job is keeping watch over the nation's food supply. Its inspectors check on plants where foods are processed and on buildings, such as warehouses and grain elevators, where foods are stored. They also inspect fresh foods and vegetables to make certain that poisonous sprays applied during the growing period no longer cling to them. During a recent typical month, the FDA kept more than 1,000 tons of unfit food from reaching consumers.

Inspection by the FDA even includes places where drugs and cosmetics are manufactured. It then watches to see that all products under its control are honestly labeled. Notice the label illustrated at the top of the next column, which was taken from a bottle of syrup. It tells the buyer that the syrup is made from 85 percent sugar and 15 percent maple-sugar syrups. With few exceptions, labels must disclose the use of artificial coloring. In this case, the color was obtained with caramel. Food imitations of any kind must be so labeled. See the illustration at the right.

Labels on drug products (except prescriptions) are required to tell what the products are for as well as how they are to be used. They must also warn

when the drug should not be used. Labels have been held to be misleading because of what they neglected to tell the buyer.

Labels on cosmetics must warn of any ingredients that might irritate the skin. Such a warning often appears on hair dyes. Products containing flammable substances must be so labeled. The warning you see at the top of page 352 was taken from a can of hair spray.

CAUTION: FLAMMABLE, DO NOT USE NEAR FIRE OR FLAME

Keep at room temperature (not over 120°F.). Do not puncture or incinerate container. Exposure to heat or prolonged sunlight may cause bursting.

DIRECTIONS: Hold container upright, 10 to 14 inches from hair. Press valve down and direct fine spray over hair. Keep spray out of eyes. Avoid inhalation.

The Federal Trade Commission

Where the work of the Food and Drug Administration ends, other Federal agencies take over. One of these agencies is the Federal Trade Commission. The Federal Trade Commission was formed in 1914 to preserve business competition. Until 1938 any protection it provided for consumers was the indirect result of its efforts to safeguard competition. That year, however, Congress gave the FTC power to halt practices designed to trick consumers, whether or not such practices hurt competition.

Most of the Commission's work is devoted to the elimination of false and misleading advertising. Advertising is false or misleading if it misrepresents in any way. As an example, one manufacturer of refrigerators claimed his refrigerator had been tested and found superior to other makes, when the tests did not show this to be true.

A common form of deception in advertising is known as "fictitious pricing." This is a way of advertising so that consumers are led to believe the seller has reduced his price. One store, for example, advertised luggage for "$9.95 marked down from the regular price of $13.98." The regular retail price of the luggage was actually only $9.95.

As you can see, by misrepresenting his product one producer can gain an unfair advantage over his competitors. Furthermore, it is estimated that false and misleading advertising causes the American public to waste more than a billion dollars a year on foods, drugs, and lotions that have no real benefit.

When the FTC finds evidence of deceptive advertising, a formal complaint is sent to the advertiser. If he does not agree to stop the deceptive practice, the Commission has the power to issue an order forbidding further use of the advertisement. This is called a *cease and desist order.*

The Department of Agriculture

People usually think of the United States Department of Agriculture as an agency concerned only with the problems of farmers. The truth is that much of its work is of direct benefit to consumers. One of its most important services is its inspection of meat. All meat and poultry shipped from one state to another must be inspected for wholesomeness by the Department of Agriculture. Meat approved for sale is then stamped with a purple circle that contains these words "U.S. Insp'd and P's'd." This is the consumer's assurance that the meat comes from healthy animals. Even though 80 percent of all meat produced in this country carries this stamp of government approval, consumers who buy their meats already cut and packaged may seldom see it.

The Department of Agriculture also provides a grading service, which you read about in Part 14. Food grades, you remember, are an indication of quality and help the consumer to compare quality and price. You have no doubt seen the U.S.D.A. grade mark on canned or frozen foods, butter, eggs, or meat. It is always enclosed in a shield as shown by the examples on page 353.

Food grading, unlike meat inspection, is ***voluntary;*** that is, food products are graded only when producers request and pay for this service. Canned and frozen foods that carry the U.S.D.A. grade mark must be processed under the continuous inspection of the Department of Agriculture. Processors who make use of this service are not required to display the grade on their products, however. If they wish, they may use only the shield you see at the right below.

The I. Q. sorter being demonstrated here electronically determines the internal quality of potatoes and apples and sorts them according to quality.

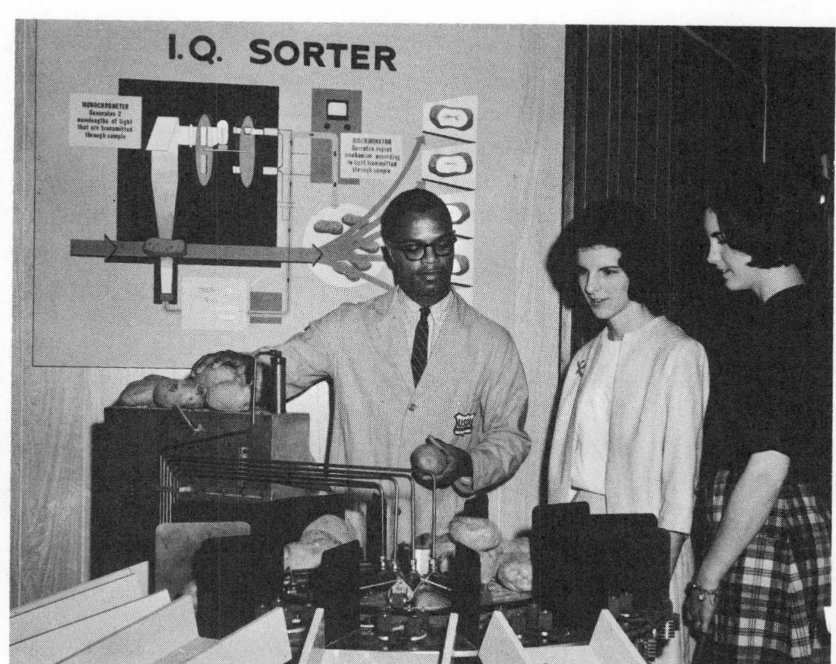

Courtesy U.S. Department of Agriculture

USDA GRADE MARKS

and the Foods on Which They Are Used

The grade names on the various grade marks shown here are merely illustrative. There is a range of grades for each of these products but different grade names are used. For a list of grades see "Grade Names Used in U. S. Standards for Farm Products" (AH–157) and "Shopper's Guide to U. S. Grades for Food" (HG–58).

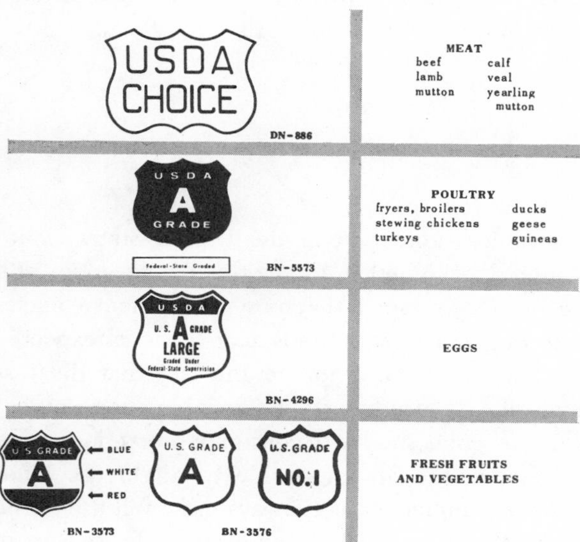

The Post Office Department

One of the most effective agencies in protecting the consumer is the U.S. Post Office Department. You have probably heard the expression "using the mails to defraud" which means to trick, cheat, or deceive. One of the jobs of the U.S. Post Office Department is to uncover and stop ***fraudulent*** use of the mails. Sellers of fake medical cures are the most frequent offenders. Other examples of attempts to defraud are job offers in foreign countries; matrimonial schemes; lotteries of all kinds (horse-race tickets, chain letters, etc.); work-at-home schemes; unordered merchandise; and appeals for donations to fake charities.

The Securities and Exchange Commission

Newest of the Federal agencies described in this part is the Securities and Exchange Commission, which was established in 1934. As you might guess from its name, this agency regulates the sale of corporate stocks and bonds.

For example, most corporations whose stock is sold to the public must provide the Securities and Exchange Commission with information about the corporation and its stock. It is the Commission's job to see that the information provided to investors about corporations is truthful. The reason is that this information is used by investors in deciding whether or not to buy stock in a particular corporation. The fact that a corporation's stock is registered with the Securities and Exchange Commission, however, does not necessarily mean that it is a good investment. It only means that the information published to promote the sale of the corporation's stock does not misrepresent its value. The work of the Securities and Exchange Commission has greatly reduced the sale of worthless stocks and bonds to the public.

STATE AND CITY GOVERNMENTS PROTECT CONSUMERS

Except for the Post Office Department, Federal agencies have authority to act only when products are sold in interstate commerce. ***Interstate commerce*** is trade between states. In other words, a product is sold in interstate commerce if it is sold in at least one state other than the one in which it is produced. All the work of protecting the consumer, therefore, cannot be left to the Federal government. Some must be done by agencies of state and city governments. Many states have food and drug laws patterned after the Federal law. And in a few, grading of certain food products, such as butter, milk, and eggs, is ***compulsory.*** To be sure that consumers get all they pay for, most cities check all weighing and measuring instruments regularly. These include not only the scales in the grocery store, but gasoline pumps, taximeters, and devices used for measuring yard goods.

The amount of consumer protection provided by city and state governments varies widely, however. Do you know what is being done in your community to help the consumer spend his money wisely?

BETTER BUSINESS BUREAUS PROTECT CONSUMERS

One of the best examples of a private agency whose work protects consumers is the Better Business Bureau. A Better Business Bureau is a nonprofit organization operated by business firms who are its members. There are more than 100 of these organizations in major cities throughout the United States. Their purposes are (1) to promote fair advertising and selling practices; (2) to protect the public against deceptive schemes; and (3) to establish public goodwill toward business.

Better Business Bureaus work in three ways to achieve their purposes. One way is by handling complaints of consumers against business concerns. For example, if a consumer feels that he has been treated unjustly by a business concern, he can register a complaint with the Better Business Bureau. The Bureau then asks the business firm for its side of the story. On the basis of all information collected, the Bureau attempts to work out a satisfactory solution. Second, to protect consumers from financial loss, the BBB invites them to ask for information about businesses or selling schemes whenever they are in doubt. Third, the BBB enlists the cooperation of business firms to be truthful in their advertising. In other words, it is an agency through which business regulates itself.

CONSUMERS CAN HELP TO PROTECT THEMSELVES

Consumer protection in the United States is undoubtedly the best in the world. Yet deception still occurs. One reason is that most government agencies are not given enough funds to do the work expected of them. If it were not for the fact that the vast majority of producers are reliable, government agencies concerned with consumer protection would be faced with an impossible task. On the other hand, consumers do not always make full use of the protection they have. As an example, even though the law requires honest labeling of drug products, consumers waste a billion or more dollars each year on useless drugs. Why? Because they do not pay attention to the labels. Recently it was estimated that more than $100 million was spent annually for worthless weight reducers alone.

One simple way a consumer can avoid being cheated is to shop around and compare prices and quality before he buys. If he should happen to be deceived, then he should do something about it. He might begin by complaining directly to the seller. If this does no good, he should report the deception to one of the agencies concerned with protecting consumers. Consumer complaints often help these agencies to uncover and stop deceptive practices.

BUILDING YOUR VOCABULARY

On a separate sheet of paper, list the figures 1 to 6, numbering down. For each term given below at the left, choose from the definitions on the right, the one that best matches it in meaning. Write this definition following the appropriate number.

1. compulsory	*a.* Trade within a state
2. fraudulent	*b.* By chance
3. interstate commerce	*c.* A government agency
4. private agency	*d.* Required by law
5. public agency	*e.* Trade between states
6. voluntary	*f.* Intended to deceive
	g. An organization open to anyone who wants to join
	h. By choice
	i. Accidentally misleading
	j. An agency not officially connected with the government

CHECKING YOUR READING

1. Why is there a need for agencies to protect consumers?
2. Why does the major responsibility for protecting the consumer rest with the Federal government?
3. What is the purpose of the Food, Drug, and Cosmetic Act?
4. How does the Food and Drug Administration help protect consumers?
5. What was the original purpose of the Federal Trade Commission?
6. What is the primary function of the FTC today?
7. What is meant by "fictitious pricing"?
8. What does the FTC do when it finds evidence of false or misleading advertising?
9. Give two examples of how the Department of Agriculture serves consumers.
10. What is one important difference between the Department of Agriculture's inspection of meat and its grading of food products?
11. How does the United States Post Office protect consumers?
12. Explain how the Securities and Exchange Commission helps protect consumers.
13. Why is it necessary for city and state governments to do some of the work of protecting consumers?

14. Describe some of the ways in which state and local governments help protect consumers.
15. What is the purpose of Better Business Bureaus?
16. Name three ways in which Better Business Bureaus work to achieve their purposes.
17. Why is it difficult for government agencies to give consumers complete protection against deception?
18. How can consumers help to protect themselves?

SHARING YOUR OPINION AND EXPERIENCE

1. Gregg Thomas says that if all people were honest there would be no need for agencies to protect consumers. Do you agree or disagree? Why?
2. The present Federal Food, Drug, and Cosmetic Act was passed in 1938. However, the first Pure Food and Drug Act became law in 1906. Why do you think cosmetics were not included in the original act?
3. There was less need for inspection of the nation's food supply 100 years ago than there is today. Do you agree or disagree with this statement? Give your reasons.
4. Why do you think the law requires that labels disclose the use of artificial coloring in foods?
5. In this part you learned what interstate commerce is. What is *intrastate* commerce?
6. Approximately 80 percent of all meat produced in this country is inspected by the United States Department of Agriculture. Why is the remaining 20 percent not inspected by the USDA?
7. Some packaged foods carry a statement explaining that the container was full when packaged, but in shipment the contents may have shaken down so that it appears to be only partially filled. What is the purpose of such a statement?
8. How are honest dealers as well as consumers protected by regular inspection of weighing and measuring instruments?
9. Why do you think a canner who uses the inspection service of the U.S. Department of Agriculture would carry only the shield and not the grade of his product on the label?

PROJECTS AND PROBLEMS

1. Copy the following list of items on a separate sheet of paper. Next to each item write the name of the consumer protection agency that would be primarily concerned with it: labels on aspirin tablets, barbershop inspection, listing of the sale of corporate bonds, grade label on a can of peaches, meat-market scales, milk, unordered merchandise, false magazine advertisements, labels on clothing, fake charities, ingredients in lipstick, door-to-door selling rackets.
2. The article on the next page appeared recently in a local newspaper. Read it and answer the questions relating to it.

CHECK LABELS ON CANS, CONSUMER IS ADVISED

Be sure to read the labels! This was underscored for women shoppers today at a consumer seminar sponsored by the Federation of Women's Clubs.

Canned and packaged foods must meet standards of labeling, weight, and quality set up by the U.S. Food and Drug Administration, the women were told. "If a housewife finds a can contains less than the label says it does, she can call the food and drug representative in the area," said Miss Theresa Adams, specialist with the district FDA.

"Ninety-five percent of the manufacturers correctly label cans of food and are concerned about the quality of their food. But the other 5 percent are either ignorant of standards or are deceptive," Miss Adams said.

Inspectors and chemists of the FDA spot-check goods to protect the consumer and the manufacturer. These inspections have corrected such things as incorrect labels and food packaged in greatly oversized boxes.

▪ *a.* Who was advised to read the labels on food cans? ▪ *b.* Who gave the advice? Whom did she represent? ▪ *c.* What three standards of the FDA were mentioned in the article? ▪ *d.* What were the listeners advised to do if they found less food in a can than the amount shown on the label? ▪ *e.* According to the speaker, what percent of food manufacturers uses incorrect labels? ▪ *f.* What two reasons were given for the incorrect labeling? ▪ *g.* What does "spot-check" mean? ▪ *h.* Who does the checking? ▪ *i.* Who is protected by the inspections? ▪ *j.* What deceptive practices have been corrected as a result of FDA inspections?

3. One way that state and local governments help protect consumers is by regulating entry into certain occupations. Persons who wish to work in these occupations must first obtain a license from a state or local agency. Usually the license is granted only after the applicant has passed an examination that demonstrates his ability to do the work. Below are listed 20 occupations. Select from the list those for which persons are usually required to be licensed. Write these occupations on a sheet of paper, and following each one, state in what way you think the license requirement helps to protect consumers.

bank teller	insurance broker	physician	stenographer
barber	lawyer	plumber	telephone repairman
business manager	machine operator	public accountant	truck driver
dentist	minister	real estate broker	typist
electrician	newspaper editor	salesman	waiter

4. Medical quackery, or the sale of fake remedies for physical ailments, is one of the most widespread forms of deception being practiced today. List as many reasons as you can why you think this is so.
5. Find out what services are provided in your community for the protection of consumers. For example, who inspects milk and dairy products? restaurants? beauty and barber shops? Write a brief report on all services you learn about.

6. Good consumers are informed about the agencies that work to protect them and cooperate with these agencies. A consumer who is well informed is able to distinguish opinion from fact. How about you? Which of the following statements do you think are opinions and which are facts?

   ▪ *a.* Private agencies protect consumers better than public agencies do. ▪ *b.* Agencies that protect consumers discourage competition. ▪ *c.* The work of the Federal Trade Commission aids honest advertisers as much as it does consumers. ▪ *d.* The Federal government does a better job of protecting consumers than state and local governments do. ▪ *e.* All meats that are inspected and passed by the United States Department of Agriculture are equally wholesome. ▪ *f.* More businesses in the United States would try to take unfair advantage of consumers if there were no agencies working to prevent it. ▪ *g.* Even though a product is honestly labeled, it may be worthless.

CHALLENGE PROBLEMS

1. Ron Jackson believes that the Securities and Exchange Commission should advise investors as to which corporation stocks are good investments. Do you agree or disagree? Give reasons to support your point of view.
2. Explain how a label could be misleading because of what it neglected to tell the buyer.
3. As you learned in this part, the Food and Drug Administration sets certain standards for foods, drugs, and cosmetics. What is a standard?
4. Why do you suppose labels are not required on prescription drugs?
5. Not all businesses in a community are members of the Better Business Bureau. Why do you think some firms do not join?
6. How can you make sure you are not being deceived by fictitious pricing?

PART 39 LAW AND YOUR BUSINESS TRANSACTIONS

FROM time to time throughout this book you have read about various ways in which business activity is regulated by law. Many of these laws protect us as consumers, even though we have little or no knowledge of them. The food and drug laws and laws regulating banks and insurance companies are examples. There are also laws governing our everyday business transactions that are intended to prevent misunderstandings between buyers and sellers. Ignorance of these laws may deprive you of the protection they provide.

A business transaction, as you know, is simply an agreement involving an exchange of goods and services. When you make a purchase, you agree to pay the seller for the good or service you want. In exchange he agrees to provide the good or perform the service. When a business firm hires a worker, the business agrees to pay him a certain wage or salary. In exchange he agrees to perform certain tasks. One of the basic freedoms in a free enterprise system is the right to make such agreements. This right is known as the *freedom of contract.*

Why is the right to make business agreements called freedom of contract? What types of business transactions might require the help of a lawyer?

EVERY BUSINESS TRANSACTION INVOLVES A CONTRACT

When you buy a magazine, have your hair cut, take a job, or enter into a business agreement of any kind, you make a contract. A ***contract*** is a binding agreement between two or more persons to do or not to do some particular thing. Those who make the agreement are called *parties* to the agreement or contract.

A contract is very often an oral agreement; that is, it is made in conversation. Many contracts, however, are merely understood. For example, you

Every business transaction involves a contract.

Ewing Galloway

might board a bus and drop your fare into the coin box without even speaking to the driver. Nevertheless, your actions indicate certain things. In boarding the bus you indicate that you will pay to ride it. By accepting your fare, the bus driver indicates that he will provide the service for which you paid. An understanding of this kind is an ***implied contract.***

Because oral and implied contracts are hard to prove, important contracts are put in writing. A life insurance policy is a written contract. An installment purchase agreement is a written contract. A promissory note is a written contract.

WHAT CONSTITUTES A LEGAL CONTRACT?

Under the law, each party to a contract has a right to whatever the other party promised. In order to be enforceable by law, however, a contract must meet certain requirements.

1. The parties involved must be competent.
2. There must be mutual assent.
3. Something of value must be involved.
4. The agreement must be lawful.
5. Some contracts must be in writing.

The Parties Must Be Competent

According to the law, a contract cannot be enforced unless all parties to the agreement are ***competent.*** In other words, they must be able to understand clearly what it is they have agreed to. This is to protect those who, for one reason or another, are not considered capable of looking after their own interests.

In general, minors (persons under 21)* are not considered competent to make enforceable contracts. An agreement made with a minor, therefore, is not a ***valid*** contract. If the minor refuses to carry

* In some states young people lose their minor status upon reaching the age of eighteen.

out his part of the agreement, the contract cannot be enforced. There are exceptions, however. Minors or their parents may be held to contracts involving necessities such as food, shelter, clothing, medical care, etc.

There Must Be Mutual Assent

Before a contract can be enforced, there must be what is known as a *meeting of the minds.* This is another way of saying that the parties to a contract must be in complete agreement.

Suppose that Mary said to Alice, "I'll sell you my bike for $25." Alice replied, "I'll give you $20." Since Mary and Alice were not in agreement, no contract would result. Complete agreement exists only when one person indicates his willingness to accept a specific offer made by another. Alice's offer to pay $20 for the bicycle amounted to a refusal of Mary's offer to sell it for $25.

Suppose, however, that when Mary offered to sell the bike for $25, Alice had said, "I'll take it." Then there would have been complete agreement, or ***mutual assent.*** Or had Mary accepted Alice's offer to pay $20 for the bicycle, this too would have constituted an agreement. In either case, a contract would have been made.

Something of Value Must Be Involved

To make a contract binding, each party must give something of value in exchange for what the other has promised. It may be money, goods, services, or a promise to do or not to do some particular thing. Whatever each party gives in exchange is his ***consideration.***

Suppose that George promised to pay Fred $25 if he sold George's automobile for him for $250. George's consideration is his promise to pay Fred $25. Fred's consideration is the selling of the car. Should Fred sell the car for $250, George would have to pay him $25, because the contract would be binding.

But suppose George said to Fred, "I will give you $25 if I sell my car for $250." This would not be a legal and binding contract since it involves no consideration on Fred's part. A contract cannot be enforced when one party to the agreement receives something for nothing.

The Agreement Must Be Lawful

A contract is not enforceable if either party agrees to do something unlawful. Suppose that Tom Wilson promised to pay Jack Garvey $50 if he would steal a new set of tires for him. Jack stole the tires and delivered them to Tom who refused to pay. Jack could not collect because this was an unlawful agreement.

Illegal contracts include those involving gambling, crime, or persons doing business without a license where the law requires a license.

Some Contracts Must Be in Writing

Most everyday business transactions involve oral or implied contracts that are as binding as written ones. Some kinds of contracts, however, are not enforceable unless in writing. For example, a person who guarantees the debt of another cannot be made responsible for payment of the debt unless he has signed a written agreement. Any contract that is to run longer than a year also must be in writing. All contracts for the sale of real property must be in writing. And most states require a written agreement covering the sale of personal property exceeding a fixed amount (usually $50). The difference between personal and real property, remember, is movability. Buildings, land, and things permanently attached to the land such as trees, shrubs, or fences are real property. Movable possessions such as cameras, furniture, and cars are personal property.

All Important Agreements Should Be in Writing. Written contracts remove all doubt as to exactly what has been agreed upon. For this reason, all important transactions should be covered by written agreements whether required by law or not. The agreement must be signed by all parties involved, and each party should receive a copy of the contract.

Your signature on a contract means that you have agreed to what it says. It is important, therefore, to read and be sure you understand all terms of an agreement before you sign it. This includes the fine print. There is an old saying that warns, "The finer the print, the more reason for reading it." If there is anything in a contract you do not understand, do not sign until you have found out what it means. The fact that you did not read or understand the contract will not free you from the responsibility of carrying out your part of it.

Furthermore, the court assumes that a written contract contains everything to which the parties have agreed. Any oral promises made in addition are not considered binding and therefore cannot be enforced.

A KNOWLEDGE OF YOUR RIGHTS AND RESPONSIBILITIES IS IMPORTANT

As a consumer, the law gives you certain rights and responsibilities. Obviously it would be impossible to explain them all in a few pages. On the other hand, some knowledge of the law as it applies to the most common business situations can help you to avoid trouble. It can also help you to realize when you need the services of a lawyer.

You Do Not Have to Accept Unordered Goods

Someday you may receive in the mail a package containing goods you did not order. This is a method some sellers use to tempt people to buy. With the unordered package, there is usually a request for payment of the goods or their return. As long as you do not use the goods, however, you are not obligated to pay for or return them.

You can return the package to the post office or the mailman. You can let the sender know that you do not want the article and ask him to make arrangements for its return; or you can keep it for a reasonable length of time and then dispose of it. But if you use the article in any way, your actions indicate an acceptance of the sender's offer to sell it. You are then obligated to pay for it.

Ownership of Property Involves Rights and Responsibilities

Whatever a person owns, he has title to. ***Title*** means ownership or evidence of ownership. When property of any kind is sold, title passes from the seller to the buyer. Only when a person actually owns property, may he legally transfer title to someone else. If a person buys stolen goods, he cannot receive title to them because the seller has no title to transfer.

As a rule, ownership of property carries with it responsibility for loss or damage. But there are exceptions. One of the exceptions is when goods are purchased on installments. When goods are sold for cash, the buyer receives title to them at once. This is also true of goods purchased on an open charge account. When an item is bought on installments, however, the seller usually remains the owner until all payments have been made, even though the buyer has the item in his possession. But the buyer is responsible for the article. Should it be destroyed or damaged in any way, the buyer is still obligated to make full payment for it according to the contract covering the purchase.

LEGAL ADVICE MAY BE NEEDED IN SOME CASES

As you can see, even the laws relating to everyday business transactions are often complex. Chances are that someday you may be in a situation and not know what your rights are. Then you should obtain the advice of a lawyer. Laws are for your protection. To take no action when your rights are being violated is to encourage those who are acting out-

Getting legal advice, especially when buying a house, is very important and can save the buyer money in the long run.

A. Devaney, Inc.

side the law to continue doing so.

People sometimes put off going to a lawyer because they think his services may cost more than they can pay. What they fail to realize is that a lawyer can often keep them out of trouble and save them money in the long run. Moreover, it is perfectly all right to ask a lawyer what his fee will be. Some lawyers charge more than others. If a person really cannot afford a particular lawyer, he will be referred to another lawyer or agency that charges fees within his means. For example, in over 140 cities and counties, there are legal aid societies that provide legal advice to persons unable to engage a lawyer. These agencies are usually financed by public contributions to community-fund drives.

Transactions Involving Real Property Require the Help of a Lawyer

No major business transaction, such as the buying or selling of real property, should ever be undertaken without the help of a lawyer. Yet it is unbelievable how many people buy homes costing thousands of dollars with no regard for the legal problems involved. The most important service a lawyer can perform for the home buyer is to make certain that he obtains a clear title to the property. Sometimes there are claims against property. The owner may have failed to pay his taxes sometime in the past; or he may not have paid for work done on the property. Anyone who buys property with claims against it becomes responsible for paying them.

BUILDING YOUR VOCABULARY

List the figures 1 to 7 on a sheet of paper, numbering down. Read the seven statements given below at the right; then, for each statement, select from the column at the left the term that best matches it in meaning. Write this term next to the appropriate number.

competent	1. A binding agreement between two or more persons
consideration	2. An agreement that is understood because of the actions of the persons involved
contract	3. Legally capable of understanding an agreement
implied contract	4. Complete agreement between two or more persons
mutual assent	5. Something of value that each party to a contract gives to the other to make the contract binding
title	6. Evidence of ownership
valid	7. Legally enforceable

CHECKING YOUR READING

1. Explain what is meant by the right of freedom of contract.
2. Give some examples of common contracts that most people enter into every day.
3. What five requirements must a contract meet in order to be enforceable?
4. What is the purpose of the requirement that all parties to a contract must be competent?
5. Why are most contracts made by minors not valid?
6. What types of contracts made by minors are legally enforceable?
7. When does complete agreement exist between two parties?
8. Give examples of some things that may be given as consideration.
9. Name some kinds of contracts that must be in writing in order to be enforceable.
10. Why is it wise to have all important contracts in writing?
11. What does a person's signature on a contract indicate?
12. Why is it important to be sure that a written contract contains everything to which the parties have agreed?
13. Under what circumstances may a person be obligated to pay for merchandise he did not order?
14. Who may legally transfer title to property?
15. Who is responsible for the care and safety of an item purchased on installments?
16. When should a person seek the advice of a lawyer?
17. What is the purpose of legal aid societies?
18. What is the most important service a lawyer can provide for a person who is buying a home?

SHARING YOUR OPINION AND EXPERIENCE

1. Why do we need laws to govern our business transactions?
2. Why is it important that a person understand what is required to make a valid contract?

3. Describe a situation in which someone was deprived of his legal rights because he did not know what they were.
4. Could you, as a minor, buy a car on installments? What are your rights in such a contract? What are the seller's rights?
5. Why do you think contracts involving unlawful acts are not enforceable?
6. Do you believe all contracts should be in writing? Give reasons for your answer.
7. Why must all contracts for the sale of real property be in writing?
8. What is a bill of sale? Why do most states require a person applying for an automobile license to show a bill of sale for the automobile?
9. Why do you think people are advised to give special attention to the fine print in a contract?
10. Why should each party to a written contract receive a copy?
11. Give some examples of how a lawyer may be able to save money for the people he advises.

PROJECTS AND PROBLEMS

1. Name at least three contracts you have made recently and answer the following questions about each.

   ▪ *a.* Who were the other parties to the contract? ▪ *b.* What consideration was given by each party? ▪ *c.* Was the contract oral, written, or implied?

2. Write the letters *a* through *f* down the left-hand side of a separate sheet of paper. After each letter write either "yes" or "no" to indicate your decision in each of the cases described below. Then give the reason for each answer.

   ▪ *a.* Harold McCarthy agreed to sell a lot he owned to Bill Henry for $2,500. The agreement was written and signed by both parties on October 22, at which time Mr. Henry paid Mr. McCarthy $300. On October 23, Mr. Henry changed his mind and wanted his money back. Did Mr. McCarthy have an enforceable contract? ▪ *b.* Dan Serrino, who is 17 years old, decided to buy a new bicycle to use on his newspaper route. He paid Fred's Bicycle Shop $15 down and agreed to pay $3 a week until the balance of $30 was paid. After three weeks, Dan gave up his newspaper job. His parents then told him to return the bicycle and get back the money he had paid. Can Fred's Bicycle Shop enforce the contract with Dan? ▪ *c.* Larry Gould agreed to sell a set of golf clubs worth $150 to Alan Sifert for $60 cash. When Mrs. Gould learned of the agreement, she objected because she felt the $60 was not enough. Her husband then refused to carry out the transaction. Did Sifert have an enforceable contract? ▪ *d.* While on a hike through the mountains, Herb Schlacter, aged 15, cut his foot and went to a nearby doctor for treatment. When the doctor sent his bill, Herb refused to pay it on the grounds that he was a minor. Can the doctor enforce the agreement? ▪ *e.* Carl Mathews promised Dick Runyon $5 if Dick would score a touchdown in Saturday's game. Dick scored two touchdowns. Can he force Carl to pay him the $5? ▪ *f.* Ned Garver offered to sell his motorboat to Steve Britton for $350. Steve replied that he would pay only $300 for the boat and Ned refused to sell. A few moments later, Ned said he had changed his mind and would take the $300. Is there an enforceable contract?

3. The following are points of law concerning installment sales. Tell in your own words what each statement means.

   ▪ *a.* In a regular sale, title passes when an agreement is made; in a conditional sale, title does not pass until the goods are paid for. ▪ *b.* In a conditional sale, the buyer has the right of possession as long as he keeps up his payments. ▪ *c.* In a conditional sale, the risk of loss is on the buyer. ▪ *d.* When the installment buyer defaults in his payments, the seller may repossess the goods. ▪ *e.* The basic right of the seller on default is to collect the balance of the purchase price.
4. As you learned in this part, some contracts are made orally, some are written, and some are implied. Following are eight common business transactions. Write the letter of each transaction in a column on a sheet of paper. After each letter write either "oral", "written", or "implied" to indicate the way in which agreement usually is reached in such a transaction.

   ▪ *a.* Purchase of a record player for cash ▪ *b.* Purchase of a newspaper at a newsstand ▪ *c.* Borrowing money at a bank ▪ *d.* Purchase of a refrigerator on installments ▪ *e.* Getting a haircut ▪ *f.* Having a television set repaired ▪ g. Sale of personal household goods worth $450 ▪ *h.* Attending a movie

5. Examine the conditional sales contract on page 138. In separate columns list the rights of the buyer and of the seller.
6. The following legal terms are often used in relation to contracts: duress, guaranty, infant, majority, offer, option, undue influence, unilateral contract. Use a business-law textbook or a law dictionary to find out their meanings. Copy the terms on a sheet of paper. Following each one, write its meaning.

CHALLENGE PROBLEMS

1. Does a minor have a moral obligation to carry out his agreements even though his contracts are not legally enforceable? Explain.
2. Why do you think a minor is legally responsible for contracts involving necessities?
3. If two parties reach additional agreements after they have signed a written contract, what should they do?
4. What is a lease? Why is it important that it be in writing?
5. What is a small-claims court? Why do you think so many states have them?

PART 40 SOURCES OF CONSUMER INFORMATION

WENDY MILLER was in the school library working on an assignment for English class. Several times she stopped writing to look up a word in the dictionary. The dictionary was her *source of information.* It told her what she wanted to know. What an important part sources of information play in our lives! Like Wendy, you probably turn to the dictionary when you want to know how to spell or pronounce a word or learn its meaning. You use the telephone directory to find the number of a friend. You check the newspaper for tomorrow's weather forecast or to find out what movies are showing at local theaters. You consult a road map when you travel by car; a timetable when you go by bus, plane, or train. For almost anything you want to know there is a source of information. This part is about sources of consumer information.

What kinds of information might consumers want? Of what value is such information? What are some important sources of information for consumers?

SOURCES OF INFORMATION HELP CONSUMERS TO SPEND WISELY

Surely you know by now that a wise consumer is a well-informed consumer. The more you know about the things you buy, the more satisfied you are likely to be with your purchases. Business produces such a wide variety of goods and services, however, that it is not possible for anyone to have a knowledge of them all. Besides, many products are so complex that it is hard to judge whether one is better than another or whether it is worth the price. But there are sources of information consumers can use to overcome these problems. In fact, sources of consumer information are so numerous that only a few of the most widely used ones can be covered in this part. Once you develop the habit of using sources of information in your buying, however, you will discover others for yourself.

Unfortunately, some sources of consumer information are not reliable. And it is not always easy to distinguish between those that are and those that are not. One way to judge the reliability of information is to ask yourself two questions. Who provided it? And why? Suppose a booklet on "How to Choose a Vacuum Cleaner" is put out by a manufacturer of vacuum cleaners. You could be reasonably certain that whatever information the booklet contained would favor his cleaner. On the other hand, suppose that information on how to buy or care for a product is provided by an organization that does not profit from the sale of the product. Then the information is likely to be more helpful. For example, a manufacturer of vacuum cleaners might publish information on the selection and care of carpets.

SEALS OF APPROVAL ARE A SOURCE OF INFORMATION

One valuable source of consumer information is a good label, as you already know. A good label can help you to choose the goods that best fit your purpose. One advantage of labels as a source of information is that they provide the information at the very time you are going to buy. A second advantage of labels is that the law requires whatever information they carry to be truthful.

A special kind of label found on some products is a seal of acceptance or approval. This is a label indicating that some agency has accepted or approved the product. An example is the label of the Underwriters' Laboratories. It may be seen on electrical products including such household appliances as toasters, irons, stoves, fans, and mixers.

An ***underwriter*** is someone who assumes risks—an insurer. The Underwriters' Laboratories is a testing organization maintained by the National Board of Fire Underwriters, an association of fire insurance companies. Its main concern is the safety

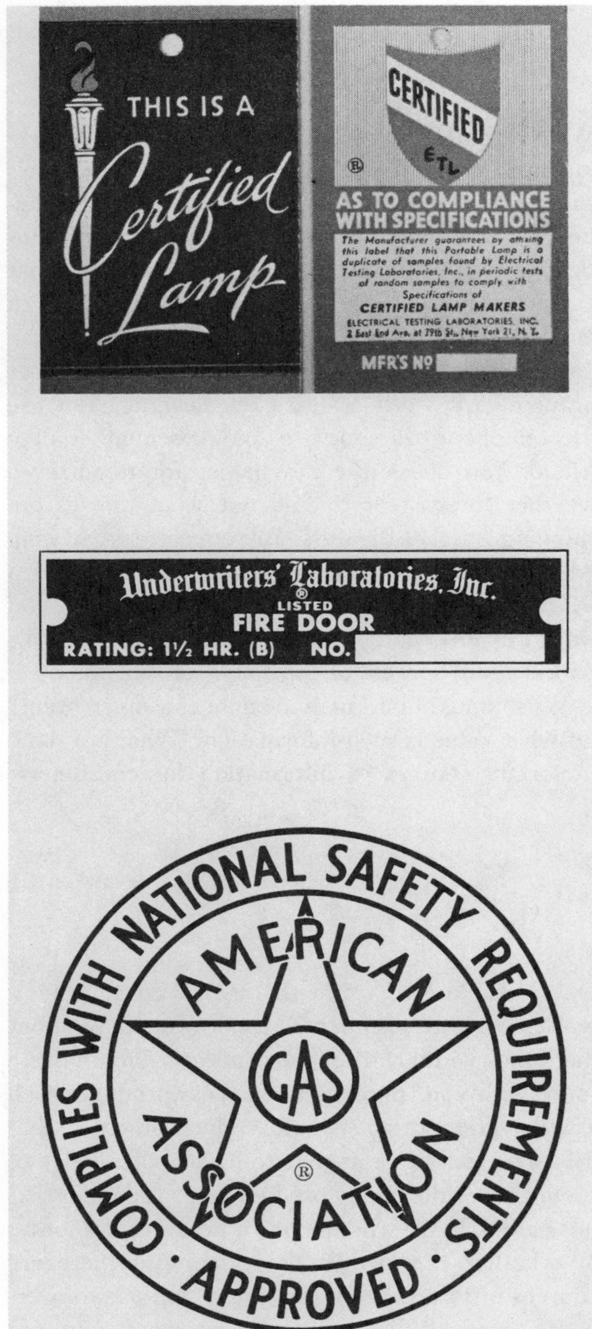

Labels like the three shown on this page assure the buyer that the product has passed the tests and meets with the approval of the testing laboratories.

of all devices or building materials that might be a fire hazard. Its label on a product means that the product meets the standards for safety established by the Underwriters' Laboratories. The label is usually in the form of a seal attached to the product; but it may take other forms like the one in the center of the facing page.

Some trade associations also operate testing laboratories and issue approval seals. A ***trade association*** is an organization of producers engaged in the same kind of business. Members of the American Gas Association, for example, are manufacturers of gas-operated equipment and appliances. This association tests such products for durability, safety, and efficiency. Products that pass the tests bear the round blue seal of the American Gas Association illustrated at the bottom of the facing page.

CONSUMER TESTING ORGANIZATIONS ARE A SOURCE OF INFORMATION

A seal of acceptance or approval on a product indicates only that the product meets certain minimum requirements. It does not mean that all brands of a product carrying the same seal are of equal quality. To learn how different brands of products compare in quality, consumers use the services of an agency like Consumer's Union, Inc. This nonprofit organization tests products and then rates them on the basis of their quality. The results are published in a monthly magazine called *Consumer Reports*.

Different products are reported on each month. For example, the contents of one issue included ratings by brand names of 24 refrigerator-freezers; 14 laundry bleaches; 17 interior wall paints; 10 white glues; 34 ironing-board covers; 2 battery-powered TV sets; and 4 automobiles. In addition, every issue of the magazine contains the following: ratings of movies currently being shown around the country; a report of actions taken by government agencies to enforce consumer protection laws; and articles of general interest to consumers.

One thing that never appears in *Consumer Reports* is advertising. Moreover, Consumer's Union does not permit manufacturers of products to use its test results in advertising their products. The organization's work is financed by the consumers who subscribe to the magazine.

BUSINESS PROVIDES CONSUMER INFORMATION

Some of the agencies you read about in Part 38 that work to protect consumers also work to inform consumers. One of these is the Better Business Bureau. The purpose of this organization, remember, is to eliminate fraud and misrepresentation in business. The more informed consumers are, the less likely they are to be deceived. For that reason, the Bureau publishes a series of *Fact Booklets* covering a wide range of topics. The following are only a few examples: *Facts You Should Know About Buying or Building a Home; Health Quackery; Home Fire Protection; Securities; Investment Companies; Life Insurance; Buying New or Used Cars; Credit; Savings.* These booklets can be obtained for a few cents each from your local Better Business Bureau or the National Better Business Bureau, Chrysler Building, New York City.

The Better Business Bureau is an organization that represents many businesses. A single business concern that provides consumer information is the Household Finance Corporation, a personal loan company with offices in all but a few states. This company also publishes a series of booklets covering different types of consumer expenditures. The purpose of these booklets is to help consumers manage their money wisely.

For example, the one called *Your Clothing Dollar* explains how to plan your clothing needs by making an inventory of your present wardrobe; how to budget your clothing purchases; how to shop for different articles of clothing; and how to care for clothing. Other Money Management booklets include: *Your Food Dollar, Your Shelter Dollar, Your Savings and Investment Dollar, Your Health and*

Recreation Dollar, Your Automobile Dollar. There are a total of 12 booklets in the series.

Why do you think a lending agency would publish information of this kind? Could the reason be that people who manage their money wisely are good credit risks who pay their debts promptly?

GOVERNMENT PROVIDES CONSUMER INFORMATION

No organization or agency, public or private, publishes more information for consumers than the United States Department of Agriculture. Altogether this agency has prepared more than 100 bulletins* written especially for consumers. Some contain buying tips, such as *How to Buy Eggs; Buying Your Home Sewing Machine;* and *Men's Suits—How to Judge Quality.* Some deal with the care and repair of clothing and household articles like the one on *Removing Stains from Fabrics.* And some deal with money management like the one called *Helping Families Manage Their Finances.*

MAGAZINES ARE A SOURCE OF CONSUMER INFORMATION

When a new product reaches the market, you often read about it first in a magazine. That is just one type of consumer information carried by magazines, however. Many carry articles on money management such as "How to Budget"; "How to Save and Invest"; "How to Buy Life Insurance." Also popular are articles on the care and repair of such products as household equipment, clothing, and cars. Since proper care extends the life of our possessions, information of this type is as valuable to consumers as buying information.

When you want information about a particular subject or product, you can find out whether or not it is available in a magazine by consulting the *Readers' Guide to Periodical Literature.* A ***periodical*** is a magazine. *The Readers' Guide to Periodical Literature* is an index of articles appearing in about 125 of the most popular magazines. Articles are indexed in three ways: by the author's name, by the title of the article, and by the subject of the article.

*For a complete list of these publications, write to Office of Information, U.S. Department of Agriculture, Washington, D.C. 20250

NEWSPAPERS ARE A SOURCE OF BUSINESS AND CONSUMER INFORMATION

The newspaper that does not carry any kind of consumer information is most unusual. It may be nothing more than advertising. But advertising, as you know, can be a very important source of consumer information. Like magazines, newspapers sometimes report on new products; and many print tips on how to care for the things you buy. One kind of information carried by most newspapers, however, is of interest to both producers and consumers. That is business and financial news. The stock-market quotations that appear in major newspapers are just one example.

From your study of investments, you know that the dollar value of corporate securities is subject to change; that is, their prices may rise or fall. The price of a stock may change only a few cents from one day to the next. Or it may increase or decrease by several dollars. If you want to know the price of a particular stock or stock prices in general, you can check the stock-market tables in your newspaper. Stocks traded through an exchange are listed in the table of stock transactions for that exchange. A complete listing of the New York Stock Exchange, for example, would include about 1,300 stocks. Stocks traded over-the-counter are listed in a separate table.

Newspapers vary in their stock-market coverage. Some devote a great deal of space to it. Others print only partial listings. Their tables also differ in some ways. The illustration on page 371 shows how stock transactions are reported in one large city newspaper. It may not be exactly like the one in your newspaper.

1965 High.	Low.	Stocks and Div. In Dollars.	Sls. 100s.	First.	High.	Low.	Last	Net Chge.
27⅛	24½	Eagle P 1.20	15	25	25¼	25	25¼	+ ⅜
70¾	41⅛	East Air Lin	138	58¼	58½	57	57	− 1⅜
106	86¼	EastGF 2.47f	7	94	94½	94	94½	+ 1
18	15½	East S Stl .90	10	15½	15¾	15½	15¾	+ ¼
84⅜	75¾	East Kod 1.40	183	77⅞	79¼	77⅝	79	+ 1½
56¼	42⅝	Eaton Mf 2.20	20	50⅜	51	50⅜	50⅝	− ⅛
32½	28⅛	Eaton pf 1.19	2	30	30¼	30	30¼	+ ¼
13⅞	11⅜	Echlin Mf .40	3	13½	13½	13¼	13⅜	...
36½	30¼	Edis Bros 1.10	5	33¼	33¼	33¼	33¼	− ¼
46¼	35	Ekco Pd 1.60	1	44½	44½	44½	44½	...
33½	26¼	Elas Stop 1.40	2	31⅜	31⅜	31⅜	31⅜	+ ⅜
39⅝	35½	El Bonds 1.55	16	36	36⅜	35⅞	36⅞	+ ⅜
4	3⅛	El Music .049	33	3¼	3¼	3¼	3¼	...
54	47	El Stor Bt 1.80	7	51½	52	51¼	52	...
27	16¾	El Assoc .54f	44	23¼	23⅜	22⅝	22⅝	− ⅜
25⅜	19	Electron Sp	38	23¾	24⅛	23⅜	23¾	...
10⅝	8	Elgin Watch	6	8¾	8¾	8½	8½	− ¼
24⅛	19¾	El Paso NG 1	33	20¼	20⅜	20¼	20⅜	+ ⅛
40¼	29½	Eltra Cp 1.40	30	34⅝	35⅛	34½	35⅛	+ ½
40	32½	Eltra pf 1.40	1	34⅜	34⅜	34⅜	34⅜	+ ⅛
50⅜	38⅝	Emer El 1.20	38	47¼	47⅜	46⅞	47⅜	+ ½
16⅞	10⅜	Emer Rad .40	36	14¾	14¾	14	14⅛	− 1⅞
46½	34½	Emery Air .80	13	42½	42½	41⅝	41⅝	− ⅝
33¾	27⅝	Emhart Cp 1	21	29⅜	30	29⅜	30	+ ¾
40⅜	35¼	Emp Dist 1.32	4	35⅝	36	35¼	36	+ ⅜
65	53½	Empor 1.20b	1	60	60	60	60	+ ¼
33⅜	23⅞	End John	6	26⅜	26⅜	26⅜	26⅜	+ ¼
36	22¼	Engel Ind 1	14	30⅝	31½	30⅝	31¼	+ ¾
45⅜	40½	Equ Gas 1.85	5	42	42⅛	41⅞	41⅞	− ⅛
10¼	5¾	Eric Lack RR	35	7⅞	8	7¾	7¾	+ ⅛
32⅝	22½	Erie Lack pf	120	24½	24⅛	24½	24⅛	+ ⅛
35⅜	26⅛	Essex Wire 1	26	27⅞	28⅜	27⅜	27⅜	− ⅛
16¼	12½	Eurofnd .10g	13	13⅛	13⅛	12⅞	13⅛	+ ¼
61⅝	41¼	Evans Pd .30d	26	50⅛	50⅛	49⅜	49⅜	− ⅜
28¼	19	Eversharp 1	27	22⅞	23	22¾	23	+ ⅛
49	39¾	ExCello 1.80	27	44⅜	44¾	44⅛	44⅛	− ⅜

1. The abbreviated name of the corporation issuing the stock—in this case, Eastern Air Lines.

2. The letters "pf" following the name of a corporation indicate a preferred stock.

3. Numbers following the name of a corporation show the annual dividend paid—on this stock, $1.40. Unless indicated otherwise, this amount is estimated on the basis of dividends already paid.

4. Columns showing the highest and lowest prices paid for a stock during the year—in this case, $40.25 and $29.50. (Stock prices are usually quoted in dollars and fractions of a dollar.)

5. This column shows the number of shares traded for the day reported. Sales are usually stated in the hundreds. The "21" shown here means that 2,100 shares of this stock changed hands that day.

6. The price paid for the first shares of this stock traded on the day reported was $24.50 per share. This is called the ***opening price.***

7. Amounts shown in these two columns indicate the highest and lowest prices paid for the stock during the day. Highest in this case was $23; lowest, $22.75.

8. The price paid for the last shares of this stock traded during the day was $8.50. This is called the ***closing price.*** This was 25¢ less than the closing price of the previous day. This is indicated by the −¼. An increase in the closing price is indicated by a plus sign.

EVERYONE SHOULD HAVE A FILE OF CONSUMER INFORMATION

The real value of consumer information lies in its use. It is most likely to be used if it is available when needed. The only trouble is that you sometimes run across information when you have no particular need for it. Later, when the information would be useful, you can no longer remember it. And usually you are unable to locate it again. For that reason, it pays to keep a file of consumer information to which you can refer when the need occurs.

Items you might keep in your file are clippings from newspapers and magazines as well as pamphlets. Certainly you will want to save labels that tell how to use and care for products you have purchased. Most of all, you will want to organize these materials in some systematic way so that, when you want information, you can locate it quickly and easily.

BUILDING YOUR VOCABULARY

For each of the five sentences given below at the right, select from the five terms listed on the left, the one that completes it correctly. Then copy the sentences on a sheet of paper, replacing the question mark with the appropriate term.

closing price
opening price
periodical
trade association
underwriter

1. A magazine that is published regularly is called a ?
2. An organization of producers engaged in the same kind of business is a ? .
3. The price paid for the last shares of a corporation's stock traded on a particular day is the ? .
4. One who provides insurance against risks is an ? .
5. The price paid for the first shares of a corporation's stock traded on a particular day is the ? .

CHECKING YOUR READING

1. What is a source of information? Give examples.
2. Explain why it is so important for today's shoppers to use sources of consumer information.
3. What questions can you ask yourself that will help you judge the reliability of consumer information?
4. What are the advantages of labels as a source of consumer information?
5. What is the purpose of Underwriters' Laboratories? What does its label on a product mean?
6. What kinds of products does the American Gas Association test? What does it try to find out about these products?
7. What does a seal of approval on a product tell you about the product?
8. How can consumers find out how different brands of products compare in quality?
9. What kinds of information may be found in the magazine *Consumer Reports?*
10. How does the Better Business Bureau help to inform consumers?
11. What is the Household Finance Corporation? What kinds of consumer information does it provide?
12. Name a department of the Federal government that publishes information for consumers. How can you get copies of its publications?
13. Give examples of the kinds of consumer information that may be found in magazines.
14. What is the purpose of the *Readers' Guide to Periodical Literature?*

15. Give examples of the kinds of consumer information that may be found in newspapers.
16. If you wanted to know the price of a particular corporation's stock on a given day, how could you find it?
17. What can you do to make sure you have the consumer information you need *when* you need it?

SHARING YOUR OPINION AND EXPERIENCE

1. What is a trademark? How does it differ from a seal of approval?
2. Why do you suppose insurance companies are willing to pay the cost of operating a testing organization such as Underwriters' Laboratories?
3. Why does the magazine *Consumer Reports* not carry advertising or allow manufacturers to use its test results in advertising their products?
4. Why do popular magazines carry articles that provide consumer information?
5. What are the advantages and disadvantages of newspaper advertisements as a source of consumer information?
6. Why would a manufacturer of vacuum cleaners publish information on the selection and care of carpets?
7. Do you think any one of the sources of consumer information discussed in this part is more valuable than the others? Why?
8. Why do you think newspapers use so much space every day just to carry stock-market tables?
9. If all buyers used the information available to consumers, would there still be a need for laws and agencies to protect them? Explain.
10. What responsibility, if any, do consumers have to keep themselves informed?

PROJECTS AND PROBLEMS

1. Make a list of the sources of information that you have in your home. Following each source, state briefly what kind of information it provides. Rank the sources according to how much they are used, numbering the most used source 1, the next 2, and so on.
2. Study the illustration of stock-market transactions on page 371 and answer the following questions:

   ▪ *a.* Which stock sold for the highest price on the day reported? ▪ *b.* Which stock sold for the lowest price? ▪ *c.* Which stocks reached their highest price of the day on the last sale? ▪ *d.* Which stocks "closed" at their lowest price of the day? ▪ *e.* Which stock increased most in price over the previous day? ▪ *f.* Which stock decreased most in price since the previous day? ▪ *g.* Which stock pays the highest annual dividend? ▪ *h.* Which stocks pay no annual dividend? ▪ *i.* Which of the stocks listed are preferred stocks? ▪ *j.* Which stock had the greatest number of shares traded during the day? How many shares were traded?

3. In a recent issue of *Consumer Reports* the following comparisons were made between three well-known automobiles. Use the information in the table to answer the questions following it.

Features	*Car A*	*Car B*	*Car C*
Price	**$3,075**	**$3,074**	**$3,100**
Overall length (inches)	**213**	**210**	**209**
Overall width (inches)	**80**	**77**	**78**
Weight (pounds)	**3,745**	**3,620**	**3,935**
Luggage capacity (number of suitcases)	**10**	**10**	**8**
Overall gas mileage (miles per gallon)	**12**	**12.5**	**12.5**
Motor-oil consumption (miles per quart)	**1,050**	**1,275**	**925**

▪ *a.* What is the difference in price between the most expensive car and the lowest priced car? ▪ *b.* Which car uses the most gasoline? ▪ *c.* What is the difference in weight between the heaviest and the lightest car? ▪ *d.* What is the overall length of the longest car? the shortest? ▪ *e.* Which car uses the least motor oil? ▪ *f.* Is the longest car also the one with the greatest width? ▪ *g.* Which car(s) has the largest luggage capacity? ▪ *h.* What is the price of the most expensive car? ▪ *i.* Do you think the difference in the prices of these cars is great enough to be important in selecting a car? Explain. ▪ *j.* Why would a buyer want to know the length and the width of a car?

4. Using a recent issue of the *Readers' Guide to Periodical Literature,* make a list of magazine articles that you think would be of particular interest to consumers. They may be articles containing buying information or suggestions on the use and care of products. Or they may be articles pertaining to money management —budgeting, saving and investing, or buying insurance. Limit your list to ten, but include as many different magazines as you can. Use a form similar to that shown below. Read and be prepared to make either an oral or a written report on one of the articles.

Title of Article	Name and Date of Magazine

5. Assume that you have $1,000 to invest in stocks. Select a stock listed on the financial page of your daily paper or the paper in your school library. Using a form similar to that shown below, keep a record of the changing values of your investment for the next six weeks. Use Wednesdays as the day for reporting.

Name of stock: *Example: Centerville Brick and Tile Company*

Number of shares purchased: *Example: 100*
(to the nearest whole number)

Market price: *1st week* *2d week* *3d week* *4th week* *5th week* *6th week*

After completing your record, write on it the answers to these questions.

▪ *a.* At the end of the period, is your stock worth more or less than you paid for it? ▪ *b.* If you were forced to sell your shares at the end of the six weeks, how much would you gain or lose, not counting broker's fees?

6. Bring to class labels that indicate a testing laboratory or other nongovernmental organization has approved the products bearing them. If you cannot find a sufficient number of labels, clip magazine and newspaper advertisements containing claims that the products advertised have been tested or approved by some agency. Make a poster or scrapbook of these labels or clippings.

CHALLENGE PROBLEMS

1. The table in problem No. 3 on page 374 compared seven features of three well-known cars. Which of these features do you think are most important in selecting a car? Give your reasons. Would you like more information about the cars before making a choice? If so, what features would you like to know more about?
2. If you wanted to know the price of a stock not listed in the tables in your newspaper, where could you get this information?
3. Is a well-informed consumer always a wise one? Explain.

CONTENTS OF UNIT 9

Unit 9 / The Financing of Government

PART 41 SHARING THE COSTS OF GOVERNMENT

NEXT to consumers, the biggest spender in our economic system is government. In a recent year, our national, state, and local governments together spent more than $135 billion. This was one-fifth of all spending and more than consumers spent on food, clothing, and medical care that year. Where did all this money come from? Most of it came from taxes paid by individuals and business firms. Taxes are the main source of government income, or ***revenue,*** as government income is sometimes called. Some other sources of revenue are highway and bridge tolls; income from government-owned enterprises such as water companies, transportation systems, and the post office; fees charged for a special privilege such as a license to drive, to hunt, or to marry; and sales of government-owned property. All levels of government, however, depend mainly on taxes for their incomes.

What do taxes buy? How do taxes differ from other kinds of spending?

WHY ARE TAXES NECESSARY?

Ewing Galloway

In the United States, privately owned business firms produce about 90 percent of all goods and services produced. Or to put it another way, they produce 90 percent of the gross national product. The other 10 percent is produced by our three levels of government. This 10 percent consists of such things as national defense, highways, education, and fire and police protection. Most of them are goods and services that privately owned business enterprises could not produce at a profit. Many of them are goods and services that the majority of people could not have if they had to obtain them in some other way. And some of them are goods and services which people might not buy otherwise. Unbelievable as it may seem, there are families who would not educate their children or buy fire-fighting equipment if the choice were left to them.

Some people have the mistaken idea that goods and services provided by government are free. You sometimes hear them speak of *free* schools, *free* parks, and *free* highways. But these and other government services are no more free than the goods and services produced by business. They are bought with taxes. In other words, by paying taxes people share the cost of the goods and services provided by their local, state, and national governments.

Paying taxes differs from other kinds of spending in several ways. An important one is the matter of choice. That is to say, people make their own decisions about whether or not to spend for other things. They have no choice when it comes to paying taxes. Anyone who fails to do so may lose his property, be fined, or be sent to prison. A ***tax,*** then, is a compulsory payment for government services.

TAXES INCREASE WITH GOVERNMENT SPENDING

Even people who realize the need for taxes often complain about paying them. And the reason they complain is because taxes keep taking a bigger and bigger bite of their incomes. In 1939, our three levels of government collected a total of $14 billion in taxes, or about 20 cents out of every dollar of income. In 1964, taxes took about $135 billion, or 30 cents out of every dollar of income. This increase in taxes has a simple explanation, which is that government spending has increased. From 1939 to 1964, government spending rose from about $100 a person to more than $800 per person. The more any level of government spends, the more it must collect in taxes.

Why Has Government Spending Increased?

Part of the increase in government spending is the result of inflation, or a general increase in prices. It

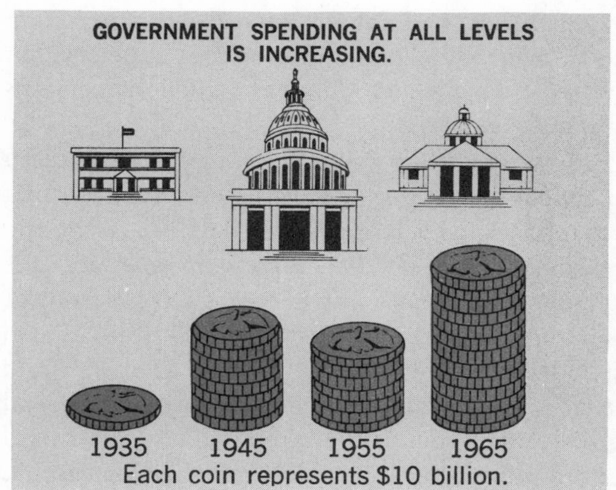
GOVERNMENT SPENDING AT ALL LEVELS
IS INCREASING.
1935
1945
1955
1965
Each coin represents $10 billion.

is estimated that between 1939 and 1964, prices in general more than doubled. Wages and salaries, which are really prices paid for labor, also doubled. The goods and services government buys, therefore, cost more today than they did 25 or 30 years ago, just as the things that families buy cost more.

A second factor behind the increase in government spending is the large increase in our population. From 1939 to 1964, the population of the United States rose from 130,000,000 to 192,000,000. It is expected that, by 1970, the number will reach 210,000,000. An increase in population swells the demand for almost every kind of government service—mail service, police and fire protection, parks, playgrounds, teachers, and schools. Total expenditures for education alone have more than doubled just since 1952. Not only are there more children to educate, but they stay in school longer.

People have come to expect more from government than they did a generation or so ago, and they are getting it. This is a third reason for the increase in government spending. The government now provides both income and hospital insurance through social security. It is building wider highways to accommodate today's bigger and faster cars. The cost of building new highways is one of the biggest items of expense for state governments. In one midwestern city the number of services provided citizens by local government has grown from 24 to over 300. Among the services added within recent years are such things as symphony concerts and golf courses.

If any one thing could be blamed for increased spending on the part of government, it is the rising cost of national defense. National defense is the sole responsibility of our Federal government, and it is at this level where the increase in government spending has been greatest. In 1900, total federal spending amounted to about half that of state and local governments combined. Today the Federal government spends more than all state and local governments together. Most of this increase in federal spending is the result of wars or war threats.

There is another important reason why spending by the Federal government has increased, however.

Spacecraft development is an important and costly part of the national defense program.

Courtesy NASA

Some activities that once were performed by state and local governments have become the responsibility of the Federal government. For example, the Federal government is now helping states and cities to pay the cost of highways, of education, and of housing for low-income families.

GOVERNMENTS ALSO BORROW

Income from taxes varies with business conditions. When production among private producers is high, employment is high; and personal and business incomes are high. Then tax collections are also high. If production falls so that fewer people have jobs and incomes, tax collections fall.

Government expenses also vary. Sometimes they are more than the government collects in taxes; sometimes less. When a government spends more than it collects in taxes, it must borrow. Borrowing, of course, means going into debt. A debt owed by any level of government is called a ***public debt.*** Any year in which a government collects more in taxes than it spends, it has a surplus. Slight differences between spending and tax collections from year to year usually balance each other out over a period of time. In other words, a surplus one year can be used to repay the debt of another year.

Sometimes, however, a government incurs a large-size debt. During a war, for example, expenses of the Federal government take such a big jump that tax collections are never enough to pay them entirely. During a recession, on the other hand, tax collections shrink for all levels of government. But government spending must go on as usual. In fact, the Federal government may increase its spending during a recession or depression, as you know. Mainly as a result of World Wars I and II and the depression years of the 1930's, the Federal government now owes a debt of more than $300 billion. Although this debt, which is called the *national debt,* is the one you hear most about today, state and local governments together also owe more than $50 billion.

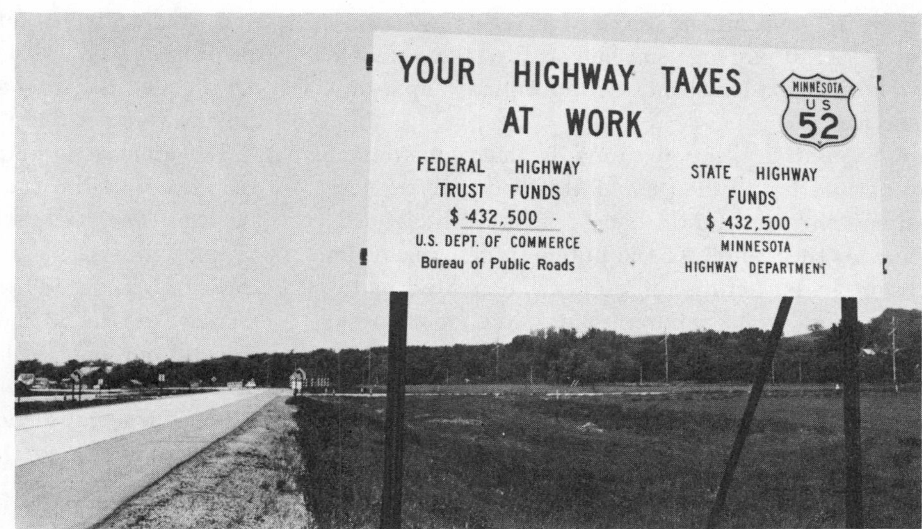

Federal and state taxes are used to build many modern superhighways.

Courtesy Minnesota State Highway Department

The money owed by state and local governments has usually been used for durable capital goods such as schools, hospitals, sewage systems, and highways. Even though the cost of these things is spread over a period of years, people are able to benefit from their use while paying for them. It is somewhat like purchasing consumer goods on installments.

Debt Increases the Expenses of Government

One of the disadvantages of any debt, public or private, is that interest must be paid on it. Some of the money collected in taxes, therefore, must be used to pay the interest on public debts. The higher the debt, the greater the interest. During a recent year $9 billion of the tax money collected by the Federal government went to pay interest on the national debt.

Some public debt cannot be avoided, for reasons already given. Nevertheless, careless use of credit holds the same dangers for government as it does for an individual or a family. It may lead to wasteful spending, which would increase the expenses of government unnecessarily.

TAXES ARE NOT PRICES

The amount a person pays in taxes does not depend on the value of what he receives in return. In other words, taxes are not prices in the usual sense. If a ticket to a certain movie costs $1, everyone who buys a ticket pays $1 and sees the same movie. Not so with taxes. Although everyone pays taxes in one form or another, some people pay more than others. Yet everyone living in a community is entitled to police and fire protection and the use of the public library regardless of how much he pays in taxes. A family with four children attending the public schools may not pay any more in taxes than a family with two children. The larger family may pay even less. This may seem unfair until you examine the problem more closely.

For one thing, it is usually difficult to measure accurately how much an individual benefits from a government service. How could you possibly determine who receives the most benefit from a court of justice, from the enforcement of pure food and drug laws, or from the exploration of outer space? On the other hand, suppose it were possible to measure the extent to which individuals benefit from a government service. If each one were expected to pay for what he got, then those unable to pay would have to do without many important services.

A point to keep in mind is that government functions for all the people. Its goods and services are not provided for the benefit of certain individuals but for the benefit of the public in general. As an example, an entire community is benefited by the education of its children. But if the public is to benefit from government services, then these services must be available to everyone, whether he can afford to pay for them or not. And as long as there are some who cannot pay their share of the cost, then some people will have to pay more. There is no other way.

HOW ARE TAXES DETERMINED?

It has long been the custom for governments to collect taxes by putting a tax on some particular thing or activity. This is referred to as *levying* a tax. In the United States, for example, a tax is levied on property. Whatever serves as the basis for the tax is called the ***tax base.*** In the case of a property tax, the value of the property is the tax base.

The amount to be paid in taxes is usually some proportion of the tax base. This proportion is the ***tax rate.*** The tax rate is very often stated as a percent of the base. You may recall that the social security tax in 1966 was 8.4 percent of a worker's earnings up to $6,600. The tax rate in that case was 8.4 percent. To figure the amount to be paid in taxes, you multiply the rate times the base. When the social security tax rate was 8.4 percent, the actual amount of the tax was $8.40 for each $100 of earnings (.084 × $100 = $8.40).

Sometimes the tax rate is expressed as a certain number of dollars. For example, property taxes are often stated as the number of dollars that must be paid for each $100 or $1,000 of value, such as $5 per hundred or $30 per thousand. If property is taxed at the rate of $30 per thousand, the actual tax on property valued at $10,000 would be $30 times ten, or $300.

BUILDING YOUR VOCABULARY

On a separate sheet of paper, list the figures 1 to 5 numbering down. For each term given below at the left, choose from the definitions at the right, the one that best matches it in meaning. Write this definition following the appropriate number.

1. ***public debt***
2. ***revenue***
3. ***tax***
4. ***tax base***
5. ***tax rate***

a. Whatever serves as a basis for a tax
b. A compulsory payment for government services
c. A debt owed to the government
d. A payment made by the government in exchange for services
e. Income received by the government
f. A debt owed by the government
g. The proportion of the tax base used to figure the amount of taxes to be paid

CHECKING YOUR READING

1. Why do governments need money?
2. What is the main source of government income?
3. What are some other sources of government revenue?
4. What kinds of goods and services do the three levels of government in the

United States produce? Why do they produce them?

5. Explain why the goods and services provided by government are not free.
6. How does paying taxes differ from other kinds of spending?
7. Why have taxes increased over the years?
8. Give five reasons why spending by the Federal government has increased.
9. Why is it sometimes necessary for governments to borrow?
10. What three events are chiefly responsible for the large debt the Federal government now has?
11. For what purposes do state and local governments usually borrow?
12. Explain how debt increases the expenses of government.
13. Why should governments avoid excessive use of credit?
14. Explain why taxes are not prices.
15. Why do some people have to pay more taxes than others?
16. How are the tax base and the tax rate used to figure the amount of tax to be paid?

SHARING YOUR OPINION AND EXPERIENCE

1. Money borrowed by government is not considered revenue. Why?
2. Why are most elementary schools and high schools in this country called *public* schools?
3. Why do you think the payment of taxes is compulsory rather than voluntary?
4. Dick Ammerman feels that government spending is now great enough and should not be allowed to increase further. Do you agree or disagree? Why?
5. Our Federal, state, and local governments now owe a debt of more than $350 billion. To whom do they owe this money?
6. Do you think a person should be entitled to government services even though he cannot pay for them? Explain.
7. How do you think a couple who has no children benefits from the public schools?
8. One principle of taxation is that people should be taxed according to their ability to pay. Do you agree or disagree with this principle? Give your reasons.
9. Are there any goods or services now provided by government that you think privately owned businesses could produce better? Explain.
10. Why do you think people expect more from government today than they did thirty or forty years ago?

PROJECTS AND PROBLEMS

1. The taxes your family pays help to provide a variety of government services such as the following: public schools, police protection, fire protection, public housing, hospitals, highways, public libraries, public parks, national defense, airports, street maintenance, sewage disposal. Some of these services benefit you directly, others indirectly.

   On a separate sheet of paper, draw a form similar to the one illustrated on page 384. In the left-hand column, copy the list of services. After each service, place a check mark in the proper column to indicate whether it benefits you directly or indirectly.

Government Service	Benefits	
	Directly	*Indirectly*

2. The table below shows the expenditures of the Federal government for fiscal years 1964, 1965, and 1966. "Fiscal" is similar in meaning to "financial." A fiscal year is a 12-month accounting period. It may or may not be the same as a calendar year. The fiscal year of the United States government, for example, begins on July 1 of each year and ends June 30 of the following year. A record of its expenditures for fiscal year 1964 includes expenditures made during the 12 months from July 1, 1963 to June 30, 1964. Following the table are some questions for you to answer.

FEDERAL GOVERNMENT EXPENDITURES
(in billions of dollars)

Item	Fiscal Years		
	1964	*1965**	*1966**
National defense	**54.2**	**52.2**	**51.6**
International affairs	**3.7**	**4.0**	**4.0**
Space	**4.1**	**4.9**	**5.1**
Agriculture	**5.6**	**4.5**	**3.9**
Natural resources	**2.5**	**2.7**	**2.7**
Commerce, transportation, housing, urban affairs	**3.0**	**3.1**	**2.8**
Health, labor, welfare, veterans	**11.0**	**11.6**	**12.9**
Education	**1.3**	**1.5**	**2.7**
General expenses and interest on debt	**13.1**	**13.7**	**14.1**

Source: Business Week **estimated*

▪ *a.* What period of time did fiscal year 1965 cover? ▪ *b.* Did total Federal spending increase or decrease between 1964 and 1966? ▪ *c.* Spending for national defense was what percent of total Federal spending in 1964? in 1965? in 1966? ▪ *d.* For which items did spending increase each year from 1964 to 1966? ▪ *e.* For which items was spending less in 1966 than in 1964? ▪ *f.* For which item was the percent of increase in spending greatest between 1964 and 1966? What was the approximate percent of increase? (Answer these questions without figuring percents for all items in the table.) ▪ *g.* Approximately what percent of total Federal spending in 1966 was for education? ▪ *h.* What do you think spending for "space" included? ▪ *i.* What do you think was included in the spending for agriculture?

3. You learned in this part that government spending has increased in amount over the years. Another way to look at government spending is to compare it with the nation's total output of goods and services year by year. Only in this way can you tell whether government is purchasing a larger or smaller share of the nation's gross national product. The graph on page 385 shows what percent of GNP was

bought by the Federal government each year from 1942 to 1966. In 1950, for example, the Federal government bought approximately 15 percent of all goods and services produced. Following the graph are some questions for you to answer.

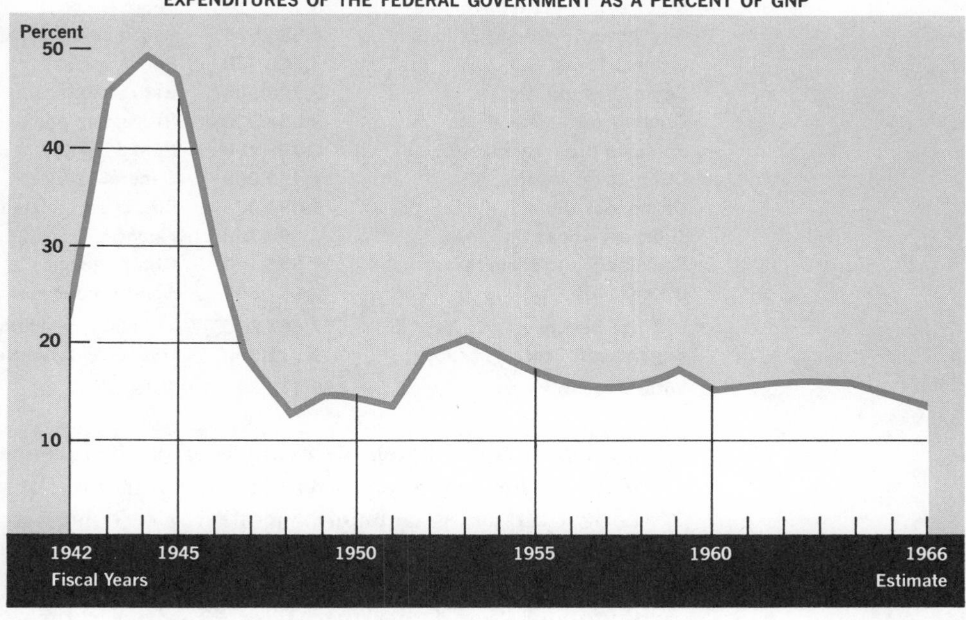

▪ *a.* Approximately what percent of GNP was bought by the Federal government in 1942? in 1950? in 1960? in 1966? ▪ *b.* In which year was the percent of GNP bought by the Federal government largest? What percent went to the Federal government that year? ▪ *c.* In which years did Federal spending amount to a larger percent of GNP than it had the preceding year? ▪ *d.* What do you think accounted for the large "hump" in the graph in the early 1940's? ▪ *e.* What was the cause of the smaller "hump" in the early 1950's? ▪ *f.* In general has Federal spending been increasing or decreasing in recent years in proportion to GNP?

4. Sometimes a tax rate is stated as a percent of the base. Sometimes it is expressed as a certain number of dollars for each $100 or $1,000 of the base amount. For each case listed below, determine the amount to be paid in taxes.

Tax Rate	*Tax Base*	*Tax Rate*	*Tax Base*
▪ *a.* 3.8%	$ 6,500	▪ *d.* 14%	$ 5,400
▪ *b.* $3 per hundred	8,000	▪ *e.* $15 per thousand	22,500
▪ *c.* $32 per thousand	15,200	▪ *f.* $2.50 per hundred	13,400

5. Illustrated on page 386 is a proposed budget for a medium-sized city. In it you will find the information to answer the questions that follow.

PROPOSED BUDGET FOR CITY
for 1965–66

Estimated Revenue		Estimated Expenditures	
Real estate taxes	$16,475,900	Public schools	$14,629,500
Sales tax	8,891,660	Public welfare	9,304,600
State and Federal payments	8,145,310	Debt service	7,612,650
City government operations	4,580,595	Public safety	7,154,600
License taxes	4,540,480	Public works	5,122,200
City owned utilities	3,728,900	Retirement	2,149,800
Utility taxes—general	3,634,300	Recreation and parks	1,967,600
Personal property taxes	2,776,460	Public health	1,588,400
Utility taxes—water	1,495,000	General services	1,343,100
Delinquent taxes	1,094,000	Courts and related agencies	1,188,350
Judiciary—fines and fees	965,700	Finance	644,400
Machinery and tools taxes	651,100	Other agencies	2,146,620
Other taxes	687,600	Appropriated reserves	2,159,200
Total Revenue	$57,667,005	Total Expenditures	$57,011,020
Beginning Balance 7/1/65	1,511,344	Unappropriated Reserve	2,167,329
Total Available	$59,178,349	Total	$59,178,349

▪ *a.* How many different items are listed on the revenue side of the budget? How many of them represent taxes of some kind? ▪ *b.* For what purpose did the city budget the largest amount of money? ▪ *c.* What percent of its total estimated expenditures was to be spent for this purpose? ▪ *d.* For what purpose did the city budget the second largest amount? What do you suppose was included in this item? ▪ *e.* Other than taxes, what were the city's sources of revenue? ▪ *f.* Did the city expect to spend more or less than its income for the year? How much more or less?

6. The three circle graphs below show what percent of the total taxes collected in three different years went to each of the three levels of government. Study the graphs and answer the questions following them.

DISTRIBUTION OF TAXES COLLECTED IN 1927, 1947, AND 1963

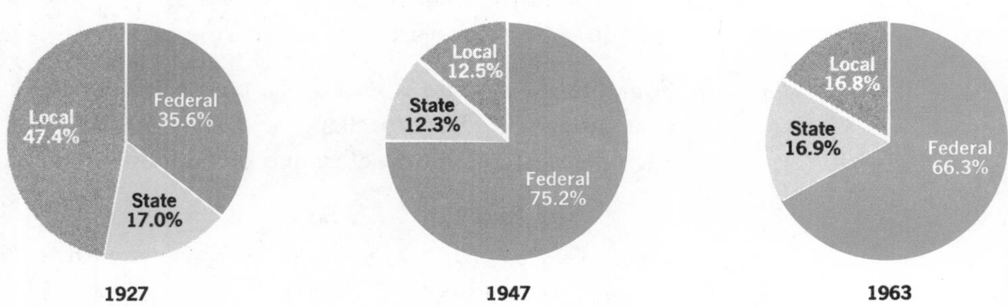

▪ *a.* Which level of government received the largest percent of the taxes collected in 1927? in 1947? in 1963? ▪ *b.* Was the percent that local governments received smaller or larger than the state governments received in 1927? in 1947? in 1963?

■ *c.* Approximately what fraction of the total taxes collected did the Federal government receive in 1927? in 1947? in 1963? ■ *d.* If total tax collections in 1927 amounted to $9 billion, how much did each level of government receive? ■ *e.* If total tax collections in 1963 amounted to $131 billion, did local governments receive more or less money than they did in 1927? How much more or less? ■ *f.* In 1947 tax collections totaled $47 billion. How much did state and local governments together receive?

CHALLENGE PROBLEMS

1. Although the primary purpose of taxes is to provide government income, they are sometimes used to regulate business activity. Explain.
2. Do you think the cost of government is likely to increase in the future? Why or why not?
3. A term frequently used in connection with the financing of government is "deficit spending." What is deficit spending?
4. The graph used in Projects and Problems No. 3 shows that the percent of GNP bought by the Federal government has generally been decreasing since 1943. Yet Federal spending has been increasing, as you know. How can both things be true?
5. If all threat of wars suddenly disappeared, what do you think would happen to government spending?
6. One economist has said that "Any government service or activity is worthwhile if, and only if, the services or goods it provides give taxpayers a larger benefit than they could get by spending the money themselves." Explain this statement and give examples.

PART 42
KINDS OF TAXES

A LIST of things on which taxes have been levied down through the centuries would include many unusual items such as hats, beds, baths, marriages, and funerals. At one time England levied a tax on sunlight by collecting from every household with six or more windows. And history tells us of a Turkish ruler who collected a tax each time he dined with one of his subjects. Why? To pay for the wear and tear on his teeth.

In a democracy one of the most difficult decisions governments have to make is what kinds of taxes to levy. It is doubtful whether lawmakers could design a tax that would meet with everyone's approval. On the other hand, a tax that is not acceptable to most people could prove politically unpopular. Those responsible for enacting the tax might be replaced at the next election.

How many different kinds of taxes can you name? What are the characteristics of a good tax?

WHAT KINDS OF TAXES ARE USED IN THE UNITED STATES?

Anyone who pays a tax is said to "bear the burden" of the tax. One fact about taxes is that the burden of a particular tax tends to fall more heavily on some persons than on others. To spread the burden of taxes among as many people as possible, therefore, the three levels of government in this country use a number of different kinds of taxes. From the standpoint of their use, the most important ones are income taxes; property taxes; sales taxes; and estate, inheritance, and gift taxes. Some of these have been used for a long time; some are fairly new. Some are used by only one level of government; others by two or even all three levels. Together these different taxes make up what is called our *tax system.*

Income Taxes

As its name indicates, an ***income tax*** is a tax on earnings. Both individuals and business corporations pay income taxes. For tax purposes, the incomes of unincorporated businesses (single proprietorships and partnerships) are treated as income for their owners. In other words, income earned from these businesses is taxed the same as individual incomes. Compared to some other kinds of taxes, the income tax is fairly new, dating back to 1913. Today it is the principal source of revenue for the Federal government, providing more than three-fourths of its total income. Nearly two-thirds of the states and the District of Columbia also tax incomes.

Property Taxes

The oldest of the different kinds of taxes used in the United States today is the property tax. It provides most of the income for local governments and at least a part of the income for all but a few states. It is not used by the Federal government.

A ***property tax*** is a tax levied on any kind of property. It may be real property such as land and buildings; or it may be personal property such as automobiles, furniture, jewelry, stocks, and bonds. Personal property also includes items owned by business firms such as machines and equipment. It even includes goods in production and finished goods belonging to manufacturers, wholesalers, and retailers that have not yet been sold.

State laws control the kinds of taxes local governments may use, and state laws differ as to what kinds of property can be taxed. Real property is taxed in all states. A tax of this kind is known as a *real estate tax.* On the matter of taxing personal property, however, states vary greatly.

Sales Taxes

A ***sales tax*** is a tax levied on the sale of goods or services. Actually there are several different kinds of sales taxes, but only three of them are described here: general sales taxes, excise taxes, and tariffs.

A general sales tax is a tax that buyers pay on most of their purchases. This is the type of tax that people usually have in mind when they speak of a sales tax. Some form of general sales tax is now used by at least three-fourths of the states. It is also a source of income for many cities. In some cases only consumers pay the tax; in others, business as well as consumers pay it. The rate of tax varies from one state to another, ranging from 2 to 4 percent of the amount of the purchase. For example, suppose you bought a coat in a state where the sales tax is 3 percent. If the price of the coat was $40, you would have to pay an additional $1.20 for the tax.

The Federal government does not levy a general sales tax, but it does collect excise taxes. An ***excise tax*** is a sales tax levied on a specific good or service such as gasoline, cigarettes, and air travel. Excise taxes are sometimes collected by means of stamps that are attached to the items taxed. These stamps, which are evidence that the tax on an item has been paid, can be found on playing cards and tobacco. Excise taxes are used by all three levels of government and in some cases, the same item may be taxed by all three.

A third kind of sales tax is a tariff. A ***tariff*** is a tax on goods imported from other countries. Only the Federal government has the right to collect such a tax, which is also known as a *customs duty.* In fact, at one time tariffs provided most of the income needed by our Federal government. Today less than 2 percent of federal income is provided by this tax.

Estate, Inheritance, and Gift Taxes

Three closely related taxes are estate, inheritance, and gift taxes. The first two are sometimes called *death taxes* because they are levied following someone's death. All three are really a kind of property tax as you will see.

Everything a person owns, including both real and personal property, makes up his *estate.* When

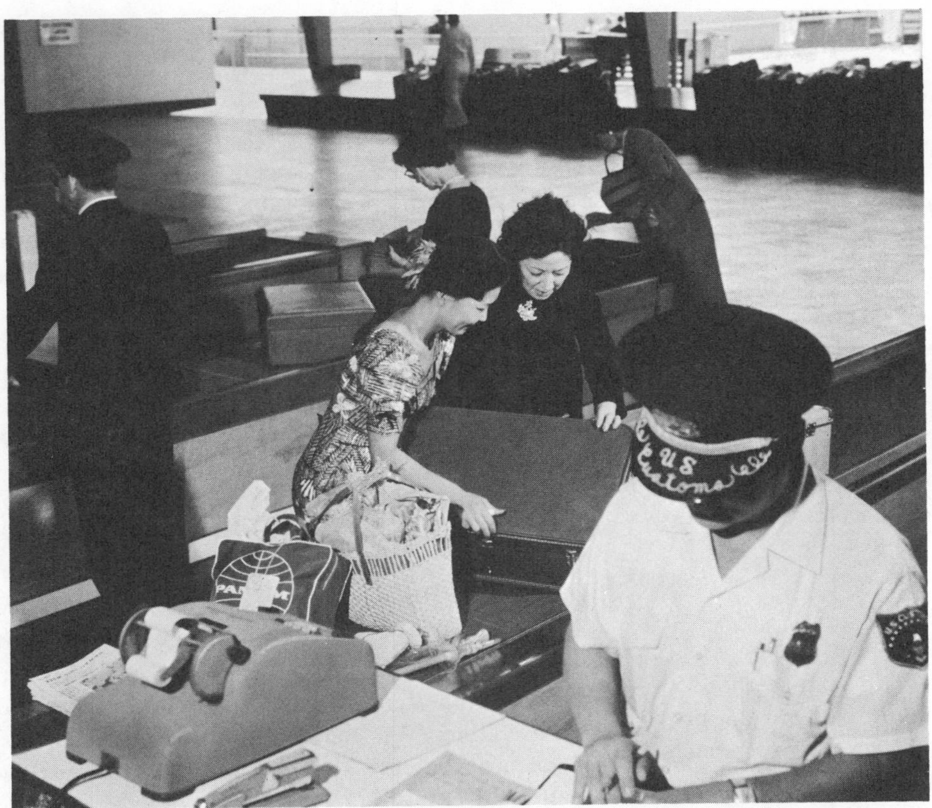

Courtesy U.S. Treasury Department

Travelers arriving at the Honolulu airport have their baggage examined for goods for which a customs duty is to be collected.

someone dies, ownership of his property or estate passes to one or more individuals or organizations. Before such property is transferred, however, it is subject to an ***estate tax*** if its total value exceeds a certain amount.

An *inheritance* is property received by one person from the estate of another person following that person's death. An ***inheritance tax*** is a tax based on the value of the property inherited. Each person receiving an inheritance pays the tax. If an estate is divided among ten people, each one is taxed according to his share.

A person might escape payment of estate and inheritance taxes by giving most of his property away before his death. He might, except for one thing—the gift tax. A ***gift tax*** is levied on any gift of property that is valued over a certain amount.

The Federal government and several states use both estate and gift taxes. Some states use the inheritance tax instead of the estate tax; a few use both.

Social Security Taxes

As you already know, the earnings of most workers are taxed to pay for old-age, survivors, and disability insurance. Some people claim that this is not really a tax, but an insurance premium. Nevertheless, because it is compulsory and because the money is used to pay for benefits received from government, it is called a tax.

WHAT ARE THE CHARACTERISTICS OF A GOOD TAX?

The purpose of taxes is to raise the money needed to pay the costs of government. The fact that taxes are necessary, however, does not mean that every tax is a good one. A good tax has these characteristics: it is fair; it is easy to collect; it is a direct tax; it does not have harmful economic effects.

A Tax Should Be Fair

A tax is usually considered fair if it is imposed on each person according to his ability to pay. Yet there is really no easy way to judge a person's ability to pay a tax. Even the fact that two people have the same incomes does not mean that they have the same tax-paying ability. For example, one man with an annual income of $8,000 may have four children. Another with the same amount of income may have only one child. In addition, the first man might have extraordinary medical expenses; the second none, and so on. Certainly the first man's ability to pay taxes would be less than the second man's. As you can see, income alone is not an accurate measure of ability to pay taxes. Neither is the amount of property a person owns nor the amount of money he spends.

A Tax Should Be Easy to Collect

When applied to taxes, the term "easy to collect" has several meanings. One meaning is that the tax should be easy to enforce. If people can find ways to get out of paying a tax without being caught, then it is not easy to enforce. Furthermore, if some persons do not pay their share of a tax, the burden of the tax falls unjustly on those who do pay.

"Easy to collect" also means that the tax should be economical to collect. The expense of collecting taxes is one of the costs of government. It must be paid out of taxes the same as the other expenses of government. The more it costs to collect a tax, therefore, the higher the tax must be.

Another thing "easy to collect" means is that payment of taxes should be convenient. In other words, the taxpayer should not be put to a lot of bother or extra expense in order to pay his taxes.

A Tax Should Be Direct

The person on whom a tax is imposed is not always the one who actually pays it. The reason is that some taxes can be shifted; that is, the person taxed is able to pass the tax on to someone else. A tax that can be shifted to someone else is called an ***indirect tax.*** The one who actually pays the tax pays it indirectly. For example, with the exception of income taxes, most taxes paid by business firms are counted as a cost of production. As a cost of production, they are included in the prices charged for goods and services produced by business. They are often called *hidden taxes* because people pay them without being aware of it. All indirect taxes are not hidden, however. The stamp on playing cards or cigarettes clearly indicates that a tax has been paid on those products and that the tax is included in the prices charged for them.

A tax that cannot be shifted is a ***direct tax.*** Income taxes and inheritance taxes are two examples. There are two reasons why it is better if taxes are direct rather than indirect. One is that a direct tax can be based more nearly on ability to pay. When a tax can be shifted, it is not possible to know who will actually pay the tax.

Another reason why direct taxes are better than indirect taxes is that people know they are paying them. When people know how much they pay in taxes, they are likely to take an interest in how their money is spent. This is important in a democracy where citizens are able to influence the decisions of government. Indirect taxes give rise to the mistaken belief that government services are free or that they cost very little.

A Tax Should Not Have Harmful Economic Effects

All taxes affect the operation of our economic system in some way. If they do nothing else, they reduce the amount consumers and business firms can spend as they please. But in some cases, they do much more. As you have seen, taxes on business increase the prices of goods and services produced by business. A tax on a particular good or service may even reduce the demand for that good or service. Heavy property taxes in one community may discourage business firms from locating there. A sales tax in one state may send people living near the state line to the next state to do their shopping. In judging whether or not a tax is a good one, therefore, it is necessary to consider what its economic effects are. If it interferes seriously with the economic decisions of consumers and business, it is not a good tax.

BUILDING YOUR VOCABULARY

List the figures 1 to 10 on a sheet of paper, numbering down. Read the ten statements given below at the right; then, for each statement, select from the column at the left the term that best matches it in meaning. Write this term next to the appropriate number.

direct tax	1. A tax on the sale of goods or services
estate tax	2. A tax on large amounts of property that are given away
excise tax	3. A tax on goods imported from other countries
gift tax	4. A tax levied on property received from the estate of someone who has died that is paid by the person who receives the property
income tax	5. A sales tax that is levied on a specific good or service
indirect tax	6. A tax on real estate or personal items such as automobiles or household goods
inheritance tax	7. A tax that can be shifted to someone else
property tax	8. A tax that cannot be shifted to someone else
sales tax	9. A tax levied on property left by someone who dies that must be paid before ownership of the property is transferred
tariff	10. A tax on earnings

CHECKING YOUR READING

1. What are some of the unusual items on which taxes have been levied in the past?
2. In a democracy, what may happen if a tax is unacceptable to a majority of the people?
3. From the standpoint of use, which taxes are the most important ones in this country?
4. Who is required to pay income taxes?
5. How is the income of single proprietorships and partnerships taxed?
6. What is the principal source of revenue for the Federal government?
7. What is the oldest kind of tax used in this country today? Which levels of government use it?
8. Which levels of government use the general sales tax? Who pays the tax?
9. How does an excise tax differ from a general sales tax? Which levels of government use the excise tax?
10. Which level of government has the right to collect tariffs?
11. How do estate, inheritance, and gift taxes differ?

12. Why are the payments that workers make to the old-age, survivors, and disability insurance program called taxes?
13. What is the primary purpose of taxes?
14. Name four characteristics of a good tax.
15. When is a tax usually considered to be fair?
16. Why is it difficult to judge whether a tax is fair?
17. What does the term "easy to collect" mean when applied to taxes?
18. Why are some taxes called hidden taxes?
19. Why is it better if taxes are direct rather than indirect?
20. Explain how taxes may affect the operation of our economic system.

SHARING YOUR OPINION AND EXPERIENCE

1. The text says "everyone pays taxes." How do you pay taxes?
2. Why is it so difficult to design a tax that will satisfy everyone?
3. Do you think everyone who has an income should be required to pay income taxes?
4. Andy Weaver says that some people who do not own property are required to pay property taxes. Do you agree or disagree? Explain.
5. Why do you suppose the Federal government does not use the property tax?
6. Does your state have a general sales tax? If so, what is the rate of the tax?
7. Since the government receives such a small percent of its income from tariffs, why does it still use this tax?
8. Why do you think an estate tax is collected only when the value of the property exceeds a certain amount?
9. Which of the following do you consider the best basis for determining a person's ability to pay taxes: (*a*) income, (*b*) value of property owned, (*c*) amount of money spent?
10. Income taxes paid by a corporation cannot be passed on to its customers, but they are paid indirectly by individuals. Explain.

PROJECTS AND PROBLEMS

1. On a separate sheet of paper, copy the form illustrated below. In the left-hand column, list the kinds of taxes that were described in this part. Place check marks in the appropriate columns to indicate which levels of government use each tax.

Kind of Tax	Used by the Federal Government	Used by State Governments	Used by Local Governments

2. For each tax listed in the preceding problem, indicate whether or not the person on whom it is imposed can shift the tax to someone else. Use a form similar to the one shown on page 394.

Tax	Can Be Shifted	Cannot Be Shifted

3. The income that governments receive from some taxes increases or decreases with the ups and downs in business activity. On the other hand, changes in business activity have little effect on the income from some taxes. Divide a sheet of paper in half lengthwise. On the left side, list the taxes that provide different amounts of income as business activity goes up or down. On the right half, list the taxes that provide about the same income regardless of changes in business activity.

WHERE THE FEDERAL DOLLAR WAS TO COME FROM IN 1966

4. The circle graph at the right shows the different sources from which the Federal government expected to receive money in 1966. Excise taxes, for example, were to provide 10 cents of each dollar received. Answer the questions following the graph.

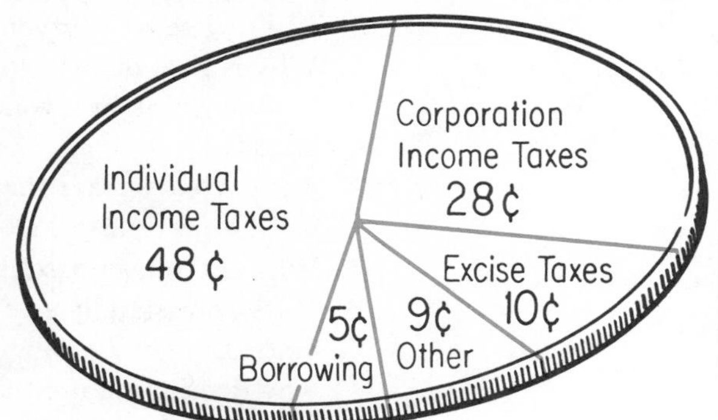

▪ *a.* What source was to provide the largest portion of each dollar the government received? ▪ *b.* Approximately what fraction of each dollar was to come from income taxes? ▪ *c.* How much of each dollar would not be considered revenue? Explain. ▪ *d.* What are some sources of income that might be included under "Other"? ▪ *e.* The total amount the government expected to receive in 1966 was $94.4 billion. How much of that amount came from each source shown in the graph?

5. In the table below are listed the amounts of income that state and local governments received from various sources in a recent year. Following the table are some questions for you to answer.

STATE AND LOCAL GOVERNMENT REVENUES

Source of Income	*Amount (billions of dollars)*
Property taxes	**20.6**
Sales taxes	**13.5**
Personal taxes	**9.7**
Federal grants	**9.0**
Other receipts	**11.6**

▪ *a.* What are federal grants? Where did this money come from originally? ▪ *b.* What do you think personal taxes include? ▪ *c.* From what source did the state and local governments receive the largest amounts of income? ▪ *d.* What was the total amount of income the state and local governments received? ▪ *e.* Approximately what fraction of the total income came from property taxes and sales taxes combined? ▪ *f.* Can you tell from the table how much of the total revenue came from taxes? Explain.

6. Using the information from the table in problem No. 5, figure the percent of state and local government revenues that came from each source. Then prepare a bar graph similar to the one in problem No. 2 of the Projects and Problems section of Part 33. (see page 309)
7. Appoint a committee to find out from what source your local government receives its income. From the information gathered by the committee, prepare a circle graph similar to that used in Problem No. 4.

CHALLENGE PROBLEMS

1. Why do you suppose the number of windows in a person's house was once the basis for a tax?
2. Frances Sellitto overheard some of her father's friends discussing double taxation. What is double taxation?
3. Why is a direct tax more nearly based on ability to pay than an indirect tax?
4. If direct taxes are considered better, why do we still have indirect taxes?
5. Interest earned on United States savings bonds is taxed as income. Interest earned on bonds issued by a state or local government, however, is not taxed. Do you consider this fair? Why or why not?
6. Is a tax on business profits considered a cost of doing business? Explain.

PART 43 HOW GOOD IS OUR TAX SYSTEM?

JUST from what you already know about taxes, one thing must be apparent. None of the taxes used in the United States has all the characteristics of a good tax. This is because it is not possible to design such a tax. Good features, you see, have a way of interfering with one another. A tax that is easy to collect may not be fair. And any attempt to make it fair may make it more difficult or more expensive to collect. Every tax, therefore, has its good points and its bad points. In many cases, however, the good points of one tax tend to make up for the defects of another. That is why a tax system cannot be judged on the basis of a single tax. It is also another reason why it is better to have several kinds of taxes rather than one.

Which of the taxes used in the United States today would you say comes closest to being a good tax? Why is it difficult to make changes in our tax system? What is meant by the statement that some taxes are used for nonrevenue purposes?

Courtesy Northern Indiana Public Service Company

THE INCOME TAX HAS MANY CHARACTERISTICS OF A GOOD TAX

Of the taxes used in the United States today, the federal income tax probably comes the closest to being a good tax. Some states have income taxes similar to that used by the Federal government. Because others tax incomes somewhat differently, however, only the federal income tax is discussed here.

The Income Tax Is Fair

Even though income alone is not a true measure of a person's ability to pay taxes, it is the best that we have. To make its tax as fair as possible, the Federal government allows a taxpayer an exemption of $600 for himself and for each of his dependents. A ***tax exemption*** is an amount of money that is not

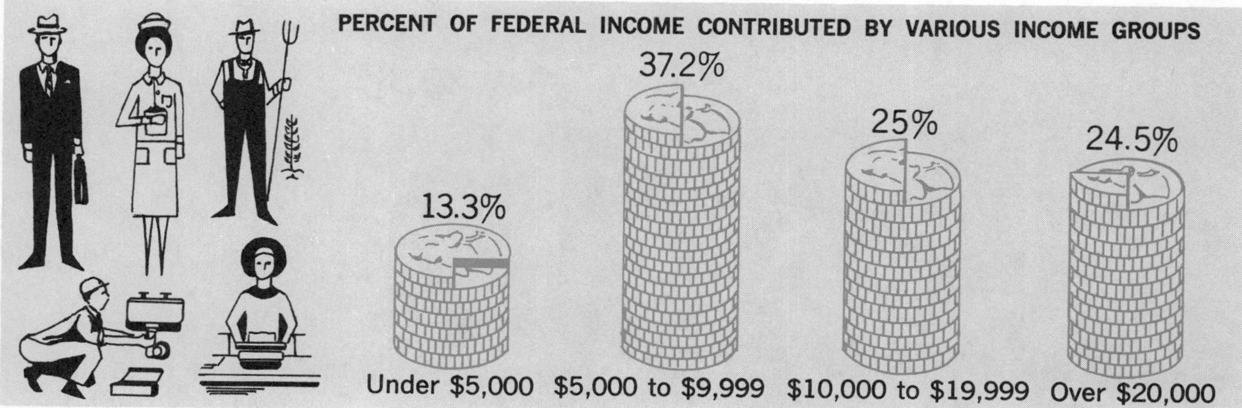

subject to tax. Thus, a man with a wife and three children has exemptions amounting to $3,000.

In addition to exemptions, individual taxpayers are permitted to deduct certain kinds of expenses from their total earnings, such as contributions to churches or charitable organizations, taxes paid to other levels of government, interest paid on debts, and medical expenses over a certain amount. The Federal government taxes only income that remains after all exemptions and deductions have been subtracted from total earnings. This is ***taxable income.*** If a man has an income of $7,500 a year, exemptions of $2,400, and deductible expenses of $825, his taxable income is $4,275 ($7,500 – $3,225 = $4,275).

The federal income tax is also progressive. A ***progressive tax*** is one for which the rate increases as the ability to pay increases. In the case of the income tax, this means that the tax rate increases as the amount of taxable income increases. Recently, for example, an unmarried person paid a rate of 16 percent on the first $500 of taxable income; $16\frac{1}{2}$ percent on the next $500; $17\frac{1}{2}$ percent on the next $500, and so on. The highest rate of tax on personal incomes that year was 77 percent. The argument in favor of these progressive rates is that as income rises, less sacrifice is involved in the payment of taxes. One of the objections most often raised against the federal income tax, however, is that the rates rise too sharply in proportion to incomes.

The Income Tax Is Easy to Collect

To make the federal income tax easy to collect, employers are required to hold back a portion of each worker's earnings and send it to the government. This method of collecting the tax is known as *withholding*. Persons who are self-employed must estimate the amount they expect to earn each year. They then pay tax on the estimated amount directly to the government, either in a lump sum or in quarterly installments during the year. Once each year, every taxpayer must file an *income tax return*. At that time any balance owing the government must be paid. If a taxpayer has already paid more than he owes, he can claim a refund.

The withholding method of collecting income taxes helps the government to enforce payment of the tax. It also makes payment of the tax easier for the taxpayer, because payment is spread over the entire year. Attempts to make the income tax fair, however, have made it so complicated that many people now need help in preparing their income tax returns.

PROPERTY TAXES HAVE MANY FAULTS

When discussing property taxes, it is necessary to keep in mind that there are two kinds—real estate and personal property taxes. What people object to

This National Computer Center will soon contain a record of every taxpayer in the nation.

Courtesy U.S. Treasury Department

most about the property tax is that local governments depend too heavily on it for income. This puts the burden of local taxes almost entirely on property owners. On the other hand, it is often argued that property owners benefit most from such government services as fire and police protection and street maintenance.

Property Taxes Are Not Based on Ability to Pay

Both real estate and personal property taxes are based on the idea that owning property of any kind is a sign of wealth. And at one time that was true. Today, however, because of our widespread use of credit, almost everyone owns some durable goods such as cars, TV sets, jewelry, and household appliances. Many people of average means own homes, while some with high incomes may not own any real property at all. The fact that a person owns property, therefore, is not a true measure of his ability to pay taxes.

Property taxes are almost always proportional. A ***proportional tax*** is one for which the rate is the same for all who pay the tax. If real estate in one community is taxed at the rate of $30 per $1,000, the tax on a house and lot valued at $12,000 would be $360. The tax on a house and lot in the same community valued at $24,000 would be $720, exactly twice as much. The amount of taxes to be paid increases with the value of the property; the rate of tax remains the same. Each owner is taxed in proportion to the value of his property. Property taxes, however, make no allowance for differences among property owners, such as the fact that some have small families and few expenses while others have large families and a great many expenses.

One other fault of this tax is that it is based on the *assessed valuation* of the property. This is a percentage of its market value, as determined by a government employee called a *tax assessor.* Estimating the exact value of personal possessions, a house, or piece of land is often very difficult. Sometimes two pieces of property the same in value are taxed differently.

All Property Taxes Are Not Easy to Collect

Although most states still tax personal property belonging to business firms, many no longer tax household goods and other items belonging to individuals. One reason is that dishonest persons could escape paying a big part of the tax by hiding such things as jewelry and furs and by denying that they owned any stocks or bonds. Also the tax is expensive to collect in terms of the amount of revenue it provides.

The real estate property tax, on the other hand, is easy to enforce. A building or piece of land can hardly be concealed. Moreover, failure to pay the tax gives the government the right to seize the property and sell it for payment of the tax. To make the payment of real estate taxes easier, some communities now collect them every three months rather than once a year or semiannually. Many of the lending agencies that make mortgage loans also take care of paying the taxes on the mortgaged property. The borrower's monthly payment then includes a certain amount for taxes in addition to the amount he has to pay regularly on the mortgage.

The Property Tax Can Be Shifted

Some people think that because they do not own property, they escape the property tax. What they fail to realize is that it is hidden in their rent. The property tax can be shifted. When property is rented, therefore, it is the renter rather than the owner who bears the burden of the tax. In some cases he may be the one least able to pay it.

SALES TAXES HAVE ONE BIG FAULT

Each year the list grows of states and cities that have sales taxes. Governments like the general sales tax in particular because it provides a large amount of revenue at a low tax rate. In addition, because it takes from everyone, a general sales tax helps to spread the cost of government among more people than any other kind of tax. Nevertheless, a general sales tax has one major fault: The burden of the tax falls most heavily on those persons who are least able to pay it.

Sales Taxes Are Regressive

Sales taxes are proportional. Everyone, rich and poor alike, pays the same rate of tax on his purchases. On the other hand, because everyone pays the same rate of tax, sales taxes are also regressive. A ***regressive tax*** is one that takes a higher portion of low incomes than of high ones. The less income a person or family has, remember, the more of it must be spent in order to live. As the portion of income spent increases, the portion that must be paid in sales taxes increases. Suppose, for example, one family has an annual income of $5,000 and spends all of it. Another family with a $10,000 income spends only $9,000 of it and saves the rest. This means that the first family would have to pay tax on a bigger share of its income than the second family.

To remedy this fault of the general sales tax, some states exempt certain items from tax. For example, nearly one-third of the states that levy such a tax do not tax food purchases.

Excise taxes, which are also a sales tax, are levied only on certain items. Many of them are considered luxuries, and for that reason some people feel that excise taxes are more fair than a general sales tax.

Sales Taxes Are Easy to Collect

From the standpoint of the government, sales taxes are easy to collect. It is difficult for anyone to escape paying them, and the cost of collecting is low compared to the amount collected. In cases where local and state governments have a general sales tax, collection for both can be made at the same time. From the standpoint of the taxpayer, sales taxes are easy to pay because they are paid in small amounts over a long period of time. On the other hand, the fact that people have to pay the tax every time they buy something makes it a nuisance.

Sales Taxes Are Both Direct and Indirect

Some people mistakenly believe that all sales taxes

The people seated at tables are receiving help in filling out their federal income tax returns at one of the district offices of the Bureau of Internal Revenue.

Courtesy U.S. Treasury Department

are indirect. This belief arises from the fact that those who actually pay them do not pay them directly to the government. A tax is indirect, however, only when it is actually paid by someone other than the one on whom it is imposed. A general sales or excise tax paid by a business firm on its purchases can be shifted to consumers. A sales tax on retail purchases, however, is a tax imposed on consumers. Sellers are responsible only for collecting the tax for the government. In fact, such a tax is often called a *consumption tax*. Its burden cannot be shifted. Moreover, the consumer is reminded of the tax every time he buys something.

TAXES ARE SOMETIMES USED FOR THEIR ECONOMIC EFFECTS

In the previous part you learned that all taxes have economic effects. In levying taxes, therefore, lawmakers should try to avoid those that would have undesirable effects. Sometimes, however, taxes are used mainly for their economic effects. For example, the purpose of tariffs is to protect manufacturers in this country from foreign competition by encouraging the sale of goods produced in this country. The purpose of inheritance and gift taxes is to prevent most of the nation's wealth from falling into the hands of a small number of people. During World War II, the Federal government levied excise taxes on many consumer goods and services to discourage spending for anything but necessities. The reason was that consumer spending would have encouraged the production of consumer goods, and at that time most of the nation's resources were needed for the production of war goods.

Taxes levied for nonrevenue purposes frequently become important sources of revenue. They then continue to be part of our tax system long after they have served their original purpose. Many excise taxes levied during World War II were not removed until 1965. A few are still in effect.

THE PROBLEM OF TAXATION IS NOT EASY TO SOLVE

By now you must realize that taxes are a problem for

both those who pay them and for those who levy them. Even though our tax system might be improved, this is more easily said than done. Regardless of how many faults a particular tax may have, it cannot simply be eliminated. Some other means of raising the same amount of revenue must first be found to take its place. One reason for the continued use of high property taxes is that local and state governments have not found a substitute for them. At least they have not found a substitute that most people will accept. It seems that someone always objects to a new tax, even if it is to replace an old one.

BUILDING YOUR VOCABULARY

List the figures 1 to 5 on a sheet of paper, numbering down. Read the five statements given below at the right; then, for each statement select from the column at the left the term that best matches it in meaning. Write this term next to the appropriate number.

progressive tax
proportional tax
regressive tax
tax exemption
taxable income

1. The amount of earnings subject to tax after exemptions and deductions are subtracted from total earnings
2. An amount of income that is not subject to tax
3. A tax for which the rate remains the same regardless of the value of the tax base
4. A tax for which the rate increases as ability to pay increases
5. A tax for which the rate decreases as ability to pay increases

CHECKING YOUR READING

1. Explain why it is difficult to design a tax that has all the characteristics of a good tax.
2. Why is it better to have several kinds of taxes rather than just one?
3. Which tax now in use in the United States comes closest to having all characteristics of a good tax?
4. What features of the federal income tax are intended to make the tax as fair as possible?
5. What is the argument in favor of progressive income taxes?
6. What is the objection most often raised against the federal income tax?
7. What is the purpose of the withholding method of collecting income taxes?
8. Name two kinds of property taxes.
9. What do people object to most about property taxes?
10. One fault of the property tax is that it is based on the assessed valuation of the property. Why is this a fault?
11. Why is it sometimes difficult to collect personal property taxes?
12. Why is the real estate tax easy to enforce?
13. Explain how the real estate tax can be shifted.
14. Give two reasons why state and local governments like the general sales tax.
15. What is the major fault of the general sales tax?
16. What have some states done to try to remedy this fault?
17. Explain how sales taxes can be both direct and indirect.

18. Give examples of taxes that are used mainly for their economic effects. Describe the effect that is desired in each case.
19. Why is it difficult to improve our tax system?

SHARING YOUR OPINION AND EXPERIENCE

1. Some people claim that the withholding method of collecting the income tax tends to make it a hidden tax. Do you agree or disagree? Give your reasons.
2. If you earned money from a part-time job, would you be required to pay federal or state income tax? Explain.
3. Is there an income tax in your state? If so, is it a progressive or a proportional tax?
4. Which do you consider more fair—a proportional tax or a progressive tax? Why?
5. A man who earns $11,500 a year may pay less income tax than one who earns $8,000. Explain why.
6. Some lending agencies that make mortgage loans collect monthly from home buyers enough to cover the real estate taxes on the mortgaged property. The lending agency then pays the taxes. What is the reason for this practice?
7. Do you think property owners benefit more from local government services than persons who own no property? Explain.
8. Why are excise taxes considered to be less of a burden on low-income families than general sales taxes?
9. What is the meaning of the term "take-home pay"?

PROJECTS AND PROBLEMS

1. You learned in Part 42 that a good tax is fair and that it is easy to collect. In this part, you learned that some taxes have both of these characteristics, some have one of them, and some have neither. Indicate whether each kind of tax listed below is based on ability to pay and whether it is easy to collect. Use a form similar to the one illustrated.

▪ *a.* Estate tax
▪ *b.* Excise tax
▪ *c.* General sales tax
▪ *d.* Gift tax
▪ *e.* Income tax
▪ *f.* Inheritance tax
▪ *g.* Personal property tax
▪ *h.* Real estate tax
▪ *i.* Tariff

Tax	Based on Ability to Pay	Easy to Collect

2. The proposed city budget used in Part 41, Problem No. 5 on page 386 indicates that the city expected to receive income from at least eight different kinds of taxes. Refer again to the budget and answer these questions:

▪ *a.* Which taxes used by the city are based on the ability-to-pay principle? ▪ *b.* What kind of tax is a utility tax? ▪ *c.* What kind of tax is a machinery and tools tax? ▪ *d.* What are delinquent taxes? ▪ *e.* From which tax did the city expect to receive the largest amount of income? What percent of its total revenue did the city expect to receive from that tax? ▪ *f.* How much did the city expect to receive from real estate taxes, sales taxes, and personal property taxes combined? Approximately what fraction of the city's total revenue did this amount represent? ▪ *g.* In the column headed "Estimated Revenue" the next to the last item listed is "Beginning Balance 7/1/65." What is meant by a "beginning balance"?

3. Mr. Herrmann bought a new house for $17,500. When he got his first property tax statement, he learned that its assessed valuation was $10,500.

▪ *a.* The assessed valuation was what percent of the purchase price? ▪ *b.* The tax rate in his city is $37 per $1,000 of valuation. How much will Mr. Herrmann have to pay in property taxes? ▪ *c.* What will his property tax be if the rate is changed to $38.10 per $1,000 of valuation? ▪ *d.* What will the amount of the tax be if the rate remains $37 per $1,000 of valuation but the valuation is changed to $11,250?

4. Most workers receive a statement of earnings and deductions along with their paychecks. The statement below is for Don Minke, an employee of the Centerville Brick and Tile Company. Following the statement are some questions for you to answer.

CENTERVILLE BRICK AND TILE COMPANY
Centerville, U.S.A.

STATEMENT OF EARNINGS AND DEDUCTIONS

507263	74155	Jun 15 1965	450.62	91.36	359.26
Check No.	**Empl. No.**	**Pay Pd. Ending**	**Gross Pay**	**Tot. Deduct.**	**Net Pay**

40.20	16.50	11.18	2.30	14.18
Fed. W/H	**State W/H**	**Soc. Sec.**	**Insur.**	**Hospital Ins.**

5.00		2.00		
Cr. Union	**Charity**	**Union**		

▪ *a.* How many different deductions were made from Don Minke's check? ▪ *b.* How much was deducted altogether? ▪ *c.* What does Fed. W/H mean? State W/H? ▪ *d.* Other than taxes, what were the deductions for? ▪ *e.* How much did Don actually earn during the pay period covered by the check? ▪ *f.* What was the amount of the check he received? ▪ *g.* Approximately what percent of his earnings was withheld for taxes?

5. Examine a pamphlet explaining regulations and procedures for filing federal income tax returns, and answer the following questions:

   ■ *a.* Who is required to file an income tax return? ■ *b.* Are minors excluded from filing federal income tax returns? ■ *c.* What is the difference between Form 1040 and Form 1040A? Who may use Form 1040A? ■ *d.* What is the amount allowed for each exemption? ■ *e.* What is a joint return? ■ *f.* List four types of expenses that may be deducted by those who wish to itemize deductions on their income tax forms.

6. Mr. Friedman's total earnings for the past year were $9,217. His deductions for federal income tax purposes were: state and local taxes, $340; contributions, $410; interest paid on mortgage and other debts, $761; allowable medical expenses, $206.

   ■ *a.* What were Mr. Friedman's total deductions? ■ *b.* Mr. Friedman is permitted an exemption of $600 each for himself, his wife, two children, and a mother who depend on him for support. What is the total of his exemptions? ■ *c.* What is the amount of his taxable income? ■ *d.* According to the tax-rate schedule, Mr. Friedman must pay $680 plus 20 percent of that part of his taxable income that exceeds $4,000. How much income tax did he have to pay?

7. The following article appeared in the Centerville newspaper in late fall of a recent year. Read the article and answer the questions following it.

   HIGHWAY LITTERBUGS JUST ROBBING THEMSELVES

   Do you like to throw money out of your car window? Maybe you think you don't. But each time you toss debris out, you're taking money out of your own tax pocket.

   The state highway department has come up with a study of costs required to pick up debris in one maintenance district.

   The study, of the 11th district headquartered at Centerville, showed that since the beginning of the year 2,730 truck hours and 8,867 man hours were charged against the picking up of 900 loads of refuse scattered by unthinking motorists.

   At an average cost of $20.85 per load, $18,760 was spent which could have gone into new highways or improvements. Projecting this expenditure on a statewide basis, it came to approximately $200,000 for the year.

   ■ *a.* What is a highway litterbug? ■ *b.* Why is the person who throws debris along the highway throwing his money away? ■ *c.* How many hours of work were required to pick up the refuse along the highway in the 11th district? ■ *d.* How much did it cost to pick up the refuse in the 11th district? ■ *e.* Had it not been necessary to clean up the litter left along the highways, what might the citizens of this state have had instead? ■ *f.* For the entire state, what was the estimated cost of picking up debris along the highway for the year? ■ g. To the nearest 1,000, how many loads of debris did the state highway department estimate would have to be picked up throughout the state during the year?

CHALLENGE PROBLEMS

1. In recent years, some people have proposed that the federal income tax be eliminated. Do you think this is a good idea? Why or why not?
2. The government sometimes reduces taxes or increases them to bring about a desired economic effect. Do you think a general reduction in taxes would cause an increase or a decrease in production? Explain.
3. Harvie Wilkerson says that the property tax on homes is regressive. Explain why this might be so.
4. Do you think a progressive income tax discourages people from attempting to rise to the top in the business world? Why or why not?

CONTENTS OF UNIT 10

Unit 10 / Measuring the Performance of Our Free Enterprise System

PART 44 HOW OUR ECONOMY HAS GROWN

ALL economic systems, as you know, are simply arrangements for using productive resources; that is, natural resources, capital, and labor. Through its economic system each nation decides what and how much is to be produced; how it is to be produced; and how it is to be divided. But no two nations make these decisions in exactly the same way. In some countries government decides what shall be produced and who shall get it. In this country the decisions are made by the people as consumers, as producers, and as voters.

Regardless of the kind of economic system a nation has, however, its standard of living depends on how well its economic system works. Some, of course, perform better than others. But one mark of all successful economies is growth. One way to find out how well our nation's economy is performing, therefore, is to measure our economic growth.

What is economic growth? How is it measured? What is this country's record of growth?

WHAT IS ECONOMIC GROWTH?

The term, economic growth, is not new to you. It means a continued increase in a nation's total production, or ***output,*** as production is sometimes called. A nation's standard of living, remember, depends on its total production. The more goods and services a nation produces in proportion to its population, the larger will be the share for each person. As a nation's population increases, its production must increase at least as fast. Otherwise, its people will have less than before and its standard of living will fall. A nation's standard of living will improve only if its production of goods and services increases at a faster rate than its population. In other words, its economic growth must be greater than the growth of its population.

Courtesy Engineering News Record

You could probably tell whether or not you have grown during the past year by the way your clothes fit. But if you wanted to know exactly how much you had grown, you would have to compare what your measurements are now with what they were a year ago. So it is with economic growth. We can tell in a general way how well our economic system is working by such things as the number of people employed; the amount collected in taxes; the amount and kinds of goods consumers buy; and so on. But if we want to know exactly how fast our economic system is growing, we need some basis for comparison. One basis used is gross national product, or GNP.

Our gross national product, as you know, is the total value of all goods and services produced in this country in any given period. It includes things produced for business such as machines and factories. It includes all goods and services produced for consumers such as automobiles, food, greeting cards, haircuts, dry cleaning, and taxi rides. And it includes all goods and services provided by government such as schools, roads, police and fire protection, mail service, and national defense. GNP is estimated by adding up the prices of all these different items.

To avoid counting any product twice, only the value of final goods is counted in figuring GNP. ***Final goods*** are products purchased for use rather than for resale. This means that raw materials or parts used in making products are not counted separately in figuring GNP. They are counted in the value of the finished products. For example, the price or market value of a pair of shoes includes the cost of the leather and other materials used in their production. If the value of these materials and the value of the finished shoes were both counted in estimating GNP, however, the materials would be counted twice. For that reason, only the selling price of the shoes is counted.

In the United States the gross national product is estimated every three months by the Department of Commerce. The table below shows GNP for every fifth year from 1940 to 1965. Notice that amounts are in billions. In 1955, for example, GNP was $398,000,000,000.

Year	*Amount (in billions)*	*Year*	*Amount (in billions)*
1940	$101	1955	$398
1945	214	1960	504
1950	285	1965	670*

*Estimated

By comparing GNP figures for different years, it is possible to tell whether total production increased or decreased.

Figures Must Be Adjusted for Price Changes

Measuring production in prices has one serious disadvantage. Prices change. A dollar may buy more or less from one year to the next. A general increase or decrease in prices will cause an increase or decrease in GNP figures even though the amount produced remains the same.

The figures in the above table, for example, show GNP measured in prices for each of the years listed. In other words, GNP for 1940 is valued at 1940 prices; GNP for 1950 is valued at 1950 prices, and so on. On the basis of these figures, it appears that there was an increase in GNP of $569 billion during the 25 years from 1940 to 1965. Was total production in 1965 actually more than 5½ times greater than in 1940? Or was some of this increase the result of an increase in prices?

To find the answer, GNP figures must be adjusted for any change in prices. This is done by estimating GNP for different years by using prices for only one year. As an example, suppose that all goods and services produced in each of the years listed in the table above were valued at 1964 prices. The GNP figures for each year would then be as shown in the first table on page 410.

Year	Amount (in billions) in 1964 Dollars	Year	Amount (in billions) in 1964 Dollars
1940	$246	1955	$473
1945	393	1960	531
1950	380	1965	657*

*Estimated

When GNP figures are adjusted for price changes, we see that total production was a little over $2\frac{1}{2}$ times larger in 1965 than it was in 1940. This is the actual amount by which our economy grew during that 25-year period.

Whenever dollar amounts in a chart or table have been adjusted for price changes, the amounts are said to be *in constant dollars* or *in dollars of constant purchasing power.* Or the amounts may be shown in dollars of some particular year as in the table above. When figures have not been corrected, amounts are said to be in *current dollars.*

IT IS PRODUCTION PER PERSON THAT COUNTS

Although we know that production has been increasing, we know that our population has also been increasing. The question is, "Has production increased enough to result in more goods and services per person?" In other words, has our standard of living really improved? And if so, to what extent?

The average amount produced per person is figured by dividing GNP by the population. This amount is called ***GNP per capita*** which means production or output per person.

The table below shows GNP per capita for the same six years used in the two preceding tables.

Year	GNP per Capita in 1964 Dollars	Year	GNP per Capita in 1964 Dollars
1940	$1,864	1955	$2,864
1945	2,808	1960	2,940
1950	2,508	1965	3,369*

*Estimated

You know, of course, that goods and services are not equally divided in this way. Nevertheless, GNP per capita figures do provide a means of measuring how much living standards in general have improved in the United States as a result of economic growth.

As the figures in the last table show, most of the time since 1940 total production in the United States increased at a faster rate than the population. This means that more and more goods and services have been made available for each man, woman, and child. Moreover, these figures have been adjusted for price changes, as you will notice.

INCREASED PRODUCTION MEANS INCREASED INCOME

The money that business receives from the sale of goods and services is all paid out again eventually. Some is used to replace worn-out machines and equipment; some goes for taxes; some is used to pay rent; some is used to pay interest on borrowed money; some of it is profit for the owners of business. But most of it is paid out in wages and salaries to workers. Money paid for rent, for interest, for wages, and as profits is income for those who receive it. It is the size of a person's or family's income that determines the amount of goods and services that can be obtained.

Since income is the result of production, total income rises when total production rises. With the rise in production, therefore, personal incomes have increased, as you would expect. According to the chart on page 411, approximately 80 percent of the families in the United States had incomes of less than $3,000 in 1940. Only about $5\frac{1}{2}$ percent had incomes of $5,000 or more. By 1965, only 17 percent of families had incomes of less than $3,000, while more than 66 percent had incomes of $5,000 or more. In fact, average income per family in the United States in 1965 was about $7,000. If our economy continues to grow as it has in the past, it is estimated that by 1975 average family income will be about $9,400.

Living standards, however, are measured by the

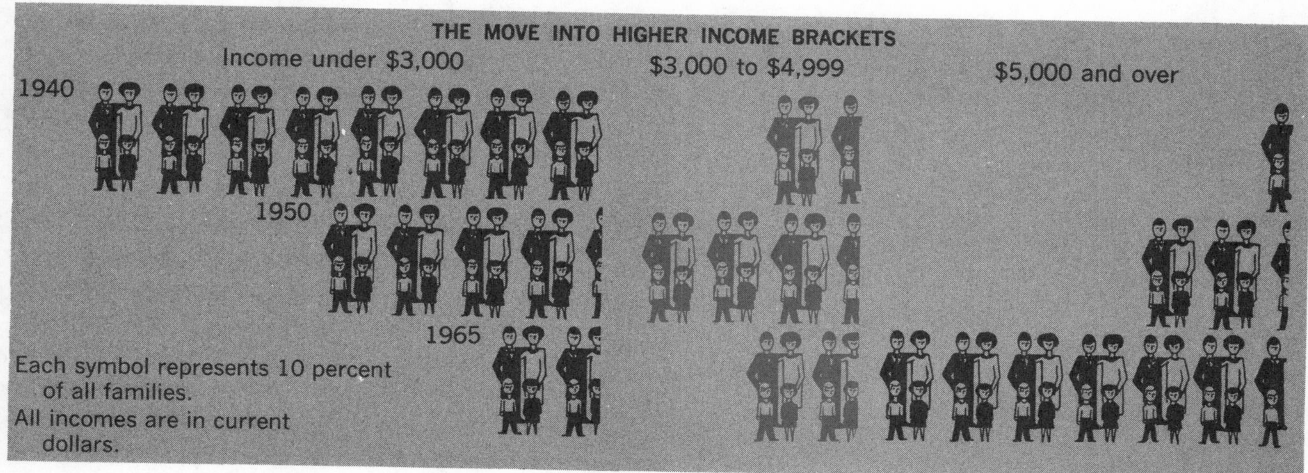

quantity and quality of goods and services people are able to buy. More important than the dollar amount of a family's income, therefore, is the amount it will buy. In terms of purchasing power, average family income in the United States was 38 percent greater in 1965 than it was in 1940. Even after paying taxes, families with average incomes could buy 26 percent more goods and services in 1965 than in 1940.

FIGURES DO NOT TELL THE WHOLE STORY

Production and income figures are useful for measuring how well our economic system is working. As you have just seen, a comparison of GNP figures from time to time will show whether production is rising or falling. But figures of this type cannot show some of the most important changes in our standard of living. One thing they do not show is the wealth of new goods available to people today that were not available a generation ago. An example is all the appliances that save work and increase the comfort of today's homes—automatic washers, dryers, floor polishers and scrubbers, food freezers, and air-conditioners. Neither do they show the increase in home ownership or the fact that most people dress better, eat better, and live longer. Nor do these figures show that within this century, the average work week has been cut from 60 hours to 40, leaving workers more leisure time. And they do not show that most workers today enjoy two or more weeks of paid vacation. Another thing they do not show is how old-age pension plans, group health insurance, and unemployment insurance have contributed to greater financial security.

Likewise, income figures do not show that in addition to what people can buy with their incomes, they have the use of goods and services provided by government. Such things as schools, parks, and libraries are available to all regardless of income.

Any way we measure its performance, the people of the United States have reason to be proud of their economic system.

Income figures do not show the increasing number of services, such as this library, that are provided by government.

Courtesy Engineering News Record

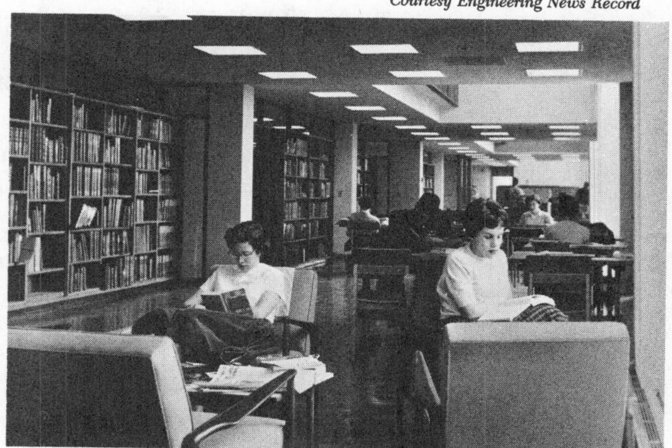

BUILDING YOUR VOCABULARY

On a separate sheet of paper, write each of the three terms listed in the left-hand column below. Read the three definitions to the right of each term. After each term, copy the definition that best describes it.

1. *final goods*
   a. Products purchased for resale to consumers
   b. Products purchased for use rather than resale
   c. Products in the final stage of production

2. *GNP per capita*
   a. The average amount produced per year
   b. The average amount produced per person
   c. The average amount produced per family

3. *output*
   a. Goods used to produce other goods or services
   b. The total amount a nation produces in a year
   c. Another name for production

CHECKING YOUR READING

1. Name one characteristic of all successful economic systems.
2. What is economic growth?
3. What is the relationship between economic growth and a nation's standard of living?
4. Name one basis used for measuring economic growth.
5. Give examples of the kinds of goods and services that are included in our gross national product.
6. Explain how GNP is figured.
7. Only final goods are counted in figuring GNP. Why?
8. What disadvantage results from measuring production in prices?
9. How are GNP figures adjusted for price changes?
10. If GNP is stated in current dollars, what does that tell you about the figures?
11. How is GNP per capita figured?
12. Why is it important to know GNP per capita?
13. Since 1940, has total production in the United States increased at a faster or a slower rate than the population? Explain.
14. Explain how personal income is affected by changes in GNP.
15. Why is the dollar amount of the average family's income not an accurate measure of a nation's standard of living?
16. In terms of purchasing power, what has happened to the average family income in the United States since 1940?
17. Give examples of important changes in our standard of living that are not shown in production and income figures.

SHARING YOUR OPINION AND EXPERIENCE

1. Why does a nation's standard of living depend on how well its economic system works?
2. What factors do you think are responsible for our remarkable economic growth?

3. Gross national product is called an "economic indicator." Why?
4. Was any of last year's GNP produced in your home? Explain.
5. Since prices change so often, why do you think we continue to measure GNP in prices?
6. A TV set made in 1965 was not sold until 1966. Should the value of the set be included in GNP for 1965 or for 1966? Why?
7. Why do you suppose the Department of Commerce estimates GNP every three months instead of only once a year?
8. In this part you learned that output per person is one important measure of the performance of our economic system. Output per man-hour is another measure that is sometimes used. What is output per man-hour?
9. Does an increase in GNP per capita mean that everybody's standard of living has improved? Explain.
10. Why might GNP also be called gross national expenditures?

PROJECTS AND PROBLEMS

1. List five ways in which young persons like you might help to increase our gross national product.
2. The bar graph below shows the GNP per capita of twelve countries in a recent year. Answer the questions following the graph.

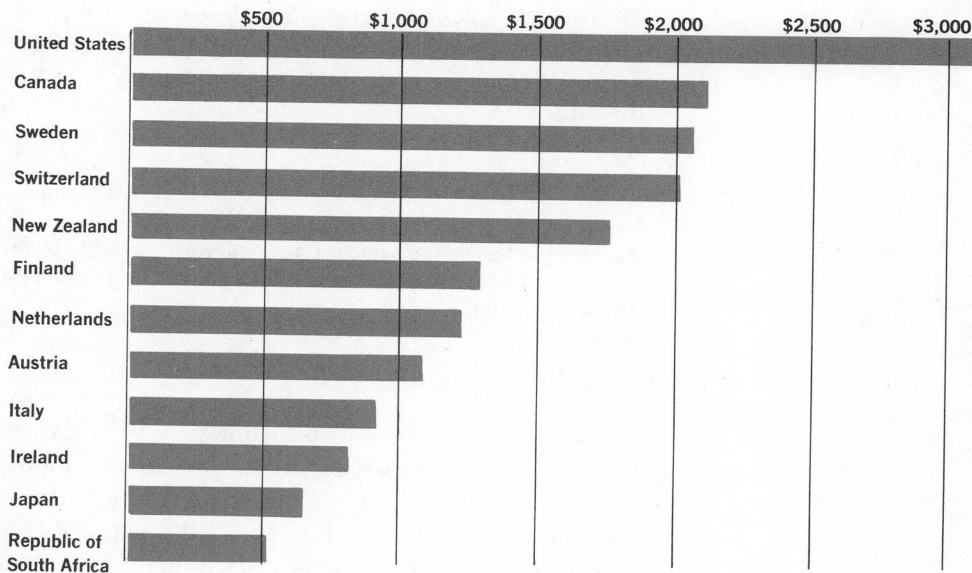

Source: National Industrial Conference Board

▪ *a.* Which country's economic system performed best in the year shown in the graph? Explain. ▪ *b.* In which countries was production per person less than half that in the United States? ▪ *c.* The GNP per capita in the United States was approximately how many times that in Japan? ▪ *d.* Can you tell from the graph whether the total output of New Zealand was larger or smaller than that of Italy? Explain. ▪ *e.* What does the graph suggest about the standard of living in Ireland as compared to Canada? ▪ *f.* Can you tell from the graph whether the economic system of any of these countries is growing? Explain.

3. Study the table at the bottom of page 410 showing GNP per capita every fifth year from 1940 to 1965 and answer the following questions.

   ▪ *a.* The GNP per capita in 1965 was approximately how many times that of 25 years earlier? ▪ *b.* During which five-year period did GNP per capita increase most? ▪ *c.* What reasons can you give for the large increase in GNP per capita during the period mentioned in question *b*? Did the increase result in a higher standard of living for the people of the United States during that period? Explain. ▪ *d.* During which five-year period did GNP per capita decline? ▪ *e.* Did our gross national product also decline during the same period? Refer to the table at the top of page 410. ▪ *f.* Did our standard of living decline during the periods mentioned in questions *d* and *e*?

4. The total annual income resulting from production is called *national income.* This income is divided among those who contribute to production. The way in which it is divided determines how the goods and services produced are shared. As you have learned, there are several ways a person might contribute to production—by working, by lending money to business enterprises, by renting property he owns, or by investing his money in a business. The table below shows how national income was divided in a recent year. Answer the questions following the table.

DIVIDING NATIONAL INCOME

Wages and salaries paid to employed workers	$361.7 billion
Income of self-employed persons (farmers, owners of single proprietorships and partnerships, and professional persons such as doctors and lawyers)	52.0
Corporation profits	57.0
Interest	26.8
Rents and royalties	12.4

   ▪ *a.* What was total national income for that year? ▪ *b.* What percent of total national income was paid in wages and salaries to employed workers? ▪ *c.* Which share of national income went to those who lent money to business enterprises? ▪ *d.* Approximately what fraction of the national income went to corporation profits? ▪ *e.* What are royalties? ▪ *f.* What part of the income paid to owners of single proprietorships and partnerships might be considered profits? ▪ g. In what ways might an employed worker share in national income in addition to wages and salaries? ▪ *h.* Do you think interest earned on a savings account would be included in national income? Explain.

5. A family's standard of living depends on the purchasing power of its income. This is known as *real income*. A family's real income depends on prices. When comparing the real incomes of families for two different periods of time, therefore, income figures must be adjusted for price changes. The table below shows a comparison of family real income for the years 1952 and 1962. Answer the questions following the table.

FAMILY REAL INCOME BY INCOME GROUPS
(in 1962 dollars)

Income Groups	*Percent of Families*	
	1952	*1962*
Under $3,000	**28**	**20**
$3,000 to $4,999	**30**	**19**
$5,000 to $6,999	**22**	**22**
$7,000 to $9,999	**13**	**21**
$10,000 to $14,999	**5**	**13**
$15,000 and over	**2**	**5**

▪ *a.* In terms of real income, which income group accounted for the largest percent of families in 1952? in 1962? ▪ *b.* Did the percent of families with real incomes of less than $3,000 increase or decrease between 1952 and 1962? What percent more or fewer families were in this group in 1962? ▪ *c.* What percent of families had real incomes between $10,000 and $14,999 in 1952? in 1962? ▪ *d.* In which income group did the greatest change occur between 1952 and 1962? ▪ *e.* In which income group did the smallest change occur between 1952 and 1962? ▪ *f.* Out of every 100 families, how many more had real incomes of $10,000 and over in 1962 than in 1952? ▪ g. Was the number of families with real incomes of $5,000 to $6,999 the same in 1952 and in 1962? Explain. ▪ *h.* What percent of families had real incomes of $5,000 and over in 1952? in 1962? ▪ *i.* Did 30 percent of the families have money incomes of $3,000 to $4,999 in 1952? Explain.

CHALLENGE PROBLEMS

1. Is it possible for a nation's standard of living to improve without an increase in its total production? Explain.
2. Our gross national product is purchased by three groups of buyers: consumers, business firms, and government. The share bought by business firms is called *investment*. Why are business expenditures called investment?
3. The economy of one nation grew 4 percent in a year while the economy of another nation grew 8 percent. Does this mean that the increase in production for the second nation was twice that for the first nation?
4. As you can see in the table on page 410, GNP measured in 1964 dollars was $13 billion less in 1950 than in 1945. This amounted to a decline of 3.3 percent. The second table on page 410, however, shows that GNP per capita declined $300, or 10.7 percent, during the same period. How do you account for the difference?

PART 45 WHY OUR ECONOMY HAS GROWN

DURING the last one hundred years production in the United States has increased at an average rate of 3 percent a year. That may not seem like much, but it is 3 percent *compounded.* In other words, it is 3 percent of a larger amount each year. In 1900, when GNP was $78.3 billion (1960 dollars), an increase of 3 percent meant an additional $2.4 billion worth of goods and services. In 1960, when GNP was $503 billion, an increase of 3 percent meant an additional $15 billion worth of goods and services. You know what happens when savings earn compound interest. At 2 percent a given amount of money will double in about 35 years. It is the same with production. Growing at an average rate of 3 percent a year, production in the United States has doubled every 20 to 25 years.

What makes this so remarkable is that it is not typical of any major portion of the world. Other economic systems have grown, to be sure; but none has a record of growth extending over as long a period as that of the United States. On the other hand, hunger is common for over half the world's population. The question is why do some economies grow rapidly; some only a little; and some not at all? What factors are responsible for the economic achievements of the United States?

ECONOMIC GROWTH DEPENDS ON MANY THINGS

If you asked ten people the reason for our extraordinary economic growth, you might get ten different answers. And all of them could be partly right. Just as the growth of crops depends on soil, sunshine, and moisture, the growth of an economic system depends on a combination of factors—so many, in fact, that only those generally thought to be most important are included here.

Courtesy Consolidated Edison Nuclear Generating Station

WE HAVE ABUNDANT NATURAL RESOURCES

Almost every success owes something to luck. In the case of the United States, you might even say it was born lucky. To produce any kind of goods, a nation must have natural resources. In distributing her resources, however, nature gave some regions more than others; and the United States happened to receive a generous share. We have rich deposits of important materials such as coal, oil, iron, and copper. We have the temperate climate that is ideal for growing many different kinds of crops. And we have a vast system of waterways that can be used for transportation as well as irrigation and electric power.

Natural resources by themselves will not make an economic system grow, it is true. Some countries have successful economies yet little in the way of natural resources. And some are poor in spite of having a good supply of them. Nevertheless, if a nation has the other things needed for economic growth, it is certainly to its advantage to have an abundance and a variety of natural resources.

WE HAVE AN EFFICIENT LABOR FORCE

One obvious reason production in the United States has increased is that the number of people working has increased. In 1900 this nation had 27.6 million workers. In 1965 it had 74.9 million employed workers. In the long run, however, the quality of a nation's labor force is more important than its size. The quality of a labor force depends on the skill of workers, their education, their health, and their attitude toward work. A lack of trained workers is one of the chief obstacles to economic growth in much of the world today.

In this country, on the other hand, the quality of labor has continually improved. Much of the credit, of course, belongs to our system of public education. Also, as our standard of living has improved in other ways, the physical fitness of workers has improved. Moreover, people in this country are not only willing to work, they want to work. It is not at all unusual for persons to hold jobs even though they have no real need for income.

Courtesy U.S. Steel

This new laborsaving machine drives 32 nails into a panel with one stroke. Developments such as this one are one of the reasons why production is increasing in the United States.

WE HAVE A WEALTH OF CAPITAL

About half the gain in our nation's production can be traced to one factor—an increase in productivity. ***Productivity*** refers to the rate of production, or the average amount produced per worker in an hour. No matter how ambitious people are, the amount they can produce in an hour is small if they work only with their hands. One of the most striking differences between wealthy and poor countries is the quantity and quality of their tools and machines. These man-made aids to production are the productive resource called *capital.*

Year after year business firms in the United States have added to their supply of capital. It is estimated that for every worker there are now 49 machines helping to produce goods and services. Moreover, they are used in almost every kind of production—in factories, on farms, and in offices. So much have they speeded up production that the average factory worker today turns out six times more in an hour than a worker did in 1850; nearly 4 times as much as in 1900. A century ago one farm worker could tend 21 acres of crops; by 1930 one worker took care of 34 acres. In 1960 the proportion was one worker to 56 acres.

The use of machines not only made it possible to produce goods in less time, it made possible a greater variety of goods and services. The reason is that, as machines took over more and more of the work load in one kind of production, workers became available for other kinds of production.

WE HAVE GOOD SYSTEMS OF TRANSPORTATION AND COMMUNICATION

Of all the machines that have helped to increase production, none have played a more important part than those used for transportation and communication—railroads, steamships, automobiles, trucks, airplanes, the telephone, telegraph, television, and radio. These, too, save work time. Good means of transportation make it possible to move a larger amount of goods more rapidly. Swift methods of communication multiply the amount of business that can be transacted in a given period of time. Both speed up production just as surely as the machines used in factories. Over the years, this country has continually improved and expanded its systems of transportation and communication to keep up with increases in other kinds of production. This has been a major factor in its economic growth.

WE HAVE LEARNED TO PRODUCE

Efficient production requires a special kind of knowledge. Without it, the usefulness of natural resources would remain undiscovered. Machines would never be invented. Coal, oil, water, and gas would never be turned into power to drive the machines. The knowledge required for production is called ***technology.*** Technology is a fund of knowledge that grows as scientists and engineers add to what is already known about production.

The United States is recognized the world over for its excellent technology. It has resulted in improved methods of production such as the assembly line used in mass production. It has led to the development of new substances such as plastics, synthetic rubber, and man-made fibers like nylon, Orlon, and Acrilan. It has brought us a seemingly endless abundance of new products. It has uncovered new sources of energy such as atomic power. And it has given us machines so automatic that they can do a whole series of operations almost without human aid. This is called ***automation.*** A familiar example of automation is the dial telephone.

The use of automated equipment is spreading rapidly throughout the business world. Banks use it to sort and handle checks. The government uses it to handle the mountains of record keeping required to operate its social security program. Hospitals and doctors use it to diagnose illnesses. Automation not only reduces the amount of time needed to produce goods and services, in many cases it does

This airplane, especially adapted to handle freight, is a part of our steadily improving transportation system.

Courtesy United Air Lines

jobs that human beings cannot do. It has made space exploration possible. It operates underwater mining equipment. It controls the temperatures in bakeries and steel mills.

WE HAVE BEEN WILLING TO SAVE

To improve or add to our supply of capital takes more than know-how. It also takes money. Where does this money come from? Most of it comes from savings. Some of it is savings that people have invested in the stocks and bonds of corporations. Some of it is savings held by banks and insurance companies that these institutions then lend to or invest in business enterprises. Another important source of money for capital is retained earnings. Perhaps you remember that a corporation does not usually pay out all of its profits to its stockholders. It saves a portion of them to reinvest in the corporation. These savings are called ***retained earnings.*** During the last twenty years or so, nearly two-thirds of the new capital goods acquired by business have been bought with retained earnings.

Courtesy NASA

Automation plays an important role in the Mercury Control Center. The large board indicates the planned orbital flight path of an astronaut.

Because individuals and business firms have been willing to save and invest, the United States has the largest and best supply of capital goods in the world today.

WE HAVE INCREASED OUR ABILITY TO CONSUME

The amount business produces depends on demand, or the amount people buy. For every increase in production, therefore, there must be an increase in demand. In other words, mass production depends on mass consumption. As our productivity increased, two things happened to boost demand. One of them you already know. It is the fact that as total production increased, workers' incomes increased. Also as productivity increased, the cost of producing goods fell. Back in the days when tin cans were made by hand, for example, one man could turn out only six an hour. Not very many people could afford to buy them; and those who could, used them over and over. Today thousands of things are packed and sold in tin cans because one machine can produce 21,000 an hour.

Higher wages together with lower prices gave consumers more purchasing power. This increased purchasing power enlarged consumer demand. It made possible the mass market needed to support mass production. Something else that made possible a mass market was an increase in the use of consumer credit, especially installment credit. It was this type of credit, you remember, that helped to enlarge the demand for automobiles and other durable goods.

Transportation and communication also contributed to the development of a mass market. As our system of transportation improved, the cost of transporting goods came down. This meant that producers could turn out goods on a large scale and sell them nationwide. It also enabled regions that specialize in the production of one or a few things to sell their products all over the country instead of just nearby. Using such mass-communication methods as newspapers, magazines, radio, and TV, producers can advertise to let millions of buyers know what they have to sell. From your own experience you know how this advertising stimulates the demand for goods and services.

OUR GOVERNMENT HAS ENCOURAGED THE GROWTH OF FREE ENTERPRISE

Ninety percent of the goods and services produced in this country are produced by privately owned business enterprises. To a large extent, therefore, it is the owners and managers of business who are responsible for economic growth. It is their decisions that determine how efficiently goods and services are produced. Nevertheless, nothing is more important to the successful operation of business than a strong and stable government. In countries where the government in power today may be overthrown tomorrow, few people would risk their money in a business venture.

The government of the United States has encouraged the growth of our private enterprise system in many ways. From the very start, the Constitution included a provision prohibiting tariffs on goods moving from one state to another. Otherwise, each state might have tried to protect its own producers from competition by taxing goods brought in from other states. As you can understand, this would have been an obstacle to trade between the various states. In the early days government provided a further boost to trade by building canals. Later it provided the land for the railroads. Today it is helping to build highways.

The government encourages risk taking by granting protection for new ideas through patents and copyrights. A ***patent*** gives its owner exclusive right to his invention or idea for 17 years. This means that no one else can make use of his idea during that time without his consent. A ***copyright*** is similar to a patent except that it protects literary, musical, or art works. In the front of this book, you will find a statement of the copyright. The purpose of patents and copyrights is to give persons who have spent money and time developing their ideas the chance to profit from their work. Only in this way is the public certain to obtain the full benefit of new goods and services.

WE HAVE ECONOMIC FREEDOM

No one knows for sure how much of our economic growth is the result of our having a free enterprise system. But neither would anyone deny that freedom to make our own economic decisions has contributed greatly to our economic progress. The effect of freedom on productivity was demonstrated not long ago in Russia where all farmland is owned by the government. In return for working on the large government-owned farms, each Russian farmer was given a plot of land, smaller than an acre, for his private use. On these plots, however, more was produced per acre than on the farms operated for the government.

If the growth of our economy proves anything, it is this. When people are free to profit from their own work and ideas, there is hardly any limit to what they can accomplish.

BUILDING YOUR VOCABULARY

Copy the sentences given below, completing each one by replacing the question mark with the appropriate term from the column at the left.

automation
copyright
patent
productivity
retained earnings
technology

1. The knowledge required for efficient production is ? .
2. The average amount produced per worker in an hour is ? .
3. The use of machines to complete a series of operations with little or no human aid is ? .
4. The exclusive right to an idea or invention is a ? .
5. The profits of a corporation that are kept and used in the business are ? .
6. The exclusive right to literary, musical, or art works is a ? .

CHECKING YOUR READING

1. Production in the United States has increased at an average rate of 3 percent a year compounded. Explain. What has been the result of this compounding?
2. Explain how luck may have contributed to the economic growth of the United States.
3. What determines the quality of a labor force?
4. What are some of the reasons why the quality of labor in this country has continually improved?
5. What single factor has been responsible for about half the gain in our nation's production?
6. What is one of the most striking differences between wealthy countries and poor ones?
7. Why has the use of machines made possible a greater variety of goods and services?

8. How do machines that are used for transportation and communication speed up production?
9. In what ways has improved technology contributed to the growth of our economic system?
10. Give examples of the uses now being made of automated equipment.
11. Where does the money come from that is used to improve and to add to our supply of capital.
12. During the past twenty years, what has been the most important single source of money for new capital goods?
13. Explain why mass consumption is necessary if we are to have mass production.
14. As our productivity has increased, what two things have happened to boost demand?
15. How did the use of credit help to create a mass market?
16. Explain how improved means of transportation and communication contributed to the development of a mass market.
17. Give examples of how the government has encouraged the growth of our free enterprise system.
18. What has the growth of our economy proved about the free enterprise system?

SHARING YOUR OPINION AND EXPERIENCE

1. Natural resources by themselves will not make an economic system grow. Why?
2. How has our system of public education contributed to the economic growth of the United States?
3. Today the average factory worker turns out four times more in an hour than a worker did in 1900. Do you think it is possible to increase productivity even more? If so, how?
4. Give examples of machines that save work time in the home.
5. Give examples of how the use of machines in your school aids both teaching and learning.
6. Is there a limit to how much the people of a nation can consume?
7. How do the stockholders benefit when some of the profits of a corporation are reinvested in the business?
8. Would economic growth be possible if people did not save? Explain.
9. How do you suppose our economic system would be affected if the government stopped granting patents and copyrights?
10. Which do you think is more important to economic growth—natural resources, labor, or capital? Give reasons for your answer.

PROJECTS AND PROBLEMS

1. One reason the economic system of the United States has grown is that we have had abundant natural resources. List 10 natural resources that have been important to our economic growth.
2. The countries of the world that have had the greatest economic growth are those in which the general level of education is highest. The fact that education

is so widespread in the United States, therefore, has played an important part in its economic growth. The number of pupils enrolled in school has increased as the population has increased. But more important, the percent of the population enrolled in school has also increased as shown in the chart below. Following the chart are some questions for you to answer.

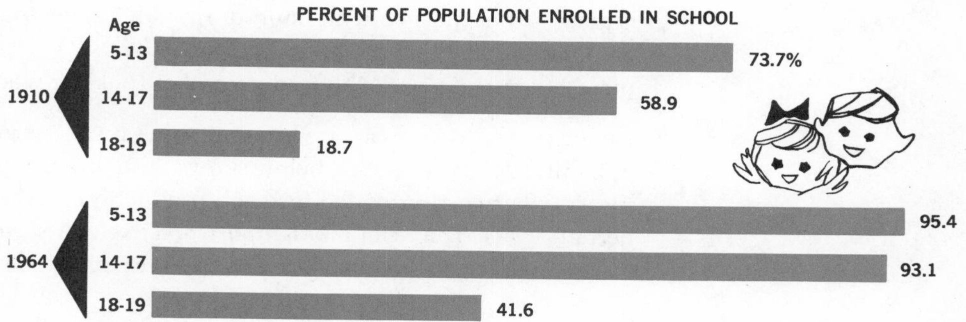

▪ *a.* Did the percent of the population enrolled in school increase for all age groups between 1910 and 1964? ▪ *b.* For which age group did the percent enrolled in school increase most? ▪ *c.* For which age group was the percent enrolled in school in 1964 more than double that for 1910? ▪ *d.* In 1910 there were 7,220,000 persons between the ages of 14 and 17 in the United States. How many of these were enrolled in school? ▪ *e.* In 1964 there were 13,978,000 persons between the ages of 14 and 17 in the United States. How many of these were enrolled in school? ▪ *f.* From 1910 to 1964 what was the increase in the percent of the age 14 to 17 population enrolled in school? ▪ *g.* The number of persons between the ages of 14 and 17 in the United States in 1964 was approximately how many times as large as that in 1910? ▪ *h.* The number of persons age 14 to 17 enrolled in school in 1964 was approximately how many times greater than the number enrolled in 1910?

3. About half of this nation's economic growth is the result of increases in productivity or output per man-hour of work. The table below shows increases in gross national product for different periods from 1909 to 1959 and increases in output per man-hour for the same periods. Answer the questions following the table.

CHANGES IN GROSS NATIONAL PRODUCT AND OUTPUT PER MAN-HOUR, 1909–1959

Year	*Gross National Product (billions of 1959 dollars)*	*Output per Man-hour (1959 dollars)*
1909	$117.0	$1.24
1929	203.6	1.68
1939	211.5	2.02
1949	328.2	2.57
1959	482.8	3.42

▪ *a.* During which period of years did gross national product increase the least? ▪ *b.* During which period of years did gross national product increase the most? ▪ *c.* During which period did output per man-hour increase least? ▪ *d.* During which period did output per man-hour increase most? ▪ *e.* Are your answers to "*c*" and "*d*" the same as those for "*a*" and "*b*"? ▪ *f.* What was the percent of increase in gross national product from 1909 to 1959? ▪ *g.* What was the percent of increase in output per man-hour during the same period? ▪ *h.* Are the dollar amounts in the table shown in constant dollars? ▪ *i.* Does the table show actual increases in gross national product and output per man-hour?

4. Increases in productivity are brought about by an increase in the use of machines or capital goods. The table below shows the average amount of capital, measured by its dollar cost, provided for each production worker in the United States for certain years. The term *production worker* refers to workers directly engaged in producing goods. Following the table are some questions for you to answer.

AVERAGE AMOUNT OF CAPITAL PER PRODUCTION WORKER

Year	*Amount (dollars)*
1930	7,741
1935	5,648
1940	5,478
1945	6,928
1950	8,280
1955	11,498
1960	18,227

▪ *a.* During which 5-year period did the amount of capital per worker increase most? ▪ *b.* What was the increase in amount of capital per worker during the 20-year period between 1930 and 1950? What was the percent of increase? ▪ *c.* How much did the amount of capital per worker increase in the 10 years between 1950 and 1960? What was the percent of increase? ▪ *d.* According to the table, during which 5-year periods did the amount of capital per worker decrease? ▪ *e.* Have the dollar amounts in the table been adjusted for changes in prices during the 30 years shown? ▪ *f.* According to the table, the average amount of capital per worker, as measured by its dollar cost, more than doubled between 1930 and 1960. Do you think the actual supply of capital per worker increased more or less than the figures in the table indicate? Explain.

5. The figures in the table at the top of page 425 show changes in the percent of work done by men, by machines, and by animals from 1850 to 1950. Present this information in the form of two circle graphs similar to those in No. 6 of the Projects and Problems section of Part 41 on page 386.

CHANGES IN PERCENT OF WORK DONE

	Percent of Work in 1850	*Percent of Work in 1950*
Men	15	4
Machines	6	92
Horses and mules	79	4

6. Another major factor in the economic growth of the United States has been the improvement in our communication and transportation systems. On the left half of a sheet of paper, list 5 types of businesses that depend on rapid communications for their success. On the right half, list 5 types of businesses whose success depends on rapid transportation.

CHALLENGE PROBLEMS

1. As the productivity of workers has increased, their wages have increased. The best measure of wages is the amount an hour's work will buy. The table below shows the average work time required to buy 12 different items in the 1960's compared with 1948. Answer the questions following the table.

AVERAGE WORK TIME REQUIRED TO BUY

Item	*1948*	*1960's*
New car	892½ hr.	975 hr.
Plane trip (New York to Chicago)	32⅔ hr.	23½ hr.
Loaf of bread	5¾ min.	5½ min.
10 lbs. potatoes	23 min.	17 min.
1 lb. bacon	34 min.	18½ min.
Man's haircut	55½ min.	45 min.
Electric refrigerator	178½ hr.	71 hr.
Washing machine	80 hr.	34½ hr.
Man's wool suit	26 hr.	17 hr.
Vacuum cleaner	37 hr.	26 hr.
Auto tire	9¾ hr.	6½ hr.

▪ *a.* In terms of work time required to buy them, did all items in the list cost less in the 1960's than in 1948? List the exception(s). ▪ *b.* For which item did the cost in work time change least from 1948 to the 1960's? ▪ *c.* For which item did the cost in work time decrease most from 1948 to the 1960's? ▪ *d.* How much less work time was required to buy a plane trip from New York to Chicago in the 1960's than in 1948? ▪ *e.* If the table showed a comparison between 1938 and the 1960's, do you think the decrease in work time required to buy the items would be greater or smaller? Explain. ▪ *f.* If the comparison were made between 1958 and the 1960's, do you think the decreases would be greater or smaller? Explain. ▪ *g.* Are workers financially better off today than they were in 1938? in 1948? in 1958?

PART 46 THE PROBLEM OF MAINTAINING ECONOMIC GROWTH

Courtesy Turner Construction Company

MAINTAINING economic growth is a problem for all nations. People everywhere want to live better than they do now. In order to have a better life, they must produce more. Considering how rapidly our economy has grown, you might wonder why future growth is a matter for concern in the United States. It is because economic growth is not something that can be taken for granted. When you hear that production in this country has been increasing at an *average* rate of 3 percent a year, you know that some years it rose more than that. You also know that some years it did not increase that much. In fact, there were years when our economy did not grow at all and years when production actually fell. This can be seen in the graph on the following page. Notice that the line representing gross national product has generally been moving upward. The rise, however, has been uneven. In other words, our economy grew for a while and then dropped back.

What caused this unevenness in our economic growth? What is being done in this country to achieve a more steady growth?

DEPRESSIONS AND RECESSIONS THREATEN ECONOMIC GROWTH

The unevenness in our economic growth is the result of business cycles. A ***business cycle*** is a series of changes in business activity. Following a period of prosperity, business activity gradually slows down until a recession or depression is reached. Eventually business picks up again until prosperity is restored. This completes the cycle. These cycles, as you know, are characteristic of our economic system.

As you might have guessed, the interruptions in our economic growth occurred during periods of recession or depression. Notice the big dip in production that took place during the depression of the 1930's. It has been estimated that the slowdown in production during that period deprived the nation of more than $600 billion worth of goods and services.

Recessions Occur When Spending Is Less Than Production

Recessions and depressions are not caused by any lack of ability to produce. They are caused by a lack of demand. In the long run, total production depends on total spending. Total spending is made up of (1) the amounts consumers spend for goods and services; (2) the amounts business firms spend for new plants, buildings, machines, and materials; and (3) the amounts Federal, state, and local governments spend for goods and services.

Most goods, of course, are produced before they are sold; and the quantity produced depends on how much business firms think consumers, government, and other business firms will buy. If they do not buy all that has been produced, some business firms will be left with more goods on hand than they can sell at a profit. When that happens, production is cut back and some workers lose their jobs and incomes. Then total spending is even less than before. In this way a recession spreads. Economic growth is halted. Some recessions are worse than others. When a recession becomes widespread and long-lasting, it is called a *depression*.

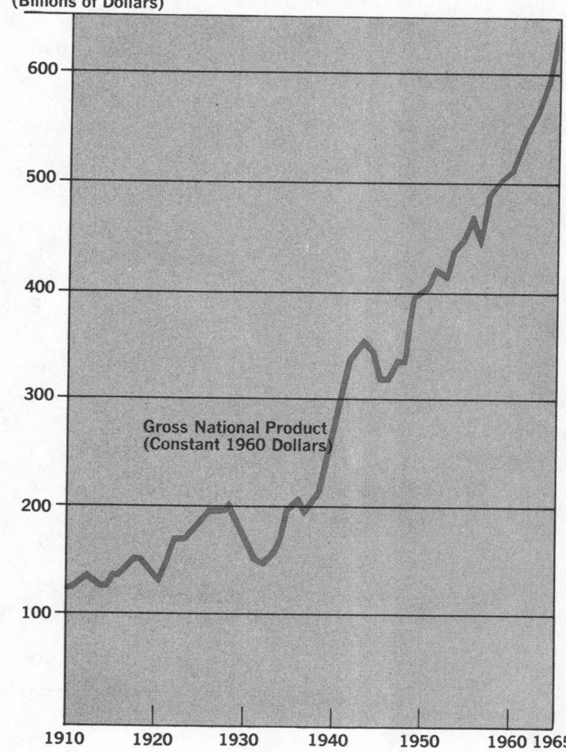

TOO MUCH SPENDING CAN RESULT IN INFLATION

Depression is the down side of the business cycle. The up side is prosperity. Growth and prosperity go hand in hand. When production, spending, and employment are rising, however, the nation has to guard against another problem—inflation, or a general increase in prices. Inflation is often described as "too much money chasing too few goods." This means that total spending by consumers, business, and government is taking place at a faster rate than the production of goods and services.

Since production takes place in response to demand or spending, production increases when spending increases. Additional workers are hired, total income increases, and spending increases still more. Business is then encouraged to increase production further. But there is a limit to how much can be produced with our present resources. When that limit is reached, additional spending pushes prices up as buyers compete with one another for the goods and services that are available. To increase production, business firms must build bigger plants and buy additional machines and equipment. But if spending is already great enough to cause inflation, this extra spending by business helps to push prices even higher.

How can spending increase faster than production? There are several ways. One is when buyers spend money that they have saved in the past. An-

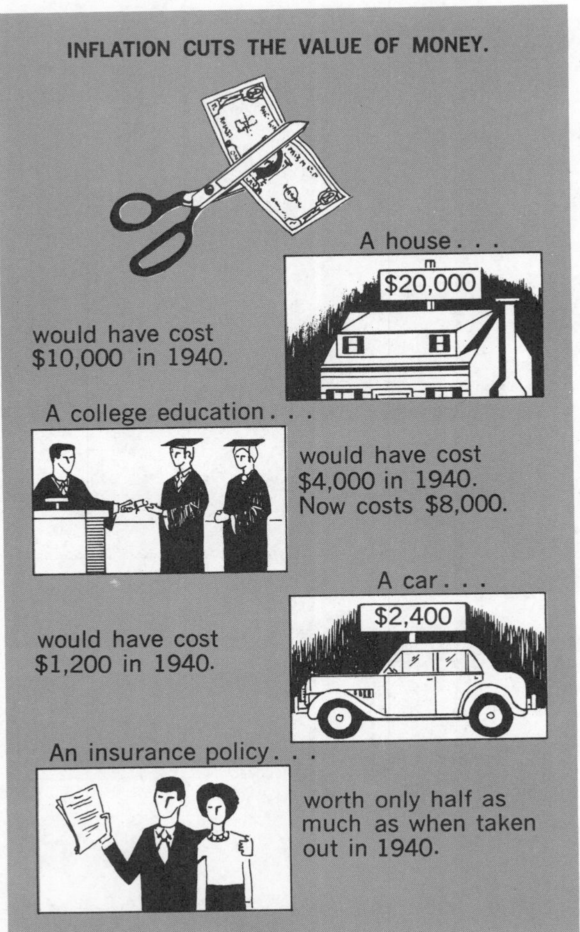

other is when they buy on credit.

INFLATION CUTS THE VALUE OF MONEY.
A house . . .
$20,000
would have cost $10,000 in 1940.
A college education . . .
would have cost $4,000 in 1940. Now costs $8,000.
A car . . .
$2,400
would have cost $1,200 in 1940.
An insurance policy . . .
worth only half as much as when taken out in 1940.

Prices may advance rapidly; or they may rise slowly over a long period. Like a recession, however, inflation can spread. As prices rise, workers may demand higher wages. If their demands are met, business firms may raise prices again to cover the cost of higher wages. This in turn leads to demands for still higher wages.

Why Is Inflation Harmful?

Inflation has many undesirable effects. One is that it changes the way goods and services are divided. When prices rise, money loses some of its purchasing power; that is to say, it will not buy as much as before. Although the incomes of many workers rise when prices rise, their living costs go up just as fast. Thus, in spite of having higher incomes, their living standards do not improve. For workers whose incomes do not keep up with rising prices and for retired persons living on fixed incomes, inflation means a lower standard of living. Only the few whose incomes rise faster than prices are able to improve their standard of living. When economic growth is accompanied by inflation, therefore, it does not mean a generally higher standard of living.

Inflation makes it difficult to build financial security. The reason is that when prices are rising, money invested in savings accounts, savings bonds, and life insurance decreases in value. In fact, continued inflation might discourage saving. This could interfere with our future economic growth. As you will recall, people's willingness to save has been one of the factors responsible for our past growth.

Perhaps the greatest danger of inflation is that, if not controlled, it could bring on a recession. When spending is heavy enough to cause inflation, business firms may overestimate the amount consumers, government, and other business firms will buy. As a result, they produce more than they can sell. Then they have to cut down on the amount they produce. As production is reduced, some workers are laid off; and the stage is set for a recession.

SPENDING AND PRODUCTION MUST RISE TOGETHER

To keep our economy growing at an even pace with no general increase in prices, production and spending must rise at the same rate. This balance is described as ***economic stability.*** Economic stability is not easy to maintain in a free enterprise system where consumers, workers, and business enterprises are permitted to make their own economic decisions. Nevertheless, through their Federal government the people of the United States are working to make their economic system more stable.

Since recession is caused by too little spending,

the measures used to check it are meant to increase total spending. Inflation, on the other hand, is the result of too much spending. The measures used to check it, therefore, are meant to decrease total spending.

Some Measures Work Automatically

Some measures to control recession and inflation are now built into our economic system. These go to work automatically. One antirecession measure that you already know about is unemployment insurance. Unemployment insurance provides income to workers who lose their jobs when production slows down. By maintaining the purchasing power of jobless workers, unemployment benefits help to prevent the spread of a recession.

Income taxes provide some control over inflation. The reason is that as personal incomes rise, they are taxed at a higher rate. As you may recall, this type of tax is called a progressive tax. Thus, when workers' wages increase, all of the increase is not available for spending.

Some Measures Must Be Put Into Effect

In addition to automatic controls, the Federal government has other means of checking recession or inflation. One way is through its power to spend and tax. As you learned earlier, for example, when recession threatens, the government may increase its own spending. Or it may put more money directly into the hands of consumers by cutting income taxes. To halt inflation, the same measures may be used in reverse. The government may reduce its own spending; or it may reduce consumer spending by raising taxes.

Spending and taxing by the government are called ***fiscal policy.*** Fiscal is similar in meaning to "financial." Fiscal policy is related to the financing of government.

The government may also encourage or discourage spending by increasing or decreasing the amount of money commercial banks may lend. This is done through the Federal Reserve system which is discussed on pages 186 and 187. Changing the amount banks may lend is called ***monetary policy.*** The word ***monetary,*** of course, pertains to money.

The measures that make up fiscal and monetary policies must be used with caution. When steps are taken to increase spending during a recession, there is always a danger that it will increase too much. Then inflation may result. Similarly, measures used

Paul E. Glines photo

These young men are receiving specialized training in a Job Corps Center to give them the kinds of skills business needs.

to slow down spending in an effort to control inflation may cause production to slow down and cause some workers to lose their jobs. As you learned in Part 7 (page 57), it is the responsibility of the President's Council of Economic Advisers to recommend when and to what extent these measures should be used.

One of the most important things to understand about fiscal and monetary policies is that they influence the actions of consumers, workers, and business enterprises. But they do not control them. Individuals are still free to make their own economic decisions.

HOW EFFECTIVE HAVE OUR EFFORTS TO ACHIEVE ECONOMIC STABILITY BEEN?

Since 1946 the United States has had several recessions. Spending slowed down, production fell in some industries, and unemployment rose. But none of these recessions developed into anything like the depression of the 30's or those of earlier years. Thus, it appears that we are making progress in our efforts to prevent depressions.

This country's record for controlling inflation, on the other hand, is not quite as good. From 1939 to 1963, the cost of living rose 119 percent. The term ***cost of living*** refers to the prices of consumer goods in general. This increase of 119 percent in the cost of living means that in 1963 a consumer needed $2.19 to buy what $1 bought in 1939. In other words, the cost of living more than doubled during that period. Most of this increase was the result of wars. Following World War II and during the Korean War, prices rose rapidly. In recent years the cost of living has been rising more slowly. From 1957 to July, 1965, for example, increases in the cost of living averaged about 1 percent a year.

At least the United States has made a start toward achieving greater economic stability. As more is learned about how our economic system works, perhaps we shall do better. Most important of all is that we have made progress without sacrificing our economic freedom.

ARE THERE OTHER OBSTACLES TO GROWTH?

Recession and inflation are not the only threats to economic growth, by any means. Several other things could keep our economy from growing at a satisfactory rate. One is taxes on profits. If profits are taxed too heavily, investment in business enterprises would be discouraged. Another thing that could slow down our economic growth is a shortage of workers with the kinds of skills business needs. But one of the most serious of all threats to economic growth is a shortage of natural resources.

Our population increases; many of our natural resources do not. Thus, our dwindling supply of materials must provide for a larger and larger number of people. Moreover, as total production in-

In order to supplement our natural resource of fresh water, desalting plants are being constructed in various parts of the country.

Courtesy U.S. Department of the Interior, Office of Saline Water

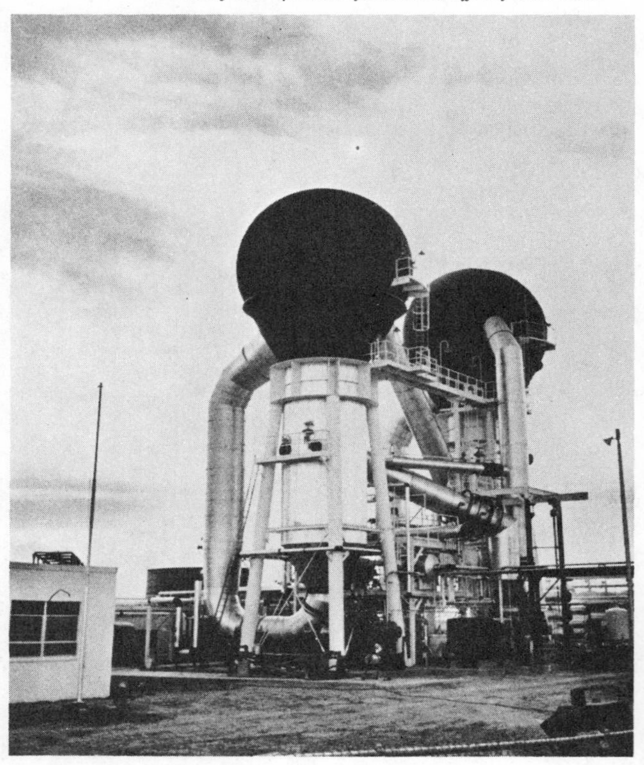

creases, our consumption of natural resources increases. How long our present supplies will continue to meet our needs will depend on how wisely they are used.

Protecting natural resources against waste is called ***conservation.*** Our state and Federal governments are working in several ways to conserve resources. The Federal government's flood control program is one example. Its attempts to convert sea water into fresh water at a reasonable cost are another. Business, too, is spending enormous sums of money in an effort to increase or extend our supply of materials. One part of these efforts is a search for new mineral deposits. Another is the development of synthetic materials that can be substituted for natural ones. Plastics are a good example. All these efforts provide additional evidence of how important technology is to economic growth.

BUILDING YOUR VOCABULARY

List the figures 1 to 7 on a sheet of paper, numbering down. Read the seven statements given below at the right; then, for each statement, select from the column at the left the term that best matches it in meaning. Write this term next to the appropriate number.

business cycle	1. Spending and taxing by the government
conservation	2. Steady economic growth with no general increase in prices
cost of living	3. A series of changes in business activity
economic stability	4. Pertaining to money
fiscal policy	5. Prices of consumer goods in general
monetary	6. Control over the amount banks may lend
monetary policy	7. Protecting natural resources against waste

CHECKING YOUR READING

1. Since our economy has grown so rapidly in the past, why should we be concerned about its future growth?
2. Explain the changes that take place in business activity during a business cycle.
3. What is one leading cause of recessions and depressions?
4. The spending of what three groups makes up total spending for the United States?
5. Who decides the quantity of goods that will be produced? On what is the decision based?
6. What usually happens when total spending is less than total production?
7. What problem does an economic system have to guard against during periods of prosperity?
8. What usually happens when total spending increases at a faster rate than total production?
9. Explain how spending can increase faster than production.
10. What are some of the harmful effects of inflation?
11. Give examples of measures that work automatically to control recession and inflation.
12. Explain how fiscal policy and monetary policy may be used to help control recession and inflation.

13. Why should fiscal and monetary policies be used with caution?
14. What is the one big advantage of fiscal and monetary policies?
15. What evidence is there that we are making some progress in our efforts to prevent depressions?
16. What has been the major cause of the inflation that has taken place in the United States since 1939?
17. What are some threats to economic growth, other than recession and inflation?
18. What is now being done to conserve our natural resources?

SHARING YOUR OPINION AND EXPERIENCE

1. Why is there a limit to how much can be produced with our present resources?
2. Does it make any difference what business produces as long as people buy what is produced?
3. Why is it important that some of our productive resources be used for the production of capital goods?
4. During World War II the Federal government controlled prices, wages, and rents by not allowing them to rise any higher than they were on a certain date. It also rationed scarce consumer goods such as sugar, coffee, meat, canned goods, butter, shoes, gasoline, and tires as well as vital producer goods such as steel. Why do you think the government did this?
5. Do you think the government should continue to control prices and wages? Give reasons for your answer.
6. Following tax cuts, tax collections by the Federal government have actually increased. Following an $11 billion tax cut in 1964, for example, Federal tax collections rose almost $4 billion. How do you explain this fact?
7. Some people are so concerned about a shortage of natural resources that they believe the nation must cut down on the amount it is now using even if it means lowering our present standard of living. Others believe that new resources and substitute materials will always be found to take care of the demands of a growing population. What is your opinion?
8. Although the nation's productive resources are limited while people's wants are unlimited, our resources are not always fully used. Explain.

PROJECTS AND PROBLEMS

1. Study the graph on page 427 and answer the following questions. ▪ *a.* How many times during the period shown on the graph did production fall? ▪ *b.* As nearly as you can determine, during which years did these interruptions in our economic growth occur? ▪ *c.* How many times during the period covered by the graph did production remain stationary; that is, it neither rose nor fell? ▪ *d.* How many of these stationary periods were followed by a drop in production? How many were followed by an increase in production? ▪ *e.* How many of the stationary periods were preceded by an increase in production? How many were preceded by decreases in production? ▪ *f.* Were any of the increases or decreases shown on the graph the result of price changes?

2. In the long run, total production depends on total spending. Because consumer purchases account for about two-thirds of total spending, consumers play an important role in determining the level of production. The bar graph below shows total consumer spending for each year, 1953 through 1964. Following the graph are questions for you to answer.

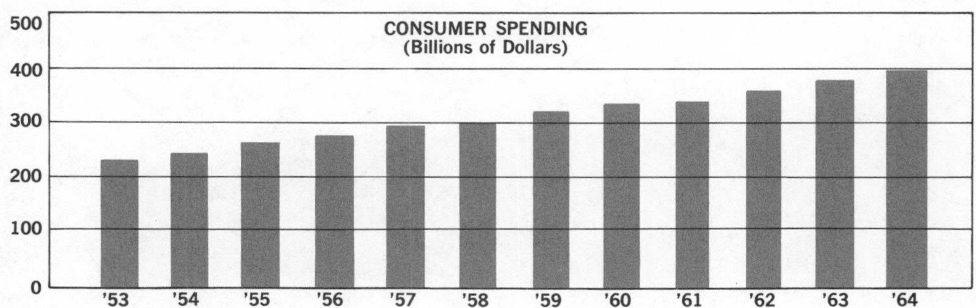

▪ *a.* Approximately how much did consumers spend in 1953? ▪ *b.* Approximately how much did consumers spend in 1964? ▪ *c.* Does the graph show any decreases in consumer spending? If so, for which year or years? ▪ *d.* Which year did consumer spending increase the most compared with the preceding year? Does the graph on page 427 show that GNP also increased during this same period? ▪ *e.* From 1953 to 1954 there was little change in consumer spending. According to the graph on page 427, what happened to GNP about that same time? ▪ *f.* The graph above shows two other periods when consumer spending changed very little, if any. Identify those periods. Does the graph on page 427 show a decrease in production during the same periods?

3. When prices in general rise, money loses some of its purchasing power. To compare prices for different periods of time, the government uses what is called a *consumer price index* or *cost of living index.* This is the average amount of money needed to buy a large assortment of consumer goods and services that are bought by most middle-income families in the United States. The cost of these goods and services is estimated monthly. It is then compared with their cost at some time in the past known as the *base period.* The consumer price index for the base period is always 100. By comparing the consumer price index for any month with the base period, it is possible to measure price changes. For example, if the consumer price index is 102 compared with the base period, it means that prices are 2 percent higher than during the base period. A 2 percent increase in prices means a decrease of 2 percent in the purchasing power of a dollar.

   The graph on page 434 shows changes in the consumer price index from 1939 to 1965. You will notice that 1957–1959 is used as the base period. This means that the price index used for comparison is the average level of prices for 1957 to 1959. Answer the questions following the graph.

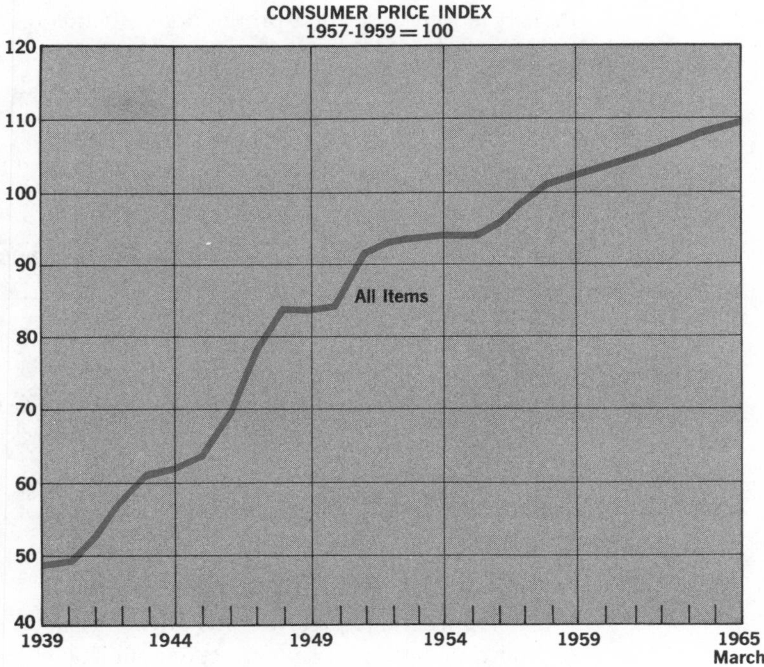

Source: National Industrial Conference Board

▪ *a.* Compared to the base period, what was the consumer price index in 1939? Does this mean that prices were higher or lower than in the base period? ▪ *b.* Approximately what year were prices double what they were in 1939? Approximately how much would a dollar have bought that year compared with 1939? ▪ *c.* When did the greatest increase in prices occur—from 1945 to 1948? from 1950 to 1951? from 1955 to 1958? ▪ *d.* The graph shows a two-year period during which prices remained fairly steady. Identify the period. ▪ *e.* Compared to the base period, what was the consumer price index in 1965? ▪ *f.* How much less purchasing power did a dollar have in 1965 than in the base period? ▪ *g.* How much did a consumer need in 1965 to buy what a dollar would have bought during the base period? ▪ *h.* How much more did a consumer need in 1965 to buy what 50 cents would have bought in 1939? ▪ *i.* Did prices rise more from 1945 to 1955 or from 1955 to 1965?

4. Few things have contributed more to our economic growth than new inventions. The invention of the steam engine, for example, started what is known in history as the *industrial revolution.* Think how the coming of the railroad stimulated trade. The automobile, the radio, the airplane, and television have all given our economic system a boost. At one time inventions were developed by one or a few individuals working on their own. Today business firms hire persons to work full time at developing new products and new ways of doing things. This work is called *research and development.* An indication of its importance is the amount of money spent on it. This is shown in the table on page 435 which lists nine industries and the

amount each spent on research and development in a recent year. Following the table are some questions for you to answer.

FUNDS SPENT ON RESEARCH AND DEVELOPMENT BY SELECTED INDUSTRIES

Industry	*Amount (million dollars)*
Food and food products	$ 108
Lumber, wood products, furniture	8
Textiles and apparel	34
Chemicals and drugs	1,151
Rubber products	126
Machinery	943
Electrical equipment and communication	2,498
Motor vehicles and other transportation equipment	858
Aircraft and missiles	4,199

Source: National Industrial Conference Board

▪ *a.* What was the total amount spent on research and development by the industries listed in the table? ▪ *b.* Which industry spent the largest amount? What percent was this of the total amount spent? ▪ *c.* Compared to the other industries listed, would you say that the one that spent the largest amount on research and development was a new or an old industry? ▪ *d.* In which industry was the smallest amount spent on research and development? Compared to the other industries listed in the table, was this a new or an old industry? ▪ *e.* Which industry spent the second largest amount on research and development? Is this industry important to the industry mentioned in question "*b*"? ▪ *f.* Approximately what portion of the total amount spent on research and development was spent by the two industries that spent the largest amount?

5. New inventions that are put to work are called *innovations.* Some innovations have a greater effect on business than others. Select some innovation of the past that has had a noticeable effect on business. Write a report about it, explaining the way or ways in which it has stimulated business activity. For example, did it create a need for other kinds of business or products? If so, how?

CHALLENGE PROBLEMS

1. During periods of war, production is at a high level. Yet war is considered an enemy of growth because it uses up valuable resources without adding to our total wealth. Explain.
2. In Projects and Problems No. 3, there is a line graph showing price changes from 1939 to 1965. Suppose the year 1939 had been used as the base period, what would the consumer price index have been in 1965?
3. Some people claim that investment in people is more important to the nation's future economic growth than any other single thing. How can a nation invest in its people?

CONTENTS OF UNIT 11

Unit 11 / Labor and American Business

PART 47 OUR LABOR FORCE

Ewing Galloway

BY now you should understand pretty well the place of business in our economic system. You should also have a good idea of how you fit into the picture as a consumer. Before long, however, you will be assuming another role—that of a full-time producer. You will become a member of what is known as the *labor force.* Almost everyone works for a living sometime in his life.

In a free enterprise system, you may choose your occupation. You may work for someone else or you may go into business for yourself. Your choice is limited in some ways, to be sure. Not everyone has the musical talent to play in a symphony orchestra. To become a doctor, lawyer, engineer, or teacher requires a long and costly preparation. Going into business takes more money than most individuals have. Nevertheless, our economic system offers countless opportunities for employment. Of all the decisions you will ever make, one of the most important will be the choice of an occupation. To choose wisely, you will need some knowledge of the world of work.

Who or what is the labor force? What effect is automation having on job requirements? Why is economic growth important to young people entering the labor force?

WHO MAKES UP THE LABOR FORCE?

Everyone 14 years of age or over who is working or looking for work, is a member of the ***labor force.*** It makes no difference whether he is a bank president or a circus clown; an astronaut or a taxi driver; a teacher or a farmer; whether he works a few hours a day or many; or whether he is working at all, as long as he is looking for a job.

In a recent year 81 million persons were in the labor force. Of this number 2.5 million were in the Armed Forces. The rest were *civilians,* which is

FUTURE EMPLOYMENT OPPORTUNITIES

Teaching

Office workers

Retail clerks

Service industries

Construction

Repair businesses

Airline stewardess

Medical care

what people not in military service are called. Among the civilian members of the labor force, 74.9 million had jobs and 3.6 million were unemployed. In the United States a person is considered unemployed if he is over 14 and without a job but looking for a job.

As the nation's population has increased, the number of persons in the labor force has increased. The percent of the population in the labor force has also increased. In 1900, for example, 36 percent of the population was in the labor force. In 1965, it was 42 percent. This increase in proportion is largely the result of an increase in the number of women working. In 1900, about one-fifth of the labor force were women. By 1965, slightly more than one-third of the labor force were women.

OCCUPATIONS OF THE LABOR FORCE HAVE CHANGED

In Part 45 you learned how technology has changed the way goods and services are produced. It has also changed the kinds of work people do. In 1900, nearly one-third of our labor force worked on farms. Since then, the proportion of farm workers in the labor force has dwindled to less than one in ten. Because of improved methods of farming and the use of mechanical equipment, fewer workers are needed to produce our food supply.

For a long time many of those who left the farm took factory jobs in the city. In recent years, however, the proportion of the labor force needed to do factory work has been decreasing. This is not because a smaller amount of goods is being manufactured. Total factory production has actually increased; but the opportunities for factory employment have not. This is because many factory jobs have been eliminated by automation.

As opportunities for employment have decreased in some occupations, they have increased in others. The demand is great for both sales and office workers. Even in manufacturing, office employment has increased. While the proportion of the labor force producing goods has declined, the proportion producing services has grown larger. In fact, there are now more people producing services in the United States than people producing goods.

A shift away from one kind of employment and toward others is called an ***employment trend.*** To persons preparing to enter the labor force, employment trends are very important.

Courtesy Florida Citrus Commission

Orange harvesting is a seasonal occupation. Many of the workers go north in the summer to harvest berries and peaches.

WHAT DETERMINES OPPORTUNITIES FOR EMPLOYMENT?

In general, employment opportunities depend on production. Jobs are most plentiful when business is good and production is high. When production slows down, fewer workers are needed. During a recession or depression, unemployment may rise quite high. In 1933, for example, more than one-fourth of the labor force was unemployed. In 1958, when there was a mild business recession, 6.8 percent of the labor force was unemployed. Unemployment resulting from a depression or recession is called ***cyclical unemployment.*** The name is taken from business cycles, the upswings and downswings in business activity that occur every so often.

THERE IS ALWAYS SOME UNEMPLOYMENT

In a free enterprise system, there is a certain amount of unemployment even during prosperity. As long as workers are allowed to choose their jobs and to change jobs if they wish, some will quit their jobs and go in search of others. Until they find new jobs, or give up looking, they are considered unemployed. The only way to eliminate unemployment entirely would be to assign workers to their jobs.

Unemployment also results from the fact that some kinds of work are seasonal. In the winter months, for example, farm jobs all but disappear, except in the far south. In late summer, automobile workers are laid off while factories are made ready for the production of the next year's models. Department stores hire extra workers before Christmas, then let them go when the rush is over. Unemployment resulting from seasonal changes in production is called ***seasonal unemployment.***

Sometimes a change in consumer demand reduces job opportunities in one firm or industry. Everyone has heard how large numbers of carriage workers lost their jobs when consumers started to buy automobiles. Where regions specialize, a lack of demand for the principal product may affect employment opportunities in an entire community. For example, when the demand for coal fell, large portions of the working population in coal-mining communities became unemployed. This, in turn, resulted in a decrease in demand for practically everything else in the community, so that there was little opportunity for any kind of employment. Regions that offer little or no opportunity for employment are called ***depressed areas.***

Some unemployment is ***technological,*** which means that workers' jobs have been taken over by machines. Displacement of workers by automation is technological unemployment.

HOW WILL AUTOMATION AFFECT OPPORTUNITIES FOR EMPLOYMENT?

Over 200 years ago, weavers in England rioted and smashed the power looms that threatened to put them out of work. This bit of history simply shows that workers have always feared the effect of machines on jobs. Today people are worried that, as automation spreads, there may not be enough jobs to go around.

It is true that automation is expected to eliminate more jobs than it has already. But it is not expected to reduce opportunities for employment. Many companies are finding they need more workers after automation than before. This is because they are able to turn out a better product at a lower price. As a result, the demand for their products has increased, and additional jobs have opened up.

While destroying some jobs, automation has created others. In 1965, for example, approximately 50,000 people were employed as "computer programmers," an occupation that was unknown until 1949. By 1970, it is estimated that the occupation of computer programmer will provide employment for another 200,000 persons. The sharp rise in office employment is largely due to an increase in the use of automated equipment in banks, insurance companies, and other businesses. Automation itself has become a whole new industry that is now one of the fastest growing in the nation. Today more than 1,000 companies are producing automatic equipment. Workers are needed not only to produce the equipment but to sell it, install it, and eventually repair it.

Courtesy Board of Education, City of New York

High school students are being trained in data processing and computer programming to help prepare them for future employment opportunities.

Automation Can Promote Economic Growth

The fact is that it is not possible to determine exactly how many jobs have been or will be lost because of automation, or how many will be created. The one thing we do know is that as our economic system has grown, the proportion of the population employed has increased. In order to provide jobs for a million newcomers to the labor force each year, as well as jobs for workers displaced by automation, the economy must continue to grow. When machines replace workers, production increases and the economy grows. Automation, therefore, is expected to be an important factor in our future economic growth. Opportunities for some kinds of employment may decline or disappear. But opportunities for other kinds will increase.

For example, the rise in business activity together with the rise in population is expected to increase the need for construction workers—carpenters, electricians, plumbers, and painters. Because of the rapid rise in our population, there is already a shortage of professional workers—teachers, nurses, doctors, dentists, lawyers, architects. As the number of households and the use of appliances grows, there is an increasing need for repair mechanics. The need for salespeople of all kinds will continue as will the need for office workers and service workers—policemen, firemen, barbers, beauticians, airline stewardesses, and so on.

THE NEED WILL BE FOR SKILLED WORKERS

Automation is eliminating mainly two kinds of jobs: the kind that do not require a great deal of skill, sometimes called semiskilled; and the monotonous kind where the worker performs the same task over and over. In factories, for example, it is the semiskilled assembly-line workers who are losing out. The complex modern machines used in production operate instead under the watchful eyes of highly skilled mechanics and engineers. In offices, automation is taking over the work of preparing payrolls, compiling sales records, figuring bills, and keeping inventory. But in spite of automation, secretaries, stenographers, receptionists, and machine operators continue to be in great demand.

The occupations that offer the best opportunities for employment have one thing in common—they require skill and training. This means that to qualify for a job, workers will need more schooling than

Morton R. Engelberg photo

An older man whose job has been eliminated by automation is being retrained for an occupation where employment opportunities still exist.

ever before. A high school education is becoming an absolute necessity as automation spreads. Many corporations will not even interview a job seeker today unless he is a high school graduate. Two to four years of schooling beyond high school are a "must" for more and more occupations.

Something for young people preparing to enter the labor force to think about is this. During a recent prosperous year, it is estimated that 4 million jobs went unfilled at the same time that 4 million persons were unemployed. Who were these people who could not get jobs even when there were jobs? More than half of them were unskilled. Many were young persons under 24 who had not finished high school. Twenty percent of the unemployed that year had not even finished the eighth grade. In short, they were persons who did not qualify for the kinds of jobs that offered opportunity for employment. You might say they were unemployable.

Retraining May Be Necessary

Tomorrow the world of work will be different from what it is today. No one really knows how different. Certain jobs will change more than others, but all jobs are likely to change some. Many workers will find that they must learn new skills to adjust to changes in their jobs. Others will have to fit themselves for new jobs that open up when old ones disappear. Some workers may have to learn as many as three or more jobs during their lifetime. For students preparing for the world of work, the most important ability to develop may be the ability to learn.

Our economic growth depends heavily on the quality of our labor force. As the need for skilled workers rises, the quality of our labor force must improve. Otherwise our economic growth could be held back by a shortage of skilled workers.

BUILDING YOUR VOCABULARY

On a separate sheet of paper, write each of the terms listed in the left-hand column below and on page 444. Read the three definitions to the right of each term. After each term, copy the definition that best describes it.

1. *cyclical unemployment*

a. Unemployment that occurs even during prosperity
b. Unemployment that affects more than 5 percent of the labor force
c. Unemployment resulting from a recession or depression

2. *depressed area*

a. A region in which automation has eliminated most jobs
b. A region that offers little or no opportunity for employment
c. A region that specializes in the production of one product

3. *employment trend*

a. A shift away from one kind of employment and toward another
b. An increase or decrease in the percent of the labor force employed
c. The reduction in employment caused by an increased use of machines

4. *labor force*
   a. Everyone 14 years of age or over who is employed and paid for at least one hour of work a week
   b. Everyone 14 years of age or over who is working but not a member of the Armed Forces
   c. Everyone 14 years of age or over who is working or looking for work

5. *seasonal unemployment*
   a. Unemployment caused by changes in the weather
   b. Unemployment caused by changes in production that occur in some industries at certain times of the year
   c. Unemployment resulting from the fact that workers are free to change their jobs

6. *technological unemployment*
   a. Unemployment among technical or highly skilled workers
   b. Unemployment that results from a lack of demand for a product
   c. Unemployment that results when machines replace workers

CHECKING YOUR READING

1. In addition to your activities as a consumer, in what way will you be taking part in our economic system?
2. What are some of the rights workers have in a free enterprise system?
3. What will you need to know to make a wise job choice?
4. Who is considered unemployed in the United States?
5. Describe some of the ways in which the nation's labor force has changed.
6. How have the occupations of the labor force changed?
7. In the long run, what determines employment opportunities?
8. Why is there some unemployment in a free enterprise system even during prosperity?
9. How might a change in consumer demand affect job opportunities?
10. Why are workers concerned about the spread of automation?
11. Is automation expected to eliminate any jobs?
12. Is automation expected to reduce opportunities for employment?
13. Why is automation considered important to our future economic growth?
14. What kinds of jobs are most affected by automation?
15. Why is education becoming more and more important for workers?
16. Why are some persons unemployed even when there are unfilled jobs?
17. What one ability will be an important one for future workers? Why?
18. How could a shortage of skilled workers hold back our economic growth?

SHARING YOUR OPINION AND EXPERIENCE

1. How will your choice of jobs affect you personally? How will your choice affect our economic system?
2. Do you think it is just as important for girls to plan and prepare for jobs as it is for boys? Why or why not?
3. In 1900 the average age of persons entering the labor force was 15. Today it has risen to 18 years. Why do you think this change has taken place?
4. Although people are living longer than ever before, the percent of persons over 65 who remain in the labor force has been steadily declining. What reasons can you give for this?
5. In the years to come, the number of unskilled jobs in our economy is expected to remain about the same as it is now. Then why is the competition for unskilled jobs expected to increase?
6. Give some examples of both seasonal unemployment and technological unemployment in your community.
7. Thanks to machines, recreation has become big business in the United States. Explain.
8. What type of job do you think you would be qualified for if you were to drop out of school right now?
9. If you are considering a business career but do not plan to go to college, what high school business subjects can provide you with direct job training?
10. Beyond high school, what opportunities for job preparation are provided within 50 miles of your community?
11. Why might it be advisable for a student to take some vocational courses even though he plans to go to college?

PROJECTS AND PROBLEMS

1. Of all the decisions you will ever make, one of the most important will be the choice of an occupation. One clue to the type of job you should choose is your interests. Your interests are simply the things you like to do best. Using a sheet of notebook paper, prepare a list of your interests using the following questions as a guide: (*a*) What are my favorite school subjects? (*b*) What home chores or part-time work have I most enjoyed doing? (*c*) What hobbies or other spare-time activities do I like best? (*d*) What clubs or other school activities interest me most?

   If you have any special interests that are not covered by the questions above, add them to your list. The more you know about your likes and dislikes, the better will be your chances of choosing an occupation that suits you. Study your list carefully. Does it indicate whether you would prefer working (1) with things such as tools, microscopes, or fabrics? (2) with people, as might be the case if you like activities involving groups such as clubs, parties, or sports? (3) with ideas, as expressed by an interest in art, science, or literature?

   Write your answer below the list and keep the paper for future reference.
2. It takes more than interest to succeed in a job, of course. You must also be able to perform whatever tasks the job requires. In addition to knowing your interests, therefore, you should know your abilities. These are the things you can do well.

Using a sheet of notebook paper, prepare a list of all things you feel you can do well. Some suggestions for such a list are shown below. You might begin by listing the school subjects in which you make your best grades. Your list of interests may suggest other abilities, since you are probably good at the things you like to do. Keep the list for future reference.

My Special Abilities

Mathematics
Art
Typewriting
Playing a musical instrument
Get along well with others
Speak well
Making things with my hands

3. As you learned in this part, the size and composition of the labor force have been changing. The table below shows expected changes in the number of workers in each group between 1960 and 1970.

CHANGES IN THE WORKING POPULATION EXPECTED DURING THE 1960'S

Age Group	*1960 (millions)*	*1970 (millions)*
Under 25	13.8	20.2
25–34	15.3	17.1
35–44	16.6	16.4
45 and over	27.9	33.4

Copy the table on a sheet of paper, adding two columns on the right. Make the heading on one "Change in Numbers"; on the other, "Percent Change." In the numbers column, show the number by which workers in each age group are expected to increase or decrease. In the percent column, show the percent of increase or decrease in each age group. Indicate a decrease by a minus sign.

4. Using the information given in the table in Problem No. 3, answer the following questions:

▪ *a.* How many workers were in the labor force in 1960? ▪ *b.* How many workers are expected to be in the labor force by 1970? ▪ *c.* How many more workers will there be in the labor force in 1970 than there were in 1960? ▪ *d.* Approximately what portion of the increase in the labor force between 1960 and 1970 will be young workers under 25?

5. Look in the "Help Wanted" section of the newspaper that serves your community to see what types of jobs are available. On a form similar to that shown at the top of page 447, list the five occupations for which workers are most in demand. Using the information given in the ads, fill in the rest of the form.

Occupation	Average Salary	Experience Required	Other Requirements: Education, Special Skills or Abilities, Physical Requirements, etc.
Example: *Accountant*	*Not Mentioned*	*Minimum of 2 years*	*College graduate with major in accounting; under 30*

6. The following article appeared in newspapers around the nation early in July, 1965. Read the article and answer the questions following it.

FACTORY JOBS TOP 18 MILLION, NEAR RECORD

Washington, D.C.—Factory jobs climbed over the 18 million mark in June and almost bettered the all-time record achieved during World War II, the Labor Department reported Monday.

A Labor Department official said manufacturing employment showed "great strength" in rising by 244,000 to 18,068,000 last month. Most of the gains came in steel, auto, and other metal working industries.

This was the highest factory job figure since the total reached 18,074,000 in November, 1943, when the economy was at its wartime peak.

The total gain in nonfarm employment in June was 759,000.

Explaining the surge in manufacturing employment, the Labor Department official said the level of demand is so high it has created a larger number of jobs.

▪ *a.* When the article appeared, approximately how many workers had factory jobs? ▪ *b.* Was this an all-time high for factory employment? ▪ *c.* Who reported the increase in factory employment? ▪ *d.* In what industries did most of the employment increases occur? ▪ *e.* What was the total rise in nonfarm employment during the month reported? ▪ *f.* Approximately what portion of this increase was in factory employment? ▪ *g.* What explanation is given for the increase in factory employment?

7. In general, the less education a worker has, the more likely he is to be unemployed. Following is the unemployment rate for workers with different amounts of education.

	Rate of Unemployment
Less than a high school education	**7%**
High school graduates	**4%**
College graduates	**2%**

Put the above information in the form of a horizontal bar graph similar to that used in No. 2 of the Projects and Problems section of Part 44, page 413.

8. As you read in this part, the need for workers will increase in some occupations and decrease in others. The table below shows the percent of increase or decrease expected in eight occupation groups by 1970. It also shows the average years of school completed by those working in these occupations during a recent year. Following the table are some questions to answer.

EDUCATION YOUNG PERSONS RECEIVE AFFECTS THEIR LIFETIME CAREERS

Employment in These Occupations	*Is Expected to Change This Much by 1970*	*People Who Work in These Occupations Have This Much Education*			
		Less Than 12 Grades	*High School Graduation*	*Some College*	*Average Years of School Completed*
Professional and technical	**Up 38%**	**6%**	**19%**	**75%**	**16.2**
Proprietors and managers	**Up 24%**	**38%**	**33%**	**29%**	**12.4**
Clerical and sales	**Up 27%**	**25%**	**53%**	**22%**	**12.5**
Skilled workers	**Up 24%**	**59%**	**33%**	**8%**	**11.0**
Semiskilled workers	**Up 18%**	**70%**	**26%**	**4%**	**9.9**
Service workers	**Up 25%**	**69%**	**25%**	**6%**	**9.7**
Unskilled workers	**No change**	**80%**	**17%**	**3%**	**8.6**
Farmers and farm workers	**Down 12%**	**76%**	**19%**	**5%**	**8.6**

▪ *a.* In which occupation group is no change in employment expected? ▪ *b.* In which occupation group is employment expected to decrease? ▪ *c.* In which occupation group is employment expected to increase least? ▪ *d.* In which occupation group is employment expected to increase most? ▪ *e.* Which occupation group requires the most education? What percent of workers in this occupation had some college education? ▪ *f.* Which occupation group had the largest percent of workers who had not finished high school? ▪ *g.* What percent of clerical and sales workers had at least a high school education? ▪ *h.* According to the table, 29 percent of proprietors and managers had some college education compared with 22 percent of clerical and sales workers. Does this tell you whether more proprietors and managers than clerical and sales workers went to college? Why or why not?

9. There is a close relationship between education and income. In general, the more education a person has, the higher his earnings. The picture graph on page 449 shows the average estimated lifetime earnings for persons with different amounts of education. Answer the questions below and following the graph.

▪ *a.* How much more is a worker with four or more years of college likely to earn than a worker with less than eight years of schooling? ▪ *b.* How much more

MORE SCHOOLING GENERALLY BRINGS HIGHER EARNINGS*

Average Lifetime Earnings of Men Workers (Based on 1958 Incomes)

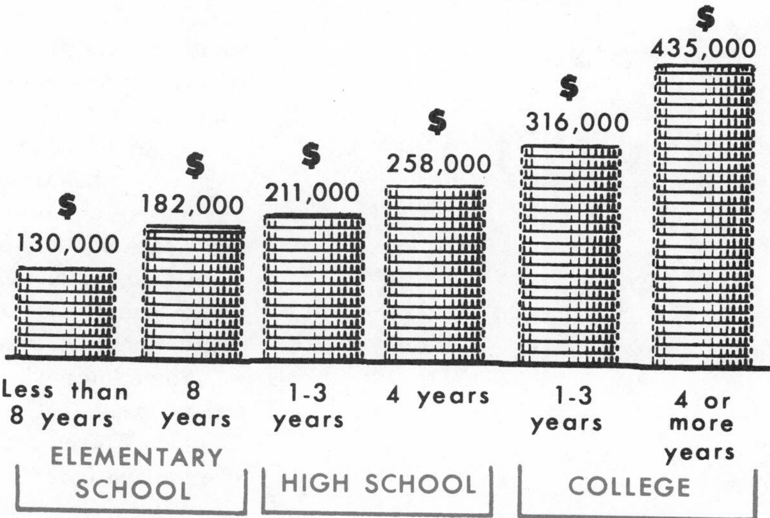

*Education is not the only factor; earnings are also affected by ability, etc.

Source: U.S. Department of Labor

is a worker likely to earn if he finishes high school than if he drops out of high school after one or two years? ▪ *c.* Assume that a person who graduates from college works 40 years. What would his average annual income be? ▪ *d.* Assume that a person who drops out of high school works 45 years. What would his average annual income be? ▪ *e.* Between which two groups of workers is the difference in lifetime earnings smallest?

CHALLENGE PROBLEMS

1. In the future, persons who remain on farms will need better education and training, the same as workers in other occupations. Why?
2. In general, would the people of the United States be better off if automation were postponed? Why or why not?
3. How might inflation cause some people to choose one occupation rather than another.
4. Competition is the driving force behind all technological advances. Explain.
5. When a worker's job is eliminated by automation, who should be responsible for training him for another job? the worker himself? the company he worked for? the local community? the Federal government? Give reasons for your answer.
6. According to the newspaper article in Projects and Problems No. 6, the same number of workers had factory jobs during the month reported as had factory jobs during World War II. Does that mean the proportion of factory workers in the labor force was the same for the two periods? Explain.

PART 48 ORGANIZED LABOR

BETWEEN 16 and 17 million members of this nation's labor force belong to organizations called ***labor unions.*** Most of them are workers engaged directly in the production of goods. About half of them are factory workers. A large number are skilled craftsmen such as carpenters, electricians, plumbers, and bricklayers. Only about one and one-half million of them are service workers. Fewer than one -half million union members work in professional and technical occupations, and most of these are either actors or musicians.

Sometimes when people use the term "labor" they mean that group of workers who belong to unions. The correct term for this group, however, is ***organized labor.***

Why do workers join unions? If there is an advantage in belonging to a union, why don't all workers join unions? What does it mean to bargain collectively?

Courtesy Benjamin Harris Company, Inc.

EMPLOYERS AND EMPLOYEES MUST AGREE ON TERMS OF EMPLOYMENT

The percent of the labor force that owns and operates businesses is probably larger in the United States than anywhere else in the world. Nevertheless, nine out of ten workers in this country earn their incomes by working for someone else. They are *employees.* Those for whom they work are *employers.*

Between every employer and employee there must be an agreement concerning such things as wages and working hours. This agreement is often the result of bargaining. For example, a worker might ask for a higher wage than the one offered him. If the employer is unwilling to pay what the worker asks, he may offer to compromise. In other words, he might offer a higher wage than he offered at first, but not as much as the worker asks.

Whatever terms the employer and worker finally agree on will depend on which one has the greater bargaining strength. If there is a shortage of workers who can do the job, the bargaining strength would be on the side of the worker. The employer would then be likely to agree to the worker's demands. But if there are other workers who could be hired for the job, the bargaining strength would be on the side of the employer. He could say to the worker, "Accept my offer or I'll hire someone else."

An agreement between an employer and employee is a contract. If either side wants to change the terms of the agreement, then further bargaining may become necessary.

WHY DO WORKERS ORGANIZE?

When men first turned from farming to other kinds of jobs, most businesses were small enterprises. Employers worked right along with their employees, and a close personal relationship existed between them. Today there are many small businesses in this country where this is still the case and where each worker bargains individually with his employer.

As the factory system of production developed, however, businesses grew larger and larger. More and more workers became dependent on one employer. In the early days of manufacturing, wages were low, often as little as 75 cents for a 12-hour day. Unsafe and unsanitary working conditions were common. But there was little an individual worker could do to bring about improvement. Anyone who dared to complain was likely to find himself out of a job. Because there were plenty of unemployed persons looking for work, all bargaining strength was on the side of the employer.

It was the inability of workers to bargain individually with their employers that finally led them to organize into unions. Then, instead of bargaining separately with the employer, they bargained together through their union. This is known as ***collective bargaining.*** Through collective bargaining, the power of workers to deal with their employers increased. An employer could easily ignore one worker's threat to quit if his demands were not met. But the possibility that all or a large portion of them might refuse to work was a serious matter. Production would certainly be slowed down during the time it took an employer to hire and train new workers, and it might stop entirely. Any decrease in production, of course, would mean a loss in profits. An employer usually preferred to try to work out a satisfactory agreement with the workers' union.

Today a single enterprise may have thousands of workers and thousands of owners. Because it would be impractical for them to bargain individually, collective bargaining is the accepted way of determining working conditions in many of these businesses.

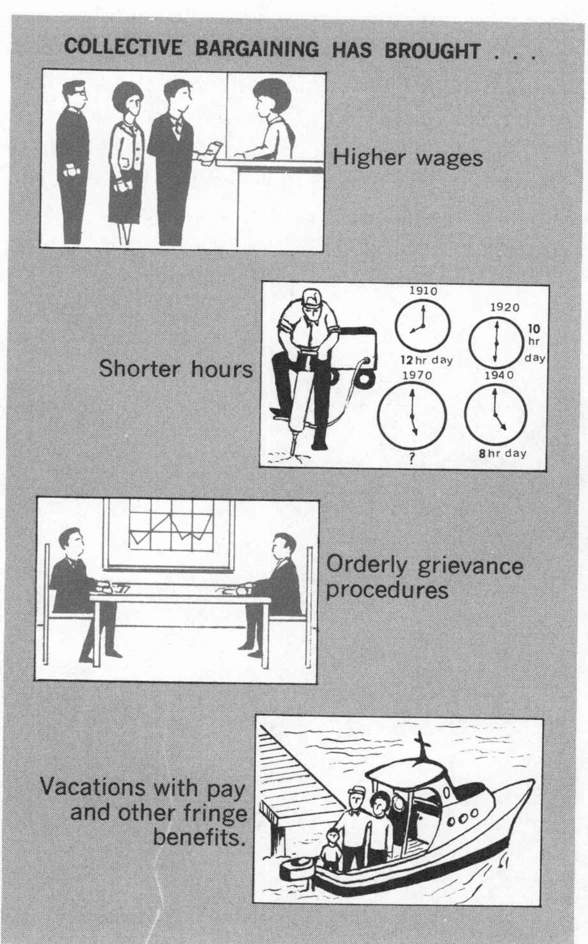

COLLECTIVE BARGAINING HAS BROUGHT . . .
Higher wages
Shorter hours
1910
12 hr day
1920
10 hr day
1940
8 hr day
1970
?
Orderly grievance procedures
Vacations with pay and other fringe benefits.

HOW DOES COLLECTIVE BARGAINING WORK?

Under the collective bargaining method, members of the union meet and decide under what conditions they are willing to work. Then someone, or a committee chosen to represent the union, meets with the employer or his representatives to discuss terms of employment. The representative of the union reports the results of these discussions to the members. If the employer offers different terms than those proposed by the union, the members vote on whether or not to accept the employer's terms. If they decide not to accept them, the bargaining continues until an agreement is reached between the employer and a majority of the union members.

After an agreement has been reached, the terms are written out and signed by representatives of both the employer and the union. This signed agreement is called a ***labor contract.*** It is binding on both sides for as long as it is in force. A contract may run for only one year or for as long as five years. At the end of the period covered by the contract, it may either be renewed or replaced by a new contract.

WHAT IS THE NATURE OF A LABOR CONTRACT?

Labor contracts differ, if for no other reason than that businesses that employ workers differ. But just as businesses are similar in certain ways, labor contracts are also similar in certain ways. Following are some of the items generally covered by a labor contract.

Wages and Hours

A typical labor contract states the wage rates for different kinds of work and hours of work. Usually it specifies a higher rate of pay for hours worked overtime. A contract that is to run longer than a year may provide for wage increases from time to time. Some provide for the raising or lowering of wages if the cost of living increases or decreases. This is known as an ***escalator clause.***

Fringe Benefits

In addition to the regular wages paid to workers,

Wide World photo

At this meeting union representatives are meeting with employer's representatives to bargain for workers.

most labor contracts provide for a certain number of fringe benefits. ***Fringe benefits*** include such things as retirement pensions, group insurance plans, paid vacations and holidays, sick leave, unemployment benefits, and coffee breaks. The cost of these extras is said to average more than $1 for every $5 workers are paid in cash.

Seniority Rights

An important provision commonly included in a labor contract is seniority rights. The term ***seniority*** refers to the length of time a worker has been employed by a firm. The worker who has been with the same firm the longest has the most seniority. This gives him special rights in connection with promotions and layoffs. For example, suppose it became necessary for an employer to let some workers go. Those who had the most seniority would be the last to be laid off. If the same workers were called back to work at a later date, seniority would determine the order in which they are recalled.

Promotions are often determined in the same way. If the opportunity for a promotion occurs, it is offered to the worker who has been with the company the longest.

Employer's Rights

In addition to granting workers certain rights, most labor contracts also define the employer's rights. For example, the employer alone has the authority to decide where the business shall be located; what and how much shall be produced; to whom its products shall be sold; and whether to schedule one, two, or three work shifts.

Grievance Procedures

A labor contract may contain as many as fifty pages. There are bound to be complaints that one side or the other is not living up to the terms of the agreement. For example, a worker might claim that he did not receive a promotion to which he was entitled. Or an employer might complain that a worker is not doing his job right. Complaints of this kind are called *grievances*. Labor contracts describe the steps to be followed in handling grievances. These are called *grievance procedures.*

ORGANIZED LABOR FOUGHT HARD FOR RECOGNITION

There have been labor organizations of one sort or another in this country since Colonial times. Yet not until this century did organized labor have an important place in our economic system. For a long time the growth of unions was held back by employers who did everything possible to keep workers from joining. Lists of union members were passed around among employers, and anyone whose name appeared on the list was not hired. Sometimes a worker applying for a job was asked to sign a statement promising not to join a union. The courts were asked to forbid union activities; and in disputes between employers and union workers, the courts were usually on the side of the employers.

The real turning point came in 1935 with passage of the National Labor Relations Act. This act, also known as the Wagner Act, guarantees workers the right to organize unions and to bargain collectively with their employers. Under this act, the workers of a company hold elections to decide whether or not they wish to belong to a union and by which union they want to be represented. Once a union is chosen to act as agent for the workers, all dealings between the workers and the employer are carried on through the union.

HOW IMPORTANT ARE LABOR UNIONS?

Following passage of the Wagner Act, union membership rose rapidly, reaching a high point in 1956 when more than 18,000,000 workers in the United States belonged to unions. Since then, the number of workers belonging to unions has decreased only slightly. But the proportion of the labor force belonging to unions has grown considerably smaller.

In 1956, it was 33.4 percent; by 1965, it was estimated to have dropped to about 30 percent. There are several explanations for this decline.

One is that union membership comes mainly from those industries where automation is eliminating jobs. As the size of the labor force increased, the proportion employed in these industries has become smaller. It is the service occupations that are growing in importance; and up to now workers in these occupations have not shown much interest in joining unions. Another explanation is that some of the reasons for joining unions no longer exist. There has been a vast improvement in working conditions and wages compared with the past. In addition, efforts to increase union membership have been hurt by the fact that some union leaders have been dishonest. This is most unfortunate because the majority of unions are run properly and for the benefit of their members.

In spite of the fact that the growth of labor unions appears to have slowed down, organized labor still holds a position of importance in our economic system. It is estimated that about one-third of the workers who could be organized are union members. Some workers do not have the kind of employment problems that unions help to solve. Farm workers, owners of business, employees of small business firms, and professional persons such as doctors, lawyers and dentists are examples. There are few large industrial firms, on the other hand, whose employees are not organized.

BUILDING YOUR VOCABULARY

On a separate sheet of paper, list the figures 1 to 7, numbering down. Read the seven statements given below at the right; then, for each statement, select from the column at the left the term that best matches it in meaning. Write this term next to the appropriate number.

collective bargaining
escalator clause
fringe benefits
labor contract
labor union
organized labor
seniority

1. An organization of workers through which they bargain collectively with their employers
2. That part of the labor force which belongs to unions
3. The process by which workers reach agreements with their employers through their union representatives
4. The length of time a worker has been employed by the same firm
5. A written agreement between a labor union and an employer stating the terms of employment for a definite period of time
6. A provision in a labor contract that permits raising or lowering of wages according to changes in the cost of living
7. Retirement pensions, hospitalization, group life insurance, paid vacations, and other extras provided workers by their employers in addition to their regular wages

CHECKING YOUR READING

1. In general what types of workers belong to unions?
2. Are most workers in the United States employers or employees? What is the difference?

3. What is the purpose of bargaining between a worker and an employer?
4. What determines the extent to which an employer agrees to a worker's demands?
5. What circumstances led to the establishment of labor unions?
6. How does collective bargaining strengthen the worker's position?
7. Why would an employer usually prefer to work out an agreement with the union than to hire new workers?
8. In what type of enterprise is collective bargaining the usual way of determining working conditions?
9. Explain how collective bargaining works.
10. What happens when a labor contract expires?
11. What are some of the items generally covered by a labor contract?
12. If a labor contract provides for seniority rights, how does this affect promotions and layoffs?
13. Give examples of employers' rights as defined by labor contracts.
14. What are grievances? What are grievance procedures?
15. What were some of the methods employers used to prevent workers from organizing in the early days?
16. What is the importance of the National Labor Relations Act of 1935 (also known as the Wagner Act)?
17. Why has the proportion of the labor force belonging to unions been growing smaller?
18. Some workers do not have the kind of employment problems that unions help to solve. Give examples.

SHARING YOUR OPINION AND EXPERIENCE

1. Some unions are *trade* or *craft unions;* some are *industrial unions.* What is the main difference between these two types of unions?
2. Do most workers in the United States bargain individually with their employers?
3. All labor contracts contain a recognition clause. What is a *recognition clause?*
4. Why do you think employers might oppose using seniority as a basis for promotions and layoffs?
5. Most office workers in the United States do not belong to unions. Why do you think they have not been organized?
6. Why are factory workers easier to organize than farm workers?
7. Does an agreement between an employer and an employee have to be in writing to be a contract?
8. Today the law requires that union members be informed how the money collected in dues is spent. Give reasons for this law.
9. Labor unions are not allowed to contribute money to any political party. What do you think is the reason for this?
10. Do you think unions have obtained higher wages for workers than they would have received otherwise?

PROJECTS AND PROBLEMS

1. Employers and workers have certain responsibilities to one another regardless of whether terms of employment are covered by a written contract. Using headings similar to those shown below, list in the left-hand column at least four responsibilities employers have to their workers. In the right-hand column, list at least four responsibilities workers have to their employers.

Responsibilities of Employers to Workers	Responsibilities of Workers to Employers

2. Using the classified section of your telephone directory, list the different types of union organizations you have in your community. If you live in a large metropolitan area, limit your list to ten.
3. The graph below is an interesting combination of a bar graph and a line graph. By means of this combination, it shows changes in union membership from 1930 to 1960 in two different ways. The line shows the number of workers belonging to unions during the 30-year period. The bars show the percent of nonfarm workers belonging to unions. Answer the questions following the graph.

UNION MEMBERSHIP

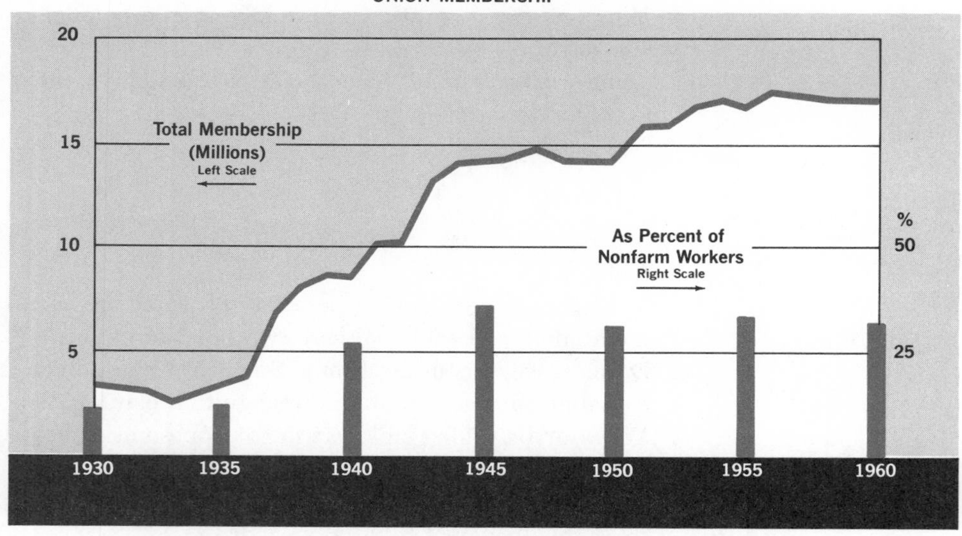

▪ *a.* In about what year was union membership the lowest? Approximately how many workers belonged to unions in that year? ▪ *b.* In about what year was union membership the highest? Approximately how many workers belonged to unions in that year? ▪ *c.* In what year was the percent of nonfarm workers belonging to unions the smallest? What percent of the workers were union members in that year? ▪ *d.* In what year was the percent of nonfarm workers belonging to unions the highest? Approximately what percent of the workers were union members in that year? ▪ *e.* In how many of the 5-year periods did the percent of nonfarm workers belonging to unions increase over the preceding period? ▪ *f.* In how many of the 5-year periods did the percent of nonfarm workers belonging to unions decrease over the preceding period? ▪ *g.* If union membership continued to rise during the 30 years shown on the graph, how could the percent of workers belonging to unions fall? ▪ *h.* If the graph showed the percent of the total labor force belonging to unions, would the bars be higher or lower? ▪ *i.* If this chart were extended to 1965, do you think the percent of nonfarm workers belonging to unions would increase or decrease?

4. During a recent year collective bargaining agreements covering seven million workers resulted in the wage increases shown in the table below. Increases shown do not include the value of fringe benefits. Examine the table and answer the questions following it.

WAGE INCREASES UNDER MAJOR AGREEMENTS

Cents Increase per Hour	*Percent of Workers*
Under 3	13
3 and under 5	16
5 and under 7	7
7 and under 9	19
9 and under 11	26
11 and under 13	9
13 and under 15	5
15 and under 17	1
17 and over	2
Not reported*	2

° *Insufficient information to compute increases*

▪ *a.* What percent of the workers received increases of less than 11 cents per hour? ▪ *b.* How many workers received increases of less than 11 cents per hour? ▪ *c.* What percent of the workers received increases of 11 cents or more per hour? ▪ *d.* What amount of increase did the largest percent of workers receive? ▪ *e.* What amount of increase did the smallest percent of workers receive? ▪ *f.* Does the table indicate what the highest amount of increase was that year? ▪ *g.* How many workers received increases of 17 cents an hour or more? ▪ *h.* Suppose a worker with a weekly wage of $75 for a 40-hour week received an increase of 5 cents an hour. What would his weekly wage be after the increase?

5. Find out all you can about the National Labor Relations Board. Write a report describing its membership, its purpose, and its important accomplishments.
6. The following acts passed by Congress contain legislation affecting labor unions: the Clayton Act, the Norris-LaGuardia Act, the Wagner Act, the Taft-Hartley Act. Look up each law, and be prepared to tell when it was passed and at least one provision it contains pertaining to labor.
7. List five outstanding labor leaders in the United States today and the name of the union with which each is associated. Prepare a brief biographical sketch of one of them, using clippings from magazines and newspapers.

8. Suppose that you are the union representative for the workers of the Pyramid Toy Company. On a separate piece of paper, indicate which of the grievances described below you think should be taken up with their employer by writing "Yes" or "No" next to the letter and then giving reasons for your answer.

■ *a.* A new automatic casting machine will permit the manufacture of certain toys, using the services of only one worker in place of the four now required. Although plans call for reassignment of any displaced workers, the employees object to installation of these new machines. ■ *b.* Workers in the trim department are often asked to work overtime at the last minute. The employees feel that this practice is unreasonable. They want to be told at least a day ahead whenever overtime work will be required so they can plan accordingly. ■ *c.* Packers in the shipping department have always been provided with assembled cartons in which to pack toys. Recently the company began having packers assemble their own cartons. The packers object, claiming this is not part of the job for which they were hired. ■ *d.* When the Pyramid factory was first built, it was located in a suburban area not served by public transportation. In order to get workers, the company provided transportation from a downtown location to its plant, using station wagons. This year public bus service was extended to the factory area, and the company transportation service was discontinued. The workers claim that they are entitled to transportation expenses unless the company service is reinstated.

CHALLENGE PROBLEMS

1. Is labor-union membership more likely to grow during recessions or during prosperity? Explain.
2. Some unions charge a very high initiation fee to persons who want to join. This keeps out many who might otherwise become members. Why do you think some unions do this?
3. Many labor unions operate on the basis of apprenticeships for new members. Select a union where this system is used and explain how it works.

PART 49 LABOR-MANAGEMENT RELATIONS

IN every business enterprise, the person or persons who make the decisions and give the orders are known as *management.* Management decides how much is to be produced and what prices to charge for the goods or services produced. Management also hires and fires workers and decides what wages they will receive. It is with management, therefore, that workers bargain.

Small business enterprises are often managed by their owners. The management of a large corporation, however, is the responsibility of persons hired for the job. In either case, the success of a business depends on the ability of its management to make wise decisions. The success of a business enterprise also depends on cooperation between workers and management. The way in which these two work together is referred to as *labor-management relations.* Good labor-management relations are not only important to a business enterprise, they are also important to our whole business system.

Why are labor-management relations important? Why is it sometimes difficult for labor and management to achieve a good relationship? How good are labor-management relations in the United States?

WHY ARE GOOD LABOR-MANAGEMENT RELATIONS DIFFICULT TO ACHIEVE?

The term "labor-management relations" is somewhat confusing because persons in management positions are also members of the labor force. As the term is generally used, however, it refers to the relationship between the management of a company and the union that represents the company's workers.

When representatives of management and a labor union bargain, they discuss a variety of matters. Some of them are matters on which workers and management find it difficult to agree. Following are brief explanations of five major issues

Wide World photo

likely to be covered in bargaining talks. After reading them, perhaps you will understand better some of the problems involved in achieving good labor-management relations.

Wages

Usually the most important topic discussed in talks between unions and management is wages. And if there is one thing, more than any other, that is likely to lead to a dispute between these two, it is wages. Businesses, remember, are organized to earn a profit. Profit is the amount of income a business has left after all costs of production have been paid. It is management's job to keep production costs as low as possible. One of the aims of a labor union, on the other hand, is to obtain as high wages as possible for its members. Wages, however, are a part of production costs. In many enterprises, wages are the biggest part. Management's opposition to wage increases, therefore, is easy to understand.

Fringe Benefits

In recent years fringe benefits have been almost as big an issue in collective bargaining as wages. Workers want pensions, group life and health insurance, and unemployment benefits because these contribute to their financial security. They argue that a holiday without pay is simply time lost from work. And a vacation without pay is the same as being unemployed for a period of time.

As you know, fringe benefits are simply an addition to wages. Management understands workers' reasons for wanting these extras. Management's complaint is that, in counting up their wages, workers tend to overlook the amount they receive in fringe benefits.

Hours

One of the first things ever demanded by a workers' union was a reduction in the working day from 12 hours to 10. Since then, hours have often been an issue in collective bargaining. The reason for this is that any change in working hours usually affects wages. Sometimes, for example, workers will demand a shorter workweek without a decrease in weekly wages. This is the same as asking to be paid a higher rate per hour. Sometimes, however, workers simply ask for a shorter basic workweek. A *basic workweek* is the number of hours of work for which workers are paid their regular hourly rate. For each hour worked in addition to the basic number, a worker is paid extra; usually time and a half. This means that if a worker's regular hourly rate is $3.50, his overtime rate is $5.25 an hour. If his basic workweek is 40 hours, he is paid $5.25 for every hour he works over 40. If his basic workweek were shortened to 35 hours, then he would receive the overtime rate for every hour he works over 35.

The union argues that a shorter workweek would help to provide employment for more workers, which might be true in some cases. But what might also be true in some cases is that a shorter workweek will increase the possibility that a worker will be required to work overtime. Management is opposed to shortening the workweek for the same reason it is opposed to increasing wages—pay for overtime adds to production costs.

Seniority

Another point of difference between labor and management that might surprise you is seniority rights. The unions, you remember, want seniority to determine layoffs and promotions. Their reason is that seniority rules prevent favoritism to workers who may be friends or relatives of management. But seniority rules do more than that. They protect older workers who often find it difficult to obtain other employment should they lose their jobs.

Management has equally sound reasons for objecting to seniority rules. One is that such rules interfere with its freedom to hire and fire workers.

GOALS OF LABOR . . .

1. Security

2. A chance to advance

3. More dignity on the job

Another is that management wants workers promoted on the basis of their ability rather than on length of employment. In bargaining talks with union representatives, therefore, management will usually ask that ability be considered along with seniority in deciding promotions and layoffs. In other words, if two workers have equal ability, the one with seniority would be promoted first.

Union Shop

One of the biggest obstacles to peaceful bargaining is organized labor's demand for a union shop. A ***union shop*** is one that requires new employees to become members of the union within a certain period of time, usually 30 days.

Why does organized labor want a union shop? Because in businesses where union and nonunion workers are employed, both receive the same benefits. But the nonunion workers contribute nothing to the financial support of the union. In time the union workers would see no advantage in belonging to the union.

Why does management not want a union shop? Because like seniority rules, a union shop lessens management's freedom in hiring workers. Also, a union shop strengthens the union's bargaining power. Obviously, a union is in a better position to bargain if all or most employees of a firm are union members than if only a small number of them are.

WORKERS SOMETIMES STRIKE TO ENFORCE THEIR DEMANDS

As you can see, before there can be agreement between a union and management, both usually have to give a little. If one or the other is unwilling to compromise, bargaining comes to a standstill. Then unions may use other methods to enforce their demands. Their best known and most effective method is the strike. A ***strike*** is a deliberate refusal on the part of the employees of a business to work. The purpose of a strike is to put pressure on the employer by stopping production and causing a loss in profits. A strike may be settled within hours or it may drag on for weeks or months.

During a strike, of course, workers receive no wages. Instead they receive financial assistance from the union in the form of payments called *strike benefits.* The money to pay strike benefits comes from funds to which all union members contribute.

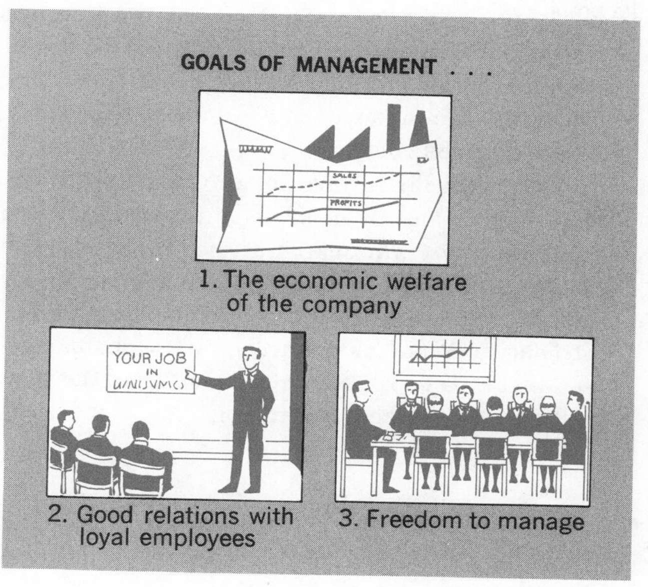

GOALS OF MANAGEMENT . . .

1. The economic welfare of the company

2. Good relations with loyal employees

3. Freedom to manage

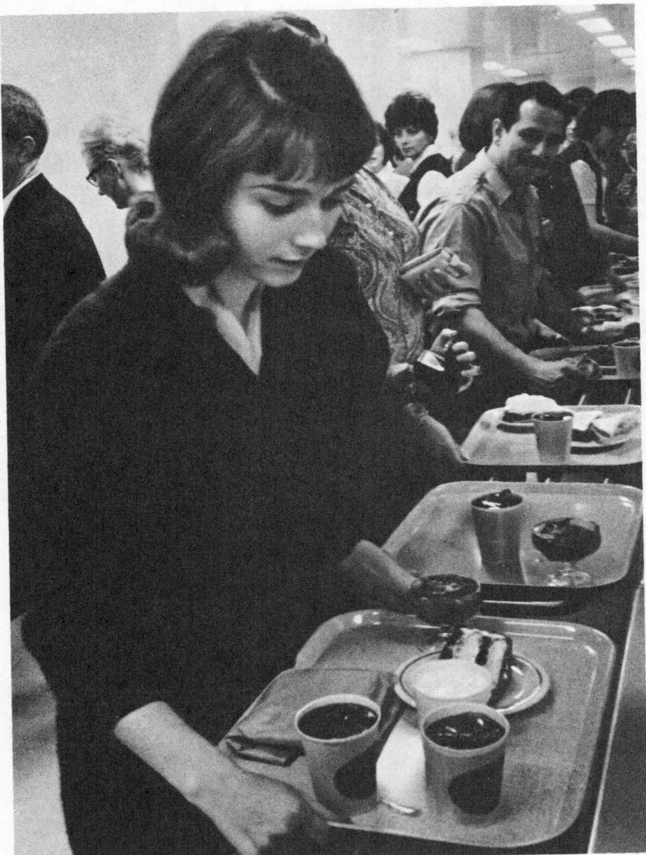

As an example of good labor-management relations, this pleasant cafeteria is provided by the company for its employees.

Occasionally workers will strike without the approval of their union. This is called a *wildcat strike.* Workers who take part in a wildcat strike do not receive strike benefits.

Strikes usually involve some form of ***picketing.*** Picketing is done by members of the striking union called *pickets,* who march at the entrance of the business involved in the dispute. Their purpose is to keep nonunion workers from taking the jobs of striking workers. Pickets usually carry signs announcing that a strike is in progress. Sometimes the signs tell why the workers are striking.

LABOR-MANAGEMENT RELATIONS ARE OF PUBLIC CONCERN

What happens in labor-management relations affects in some way even those who have no connection with either side. When workers' demands for higher wages result in higher prices for consumer goods, money loses some of its purchasing power. A strike against one business not only works a hardship on its customers, it usually results in a loss of income for other businesses. Because ours is an interdependent economy, a strike against a major industry could halt production and cause unemployment in many other industries. A strike among steel workers, for example, or a strike against a transportation industry could weaken our whole business system.

Many people wonder why such strikes are allowed. Some even question whether unions and management should be permitted to make agreements that result in higher prices. The explanation is that the more our business system is regulated by law, the less free it becomes. Sometimes, however, the government will ask labor unions not to demand wage increases. It will also ask management not to raise prices. In addition, the President can ask the Federal courts to prohibit for 80 days any strike that endangers the health or safety of the public. If no agreement has been reached at the end of the 80-day period, the union has the right to strike. If it decides to do so, the President may ask Congress to help settle the dispute.

HOW GOOD ARE LABOR-MANAGEMENT RELATIONS?

Strikes make news, particularly strikes that tie up a major industry or that inflict hardship on the public. So if all you knew about labor-management relations was what you learned from the news, you might have the wrong idea. The fact is that labor-management relations have been growing steadily better year by year. Today there are over 125,000 separate labor-management agreements in the United States. Most of them are the result of peaceful bargaining.

There is still room for improvement, to be sure. But there are also many signs of progress toward better cooperation between labor and management. Many employers believe it is to their advantage to have their workers belong to unions. They find it easier to deal with union representatives than to deal with each employee individually. In more and more business enterprises unions are assuming a share of the responsibility to make the enterprise a success. As one example the union employees of a large meat-packing plant recently agreed to accept a cut in wages. Why? Because the lower wages made it possible for the company to cut its price and thus hold its own in competition. In many industries employers and union leaders are working out time schedules so that automation will be introduced little by little. Their purpose is to reduce the difficulties that automation can cause for workers. These examples simply show what can be accomplished when labor and management work together to solve their problems.

BUILDING YOUR VOCABULARY

On a separate sheet of paper, write each of the terms listed in the left-hand column below. Read the three definitions to the right of each term. After each term, copy the definition that best describes it.

1. *picketing*
   - *a.* The stationing of striking workers at the entrance to a plant involved in a labor dispute to keep others from entering
   - *b.* A refusal on the part of union members to do business with an enterprise involved in a dispute with members of another union
   - *c.* An unlawful method of preventing an enterprise involved in a labor dispute from doing business with those not involved in the dispute
2. *strike*
   - *a.* A refusal on the part of employees to leave the establishment in which they are employed
   - *b.* The shutting down of a plant or industry to keep workers from organizing
   - *c.* A planned work stoppage on the part of employees of a plant or industry
3. *union shop*
   - *a.* A plant or enterprise in which workers may be employed regardless of whether they are union members
   - *b.* A plant or enterprise in which all new workers hired must either belong to the union or agree to join
   - *c.* A plant or enterprise in which only union members can be hired

CHECKING YOUR READING

1. With whom do workers in a business enterprise bargain?
2. Name two things mentioned in the text that are important to the success of a business enterprise.
3. To what does the term "labor-management relations" usually refer?
4. Why are wages likely to be a subject of disagreement between labor and management?
5. Explain the workers' point of view toward fringe benefits.
6. What is management's complaint concerning fringe benefits?
7. What is the union's argument in favor of a shorter workweek?

8. Why might management oppose a shorter workweek without a decrease in wages?
9. Why might management oppose a shorter basic workweek?
10. Why do the unions want seniority to determine layoffs and promotions?
11. What is management's objection to seniority rules? In addition to seniority, what does management want to use as a basis for promotions?
12. Why does organized labor want a union shop?
13. What is the purpose of a strike?
14. What are strike benefits, and where does the money to pay them come from?
15. What is a wildcat strike?
16. What is the purpose of picketing?
17. How are those not on either side affected by labor-management relations?
18. What are some ways government acts to protect the public interest in disputes between labor and management?
19. Are labor-management relations improving? Give examples.

SHARING YOUR OPINION AND EXPERIENCE

1. How can union demands affect the prices of goods and services?
2. A number of unions are asking employers for a "guaranteed annual wage." What does this mean?
3. Have you ever been inconvenienced by a strike? Explain.
4. It was once the policy of unions to ask for a "closed shop," which is now illegal. What was a closed shop? How did it differ from a union shop?
5. Some unions have been accused of "featherbedding." Explain.
6. A few years ago, the pilots of one major airline and the mechanics of another went on strike, tying up transportation during the Christmas holidays. Many people felt that the government should have prevented these strikes because the public was greatly inconvenienced as a result of them. What is your opinion?
7. How far do you think the government should go in settling labor disputes?
8. In Part 28 you read that some corporations have stock-purchase plans. These are making it possible for many workers to become stockholders in the corporations for which they work. What effect do you think this might have on labor-management relations?

PROJECTS AND PROBLEMS

1. In disagreements between unions and management, the bargaining strength is sometimes on the side of the workers and sometimes on the side of management. In each of the following situations, which side has the greater bargaining strength?

   ▪ *a.* The majority of the workers in the plant involved in the dispute are organized, but the company has other plants in which workers are not organized. ▪ *b.* The jobs of workers involved in the dispute are necessary to the operation of other industries. ▪ *c.* The good or service produced by workers involved in a dispute cannot be replaced by something else. ▪ *d.* The good or service produced by the workers in a dispute is highly perishable. ▪ *e.* The good or service produced by workers involved in a dispute can be made up and stored in preparation for a strike. ▪ *f.* The workers involved in a dispute are highly skilled and in great demand.

2. The table below shows the three major issues that led to strikes in a recent year and the number of man-days lost from work as a result. A *man-day* is the normal amount of time one worker spends at his job per day. Thus, if 100 workers went on strike, 100 man-days would be lost for each day of the strike. Following the table are some questions for you to answer.

MAJOR ISSUES INVOLVED IN WORK STOPPAGES

Issues	*Stoppages*		*Man-days Lost*	
	Number	*Percent*	*Number*	*Percent*
Wages, hours, and benefits	1,880	51	12,047,500	73
Union organization (recognition of union, union security)	601	16	1,313,500	8
Working conditions	837	22.8	2,630,000	16

▪ *a.* How many strikes were caused by the three major issues that year? ▪ *b.* How many man-days were lost that year because of strikes over these issues? ▪ *c.* Which issue led to the greatest number of strikes? ▪ *d.* What percent of the strikes during that year revolved around that issue? ▪ *e.* How many man-days were lost because of strikes over the leading issue? ▪ *f.* Which issue led to the second largest number of strikes? ▪ *g.* The number of strikes caused by the second leading issue was approximately what portion of the number caused by the leading issue? ▪ *h.* The number of man-days lost because of strikes caused by the second leading issue was approximately what portion of the number lost as a result of the leading issue? ▪ *i.* What percent of all strikes that year revolved around the three leading major issues?

3. Clip from your local daily newspaper or weekly news magazines articles reporting on labor-management disputes. Paste or tape each article to a sheet of paper. Underneath it, describe briefly:

   ▪ *a.* Who is involved in the dispute—the employer and the name of the union.
   ▪ *b.* What the workers are demanding from the employer.

4. The 275,000 workers of a major company were on strike for a period of 42 working days before an agreement was reached.

   ▪ *a.* If the company lost $300,000 a day as the result of the strike, what was its total loss? ▪ *b.* If each worker in this company lost an average of $82 for each 5 days of the strike, what was the total loss in earnings for all workers? ▪ *c.* What was the total cost of this strike to the company and to its workers combined?

5. Wages are determined by many factors, such as general business conditions, the number of workers available for a given job, and the amount produced per worker per hour. Nevertheless, there is some evidence that average annual earnings have increased more in industries employing union workers than in industries employing nonunion workers. In 1959, the Joint Economic Committee of the United States Congress conducted hearings on "Employment, Growth, and Price Levels." One of the economists who testified at the hearings presented to the committee the table below. The table compares wages for union and nonunion workers from 1946 to 1958. Answer the questions following the table.

AVERAGE ANNUAL EARNINGS IN UNION AND NONUNION INDUSTRIES

Year	*Average Annual Earnings*	
	Union	*Nonunion*
1946	$2,707	$2,226
1947	2,998	2,427
1948	3,261	2,598
1949	3,337	2,661
1950	3,572	2,793
1951	3,994	2,940
1952	4,163	3,065
1953	4,402	3,199
1954	4,507	3,319
1955	4,753	3,457
1956	5,027	3,603
1957	5,282	3,753
1958	5,468	3,882

▪ *a.* What were the average annual earnings of workers in union industries in 1946? in 1958? ▪ *b.* Approximately how many times greater were average annual earnings of workers in union industries in 1958 than in 1946? ▪ *c.* What were the average annual earnings of workers in nonunion industries in 1946? in 1958? ▪ *d.* What was the percent of increase in earnings of nonunion workers from 1946 to 1958? ▪ *e.* In which year did average earnings of workers in union industries increase most over the preceding year? (Answer this question without figuring increases for every year.) ▪ *f.* Which year did average earnings of workers in nonunion industries increase most over the preceding year? (Answer without figuring increases for every year.) ▪ g. Was there any year in which average earnings of nonunion workers increased more than the average earnings of union workers? If so, which year or years? ▪ *h.* What was the percent of difference between union and nonunion earnings in 1946? in 1958?

6. The following article appeared in the nation's newspapers on or about September 7, 1965. Read the article and answer the questions following it.

NEW STEEL CONTRACT IS SIGNED

Pittsburgh, Pa.—Steel union and industry chiefs Monday night signed a contract guaranteeing labor peace in the basic steel industry until at least Aug. 1, 1968.

President I. W. Abel of the United Steelworkers Union (USW) and the chief industry negotiator, R. Conrad Cooper, signed the contract at about 9:30 p.m., putting the final touch on the agreement made last Friday, under prodding by President Johnson, to avert a major strike. A strike would have idled some 450,000 steelworkers and shut off 80 percent of the nation's steel-making capacity.

Approved by the union's wage policy committee, the agreement gives steelworkers increased earnings and benefits estimated by the union at 47.3 cents an hour.

The government estimated the increases at 49 cents an hour, while the industry reportedly placed an even higher price tag on them.

Steelworkers already were among the highest paid industrial workers in the country, averaging $4.40 an hour in wages and benefits.

The agreement provides immediate pay raises ranging from 10 to 19 cents an hour, depending on job classification. Also included are improvements in vacations, medical benefits and life insurance.

▪ *a.* The contract mentioned in the article was an agreement between workers and management in what industry? ▪ *b.* For how long was the contract to run? ▪ *c.* Who signed the contract for the union? ▪ *d.* Who signed the contract for the industry? ▪ *e.* Who had persuaded the union and industry not to allow their disagreement to result in a strike? ▪ *f.* Had there been a strike, how many workers would have been idle? ▪ *g.* By what percent would production in the industry have fallen had the workers gone on strike? ▪ *h.* According to union estimates, how much of an increase in wages and benefits did workers receive under the new contract? ▪ *i.* According to government estimates, how much did the increases amount to? ▪ *j.* Was the industry's estimate of the increases higher or lower than the government's estimate? ▪ *k.* Based on the amount of increase estimated by the union, what will average earnings for workers in the industry be when the new contract goes into effect? ▪ *l.* What was the minimum wage increase under the new contract? the maximum? ▪ *m.* What fringe benefits were included in the new contract? ▪ *n.* Is the contract discussed in the above article still in effect? If not, has a new agreement been reached without a strike?

CHALLENGE PROBLEMS

1. Many labor contracts contain a "productivity clause." What is a "productivity clause"?
2. Some people claim that organized labor plays an important part in offsetting the power of big business. Explain.
3. Section 14(b) of the Taft-Hartley Act made it legal for states to have right-to-work laws. In 1965, a bill was introduced in the United States Congress to have this section of the Act repealed, making right-to-work laws illegal. What are right-to-work laws? Was section 14(b) of the Taft-Hartley Act repealed? In your opinion should states be allowed to have right-to-work laws?

CONTENTS OF UNIT 12

Unit 12 / You as a Citizen

PART 50 CITIZENSHIP RESPONSIBILITIES IN A FREE ENTERPRISE SYSTEM

EVER since the world began, people have been struggling to be free—free to choose their own government; free to speak and to write their own thoughts; free to worship in their own way. People in the United States have these freedoms. They also have ***economic freedom,*** which means that they have the right to make their own economic decisions as consumers, as producers, and as voters. It is easy to understand how the decisions you make will affect you personally. But more than that, your individual decisions also influence how our free enterprise system works.

Freedom is a privilege. And in exchange for privileges you must accept responsibilities. In return for the privilege of driving an automobile, for example, you have the responsibility to obey traffic regulations. Otherwise, you may lose your right to drive. In return for the privilege of making your own economic decisions, you have the responsibility to make wise decisions.

What are some of the ways in which our individual decisions affect our free enterprise system? It has been said that the success of a free enterprise system depends on an informed citizenry. What does that mean?

A. Devaney, Inc.

YOU HAVE RESPONSIBILITIES AS A CONSUMER

As a consumer you are free to choose how you will spend your money and with whom you will trade. In this way you help to decide how the nation's productive resources (natural resources, labor, and capital) are used. You also help to determine how business is conducted.

Millions of times a day consumers all over the nation tell business firms what kinds of goods and services they want and do not want by the way they spend their money. As their preferences change, resources are shifted from the production of one thing to another—from passenger trains to planes; from coal heat to oil, gas, or electric heat; from bobby sox to textured stockings.

When you make wise consumer choices, you not only benefit yourself, you also encourage the production of worthwhile goods and services. When you buy from reliable sellers, you encourage good business practices. When you shop to obtain the best possible product for your money, you encourage competition. If you make unwise choices, you waste both your own money and some of the nation's resources as well.

Seldom do consumers make unwise decisions deliberately. They make them because they lack the knowledge needed for making wise ones. One of your responsibilities as a citizen in a free enterprise system, therefore, is to be an informed consumer. An informed consumer not only knows the rules for wise buying, but he also practices them because he understands the effect of his decisions on our free enterprise system.

YOU WILL HAVE RESPONSIBILITIES AS A PRODUCER

One of this nation's most valuable resources is its workers, or ***human resources.*** When workers' abilities are not fully used, however, some skills that our business system needs are wasted. People differ in their abilities. Some have greater mechanical ability than others; some have greater mental ability; some have greater selling ability, and so on. A person's abilities determine the types of work he can do best.

For some part of your life you will be a producer helping to make or market things that people want. As a citizen in a free enterprise system, you may choose your own occupation. One of your responsibilities is to choose work that will enable you to make the best use of your abilities. Otherwise, you will not be contributing as much as you could to the successful operation of our free enterprise system.

You can begin now to help prevent waste of human resources by taking advantage of opportunities to develop your abilities through education.

Your responsibilities as a producer will not end with choosing the right job, however. If you work for someone else, you will have a responsibility to help in every way you can to make your employer's business successful. In the long run, the income and other benefits you receive will depend on his profits. If you join a labor union, you will have a responsibility to participate in the affairs of the union by attending meetings and voting on important questions. Otherwise, someone else will be making decisions for you. If you become an owner or manager of a business, you will be responsible for using productive resources efficiently. Whether you own a business or work for someone else, you will be helping to determine wages and prices. If you understand the effect of your decisions on our free enterprise system, it will help you to make wise decisions as a producer. In fact, as a citizen in a free enterprise system that is one of your responsibilities.

YOU WILL HAVE RESPONSIBILITIES AS A VOTER

In almost every election today—national, state, or local—there are economic issues to be decided. Sometimes citizens decide them directly and sometimes indirectly. In a local election, for example, citizens may vote directly for or against issuing bonds to finance the construction of new schools. In a national election, on the other hand, they usually express themselves on issues indirectly by voting for the party or candidates whose views are most like their own. Tariff legislation, tax reform, medical care for the aged, retraining of the jobless, and higher postal rates are examples of recent national issues.

In the years to come you will be helping to decide economic issues as a voter. In return for this privilege, you will have a responsibility to vote intelligently. This means, first of all, that you know what the issues are. Opportunities for learning about

Workers have a responsibility to take an active part in the affairs of their union by attending regular meetings.

Courtesy UAW SOLIDARITY photo

them are many. Before elections, issues are discussed from campaign platforms, in the newspapers, on radio and television. The purpose of most of these discussions is to persuade you to vote in a particular way. An intelligent voter, however, does not merely accept other people's opinions. He looks at all sides of an issue, then votes according to his own opinion. He can do this because he understands how our free enterprise system operates. As a voter you will have the same responsibility.

YOU WILL DECIDE WHAT THE ROLE OF GOVERNMENT SHALL BE

Early in this course you learned that our economic system is sometimes called ***modified free enterprise.*** To modify something means to change its basic form or characteristics in some way. In a completely free enterprise system all enterprises would be privately owned and all decisions would be made by individuals acting independently. But in the United States free enterprise is modified to the extent that some decisions are made through government.

For example government, rather than private enterprise, provides some of our goods and services. Government regulates business to protect the economic freedom of consumers, workers, and business owners. Government sometimes prohibits competition and controls prices. In these ways the people of this country modify their free enterprise system. The purpose of modifying free enterprise is to make it function more efficiently. And in some cases, our business system does work better as a result of government action. But this is not true in all cases.

In a ***democracy*** the economic role of government is decided by citizens through their elected representatives. In other words, you will help to determine the future role of government by supporting or opposing plans to give government greater power to make economic decisions. You will do this by the way you vote and by letting those who represent you in government know your views. One of the advantages of a free enterprise system is that citizens have an opportunity to work for its improvement. This places on each of us an obligation to weigh the possible consequences of any decision to modify the system. How will the change affect private enterprise? How will the change affect the freedom of individuals to make their own decisions?

YOU WILL HAVE RESPONSIBILITIES AS A TAXPAYER

Whatever goods and services you and your fellow citizens decide government should provide, you will help to pay for with taxes. Just as you have a responsibility as a consumer to spend your money wisely, so you have a responsibility as a taxpayer to see that your money is spent wisely.

Informed consumers apply the principle of real cost to their personal spending. Responsible citizens apply the same principle to government spending. The real cost of any choice, remember, is whatever else you might have instead. When citizens demand that government build new highways, they must either pay higher taxes or do without some other good or service that the money spent for highways could buy. Thus, the real cost of new highways might be consumer goods that people could buy for themselves. Or it might be goods they buy through government such as schools, parks, or hospitals. One of your responsibilities as a taxpayer will be to make certain that the goods and services we buy through government represent the best possible use of our money.

It will also be your responsibility as a taxpayer to see that neither your money nor the nation's productive resources are wasted. Government enterprises, unlike business enterprises, do not have to make a profit. Neither do they have to compete with other enterprises. For these reasons, there is always a possibility that they may not produce as efficiently as private enterprises. As a result some productive resources may be wasted, and some government goods and services may cost more to produce than necessary. In a democracy, citizens can influence taxing and spending policies. It is their responsibility to do so by learning about tax problems and working for a fair and sound tax system.

YOU WILL BE EXPECTED TO HELP SOLVE PROBLEMS

No nation ever succeeds in solving all of its economic problems. As some are overcome, new ones take their place. In the United States, for example, there is the problem of achieving economic stability that you read about in Part 46. There is the problem of how to get workers to move from places where there are no jobs for them to places where there are jobs. There is the problem of providing employment for men and women who lose their jobs to machines and the problem of what to do about people who have too little income for an adequate standard of living. There is the problem of labor-management relations and many others. None of them are simple problems. Neither have they simple solutions. Moreover, they are problems that individuals cannot solve by themselves.

WHAT SERVICES DO WE WANT GOVERNMENT TO PROVIDE?
National security?
Courts of law?
Generation of electric power?
Crop subsidies?
Housing projects?

Throughout the United States many private groups, such as Junior Achievement, are providing high school students with actual business experience.

Eastern Photo Service

One thing to be said for the people of the United States, however, is that they have faced up to their problems and worked together to solve them. Sometimes they solve them through private action. All over the nation, groups can be found working to improve their school systems; to beautify their communities; to aid disaster victims; to raise funds for hospitals or recreation centers; and to bring new business enterprises into their areas. Sometimes the people of the United States work through government to solve their problems. Social security is one example. The insuring of bank deposits is another. Sometimes government and private enterprise work together to solve problems. As one example, both government and business are operating training programs to help workers learn skills that will enable them to obtain jobs.

One of your responsibilities as a citizen in a free enterprise system will be to help find ways of dealing with problems that arise. To do this you will have to understand the problems. To understand the problems you will have to understand our free enterprise system.

YOU HAVE A RESPONSIBILITY FOR PRESERVING OUR ECONOMIC FREEDOM

In general, the people of the United States agree that they want a growing and stable economy, one in which income is divided fairly, and one which makes efficient use of productive resources. But more than anything else, they want their economic system to remain free. The greatest threat to economic freedom is a failure on the part of citizens to make wise economic decisions. Many of the government regulations in force today resulted from someone's failure to assume this responsibility. For example, because a few labor unions have acted irresponsibly, stricter labor laws have been put into effect. Because a few businessmen have been guilty of unfair practices, legislation has been passed prohibiting such practices. Our antitrust laws, our minimum wage laws, our pure food and drug laws are all attempts to *legislate* responsibility.

The free enterprise system of the United States is constantly changing as a result of decisions made by citizens as consumers, producers, and voters.

Yet, it is basically still a free enterprise system. As a citizen you have a responsibility for helping to preserve it and to make every effort to further improve it.

BUILDING YOUR VOCABULARY

Copy the four sentences below, completing each one by replacing the question mark with the appropriate term from the column at the left.

democracy
economic freedom
human resources
modified free enterprise

1. People who have the right to make their own decisions as consumers and producers have ? .
2. A nation's workers are its ? .
3. An economic system in which some decisions are made by government, but most are made by individuals as consumers and producers is called ? .
4. A system of government in which decisions are made by citizens through their elected representatives is a ? .

CHECKING YOUR READING

1. What responsibility does the privilege of making your own economic decisions carry with it?
2. What freedoms do you have as a consumer? How do your decisions affect our free enterprise system?
3. Why is it important that you make wise consumer choices?
4. What causes consumers to make unwise choices?
5. What is one of your important responsibilities as a consumer in a free enterprise system?
6. What happens when workers' abilities are not fully used?
7. What can you do to help prevent waste of human resources?
8. What responsibilities will you have as an employee? as a member of a labor union? as an owner or manager of a business?
9. As a producer, why is it important that you understand the effect of your decisions on our free enterprise system?
10. Voters help to decide economic issues both directly and indirectly. Explain.
11. Describe the responsibilities of a voter in a free enterprise system.
12. Why is the economic system of the United States called "modified free enterprise"?
13. What is the reason for modifying free enterprise?
14. In a democracy, how is the economic role of government determined?
15. Compare your responsibility as a taxpayer with your responsibility as a consumer.
16. How does the principle of real cost apply to government spending? Give an example.
17. Give two reasons why government enterprises may not produce as efficiently as private enterprises.

18. What are some of the problems facing the United States?
19. In what ways do the people of the United States solve their problems?
20. What is the greatest threat to economic freedom? Explain.

SHARING YOUR OPINION AND EXPERIENCE

1. Does your community have any economic problems? What are they? Why do you consider them *economic* problems?
2. Some people think that it is unpatriotic to admit that our economic system is not perfect. Do you agree or disagree? Give your reasons.
3. Give examples of laws legislating responsibility other than those mentioned in this part.
4. If government took over all businesses in this country, what kind of a system would we have? What would happen to competition under such a system?
5. Consumers in the United States are sometimes referred to as "citizen managers of our business system." What does this mean to you?
6. How can consumers become better informed?
7. What are some of the economic problems facing the United States other than those suggested in the text?
8. In what ways have you participated in activities to improve your community?
9. In recent years, the rate of our economic growth has been an important issue in national election campaigns. Do you think economic growth should be a political issue?
10. What is the purpose of the Job Corps Program that was started by the Federal government in 1965?

PROJECTS AND PROBLEMS

1. One of your responsibilities as a producer will be to choose an occupation that will enable you to make the most of your abilities. In the Projects and Problems section for Part 47, you were asked to list your interests and abilities as a first step in choosing an occupation. The next step is to find out all you can about jobs that fit your interests and abilities. For example, if you enjoy outdoor activities, you would probably want to investigate jobs that offer an opportunity to work out of doors. If your list of interests indicates that you enjoy working with things rather than with people or ideas, you will want to investigate jobs that involve working with things; and so on.

   Your school or public library probably has many sources of information about occupations such as the *Job Guide for Young Workers*, the *Dictionary of Occupational Titles*, or the *Occupational Outlook*. Using these or any other sources of information, select an occupation that you feel is closely related to your interests and abilities. Write a report about this occupation covering the following points:

   (1) The tasks performed by workers in the occupation (2) Requirements of the occupation ▪ *a.* Education ▪ *b.* Skills and special abilities ▪ *c.* Physical characteristics ▪ *d.* Special requirements (licenses, union membership, tools, or equip-

ment) (3) Working conditions ▪ *a.* Hours ▪ *b.* Travel ▪ *c.* Work done under pressure ▪ *d.* Hazards involved (4) Opportunities for employment ▪ *a.* Demand for new workers ▪ *b.* Effect of business conditions on occupation ▪ *c.* Competition for jobs in this field (5) Income ▪ *a.* Average beginning salary ▪ *b.* Average top salary (6) Opportunities for advancement ▪ *a.* Possibilities for promotion ▪ *b.* Requirements for promotion (skills, additional education, or training) At the end of your report, explain how you gathered your information.

2. At least once, and perhaps several times, during your lifetime, you will have to write a letter of application. When preparing such a letter, remember that it must represent you in selling your services. Remember, too, that it may have to compete with many others. Suppose that you are applying for a part-time or summer job with one of the business firms in your community. Prepare a letter of application, indicating the type of work for which you are applying. Make your letter brief, but include all necessary information.
3. List in a single column the courses you have taken and are now taking in high school, as well as those you plan to take next year. Some of these courses will have special value for certain occupations. Others will be general in nature, being of value to everyone regardless of the kind of work he plans to do. In a second column, after each course listed, write the name of one or more occupations in which the worker would find such training particularly useful. If you think the course has general education values only write "general" following it.

Name of Course	Course Has Special Values for
Example: Mechanical drawing	*Draftsman, toolmaker, engineer*

4. As a citizen in a free enterprise system, one of your producer responsibilities will be to follow the rules and regulations laid down by your employer, just as you now have a responsibility to follow the rules and regulations of your school. Make a list of your school rules and regulations. Following each one, write the reason for it.

5. On a sheet of paper write your answers to the following questions:
▪ *a.* Who is the mayor (or the city manager) of the city in which you live? ▪ *b.* Who is your representative in the state legislature? ▪ *c.* What are the names of the United States senators that represent your state in Washington? ▪ *d.* What is the name of the congressman from your district? ▪ *e.* What is the name of your governor? To what political party does he belong?

   As a committee project, collect the answers given by all class members and summarize them. From the results, would you say that your classmates are well informed about their leaders in government?

6. Prepare a written report telling what you have already learned from this and other courses that has helped you become a better consumer. What things do you feel you still need to learn? Arrange topics in order of their importance to you.

7. The voting record in two presidential elections was as follows:

Year	*Civilian Population of Voting Age*	*Votes Cast*
1960	**107,597,000**	**68,839,000**
1964	**112,549,000**	**70,644,000**

▪ *a.* What percent of the population of voting age voted in 1960? in 1964? ▪ *b.* By how many persons did the voting population increase from 1960 to 1964? ▪ *c.* How many more votes were cast in 1964 than in 1960? ▪ *d.* Did the percent of the population voting increase or decrease in 1964 over 1960? by what percent?

8. In a democracy, people are free to disagree over the solution to economic problems. You may find evidence of such disagreement in the "Letters to the Editor" column of your newspaper. Collect all letters you can that pertain to one problem or issue. Summarize the information contained in the letters by first identifying the issue, then listing the arguments for each side. Were there more letters favoring one side than the other? Explain.

9. Make a list of at least five private groups in your community whose purpose is either to help others or to improve the community in general. Describe briefly what you know about the work of each. Do any of them offer persons in your age group an opportunity to participate? Explain how.

CHALLENGE PROBLEMS

1. Many people have criticized the Federal government's spending the billions it will cost to put men on the moon. To support their arguments, they point to some of the other things the nation might do with the money instead. It has been suggested, for example, that the money be used to solve our transportation problems; to expand our educational facilities; or to clear our cities of slums. Those favoring the moon program, however, claim that even if the program were dropped, the citizens of the United States would probably not vote to spend the money for these other purposes. Explain why you approve or disapprove of spending the money needed for moon exploration.

2. Is a free enterprise system possible only in a democracy?

3. During the 1965 session of the United States Congress, one senator proposed that college students or their parents be permitted to deduct at least part of the cost of college education in figuring income taxes. What was the purpose of this proposal? What would the nation gain if it accomplished its purpose?

GLOSSARY

A

Accidental death benefit. (*see* Double indemnity)

Account. A bank's record of a customer's deposits and withdrawals

After-tax income. The amount of earnings a worker has for spending

Annuity. A guaranteed retirement income purchased from an insurance company

Appraisal. An estimate of the value of property

Articles of copartnership. A written agreement between two or more persons about the organization and operation of a partnership form of business

Assessed valuation. A percent of the market value of property, as determined by a government employee called a *tax assessor*

Automatic loan provision. A provision giving the insurance company authority to pay the premium with a policy loan if it has not been paid within the grace period

Automation. The use of machines to complete a series of operations with little or no human aid

Automobile liability insurance. Insurance for the automobile owner that protects against losses arising from injury to other persons or damage to property belonging to others

Average. The result of dividing the total of several figures by the number of figures

B

Balance. *In a checking account,* the amount on deposit in a bank account at a given time; *in an income and expense record,* the difference between "Money Received" and "Money Spent or Saved"

Balancing a bank statement. (*see* Reconcile)

Bank. A business enterprise that deals in money and credit

Bank statement. A report made by a bank to a depositor showing the depositor's checking account transactions

Bar graph. A graph of rectangular bars of varying length used to compare amounts

Barter. Trading goods for goods

Base period. A specific year in the past for which the consumer price index is always 100; the prices of all other years are compared to the prices of the base period

Basic work week. The number of hours of work for which workers are paid their regular hourly rate

Beneficiary. The person to whom an insurance policy is made payable

Benefits. *As used in insurance,* money or services a policyholder receives when a loss occurs

Blank endorsement. An endorsement that permits a check to be cashed by anyone

Blue Cross. A nonprofit corporation that sponsors a hospital insurance plan

Blue Shield. A nonprofit medical and surgical insurance plan sponsored by doctors

Bodily injury liability insurance. Insurance that protects against financial losses resulting from injuries to pedestrians, to persons riding in other cars, or to guests in a policyholder's car

Bond. A printed promise to pay a certain sum at a future date

Bondholder. A person who owns a bond

Borrower. (*see* Debtor)

Broken-line graph. (*see* Curve graph)

Budget. A plan for spending and saving

Business. The principal means by which we satisfy human wants

Business cycle. A series of changes in business activity

Business enterprise. Any organization that produces goods or services for sale

Buying guide. A way of getting information about a product

Buying skill. (*see* Buymanship)

Buymanship. The art of changing money into goods and services

C

Canceled checks. Checks that have been paid by the bank

Capacity. The ability to pay a debt

Capital. Often used to mean the money needed to buy the man-made things used in production (*see also* Capital goods; Wealth)

Capital gain. The profit an investor receives when he sells stock for more than he paid for it

Capital goods. Man-made things used in production (*see also* Producer goods)

Carrying charge. The charge made for installment credit

Cash value. The amount a policyholder can obtain in exchange for a permanent life insurance policy

Cashier's check. A check that a bank draws on its own funds

Certified check. A personal check for which payment is guaranteed by the bank

Character. The reputation a person has for honesty and dependability in paying his debts

Character loan. (*see* Signature loan)

Charge account. A credit plan that permits the user to charge any number of purchases and pay for them monthly

Check. An order to a bank to pay a stated sum of money to another person or business

Check stub. A form on which the depositor keeps a record of his checking account transactions

Checkbook. A bound set of printed forms used in writing checks

Checkbook dollars. (*see* Checkbook money)

Checkbook money. Money in the form of checks

Circle graph. A circle divided into sections to compare single items within a group with the entire group

Civilians. People not in military service

Claim. A request for payment of losses

Clearing. The process of collecting payment for checks

Clearinghouse. An agency that collects payment of checks for a number of banks

Closing costs. Fees and other expenses that a home buyer must pay at the start, in addition to the down payment

Closing price. The price paid for the last shares of a corporation's stock traded on a particular day

Collateral. Property used as security for a loan

Collective bargaining. The process by which representatives of labor unions work out agreements with employers

Collision insurance. Insurance that protects against losses resulting from damage to the policyholder's car regardless of who is responsible

Commodity. A good that can be transported or carried

Commodity money. A good that can be transported or carried and that is generally accepted, within a given area, as payment for goods, services, or debts

Common stock. Stock that has no preference over other stock

Compensation. Payment for a loss or damage

Competent. Legally capable of understanding an agreement

Competition. Rivalry between two or more businesses

Compound interest. Interest paid on both principal and previously earned interest

Comprehensive physical damage insurance. Insurance that pays for damages to the policyholder's car that are not covered by collision insurance

Compulsory. Required by law

Conservation. Protecting natural resources against waste

Consideration. Something of value that each party to a contract gives to the other to make the contract binding

Conspicuous consumption. The buying of goods for the purpose of impressing others

Constant dollars. Dollar amounts adjusted for price changes

Consumer. Anyone who buys or uses the goods and services of business

Consumer credit. Credit used by individuals and families for personal reasons

Consumer demand. The buying done by individuals and families

Consumer finance company. Another name for a small-loan company

Consumer goods. Goods and services that satisfy human wants directly

Consumer price index. A list of the average prices of a large assortment of consumer goods and services that are bought by most middle-income families in the United States

Consumption. The using up of goods and services

Consumption tax. A retail sales tax imposed directly on consumers but collected for the government by sellers

Contract. A binding agreement between two or more persons

Convertible (*insurance*) Term insurance that may be exchanged for another type of insurance without physical examination

Cooperative. A business enterprise owned by its customers

Copyright. The exclusive right to literary, musical, or art works

Corporate bond. A bond issued by a corporation

Corporation. A business organization in which the liability of the owners is limited to their original investment

Cosigner. Anyone who signs a promissory note in addition to the borrower

Cost of living. Prices of consumer goods in general

Cost of living index. (*see* Consumer price index)

Counterfeit. Money made by anyone other than the Federal government

Coverage. Any type of insurance protection

Covered. Protected by insurance

Credit. A means of obtaining something of value in exchange for a promise to pay at a future time

Credit bureau. An agency through which business firms exchange information about their credit customers

Credit memorandum. (*see* Credit ticket)

Credit rating. The reputation a person or business has established for meeting credit obligations

Credit service charge. (*see* Carrying charge)

Credit terms. The details covering an installment purchase, such as the down payment, number and size of payments, and service charge

Credit ticket. A record of the return of merchandise that has been purchased on credit

Credit union. A cooperative organized to make loans to its members

Creditor. One who supplies goods, services, or money on credit

Currency. (*see* Currency dollars)

Currency dollars. The coins and paper bills used as a means of payment

Current dollars. Dollar amounts not adjusted for price changes

Curve graph. A graph that consists of a series of lines drawn from one point to another, sometimes in different directions

Customs duty. (*see* Tariff)

Cyclical unemployment. Unemployment resulting from a recession or depression

D

Death taxes. Taxes that are levied following someone's death

Debt. An amount owed by one person or business to another

Debtor. One who owes for goods, services, or money obtained on credit

Decreasing term insurance. Insurance that provides a smaller amount of protection each year it is in force

Deductible insurance. An insurance agreement that makes the policyholder responsible for paying a part of the loss himself

Deflation. A general decrease in prices

Demand. The amount of a good or service that will be bought at a particular price

Demand deposits. Deposits made in a checking account

Democracy. A system of government in which decisions are made by citizens through their elected representatives

Dependents. Persons who rely on someone else for support

Deposit. Money placed in a bank for safekeeping

Deposit money. Demand deposits, or the money people have in their checking accounts

Deposit slip. A form on which a depositor lists the items to be credited to his account

Depositor. Anyone who puts money in a bank

Depreciation. A decrease in the value of property resulting from age and use

Depressed area. A region that offers little or no opportunity for employment

Depression. A widespread and long-lasting slump in business activity

Descriptive label. A statement found on a product that itemizes important information about the product

Direct tax. A tax that cannot be shifted to someone else

Disability income provision. A provision of a life insurance policy that provides a monthly income to the policyholder if he becomes disabled

Disability insurance. (*see* Loss of income insurance)

Disability waiver of premium. A provision of a life insurance policy that frees the policyholder from further payment of premiums if he should become permanently disabled

Discount. Interest deducted from the amount borrowed at the time a loan is made

Discretionary spending. Buying goods and services from choice rather than necessity

Disposable personal income. The total amount of income consumers have for spending after payment of taxes

Dividend. A share of corporation profits paid to the owners (stockholders) of the corporation

Division of labor. (*see* Specialization)

Dollar votes. (*see* Economic votes)

Dollars of constant purchasing power. (*see* Constant dollars)

Double indemnity. A provision in an insurance policy that promises to pay twice the face value of the policy if the insured dies as the result of an accident

Down payment. An amount paid on an installment purchase at the time of purchase

Drawer. The person who signs a check

Durable goods. Products that usually last three years or more

E

Earned income. Money received for work

Economic freedom. The right of people to make their own economic decisions as consumers, as producers, and as voters

Economic growth. An increase in a nation's gross national product

Economic risk. The possibility of a money loss

Economic stability. Steady economic growth with no general increase in prices

Economic system. The arrangements a country makes for using its productive resources

Economic votes. Purchases that tell producers what kinds and how many goods and services are wanted

Economical. Avoiding waste or extravagance in using money or other resources

Economize. To use money or some other resource to the best advantage

Economy. (*see* Economic system)

Emotional advertising. A way of promoting the sale of a product by appealing to the consumer's pride or fears

Employee. One who earns his income by working for someone else

Employer. One who pays others to work for him

Employment trend. A shift away from one kind of employment and toward another

Endorse. To sign one's name on the back of a check

Endorsement in blank. (*see* Blank endorsement)

Endorser. *Of a note,* a person who agrees to be responsible for payment of a loan if the borrower fails to pay

Endowment insurance. Insurance that pays the face amount to the policyholder himself if he is living when it matures

Escalator clause. A provision in a labor contract that provides for raising or lowering wages according to changes in the cost of living

Estate. Everything a person owns, including both real and personal property

Estate tax. A tax levied on property left by someone who dies that must be paid before ownership of the property is transferred

Estimate. A reasonably accurate guess

Excise tax. A sales tax that is levied on a specific good or service

Exclusions. Risks not covered by a particular insurance policy

Expenditure. An amount of money that has actually been spent

Extended coverage. Insurance that provides protection against losses due to hailstorms, tornadoes, and similar causes

Extended term insurance. Insurance purchased with the cash value of a policy that gives protection for a limited time equal to the face value of the policy

F

Face value. *Of an insurance policy,* the amount to be paid by the insurance company to the policyholder

Factors of production. Natural resources, labor, and capital

Family income policy. An insurance policy that provides both straight life and decreasing term insurance protection

Family protection coverage. (*see* Uninsured motorists coverage)

Final goods. Products purchased for use rather than resale

Finance charge. (*see* Carrying charge)

Financial responsibility laws. Laws that require an automobile owner involved in an accident resulting in bodily injury or property damage to show proof of his ability to pay for the losses

Fiscal policy. Spending and taxing by the government

Fixed capital. Producer goods that can be used over and over, such as tools and machinery

Fixed expenses. Costs that are necessary and difficult to change

Fixed-dollar investments. Investments that do not increase or decrease in dollar value

Flexible. Capable of being changed to meet changing conditions

Fraudulent. Intended to deceive

Free enterprise. A system in which individuals and businesses make their own economic decisions

Freedom of contract. Right to make binding contracts

Fringe benefits. Benefits paid to workers in addition to their regular wages, such as retirement pensions, group insurance, and paid vacations

Full endorsement. An endorsement that indicates to whom the check is transferred

Functions of marketing. Tasks that middlemen perform in the process of moving goods from the original producer to the point of final sale

G

General medical expense insurance. Insurance that covers doctor bills for illnesses not requiring surgery

Geographic specialization. A division of labor caused by the location of natural resources or raw materials

Gift tax. A tax on large amounts of property that are given away

Goods. Material objects, such as books or cameras

Grace period. A period following the date an insurance premium is due during which the premiums may be paid

Grade label. A label indicating the quality of the product that bears it

Grievance. A complaint that one side or the other is not living up to the terms of a labor agreement

Grievance procedures. Steps to be followed in handling complaints related to a labor contract

Gross national product. The total amount that a nation produces in a year

GNP per capita. The average amount produced per person

Gross profit. The difference between the money received from the sale of goods and the cost of those goods

Group life insurance. Insurance protection provided to a number of people under one policy

Guarantee. A promise that a product is as represented or will perform in a certain way

H

Hidden taxes. Taxes people pay without being aware of paying them

Homeowner's policy. A single insurance policy that covers both the policyholder's house and his household goods and other personal property

Horizontal bar graph. A bar graph in which the bars extend across rather than up and down

Hospital expense insurance. Insurance that pays all or part of the costs of hospitalization

Household inventory. A list of personal property contained in a home

Human resources. The workers of a nation

I

Implied contract. An agreement that is understood because of the actions of the persons involved

Impulse buying. Spending without thought or plan

Income. Money received by business from the sale of goods and services

Income tax. A tax on earnings

Income tax return. A form that must be completed and filed each year by every person or business whose earnings are subject to tax

Indirect tax. A tax that can be shifted to someone else

Individual proprietorship. A one-owner business

Industrial life insurance. Insurance that is usually paid for in small weekly or monthly premiums

Industrial revolution. An economic revolution marked by a rise in the production per person of industrial goods and the introduction of power-driven machinery into industry

Industry. A group of business enterprises that produce similar products or provide similar services

Inflation. A general increase in prices

Informative. Telling you what you want to know

Informative label. (*see* Descriptive label)

Inheritance. Property received by one person from the estate of another person following that person's death

Inheritance tax. A tax levied on property received from the estate of someone who has died that is paid by the person who receives the property

Innovations. New inventions that are put to work

Installment contract. A formal agreement covering the purchase of goods bought on installment credit

Installment credit. A type of credit that provides for repaying the amount owed in two or more payments

Insurable interest. A money interest in property or in a person's life

Insurance. A way of sharing economic losses

Insurance agent. A man or woman who sells insurance

Insurance company. A business enterprise engaged in providing insurance protection

Interdependence. A characteristic of an economic system in which all persons or groups rely on one another

Interdependent. To rely on one another

Interest. A charge made for the use of money

Interest rate. Interest expressed as a percent of the amount borrowed

Interstate commerce. Trade between states

Inventory. An itemized list of property or possessions

Investing. Putting savings to work to earn an income

Investment. An exchange of money for capital goods

Investment bank. A wholesaler of stocks and bonds

Investment broker. A person who buys and sells securities for others

Investment company. A corporation whose business is that of investing in securities

Investment credit. Credit used for the purchase of capital goods

Investor. One who puts his savings to work

Itemize. To list or describe fully

J

Joint account. A checking account used by two or more persons

L

Label. A tag, carton, wrapper, or seal that carries a message about the product to which it is attached

Labor. The human effort that goes into production

Labor contract. A written agreement between an employer and a labor union stating the terms of employment for a definite period of time

Labor force. Everyone 14 years of age or over who is working or looking for work

Labor union. An organization that represents a group of workers in bargaining with their employer

Labor-management relations. The way in which employees and the management of a business work together

Lender. (*see* Creditor)

Levying. Placing a tax on an item or activity

Liability insurance. Insurance that provides protection against financial losses resulting from injuries to other persons or their property for which the insured is held responsible

Limited liability. Responsibility for business debts only to the extent of the value of the business property

Limited payment life insurance. Permanent life insurance that becomes fully paid up after a stated number of years

Liquid. Easily turned into cash without loss

Living benefits. Proceeds of a life insurance policy that are paid to the policyholder himself

Loan credit. Credit that is used to obtain money

Loan shark. An unlicensed or illegal lender

Loss of income insurance. Insurance that helps to replace earnings lost as a result of disability

Lump-sum payment. The entire proceeds of a life insurance policy paid to the beneficiary at once

M

Major medical expense insurance. Insurance designed to pay expenses resulting from serious or prolonged illness

Maker. The person who signs a note to borrow money

Management. The person or persons in a business who make major decisions and provide the leadership

Man-day. The normal amount of time one worker spends at his job per day

Market value. *Of securities,* the price that securities will bring at any given time

Marketing. The process of getting goods from producers to consumers

Mass production. The manufacture of goods in very large quantities

Maturity date. The date on which the face value of a bond is to be repaid

Medical payments insurance. Insurance that pays medical expenses for persons injured while riding in the policyholder's car regardless of who is responsible for the accident

Member banks. The stockholder banks, or owners, of a Federal Reserve bank

Middleman. A business enterprise engaged in moving goods from producers to consumers

Mixed economy. An economic system in which most decisions are made by individuals acting independently but some are made jointly through government

Mobile homes. Homes on wheels

Modified free enterprise. (*see* Mixed economy)

Monetary. Pertaining to money

Monetary policy. Control over the amount banks may lend

Money. Anything generally accepted in payment for goods, services, or debts

Money capital. The money needed to buy producer goods

Money economy. An economic system in which money plays a very important role

Money order. A means of making money payments that may be purchased at post offices or banks

Monopoly. The ability to control the supply and price of a good or service

Mortgage. A loan secured by property

Mortgage loan. (*see* Mortgage)

Mutual assent. Complete agreement between two or more persons

Mutual funds. Shares of stock in investment companies that issue new shares whenever there is a buyer for them

Mutual savings banks. Banks that accept time deposits only

N

National debt. The debt owed by the Federal government

Natural resources. Things in existence that man did not produce, such as timber, oil, and iron

Net profit. The amount that remains after all costs of doing business are deducted from income

Nondurable goods. Products that are used up within a short time

Noninstallment credit. A type of credit that provides for repaying the amount owed in one payment

Nonparticipating policies. Insurance policies on which no dividends are paid

Note. (*see* Promissory note)

O

Old age, survivors, and disability insurance. An insurance plan operated by the Federal government that pays benefits when a worker retires, dies, or is disabled

Open-book credit. (*see* Charge account)

Open charge account. (*see* Charge account)

Opening price. The price paid for the first shares of a corporation's stock traded on a particular day

Option account. A credit plan that may be used as either an open account or a revolving charge account

Ordinary life insurance. Insurance sold by agents on an individual basis in units of at least $1,000

Organized labor. Workers who belong to labor unions

Output. Another name for production

Outstanding checks. Checks written but not yet paid by the bank

Overdraw. To write a check for more than you have on deposit

P

Participating policies. Insurance policies that pay dividends to the policyholders

Partnership. A business in which two or more owners share both the profits and risks

Passbook. A book used for recording deposits which serves as the depositor's receipt

Patent. The exclusive right to an idea or invention

Patronage refund. Money refunded to a member of a cooperative based on the amount of his purchases

Payee. The person to whom a check is written

Pension. A regular payment of money to a retired worker

Percent. Per 100 or parts of 100

Periodical. A magazine that is published regularly

Personal finance company. Another name for a small-loan company

Personal insurance. Insurance that provides protection against losses resulting from illness, bodily injury, or death

Personal liability insurance. Insurance that protects the property owner against claims resulting from injuries to others while on his property

Personal loan. A loan made to an individual for a period of three years or less

Personal property. Moveable property, such as furniture, clothing, or books

Personalized checks or deposit slips. Checks or deposit slips which contain the printed name of the depositor

Picketing. The stationing by a labor organization of striking workers at the entrance to a business involved in a labor dispute to keep others from entering

Pie chart. (*see* Circle graph)

Planned economy. A system in which the government makes most economic decisions

Pocketbook money. The cash that people carry in their pockets and purses

Policy. A written agreement between an insurance company and a policyholder

Policyholder. A person for whom an insurance company assumes a risk

Postal savings. A savings account system operated by the Federal government through its post offices

Preferred stock. Stock that has first claim on dividends

Premium. A payment for insurance protection

Prepayment privilege. The right of a borrower to make extra payments on a mortgage or other installment loan in order to save interest

Price. The value of anything expressed in money terms

Price competition. Rivalry between two or more businesses that is based on price differences

Price-earnings ratio. The price of stock compared with (divided by) the company's earnings per share

Principal. A sum of money that has been invested; *of a loan,* the amount of a loan

Private agency. An agency not officially connected with the government

Private debt. The total amount owed by both consumers and privately owned business enterprises

Private enterprise. An economy in which the majority of businesses are privately owned

Private pension plan. A pension plan operated by an employer for the benefit of his employees

Private property. Anything owned by an individual

Probable. Likely to happen

Proceeds. The amount paid to the beneficiary of a life insurance policy

Processing. Changing the form of things already produced in order to sell them

Producer. A person or enterprise that makes goods or provides services

Producer credit. Credit used by business firms

Producer goods. Goods used to produce other goods or services (*see also* Capital goods)

Product competition. Rivalry between two or more businesses that is based on differences in products

Production. Changing the form or location of natural things to satisfy human wants

Production workers. Workers directly engaged in producing goods

Productive resources. (*see* Factors of production)

Productivity. The average amount produced per worker in an hour

Profit. The difference between what a business earns and what it costs that business to operate

Progressive tax. A tax for which the rate increases as ability to pay increases

Promissory note. A written promise to repay a loan by a certain date

Property damage liability insurance. Insurance that pays for damages caused by the policyholder's car to any type of property belonging to others

Property insurance. Insurance that provides protection against possible financial losses resulting from damage to the insured's property

Property tax. A tax on real estate or personal items such as automobiles or household goods

Proportional tax. A tax for which the rate remains the same regardless of the value of the tax base

Prosperity. A period when business activity is rising

Provisions. Promises made in an insurance policy

Public agency. A government agency

Public debt. A debt owed by the government

Public utility. A private enterprise that provides a service so essential that its prices are regulated by the government

Public works. Construction projects, such as highways, bridges, and parks, undertaken by the government

Purchase credit. (*see* Sales credit)

Purchasing power. The amount money will buy

Q

Quarterly. Every three months

R

Rate. A price of one thing based on the amount of another

Real cost. The price of an article in terms of other goods or services the buyer might have bought

Real estate. Property of a permanent nature, such as land and buildings

Real estate tax. A tax on real property

Real income. The amount that can be bought with money earned

Real property. Land, buildings, and other things permanently attached to the land

Real wages. (*see* Real income)

Recession. A slump in business activity

Reconcile. To bring into agreement the balances shown on a bank statement and on a checkbook record

Redeem. To exchange for cash

References. Friends or acquaintances who can furnish information about your identity and character

Refinance. To arrange repayment of a debt so that payments are smaller than they were originally

Regressive tax. A tax for which the rate decreases as ability to pay increases

Renewable (*insurance*) Term insurance that may be carried for one or more additional periods without another physical examination

Repossess. To take back goods sold on credit if the buyer fails to make payments when due

Research and development. Discovering new products and new ways of doing things

Reserve account. A member bank's reserves on deposit at the Federal Reserve bank

Reserves. The portion of a bank's deposits that cannot be loaned

Resource. A means of doing something

Restrictive endorsement. An endorsement that limits the use of a check by stating the endorser's intentions

Retailer. A person or business enterprise that sells directly to consumers

Retained earnings. The profits of a corporation that are kept and used in the business

Return. The interest or other income received from an investment

Revenue. Income received by the government

Revise. To change in an effort to correct or improve

Risk. The possibility of a loss

S

Safe-deposit boxes. Boxes in bank vaults that are used to store articles of value, such as important papers, jewelry, stocks, and bonds

Salary. (*see* Wages)

Sales credit. Credit that is used to acquire goods

Sales tax. A tax on the sale of goods or services

Sales ticket. A record of a sale made by the salesclerk and given to the customer

Saving. The storing up of purchasing power

Savings. Money, or purchasing power, kept in reserve

Seasonal. Pertaining to or affected by the seasons of the year

Seasonal unemployment. Unemployment caused by changes in production that occur in some industries at certain times of the year

Secured loan. A loan that is guaranteed either by collateral or by the endorsement of someone other than the borrower

Securities. Another name for stocks and bonds

Security. Something pledged to guarantee repayment of a loan

Semiannually. Twice a year

Seniority. An employee's length of service with one firm

Service charge. A fee paid to a bank for checking account service

Service credit. Credit that is used to purchase services, such as electricity or medical care

Services. Things others do for us, like cutting our hair or repairing our cars

Settlement options. Different methods of paying life insurance benefits

Shares. Units of stock

Short-term credit. Credit extended for a period of six months or less

Signature card. The bank's record of the way a customer signs his checks

Signature loan. A loan backed only by the borrower's promise to pay

Single-payment loan. A loan that is repaid in a lump sum

Small loans. Personal loans made to consumers

Small-loan company. A business that specializes in making small loans to consumers

Sound money. Money that holds its value

Specialization. A way of dividing production so that each worker performs only one job

Standard of living. The way a family or the people of a nation live

Statistics. Facts stated in numbers

Stock certificate. A printed form representing ownership of stock in a corporation

Stock exchange. A central agency through which securities may be traded

Stockholders. The owners of a corporation

Stop-payment order. An order instructing a bank not to pay a check

Straight life insurance. Permanent life insurance on which the policyholder pays premiums for as long as he wants the protection

Strike. A deliberate refusal on the part of employees of a business to work

Strike benefits. Financial assistance from a union given to members during a strike

Subsidy. Financial assistance given by the government to a private enterprise

Summarize. To state briefly

Surgical expense insurance. Insurance that pays all or part of the doctor's fee for an operation

T

Tariff. A tax on goods imported from other countries

Tax. A compulsory payment for government services

Tax assessor. A government employee who estimates the value of property in order to establish its tax base

Tax base. Whatever serves as a basis for a tax

Tax exemption. An amount of income that is not subject to tax

Tax rate. The proportion of the tax base used to figure the amount of taxes to be paid

Tax system. All the taxes used by government

Taxable income. The amount of earnings subject to tax

after exemptions and deductions are subtracted from total earnings

Technological unemployment. Unemployment that results when machines replace workers

Technology. The knowledge required for efficient production

Telegraphic money order. A message from one telegraph office to another requesting that money be paid to a certain business or individual

Teller. A bank clerk who accepts deposits and handles withdrawals

Term insurance. Insurance that provides protection for a limited period of time

Test question. A question that is sometimes sent with a telegraphic money order to insure that the money is paid to the right person

Testimonial advertising. A recommendation for a product by persons who supposedly use it

Thirty-day account. (*see* Charge account)

Thrift. Efficient use of anything limited in supply

Time deposits. Deposits made in a savings account

Title. Evidence of ownership

Trade association. An organization of producers engaged in the same kind of business

Traveler's check. A special check that is widely accepted as a money substitute and is easily replaced if lost or stolen

Treasurer's check. (*see* Cashier's check)

Triplicate. Made in three identical copies

True interest. The percent cost of credit for a year

Trust. Money or property that a bank manages for others

U

Underwriter. One who provides insurance against risks

Unemployment insurance. An insurance plan operated jointly by the Federal and state governments that provides weekly benefits to workers temporarily out of work

Unethical. Having no regard for good business practices

Uninsured motorists coverage. Insurance that pays for all losses resulting from injuries caused by other drivers for which the policyholder is unable to collect

Union shop. A business that hires only workers who are or agree to become members of a union

Unlimited liability. Responsibility for debts to the full extent of all business and personal property

V

Valid. Legally enforceable

Value. The worth of a good or service in terms of other goods and services

Vertical bar graph. A bar graph in which the bars go up and down rather than across the page

Voluntary. By choice

W

Wages. Money that workers receive for their services

Waiting period. The length of time a policy must be in force before the policyholder may receive benefits

Wealth. *Of a nation,* the nation's stock of natural resources and man-made goods

of a person, what a person owns in the way of property: a car, jewelry, furniture, and the like

Wholesaler. A merchant who buys goods in large quantities and resells them in smaller lots

Wildcat strike. A strike that is not approved by the union to which those on strike belong

Withdrawal. Money taken out of a bank

Withholding. A method of collecting income tax in which employers are required to keep back a portion of each worker's earnings and send it to the government

Working capital. Producer goods that are used up in production, such as raw materials or office supplies

Workmen's compensation insurance. A type of insurance, required by law, designed to protect employees who may be injured on the job

Y

Yield. The rate of return on corporate securities

INDEX